AFRICAN SURVEY

AFRICAN SURVEY

Alan C. G. Best
DEPARTMENT OF GEOGRAPHY, BOSTON UNIVERSITY

Harm J. de Blij
DEPARTMENT OF GEOGRAPHY, UNIVERSITY OF MIAMI, FLORIDA

JOHN WILEY & SONS
NEW YORK SANTA BARBARA LONDON SYDNEY TORONTO

Library of Congress Cataloging in Publication Data:

Best, Alan C G
  African survey.

  Bibliography: p.
  Includes index.
  1. Africa—Description and travel—1961–
2. Africa—Politics and government—1960–   I. De
Blij, Harm J., joint author.   II. Title.
DT12.2.B44   960'.3   76-44520
ISBN 0-471-20063-8

Printed in the United States of America

10 9 8 7 6 5 4 3

PREFACE

After more than a decade of neglect, Africa once again occupies a place of prominence among American concerns. Events in Southern Africa have been chiefly responsible for this resurgence of interest, but Washington could not have long ignored the growing strength of African states in the international arena. North Africa's oil and the role of North African states in the affairs of the Middle East, Nigeria's emergence as an African power, and socialist experiments in East and Northeast Africa, coupled with the prominent role of African states in the United Nations, have all contributed to the renewal of the United States' concern over developments on the African continent.

African Survey is a thematic regional geography of Africa. In both the general introductory sections, dealing with the continent as a whole, and in the chapters that focus on individual countries, we select specific themes that are developed within a particular framework and from a particular point of view. The chapters on South Africa, Namibia, Sudan, and Nigeria (among others) are essentially essays on political geography. The chapters on Somalia, Tanzania, Rwanda, and Burundi are centered on sociocultural geography. In one way or another all chapters (though some more explicitly than others) deal with development issues. Our purpose is to present contemporary development prospects within a broad geographic framework.

This book differs in several respects from its predecessor, *A Geography of Subsaharan Africa* (1964). For practical reasons we have added a segment on North Africa; the role of North African states as members of the Organization of African Unity (OAU), and the impact of the OAU on North African issues, compel this change. The introductory section of the book has also been expanded to include much material previously discussed in the regional chapters. As a result, the regional narratives are more concise, although the majority retain their rather systematic foci.

Our principal objective is to place Africa's changing cultural landscapes in geographic context. In the process we provide a wide-ranging and current information base, so that this book can serve as a substantial introduction to Africa of the late 1970s.

This book has benefited enormously from the work of Hibberd V. B.

Kline of the University of Pittsburgh. Dr. Kline reviewed the manuscript in the greatest detail, researched persistent problems, suggested sources, expressed sometimes pungent opinions, kept our adrenalin flowing, and generally contributed in countless ways. We express our deep and permanent gratitude for an effort that went far beyond what we might have expected from a routine review.

In the time since the appearance of the original book, numerous colleagues have made helpful comment and suggestions. It is a pleasure now to acknowledge these contributions, whether made in formal review, by letter, or casually; the accumulated record proved most useful. We are grateful to J. C. Armstrong, D. J. Ballas, S. H. Bederman, S. S. Birdsall, C. H. Brooke, H. C. Brooks, D. L. Capone, H. E. Colestock III, R. J. Davies, W. DePree, W. W. Deshler, L. C. Duby, S. S. Edison, T. J. D. Fair, B. J. Garnier, R. D. Garst, J. F. Goff, P. R. Gould, W. J. Hanna, R. N. Henderson, R. K. Holz, J. R. Hooker, R. J. Horvath, R. J. Houk, J. M. Hunter, D. H. Irwin, J. W. King, D. B. Knight, D. E. Kromm, D. N. Larson, P. L. Lehrer, B. E. Logan, J. B. McI. Daniel, J. O. McKee, W. L. McKim, E. McClennen, M. P. Mensheha, E. J. Miles, S. Mokerjee, E. S. Munger, A. A. Nazzaro, B. C. Peters, P. W. Porter, F. J. Simoons, J. W. Stafford, W. R. Stanley, M. J. Swartz, D. J. Thom, B. E. Thomas, E. A. Tiryakian, D. E. Vermeer, J. A. Wolter, and B. S. Young.

We also express our appreciation to our peripatetic editor, Paul A. Lee, whose idea this project was in the first place and who worked as hard as anyone to keep it moving forward, and to Kathy DiConza, who assisted us in countless ways. We also thank Bonnie Doughty for her help. A special note of thanks is directed to Lillian B. Funk, who typed several drafts of the manuscript. We, of course, remain responsible for the book's shortcomings.

HARM J. DE BLIJ
ALAN C. G. BEST
MAY, 1976

CONTENTS

CONTENTS

LIST OF FIGURES

CONTENTS

CONTENTS

FOR
CICELY J. BEST
AND
NELLY MARGOT DE BLIJ-ERWICH

PART ONE

THE
CONTINENT

ONE

Alone among the continents, Africa is positioned astride the equator, extending beyond 35° North Latitude and nearly reaching 35° South. The continent's northernmost areas, the countries of the Maghreb, lie in the general latitude of North and South Carolina; South Africa shares its latitude with southern Brazil and Uruguay. Tunis, capital of Tunisia, lies in the approximate latitude of Richmond, Virginia and San Francisco, California. Cape Town, South Africa's second city, lies almost exactly due east of Buenos Aires, Argentina and Montevideo, Uruguay.

Coupled with this equator-straddling situation is Africa's position at the heart of the land hemisphere. Again among the landmasses, only Africa lacks a Pacific coastline. This means that Africa has a minimum aggregate distance to the world's other continents as well as a central location, which is antipodal to the Pacific (Fig. 1-1).

The African continent constitutes the second largest landmass on this planet, after Eurasia. It stretches some 5000 miles (8000 km) from Bizerte, Tunisia to Cape Agulhas, South Africa and an almost equal distance from Dakar in the west to Cape Gardafui in the east. Africa's dimensions (its area is 11.7 million sq mi or 30.3 million sq km) and its compact shape are two of its most distinctive physical characteristics. Africa's coastline is remarkably straight and unbroken over distances of many hundreds of miles; there are few really large bays or estuaries, and no substantial island arcs lie off its shores. Nor is Africa flanked by continental shelves comparable to those off Eurasia or North America. In general the ocean floor drops sharply, and quite near the coastline, to great depths. Almost equally abrupt is the sharp rise of the land, in many places as a spectacular mountain wall. The Great Escarpment, as this wall is called, exists in places as widely distributed as Sierra Leone,

THE PHYSIOGRAPHY OF AFRICA

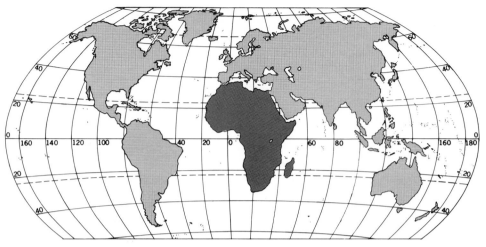

FIGURE 1-1 *Location of Africa.*

Namibia, Lesotho, and Ethiopia. The escarpment in many areas (such as Angola and South Africa) lies within a few dozen miles from the coast, so that Africa, per unit area, has relatively little low-lying territory and even less true coastal plain.

Plateau and Basins

Africa's continental physiography is that of an enormous plateau, higher in the east and south, and lower in the west and north, although the Atlas, Ahaggar, and Tibesti Mountains rise above the lower northern elevations. High Africa includes the Ethiopian Massif, where elevations exceed 14,000 ft (4250 m), the extensive East African Plateau, and South Africa's Drakensberg, which reach over 11,000 ft (3350 m). The highest point along this eastern axis of the great African plateau is Mount Kilimanjaro, a dormant volcano whose snow-capped peak exceeds 19,300 ft (5880 m). Much of the plateau of eastern Africa, however, presents a gently undulating landscape broken only by hills and ridges sustained by more resistant rocks; elevations average between 4000 and 5000 ft (1200 and 1500 m). Along the plateau's eastern margin, from the Red Sea to South Africa, lies the Great Escarpment, almost everywhere a prominent obstacle to road, rail, and water transport.

Madagascar, 250 mi (400 km) from the southeast African coast, mirrors the East African physiography. A high-elevation plateau axis forms the island's eastern backbone, with some mountains exceeding 8000 ft (2400 m) and a steep escarpment facing the Indian Ocean. Westward, elevations decline. Again, the crystalline rocks support the plateau surface, volcanics sustain the greater heights, and sedimentary rocks underlie the lower west.

To the west of Africa's great eastern upland, the continental surface subsides into several major basins separated by plateau-level drainage divides (Fig. 1-2). Astride the equator lies the Zaire (formerly Congo) Basin, a great structural depression filled with sedimentary layers and surrounded by the plateau crystallines. To the south, the Kalahari Basin occupies the area between the South African–Rhodesian *Highveld* and the high coastal ranges of Namibia. Unlike the forest-clad Zaire Basin, the Kalahari Basin is

The Great Escarpment in South Africa. To the right lies the Gondwana erosion surface of the African plateau; to the left the lower country that slopes towards the Indian Ocean. The vertical drop here exceeds 5000 feet (1500 m). (Satour)

a sandy desert and steppe, but the two depressions share the accumulations of thick sediments that weighed down the underlying crystalline floor.

North of the Zaire Basin, and beyond the North Equatorial Divide, lie three major interior basins. Easternmost is the Sudan Basin, drained by the White Nile and the Blue Nile. Much of this basin lies below 1000 ft (300 m) in elevation, and in the south it contains the Sudd, one of the world's most extensive marshlands. Here the White Nile divides into numerous distributaries as it penetrates dense masses of floating vegetation; its gradient is reduced to under 140 ft (43 m) over a distance of nearly 800 mi (1250 km).

The western boundary of the Sudan Basin is marked by the Plateau of Darfur and the Ennedi Plateau, and there the crystallines reappear in such prominent landmarks as the Marra Mountains. Still farther

THE PHYSIOGRAPHY OF AFRICA

5

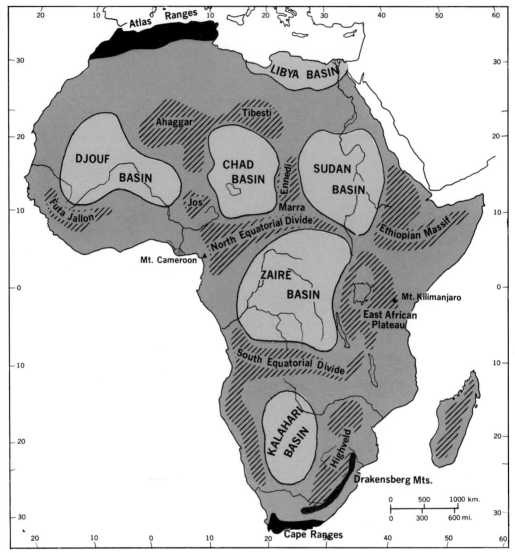

FIGURE 1-2 *Basins and drainage systems.*

to the west lies the Chad Basin, the second of the great northern depressions. The core of the Chad Basin is constituted by the Bodele Depression and Lake Chad. Formerly much more extensive than it is today, Lake Chad has dwindled to a swampy area that is inundated after heavy rains but is being encroached on by Sahara sands from the north. The Chad Basin's northern boundaries are defined quite clearly by the Tibesti Massif and the Ahaggar Mountains. The western boundary is less well expressed, although a southward extension of the Ahaggar reaches close to the plateau of northern Nigeria, the Jos Plateau.

The westernmost of the great basins, the depression of Djouf, occupies the western Sahara Desert and reaches its fullest development in the region along the Mauritania-Mali boundary. It is separated from

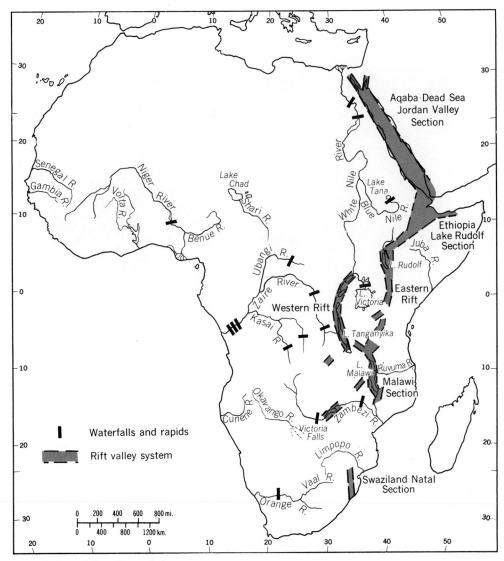

FIGURE 1-3 *Rift valleys and rivers.*

the coast by high ranges such as the Futa Jallon and forms the drainage area for the upper and middle Niger River. The heart of the Djouf Basin (like the other basins, an area of sedimentary accumulation) lies below 500 ft (150 m) in elevation.

Rift Valleys

Although the prevailing scenery in Africa is that of the flat or gently undulating plateau, the surface is broken—often in spectacular fashion—by a great system of troughs that extends from Ethiopia to South Africa (Fig. 1-3). The system's total length

Mt. Mlanje, Malawi. Hard crystalline rocks of the African shield rise above the rift valley floor. (Alan C. G. Best)

exceeds 6000 mi (9600 km), beginning in the north with the Red Sea and extending through the heart of Ethiopia to Lake Rudolf, then dividing into eastern and western segments in East Africa and continuing through Lake Malawi and Swaziland into Natal. These are East Africa's great rift valleys, oriented north–south with subsidiary faults running north–northwest and north–northeast.

It has become clear relatively recently that the African rift valley system is only a part of a worldwide system of such trenches, most of whose length exists beneath the ocean surface. Even so, some unanswered questions remain. The geologist J. W. Gregory, who was the first modern scientist to see East Africa's rifts more than a half century ago, assumed that the strips between the parallel faults had simply dropped down—creating the elongated troughs—as a result of tensional forces in the crust. Later, studies of the forces of gravity prevailing in the rift areas indicated that at least some of the strips did not simply drop down but

were, in fact, being held down by the adjacent plateau mass, so that compressional forces also appeared to be at work. Today, the rift valleys are viewed in the context of plate tectonics, and they may represent the margins of plates moving against each other. What has hitherto been known as sea-floor spreading may be affecting the African landmass along the rifts, and the continent may be in the process of breaking up along those lines of weakness and seismic activity, Madagascar's separation may represent a comparatively advanced stage; the Red Sea a less developed stage; and the interior rifts a third, initial stage.

In spite of their length, the rift valleys over great distances remain remarkably uniform, considering their dimensions. In general the rifts from Lake Rudolf southward are between 20 and 60 mi (30 and 90 km) wide, and the walls, sometimes sheer and sometimes steplike, are well defined. Hence the rift—almost wherever it may be observed, whether in Swaziland, Kenya, or Ethiopia—is unmistakable in appearance.

From the plateau rim, the land falls suddenly to a flat lowland that often possesses climatic and vegetative characteristics quite unlike those above the fault scarp. In the far distance lies the opposite scarp, and the plateau resumes.

The floor of the rift, however, is not quite as uniform. The narrow strip of land that lies depressed between the echelon faults lies far below sea level in some places and thousands of feet above it in others. The degree of variation is expressed especially well in the Western Rift of East Africa, where the floor of Lake Tanganyika is as much as 2140 ft (650 m) below sea level—but some distance to the north the rift floor lies more than 5000 ft (1500 m) *above* sea level.

The association between the rift valleys and the lakes of East Africa is so obvious that it hardly requires emphasis. The lakes of the Western Rift are larger than those of the Eastern segment, but there is evidence that lake levels have fluctuated considerably during geologic time and that the rift lakes were larger than they are at present. Raised beaches and terraces indicate higher stages during the Pleistocene, but elsewhere there is evidence of more recent (perhaps temporary) rise of lake level. In any case, the lake waters are not (not yet, at least) invasions of the ocean. Their saltiness relates to local source areas and rapid evaporation from the surface.

One prominent East African lake, Africa's largest, lies between, not within, the rifts: Lake Victoria, with an area of 24,300 sq mi (63,000 sq km). Lake Victoria is also one of Africa's shallower lakes, under 300 ft (90 m) in depth, and it does not display the attenuated shape of the other larger East African lakes. This is so because Lake Victoria lies in a broad depression rather than a rift valley. The lake's shorelines and adjacent drainage lines reveal that the area was formerly a divide, with rivers flowing eastward to the Indian Ocean and westward into the Zaire (Congo) Basin. Then this broad plateau was depressed, forming the basin now occupied by the lake. Rivers were reversed, and Lake Victoria began to empty northward, feeding the White Nile. A relationship undoubtedly exists between the rift movements (which further disrupted East African drainage patterns) and the formation of the Victoria depression, but the nature of this relationship is still unclear.

Maps of seismic activity and the incidence of volcanoes in Africa reflect another spatial relationship with the rift valley system. East Africa, from Ethiopia to Tanzania, is the continent's great volcanic zone, and while there are extinct and apparently dormant volcanoes, volcanic activity continues in several areas (Fig. 1-4).

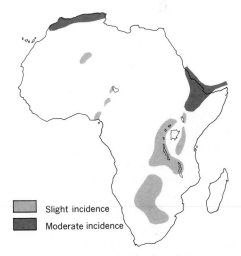

Slight incidence

Moderate incidence

FIGURE 1-4 *Seismic and volcanic activity.*

Outside the East African volcanic region, Mt. Cameroon (13,350 ft, 4000 m) is the largest active volcano in Africa (a recent eruption occurred in 1959). Mt. Cameroon lies near the coast at the point of contact between West and Equatorial Africa, and at the focus of a belt of volcanic activity that extends landward as well as seaward. Offshore, Fernando Po as well as São Tomé and Principe are volcanic islands, and inland there are areas underlain by comparatively recent volcanic rock, which, here as in East Africa, generates poductive soils. Elsewhere, the Ahaggar and Tibesti areas in North Africa also have volcanic origins, and the volcanism continued into the Quaternary. More recently, water and wind erosion have carved the volcanic rocks into jagged shapes reminiscent of moon landscapes.

But the major theater of volcanic activity lies in the east, where crustal instability is greatest. Volcanic mountains arose within the rifts (Mount Longonot, 9111, ft or 2780m), between the rift valleys (Mount Elgon, 14,178 ft or 4320 m), and outside the rift zone (Mount Kilimanjaro). Volcanic activity has continued into very recent times, and Quaternary volcanism produced such peaks as Mount Kenya (17,065 ft or 5200 m) and

Mount Meru (14,979 ft or 4570 m). Pleistocene-age volcanic lavas and ashes overlie strata containing human artifacts, and while the largest volcanoes presently appear dormant or extinct, there is widespread, continuing activity. Mount Meru showed signs of life during the 1870s and Teleki's Volcano, near the southern end of Lake Rudolf (Turkana), in the 1890s. Ol Doinyo L'Engai, near Lake Natron, remains an active volcano, and there has been other activity in recent years in northern Tanzania and western Zaire (in the Kivu region). In addition, local folklore is full of references to events involving volcanic activity, indicating other eruptions during the past several centuries. The East African sector of Africa's crustal plate is obviously under stress.

Africa's Rivers

Several great rivers drain the African continent. The White Nile, with its chief tributary, the Blue Nile, drains the northeast. The Niger, joined in Nigeria by the Benue River, traverses West Africa. The Congo (Zaire) River, with its large Ubangi tributary, flows across equatorial Africa. In Southern Africa, the Zambezi River is the major artery.

A closer look at the map of African drainage lines (Fig. 1-3) reveals that Africa's largest rivers share a number of properties, some of which are easily explained by the plateau nature of the continent, while others appear contrary to what would be expected. The Niger River is a good case in point. On a continental landmass that has been tilted quite strongly to the west, the Niger rises only 175 mi (280 km) from the Atlantic Ocean near its westernmost bulge—and then heads northeastward into the Sahara. As it penetrates the Djouf Basin, the Niger develops a network of distributaries resembling a delta, which eventually unite again into a single channel. The river now traverses the West African interior, turning 90 degrees to

flow southeastward into Nigeria, leaving the Djouf Basin. It plunges over a great falls, is joined by the Benue, and forms a large delta upon entering the Gulf of Guinea.

The course of the Nile River is similarly noteworthy. The White Nile rises in the drainage entering and leaving Lake Victoria, and on entering the Sudan Basin this river also divides into a large number of distributaries; its gradient is reduced to such an extent that, over a distance of 800 mi (1250 km), it drops only 140 ft (43 m). After traversing its vegetation-clogged Sudd, the braided Nile unites again to form a single channel. It is joined by its largest tributary, the Blue Nile (whose source is Lake Tana in Ethiopia), and on its course to the Mediterranean the Nile plunges over a series of cataracts. In the heart of the Sudan Basin the Nile's northward course is interrupted as the channel turns southwest, a direction it sustains for over 150 mi (250 km) before resuming its northward orientation. On the North African coast, the Nile forms the world's most famous delta.

In equatorial Africa, the Zaire River

The Zaire River breaking through the Crystal Mountains, Zaire just east of the Atlantic Ocean. Rapids and waterfalls are common along the river's lower and upper courses. (Sabena)

mirrors several of the peculiarities of the Nile and Niger. The most obvious of these is its course. Rising (as the Lualaba River) on the South Equatorial Divide, the Zaire River actually commences its course by flowing northeastward. It then proceeds northward for more than 600 mi (1000 km) before turning westward in the vicinity of Kisangani. Eventually it turns to the southwest, is joined by its major tributary, the Ubangi River, and cuts through the Crystal Mountains to reach its mouth. Like the Nile, the Zaire River drops over several cataracts and falls, including those in the Crystal Mountains.

Southern Africa's drainage pattern is dominated by the Zambezi River. The Zambezi's history involves also the Okavango and Kwando Rivers, predecessors of the upper Zambezi's shifting traject. The Zam-

bezi rises on the southern slope of the South Equatorial Divide in an area where drainage lines are oriented toward the Kalahari Basin rather than the Indian Ocean coast. The large delta that marked the entry of this drainage into the heart of the depression is still visible in the Okavango Swamp, as is the course that carried the water to the Zambezi's main channel above the Victoria Falls. Following its plunge over the great falls, the river traverses a deep trough now occupied by artificial Lake Kariba, crosses its rapids at Cabora Bassa in the Mozambique proruption, and develops a substantial delta on the Indian Ocean coast north of Beira. It is especially instructive to observe the behavior of the Zambezi River's northern tributary, the Kafue. From the northern Zambia boundary for 250 mi (400 km) the Kafue River flows almost due south, headed directly for the

The Victoria Falls on the Zambezi River. Immediately above the falls the Zambezi is over a mile wide; below, it cuts a deep and narrow trough through the African plateau before developing a delta on the Indian Ocean coast north of Beira, Mozambique. (Harm J. deBlij)

delta in the Okavango Swamp. Then it suddenly abandons that direction (and its course, which can be seen to continue as an empty valley) and turns due eastward, joining the Zambezi as it emerges from the Kariba gorge.

The impression conveyed by these river patterns of the African continent is that the upper courses—above the interior deltas—are oriented toward the great interior basins, while the lower courses appear directed toward existing continental coastlines. This

Aerial view of the Okavango Swamps, northern Botswana. The swamps are part of an old inland delta in the Kalahari Basin. (Alan C. G. Best)

suggestion is reinforced by a study of the rivers' longitudinal profiles: they display clear evidence of a dual genesis, two approximately graded segments separated by falls or a series of rapids. Hence the African rivers at one time appear to have entered waters that stood in the great interior basins as huge interior lakes or seas; as they did so, they formed deltas whose remnants still are visible on the map. Nor have the lakes that once filled the basins entirely disappeared: in the swampy Sudd, in Lake Chad, in the Okavango area, and in Lake Mai Ndombe (formerly Lake Leopold II) their remnants survive. When the interior lake waters were released, they rushed out along the courses of the lower segments of Niger, Nile, Zaire, and Zambezi, and in the process they carved the falls and rapids that interrupt the continent's natural waterways. As will be seen later, Africa's rivers are keys to the interpretation of Africa's past.

Mountain Ranges

From what has been said about Africa's plateau character, it should not be surprising to find that the continent is poorly endowed with linear mountains of Andean or Himalayan dimensions. Nevertheless, the world distribution of such mountain chains and their virtual absence in Africa—a landmass comprising one-fifth of the earth's land area—raises still another question in addition to those already posed by rifts, basins, rivers, and interior deltas. Every other continent is associated with a mountain backbone: South America's Andes, North America's Rocky Mountains, Europe's Alps, Asia's Himalayas, and even plateau-dominated Australia with its Great Dividing Range. No African equivalent exists; the Atlas ranges in the northwest are extensions of the trans-

The Cape Ranges, South Africa. With the Atlas Mountains of North Africa, the Cape Ranges represent the only major folded mountains in Africa. (Alan C. G. Best)

Eurasian Alpine system and occupy a mere corner of the continent. The other, much older linear mountains in Africa lie at the Cape, in South Africa. Again, the Cape Ranges are no match for an Andes or a Himalayas.

What Africa lacks, of course, is *not* mountainous topography, but fold-mountains of structural equivalence to those of the other continents. Africa's mountainous to-pography (reflected in regional identities old and new: *Abyss*inia, *Sierra* Leone, *Drakensberg*, *Kilima*njaro) owes its origins mainly to uplift and differential erosion of ancient rocks and to volcanic activity, and much less to the compression and folding of younger sedimentaries. East Africa's highlands, from Ethiopia to South Africa, are sustained by ancient crystallines, old, lava-capped sedimentaries, and volcanics.

Africa Forms the Key

It has been well over a half century since Alfred Wegener gave substance to the idea of continental drift in his book *The Origins of Continents and Oceans* (English translation, 1924), and 40 years since Alex du Toit, following in Wegener's footsteps, published *Our Wandering Continents* (1937). Wegener fo-cused attention on the jigsawlike fit of opposing Atlantic coastlines, notably between Africa and South America, and Du Toit produced a mass of evidence to support a former assembly not only of Africa and South America, but of the other landmasses of Gondwana as well (Fig. 1-5). On the fron-

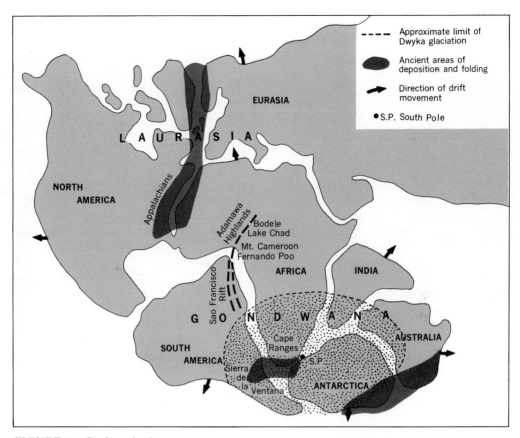

FIGURE 1-5 *Gondwanaland.*

tispiece of his volume, Du Toit states that "Africa Forms the Key."

This reference is to the surface characteristics of Africa just described, and to subsurface properties not yet enumerated. Only one hypothesis, Du Toit reasoned, could at once account for all the qualities of the African landscape: the marginal escarpment, the plateau shield (Africa lay at the heart of Gondwana), the great interior basins, filling with sediments as the rivers flowed into growing landlocked seas, the inland deltas. As Gondwana fractured and the pieces of the jigsaw puzzle began to drift away, Africa acquired its scarp-dominated coastlines, the interior seas emptied through river channels and carved gorges and falls in the process. Eventually the process of breakup affected the crystallines of the plateau itself as the rift

valleys revealed the lines of weakness, first with the separation of Madagascar, later in interior East Africa proper. Volcanic outpourings marked the original dismemberment of Gondwana; volcanism continued into recent times as crustal weakness in East Africa was evinced.

If there is indeed an essential unity to continental Africa's physiography, a unity attributable to Africa's central position to Gondwana, then the landmass should provide additional evidence for the reassembly in related contexts: in subsurface geology and the fossil record, in the distribution of mineral resources, in geomorphology and erosion surfaces, and in external structural and stratigraphic associations. And certainly the geological sequence supplies the ingredients for such a test. While Gondwana existed, a large basin of sedimentary accumulation developed, extending across Southern Africa, Madagascar, areas of southern South America, and parts of India. Two phases of accumulation are especially significant: first, a period of glaciation that witnessed the development of large ice sheets whose evidence exists in Africa as well as the other fragments of Gondwana; and second, a subsequent, deep sedimentary accumulation that concluded with the outpouring of basaltic lavas that still sustain not only South Africa's Drakensberg, but also India's Deccan Plateau and highlands in South America and Madagascar.

The Dwyka glaciation occurred during the beginning of Gondwana's last 100 million years of existence, and the ice sheets surrounded a polar core that appears to have been located not far off the southeast African coast (Fig. 1-5). They scoured the Gondwana crystalline subsurface and deposited hundreds of feet of tillite, leaving widespread evidence for their distribution. This ice age provides one of the most convincing pieces of evidence for Gondwana's former unity, for its spatial properties are easily accounted for in the context of the reassembled continents, as Figure 1-5 shows. Following this glacial age, a lengthy period of sedimentary deposition began, and we can interpret the environmental conditions that prevailed from the color and content of the accumulated strata. Southern Africa became progressively drier, and the sediments of the great Kalahari Basin were laid down as well as those of the even deeper Karroo Basin farther to the south and east; in the Karroo Basin some 25,000 ft (7600 m) of sediments were deposited, until the breakup of Gondwana was signaled by the huge fissure eruptions that built the Drakensberg, the Deccan, and much of ice-covered Antarctica.

Gondwana's fossil record provides ample evidence for the supercontinent's former existence, but perhaps none is more dramatic than that involving Madagascar and Southern Africa. Madagascar's paleontology is similar to that of southeast Africa until the Cretaceous, but with the separation begins a growing contrast that is pervasive today. Though only a matter of hundreds of miles from Africa, Madagascar today has no carnivores (lions, leopards, cheetahs) and no poisonous snakes (mambas, puff adders); it does, however, have marsupials not found on mainland Africa at all.

The distribution of prominent structural features in Gondwana still is imprinted on the continental fragments today. South Africa's Cape Ranges have their equivalent in Argentina, numerous fault lines and other linear features found in Africa continue in South America, and the Karroo depositional sequence is mirrored in Madagascar and, less perfectly, in India and Antarctica. One of the most interesting continuities begins in the Bodele Depression in the Sahara, continues through Lake Chad and the Adamawa Highlands to Mount Cameroon and to the volcanic islands in the Gulf of Guinea. These features lie in a nearly straight line—a line that may be seen to continue in South America in the São Francisco river valley, a rift feature. From the seismic incidence and volcanic activity in West Africa it may be concluded that the landmass may be in the process of breaking open there; the São Francisco rift in South America may signal the first phase of a Madagascarlike breakoff as well. The map suggests it (Fig. 1-5).

The distribution of African mineral resources should also be viewed in the context of the continent's position in Gondwana. Africa's mineral-rich backbone begins in southeast Zaire, then continues through Zambia's Copperbelt and Rhodesia's (Zimbabwe's) Great Dyke and includes the South African Bushveld Basin, where platinum and chromium occur, the Witwatersrand and Orange Free State gold fields, and the diamond areas that extend to Kimberley in the Republic's Cape Province. Diamonds that are thought to be of African origin have been found in sedimentary strata in South America, and the Transvaal and Rhodesian (Zimbabwean) coal fields form part of a belt that extends from southern Brazil to central India.

Africa's geomorphology, notably its cyclic erosion surfaces, has proven to be strongly associated with the drift sequence. After the extrusion of the basalts that covered much of Southern Africa, parts of India and South America, and a large segment of Antarctica as well, a period of erosion flattened the landscape and created the Gondwana erosion surface (King, 1957). The surface cuts across ancient crystallines and other rock strata as well as the basalts. Remnants of the surface can still be observed on uplands in Lesotho, Ethiopia, Angola, eastern Brazil, and western India. Subsequent to the fragmentation of Gondwana, the drifting landmasses experienced a sequence of cycles of erosion that are reflected in extensive erosion surfaces. Thus the formation of the African surface, a Late Tertiary phase, destroyed (through slope retreat) most of the previously formed Gondwana surface. The African surface also is extensive in Brazil, India, and Australia (King, 1951). Another Late Tertiary surface (also called the Victoria Falls cycle) began to invade the African surface, and the most recent or Quaternary surface is still of very limited areal extent. Importantly, Figure 1-6 shows both the degradational (erosional) and aggradational (depositional) arenas of these cycles.

In all this it was Africa—the heart of the African tectonic plate—that was positioned in the center of Gondwana, the only continent-to-be that possessed no outer coastline, a vast region of internal drainage whose endorheic streams filled expanding basins of deposition, basins that became huge interior seas. As the drift (or "spreading") process dismembered Gondwana, Africa began to acquire its modern physiography, but, unlike South America, India, and Australia, Africa's lateral or radial movement was comparatively slight, a circumstance that may help explain the absence of a world-scale linear mountain chain.

The African physiographic map, which was Du Toit's key interpretive element in his analysis of Gondwana's former unity, suggests that our present interpretation of a major, single African tectonic plate may be premature. In any case, it suggests that "seafloor spreading," the current appellation for the drift process, is a misnomer. The globe-girdling system of midocean ridges, the magma-producing rifts that form the foci of crustal divergence, commenced as fractures across the Gondwana landmass; only after the fragments began to drift away and intervening area widened did ocean water invade as the newly formed, separating crust became "sea-floor." The African map may once again provide the crucial insight: it appears to reveal several stages in the "crustal spreading" process (as it is better designated). Oldest is the stage that began along the Mid-Atlantic Ridge perhaps 125 million years ago and that has caused Africa and South America to diverge several thousand kilometers. The Madagascar separation suggests a more recent stage, and the Red Sea rift is just the beginning of what will eventually be a wide portion of ocean. East Africa's rift system probably resembles what the Africa-America contact looked like just before separation began, and this is a still-younger stage than that of the Red Sea. And that linear zone extending from the Bodele Depression through Lake Chad and the Adamawa Highlands to Mount Cameroon and the islands in the Gulf of Guinea could be a preliminary to the whole process. The so-called African Plate in global tectonics may consist, the physiographic map suggests, of several plates.

Africa's particular position in Gondwana, central to that landmass as it is today to the land hemisphere, accounts for the essential unity of the continent's physiography. It is no accident that the course charac-

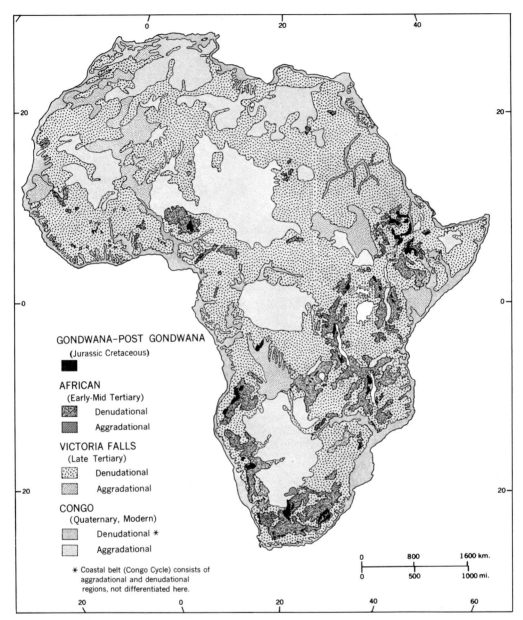

GONDWANA–POST GONDWANA
(Jurassic Cretaceous)

AFRICAN
(Early-Mid Tertiary)
　　Denudational
　　Aggradational

VICTORIA FALLS
(Late Tertiary)
　　Denudational
　　Aggradational

CONGO
(Quaternary, Modern)
　　Denudational *
　　Aggradational

* Coastal belt (Congo Cycle) consists of
　aggradational and denudational
　regions, not differentiated here.

0 ── 800 ── 1600 km.
0 ── 500 ── 1000 mi.

FIGURE 1-6 *Erosional surfaces.*

teristics and genetics of the Niger River resemble those of the Zambezi, or that rift scenery in Swaziland resembles that of Ethiopia, or that an erosion surface in South Africa is similar to one in Nigeria. Perhaps no other landmass on earth still carries so faithfully the imprint of its distant past.

Bibliography

Allard, G. O., and V. J. Hurst, "Brazil-Gabon Link Supports Continental Drift," *Science*, Vol. 163 (February, 1969), pp. 528–32.

De Blij, H. J. "Continental Drift and Present Landscapes," *Journal of Geography*, Vol. 73, No. 5 (May, 1974), pp. 24–44.

Du Toit, A. L. *Our Wandering Continents*. London: Oliver and Boyd, 1937.

Falcon, N. L., et. al. *A Discussion of the Structure and Evolution of the Red Sea and the Nature of the Red Sea, Gulf of Aden and Ethiopian Rift Junction*, Royal Society of London, Philosophical Transactions, Series A, Vol. 267, 1970.

Furon, R. *Geology of Africa*. Edinburgh: Oliver and Boyd, 1963.

Gregory, J. W. *The Rift Valleys and Geology of East Africa*. London: Seeley, Service and Co., 1921.

Hallam, A. "Alfred Wegener and the Hypothesis of Continental Drift," *Scientific American*, Vol. 232, No. 2 (February, 1975), pp. 88–97.

King, L. C. "A Geomorphological Comparison Between Eastern Brazil and Africa," *Geological Society of London Quarterly Journal*, Vol. CXII (1957), pp. 445–70.

———. *South African Scenery*. Edinburgh: Oliver and Boyd, 1963.

———. *Morphology of the Earth*. New York: Dutton, 1967.

Marvin, U. *Continental Drift*. New York: McGraw-Hill, 1971.

Mohr, P. A. "Major Volcanic-Tectonic Lineament in the Ethiopian Rift System," *Nature*, Vol. 213 (February, 1967), pp. 664–65.

Smith, A., and A. Hallam, "The Fit of the Southern Continents," *Nature*, Vol. 225 (January, 1970), pp. 139–44.

Sullivan, W. *Continents in Motion*. New York: McGraw-Hill Book Co., 1974.

Tarling, D. H., and M. P. Tarling. *Continental Drift: a Study of the Earth's Moving Surface*. New York: Doubleday, 1971.

Wegener, A. (translated by John Biram). *The Origins of the Continents and Oceans*. London: Methuen, 1967.

Wellington, J. *Southern Africa* (Vol. I, Physical Geography), Cambridge University Press, 1955.

Wilson, J. T. *Continents Adrift*. San Francisco: Freeman, 1970.

TWO

Africa straddles the equator, and much of it lies in the tropics. Consequently, the image most often associated with Africa is one of heat and humidity, and over a large part of the continent this impression is verified by the facts. The absence of any lengthy mountain chains or other weather divides permits a free circulation of tropical air over the continent, so that, in general, changes in climate from one place to another occur very gradually. This does not mean that there is little diversity. Because of the elevation and extent of the African plateau, the escarpment that forms its rim, the narrow coastal belt, and the ocean currents along the shores, there is variation, although perhaps not as much in temperature as in precipitation.

Figure 2-1 shows mean annual rainfall is highest in low Equatorial Africa, along the Guinea Coast, in the highlands of Ethiopia and Madagascar, and on parts of the East African Plateau. In these regions the mean annual rainfall generally exceeds 56 in. (1400 mm); however parts of the Cameroon Highlands receive over 300 in. (7620 mm), and Freetown (Sierra Leone) has an average annual rainfall of 157 in. (3988 mm). Mean annual rainfall is lowest in the Sahara and Namib deserts, and parts of Somalia and Ethiopia. For example, the mean annual rainfall at Khartoum is only 5 in. (127 mm), and on the Namibian coast at Swakopmund it is under an inch (25 mm). These same desert regions experience the highest variability of rainfall (Fig. 2-2).

Much of Africa has distinct wet and dry seasons: the northern and southern extremities record winter maximums; the savanna areas have a pronounced summer maximum; while the rainforest regions have a more even distribution of rain through the year. Figure 2-3 shows that in January the mean monthly precipitation is highest south of the equator, especially in Malagasy, Zaire, and

CLIMATES
OF
AFRICA

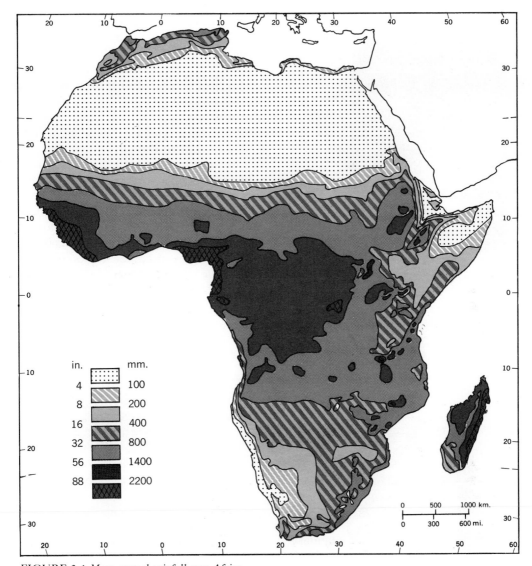

FIGURE 2-1 *Mean annual rainfall over Africa.*

Zambia, and that there is a narrow belt of rainfall along the Mediterranean coast. In July rainfall is heaviest north of the equator, especially in Ethiopia and along the Guinea Coast.

Variations also exist in temperature regimes, although in general the extremes are not as great. Interior desert regions experience the greatest temperature ranges. For example, the mean January and July temper-

atures of the town of In Salah, Algeria, are 56° F (13.3° C) and 99° F (37° C), respectively. The average daily maximum in July is 117° F (47° C), while the nighttime temperatures in winter drop below freezing. Throughout the Sahara the mean July temperature is above 80° F (26.6° C), while in winter the mean temperature ranges from 55° F (12.7° C) along the Mediterranean coast to 70° F (21° C) along the southern

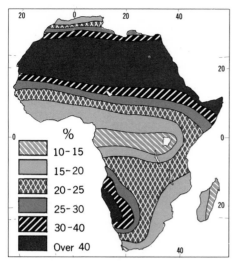
FIGURE 2-2 *Rainfall variability over Africa.*

border. In contrast in low equatorial Africa the average monthly temperatures throughout the year are about 75° F to 80° F (24°–27° C). Elevation has a modifying effect on temperature, and, since many eastern and southern areas are above 3000 ft (914 m), their temperatures are not as high as might be expected given their tropical location. On the East African Plateau, for example, Nairobi's (elevation 5450 ft–1661 m) mean July temperature is 58.5° F (14.4° C) while that of the port of Lagos, which is at the same general latitude, is 78° F (25.5° C). In the Ethiopian Highlands, Inyanga Mountains of Rhodesia (Zimbabwe), and other highland areas within the tropics, winter frosts are not uncommon.

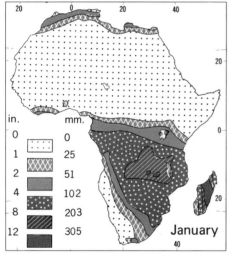
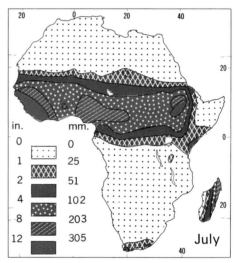
FIGURE 2-3 *Mean monthly precipitation—January and July.*

Pressure, Air Masses, and Fronts

These basic rainfall and temperature patterns are affected by permanent and semipermanent pressure systems and their associated winds and air masses. Locational changes in the pressure systems bring changes in the amount and distribution of rainfall and the intensity of heat. In January, the southern hemisphere tropical anti-

cyclones are situated at about 30° S in both the Atlantic and Indian Oceans, and the equatorial low pressure belt has shifted to the south and is linked with a weak thermal heat low of the Kalahari. Thus the entire continent south of the equator is under the influence of low pressure systems during this high-sun period, while high pressure pre-

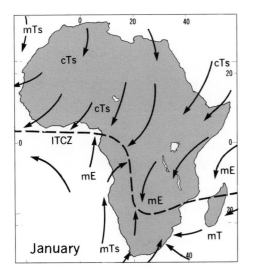
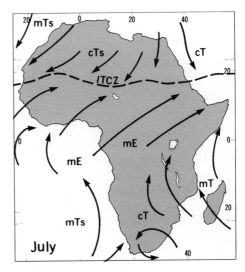

Air Masses

cT = Continental Tropical

cTs = Continental Tropical (subsident)

mT = Maritime Tropical

mTs = Maritime Tropical (subsident)

mE = Maritime Equatorial

FIGURE 2-4 *Air masses, winds, and the intertropical convergence zone—January and July.*

dominates north of the equator. In July, the pattern is essentially reversed. High pressure extends across southern Africa and the adjoining Atlantic and Indian Oceans, while an intense thermal low is situated over the Sahara to which is linked another low pressure system over southwest Asia. These conditions result in two distinct seasonal air circulation patterns across Africa (Fig. 2-4).

In January the circulation north of the equator is circular around the anticyclone, that is from the north and northeast to the south, and across the equator in the eastern regions. Along the South Atlantic coast however, the flow is around the South Atlantic anticyclone and from the south toward the equator. In July, the wind flow across Africa north of latitude 20° N is from the northeast, but the dominant flow across the rest of Africa is from south to north. Once the winds cross the equator they are drawn

in a northeasterly direction toward the low pressure areas of the Arabian peninsula.

Several types of air masses are associated with these circulation systems and play important roles in the precipitation regimes and distributions. Most of the air masses are tropical. Continental tropical (cT) air originates in the upper levels of the atmosphere above the Sahara and Kalahari deserts, and brings very dry and warm conditions to the surface in its descent. Subsident maritime tropical (mTs) air originates in the eastern sectors of the Azores and South Atlantic anticyclone cells, and it too is dry and stable. It controls the climates of Mauritania and Morocco, and the coastal areas of Namibia and southern Angola. A similar air mass dominates the Somalian coastlands although it may also be modified by continental tropical air from Asia. As the maritime tropical (mT) air masses pass over the oceans, they gather moisture, become unstable, and then appear as maritime equatorial (mE) air masses. The subsident maritime tropical air masses on the east side of the South Atlantic anticyclone cell, for example, become warmer, moister, and unstable as they are drawn toward the equatorial low pressure areas along the Guinea Coast. With uplift they can give heavy rains on reaching land, such as in the Cameroon Highlands and the Futa Jallon. Similarly, the maritime tropical air masses originating in the South Indian Ocean can bring heavy rains as they ascend eastern Madagascar and the mainland's southeast coast.

When two different types of air masses converge, a front is formed, along which there can be unsettled weather. In the mid-latitudes, frontal activity is common where cold and warm air masses meet. In the Mediterranean regions, and along the South African coast, there are frequent fronts during the winter months as modified polar air meets warmer tropical air. Cloudy and rainy conditions prevail, followed by clearing. In tropical Africa, however, the nature, extent, and frequency of frontal activity are still not certain, but most climatologists agree that the most important is associated with the Intertropical Convergence Zone (ITCZ).

Wet Equatorial Climates (Af and Am)

A large part of equatorial Africa from the Zaire Basin west along the Guinea Coast to Guinea, has tropical humid or wet equatorial climates (Fig. 2-6). In the eastern sections the climate is known as tropical rainforest (Af). There the seasons pass virtually unnoticed as the unbroken monotony of hot, humid rainy days is only slightly ameliorated by the nightly drop in temperatures of about 15° F (9.4° C). Even so, "night is the winter in the tropics," for the annual temperature range (the difference between the means for the warmest and coolest months) is less than the daily range. Tropical rainforest climate is characterized by continuously high temperatures, no month below 68° F (20° C), and an annual rainfall

exceeding 50 in. (1270) mm) without any dry season. Temperature and rainfall data for Barumbu, Zaire, a typical tropical rainforest station, are shown in Table 2-1.

Like most rainforest stations, Barumbu receives heavy rains each month, although there is a distinct period of maximum precipitation (Fig. 2-7a). In several places, because of the migration of the heat equator and associated features (e.g., the ITCZ), there is a double maximum of rainfall. Throughout much of the rainforest regions, there are frequent, almost daily, late afternoon thundershowers derived from heat-of-day thermal convection. The heaviest falls are found where mountains force the unstable air to rise, as in the Cameroon Moun-

Table 2-1 TEMPERATURE AND RAINFALL DATA, RAINFOREST (Af)

	J	F	M	A	M	J	J	A	S	O	N	D	Year
BARUMBU, ZAIRE (1378 FT–420 M)													
° F	77.5	78	78.5	79	78	77.5	76.5	76.5	77	76.5	76.5	76.5	77
In.	2.8	3.5	5.6	7.0	6.1	5.7	6.9	6.5	7.3	8.1	7.2	4.1	70.8
ENTEBBE, UGANDA (3863 FT–1177 M)													
° F	71.1	71.1	71.3	70.3	69.8	69.4	68.6	68.6	69.4	70.1	70.1	70.2	70.0
In.	2.6	3.6	5.8	9.7	8.5	5.1	2.9	3.1	3.1	3.5	5.0	5.1	58.0

The ITCZ oscillates north and south across Africa between latitudes 20° N and 20° S. In July it extends across the continent at the southern margins of the Sahara, although its position varies considerably from year to year. In January it parallels the Guinea Coast at about 5° N and then turns sharply southward to about 20° S from where it trends northeast across Rhodesia to northern Madagascar. Its irregular movement is of critical importance since rainfall is associated with the front.

In July the ITCZ represents the boundary between the hot, dry Saharan air of anticyclonic origin and the cooler maritime equatorial air from the south. The hotter, more stable, and less dense air of the Sahara is forced to rise at a low angle of inclination over the cooler, moister air from the south (Fig. 2-5). But the dry and stable Saharan air precludes the development of precipitation as it rises; the underlying moister air becomes drier as it moves north. Cumulus clouds that may develop are soon desiccated as they break into the overriding Saharan air, so that little or no rain falls as the front advances. However, further to the south, where the maritime air is sufficiently deep to allow the development of cumulonimbus clouds, heavy rains may occur.

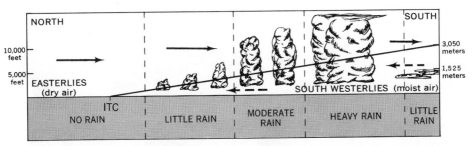

FIGURE 2-5 *Cross section of the ITCZ in Africa—July.*

The ITCZ, therefore, does not resemble midlatitudinal warm or cold fronts that frequently bring rain. Its behavior is less predictable than the cyclonic fronts of the westerlies. Its migration is the result of contrasts in strength between the humid and dry air masses, and in West Africa its frequent failure to move northward, preventing the penetration of moist air inland, is a prime cause of unreliable precipitation only short distances from the coast. In East Africa, the ITCZ forms the zone of convergence between air masses flowing in from the northeast and southeast. Here, however, its movement is restricted and modified by the high plateaus, and it has proved a far less useful tool for the interpretation of weather phenomena and for predicting rainfall than in West Africa.

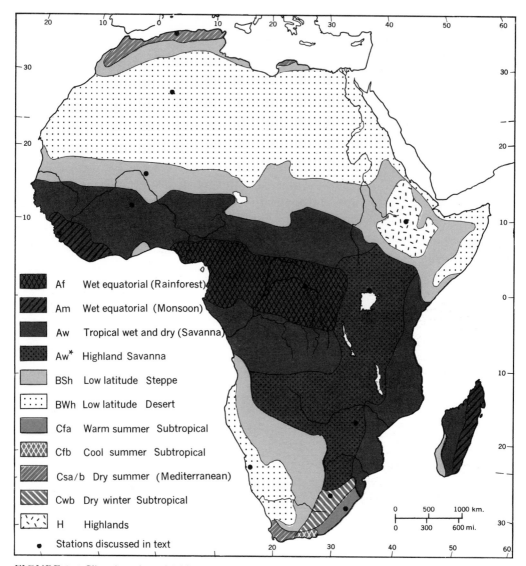

FIGURE 2-6 *Climatic regions of Africa.*

tains. It is a common misconception that the hottest temperature recorded are those of the tropics. In fact, in the tropical rainforest areas, daytime temperatures rarely rise above 100° F (37.7° C); they are usually about 84–86° F (30° C).

In the region of the Zaire Basin, two major air circulations have been recognized as important in creating the conditions described above. There is a constant inflow of maritime equatorial (mE) air from the south-

west, while the trade winds blow in from the northeast. Because of the higher elevations east of the Zaire Basin, tropical rainforest conditions do not extend to the Indian Ocean, but parts of southern Uganda have a modified rainforest climate. Entebbe, Uganda, for example, has the characteristically small annual range of temperature, but the warmest month averages only 71° F (21.6° C) (see Table 2-1 and Fig. 2-7b). Like Barumbu, its rainfall is heavy and there are

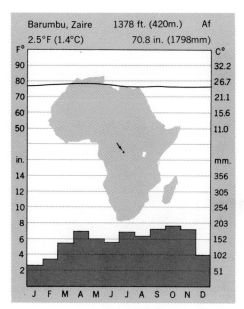

FIGURE 2-7a *Barumbu, Zaire. Tropical rainforest (Af).*

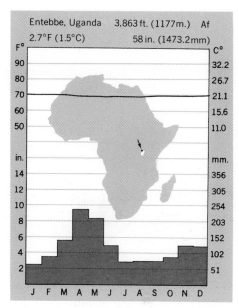

FIGURE 2-7b *Entebbe, Uganda. Tropical rainforest (Af).*

two peaks—one in April–May, and the other in November–December.

Towards the western end of the Guinea Coast, and along the Madagascar escarpment, there are narrow zones of monsoon climate (Am) (Fig. 2-6). There the annual rainfall is heavy, but there is a marked dry season and a very pronounced wet season. Freetown, Sierra Leone, has a monsoon climate. Its dry season extends from December through March when less than 4 in. (100 mm) of rain are recorded, while from June through September over 120 in. (3048 mm) of rain falls (Table 2-2). Monthly temperatures throughout the year are above 78° F (25.5° C), the highest occurring immediately before and after the heavy rains (Fig. 2-8). At Tamatave, Malagasy, the monsoon rains begin in December and extend through March, the high-sun period in the southern hemisphere, but the dry season is less pronounced than in West Africa. In both regions there is orographic precipitation as

FIGURE 2-8 *Freetown, Sierra Leone. Monsoon (Am).*

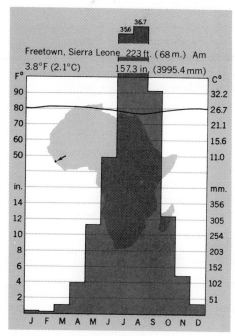

	J	F	M	A	M	J	J	A	S	O	N	D	Year
°F	81.3	82.3	82.4	82.4	81.5	80.3	78.6	77.9	79.1	80.1	81.2	81.4	80.7
In.	0.4	0.3	1.2	4.1	11.5	20.0	35.6	36.6	28.5	12.6	5.1	1.4	157.3

the moist air masses cross from the oceans onto the plateaus, but there is also thermal convectional rainfall and rainfall associated with fluctuations in the ITCZ.

Tropical Wet-and-Dry Climate (Aw)

On either side of the wet equatorial climates, lies one of the most widespread and distinctive African climates known as the tropical wet-and-dry, or savanna climate (Fig. 2-6). The major difference between rainforest and savanna conditions lies not so much in temperature as in the amount and distribution of precipitation. Temperature conditions show a slightly greater annual range that is usually less than 15° F (9° C). At Ouagadougou, Upper Volta, for example, the mean annual temperature range is 13° F (10° C) and the hottest month is April (Table 2-3 and Fig. 2-9a). Daily maximums at this time of year average 107° F (41.6° C).

Total annual precipitation is considerably less than in the wet equatorial areas and there is a distinct dry and wet season. At Ouagadougou, and throughout the savanna belt of West Africa, the rainy season corresponds with the high-sun period beginning generally in May and terminating in September. Rainfall becomes lighter and more variable with distance from the equator. There is no sharp break between the wet equatorial and tropical wet-and-dry areas, so that the inner margins of the latter resemble the rainforest. The heart of the savanna, nonetheless, displays seasonally dry conditions that are absent from the wet rainforest.

There are three general areas of tropical wet-and-dry climate (Fig. 2-6). The first lies north of the rainforest in West Africa, and extends from Senegal to the southern Sudan. There, rainfall decreases appreciably from south to north. During the dry winter months, the Harmattan winds blow from northeast to southwest, whereas in summer tropical maritime air is transported inland from the southwest. The second region lies south of the Zaire Basin and covers much of the Bihé Plateau. The third, and largest, zone occupies the eastern highlands and coastal areas from Kenya to the South African border. Since a large portion of the East Africa savanna lies at considerable elevations, temperatures are generally lower than in the West Africa savanna belt. At Salisbury, Rhodesia (Zimbabwe), for instance, situated at an elevation of 4900 ft (1494 m) and well within the tropics, the mean annual temperature is 65.3° F (18.4° C), and the warmest month averages only 70.7° F (21.6° C). Its rainfall regime, however, is typically savanna (Table 2-4 and Fig. 2-9b).

Table 2-3 TEMPERATURE AND RAINFALL DATA, SAVANNA (Aw) OUAGADOUGOU,
UPPER VOLTA (991 FT–302 M)

	J	F	M	A	M	J	J	A	S	O	N	D	Year
°F	77.5	82.3	87.4	90.4	87.8	83.5	80.6	78.8	80.0	84.2	83.3	78.2	82.8
In.	0.0	0.1	0.6	0.8	3.1	5.3	8.4	10.4	5.6	1.0	0.0	0.0	35.3

Harmattan

During the winter months, the coastal regions of West Africa are influenced by northeasterly winds emanating from the subtropical high-pressure region over the Sahara Desert. The excessively moist conditions of the coasts are driven away, to be replaced by the dry, often cool air from the interior. Relative humidity percentages may drop to between 10 and 20, skies clear, and the general effect is one of relief for the inhabitants. Known as the *Harmattan*, this outflow of air may be strong and very persistent, affecting not only the coastal regions but continuing far out into the Gulf of Guinea.

While bringing relief to the coasts, the Harmattan is often hot, dust-laden, and stifling in the steppe interior. Its effect on man, animals, and vegetation can be disastrous when its reign is unbroken for long spells. Swirling dust storms and severe droughts occur, and the failure of vegetation and consequent overgrazing result in destruction of the vulnerable grass cover and much-feared desert encroachment.

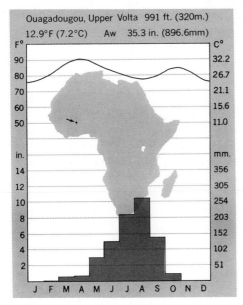

FIGURE 2-9a *Ouagadougou, Upper Volta. Savanna (Aw).*

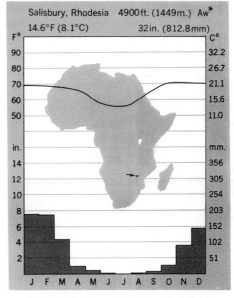

FIGURE 2-9b *Salisbury, Rhodesia (Zimbabwe). Highland savanna (Aw).*

Table 2-4 TEMPERATURE AND RAINFALL DATA, HIGHLAND SAVANNA SALISBURY, RHODESIA (4900 FT–1394 M)

	J	F	M	A	M	J	J	A	S	O	N	D	Year
°F	69.7	68.8	68.2	65.7	60.6	56.9	56.1	60.2	66.4	70.7	70.7	69.6	65.3
In.	7.5	7.4	4.5	1.0	0.5	0.1	0.0	0.1	0.3	1.1	3.7	5.8	32.0

Mudcracks in an intermittent stream in Senegal, West Africa, an area of recurrent droughts and prolonged dry seasons. (UN)

The air masses that affect this part of Africa originate in three separate areas. In the heart of savanna East Africa, the annual migration of the wind and pressure belts is reflected by the alternation of northerly winds (during the period from October to March, the Southern Hemisphere summer) and southeasterlies (during the Northern Hemisphere summer). In addition, there is an occasional westerly component, carrying air from the South Atlantic Ocean across the Zaire Basin and into the eastern highlands.

Thus, the air reaching the eastern part of Africa from South Africa to southern Ethiopia would appear to possess all the characteristics favorable to precipitation, and yet relatively little rainfall is recorded. Several factors might explain this apparently anomalous situation. As is indicated below, there are reasons to believe that the inflow of air from the northeast as well as the southeast takes place in a rather thin layer, above which there is air that is much drier. In the case of South Africa, the trades that hit the

Great Escarpment may have a vertical extent of less than 10,000 ft (3000 m) and thus fail to cover the interior highlands. In East Africa also, the air mass would have to be of great depth in order to carry much moisture onto the plateau. Of course, if there is indeed a drier layer of air overlying the trade-wind layer, the vertical development of clouds and, consequently, the rainfall would be inhibited.

In addition, attention has focused on the actual path of these "monsoon" winds from the east. Actually, the northeast trades have traveled great distances across land rather than water; some of the air flowing in from the north has moved around the western side of the Ethiopian Plateau. Those winds coming from the northeast travel parallel rather than into the land, and this has the effect of reducing the precipitation. The moister air flowing in from the south has moved long distances across warm water but, as it approaches the coast, its trajectory too, becomes more meridional. If these air masses struck the coast at right angles, considerable precipitation would result. Their paths, however, appear to be among the causes underlying East Africa's rainfall deficiency.

Surface divergence and subsidence of air also create dry conditions. This situation appears to prevail over much of the eastern savanna land of Africa, and it is a contributing factor in the picture of dryness. Possibly the island of Madagascar affects the mainland. It is high, with a steep eastern slope directly in the path of the southeast trades. Indeed, Madagascar's eastern escarpment shows the sort of precipitation to be expected in windward equatorial regions (around 100 in. or 2540 mm annually). But western Madagascar receives less than 30 in. (762 mm) over extensive areas, and a large part of the African continent lies in the lee of the great island mass. There, the winds become more meridional, the air subsiding and divergent, and again the situation is one of rainfall deficiency.

Exactly what does produce the rainfall on the savanna lands of eastern Africa is still uncertain. Nairobi (40 in./1016 mm) and Dar es Salaam (45 in./1143 mm) are near the lower limit of savanna moisture conditions, and yet one city lies in what would appear to be an orographically favorable position, and the other is on the coast. It is much less easy in these areas to trace the effect of zones of convergence than it is in West Africa. Lines of disturbance have been noted forming in the air mass when it is still over the ocean, and these then move toward the coast in a west-northwesterly direction. Since a situation seems to prevail that is not entirely dissimilar to that recorded in West Africa (a moist lower layer overlain by a drier air mass), the disturbance may similarly be of the character of an easterly wave. It is also possible that surges of air from the south, invading the southeasterlies, produce the disturbance recorded. In the interior, the western part of East Africa's plateau may be affected by invasions of air from the Zaire Basin and, ultimately, the South Atlantic Ocean. Finally, the great South African anticyclone may influence the weather of the savanna lands of East Africa.

Low-Latitude Steppe (BSh) and Tropical Desert (BWh)

Africa's low-latitude steppes lie on the drier margins of the savanna, and in a narrow band north of the Sahara (Fig. 2-6). The steppe zone that extends across the continent south of the Sahara is known as the *Sahel* (Arabic for "border"). This region suffered a four- to six-year drought in the 1960–1970s when an estimated five million head of livestock and 300,000 persons perished for lack of water and food. Recurrent drought is a feature of Africa's steppelands, and as long as the human and livestock populations grow at their present rates, the consequences will be catastrophic. In the Sahel, overgrazing, poor groundwater management, and continuous cultivation of the land without rotation have produced dustbowl conditions and desert encroachment. The steppelands are not devoid of tree growth, and particularly in the Kalahari, a thorny acacia manages to survive on the generally poor and shallow soils. Its existence is of great importance to the cattlemen, for without the shade trees, the cattle would not survive.

The steppe is characterized by light and unreliable precipitation, dry, warm winters, and very hot summers. Average annual precipitation rarely exceeds 20 in. (508 mm) and because evapotranspiration rates are high, the effectiveness of even this moderate amount is reduced. The rain is almost always concentrated in the high-sun season, with the winter period being extremely dry. At Gao, for example (Table 2-5 and Fig. 2-

Table 2-5 TEMPERATURE AND RAINFALL DATA, STEPPE (BSh) GAO, MALI (902 FT–275M)

	J	F	M	A	M	J	J	A	S	O	N	D	Year
°F	72.9	76.1	84.2	90.0	94.4	95.0	89.8	85.7	88.6	90.2	83.3	75.1	85.4
In.	0.0	0.0	0.1	0.3	0.6	1.2	3.0	3.8	1.5	0.4	0.0	0.0	10.9

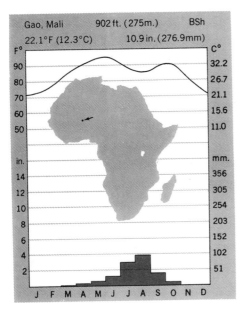

FIGURE 2-10 *Gao, Mali. Steppe (BSh).*

Five years of subnormal rainfall brought severe drought and widespread starvation to the Sahelian states of West Africa during the late 1960s. The amount of rainfall received depends in part on the position of the Intertropical Convergence Zone (ITCZ). (UN/FAO)

10), almost all the rain falls between June and September, and during this period the daily maximums are over 100° F (37° C), so that evaporation rates are high. Even during the cooler drier season the daily maximums are approximately 90° F (32.2° C).

Adjoining the steppe regions are the tropical deserts (Fig. 2-6). The Sahara is the largest hot desert in the world, and stretches from the Atlantic to the Red Sea, and from the southern Mediterranean to the Sahel. Its aridity is due to the extremely stable continental tropical air mass that dominates the region. The air almost continuously descends from the upper levels of the atmosphere. The infrequent and isolated rain storms that occur, more especially in summer, come from the inflow of unstable maritime air masses from the northwest, or the occasional inflow of maritime tropical air (mT) behind the ITCZ from the south. This rain falls from convectional storms in these air masses, and is very localized so that average rainfall figures mean very little. Few stations record more than 4 in. (102 mm), and most only a trace. In Salah (Table 2-6 and Fig. 2-1 la), the average annual precipitation is only 0.6 in. (15 mm); Cairo receives only 1.1 in. (28 mm) and Khartoum 5.1 in. (130 mm) on the average. A desert characteristic is temperature extremes. Hot days may be followed by cold nights as the cloudless sky permits the loss of great amounts of long-wave radiation in short periods of time. In summer, daytime temperatures have been

Table 2-6 TEMPERATURE AND RAINFALL DATA, DESERT (BWh)

IN SALAH, ALGERIA (919 FT–280 M)												
	J	F	M	A	M	J	J	A	S	O	N	D	Year
°F	56	61	68	77	84	95	97.5	96.5	91	80	66.5	58	77.5
In.	0.1	0.1	0.0	0.0	0.0	0.0	0.0	0.0	0.0	0.1	0.2	0.1	0.6

SWAKOPMUND, NAMIBIA (20 FT–6 M)												
°F	62.6	63.1	63.3	59.9	60.6	58.5	56.5	54.9	56.1	58.1	58.6	61.5	59.5
In.	0.0	0.1	0.2	0.0	0.0	0.0	0.0	0.0	0.0	0.1	0.0	0.0	0.6

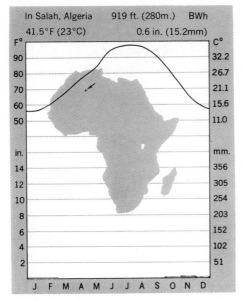

FIGURE 2-11a *In Salah, Algeria. Hot desert (BWh).*

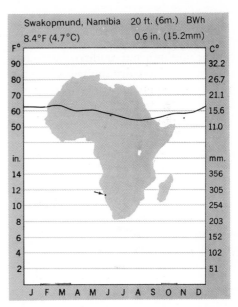

FIGURE 2-11b *Swakopmund, Namibia. West coast desert.*

known to exceed 130° F (54.4° C) while in winter there are often subfreezing temperatures.

Desert conditions extend south from the Red Sea to northern Somalia. These regions lie in the rain shadow of the Ethiopian Massif and thus do not receive moisture that falls from the maritime equatorial air masses that originate in the southwest in the high-sun period. During the low-sun period (January), they receive dry tropical continental air from Arabia that absorbs very little moisture as it crosses the Gulf of Aden. Again,

rainfall is generally less than 4 in. (102 mm) and temperatures are high.

The third area of desert climate stretches along the coast of Namibia (Fig. 2-6), one of the most barren and desolate regions on earth. A combination of factors produces this aridity. The Namib Desert lies in the northwestern and southwestern (dry) quadrants of the Kalahari anticyclone, so that the pressure situation prevents precipitation. In addition, the coastal margin (to a width of only a few miles) is influenced by the cool Benguela Current that produces rel-

CLIMATES OF AFRICA

atively cool temperatures, and, not infrequently, a fog that forms over the water and drifts slowly inland. Namib conditions are typified by Swakopmund (Table 2-6 and Fig. 2-11b). Similar climatic conditions prevail along the Mauritanian coast because of the cooling effect of the Canary Current. Nouadhibou, for example, receives only an inch (25 mm) of rain on average, and the warmest month is only 60° F (20.5° C).

The interior of the Namib Desert,

merging into the western Kalahari, is a little moister than the coast. Five inches (127 mm) of rain are recorded on average about 70 mi (113 km) east of Swakopmund, and the region around Windhoek, Namibia's capital, actually gets about 15 in. (380 mm). The coastal regions of the southwest are the driest, but, with the ascent of the plateau, the precipitation totals rise, to drop again toward the heart of the Kalahari.

Dry Summer Subtropical (Csa and Csb)

The northern and southern extremities of Africa experience dry summer subtropical climates, commonly known as Mediterranean (Fig. 2-6). Both come under the influence of dry subsiding anticyclonic air in the summer, and modified maritime polar air with its associated frontal disturbances in winter. At Algiers (Table 2-7 and Fig. 2-12) the mean temperatures for June, July, August, and September range from 71.6° F to 78° F (22–26° C), with the total rainfall for these same months is only 2.4 in. (61 mm). In the six months from October through March, however, there are approximately 24 in. (610 mm) of rain. A small area of Mediterranean climate is found around Cape Town, where the annual range of temperature is only 15° F (9° C) which is considerably less than along coastal Algeria. In winter, especially in July and August, the westerly wind belt migrates northward bringing with it the cyclonic storms that produce rain and many gray, overcast days. In summer, strong southeasterly winds originating over the cool ocean may produce

a "tablecloth" of cloud on Table Mountain that dominates the Cape Town skyline.

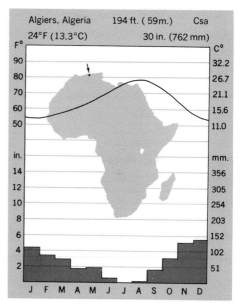

FIGURE 2-12 Algiers, Algeria. Mediterranean (Csa).

Table 2-7 TEMPERATURE AND RAINFALL DATA, MEDITERRANEAN (Csa) ALGIERS, ALGERIA (194 FT–59 M)

	J	F	M	A	M	J	J	A	S	O	N	D	Year
°F	54	55	57.5	61.5	66	71.6	76.5	78	75	68.5	61	55.5	65
In.	4.4	3.3	2.9	1.6	1.8	0.6	0.0	0.2	1.6	3.1	5.1	5.4	30.0

Humid Subtropical Climate (Cfa)

Along the southeast coast of South Africa lies a narrow region of humid subtropical climate, characterized by summer maximum precipitation. Somewhat cooler than the tropical savanna to the north, summers in this area are nevertheless hot, with lower temperature conditions mainly in the winter period. The region is limited by the rapid rise of the plateau slopes toward the interior. Except for some frost due to air drainage, which is confined to valley lowlands, subfreezing temperatures do not occur.

In terms of precipitation, the contrast between summer and winter is not as great as in the interior. Although most rain comes during the summer, there is no month with less than one inch of rain. Rainfall is orographic, as might be expected from the topography of the area and the prevailing winds, but, of course, convectional storms occur in the summer. The coasts are influenced by the warm Mozambique Current, and the southeast trades arrive laden with moisture from these waters. In winter, when the entire system moves to the north, it is the coasts of Mozambique and Madagascar

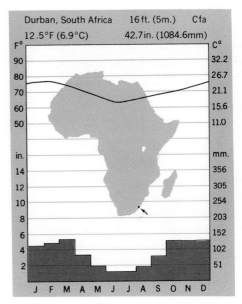

FIGURE 2-13 *Durban, South Africa. Humid subtropic (Cfa).*

that continue to benefit from the moisture (particularly exposed Madagascar), and the drier period sets in further south. The situation is illustrated by the climatological data of Durban (Table 2-8 and Fig. 2-13)

Table 2.8 TEMPERATURE AND RAINFALL DATA, HUMID SUBTROPICAL (Cfa) DURBAN, SOUTH AFRICA (16 FT–5 M)

	J	F	M	A	M	J	J	A	S	O	N	D	Year
°F	76.3	76.8	74.9	71.8	67.8	64.8	64.3	65.8	67.6	69.5	72.0	74.6	70.5
In.	4.6	4.9	5.4	3.4	1.9	1.2	1.2	1.7	3.2	5.1	5.0	5.1	42.7

Dry Winter Subtropical (Cwb) and Highland (H)

The plateau of South Africa is known as the *Highveld*, suggesting its elevated nature and grassland vegetation. There is justification for singling out this region climatically, as its latitudinal location (well outside the tropics) and altitude combine in creating a temperate climate.

Extremes are considerable on the plateau. Summer days can be oppressively hot, while frosts occur in winter. In high regions such as the Drakensberg, snowfalls are not infrequent. Winters are dry, and, after sunny days, rapid radiation losses cause inversions of temperature. Jackson (1952) has

Table 2-9 TEMPERATURE AND RAINFALL DATA, DRY WINTER SUBTROPICAL AND HIGHLAND

	J	F	M	A	M	J	J	A	S	O	N	D	Year
JOHANNESBURG, SOUTH AFRICA (5750 FT–1753 M)													
°F	65	64	62	59	55	50	50	55	59	61	63	65	59
In.	5.6	5.0	3.8	1.3	0.7	0.1	0.3	0.6	0.9	2.7	5.1	4.8	30.9
ADDIS ABABA, ETHIOPIA (8000 FT–2438 M)													
°F	60.1	62.4	64.8	64.4	65.7	63.5	61.7	61.0	61.3	61.7	59.2	58.6	62.0
In.	0.6	1.9	2.8	3.4	3.0	5.7	11.0	12.1	7.6	0.8	0.6	0.2	49.7

disproved the long-accepted assertion that Southern Africa is under the influence of cyclonic conditions during the summer and anticyclonic conditions during the winter. It has become clear that the circulation over the plateau is essentially the same throughout the year, namely, a rather weak anticyclone centered over the eastern margin of the subcontinent. In winter, this cell is somewhat stronger than in summer, when it is forced to move southward. During the dry winter season, the result is a high frequency of westerly and northwesterly winds.

In summer, the anticyclonic circulation transfers maritime, potentially unstable air from the region of the Limpopo mouth and further north onto the plateau. The actual mechanism producing the rainfall, which is particularly heavy in the east, probably lies in the convergence between the plateau anticyclone and adjacent oceanic anticyclones. In the interior, convectional storms are common, with the formation of cumulonimbus clouds, severe thunderstorms, and rapid clearing. Summer days on the plateau are hot, but they are tempered by the elevation. Conditions at Johannesburg (Table 2-9 and Fig 2-14*a*) illustrate the situation.

A second region of warm, temperate climate in a highland environment occurs in Ethiopia, although the specific climatic characteristics and causes differ substantially from those in South Africa. Ethiopia has great topographical and altitudinal variation so that different climates exist short distances from one another, and the major distinctions are caused by altitude. In the low-lying Danakil Depression and in Eritrea are found desert conditions similar to the Sahara; and on the lower slopes of the highlands below 5000 ft (1520 m), warm tropical conditions persist. But between 6000 and 9000 ft (1830–2740 m), in what is known as the *woina dega*, or wine highlands, the climate is temperate; summers are warm and rainy. At Addis Ababa (Table 2-9 and Fig. 2-14*b*), the mean monthly temperatures vary from 59° F to 66° F (15°–19° C), and the rainy season extends from June to September. The rains are brought by maritime equatorial air from the southwest in association with the northward movement of the ITCZ, while for the remainder of the year the Ethiopian Highlands are affected by dry continental tropical air from Arabia. Above the *woina dega* lies the *dega* (highlands) where temperatures are lower, and on the peaks above 13,000 ft (3960 m) there are occasional winter snows.

Climate and Man

Climate, especially the precipitation factor, has clearly affected the distribution of man and his activities. Stamp (1972) has claimed that the "key to the whole of

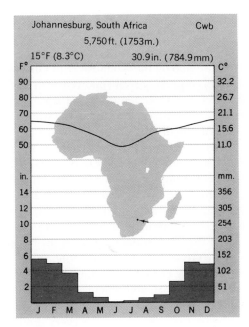

FIGURE 2-14a *Johannesburg, South Africa. Dry winter subtropic (Cwa).*

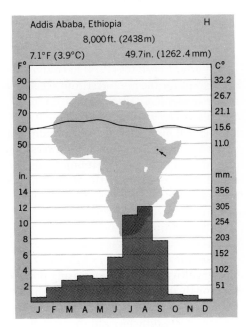

FIGURE 2-14b *Addis Ababa, Ethiopia. Highland (H).*

Africa's development is control of water." While many geographers may not accept this statement, most would agree that water supply and management are important issues for a great many developing states. Water issues concern all those who live on the land, and not infrequently those who live in cities. Compared to other tropical areas, the percentage of land in Africa that receives a high annual precipitation is relatively small, and a large part of the region that does receive much rain is rather sparsely populated. Most Africans live in the climatic zone defined as savanna, and again, the savanna is subhumid over vast areas. A marked dry season brings serious problems for the pastoralist, and somewhere in Africa thousands of livestock die every year as wells and streams run dry and fodder becomes unavailable. For the farmer, much depends on the amount of moisture the preceding wet season has brought: adequate rainfall and good crops render survival easier during the lean, dry season. But, over much of Africa, rainfall variability is high, and a failure of the rains

during the wet season brings hunger during the ensuing dry season. The bulk of east Africa's savanna lands, for instance, receive their annual average rainfall in only one year out of three.

Even when the rains do come, their effectiveness is vastly reduced. Often the rains arrive in severe storms after the sun has parched the countryside for months and has baked the soil's upper layer into a hard, dry crust that defies all farm implements. The result is that much of the rainfall, rather than seeping down into the soil's lower layers, becomes useless runoff—worse than useless, for it contributes to erosion, breaks through the crust to create gullies, and carries great quantities of valuable soil off to the ocean.

After the initial onslaught, when the soil has been softened and the water begins to seep down, its effectiveness in stimulating plant growth continues to be reduced because, most of the time, there simply is not enough water available. Africa, by virtue of its latitudinal location, receives a great amount of radiation, and the high temperatures cause the evaporation of much of the badly needed water brought by the rains. D. B. Carter's analyses (1954) have shown that, except for the rainforest, the vegetation cover requires more than the entire annual precipitation *before* runoff and evaporation. In the global heat balance, low-latitude areas experience the greatest amount of excess insolation (over outgoing radiation). Thus, a rainfall figure of 40 in. (1016 mm), considerable in the middle latitudes, may be only one-third as effective in equatorial regions.

The traditional method by which the African has countered the problems posed by these climatic restrictions has been that of shifting cultivation. With increasing population growth and pressure and the expansion of cash cropping, this process has become more and more difficult, and the introduction of change in an organized fashion, however problematic, has become imperative. Although shifting cultivation ought not to be dismissed as wasteful and ignorant, as Europeans unaware of its background have done, its effects are undesirable. It is destructive and promotes soil erosion, often ruining areas beyond repair and initiating gullying that cannot be halted.

The introduction of changes, however, is a difficult process. Changes must come in land-tenure systems, techniques of cultivation must be improved, and the regular use of fertilizers, in areas where these are applicable, must be encouraged. But changing peoples' association with their lands is difficult, foreign agricultural techniques may be completely unsuccessful in Africa, and the presence, over extensive areas, of the tsetse fly precludes the raising of cattle and, therefore, the local production of fertilizer. Means to store and conserve water must be established under local responsibility, a practice remarkably absent in Africa in spite of its difficult environment.

Among the most spectacular changes introduced have been those involving irrigation schemes, whether the barrages were built specifically for the purpose of irrigation (as at the Gezira scheme on the Nile) or initially for the production of electric power (as at Akosombo on the Volta River in Ghana). Africa is especially well endowed with hydroelectric potential, totaling perhaps twenty-three percent of that of the world, and many hydroelectric projects have associated benefits in that they facilitate the irrigation of adjacent lands. On these irrigated lands are examples of individual land tenure, cash cropping, mechanization, cooperative ventures, and other aspects of progress that must come to agriculture in Africa. In the case of the Sansanding scheme on the Niger and the Gezira scheme on the Nile, these projects have come to form the economic core areas of Mali and Sudan, respectively. But even the smallest dam built of mud and branches is of significance, for every drop of Africa's water must be put to use.

Irrigation projects do not escape the environmental obstacles Africa puts in the way of progress in agriculture. The number of acres that can be irrigated depends on the number of square miles of catchment area, the amount of rainfall received there and its reliability, and the climatic conditions at the irrigated area, among other factors. Much depends also on the physical characteristics of the storage reservoir, the loss of water by evaporation from it, and the efficiency with which the irrigation water can be distributed to the cropped areas. This, of course, is true of any irrigated area, but the particular vagaries of the African climate emerge again as major problems. A very small rainfall during a wet season in the catchment area, and consequent inadequate replenishment of the water in the storage reservoir, can mean disaster in the intensively cultivated lands, and the low reliability of rainfall has already been emphasized. Just as it is possible to estimate the amount of moisture required by the vegetation cover on the savanna, so the number of acre-feet required by a planted crop can be calculated. The acreage that can be irrigated is related to the amount of water

High winds sweeping across the Highveld of Southern Africa and into the mountains of Lesotho, causing severe soil erosion in a land of limited agricultural potential and high population pressure. (Alan C. G. Best)

provided by the catchment area; if it fails to produce that water, and the storage reservoir empties, crop failures result. Thus, what may happen on the smallest scale to an individual's grazing land somewhere on the plateau can be paralleled by major problems in large irrigation projects. The dams are built to regulate the water supply and raise the water level for purposes of distribution, but in the end that supply is still dependent upon the annual precipitation and its variability.

Every country in Africa shares in some measure in the severe problems presented by the climatic environment. Although it is indeed possible, on a continental scale, to marshal a number of exceptions that would seem to give cause for optimism, these are islands in a sea of difficulties. Only one country, South Africa, shows a really significant degree of climatic and pedologic diversification, but it lies almost entirely outside of tropical Africa. More money has been spent on the improvement of agriculture in South Africa than in any other African country, yet even there droughts, soil erosion, vegetation depletion, low yields on farmland, and desert encroachment rank among the major concerns. Improving the use made of the limited opportunities for agriculture provided by the climatic environment over much of Africa is a slow and difficult process. It involves far more than the study of meteorology and pedology and the understanding of the mechanisms behind the processes observed. It involves more even than the introduction of fertilizers and improved farming methods. Many aspects of the African peoples' ways of life are responses to the rigors of the environment. To counter the consequences of that environment is but one step. It must be accompanied by changes in those ways, and that is quite another.

Bibliography

Bargman, D. J. (ed.). *Tropical Meteorology in Africa.* Nairobi: Munitalp Foundation, 1962.

Barry, R. G. and A. H. Perry. *Synoptic Climatology: Methods and Applications.* London: Methuen and Co. Ltd., 1973.

Carter, D. B. "Climates of Africa and India According to Thornthwaite's 1948 Classification," Publication C, 1954.

Griffiths, J. F. (ed.). *Climates of Africa.* New York: Elsevier Publishing Co., 1972.

Jackson, S. P. "Atmospheric Circulation over South Africa," *South African Geographical Journal*, Vol. XXXIV (December, 1952), pp. 48–60.

———. *Climatological Atlas of Africa.* Johannesburg: University of the Witwatersrand, 1961.

Richards, P. (ed.). *African Environments: Problems and Prospects.* London: International African Institute, 1975.

Riehl, H. *Tropical Meteorology.* New York: McGraw-Hill, 1954.

Stamp, L. Dudley and W. T. W. Morgan. *Africa: A Study in Tropical Development.* Third Edition. New York: John Wiley and Sons, Inc., 1972.

Thompson, B. W. *The Climate of Africa.* Nairobi: Oxford University Press, 1965.

Trewartha, G. T. *The Earth's Problem Climates.* Madison: University of Wisconsin Press, 1966.

THREE

The vast majority of Africa's people depends on agriculture and pastoralism for its livelihood. Thus the natural environment plays an important but not necessarily decisive role in influencing the distribution and density of rural activity. This chapter describes and explains the major distribution patterns of Africa's vegetations, soils, and common noncommunicable diseases.

Vegetation

Few extensive areas remain in Africa where the natural vegetation has not been modified by man and his livestock. For centuries pastoralists and cultivators have cleared the grasslands and forests by fire and hoe, and hunters (in places such as the Kalahari Desert) have burned the scrublands to drive out the game. Areas once covered with thick forest or tall grasses now stand open, exposed to the sun, wind, and rain. Excessive grazing in the Sahel, for example, has destroyed the natural ecology and promoted desert encroachment. Microclimatic changes in turn have produced different vegetation covers.

It is impossible, perhaps pointless, to describe and analyze Africa's "natural vegetation." Instead, what follows is a discussion of the existing vegetation types and their distributions, and not the presumed climax types. Figure 3-1 is based on the works of Keay (1959) and Rattray (1960). Areas under cultivation are not shown on the map. The classification used is physiognomic in that it is concerned with the appearance of the vegetation, rather than with its species although

VEGETATION, SOILS, AND DISEASES

41

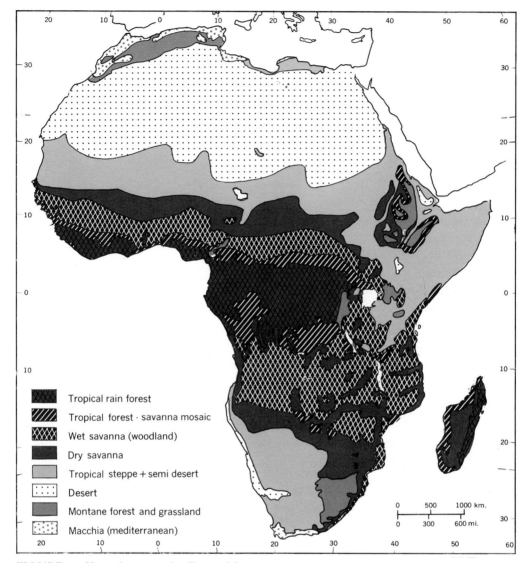

FIGURE 3-1 *Vegetation types (after Keay and Rattray).*

species are used to subdivide the major groups. The basic distributional pattern of vegetation types, as might be expected, corresponds quite closely with that of climatic types, but is modified by local soil, drainage, topographic and bedrock conditions and by the incidence of fire, cultivation, and pastoralism. The main zones from the moister to the dries regions are tropical rainforest, woodland savanna, dry savanna, grass steppe, thornbush, and desert. A mixture of forests and grasslands occupy the highland regions where altitude rather than latitude is the dominant control factor.

Tropical rainforest covers low-lying areas of the Zaire Basin, the lower altitudes of the Cameroon Highlands, the Niger Delta, and the Guinea Coast east of Sierra Leone. It is far less extensive than at one time believed, perhaps because early reports were based on observations made from rivers, the banks of which were covered in thick luxuriant forest encouraged by exposure to the sun, light, and water, whereas only short distances away the vegetation was less dense. The tropical rainforest develops in tropical climates where the rainfall exceeds 55 in. (1397 mm) a year, and where at least 2 in. (51 mm) fall in every month. In general, the warmer and wetter the climate, the more luxuriant the forest, although excessive rain, cloud cover, and poor drainage may inhibit growth.

Typical rainforest contains a great many species of trees, bushes, and ferns, and characteristically there are three layers of vegetation: a ground cover of shrubs and ferns from 6 to 10 ft (2–3 m) tall; a middle story of trees, palms, and woody climbers or lianas that reach about 60 ft (18 m) in height; and a dominant top canopy of broad-leaved evergreens of up to 150 ft (45 m) high with spreading crowns that permit only a little light to filter through to the ground. Hence the ground cover is not especially dense, but the lianas and epiphytes that are attached to the trunks and branches may give that appearance. As many as 3000 species of plants may be found in a square mile, and rarely are there extensive homogeneous stands, thus making specialized lumber extraction almost impossible. Among the principal trees with considerable commercial value are mahogany, rubber, silk-cotton, and the Guinea oil palm. On certain low-lying, swampy areas such as the outer delta of the Niger, and the mouth of the Zaire, Zambezi, and Ravuma rivers, there are stretches of mangrove swamps composed of trees whose stilted roots entrap the river sediments and extend the land and hinder transport.

The great problem of using rainforest areas does not lie in clearing the dense vegetation. It involves the soil quality, the high incidence of disease stimulated by the heat and humidity, and the absence of a dry period to harvest grain crops. Malaria, yellow fever, sleeping sickness, schistosomiasis, and a host of other plagues afflict all tropical regions. For all practical purposes, pastoralism is impossible, and agriculture has developed in a shifting form that is an adaptation to the environmental limitations of the region.

There is no sharp outer boundary to the rainforest, but instead there is a zone of transition into the surrounding savanna grasslands. Here there are patches of forest (especially along streams) and tall broad-leaved grasses such as the "elephant grass." The reasons for this mosaic are not altogether known, but the combination of climate and the burning of the vegetation is undoubtedly the most important.

The most distinctive and widespread vegetation association in Africa is the savanna. The various savanna types stretch in a series of belts across West Africa to the upper reaches of the White Nile, and then form a broad zone from Angola to the Indian Ocean, and southward to the lowvelds of Rhodesia (Zimbabwe) and South Africa, including those of the Zambezi and Limpopo valleys. On the wetter margins both the grasses and deciduous trees may be dense enough for a wooded savanna to prevail, but toward the drier limits, tree growth becomes restricted and the grasses predominate. Characteristic of the savanna belt are the flat-topped acacia trees and the large barrel-shaped drought-resistant baobab trees, which along with bushes and shrubs are scattered throughout the grasslands giving an open "parkland" appearance. Grasses instead of trees predominate not only because of the marked seasonal rainfall, but because of the widespread practice of burning, especially during the dry season when the old "bush" is deliberately set on fire. This is to dispose of the old growth and to stimulate new, or as a means of clearing the land prior to cultivation. Only fire-resistant trees survive, and if burning were discontinued for long periods, there would be a reinvasion of woodland species. When rainfall is high, the

Logging operations in Gabon's tropical rain forest (World Bank)

Fires are deliberately set to the savanna grasslands to destroy the pests, burn off the old and dry cover, and encourage new growth at the onset of the rainy season. However, the root system may be destroyed or permanently damaged. Savanna fire in central Malawi. (Alan C. G. Best)

Parkland Savanna in Southern Africa. Note the trees with clear trunks, spaced well apart, and the virtual absence of undergrowth. The average annual rainfall in this area is about 30 in. (760 mm). (Harm J. deBlij)

savanna grasses may reach heights of 10 to 12 ft (4 m). Although hard and not particularly nutritious, these grasses sustain the bulk of Africa's cattle population. This is also the land of the great herds of antelope, wildebeest, buffalo, elephants, and giraffe, now protected in a number of world-famous game reserves such as Serengeti (Tanzania) and Wankie (Rhodesia).

Progressing still further toward the more arid regions, the dry savannas give way to grass steppes, which give way to the subdesert steppes or thornbush. The thorny acacias and grasses become shorter and more sparse, and no longer form a continuous sod cover. In these regions of the Sahel, the East African Plateau, the Kalahari, Namibia, and the South African Karoo, the average annual rainfall varies from approximately 4–15 in. (100–380 mm), and the reliability is very low, so that with prolonged and repetitive drought there can be serious overgrazing and severe stock losses such as occurred in Bo-

tswana throughout the 1960s and in the Sahel, Ethiopia, and Somalia in the early and middle 1970s. In these subdesert areas, rainfall is both insufficient and too poorly distributed in time to permit a continuous vegetation cover, so that open spaces of ground separate the low shrubs and grasses that may be green only a few weeks in the year following rain. The true desert regions themselves are virtually devoid of vegetation other than widely scattered xerophytic plants such as the *stipa* grass, the *tamarisk*, and date palm.

Beyond the tropics and coinciding with the Mediterranean climate areas of South Africa and the Atlas Mountains, is a very distinctive vegetation type composed of hard-leaved evergreen shrubs and trees known as sclerophyll forest that is well adapted to the summer drought conditions. Short, stunted junipers and pines are common, as are species of cork, oak, cedar, and olive. Tree growth is generally insufficient

The Baobab tree, commonly known as the "upside down" tree on account of its short and stocky branches, is found in the steppe areas and the drier margins of the savanna. (UN/FAO)

for extensive cutting, and the vegetation performs an important soil maintenance function on the steeper slopes, which in Morocco, Tunisia, and Algeria are all too frequently overgrazed by goats and sheep.

In the highland areas of Africa there is a great diversity of vegetation types reflecting the diversities of climate, soil, drainage, and exposure. On the South African highvelds above 3500 ft (1100 m) there are vast expanses of temperate grasslands mixed with occasional stands of acacia. These grasslands especially the "sweet velds" provide good grazing, although in winter the grasses are generally less palatable. In the highlands of East Africa and Ethiopia, both montane grasslands and montane forest occur in scattered locations. The latter resemble temperate deciduous forests found at lower elevations further poleward and contain many different species of plants and trees. Above 10,000 ft (3048 m) where nightly frosts do ocur, the vegetation type is made up of associations of many heath plants, sedges, and tussock grasses.

Soils

It is unfortunately true that few areas of Africa possess fertile soils, and that most soils are decidedly unproductive. High temperatures, torrential rainfalls, and the parent materials have combined to produce a pedology that is marked by poverty in lime, potash, magnesia, and phosphorus. The lack of organic material (humus) and the tendency to form "hardpan" layers also contribute to render many African soils low in fertility and extremely difficult to work for agriculture.

Most of these problems stem from the climatic environment under which the soils have evolved. The high temperatures accelerate bacterial activity to the point where much of the product (nitrates of various kinds) is lost before it can be used up by the living vegetation. The nature of the precipitation and the high temperature of the rain water contribute to produce deep soils, leached in their upper horizons of the materials so badly needed there. What remains after the wet season is the evaporated content of the rapidly percolating waters: compounds rich in aluminum and iron. These are the materials that help constitute the "hardpan," through which roots penetrate with difficulty and which facilitate the runoff and loss of surface water. These iron and aluminum compounds color the soils, called *latosols* by pedologists, the familiar reddish-yellow of the tropics.

Practically every aspect of these latosols is disadvantageous to agriculture. As deep weathering takes place, the waters carry the valuable nutrients to horizons farther and farther from the root level of the plants above. With time, the processes affecting the soil make it worse, not better, for more and more of the essentials are carried downward and, eventually, what is left depends on the composition of the parent material. If it was rich in quartz, a sandy soil remains; if there was much feldspar, a clayey latosol. Both react badly to attempts to use machines in farming. In the case of the sandy soil, compaction is often the result, while the clay variety is extremely difficult to work because of its hardness after exposure and its stickiness when moist.

To be sure, there are some areas where better soils have evolved, and where soils have been found capable of artificial improvement. As is true elsewhere in the world, alluvial soils are among the best in Africa, and in some areas extensive deposits have been laid down by the great rivers. The Niger becomes braided between Bamako and Timbuktu, and there the alluvial soils form the basis of an extensive irrigation scheme. Similarly, alluvial soils lie between the White Nile and its tributary, the Blue Nile, and another such scheme, the Gezira, has been developed there. Projects on a larger or smaller scale can be found along almost every sizeable river in Africa: the Juba in Somalia, the Zambezi in Mozambique, and the Senegal in West Africa.

Certain nonalluvial soils also have been found to be of good quality, such as those on the South African Highveld, the Rhodesian Plateau, and the Highlands of Kenya, as well as on the slopes of the Cameroon Highlands. These soils have resulted from particular parent materials or unusual climatic conditions, and they support the few really important cash-cropping regions of the continent. But there is nothing in Africa to compare with the agricultural cores of Europe and Anglo-America in terms of size and yields per acre, and in a continent where the vast majority of the people still make their living off the land, this is a somber reality.

We are only now beginning to understand soil characteristics, soil formation processes, and soil distributions in Africa. It will be many years before accurate maps for the continent as a whole are constructed. Soil surveys are costly, time consuming, and most often confined to only small areas. Frequently soils are used without adequate knowledge of other environmental conditions such as vegetation and climate. The consequences can be far reaching. In Tanzania, for example, about 2.4 million acres (942,000 ha) of land were temporarily destroyed in the East African Groundnut Scheme of the late 1940s. After only superficial surveys of the soil, climate, drainage, and other production factors, the land was stripped of its vegetation and planted to

Severe gully erosion from overgrazing in the Oued Lallouf hills, Tunisia. (UN)

groundnuts. Exposed to the sun and rain, and turned over by inappropriate machinery, the soil quickly deteriorated, and the project had to be abandoned.

Several soils classifications are in use; one of the most widely adopted for Africa is that of D'Hoore (1965). It is based on the known properties of the soils themselves, on a recognition of the processes and regimes that created them, and a consideration of factors under the influences of which these processes originated and developed. Great importance is given to parent material, and not to climate. Yet, as Figure 3-2 shows, there is a striking similarity between soil and climatic regions.

The first soil type in the D'Hoore system is actually a nonsoil in that it consists of rock and rock debris, ferruginous and calcareous crusts, and desert detritus such as sand, ergs, and desert pavement. These raw mineral "soils" cover almost one-third of Africa and center on the Sahara and Namib Deserts, and parts of the Afar Depression of

Ethiopia. Here the soil-forming processes are too weak to produce real soil. Adjoining them are weakly developed soils that are shallow and contain little humus but excessive soluble salts, such as calcium carbonate. Lime crust or *caliche* may form near the surface during prolonged dry periods when ground waters may rise by capillary action and evaporate near the surface. The Brown soils of the Sahel, Kalahari, and other steppe regions are somewhat deeper but contain many fragments of parent material throughout the soil layer. The texture is often coarse and its color indicates small qualities of humus. With irrigation, the Brown soils can be productive.

Coinciding largely with the savanna and tropical wet climate areas, and developing on a great variety of rock types, lies a diversity of soils that in general are richer, have deeper profiles, and may contain more humus. These are the iron-rich tropical soils frequently referred to as latosols or lateritic soils because of the high concentrations of

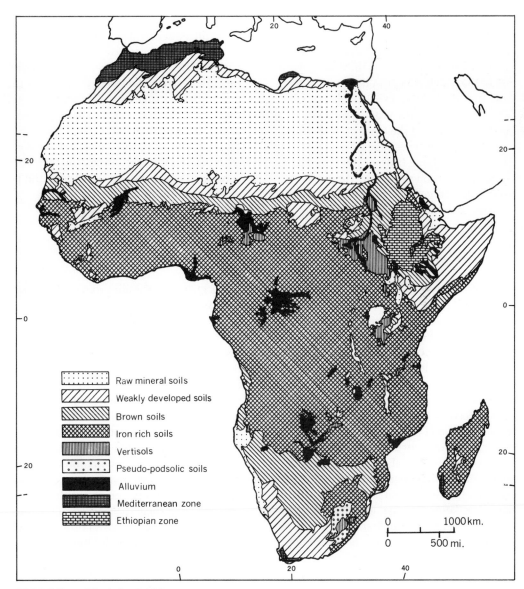

FIGURE 3-2 *The Soils of Africa.*
L. D. Stamp and W. T. W. Morgan. Africa: A Study in Tropical Development.
3rd edition. New York: Wiley, 1972. After D'Hoore. Reprinted by permission of John
Wiley & Sons, Inc.

sesquioxides of iron and aluminum and the almost complete removal by leaching of silica because of high rainfall. Related to them are the vertisols that are also derived from calcareous rocks and rocks rich in ferromagnesian minerals. However, the vertisols are darker or black in color and occur in poorly drained regions such as the southern Sudan where, during the dry season, the soils develop deep cracks but become sticky and difficult to work in the rainy season.

Beyond the tropics and the arid regions,

only the red-brown Mediterranean soils cover any appreciable area. The mountainous terrain of both the Atlas and the Cape Ranges has prevented the accumulation of thick soils except in the valley bottoms, and the light and seasonable rainfall has restricted both the vegetation cover (hence humus), and the amount of weathering. Distinct soil types may be coorelated with the underlying bedrock, such as the sandy acid soils on the Table Mountain Sandstones. In general, the Mediterranean soils are acid and of low fertility.

In contrast, the alluvial soils tend to be fertile although they can be poorly drained and waterlogged. They coincide with Africa's major river systems, especially the Nile, Niger, and Senegal, and with the interior basins such as the Zaire, Chad, and Okavango. As previously indicated, with proper management and capital, they can become some of Africa's most productive areas, and in the case of the Nile they have supported many millions of agricultural people over several millenia.

Pests and Diseases

A great many Africans are habitually unwell, and countless millions spend their lives fighting sickness from the day they are born to the day they die. Sickness and disease, like poverty and ignorance, are two of the major obstacles to widespread and rapid betterment of society. In part these are due to poor diet, insufficient food, seasonal variations in food intake, and the avoidance of certain foods and the preference of others that may be less nutritious all of which may have deep-rooted social, cultural, and economic causes. Frederick Simoons (1967) for example, has shown that among the Galla, Somali, Kikuyu, Chagga, and other East African peoples, either the flesh of chickens or chicken eggs, and sometimes both, are not eaten, eggs being considered the excrement of fowls, and the flesh being offensive. In theory at least, man can individually and collectively ameliorate some of these deficiencies; he can change the system so that he can eat a better diet, build resistance to disease and sickness, and expend more energy on maintaining his improved position.

At the same time, however, man's health and well-being are also affected by certain elements in the natural envionment over which he lacks complete control. These include diseases borne by flies, mosquitoes, worms, and parasites, which directly affect man's energy and ability to work, and pests such as locusts, rats, termites, and birds, which destroy or limit his food supply. In most areas, both systems operate simultaneously, and many different diseases may be found together. Indeed, it is not uncommon for a person to be suffering from malaria, sleeping sickness, worm infections, and malnutrition all at the same time. Sickness and disease in Africa are not merely local and regional problems, they are international in their occurrence and require international control. Unfortunately many states jealously guard their territory and resent their neighbors violating their space, even in the interests of controlling disease. Through the efforts of the World Health Organization (WHO), other international groups and local concerns, the war on insects and pests appears to be succeeding, but the assault on malnutrition is far more complex and less promising.

Although accurate, uniform, and current data on disease are by no means complete and available, there is sufficient evidence of the seriousness and general distributions of most diseases. It can be safely assumed that only a small proportion of all cases are reported to health authorities, and an even smaller proportion of deaths attributed to a specific disease get recorded.

Table 3-1 SELECTED COUNTRIES IN WHICH MALARIA WAS
THE MOST COMMONLY REPORTED DISEASE, 1969

Country	Number of Reported Cases	Estimated Population in 1969
Sudan	808,644	15,186,000
Uganda	707,288	9,526,000
Mali	664,335	4,831,000
Upper Volta	582,937	5,128,000
Senegal	539,158	3,780,000
Nigeria	369,397	65,820,000
Cameroon	366,349	5,680,000
Kenya	279,022	10,942,708
Togo	241,434	1,955,916

SOURCE. *United Nations:* World Health Statistics, 1969, *Vol. II, WHO, Geneva, 1972.*

Thus data, official or not, should be treated with caution. WHO, for example, in its annual reports on infectious diseases does not list all diseases for all countries (and not all countries are listed), but the data do show that malaria, measles, dysentery, influenza, and amoebiasis are the most commonly reported diseases. Malaria was the most commonly reported disease in 22 African states in 1969.

MOSQUITOES

Malaria is undoubtedly the most common disease in tropical Africa. It is estimated that almost 500,000 infants and children die yearly fom the direct effects of the disease, and tens of thousands die from it indirectly. It is a debilitating disease that lowers resistance to other diseases and reduces general efficiency. Table 3-1 shows the number of reported cases of malaria in selected countries. It may be safely assumed however, that three-fourths of their populations is affected by malaria. In parts of eastern Senegal for instance, a survey showed that 80 percent of the population had parasitic evidence of malaria (Hughes and Hunter, 1970).

Malaria is caused by a parasite carried from man to man by mosquitoes, especially *Anopheles gambiae*, which along with other species of *Anopheles* is found in all but the continent's dry regions (Fig. 3-3a). The mos-

quitoes usually breed in standing waters of swamps and rivers, and even in small rain pools and water trapped by leaves of trees. Discarded oil drums and containers and clogged drainpipes make ideal breeding grounds that unfortunately may be in villages and other population concentrations. Their larvae can be destroyed by draining these pools and spraying insecticides (chiefly DDT), the oil of which forms a thin film over the water, preventing the larvae from breathing. Drugs can be given to those infected, but this is costly and not always logistically possible, so that the first concern should be the eradication of the parasite and the mosquito.

Another type of mosquito, *Aedes aegypti*, is the carrier of yellow fever, one of Africa's most dreaded diseases. It is commonly fatal, but WHO lists few reported cases and very few fatalities. In 1961 there was a serious epidemic in Ethiopia with 3000 deaths, and the 1965 Senegal epidemic claimed as many as 20,000 cases with about 200 deaths. Fortunately the control by vaccination and insecticides is not too difficult providing action is taken immediately after the disease has been confirmed. Yellow fever is endemic within the wetter areas of the tropics, but in regions far smaller than that affected by malaria. Many Africans build up immunity to it and other diseases through mild attacks in childhood, and millions have now received prophylactic treatment. Other mosquito-borne diseases are dengue or "break-bone" fever and elephantiasis.

PARASITIC WORMS

There are many different kinds of parasitic worms that affect countless millions of Africans. The hookworm, which lives in the intestine and feeds on the blood of its host, produces anemia. The worm hatches from eggs contained in human excreta and then enters the skin through the feet of those walking in contaminated areas. In Tanzania, among the Wagogo people, the hookworm incidence is 37 percent. In Angola a study showed the total intestinal parasite incidence was 74 percent, of which hookworm was 41 percent, while in the city of Lagos, Nigeria, one quarter of the population may be infected (Hughes and Hunter, 1970). Another common parasitic worm, which is particularly widespread in West Africa, is the Guinea threadworm. It lives under the skin, causing ulceration of the legs and much discomfort, and is most frequently picked up from drinking unboiled water.

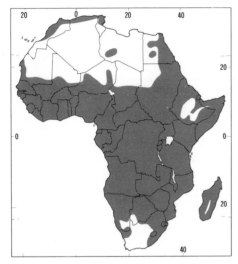

FIGURE 3-3a, Malaria;

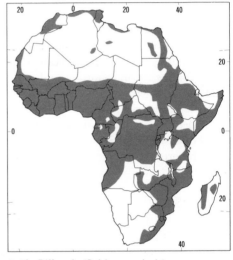

3-3b, Bilharzia (Schistosomiasis);

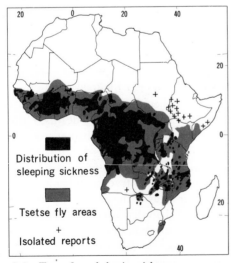

Distribution of sleeping sickness

Tsetse fly areas

+ Isolated reports

3-3c, Tsetse fly and sleeping sickness;

One of the most debilitating and widespread diseases is schistosomiasis or bilharziasis (Fig. 3-3b). It is endemic in all countries except Lesotho, and possibly affects one out of two persons in the continent. Egypt is the most heavily infected state where more than 15 million persons are affected. One study in Mozambique showed infection in 66 percent of a sample population aged 3–24 years, while another showed that in children 3–16 years, between 80 and 83 percent were infected and parasitic association was present in half of the cases (Hughes and Hunter, 1970). Very high incidences have been confirmed in the West Nile District of Uganda and in Mauritania, Nigeria, Tanzania, Ivory

Coast, Zululand (South Africa), and parts of the Sudan.

Schistosomiasis is caused by several strains of a parasitic blood fluke of the genus *Schistosoma*, the most common being *S. haematobium* and *S. mansoni*. The schistosoma are carried from man to man through an intermediate host, a water snail, that lives in rivers, lakes, and irrigation canals. They are readily picked up while bathing, washing clothes, or drinking infected water. One of the unfortunate corollaries of development, especially that based on irrigation works, is the spread of schistosomiasis. As man constructs dams and irrigation ditches to alleviate his hunger, he sets up the ideal conditions for the spread of schistosoma. Such schemes tend to foster dense populations (of both humans and snails), and attract migrant workers who may come from endemic regions and thus act as agents in the diffusion of the disease. When the Aswan Dam was built, for example, in four selected areas in a three-year period, bilharzia infection rates increased as follows: from 10 to 44 percent, from 7 to 50 percent, from 11 to 64 percent, and from 2 to 75 percent. Similarly, at the Sudan's Gezira Irrigation Scheme near the confluence of the White and Blue Niles, field investigations in 1947 showed a mean incidence of 21 percent among adults and 45 percent among children, whereas prior to the Scheme's construction, neither bilharzia nor the host snail were present. It is believed the disease was introduced to the areas by migrant workers from West Africa (Hughes and Hunter, 1970). Other major irrigation schemes reporting bilharzia include the

A boy guides two blind men, victims of onchocerciasis *(river blindness) in Upper Volta. More than 20 million persons (mainly in West Africa's savanna belt) suffer from* onchocerciasis, *a disease spread by the* simulium *fly, and being combated by the World Health Organization.* (UN)

VEGETATION, SOILS, AND DISEASES

Mbarali on the Rufiji River, Tanzania; the Bacita near Jebba, Nigeria; and the Volta Project in Ghana.

Another common disease found in the vicinity of rivers is *onchocerciasis* or river blindness, caused by a parasitic worm transmitted by a small black fly called *Simulium damnosum*. Onchocerciasis is endemic in the savanna belt south of the Sahara from Senegal to Kenya, and was carried by African slaves to Mexico, Venezuela, and Guatemala where it is endemic today. It is hyperendemic along stretches of the upper tributaries of the Volta River of Ghana, where it has been estimated that the incidence of blindness is 3000 per 100,000 as compared with about 200 in Europe (Hunter, 1966). Almost half of the cases in northern Ghana are the result of onchocercal infection, and where the local incidence is 10 percent or more, 9 out of 10 cases are due to onchocerciasis.

The simulium fly breeds along river banks, and when the rivers are not flowing, it disappears without trace; but once the summer rains begin, the fly reappears and usually concentrates within 12 miles (19 km) of the rivers themselves. The incidence of onchocerciasis is highest close to the rivers and decreases with distance from water into the interfluves. Lands adjoining the infected regions are frequently abandoned, and there is ample evidence that settlement has retreated as onchocerciasis has encroached. Thus valuable land may lie idle while undernourished and malnourished peoples live only short distances away, unable to farm and irrigate until the disease is eliminated.

TSETSE FLY

There are about 20 species of tsetse fly that transmit the single-celled organism known as *Trypanosoma gambiense*. When the tsetse fly takes blood from an infected person or animal, the trypanosomes pass into the fly where they develop; then they are passed into the blood of the man or beast on which the fly may next feed. The resulting disease in man is called *trypanosomiasis* or sleeping sickness, while that of livestock is called nagana.

The tsetse fly *glossina* is found in much of the tropical rain forest and savanna areas and is concentrated in belts along the margins of forest and bush near rivers and lakes (Fig. 3-3c). It is less common in the more open savanna where summer temperatures are very high, and in the higher elevations of East Africa where it is too cool. Sleeping sickness is known to have existed in West Africa during the fourteenth century, and was probably confined to that region until the end of the last century when it spread east and south. It was first recognized in Uganda in 1901, and four years later about 200,000 persons died of sleeping sickness in the Busoga Province of Uganda alone. Since then it has spread as far south as Mozambique and South Africa, leaving in its wake extensive areas of sparse population and limited pastoral activity. The Gambian variety is most frequently hosted by man, whereas Rhodesian sleeping sickness is usually associated with game tsetse and a wild animal reservoir.

Control of the fly and disease are both difficult and costly, and different methods of eradication must be adopted according to the species of *glossina* present, since each species has its own feeding and breeding habits. Spraying, innoculation, and bush clearing are the principal methods of control, although spraying may kill useful insects and be ineffective against the pupae which lie hidden in the soil. In parts of northern Nigeria, dieldrin was completely successful in controlling tsetse fly; in Rhodesia, DDT has been successfully used. In Kenya and Nigeria the cost of eradicating tsetse from rivers by insecticide was from one-tenth to one-fifth the cost of clearing (Knight, 1971). Bush clearing is common and involves the destruction of vegetation in a band perhaps 3 miles wide (5 km) and scores of miles in length. This has been done in parts of Uganda, Tanzania, and Rhodesia (Zimbabwe) where in conjunction with this, thousands of game animals (especially antelope), carriers of trypanosomes, have been destroyed. Innoculation is the immediate but costly solution, whereas the ultimate control will only come with the destruction of the tsetse habitat and wild life reservoirs through the clearing of thickets and the establishment of denser human and livestock populations.

The presence of tsetse fly has influenced the geographical distribution and density of pastoralism and of mixed crop and livestock farming. Cattle have been restricted to tsetse-free areas, many of them arid and thus subject to overgrazing, soil erosion, and general land deterioration. In the past, agriculture was commonly concentrated on the arid but tsetse-free margins of the savannas where food shortages were not infrequent. The fly has been a determinant of seasonal migration patterns in both East and West Africa. For example, the Fulani of West Africa trek their cattle northward as the rains and tsetse fly spread from the south, and return to areas of permanent pasture during the dry season. Centuries ago, cattle was driven south of the Zaire basin, the major route being in the highlands between Lakes Tanganyika and Malawi and onto the southern plateaus.

It is now generally agreed that sleeping sickness was responsible for the absence of the plow and animal-drawn carts in precolonial Africa (Knight, 1971). Sleeping sickness also limited the extent of early European penetration into tropical Africa, while the spread of Islamic horsemen and militia was checked in the tsetse-infested areas of precolonial West Africa. The disease has been spread inadvertently by shifting cultivation, the expansion of plantation agriculture into new areas, and by resettlement schemes. During the 1920s, for example, the British government resettled Napore and Nyaneya pastoralists from Uganda's northern border and the Sudan to control intertribal warfare. However, as the pastoralists left, both game and the tsetse fly moved in.

Within a very short time, about 1500 sq mi (3885) sq km) became infested, forcing the pastoralists to migrate into poorer country, and increasing the problems of overgrazing, soil erosion, and population pressure. Following a tsetse fly clearance program two decades later, the land was reclaimed and both tillage and grazing resumed (Deshler, 1960).

RINDERPEST

Another cattle disease is rinderpest, which was first introduced to Africa by Italian armies in present-day Somalia and Ethiopia during the late 1880s. British explorers and settlers introduced it to Kenya a little later, and by the turn of the century it had greatly reduced the cattle numbers throughout East Africa, and had spread southward to Tanzania, Malawi, Angola, and South Africa. Having no immunity to this exotic disease, the cattle quickly succumbed; over 90 percent of the Ugandan cattle died of rinderpest in 1889 following its introduction from Ethiopia. It also spread across the savanna belt into West Africa, where today it is more common than elsewhere in Africa, but it is now being brought under control by internationally funded inoculation programs.

LOCUSTS

Perhaps the greatest damage to crops and grazing land is caused by locusts. They can strip the countryside of its greenery in a few hours, and bring hunger and despair to millions dependent on farming and livestock. Locusts are capable of consuming their own body weight of food daily, and an average size swarm contains an estimated 60 million individuals. In a heavy infestation in Somalia in which the total swarm area was considered to be about 800 sq. mi., locusts consumed more than 150,000 tons of vegetation per day. In 1958, in the Tigre Province of Ethiopia, locusts consumed enough grain to feed more than a million people for a year, and 15,000 persons starved as a direct consequence. Seventy percent of Kenya's crops was ravaged during the 1931 locust invasion,

A plague of locusts in Morocco. (UN/FAO)

and during a six-week period in the winter of 1954–55 over $13 million worth of crops were destroyed in Morocco. Although it is not possible to determine precisely the damage done by locusts to crops and grazing lands in Africa, the FAO has estimated it to be in excess of U.S. $1 billion per annum (May, 1973). But this is no true reflection of the situation since it ignores the costs of famine, the disruption of trade and food processing, the diversion of labor, and the heavy expenditures for control measures.

Four different kinds of locust are present in Africa: desert, migratory, red and brown. The desert locust breeds in the Maghreb, the Horn of Africa, and the Arabian peninsula from March to June; across the Sahel in August and September; and in the Horn and East Africa again from October to January. From these regions they can spread throughout the Sahara and the savanna belts of East and West Africa (Fig. 3-3*d*). A swarm that originated in the Arabian peninsula during the spring of 1950, was carried by the trade winds as far as Mauritania in only 11 weeks, while another reached Niger in only a month. Desert lo-

custs hatching in the Sahel may be transported by winds associated with the ITCZ, and variations in the extent of desert locust invasions can be correlated with the migration of the ITCZ. Throughout the 1960s desert locust invasions were especially severe in the Sudan and Ethiopia, following unusually heavy rains in Somalia, Saudi Arabia, and Yemen. There the locusts had lain their eggs in dry sandy soils to hatch following these heavy rains.

The African migratory locust has been recorded in all of tropical Africa except in coastal Angola and Gabon (Fig. 3-3*e*). The last invasion on a continental scale began in what is now Mali in 1928, and spread to Ethiopia and South Africa by 1932. Smaller invasions were reported in the 1940s, which prompted the colonial governments of Britain, France, and Belgium to take joint action in locust research and control. Most of Africa south of the Sahara is liable to infestation by the red locust (Fig. 3-3*f*). Four plagues, each of 10 to 15 years duration, have been recorded since 1792 at varying intervals of about 30 years. Six outbreak areas have been identified: three near Lake Rukwa in south-

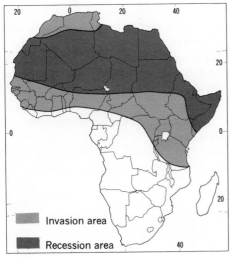

3-3d, *Desert locust;*

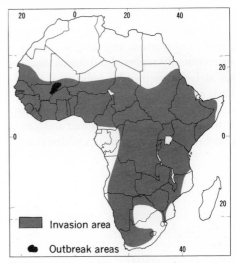

FIGURE 3-3e, *African migratory locust;*

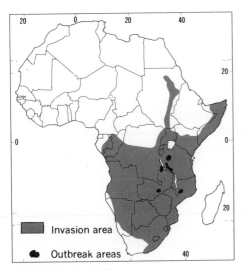

FIGURE 3-3f, *Red locust.*

western Tanzania, two in Zambia, and one in the Chilwa plains of Malawi. All are open savanna plains that are subject to seasonal flooding. The brown locust is restricted to the desert and semidesert regions south of the Zambezi. They have appeared most frequently in the Orange River Valley of South Africa, and on a considerable scale between 1962 and 1969 when drought conditions were particularly severe.

Effective locust control is costly, requiring considerable capital outlay in aircraft and insecticides, and is especially burdensome on the poor countries that are most frequently struck by the pest. Since locust infestation is so widespread and serious, international cooperation is essential in locust control and breeding research. The antilocust programs established by the British and French colonial governments during World War II, have since been emulated by other governments and are now coordinated under the supervision of the UN-FAO. Four regional organizations representing Northwest Africa, the Sahelian states, East Africa, and the Near East including the Sudan and Egypt, have been established with funds administered by the FAO. An international fund has been established, and the Anti-Locust Research Centre in London is the nerve center for locust control in Africa.

Similar approaches must be adopted toward the many other pests and diseases that afflict so many peoples and regions. Ticks, lice, and flies are the vectors of relapsing fever, the plague, tularemia, scrub typhus and others, which have taken countless thousands of lives especially in the more densely populated parts of Africa, and which have yet to be brought under control. Rats are the host of murine plague, while mosquitoes are the vectors of filariasis and dengue. The most commonly reported infectious diseases (after malaria) are measles, influenza, trachoma, and the gonococcal and respiratory diseases. Tuberculosis is endemic throughout the tropics, while pneumonia and yaws take the lives of thousands of children each year. Communicable diseases appear on the rise in urban centers where housing and sanitary facilities are frequently substandard, and population densities high. Diseases once confined to small geographic areas are now more widespread because of the increased mobility of the populations and the seasonal labor migrations that are becoming more common.

Bibliography

A. SOILS AND VEGETATION

Batchelder, R. B. and H. F. Hirt. *Fire in Tropical Forests and Grasslands.* Technical Report 67–41–ES, U.S. Army Natick Laboratories, 1966.

Bridges, E. M. *World Soils.* Cambridge: Cambridge University Press, 1970.

deVos, A. *Africa, The Devastated Continent? Man's Impact on the Ecology of Africa.* The Hague: Dr. W. Junk. b.v. Publishers, 1975.

D'Hoore, J. L. *Soils Map of Africa.* Lagos: Commission for Technical Cooperation in Africa, 1965.

Keay, R. W. J. *Vegetation Map of Africa South of the Tropic of Cancer.* London: Oxford Univerity Press, 1959.

Moss, R. P. (ed.). *The Soil Resources of Tropical Africa.* Cambridge: University of Cambridge Press, 1968.

Owen, D. F. *Man in Tropical Africa: The Environmental Predicament.* New York: Oxford University Press, 1973.

Rattray, J. M. *The Grass Cover of Africa.* FAO Agricultural Studies, No. 49, Rome: FAO, 1960.

Stamp, L. D. *The Geography of Life and Death.* Ithaca: Cornell University Press, 1964.

Strahler, N. *Physical Geography.* Fourth Edition. New York: John Wiley and Sons, Inc., 1975.

B. PESTS AND DISEASES

Bruce-Chwatt, L. J. "Movements of Population in Relation to Communicable Disease in Africa." *Rural Africana.* No. 17, Winter 1972, pp. 39–48.

Deshler, W. "Livestock Trypanosomiasis and Human Settlement in Northeastern Uganda." *The Geographical Review.* Vol. L, No. 4 (October, 1960), pp. 541–54.

Hughes, C. C. and J. M. Hunter. "Disease and 'Development' in Africa." *Social Science and Medicine,* Vol. 3, No. 4 (April, 1970), pp. 443–93.

Hunter, J. M. "River Blindness in Nangodi, Northern Ghana: A Hypothesis of Cyclical Advance and Retreat." *The Geographical Review,* Vol. LVI, No. 3, (July, 1966), pp. 398–416.

Knight, C. G. "The Ecology of African Sleeping Sickness," *Annals, A.A.G.,* Vol. 61, No. 1 (March, 1971), pp. 23–44.

McKelvey, J. J. *Man Against Tsetse: Struggle for Africa.* Ithaca: Cornell University Press, 1973.

May, I. R. *The Locust Threat to Africa.* Occasional Paper No. 34. Africa Institute of South Africa, 1973.

May, J. M. (ed.). *Studies in Disease Ecology.* New York: Hafner Publishing Co., Inc., 1961.

Prothero, R. M. *Migrants and Malaria in Africa.* Pittsburgh: University of Pittsburgh Press, 1965.

―――. "Population Mobility and Trypanosomiasis in Africa." *Rural Africana*, No. 17, Winter 1972, pp. 56–66.

Simoons, F. J. *Eat Not This Flesh.* Madison: University of Wisconsin Press, 1967.

United Nations, *World Health Statistics*, 1969. Vol. II. Geneva: WHO, 1972.

FOUR

Africa's early history is known only in fragments, due to the paucity of documentation. During the last few years, however, a concentrated effort has been made to reconstruct the African past. This is partly because of the unprecedented involvement of academicians in the African field, and it is also a consequence of independence for Africa's political entities. Africans themselves desire to reestablish their links with a history full of achievements which was interrupted by the colonial episode. Still held by some observers of the African scene, however, is the opinion that Africa at the time of colonization was a continent completely devoid of political sophistication, economic organization, and artistic achievement. This false image is now being destroyed.

Indeed, the very lateness of the European invasion of Africa is evidence for the degree to which Africans were organized. While sometimes at enmity with one another and even willing to cooperate with European and Arab in the evil of slavery, they protected their inland trade routes effectively. For example, in the hinterlands of the Gold Coast trading stations and in the gold-producing areas of Rhodesia, the African middlemen successfully repelled for centuries European efforts to encroach.

Early Man in Africa

If it cannot be clained that Africa during the past several hundred years was in the center of the world stage, it must be emphasized that during hundreds of thousands of years previously, Africa was indeed the heart of the inhabited world. There, the evolution of Homo sapiens has been traced from very early beginnings, when the making of tools

AFRICAN POLITICAL HEARTHS: AN HISTORICAL GEOGRAPHY

commenced. Africa's Pleistocene stratigraphy has yielded an orderly sequence of objects made by man's ancestors, ranking from the earliest stone pebble tools to hand axes. At Olduvai Gorge in Tanzania, a sequence covering about two and a half million years has been found. Perhaps during the later phases of the Pleistocene glaciation, which was felt in East Africa as a series of wet and dry periods and was reflected by variations in the Rift Valley lake levels, the use of fire was discovered. That may have been 50,000 years ago, during a dry period that probably coincided with a glacial advance and possibly brought colder weather to equatorial regions. Man sought shelter in caves, began to make new and different tools, including many with wooden handles, and started to use bone and wear skins. Finally, Homo sapiens appeared on the scene—in Africa probably an early ancestor of the present-day Bushman. The entire sequence is recorded in Africa more perfectly than anywhere else, and "there is little doubt that throughout all but the last small fraction of [the] long development of the human form, Africa remained at the center of the inhabited world." (Oliver and Fage, 1962)

Africa's first occupants were hunters and gatherers who lived a precarious existence in constant search of food. The Bushman peoples of the Kalahari, and the Pygmies of the Ituri Forest, Zaire, today exemplify the types of societies and economies that once prevailed over much of the continent. The Bushman live in small bands under the leadership of the most skillful hunter, and move from place to place in search of antelope, giraffe, ostrich, and other game that they hunt with spears, bows, and arrows. They read the veld like a book and are able to locate animals by the most minute bits of evidence. Smaller game is taken in snares and traps, and roots and berries are gathered most frequently by women and children. Their shelters, or werfs, are simply made of branches and grasses gathered

from the veld, and are abandoned when the game is depleted. In the past, the Bushman lived in rock shelters where much can be learned of their culture from the rock paintings they have left behind.

The Bushman in all probability was not the only occupant of the African stage at this early time. It is thought that a distinct Negroid type appeared in the forests of the west (whereas the Bushman occupied the eastern highlands), and in northeastern Africa a later arrival was a Caucasoid, proto-Hamitic type. This last representative migrated into northern and eastern Africa, along the Mediterranean coast and the East African lakes, and made major contributions to the cultural development of the continent by introducing the idea of barbs for spears and arrows, special chiseling tools for wood and bone, and pottery.

Archaeologists, anthropologists, linguists, and historians have attempted to reconstruct the events that followed the arrival of man on the African scene. Using linguistic phenomena in present-day Africa as their guide, they suggest that, in addition to the Semitic-Kushitic languages of the northeast and the Khoisan languages of the southern Bushman, two major ancient language stocks existed in the Africa of about 5000 years ago. To the south and west of Lake Chad was the Niger-Congo stock (formerly known as West Sudanic), while to its east and north was the Sudanic stock. When one studies the individual languages within each group, it quickly becomes clear that they have been developing in separate ways for many centuries, because they differ greatly from each other. When this situation is compared to that prevalent among the Bantu group of languages predominant in Africa south of the equator, it is noted that these Bantu languages are much more closely related to each other, so that they may be considered to be much younger. From this and other data, it is deduced that the peopling of Africa to the north of the equator, east and west of Lake Chad, took

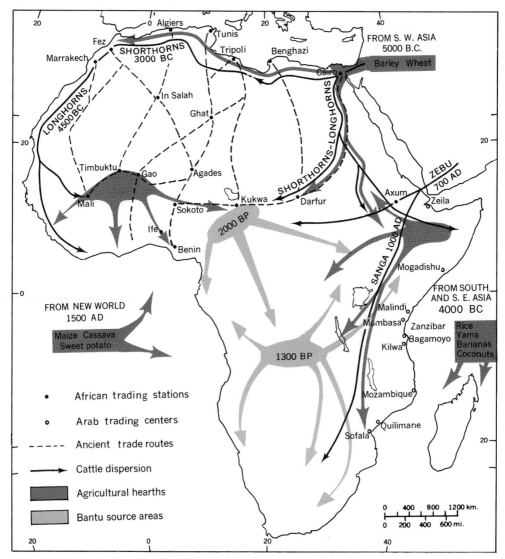

FIGURE 4-1 *Agricultural hearths, and early migrations and trade routes.*

place long before that of southern Africa. That is, the arrival of the modern inhabitants of southern Africa and the displacement of the Bushman and Pygmies by Bantu peoples occurred possibly after A.D. 1, while agriculture and its consequent expansion of population had been felt for more than 3000 years previous in Sudanic Africa.

The agricultural revolution experienced by tropical Africa came in several distinct phases. In the savanna lands, the growing of cereals probably was first learned in the west and then spread to the east. The noted anthropologist George Murdock maintains agriculture was invented in West Africa independently of other areas such as Southwest and Southeast Asia (Murdock, 1959). But many of the crops found in other parts of Africa were introduced from other continents and probably did not arrive until after the beginning of the Christian era. Bananas and yams, for instance, came from

Asia (Fig. 4-1), possibly during the first centuries A.D., and the present-day staples of corn and cassava came from the Americas as late as the sixteenth century. Thus, the southern part of tropical Africa apparently lagged some 3000 years behind the Sudanic regions in this field, perhaps the major reason why the dispersion of the Bantu-speaking peoples came so late.

Contact with Asia brought more than food crops to tropical Africa. Immigrants arrived from Southeast Asia, including Indonesia, and they settled along the East African shores, later to migrate to Madagascar, where they became the ancestors of a sector of the present-day Malagasy people.

One of the remaining questions connected with the peopling of Africa south of the Sahara involves the location of the core region from which the Bantu-speaking peoples spread. While linguists and historians once favored the theory that this dispersal originated from the southern margins of the equatorial forests, most now believe it began not much more than 2000 years ago from the areas in which the most closely related languages of the Benue-Niger substock are at present spoken in east central Nigeria. While this migration was in progress, the use of iron was probably discovered, and the early hunting, fishing, and gathering Bantu-speaking peoples were superseded by the expanding agricultural and pastoral peoples. These later representatives conquered and absorbed the Bushman and Pygmies, but their competition with the more stubborn Caucasoid peoples of the east was lengthy and less successful. There, too, much intermixture took place, and eventually the Caucasoids were displaced or absorbed also, leaving linguistic and somatic evidence of their former hegemony.

Early States of North and Northeast Africa

While all these changes were in progress in tropical Africa, and the coming of cultivation and iron implements was producing major population growth and migrations, the focus of an even more important transformation lay in the northeast of the continent, whence the concept of organized agriculture had spread. For there in Egypt, urban centers began to develop, great strides were made very rapidly in political and religious thinking, great artistic achievements occurred, and economic activity was carried farther than ever before. In an amazingly brief period, political unity was achieved in the most highly complex, most densely populated state of its time. For several thousand years, Dynastic Egypt was the heart of power and the source of ideas for Africa and the world (Fig. 4-2).

The Old Kingdom (2650-2350 B.C.) was the period of the great pyramids and tombs, when Egypt had a strong government that exercised control over the annual floods of the Nile and constructed a vast system of dikes and irrigation channels. The regular surplus of food supported an expanding population, stimulated commerce, and paid for the Pyramids and other great monuments. During the Middle Kingdom (2130-1650 B.C.), the Egyptian Pharaohs looked westward into Libya, and their armies moved southward up the Nile and through the Red Sea to subjugate the inhabitants of the Middle Nile, and to return with new treasures and slaves. By the year 2000 B.C. Egyptian power had been extended to Aswan and during the New Kingdom (1985-1580 B.C.), Rameses II built the famous temple of Abu Simbel in Nubia. By the last millennium B.C. lower Egypt had begun to lose power, and it was eventually overrun by Assyrians, Persians, Greeks, and Romans, so the center of royal authority moved southward into Nubia.

By the beginning of the Christian era there were several important centers of in-

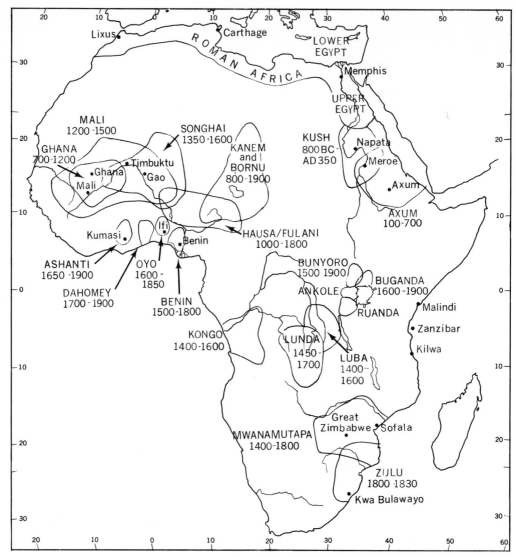

FIGURE 4-2 *Pre-European states of Africa.*

novation, technology, and political power that would have a profound impact on the course of African culture and development south of the Sahara. Kush, Carthage and its associated Libyan-Berber states, and Axum are among the most important: Kush for its iron technology and art that diffused both south and west across the Sahel into West Africa; Carthage for its metal products, commercial links with early West African states, and its religious influence throughout the Saharan realm and south into the savanna zones; and Axum for its massive dry-stone buildings, hillside terracing, and irrigation that have diffused throughout East Africa and possibly as far south as Rhodesia (Zimbabwe).

The state of Kush centered around the towns of Napata, Meroë, and Naga, situated between the fourth and sixth cataracts of the

Nile near the present-day cities of Atbara and Khartoum, Sudan (Fig. 4-2). From their capital in Napata, the Kushites extended their sphere of influence up the rivers to the borders of modern-day Ethiopia and Uganda. By 725 B.C. they had successfully embarked on the conquest of Egypt itself. When the Assyrians invaded lower Egypt in 666 B.C. the Kushites were unable to repel them primarily because of their inferior weapons; they retreated southward and a century later transferred their capital to Meroë. The reasons for this transfer are not entirely clear, but it is likely that the Kushites were unable to produce sufficient food in their original stronghold because of increasing desert encroachment. For centuries much of the Sahara had become increasingly more arid and the human and livestock populations were being forced to retreat to the desert margins, oases, and certain sections of the Nile. But other reasons for the change of capital were possibly equally important. Meroë lay closer to the caravan routes along the Atbara River leading to Ethiopia and indirectly to the Indian Ocean. For the next 800 years, Kush—and especially Meroë—was the center of the largest iron-smelting industry in Africa, and according to many historians, one of the most important cradles of innovation whose impact was to be felt across Africa in the centuries that followed (Davidson, 1972). Kush was to Africa south of the Sahara what the civilizations of the Mediterranean had been to northern Europe a few centuries earlier.

The kingdom of Kush itself was vanquished by the rulers of Axum soon after 300 A.D. The founders of Axum were Yemeni Arabs who first settled the African continent during the first century B.C., and later extended their authority over the northern half of present-day Ethiopia and eastern Sudan. They maintained trade relations with Greek and Syrian merchants who came to buy ivory, gold, and incense from the African interior, and it was through this that Axum was able to defeat the Kushites. The importance of Axum lies in its adherence to Christianity after the fourth century, and the spread of the Coptic Christian Church to much of Ethiopia and parts of Nubia. With the simultaneous spread of Islam in the surrounding states, Axum became an island of Coptic Christianity that proved to be a religious, cultural, and political barrier to the passage of Islamic ideas and practices. However, toward the end of the tenth century, the Kingdom of Axum disintegrated, and there followed a period of struggle between Christian and Moslem that continues to the present.

Two important contributions of Axum to the African landscape, other than the religious aspects, are the art of massive drystone building, that is, building without mortar, and the practice of terracing and irrigation. Large stone structures are found in several locations of east and southern Africa, and the famous Zimbabwe ruins of Rhodesia may in some way be linked with this early culture hearth. Hundreds of thousands of acres of abandoned hillside terraces and irrigation have been identified in the Darfur Mountains of western Sudan, and from Ethiopia to Rhodesia. The practice is thought to have been diffused from Axum (Davidson, 1959).

The history of the Saharan and North African hearths is long and complex, yet a number of themes and events need to be reviewed to understand their role in the cultural and political development of Africa as a whole but, more especially, the development of West Africa. In the second millennium B.C. Phoenician adventurers established a number of city-states along the Maghreb coast from the Gulf of Sirte to the Atlantic coast of Morocco (Figs. 4-1 and 4-2). The largest and most important of these was Carthage, which may have had a population exceeding a half million people at its zenith. Like other cities, Carthage was dependent on trade and the surrounding regions for grain, and as the Phoenician populations increased, additional coastal lands had to be

The Great Sphinx and Pyramids at Giza built during the Fourth Dynasty or the Old Kingdom (c. 2650–2350 B.C.). (UN/FAO)

St. George's Church, one of several hewn from the solid rock at Lalibela in north-central Ethiopia during the Zagwe dynasty of the 13th century. (Alan C. G. Best)

THE CONTINENT

cultivated, but there was no need for expansion inland. However, following the fall of Carthage in 146 B.C., the Roman victors, faced with the need to produce grain for its metropole, pushed southwards into the steppe lands. There they irrigated the land (especially in Numidia, the eastern half of modern Algeria), and established a settled agricultural way of life among the Berbers to whom they also introduced Christianity. By the fifth century, Roman power was declining and the more nomadic Berbers undertook systematic raids on the agricultural communities, and pastoralism thus once more expanded.

Neither Carthaginian nor Roman rule ever reached across the Sahara, and while the Carthaginian empire was never really territorial, it had, like the Roman Empire, well-defined commercial links with points to the south. Carthage was linked with Gao, while the Roman city of Leptis Magna, close to modern Tripoli, was the northern terminus for the trans-Saharan caravan routes through the Fezzan; and Marrakech was the Moroccan terminus of a trade route across the Mauritanian desert (Fig. 4-1). Berber pastoralists were the agents in this contact and, quite likely, had been so even prior to the Mediterranean civilizations. Throughout the centuries, the main exports of the Western Sudan were gold, slaves, ivory, ostrich feathers, and hides, while salt, cloth, iron, and copper goods were imported from the north.

Trans-Saharan trade would have provided no extreme hardship several millennia ago when much of the Sahara was more humid than now and supported rich grasslands for the Berber pastoralist traders but, as the Sahara became more arid, the routes became more selective and the journey more hazardous. With the gradual desiccation of the landscape through overgrazing and climatic change, the Negroes of West Africa retreated to the south, leaving most of the Sahara to Berber nomads, although residual Negro groups remained in the oases and Tibesti Mountains.

The final phase of occupation and control of the Saharan and North African realms came with the Arabs in the seventh and eighth centuries, and like their predecessors in the western regions, they initially confined themselves to the Mediterranean lands, only entering the Sahara proper in significant numbers during the twelfth century. The Arabs brought with them Islam, giving profound unity to this otherwise heterogeneous region, which, since the end of the Roman occupation, had never been a unified political or even cultural area. Arab diffusion through the Maghreb met with widespread resistance from sedentary and nomadic Berbers alike, and from Byzantine armies, but nevertheless an Arab empire was established and Islam prevailed. By the tenth century, the empire collapsed to be later reorganized by the Moslem Ottoman Turks.

Early States of the Western Sudan

The earliest of the West African states about which much information has been gathered is *Ghana*. It was located in the western part of present-day Mali, to the north of the major headwaters of the Senegal and Niger rivers (Fig. 4-2). It has not been possible to date the origins of the Ghana state with exactness, but it probably was in existence about the fourth century A.D. Its eco-nomic foundations, however, are quite well understood. The river valleys to the south contained alluvial gold, much of which was mined and exported northward. The actual mining was done by Mandingo people, who lived outside the sphere of Ghana proper, but these people exchanged the gold for salt and other products they required. Also taken from the south were slaves, to be sold on northern markets. From the north, caravans brought copper, dried fruit, cowries, and other merchandise which was exchanged in Ghana and then distributed throughout the Sudan.

It is easy to see that Ghana's situation was an extremely favorable one from the economic point of view, and that control of its area would yield great profits. This was possibly first recognized by immigrants from northern parts of Africa who came to settle among the Soninke (Negro) peoples and founded a dynasty. As was mentioned previously, the beginnings of the Ghana state are shrouded in mystery, and the identity of the earliest rulers is not even certain. But if the earliest kings were not Soninke, those of later centuries were. Indeed, under these kings the state appears to have thrived under strong central government and experienced at least 200 years of relative stability. The non-Soninke dynasty was overthrown toward the end of the eighth century A.D., and Negro kings ruled until the empire began to crumble during the eleventh. Under their rule the state achieved its greatest territorial expansion, extending from Timbuktu in the east to the borders of present-day Senegal in the west, and from the headwaters of the Senegal and Niger in the south to the land of the Berbers in the north. Moreover, in the very creation of the state and in its perpetuation, the recognition of the economic advantages was a major factor. Thus, Ghana relied less on military conquest and imposition than most other African states, and in consequence it was more stable and survived longer.

The wave of Islam spreading west from the land of the Arabs eventually reached Ghana, though indirectly: the people of the northern desert, converted to a version of this faith, launched a war against pagan Ghana about 1062. Ghana did not, however, fall apart immediately after the first onslaught, as was the case in so many of the other states that existed during this period. On the contrary, the leaders and people of the empire fought stubbornly, and it was not until 14 years later that the capital (also named Ghana) was destroyed. Even after its defeat, Ghana's momentum continued; the victorious tribes from the north had little idea how to run the country, and in 1087 a successful rebellion by the Soninke brought the state renewed independence. But the invaders had ruined the agricultural areas, and although ousted from Ghana, they continued to cut the state off from its northern trade connections. Having been the foundation of the state, the weakened economy was no longer a cohesive force, and it was not long before Ghana began to break up into various smaller kingdoms and tribal entities.

The destruction of Ghana did not end the efforts to establish states and empires in West Africa. After a relatively brief period of instability, during which the penetration by Islam continued, a new and even more impressive empire arose during the middle of the thirteenth century. This was the state of *Mali*. Like Ghana, Mali's strength depended on the caravan routes to the north, but unlike Ghana, its area incorporated the gold-producing territories, which gave the state greater security. Its relations with the Islamic peoples of the desert and the north were good, because Mali's leaders were Moslems, the *Jihad* (Holy War) of conversion having been successful in these parts.

Many of the characteristics of Ghana were repeated in the empire of Mali. There was comparative stability, and a succession of rulers managed to hold the empire together. During the first quarter of the fourteenth century, the state reached its zenith. Territorially, it extended from Gao and the middle Niger in the east to the ocean in the west, covering the entire savanna belt, and from the Futa Jallon in the south to areas deep in the Sahara Desert (Fig. 4-2). Trading caravans came from as far afield as Egypt and Morocco. The cities of Mali (Niani), about a hundred miles below present-day Bamako on the Niger River, and Timbuktu became urban centers of renown.

Architectural improvements were made and great mosques constructed, an institution of higher learning was established at Timbuktu, and leaders made pilgrimages to Mecca.

But the adjutants of Mali's leaders extended the empire farther than control could be effective, and the fourteenth century saw the beginning of the end. The Tucolor of the west, the Tuaregs of the northern desert, and the Mossi of the south raided with success, and by the beginning of the fifteenth century the kings of the Songhai had also broken away. But again, the principles of state organization were not lost on those who rebelled against the weakening central authority in Mali. Other empires soon appeared.

In the region of Gao, on the middle Niger, the land and people were long subject to the rulers of Mali. When Mali fell apart, however, another state of significance, *Songhai*, arose in this area. Songhai was located farther to the east than either Ghana or Mali, so that its influence in the far west was probably less. But the tradition of greatness of the central city continued, as Gao replaced the town of Mali, which itself had taken over from the town of Ghana. From the environs of Gao, the leaders of Songhai set about extending the domain of the state, which by the early sixteenth century encompassed the lands of the Hausa in the east almost as far as Bornu, in the north extended to the very margins of Morocco, in the west almost to the ocean, and in the south well into the forests. Only in the south did some of the Mossi states manage to hold their own against the Songhai armies. Meanwhile, trade and agriculture flourished, and the heart of the empire during the first quarter of the sixteenth century experienced stability and order.

Songhai, however, suffered from intrafamily rivalries for the leadership and from competition among the various generals of the successful armies. These were the seeds of weakness which during the later 1500s,

began to affect the state. By 1600, Moroccan invaders from the north captured the salt mines, while internal rebellions fragmented the empire. But Songhai had continued to spread Islam among those peoples it had subjected, it had continued to keep close ties with the Arab world of Islam, and its effects were felt long after it fell.

Viewing the sequence from a spatial perspective, it is notable that Mali arose well to the south and somewhat east of Ghana, and that Songhai subsequently developed east of Mali. These shifts had several causes and consequences. The general easterly migration of the core areas may have been related to the events taking place in North Africa, where the center of power moved from Morocco to Tunis during the same period. Doubtless, the invasion of Ghana and the breakup of the westerly trade routes led to a search for new, necessarily more eastern crossings of the Sahara. Mali's more southerly location rendered it less vulnerable to the onslaughts of the desert peoples whose raids had been fatal to Ghana, and, Mali, being Moslem whereas Ghana was pagan, naturally had many ties to the east. This factor no doubt also played a role in the rise of Songhai. Since Gao lay some seven hundred miles downstream on the Niger from Mali, goods began to move along the Niger trade route to Timbuktu and Gao, and even beyond, and the whole orientation of the region was more and more toward the central Sahara and the eastern parts of the north.

With the invasion of Songhai by the Moroccans and the ensuing chaos, the center of African power shifted southward, toward the region between the forests and the steppe in the elbow of the Niger River. There, some smaller but remarkably stable political entities, known as the Mossi-Dagomba states, survived until the Europeans entered the scene in numbers. In the far east, between Songhai and Lake Chad, the kingdoms of the Hausa and the state of Bornu also had some organization and stability. Possibly, the Kushitic influences played an indirect role there. Much later, these Hausa kingdoms were overthrown by the rising group of Fulani, who had come from the west to live in Hausaland and brought with them a strict adherence to Islam. This was another Holy War and had important repercussions all through the West African savanna belt.

Early States of the Guinea Coast

The sequence described above is, of course, a very generalized one. Many states about which something is known—and probably others about which little or nothing has been learned—have not been included in the story of the complex political transitions in West Africa. It is even more difficult to comprehend the political changes going on at the same time in the Guinea area, the region between the savanna-steppe of the north and the coast.

For a variety of reasons, some of the political ideas of Ghana, Mali, and Songhai were carried southward. Defeated leaders sought refuge in the south, and the invasion of aggressive northern tribes sent whole populations migrating in that direction. Nor were war and revolution the only causes of a shift to the south. During the two millennia of political change, this part of Africa was also undergoing environmental changes. Put most simply, the Sahara Desert was progressively becoming drier. Agriculture became increasingly difficult along the northern fringes of the savanna, and with the increasing drought in the interior, the whole of

The Dogon village of Sangha, Mali. During the 16th century the Dogon were part of the Songhai empire that centered on Gao, an important Sahelian town on the middle Niger River. The block structures are houses, the thatch-roof structures are granaries. (UN)

West Africa was affected, for the moister belts to the south received proportionally less rainfall.

Details of the Guinea states are even harder to obtain than those of the savanna states. After all, the ties between the Arab world and the West African countries were close, and if the Negroes themselves did not write, the Arabs did; much of what is known about Ghana, Mali, and Songhai has been gleaned from Arab writings. But the southerly states were beyond the orbit of the Arabs, and the reconstruction of their past is a far more difficult problem. When the Europeans arrived, they began to report on the political entities, but they had been in existence long before the first whites came.

Actually, the Europeans contributed considerably to strengthening some of these southern states. While the savanna states ruled supreme, the forest people were at the mercy of slave raiders. In those days, the forests, especially the northern margins, were merely tributary areas from which products were to be extracted. The local chiefs could do very little against the powerful armies of the empires, so that their only protection was to move deeper into the forest to avoid slave raids and the cavalry of the kings. Very little forest was actually controlled by the savanna empires, for the kings' forces simply were not suited to fight in the dense bush. The great armies were effective on the savanna, on the open lands, where grazing was available for the horses, but in the dense undergrowth they ran the risk of annihilation. Armed slave-raiding and punitive parties did enter the forest, but left again with their loot. They could maintain no effective government there.

Naturally, political organization in the forest was a difficult process, and in this respect the savanna lands experienced progress first. But then the Europeans came to the coasts, built trading stations there, and demanded the same products that the caravans had so long carried north across the desert. Furthermore, they brought firearms to the people of the forest. Suddenly, these people found themselves with economic and military advantages, and from those days on, the might of the savanna empires was on the wane.

Having brought some advantages to the people of the forests, the Europeans also introduced their version of an evil long perpetrated by the Arabs: the slave trade, which led to war and chaos among the african peoples. Yet while this very practice prevailed, some of West Africa's most important Negro states thrived.

It must be remembered that many of the political ideas incorporated in the Guinea states had been introduced from the north, so that the coastal forest states were bound to have certain features in common. Generally, it is thought that the first state of this kind was *Ife,* which may have arisen as early as the tenth century A.D. From Ife, ideas spread which led to the foundation of several states populated by the Yoruba people. Perhaps the best example of the type was *Oyo* (Fig. 4-2), located in the north of what is today the Western State of Nigeria, and including sections of Benin. Oyo, like other forest empires, probably had its beginnings along the northern fringes rather than within the forests, and was extended southward as time went on. Oyo was noteworthy for several reasons: it was among the first of such states to form, it survived for a long time, and it brought such stability to the Yoruba people that they withstood the European impact from the south for many years.

The core areas of these Yoruba states consisted of urban centers of considerable size, surrounded by a wall that usually included some farmland within its confines. Thus, the town could withstand a siege, the enclosed farmland being just sufficient to supply some food to the people seeking shelter. There was much military activity in the expansion of the Yoruba states: the leaders of Oyo, for instance, sought to incorporate not only all Yoruba people, but non-Yorubas as well. Eventually, it was this enforced tribute and strife resulting from the slave trade that caused internal fragmentation. Oyo was paramount in its region from the seventeenth century until the first decades of the nineteenth, and had been growing in significance and influence long before that.

Another offshoot of Ife was the state of *Benin*. Originally a group of states, in the fifteenth century it was consolidated by the first of a strong dynasty of kings. Benin is known, among other things, for its fabulous bronzes and other works of art, products of skills introduced from Ife. The state centered on the city of Benin, which grew in importance with European contact and trade. Benin's merchants became the important middlemen between the whites and the Yorubas of the interior, and through the city passed pepper, cotton cloth, slaves, and beads. The power of the merchants was increased by their procurement of firearms, and Benin's armies raided farther and farther into the interior. The kingdom reached its zenith during the late sixteenth and early seventeenth centuries, but eventually the devastation of the hinterland proved fatal. Fewer products and slaves reached the capital, fewer Europeans called there, and by the end of the nineteenth century the state was in decay.

The state of *Dahomey* never reached the importance of Benin or Oyo, and its consolidation was largely the result of economic conditions created by the slave trade. Dahomey was internally divided, the Europeans encouraging this division by their support of whatever parties would deliver the slaves to the coast most efficiently. From the outside, Dahomey was threatened by Oyo and encroached upon by *Ashanti*, a state of major proportions far more powerful than Dahomey. Like the kingdoms of the Yoruba, Ashanti, located in the interior of what came to be called the Gold Coast (Fig. 4-2), resulted from a union of a number of states under a powerful ruler who was succeeded by equally effective kings. In this case, a common effort on the part of Akan-speaking people to prevent the invasion of competitors led to a further combined effort to throw off the yoke of tribute imposed by a state called Denkera. Thus, the Ashanti nation was forged, with headquarters in Kumasi, under the leadership of the *Asantehene*, guardian of the Golden Stool, the symbol of national unity.

Ashanti grew during the eighteenth century, and, by the beginning of the nineteenth, the empire was encroaching on the coastal states of the Fante, where the Europeans had their forts and trading stations. Slaves and gold were exchanged for arms and ammunition. Eventually, Ashanti invaded the nominal British protectorates along the coast. The termination of the slave trade had removed one of the economic mainstays of Ashanti, and relations between the Ashanti and the British had steadily deteriorated. Ashanti's attack, which came in 1863, was not repaid until several years later, and then ineffectively. It is a measure of Ashanti resilience that the state survived the 1874 punishment inflicted by Britain and required reoccupation in 1896. In 1900, when the British governor demanded the surrender of the Golden Stool, Ashanti rose for the last time in a hopeless rebellion. Only as late as 1901 did Ashanti territory become part of a British Crown colony.

Early States of Equatorial and Southern Africa

Large, militarily strong, and economically diversified states also existed in equatorial and southern Africa during these same times (Fig. 4-2). When the Portuguese penetrated the coast near the mouth of the Zaire River at the end of the fifteenth century, they found the flourishing state of *Kongo* centered on Mbanza located near present-day

São Salvador, Angola. The Bakongo king willingly entered into trade with the Portuguese, exchanged ambassadors with Lisbon, and permitted Christian missionaries to proselytize among his subjects. At the same time, however, he allowed the Portuguese to remove countless thousands of slaves, which, together with internal wars, contributed to the kingdom's decline by the end of the seventeenth century.

East of the *Kongo* kingdom in the light woodland regions bordering on the southern rim of the Zaire Basin, where conditions favored prosperous agricultural and fishing economies, were similar societies including the *Bushongo* of the Kasai, and the *Luba-Lunda* of Katanga (Shaba). The Bushongo were skilled in weaving and iron and copper smelting, and they developed a sophisticated hierarchical system of chiefs and political behavior, and a division of labor. The rich mineral deposits of the Katanga, mined as early as the eighth century A.D., provided the economic base of the Luba-Lunda states. These states reached their climax in the late sixteenth century, and while their capitals were not as permanent as those in West Africa, they were considerable centers of government and trade. Court officials and skilled craftsmen—smiths, weavers, carvers, and others—congregated around the capitals and lived off the tribute paid in foodstuffs from the surrounding countryside. They controlled a prosperous business in ivory from Lake Bangweulu to the Benguela coast.

A series of kingdoms existed in the vicinity of the West Rift Valley between Lake Albert and Lake Tanganyika (Fig. 4-2). They included *Buganda*, *Bunyoro*, *Ankole* (all within the present-day boundaries of Uganda), and *Karagwe*, *Rwanda*, and *Burundi*, each quite likely having at its zenith populations of half a million or more people. As with the pre-Islamic states of the Sudan, they were ruled by divine kings who governed through an elaborate hierarchy of court officials and provincial chiefs.

Throughout the centuries the East African highlands attracted waves of foreign traders and conquerors, mainly from the Ethiopian borderlands and the southern Nile region. Slave traders periodically pushed southward up the Nile, and by the middle of the nineteenth century, Arab merchants had visited the court of Buganda to obtain ivory and slaves in exchange for cloth and guns. The main trade route ran from the coast to Tabora, through Karagwe and on to Ankole, Buganda, and Bunyoro. The Buganda kingdom was the largest and most powerful in the region and occupied a strategic location on the north shore of Lake Victoria. Its warriors not only controlled its lakeshore stronghold, but regularly crossed Lake Victoria to control trade to the south. Like most kingdoms of its time, Buganda succumbed to colonial domination by the turn of this century.

Two contrasting state systems remain to be discussed: one about which there is a great deal of speculation and controversy surrounding the origin and purpose of its massive stone edifices and structures and the other about whose military might and plunder there is considerable oral and written history. The first centers on a series of Iron Age states situated on the Rhodesian highveld in and around *Great Zimbabwe*, while the second concerns the aggressive *Zulu* under Shaka and Dingaan.

At the time the states of Mali, Ghana, and Songhai flourished in West Africa, there existed between the Zambezi and Limpopo Rivers a number of Iron Age states that had well-established trade connections with the east coast and points beyond, possibly India and China. The *Mwanamutapa* states of the people called Shona Karanga were the most significant, and the most imposing remnants are those of Zimbabwe. Zimbabwe is a group of stone ruins a few miles southeast of Fort Victoria, Rhodesia,* which, in view of their massive walls and towers, rounded gateways and strategic siting, are evidence of

* The national name for Rhodesia is Zimbabwe.

Zanzibar, once an Arab city-state, was the largest slaving port in East Africa until the mid-nineteenth century when approximately 45,000 slaves were sold each year. Today it is part of Tanzania, and is known for its clove exports. (Harm J. deBlij)

power and ordered settlement. The so-called "Acropolis" occupies an almost impregnable position atop a granite hill, while on the plains below stands the "Temple" or "Elliptical Building" both made of local granite blocks, and structurally showing striking similarity to fortifications in Axum. The "Temple" measures some 300 ft by 220 and its girdling walls stand 30 ft high and over 20 ft thick. The total complex gives a sense of power, skill, and permanence.

The precise chronology of the Zimbabwe complex is still unknown but it was probably built and rebuilt by at least three successive occupants. The oldest part of the ruins date back to the fifth century when simple structures of wood and straw predominated. Zimbabwe may then have been the capital of the Guruuswa (Urozwi) kingdom, and by the twelfth century it had commercial links with Sofala and other coastal city-states through which it exchanged gold and ivory for porcelain, copper coins, glass beads, and other luxuries. By the middle of the fifteenth century, the focus of power had shifted northward to the Zambezi and Inyanga Mountains bordering modern Mozambique. There smaller stone structures were built, the hillsides were terraced, and gold and other metals were mined. But by the seventeenth century control over this vast and rich interior was threatened by Arab and Portuguese entrepreneurs, the Portuguese eventually installing a puppet king over the Mwanamutapa in 1630. An outlier of the Zimbabwe-Mwanamutapa cultures existed south of the Limpopo at Mapungubwe, which was intermittently occupied by different peoples from before the ninth century until the eighteenth century when Nguni invaders from the south destroyed the state.

The "Temple" or "Elliptical Building" of Zimbabwe, Rhodesia (Zimbabwe). These and other local stone structures may date back to the 12th century when its occupants were trading gold and ivory for porcelain, glass beads, copper coins and other luxuries imported through the East African port of Sofala. (Rhodesia Ministry of Information)

Finally, a powerful nineteenth-century military empire was situated in Zululand, South Africa. First under Dingiswayo, and later under Shaka and Dingaan, the Nguni-speaking *Zulus* controlled an extensive pastoral and game-rich region from Natal north to the Zambezi, while the Zulu core area itself focused on the Tugela River (Fig. 4-2). Shaka Zulu amassed great regiments of warriors well trained in hand-to-hand fighting to extend his control over weaker groups, and was the most widely feared of the Zulu leaders who, in the course of his 10-year reign, may have slaughtered up to a million people. His first capital, located near Babanango, was appropriately called Kwa Bulawayo or "The Place of Killing." He later established another capital, also called Kwa Bulawayo, near Eshowe. An even larger military capital, Kraal Dukuza, was built near

Stanger. Shaka Zulu had a small group of councillors, but he personally made every important decision. He was the commander in chief, the high priest, ultimate court of appeal, and the sole source of laws. He was the wealthiest man in the kingdom, owning thousands of cattle and commanding the services of thousands of warriors and hundreds of women. He ruled by fear, and fear became an important nation-building factor as he amalgamated many separate tribes into the strongest single nation in Southern Africa. Following his assassination in 1828, the Zulu kingdom lost its impetus, and under another tyrannical leader, Dingaan, the Zulus gradually succumbed to British rule.

From this brief review of early state organization in Africa, a number of general conclusions may be drawn. It should be clear that much of the continent has enjoyed a long and rich history, a history of diverse sociopolitical organization. Like states of today, the pre-European states of Africa had towns and cities, clearly defined divisions of labor, class structures, communications networks, and spheres of influence and possession. Commonly they were imposed by conquest, by militarily superior invaders imposing their will on peoples with different customs and languages, and they survived only as long as the conquering minority could manage to extract tribute from their subjects. Sometimes there was little cohesion in the state, the only real bond being the periodic collection of tribute by the ruler and his agents. Often the state would take the form of a cluster with a strong central kingdom and less effectively controlled provinces around the periphery. But internally, these states were not ruled in a hereditary fashion by a succession of descendants of a privileged family. They were not normally feudal in character—although Africa has seen feudalism, for instance in Ethiopia—and the great administrative force serving the divine king was a sometimes endless array of viceroys, officials, chiefs, and other agents.

Northeast Africa's role in the emergence and character of these pre-European states was crucial. From Kush and Axum, iron technology, stonemasonry, and other crafts and skills diffused as far west as the Niger and south beyond the Limpopo; from the Nile and Mesopotamia came grains and cattle, staples in so many regions today; and from the north, Islam was spread through and across the Sahara and Sahel, and down the east coast. For centuries peoples and cultures moved across Africa, the movement of Bantu-speaking peoples from the Lake Chad-Cameroon Highland area eventually affecting all areas to the south and east. Commercial linkages were widespread, East African cowrie shells being a medium of exchange as far west as Mali and Songhai.

Bibliography

Davidson, B. *The Lost Cities of Africa*. Boston: Little, Brown and Co., 1959.

———. *Africa: History of a Continent*. New York: The Macmillan Co., 1972.

Fage, J. D. *An Atlas of African History*. London: Edward Arnold Ltd., 1958.

Greenberg, J. H. *The Languages of Africa*. Second Edition. Bloomington: Indiana University Press, 1966.

Hallett, R. *Africa to 1875: A Modern History*. Ann Arbor: University of Michigan Press, 1970.

———. *Africa Since 1875: A Modern History*. Ann Arbor: University of Michigan Press, 1970.

Klein, M.A. and G. W. Johnson (eds.). *Perspectives on the African Past*. Boston: Little, Brown and Company, 1972.

Murdock, G. P. *Africa: Its People and Their Culture History*. New York: McGraw-Hill, 1959.

Murphy, R. "The Decline of North Africa Since the Roman Occupation: Climatic or Human?" *Annals, A.A.G.*, Vol. 41, No. 2 (June, 1951), pp. 116–32.

Oliver, R. and A. Atmore. *Africa Since 1800*. Cambridge: Cambridge University Press, 1967.

Oliver, R. and J. D. Fage. *A Short History of Africa*. Baltimore: Penguin Books, 1962.

Skinner, E. P. (ed.). *Peoples and Cultures of Africa*. Garden City: Natural History Press, 1973.

FIVE

The course of African history was profoundly changed by the colonial powers of Europe. Each power came for its own reasons with its own values, perceptions, and institutions; and each left its mark on the peoples and landscapes in the form of language, education, law, technology, and so on. To understand Africa's contemporary political and economic geographies, it is necessary to have an appreciation of the ways in which colonial Europe partitioned Africa, viewed its peoples and resources, and brought to Africa instruments of change. This chapter emphasizes these processes in Africa south of the Sahara, where the colonial interlude was most complex.

Early Portuguese Interests

Portuguese navigators made contact with West Africa in the first half of the fifteenth century. There they carried on what the Arabs had initiated in East Africa: a profitable traffic in slaves, for many centuries Africa's major export. While fewer slaves were shipped to the Iberian Peninsula than from East Africa to the Middle East and South Asia, the trade was nevertheless significant and set the stage for further human exploitation to be extended to the New World.

The fifteenth and sixteenth centuries in Africa may well be called Portugal's centuries, although they were not only Portugal's. It was the Portuguese, however, who first rounded the Cape of Good Hope and sailed past the tip of Africa into the Indian Ocean, settling along the east coast and disputing possession of the lands of the east with the Arabs.

THE COLONIAL INTERLUDE

Although some individual explorers penetrated far inland, the Portuguese settlements were mainly peripheral. The city of Benguela, Angola, dates from this period, as does Lourenço Marques (now called Maputo), Mozambique, although settlement on Delagoa Bay was intermittent until the eighteenth century.

Initially, the voyages of Bartholomew Diaz and Vasco Da Gama produced friendly contact with the Arabs, and it was an Arab guide who first led the Portuguese to the Indies. Soon, however, Portuguese power subjugated the Arab holdings on the East African coast and spread as far north as Arabia. By not consolidating their settlements, but maintaining real interest only in the route to the Indies, the Portuguese made the error that was eventually to lead to their defeat. As the sixteenth century drew to a close, the Portuguese Empire in Europe was declining, and the Arabs began systematically pushing the invaders from East Africa. Mombasa was beleaguered and bombed numerous times, as both sides took and lost the city repeatedly. Shortly after 1700, the Portuguese had lost all the land they once held north of Cape Delgado, the present northeastern extremity of Mozambique.

In West Africa, meanwhile, the Portuguese slave-trading stations, thriving from Senegal to Angola, also shared in the decline of Portuguese power, and Britain, the Netherlands, and France appeared on the scene. A glance at the seventeenth-century map reveals that by this time other products were being taken: in addition to the Slave Coast, the map shows a Gold Coast and an Ivory Coast. The slave trade, however, remained the most profitable of all, stimulated by the demand in the Americas. Nevertheless, few real European settlements were established. Along the coast of West Africa, there were some forts, but they were there primarily for the protection of the trade. Slave traders associated with Africans who helped carry out the capture of slaves, and thus the real penetration of Africa by the white man continued to be delayed. In tropical Africa, it was not until late in the eighteenth century that the age of exploration commenced, as the slave trade began to wane. To all intents and purposes, the accumulation of knowledge concerning interior Africa began only during the nineteenth century.

Hollanders and British at the Cape

Portugal yielded its power position in Europe and on the seas to Holland, which had emerged undefeated from 80 years of war with Spain. During the period of slave trading and intermittent, peripheral white settlement in tropical Africa, the Dutch established a revictualling station for their ships at a place neglected by the Portuguese, Table Bay. Founded in 1652, the settlement at the foot of Table Mountain was the first and for many decades the only European base to possess some characteristics of permanence. Out of it grew the city of Cape Town, today second in size only to Johannesburg in Southern Africa.

The Dutch, failing to oust the Portuguese permanently from Benguela, chose the site of Cape Town mainly because it had not been taken by others, and they found themselves in possession of one of Africa's best natural harbors. In the centuries to come, it became clear that Cape Town dominated what is economically the richest part of Africa, the south, but initially the Hollanders were not interested in the colonization of the Cape. Having learned from the Portuguese the need for a revictualling station, they established one, but white immigration was actually discouraged, as it was feared that a large Cape colony would become an administrative liability. Thus Cape Town's growth was retarded, and it has been estimated that a century and a half later, in 1800, the total white population of the city and the colony which had inevitably developed was only about 25,000.

The Dutch East India Company, engaged on behalf of the Netherlands government in the trade with the Indies, introduced a number of crops to the Cape, traded with the local Hottentots for meat, and imported a large number of slaves from Madagascar, Malaysia, and even West Africa, when local labor ran in short supply. The company was unable to contain the Dutch citizens who had fulfilled their tour of duty with the government as farmers or employees and who refused to return to Europe, however. Many of these white people left the environs of Cape Town and trekked into the interior, warring with Bushman and Bantu over the lands they desired. There, before the end of the eighteenth century, whites were entering Africa's interior, and for some time the southern tip of the continent was better known than most other regions.

Like Portugal before it, Holland declined from its position as the leading sea power of Europe. After a brief temporary wardship, Britain in 1806 took permanent possession of the Cape, finding it a stagnating, backward settlement and an asset mainly as a means of preserving sea power. Britain also showed little interest in the interior. In this hinterland of Southern Africa, meanwhile, a most significant event was taking place. Among the many Bantu peoples which had migrated southward were the Zulu, who settled in Natal (Fig. 5-1). Strong leadership by a succession of chiefs who developed a degree of military organization the like of which Bantu Africa had never seen thrust the Zulu empire into prominence as the most powerful on the subcontinent. Waging war on tribal peoples in every possible direction, the Zulu decimated the African population on the plateau, defied only by the Basuto and the Swazi.

With the whites confined mainly to the Cape and the powerful Zulu concentrated in Natal, direct conflict did not seem inevitable. Events in Britain, however, resulted in a mass exodus of white Dutch settlers from the Cape into the regions over which the Zulu held sway. The efforts of William Wilberforce, aimed at the elimination of the slave trade, were reaching the public conscience in Britain, and, in 1833, slavery was abolished throughout the British Empire, of which the Cape Colony was a part. The Dutch settlers who remained after the demise of the Dutch East India Company had shown increasing dissatisfaction with Britain's efforts to anglicize the Cape, and the termination of the practice of slavery was the last straw. So began, in 1836, the mass movement of whites, most of Dutch ancestry, onto the plateau of Southern Africa in what has become known as the Great Trek (Fig. 5-1). It was the vanguard of a series of waves of white immigration, resulting in the only really large white population accumulation in all Africa.

The Great Trek eventually brought white and Zulu into conflict, the decisive battle being fought at Blood River in Natal, where the Zulu, although numerically greatly in the majority, were defeated. It was the desire of the Dutch ("Boers," as they were often called) to establish beyond the borders of the British Cape Colony, pastoral republics where they might retain their cultural and religious heritage. Having defeated the Zulu, the Boers seemed a step closer to their ideal, and although Britain invaded Natal and removed the Dutch from that region, they remained on the plateau itself. There, the Orange Free State Republic and the Republic of South Africa (Transvaal) were founded by independence-minded frontiersmen of Dutch origin. Although there were some border skirmishes and occasional friction with Africans, the Boer republics were recognized by Britain, and it appeared that the goal of the trekkers had been achieved.

The temporary *status quo* was disturbed

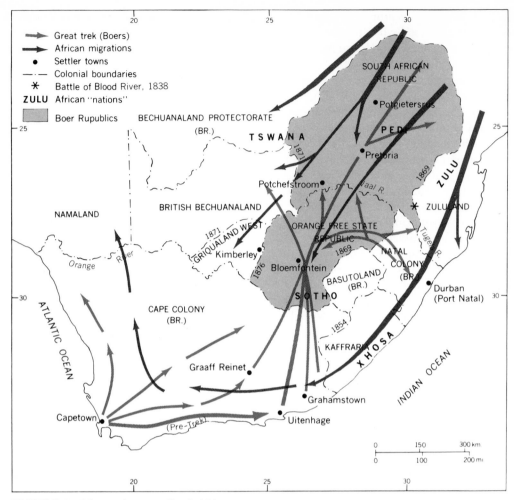

FIGURE 5-1 *Nineteenth century South Africa.*

in 1867 by the discovery, on the banks of one of Southern Africa's great rivers, the Orange, of diamonds. The richness of the fields and their relative accessibility brought fortune hunters not only from all parts of South Africa but also from overseas, producing a second Great Trek, this time initiated by economic causes. Kimberley became the economic capital of Southern Africa, and the building of railroads into the interior was begun. The British annexed the diamondiferous region to the Cape Colony, thus being enabled to administer the new city and its inhabitants (Fig. 5-1). Although dis-

pleased with this action, the leaders of the Boer republics did not attempt seriously to alter it, largely in order not to threaten their continued existence.

Another mineral find, this time a much more significant one, occurred in 1884, when gold was discovered in the South African Republic near what is today the city of Johannesburg. This brought a third Great Trek, but there was no way in which the British at the Cape could annex this territory without war. The republic was unequipped for the mass of foreign intruders, and administrative chaos resulted. Johannesburg began its uncontrolled growth, within 10 years reaching 100,000, while the capital, Pretoria, was eclipsed. Johannesburg became the economic capital of the region, a position it has retained to this day. President Paul Kruger and his stubborn Afrikaner (Boer) government, resentful of the disruption created by Johannesburg's large foreign population, continually refused to cooperate in city development and denied the allocation of funds for necessary amenities. Friction between the Afrikaners and foreigners was rife. Britain, meanwhile, partly on the advice of such people as Cecil Rhodes and Dr. Leander Starr Jameson, continued to cast covetous eyes on this rich economic prize. Troops massed on the republic's borders, and in 1899 war broke out.

In the Anglo-Boer War, white faced white on a scale unprecedented in Southern Africa. Britain, after some initial setbacks, at length defeated the Boers, who maintained a guerrilla campaign when defeated on the battlefield. Having finally subdued the obstinate Afrikaner opposition, the British made an effort to grant the Boers some participation in the affairs of what had once been their country. In 1910, the Union of South Africa came into being, joining the two British colonies (Cape and Natal) and the two defeated republics (Orange Free State and Transvaal). Although victorious, the British gave in to several of the Afrikaners' desires when this Union was created. One of these was the elimination from the political scene of all African and other nonwhite elements: the Union became a state ruled by an all-white electorate. Nonwhites at first retained some indirect representation, but this was subsequently discontinued. The Union survived for just over half a century, for the Afrikaners came to dominate the white electorate, and in 1948 an Afrikaner government was returned to power. It promised economic development, racial segregation, and a revival of the republic; by 1961, the three promises had all been kept, as on May 31 of that year a new Republic of South Africa came into being.

The Explorers

The developments which took place in South Africa did not mirror the sequence of events in tropical Africa. White penetration of the south came early, and numbers were comparatively large. Northward, it was long left to a few explorers to investigate the interior. Some, in spite of heroic deeds, have fallen into relative obscurity, like James Bruce, who entered what is today Ethiopia and the Sudan, following the Blue Nile to its confluence with the White Nile (Fig. 5-2). Among the early explorers to achieve fame was Mungo Park, who attempted to solve the riddle of the Niger River. On many early maps, the Niger is seen to flow from east (the general vicinity of Lake Chad) to west, reaching the ocean as the Gambia. Park, in 1795, traveled up the Gambia, hoping to find an actual link with the Niger. On his first journey, he did indeed find the Niger and became aware that its flow is eastward, not west, but he was unable to follow the great river to its mouth, as he had intended. Having disproved the Gambia-Niger connection, Park in 1805 set out again in an effort to trace the Niger to its mouth which, it is thought, he believed to be the Zaire. The great explorer met his death in the waters of the river that was the object of his search: he drowned during a battle with local Nigerians. Only in 1830 did Richard Lander complete Park's task and prove that the Niger flows into its delta on the Guinea Gulf.

While explorers like Hugh Clapperton, René Caillé, and Lander were traversing the western part of Africa, equatorial Africa remained barely touched (Fig. 5-2). South of

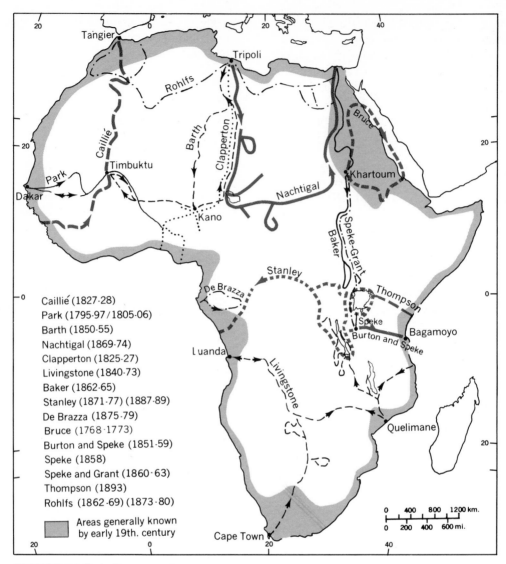

Caillié (1827-28)
Park (1795-97 / 1805-06)
Barth (1850-55)
Nachtigal (1869-74)
Clapperton (1825-27)
Livingstone (1840-73)
Baker (1862-65)
Stanley (1871-77) (1887-89)
De Brazza (1875-79)
Bruce (1768-1773)
Burton and Speke (1851-59)
Speke (1858)
Speke and Grant (1860-63)
Thompson (1893)
Rohlfs (1862-69) (1873-80)

Areas generally known by early 19th. century

0   400   800   1200 km.
0   200   400   600 mi.

FIGURE 5-2 *Early European explorers.*

the Zaire River was the Kingdom of Kongo, which was entered by a number of Portuguese from the coastal settlements during the sixteenth and seventeenth centuries, but the Katanga region was not reached until 1798, when the Portuguese explorer Lacerda penetrated it. Although there were sporadic efforts by Portuguese and Arabs to enter the interior, the real age of the explorers in equatorial Africa did not begin until the middle of the nineteenth century with the travels of the most famous of all, David Livingstone, who covered extensive areas.

Livingstone was one of the emissaries of the London Missionary Society, an organization which was very active in Southern Africa. He arrived in Cape Town in 1841 and traveled to Bechuanaland (now Botswana). There began his first series of traverses, and in 1849 he reached Lake Ngami, a part of the Makadikgadi-Okavango swamp and delta complex in the Kalahari Desert.

Subsequently, he crossed Angola to Luanda, which he reached in 1854. The next year, he returned to the region of the upper Zambezi River, intending to follow the stream to its mouth. In the process, he came upon the stupendous falls which he named Victoria Falls, and in 1856 he succeeded in reaching the Zambezi delta.

In 1858, the second phase of Livingstone's explorations began, as he traveled up the Zambezi from its mouth, past the rapids to the Shiré confluence. He then proceeded along the Shiré until he reached Lake Nyasa (now Lake Malawi). The lake may have been seen previously by Portuguese and Arabs, but it was Livingstone whose vivid descriptions made these areas known to the outside world.

For many years, the problem of the source of the (White) Nile had been unsolved, and Livingstone set out to find it in 1865, in his third series of traverses. This was the period during which the great explorer was lost, his fate unknown to the world for half a decade. After Henry Morton Stanley succeeded in locating Livingstone in 1871 at Ujiji on Lake Tanganyika, the two explorers together sought the origins of the Nile, traversing the area around the south end of Lake Tanganyika. Soon after Stanley's departure, in 1873, Livingstone died, weakened by malaria and other diseases.

The Nile problem was solved by John Speke, who had entered East Africa in 1857, crossed the plateau, and, with Richard Burton, reached Lake Tanganyika in 1858 (Fig. 5-2). Subsequently, without Burton, Speke traversed the region about Lake Victoria, although he did not on that first journey discover the Nile outlet of the lake. In 1860, after having been taken prisoner by the Baganda, he did locate the outlet, realizing that the question of the Nile's origin had finally been solved, unless there should be a southerly connection between Lakes Victoria and Tanganyika. Samuel Baker in 1863 placed the Nile outlet of Lake Victoria beyond doubt by traveling up the Nile through the Sudd, meeting Speke and his companion, James Grant, who were coming down the same river.

Stanley returned to Africa in 1874 and proved that the rivers west of Lake Tanganyika which he and Livingstone had seen were in the drainage basin of the Congo and could be followed to the Atlantic Ocean. It so happened that in 1876 King Leopold II of Belgium convened a meeting of geographers with knowledge of equatorial Africa, and Stanley, who reported on the nature of the Congo in the heart of the continent, impressed Leopold with the potentialities of a transportation route there. Consequently, Stanley in 1879 mounted an expedition into the Congo on behalf of the king. Obtaining concessions and treaties, within five years he accumulated for Leopold a tremendous territory that came to be known as the Congo Free State. Stanley thus changed from explorer to land hunter, and as such he played a significant role in the great struggle for Africa's territory.

The diaries of these explorers contain vivid descriptions of Africa's landscapes and peoples and did much to arouse the interest of missionary societies bent on spreading the gospel and eliminating slavery and human suffering. They also stirred the imagination of the monied class who urged their respective governments to act on their behalf in establishing control of the newly found riches and regions. But for the majority of peoples in Europe and America, the diaries meant little more than excitement and drama set on a totally foreign and exotic stage.

The "Scramble for Africa"

While exploration was still in progress in equatorial Africa, the struggle among European powers for possession of Africa's land—a struggle that was to lead to the colonial partition of virtually the entire continent—had already begun elsewhere. As early as 1857, France and Britain came to an agreement in which France recognized Britain's sovereignty over the Gambia River and its valley, while Britain consented to France's occupance of the area around the Senegal River. Thus was the concept of "spheres of influence" born. The only territories to escape Europe's nineteenth-century invasion of Africa were coastal Sierra Leone, itself a British colony but established in the 1790s, with the special purpose of providing a home for freed slaves, and Liberia, founded by American interests for a similar purpose in the 1820s. Even Ethiopia, the feudal empire that had survived the upheavals of Africa over several centuries, was eventually overrun in the twentieth century by the European state last in colonial expansion, Italy.

The French were probably the first to recognize the value of a continuous, interconnected empire in Africa; in any event, the French dream of "Africa French from Algeria to Congo" preceded the British ideal of "Africa British from the Cape to Cairo." Thus, France concentrated her efforts in West Africa and the Maghreb and made considerable headway at an early stage. Britain continued to view her African possessions as isolated stations rather than as a contiguous empire, and then France's expansionism was temporarily halted by the war with Germany. After her 1871 defeat and some territorial loss in Europe, France, stimulated by the need for a revival of national pride and prestige, again focused her interest upon West Africa. By then, however, Germany and especially Britain were also engaged in the struggle for land in this region. Viewing with concern the spread of French power across the Sudan, the British decided to acquire the hinterland of their coastal trading stations, which, they feared, might be cut off from the interior upon which they depended for survival. Thus, Britain penetrated the interior of Sierra Leone, the Gold Coast (now Ghana) and Nigeria.

In Nigeria, the British sphere of influence was expanded by the Royal Niger Company, formed by British trading interests and supported by the British government. Its forerunner, the United Africa Company, established in 1879, was instrumental in containing the latest European power to enter with colonialist designs, Germany. Although individual land hunters were active on behalf of the German state earlier, it was only in 1884 that Lomé on the Togoland coast was proclaimed German territory. A narrow strip of hinterland was also claimed, effectively separating the Gold Coast sphere of influence from the Nigeria region. Clearly, the major object of German claims there was the obstruction of the designs of the rival colonial powers.

In equatorial Africa, the Belgian sphere of influence was in the west, and during the first half of the nineteenth century Arab power continued to dominate the east. While Stanley was gathering treaties and concessions on behalf of the King of the Belgians, creating the Congo Free State, East Africa remained under Bantu domination in the interior and Arab hegemony in the littoral. Arab power centered on the island of Zanzibar, which had long been a focus of Arab activity. During the first half of the nineteenth century, the Sultanate of Zanzibar was associated politically with Arabia, but in 1861, shortly after the Speke-Burton explorations of the interior had begun, these ties were severed. With the opening of the Suez Canal in 1869, the sultanate attained unprecedented importance, and the sultan laid claim to large sections of the African coast. Although both Britain and Germany were somewhat interested in East Africa by this time, largely because of the reports of the explorers, the sultan's claims were recognized. Britain was less concerned with obtaining territory than with the elimination of the slave trade, and she sought good relations with the Zanzibar rulers to achieve this end. It was not until the 1880s that the British were finally successful in their efforts, and by then the sultanate had begun to crumble.

The interest shown by various European colonial powers in Africa was due to a great extent to the efforts of the explorers. The success of colonization, however, must in large measure be attributed to individuals who could also be called explorers, though less in search of truth than of gain. Stanley, an explorer at first, became such a land hunter, and some of the others became as famous as their predecessors. For Germany, Robert Flegel in West Africa (especially the fringes of the Nigeria sphere of influence) and Karl Peters in East Africa obtained concessions from local chiefs. De Brazza worked for France in the region which was to become French Equatorial Africa. For Britain, Rhodes penetrated Zambezia, later to be named after him, and obtained vase concessions. It is due to these men more than any others that the spread of European influence in various parts of Africa was rapid once it began.

As the spheres of influence of the colonial powers expanded and rival claims were made to certain parts of the continent, it became clear that a discussion of Africa's colonial partition was necessary. There was real danger of open hostilities in some areas, and in others, the local chiefs had ceded their land more than once, first to the representatives of one colonial government, then to those of another. Hence, in 1884, the Germans convened a conference in Berlin, lasting into 1885, at which various colonial possessions were consolidated, problematic boundaries defined and delimited, and some sections of land exchanged. Rules for the "effective occupation" of the territorial claims were established, and some order was brought out of the political chaos into which the continent had been thrown.

The story of East Africa during the last decades of the nineteenth century and the beginning of the twentieth is one of rivalry and friction between Britain and Germany.

In the south of this region, Karl Peters, an emissary of the German Colonization Society, traveled through what is today Tanzania, obtaining treaties and concessions from African chiefs. Even chiefs who were already under the jurisdiction of the Zanzibar sultanate gave Peters concessions, so that by 1885 he had claimed for Germany most of the area of Tanganyika (now Tanzania). Having become aware of his activities, the Sultan of Zanzibar objected to Peters' claims to land belonging to the sultanate, but Germany responded by sending a fleet to support them. Although the threat of naval bombardment forced the sultan to yield, there were uprisings by both Arabs and Africans in Tanganyika itself, and some years were to elapse before German power was undisputed. The Arabs rose because they feared that the slave trade would be ended by German occupation, and subsequent revolutions were sustained by Africans who had been affected by slavery but never by actual territorial subversion. Among the African peoples, the Hehe distinguished themselves by courage and perseverance. The last uprising was the famous "Maji-Maji" rebellion of 1905–1906, involving most of southern Tanganyika, which was put down with great bloodshed. Germany's activities in East Africa and South West Africa (now Namibia), where she was involved in a bloody campaign against Herero people, are among the darkest chapters of European history in Africa, rivaling the atrocities committed in the Congo and Portuguese-Arab terror in sustaining the slave trade.

While Tanganyika came under German control, Britain was engaged in the colonization of other areas. In 1888, the British East Africa Company was created, with aims similar to those of the Royal Niger Company but with substantially less capital. Leaders of the company were aware that the Baganda people were likely to play a dominant role in a developing East Africa, and a railroad was begun to connect Mombasa, on

One of the first undertakings of the colonial governments to gain greater control of their new possessions, was the building of railways from the coasts to the interior. The photo shows a steam train on the Mombasa-Nairobi line, Kenya. (World Bank)

the Kenya coast, with Kisumu, on the shores of Lake Victoria. In 1890, the failing Sultanate of Zanzibar became a British protectorate, which included a strip on the Kenya coast but not the portion that had been claimed by Germany. Thanks to the efforts of the company, this territory in 1893 also became a part of the British sphere of influence as a protectorate.

The British East Africa Company, unlike the British South Africa Company and the Royal Niger Company, did not thrive on rich mineral finds and agricultural development. Burdened with a multitude of administrative functions which London was reluctant to take over, the company was frequently in financial difficulties, as when it was building the railroad to Uganda. In-

deed, its charter was terminated in 1895, eight years before the railroad reached the shores of Lake Victoria. At the turn of the century, nevertheless, a British protectorate existed over Uganda, Kenya, and Zanzibar, and the company had made a major contribution in bringing this about.

In Southern Africa, the events leading to the formation of the Union of South Africa had occupied the center of the stage to such an extent that the huge territory of South West Africa was virtually neglected until German claims to it were substantiated by armed force. A war had long been in progress between the Hottentot and the Herero, a Bantu people, and the lives of white missionaries and traders were endangered. Appealing for protection, these people failed to get support from London or Cape Town. There were a number of whites of German nationality living in South West Africa, and the German rulers took a sympathetic interest in their plight. In the 1880s, German claims in the region were expanded through the efforts of Adolph Lüderitz, and the appearance of German ships off the shores of the territory removed all doubt that Germany's presence was to be permanent. At the 1884–1885 Berlin Conference, the Germans insisted upon connecting their territory with the Zambezi River, and thus the Caprivi Strip came into being, extending eastward from the northern edge of the main body of German South West Africa.

One of those regions whose ownership was not settled was Zambezia, the area around the great Zambezi River, lying between Angola and Mozambique, north of the Transvaal and south of the Congo and Tanganyika. In 1886, France and Germany appear to have agreed that Portugal should extend her possessions in coastal Angola and Mozambique across the entire continent in order to link these two portions of her empire. This agreement was less an act of friendship toward Portugal than an effort to obstruct British imperialism in the south, but Rhodes and his supporters helped foil this plan. The Pioneer Column, a vanguard of white settlers equipped by Rhodes, penetrated Matabeleland in 1890 and began a white immigration which was to reach sizeable proportions. The British South Africa Company obtained concessions from African chiefs, and Portuguese expansion into the interior was limited by agreement.

In the northeast, including the "Horn" and the Sudan, the center of the historico-geographical stage during the last decades of the nineteenth century was occupied by Britain and several powerful local rulers. Also interested in this area were France and Italy. France wished to extend her West African domain to the Red Sea and the Gulf of Aden, and Italy, having occupied coastal sections of Eritrea and Somaliland, desired the Abyssinian (Ethiopian) interior. Britain's protectorate over Egypt helped lead to British subjugation of a region that had long been the object of Egyptian expansionism, the Sudan.

The process of colonization in the northeast was only partially completed. Ethiopia was consolidated under a powerful leader, Menelik, who was also a skillful negotiator and military tactician. While the colonial powers were encroaching upon this part of Africa, Menelik himself embarked on a program of Ethiopian expansionism, and the boundaries he pushed far beyond the limits of the Ethiopian Plateau were eventually recognized. He defeated the Italians in battle (Adowa, 1896) and laid the foundations of the Ethiopian state. In the Sudan, joint British-Egyptian control was interrupted in 1881 by the Mahdist revolt, led by Muhammad Ahmad, and was not reestablished until Kitchener defeated the remainder of the Dervish Army in 1898. Immediately afterward, French encroachment on the Sudan was repudiated by a show of force, and joint British-Egyptian government of the region took effect once more.

Colonial Policies

The European nations partitioned Africa primarily to ensure that they would not be excluded from areas that might prove valuable in the future. Few areas were expected to produce immediate wealth, so that pace of "development" was slow. The colonial powers felt their primary responsibility was to maintain law and order, at minimum cost to the European taxpayer. Thus the first two decades of colonial rule were characterized by the definition and delimitation of administrative boundaries, the establish-

Cotton harvest from the Gezira Scheme, Sudan. Cotton was a common and profitable colonial cash crop in the savanna regions. (UN)

ment of government machinery, the in-migration of administrators, missionaries, and settlers, and the building of railways and other strategic services that later facili-tated the exploitation and development of Africa's resources and peoples. Each colonial power approached these and other issues from its own particular political and cultural perspective. Their policies changed through time and differed from place to place. These are highlighted in the paragraphs that follow and are developed more fully in subsequent chapters.

GERMANY

Germany's colonial tenure in Africa was short lived and unsuccessful: what Germany acquired by conquest and treaty after 1885, it lost to its conquerers following World War I. In West Africa the Germans established themselves in Togoland, a narrow finger of land separating British Nigeria from the Gold Coast; and in Cameroon where they pushed far northward and came close to

fragmenting the extensive French West Afri-can realm. In East Africa they obtained a part of what is today Tanzania, thus dealing a blow to British intensions of a Cape-to-Cairo axis, while in Southern Africa, Ger-many acquired the desert lands of South West Africa, today called Namibia (Fig. 5–3a).

Germany's economic and political inter-ests in Africa were pursued with a fervor un-matched by other colonial powers. In South West Africa, Germany conducted a cruel and oppressive campaign against the Herero people, while its infrastructural investments in Cameroon and German East Africa made these two territories profitable possessions by 1914. Germans were encouraged by their government and colonial societies to settle their African territories; land was set aside for them, particularly in areas destined to be opened up by railways. These included highland areas in southern Cameroon and in the vicinity of Mt. Kilimanjaro. A railway was built from Dar es Salaam to Lake

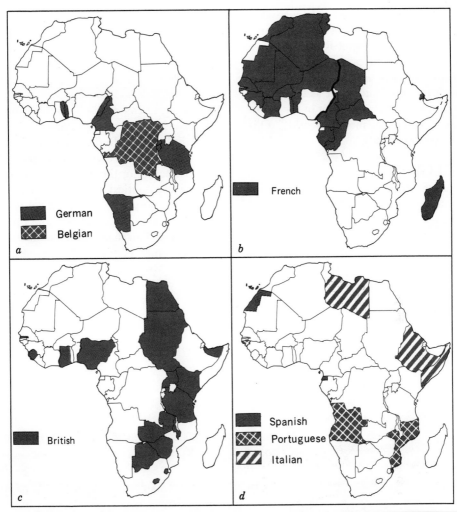

FIGURE 5-3 *Colonial possessions in Africa.* A, *German and Belgian;* B, *French;* C, *British;* D, *Portuguese, Italian, and Spanish.*

Tanganyika to compete with British interests, while in both Togoland and Cameroon powerful monopoly companies were chartered to operate in and develop each protectorate. However, they suffered from insufficient capital and poor organization. Full political power, even at the local level, was in the hands of German colonial authorities, and the German Reichstag believed that the colonial governments should be self-supporting. Consequently, development grants were rare, and revenues were derived primarily from head taxes, import duties, and the sale

of commercial franchises.

Following World War I, Germany's colonies were divided among the victor nations according to principles established by the League of Nations. South West Africa was entrusted to the Union of South Africa as a Class C Mandate, which meant that it would be administered as an integral part of South Africa. Cameroon was similarly partitioned, the smaller British section being administered with Nigeria, and the larger share being made a mandate of France. Most of German East Africa became a Class B Mandate of Britain under the name Tanganyika, while Belgium took charge of a small mountainous section consisting of Ruanda and Urundi. Those countries undertaking the task of administrator agreed to govern their new territories until such time as they were "able to stand on their own feet in the strenuous conditions of the modern world." (Oliver and Atmore, 1967).

BELGIUM

Apart from the mandate and trusteeship over Ruanda-Urundi, the Belgians possessed only one colony: The Congo (now Zaire), once the personal property of King Leopold II (Fig. 5-3a). In 1907, following reports of merciless exploitation of Congolese labor to meet quotas of ivory and rubber, the Congo's administration was taken over by

the Belgian state. Belgium saw its colonial task as a paternal one. It never viewed the Congo as an "overseas Belgium," and it never intended to make Belgians of the Congolese people.

Belgian colonial policies were such that decisions regarding the Congo were made only in Brussels. In the Congo itself, neither the European representatives of the Belgian government, nor the white settlers, possessed any political rights or voice in the fate of the territory. Neither, until a matter of months before independence, did the local Congolese. Paternalism extended also into the economic, educational, and social spheres. Much progress was made in elementary education, but higher education for Africans was virtually nonexistent, and

Open-pit copper mine, Shaba (formerly Katanga), Zaire. Copper was the former Belgian Congo's principal export for many years. (Gécamines, Zaire).

The Port facilities of Kinshasa (formerly Leopoldville), Zaire. The downtown area is in the background, while a "train" of river-barges pulls away from the sheds and railway terminal of this, Africa's largest river port. (Belgo-American Development Corporation)

when independence came (1960) the new state had only 30 Congolese university graduates. A broad elementary education was preferred to one that produced a highly educated African elite, and even the small group of *evolués* (middle class "evolved" Africans) could not aspire to Belgian nationality and equality, and was viewed as in need of paternal restrictions.

Belgium, not the Congo, benefited most from the Congo's output of industrial diamonds, copper, cobalt, and forest products. While Belgian financial interest groups thrived in the Congo, the colonial administration struggled to overcome the internal diversity of the country, usually with inadequate resources. In the tripartite power structure of the colonial government, the Roman Catholic Church, and mining-industrial concerns, each had its own goals, but paternalism was the common denominator. The transport system was designed for the coastward transit of interior products. The churches and missions, while accomplishing

much in primary education and medicine, strengthened the image of the white man as the "father" of the African masses. And under the colonial administration, little attempt was made to produce a homogeneous people in a unified state.

To administer its policies in a land 80 times its own size, Belgium created six major provinces, each with a capital, and each subdivided into districts. The provincial capitals became places of power under lieutenant governors, and the provinces in some ways became separate colonies, with Leopoldville (now Kinshasa) the capital being both physically and psychologically removed. Following independence, the provincial capitals themselves became centers of control for secessionist leaders who failed to heed Leopoldville's dictates.

FRANCE

France possessed the most extensive colonial empire in Africa (Fig. 5-3*b*). It extended in a continuous block from Tunisia,

Algeria, and Morocco across the Sahara to the Guinea Coast and south to the Zaire Basin. Together with the two outliers of Madagascar and French Somalia, this empire encompassed, at the height of French power, more than 4 million sq mi (10.4 million sq km) and 65 million people. A great diversity of peoples, institutions and environments comprised this empire, yet France imposed a remarkably uniform colonial policy. Colonial administration was to be financially self-supporting, and the colonies themselves were to provide France with raw materials and with markets for French manufactured goods. To finance the administration of French West Africa (Mauritania, Senegal, Upper Volta, Niger, Ivory Coast, French Guinea, Dahomey, and French Sudan), a head tax was imposed; to pay for it the Africans were forced to enter the cash economy by growing groundnuts, cotton, and other commodities or by providing labor and services required by the French. In French Equatorial Africa (Chad, Ubangi-Shari, Gabon, and Moyen Congo), much of the finances were generated by large concessionaire companies having commercial monopolies over extensive areas, and the power to use local labor as it chose.

France's ultimate objective in Africa was the assimilation of Africans into French culture through the adoption of the French language and education system. Unlike the Belgians, the French desired the quick development of an educated, acculturated elite, which would have French interests at heart and French culture to boast. This elite, it was reasoned, would support the French presence in the empire as a matter of self-protection, for by accepting and adopting French values and ways of life, these people often separated themselves from their own countrymen, most of whom remained bound to local tradition. French colonial subjects, then, were to be assimilated in the greater French Empire, and they could obtain a voice in the politics of the French realm through representation in Paris.

Important changes in French colonial policy came with the passage of the *Loi Cadre* (Outline Law) of 1956. France kept control of foreign policy, defense, and overall economic development of the French territories, but all other aspects of government became the responsibility, not of the existing federal governments of French West and French Equatorial Africa, but of the 12 individual colonies of which they were composed. Two years later, the concept of a *France d'Outre Mer*, an overseas France, was largely abandoned when President De Gaulle established a new French constitution, and offered the colonial peoples the choice between autonomy (self-government) as separate republics within a "French Community," or immediate independence with the severance of all links with France. Only Guinea chose complete independence outside the Community, while the others chose autonomy buttressed by continuing French economic aid. By 1960, they too had received their independence while retaining close economic ties with France.

Throughout the post-World War II period, Algeria occupied a very special position in the decolonization program. Because of Algeria's almost one million European settlers (*colons*), its rich deposits of iron ore, oil, and natural gas, and its proximity and effective communications with the metropole, France was reluctant to withdraw. However, following a period of uprising, turmoil, and eventually eight years of war, nationalist demands were met, and Algeria was granted its independence in 1962. Morocco and Tunisia were neither territories nor parts of France; they were protectorates that meant French policy attempted to combine French interests with those of the local people. No overt attempt was made to replace traditional institutions with those of France. Frenchmen were encouraged to settle as *colons*, and much of the economic development that took place under French rule may be attributed to these immigrants, although their presence caused political and social difficulties. They not only occupied good land, but competed for jobs with the local Muslim peoples.

UNITED KINGDOM

Britain, like France, was responsible for a multiplicity of peoples and cultures operating under an incredible diversity of environmental conditions and traditional systems, but, unlike the French, the British formulated policies that were often adapted to the specific requirements of the individual dependencies. The basic premise was indirect rule, and flexibility was an essential ingredient. The principle of indirect rule was intended to prevent the destruction of indigenous culture and organization and to facilitate effective British control. In such fields as tribal authority, law, and education, the British often recognized local customs and permitted their perpetuation, initially outlawing only those practices that constituted, in British eyes, serious transgressions of human rights. Then the people were slowly introduced to the changes British rule inevitably brought. There was rarely any sense of urgency and need for radical change. Despite this policy, Britain professed from almost the beginning that her ultimate goal was the independence and self-determination of the Africans under the colonial flag. This was a major difference between British policy and all others, that were either directed at converting the colonies into integral parts of the metropoles, or bent on preserving the status quo indefinitely.

British policy was strongly influenced not only by traditional systems, but by the size and character of the European settler populations. In Kenya and Rhodesia where the settler populations at their maximum were large and powerful (70,000 and 225,000, respectively) the desires of London were often overridden by those of the local whites. But in the Sudan, Ghana, Nigeria,

and elsewhere, white colonists presented fewer obstacles to the administration and to the path toward independence.

British policy also differed according to the political status of the dependencies. Territories that were conquered and settled by white immigrant groups became colonies, such as Kenya, implying a considerable amount of self-determination from the settler population. However, those territories like Bechuanaland (Botswana), whose indigenous leaders had requested and been granted Crown "protection" became protectorates. While the principle of indirect rule in the white-controlled colonies was mainly replaced by local European control, the principle was adhered to quite strictly in any territory that had been granted protectorate status. Southern Rhodesia, by virtue of conquest from the south became a British colony, while Northern Rhodesia (Zambia), somewhat more isolated by the Zambezi River, became a protectorate. In Nigeria, two different kinds of administrative control prevailed simultaneously: southern Nigeria, which had a long contact with Britain, became a colony, while northern Nigeria remained under indirect rule. Indirect rule fostered a greater sense of individuality among the various colonies than was possible under the French regime, and thus not unexpectedly, the timing and consequences of independence differed, and more about this is said in subsequent chapters.

The geographical contiguity of the three East African possessions (Kenya, Uganda, and Tanganyika) permitted closer economic, monetary, and customs links than in West Africa where the British possessions were geographically separated from one another (Fig. 5-3c). The three landlocked territories of Swaziland, Bechuanaland, and Basutoland, were joined in a Customs Union with South Africa (1910) which drew them economically into the South African sphere of influence, while their political administrations remained separate from South Africa.

Not all the possessions were economic assets (Bechuanaland and Lesotho, for example), while others including Kenya and Ghana yielded valuable agricultural products and minerals required in Britain.

PORTUGAL

Portuguese rule in Africa came to an end in 1975 after more than four centuries of neglect and exploitation by Lisbon, and after two decades of struggle for liberation in the territories themselves. Portugal looked on Mozambique, Angola (including Cabinda), Portuguese Guinea, and the offshore islands of São Tomé, Principe, and the Cape Verde Islands (Fig. 5-3d), as reservoirs of human and natural resources to be exploited for the benefit of the metropole. Little or no concern was shown for the welfare of the peoples themselves. Angola and Mozambique in particular were viewed as richly endowed but sparsely populated lands that would take care of Portugal's excess population, and provide the fragile Portuguese economy with much needed revenues, foods, and industrial resources. By the early 1970s there were over 400,000 Portuguese settlers in Angola and 150,000 in Mozambique, and large-scale agricultural and mining projects remained firmly in European hands. The widespread poverty and the social and political backwardness that characterized these regions merely reflected the state of Portugal itself, the poorest of Africa's rulers.

Portugal adhered to the legal position that its African possessions were, in fact, "provinces" of the metropolitan Portuguese state whose residents could aspire to Portuguese citizenship and to representation in the Portuguese government. Like the French, the Portuguese encouraged a small elitist class who could gain virtual equality with whites, provided a number of educational, economic, and religious qualifications were met. Only a very small number (perhaps 70,000 out of a total population of 12 million), became *assimilados*, but those who did were accepted by the Portuguese citizenry in a manner unique in Southern Africa. The vast majority of the population were *indigenas* (natives) whose main function in the eyes of the administration was to provide labor for the mines, agricultural schemes, and other government projects.

Control over the populations and local economies was maintained by dictatorial means just as at home in Portugal. The "provinces" were subdivided into a number of districts where decisions, made in Portugal and transmitted through governors-general situated in the capital cities, were implemented. They were also divided into numerous economic units or circumscriptions controlled by administrators and assisted by "chiefs of post" who were given extraordinary powers over the essentially rural populations. The administrators had absolute jurisdiction over the amount of land to be placed under crops, the types of crops to be grown, the prices to be paid for the crops, and they formulated and enforced the labor laws that guaranteed the state a permanent and low paid work force. The system fragmented an already tribally heterogeneous population, prevented effective communication between groups and regions, seriously hindered the emergence and development of African nationalism, and left the Africans poorly prepared for an independence never foreseen in Portugal.

ITALY

Italy was the last of the European states to participate in the "Scramble for Africa" primarily because of the late unification of Italy itself. In 1883 Italian troops occupied part of the Eritrean coast of the Red Sea, and soon after Italy laid claim to the eastern Somali coastline, then part of the Sultan of Zanzibar's domain (Fig. 5-3d). In 1889 Italy signed the Treaty of Wishale, which defined the boundary between Ethiopia and Italian Eritrea, and in 1896 Italy tried unsuccessfully to occupy Ethiopia. It failed to capitalize on its position in Eritrea, and Italian commercial companies in Somaliland went bankrupt by 1904.

Italy turned next to Libya, ousting the Turks in 1912, and for the next 27 years Italian occupation became more militaristic and, under Mussolini, more fascistic. An even more aggressive attitude was taken toward what became Italian East Africa—composed of Ethiopia, Eritrea, and Somaliland. In Ethiopia, the Italians immediately set about improving the communications system, realizing that development depended on it and her political control would also be strengthened. Indeed, it was Italian-built roads from Massawa in Eritrea, and Mogadishu in Somaliland, completed earlier this century that facilitated Italy's occupation in 1936. In Somaliland, the Italian interests focused on government sponsored agricultural schemes geared to Italian markets, while little attempt was made to improve the education levels, health standards, economic well-being, and political awareness of the majority.

SPAIN

Of all the colonial possessions in Africa, Spain's were the smallest in area and population (Fig. 5-3d). They also derived little benefit from Spain despite a long history of Spanish control. For more than four centuries, parts of the northwest coast belonged to Spain, and even today there are city-sized colonies (Cueta and Melilla) or *"presidios."* The largest Spanish possession was Spanish Sahara, once a protectorate and then an Overseas Province of Spain until its incorporation into Morocco and Mauritania in 1976. It and the other coastal outliers were poor and treated as integral parts of Spain. Further south, wedged between Gabon and Cameroons, was Spanish Guinea composed of mainland Rio Muni and the island of Fernando Po. It provided Spain with forestry products, cocoa, coffee, and other tropical products, and until independence (1968), its administration (like that of Spain itself) was highly centralized and autocratic.

The "Wind of Change"

The "Scramble for Africa" was completed in less than two decades after 1884–1885, and for the next half century the European powers consolidated their positions, formulated their policies, and in general reaped the rewards of their investments. In an equally short time, beginning soon after the close of World War II, the colonial powers withdrew from Africa, and their colonies and possessions became independent states. While independence has yet to be granted to Namibia, the French Territory of the Afars and Issas, and the Spanish *presidios*, and has yet to be recognized in Rhodesia, it has been completed elsewhere and with remarkable speed and relative calm. Few political observers foresaw this rapid transformation from colonialism to independence, least of all the colonial governments themselves, and especially the Portuguese

who, until 1974, saw their African possessions as permanent and integral parts of European Portugal.

This "Wind of Change," so named by the late British Prime Minister Harold MacMillan, began in northern Africa with the independence of Libya (1951) and then swept south fanned by an increasing awareness of African nationalism, and the desire for self-determination. It was ushered in by the declining strength of the European powers following World War II, and the shift in world power to two professedly anticolonial nations—The United States and the Soviet Union. In 1945 only four independent states existed in Africa: Ethiopia, Liberia, Egypt, and South Africa, and of these both Ethiopia and Egypt had some colonial rule this century, while South Africa was created in 1910 out of two Boer Republics and two British

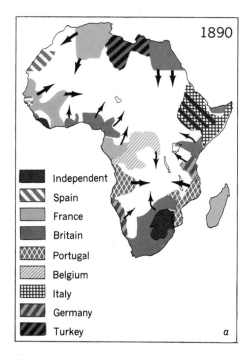

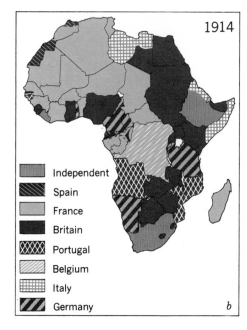

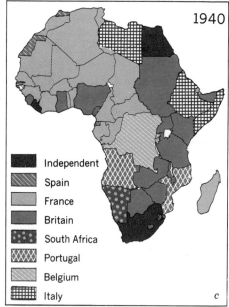

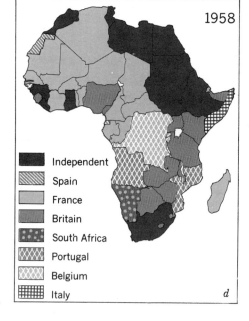

FIGURE 5-4 *The changing map of Africa.*

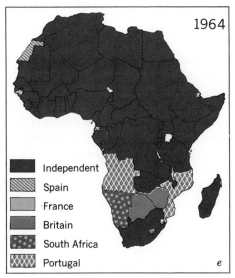 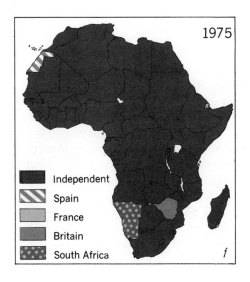

FIGURE 5-4 (*continued*) *The changing map of Africa.*

colonies without approval of the African majority. Following the independence of Libya, the Sudan was liberated from Britain and Egypt in 1956, and later in the same year France withdrew its administrations from Morocco and Tunisia.

The second wave of the wind of change began in West Africa with the independence (1957) of Ghana (formerly the Gold Coast), and quickly spread east and south (Fig. 5–4). Guinea became the first black African territory to gain its independence (1958) from France, and in 1960 all of former French West Africa and French Equatorial Africa made the transition. Of the 18 independent states created in the world in 1960, 17 were in Africa, and 14 were formerly French. In the same year Britain relinquished Nigeria, the Italian trusteeship over Somalia was terminated, and the Belgians withdrew from the Congo. In most cases the transfer of authority was completed without major incidence, but in the Congo separatists movements vied for control, and the economy and administration collapsed.

Sierra Leone received its independence from Britain in 1961, as did Tanganyika. After almost eight years of civil war, Algeria received its independence in 1962, and dur-

ing the same year, independence was granted to Rwanda, Burundi, and Uganda. In 1963 the ill-fated Central African Federation of Northern Rhodesia, Southern Rhodesia, and Nyasaland was dissolved, and Nyasaland became the independent state of Malawi. The following year Tanganyika and Zanzibar joined to form the United Republic of Tanzania, and the British protectorate of Northern Rhodesia became the independent Republic of Zambia.

Thus by 1964 (Fig. 5-4), the wind of change had reached the Zambezi River, there to be checked temporarily by colonial interests of Britain and Portugal. Further south lay white-ruled South Africa and its mandated territory of South West Africa, and the three British High Commission Territories of Bechuanaland, Basutoland, and Swaziland. In 1966, Buchuanaland became Botswana, Basutoland became Lesotho, and two years later Swaziland achieved independence and chose to retain its old name. The ruling white minority of the self-governing colony of Southern Rhodesia declared its independence unilaterally (UDI) in 1965 and renamed the territory Rhodesia. After years of revolutionary warfare by liberation units in the Portuguese possessions, Guinea

Bissau became independent in 1974, and Mozambique, São Tomé, Principe, the Cape Verde Islands, and Angola followed in 1975.

African independence was brought about by many forces emanating from within and beyond the continent. Local nationalist groups emerged in opposition to colonial injustices, and were championed by articulate leaders; where necessary liberation movements resorted to violence. The wind of change was quickened by effective debate in the United Nations where the newly independent states took their place to argue for the self-determination of all Africans. And supranational organizations, especially the Organization of African Unity (OAU) and the Arab League, became effective platforms for anticolonialism and pro-African ideals. Colonialism's impress on the landscape is unmistakable and not erasable: the roads and railways, mines and factories, cities and rural development schemes, schools and churches, all begun within a colonial framework are there to stay. So too are the European languages, political institutions and boundaries, legal and educational systems, besides many far less tangible legacies. These are the subjects of the following chapters.

BIBLIOGRAPHY

Chamberlain, M. E. *The Scramble for Africa.* London: Longman, 1974.

Davidson, B. *Africa: History of a Continent.* New York: The Macmillan Co., 1972.

de Blij, H. J. *Systematic Political Geography,* Second Edition. New York: John Wiley & Sons, Inc., 1973.

Hallett, R. *Africa Since 1875: A Modern History.* Ann Arbor: University of Michigan Press, 1970.

Hodgson, R. D. and E. A. Stoneman. *The Changing Map of Africa.* Second Edition. Princeton: D. Van Nostrand Co., Inc., 1968.

Oliver, R. and A. Atmore. *Africa Since 1800.* Cambridge: Cambridge University Press, 1967.

Oliver, R. and J. D. Fage. *A Short History of Africa.* Baltimore: Penguin Books, 1962.

Wilson, M. and L. Thompson (eds.). *The Oxford History of South Africa.* Vol. I. New York: Oxford University Press, 1969.

SIX

When the states of Africa gained their independence, they inherited a number of important political and economic institutions from former colonial powers, which have, of necessity, provided the basis of operation and development in the postcolonial era. While there have been changes in response to changing political and economic conditions both within and beyond the various state boundaries, the fundamental economic patterns and, to a lesser extent, the political institutions, have remained essentially the same. This is not unexpected in view of the communications systems, administrative networks, educational systems, economic frameworks, and political structures either implanted or fostered by the colonial governments in their half century or more of tenure. All of these contemporary systems operate within yet another set of inherited phenomena, the political boundaries established in the colonial period, and since the boundaries were drawn to satisfy colonial *raisons d'être*, they may not necessarily satisfy the needs and desires of the respective independent states of today.

This chapter briefly reviews several essential elements of the state that were partly prescribed during the colonial era, and then examines the ways in which the independent states have attempted to overcome some of these limitations to better meet their own *raisons d'être*. The principal politico-geographic components of the state reviewed are boundaries; the size, shape, and location of states; capital cities and core regions; and political ideals, systems, and supranational organizations. During the colonial period, the map of Africa showed broad regional power blocs, and while these have disappeared they have nevertheless been replaced by others, some political, others cultural-ideological, and still others economic.

THE CONTEMPORARY MAP OF AFRICA

FIGURE 6-1 *African independence.*

Boundaries and Territories

Many of the international boundaries of contemporary Africa, and especially Africa south of the Sahara, were defined by the Berlin Conference of 1884–1885 by land hungry governments without real knowledge of, or concern for, the peoples and regions which were being divided. At the time, only superficial knowledge gained from records of missionaries, explorers, and traders, existed about Africa's rivers, natural divides, resources, cultural patterns, and the territorial extent of traditional political systems. Nevertheless, boundary lines were defined by treaty, demarcated on maps, and some were later delimited in the landscape. Where practically no information existed about the region, such as the Sahara and the interior regions of Southern Africa, geometrical boundaries following lines of longitude, latitude, and directional compass bearings were superimposed on the map. Most traverse sparsely populated regions, and most were drawn as a matter of expediency.

Geometric boundaries separate Somalia from Kenya and Ethiopia (Fig. 6-1) and were drawn without concern for the local pastoralists who for generations had freely migrated from highland to lowland across the region. The straight-line boundary between Angola and Zaire was superimposed on the Bakongo peoples, making some subject to Portuguese rule, and others to Belgian. The initial consequence was local population redistribution, and social-political unrest. The pattern was repeated literally hundreds of times over across Africa, and the consequences were similar. Gambia is enclosed by geometric boundaries, and is the most artificial of all African states. There a series of arcs were drawn with the compass placed at regular intervals along the Gambia River, and two parallel lines were extended from near the mouth of the river to connect with these arcs. Thus the state of Gambia in no way corresponds with the natural hinterland of the river, which includes much of the surrounding state of Senegal, a former French possession.

Physical features including rivers, mountain ranges, escarpments, and lakes became international boundaries primarily because they were readily identifiable and rarely needed delimiting. Rivers were seen as natural dividers between peoples and regions, whereas, in fact, rivers can be integrating or binding elements of the landscape and thus very unsatisfactory boundaries. Some of Africa's large rivers, such as the Zambezi, Limpopo, and Ravuma, chosen as international boundaries, have always been effective obstacles to movement and historically have separated different culture groups. In contrast, the Zaire and its tributary the Bangui, which separate Zaire from the Congo Republic and the Central African Republic, and the Senegal River, which divides Mauritania and Senegal, are navigable for considerable distances and have tended to draw together people on both sides of the rivers. In West Africa, rivers form boundaries between Liberia and its coastal neighbors, Sierra Leone and the Ivory Coast, while shorter stretches of rivers partially bound Upper Volta, Togo, Dahomey, Niger, Negeria, Mali, Chad, Guinea, and Ghana. Indeed, river boundaries are common in Africa, and rarely have they been contested.

International boundary lines have been drawn through lakes and along escarpments and mountain ranges. Lakes Victoria, Rudolf, Albert (Mobutu Sese Seko), Edward (Idi Amin), Kivu, Tanganyika, Nyasa (Malawi), and Chad were selected for matters of convenience and then divided by geometric lines. The boundaries between Zaire and the Sudan, the Central African Republic and the Sudan, and Malawi and Mozambique follow natural divides (watersheds), while the Great Escarpment forms the eastern boundary of Lesotho.

Since the international boundaries were defined and adopted as quickly as possible, few cultural criteria were used in the selection process. Compare, for example, the contemporary map of Africa (Fig. 6-1) with Murdock's ethnic map (Fig. 6-2) which is a very complex mosaic. Nevertheless, in the case of Lesotho and Swaziland, the boundaries today define ethnically homogeneous regions, but there the people adjusted to the boundaries as much as the boundaries respected the cultural patterns. Internal or provincial boundaries, such as those in Zaire, more frequently corresponded with tribal or ethnic lines, since the colonial governments found this facilitated their administration.

Independent Africa inherited not only unsatisfactory international boundaries, but grossly misshapen and unfortunately positioned territories. In West Africa, boundary lines were extended inland only short distances around strategic river courses and traditional settlements, and defined relatively small areas (other than Nigeria), and in the case of Gambia, Togo, and Dahomey, they defined small elongated states. This resulted in a vast residual interior that was subsequently divided into five landlocked states (Niger, Upper Volta, Mali, Chad, and the Central African Republic) that were all part of former French Africa. Similarly, following the initial partition of the coasts further

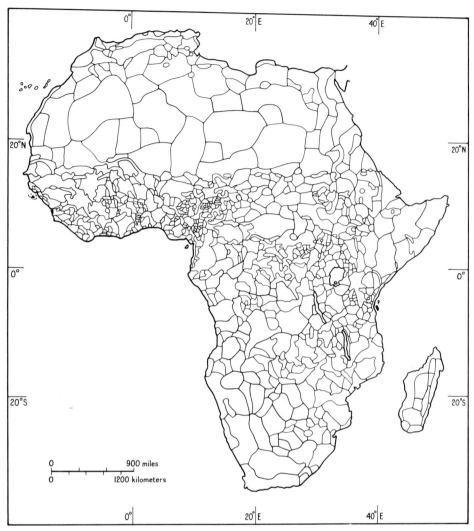

FIGURE 6-2 *Ethnic map of Africa.*
Compare the boundaries with the Contemporary Map of Africa (Figure 6-1).
L. D. Stamp and W. T. W. Morgan. Africa: A Study in Tropical Development.
3rd edition. New York: Wiley, 1972. After G. P. Murdock, Africa: Its Peoples and
Their Culture History. *McGraw-Hill Book Company. Reprinted by permission of John
Wiley and McGraw-Hill Book Company.*

south and east, nine other landlocked countries were created: Uganda, Malawi, Zambia, Rhodesia, Botswana, Lesotho, and Swaziland, all of which were British, and Ruanda and Burundi, once mandates under Belgian administration.

A landlocked state is in a disadvantaged position unless it is guaranteed the right to use the high seas like the coastal states, the right of innocent passage in other states' territorial waters, a share of port facilities along suitable coasts, and a means of transit from that port to the state territory for its external trade. Furthermore, landlocked states have no claims to the continental shelves, some of which are proving to be rich in mineral and food resources. In theory, landlocked states have access to the coast and the high seas by three means: by international rivers, land corridors, and free transit rights. Any navigable river that traverses both the landlocked state and the coastal state may be declared by agreement an international river similar to the high seas in its freedom. The Zaire, Niger, Zambezi, and Shiré were declared international rivers. In theory this provided Upper Volta, Niger, Zaire, Rhodesia, Malawi, and Zambia access to the sea, but since only portions of these rivers are navigable it does not truly alleviate the problems of location.

Land corridors have not been widely adopted. Zaire, has a vital corridor to the Atlantic via the Zaire River. The Belgian government exchanged land with the Portuguese as late as 1927 in order to provide the-then Belgian Congo more effective access to the sea along that corridor. The Belgians acquired a little more than a square mile for the development of the ocean port of Matadi, in exchange for 480 sq mi (1,243 sq km) elsewhere. In another case the Portuguese acquired from the British a corridor up the Zambezi as far as Zumbo.

All the landlocked states of Africa have free transit rights to the coast, the terms of which have been defined by international treaties. Nevertheless, coastal states have the upper position, and can affect the amount and composition of traffic bound to and from the interior states. The landlocked states of West Africa under French control used the ports of Dakar and Abidjan without restriction, but since independence and because of local political friction, Mali has diverted its traffic through the far less convenient port of Abidjan, and Niger now uses the more suitably positioned ports in Nigeria. Zambia's main links with the outside world are through Tanzania, Mozambique and Angola, although during the postindependence Angolan civil war, the Angolan outlet via the Benguela Railway was temporarily closed. When Mozambique was Portuguese, white-ruled Rhodesia depended almost exclusively on Beira and Lourenço Marques (Maputo), but Mozambique's revolutionary wars of independence spurred Rhodesia into building a railway to South Africa. Rhodesia's other rail link to the sea is through Botswana and South Africa.

Landlocked Botswana, Lesotho, and

Maputo (formerly Lourenço Marques) is the capital and primate city of Mozambique. Its port is linked by rail with landlocked Swaziland and Rhodesia (Zambabwe) and with the Witwatersrand, South Africa's major industrial core. (Harm. J. de Blij)

Swaziland face particularly difficult problems because of their location and opposition to *apartheid* in neighboring South Africa. Lesotho is completely surrounded by South Africa, and Botswana is virtually enclosed by white-controlled territory: South Africa, Namibia, and Rhodesia. Both countries are totally dependent on South African ports for access to overseas markets, and on occasion South Africa has refused to permit certain goods and individuals to cross its space. Swaziland has a slightly less vulnerable position, in that it shares a boundary with Mozambique and has rail links with Maputo.

Landlocked Malawi has always depended on the ports of Mozambique, especially Beira and Nacala, and throughout Portugal's tenure in Africa it had to place its economic interests before international opinion. An independent Mozambique has removed that particular issue, but not the general problem of access. Uganda's only practical exit is through the Kenyan port of Mombasa, and for many years Uganda has been guaranteed the right of transit across Kenya. In 1976, however, Kenya threatened to block all Ugandan transit trade following the slaughter of Kenya nationals residing in Uganda. Finally, Rwanda and Burundi have transit rights across Tanzania, while Chad has rights to use Nigerian and Cameroonian ports, and the Central African Republic uses Pointe Noire in the Congo Republic.

The "Scramble for Africa" left a number of very small territories such as Lesotho, Swaziland, Rwanda, Burundi, Gambia, Togo, and Guinea-Bissau. It also left a number of prorupted states, that is, states possessing an extension of territory in the form of a peninsula or a corridor leading away from the main body of the territory. Such prorupt states often face serious internal difficulties, for the proruption is either the most important part of the state or a distant problem of administration. Figure 6-1 shows Zaire has two proruptions: the western one contains the capital city (Kinshasa), the port of Matadi, the mouth of the Zaire River, and the important Inga hydroelectric scheme; the eastern proruption has the economic core based on the copper resources of Shaba. Between the two areas lies the vast Zaire Basin, in many ways more a liability than an asset to the state at present.

Another example is found in Namibia where the Caprivi Strip reaches deep into the interior of black Africa. For decades it had little importance in the course of African history, but today it is an area of guerrilla warfare directed at the overthrow of white South Africa, and is a narrow arm of white-controlled territory that separates Botswana from the rest of black Africa.

Core Regions and Capitals

In the preceding chapter we discussed certain locational, functional, and structural attributes of Africa's precolonial states, and emphasized they contained an administrative center, an elite class, specialized labor, and a communications network that linked the capital with its periphery. Commonly the capital was the largest and most important place within the state area, and was supported by lower-order places over which it exerted some control. There existed a pattern of core areas and peripheries, the core being the politico-economic heart of the state, and the periphery its less developed surroundings.

Today, Africa's core regions are still not as developed as those of the industrial world, or even those of most Third World countries in Asia and Latin America. In view of the artificial nature of the states themselves, the relatively short history of economic development and modernization, and the as yet elu-

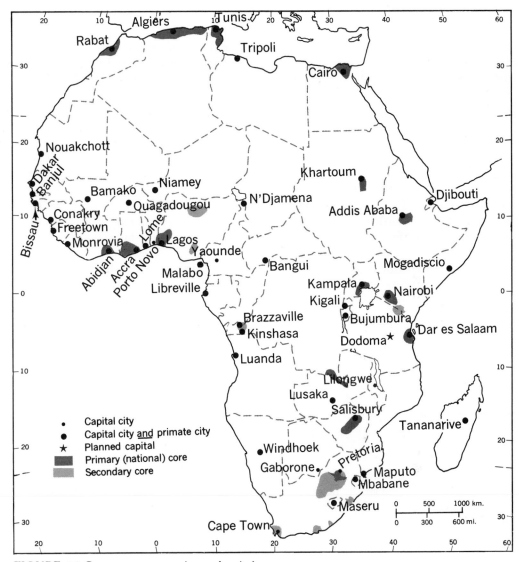

FIGURE 6-3 *Contemporary core regions and capitals.*

sive *raisons d'être* of so many states, this is not unexpected. Africa's cores differ considerably in size and composition, and in the roles they play in their respective states. In some states, such as Chad and Botswana, there are no real core areas (Fig. 6-3). In others they focus on the capital, which more often than not is also the primate city (Table 6-1), that being the largest city according to population, and the most important in terms of manufacturing, services, and political influence. They are also the country's prime generator, transformer, and distributor of the forces of change and modernization. Most are several times larger than the second city, and exert greater influence on their states' political and economic systems than would be suggested by size alone. A few core regions and capitals serve to illustrate these points and to emphasize their great diversity in origin, form, and function.

The Republic of South Africa is the only modern industrial state in Africa, and the only state to possess a truly diversified national core supported by secondary cores (Fig. 6-3). The national core centers on the primate city (but not capital city) of Johannesburg (1.5 million), and extends east and west along the minerally rich Witwatersrand. Here there are gold mining towns, iron and steel industries, several centers of higher learning, a modern transport system, the state's administrative capital (Pretoria), and a host of industries that account for almost half of South Africa's industrial output. It is supported by four secondary metropolitan cores (Capetown, Durban, Port Elizabeth, and East London), each of which is supported in turn by smaller industrial centers and agricultural areas. The industrial and economic wealth of each of South Africa's four metropolitan subcores surpasses that of most primary cores elsewhere in Africa.

Another good example of a national core where there is a high level of urban development and industrial output is to be found in Egypt. It centers on Cairo (7 million) and Alexandria (2 million)—the two largest cities in Africa—and comprises the entire delta region where almost half the Egyptian population lives. Spatially this is one of Africa's most distinct core regions, it being bounded by the coast and desert. Unlike the South African core, that of Egypt dates back thousands of years, and irrigated agriculture rather than mining was the original basis for its development.

By far the most important multicore state in tropical Africa is populous Nigeria. Its core areas are not only clearly defined, but they are also individually unique in terms of ethnic composition, economic activity, historical association, and many other aspects. Nigeria has three major core areas, each of which would do justice to any single West African state. The primary core lies in the southwest (Fig. 6-3), and includes a

number of major urban centers such as the federal capital Lagos (1.5 million), and the Yoruba towns of Ibadan (1 million), Ogbomosho, Oshogbo, and Abeokuta. This is one of Africa's most highly urbanized regions whose exchange economy is based on both agriculture (especially cocoa) and industry. Northern Nigeria is predominantly rural and Moslem, and its core focuses on the ancient cities of Kano and Zaria. The third core region lies in the southeast where population densities are among the highest in Africa, and the economy is based on petroleum, oil palm, and other products.

In these and other countries, the capital city plays an especially important role in the spatial organization of the state, the capital generally having a nodal location and being the dominant center of innovation, education, political influence, and capital accumulation. In more than half the countries, the capital and the core region are virtually one and the same (Fig. 6-3), and 40 capitals are, at the same time, primate cities. Table 6-1 gives some selected characteristics of Africa's capitals and some measures of primacy. Only seven capitals are not primates: Rabat (Morocco), Porto Novo (Benin), Yaoundé (Cameroon), Gaborone (Botswana), Lilongwe (Malawi), Dodoma (Tanzania), and Pretoria (South Africa). Four new capitals—Nouakchott (Mauritania), Gaborone, Lilongwe, and Dodoma—have been built since independence. In several other countries the capital has been moved at one time or another.

All the North African capitals predate colonial occupation and remained administrative centers under foreign rule (Table 6-1). The ancient Arab capital of Marrakech (Morocco) was superseded by another Arab city, Rabat, which from the French point of view occupied a more favorable position on the coast. In West Africa, the colonial powers selected places that satisfied their particular economic and political interests. Along the Guinea Coast that meant ports (except Porto Novo, capital of Benin), and in the in-

The National Assembly Building, Gaborone, Botswana. Before Gaborone was built in 1965, Botswana was administered from Mafeking, South Africa. (Alan C. G. Best)

View of Dar es Salaam, Tanzania's primate city and terminus of the Tan-Zam Railway. In the left distance is the central business district, and in the foreground the port facilities. Tanzania is moving its seat of government from Dar es Salaam to a more central site, Dodoma. (Tanzania Government)

THE CONTEMPORARY MAP OF AFRICA
107

Table 6-1 SELECTED CHARACTERISTICS OF CAPITAL CITIES

	Capital	Indigenous City	Ex-Colonial Capital	New Postindependence capital	Primate City	Only Major City	Main Seaport	Lake/River Port	Main Airport	Main Rail Center	Main Manufacturing City
Northern Africa											
Algeria	Algiers	x	x		x		x		x	x	x
Egypt	Cairo	x	x		x			x	x		x
Libya	Tripoli	x	x		x		x		x	x	x
Morocco	Rabat	x	x				x				
Tunisia	Tunis	x	x		x	x	x		x	x	x
West Africa											
Chad	N'Djamena		x		x	x			x		x
Benin	Porto Novo	x	x								
Gambia	Banjul		x		x	x	x	x	x		x
Ghana	Accra		x		x				x		x
Guinea	Conakry		x		x	x	x		x	x	x
Guinea-Bissau	Bissau		x		x	x	x	x	x		x
Ivory Coast	Abidjan		x		x		x		x	x	x
Liberia	Monrovia	x			x	x	x		x	x	x
Mali	Bamako	x	x		x	x			x	x	x
Mauritania	Nouakchott			x	x	x	a		x		
Niger	Niamey		x		x	x			x		x
Nigeria	Lagos		x		x		x		x	x	x
Senegal	Dakar		x		x	x	x		x	x	x
Sierra Leone	Freetown		x		x	x	x		x	x	x
Togo	Lomé		x		x	x	x		x	x	x
Upper Volta	Ouagadougou	x	x		x				x		
Cameroon	Yaoundé		x								
Central Afr. Rep.	Bangui		x		x	x		x	x		x
Congo	Brazzaville		x		x			x	x		x
Equatorial Guinea	Malabo		x		x		x		x		
Gabon	Libreville		x		x		x		x	x	x
Zaire	Kinshasa		x		x			x	x		

terior it meant either river locations with some nodality (Bamako and Niamey) or some densely populated area (Ouagadougou and N'Djamena). As the colonial systems developed, so did the ports. Today in 11 of the 16 West African states, the capital city is both the primate and the only major city of the state. Advantages accrued to the colonial capitals have in most cases persisted to the present.

The capitals of East Africa and the Horn are markedly more central with respect to their populations and territories, than those of West Africa. Nairobi and Kampala are central within their respective and well-defined core regions, while Bujumbura and Kigali are the only significant towns within compact, small, and very densely populated mountain states. The Ethiopian capital of Addis Ababa occupies a commanding position in the densely populated highlands, and was established in 1889, the year Menelik became Emperor. It is more than three times the size of its second city,

Table 6-1 (continued)

		Indigenous City	Ex-Colonial Capital	New Postindependence capital	Primate City	Only Major City	Main Seaport	Lake/River Port	Main Airport	Main Rail Center	Main Manufacturing City
Southern Africa											
Angola	Luanda		X		X		X		X		X
Botswana	Gaborone			X					X		
Lesotho	Maseru		X		X	X			X	X	
Malagasy	Tananarive	X	X		X				X	X	X
Malawi	Lilongwe			X							
Mozambique	Maputo		X		X		X		X	X	X
South Africa [b]	Pretoria										
Swaziland [b]	Mbabane		X		X						
Zambia	Lusaka		X		X				X		X
East Africa											
Burundi	Bujumbura		X		X	X		X	X		X
Kenya	Nairobi		X		X				X	X	X
Rwanda	Kigali		X		X	X			X		X
Tanzania	Dodoma [a]			X							
Uganda	Kampala		X		X			X			
Horn and Sudan											
Ethiopia	Addis Ababa	X			X				X	X	X
Somalia	Mogadishu		X		X	X	X		X		X
Sudan	Khartoum		X		X				X		X
Dependencies											
Afars Issas	Djibouti				X	X	X		X	X	X
Namibia	Windhoek				X				X	X	X
Rhodesia	Salisbury				X				X		X

[a] *Under construction.*

[b] *More than one capital. Administrative capital given.*

Asmara, capital of the recalcitrant district of Eritrea. Mogadishu is virtually the only urban center and port in Somalia, and because of the country's peculiar shape, it is peripheral and not readily accessible from the northern regions. Finally, Khartoum, which adjoins the indigenous city of Omdurman, is central within a very large area and exhibits the blend of traditional and foreign influences so typical of African capitals.

Three of Africa's new (postindependence) capitals have had insufficient time to develop into primate cities, and because of their locations and the level of development elsewhere in their respective states, they are unlikely to become the largest cities or anything more than administrative centers. Gaborone was built in 1965 to meet the needs of the newly independent state of Botswana. Under British rule, the then Bechuanaland Protectorate was administered from Mafeking, located not in the protectorate itself, but in neighboring South Africa. In order not to favor one ethnic group over another, none of the local administrative centers was chosen to become the capital, and a new town was built. It has failed to attract much industry and is smaller than both Serowe, the traditional headquarters of the country's largest ethnic group, and Francistown, a fast-growing commercial-industrial town near Botswana's mining areas.

Malawi's capital was shifted from Zomba to Lilongwe in 1975 to encourage economic development in the less populous and poorer areas of the center and north. To date most development has occurred in the south around Blantyre, the primate city. Tanzania is moving its capital from its largest port and primate city, Dar es Salaam, to the smaller town of Dodoma located 250 mi (400 km) farther west. The move is part of Tanzania's effort to decentralize development, to stimulate growth in a peripheral area, and to dispel the colonial image still associated with Dar es Salaam. The fourth new postindependence capital is Nouakchott, capital of Mauritania. It has grown from a small nomadic camp into a modern city of 80,000 people and, like most African capitals, it is unable to provide adequate jobs and housing for those who have drifted to it from the periphery.

Other states whose present capitals are not the original seats of administration are Niger, the Congo Republic, Zambia, Zaire, Ivory Coast, and Cameroon. In 1926, Niger's capital was shifted from Zinder to Niamey; the Congo Republic's first capital was Pointe Noire; Zambia's capital was moved in 1929 from the peripherally situated town of Livingstone to the more centrally situated Lusaka; Kinshasa replaced Boma as the capital of Zaire in 1929; Abidjan became the capital of the Ivory Coast in 1934 following brief tenures in nearby Grand-Bassam and Bingerville; and Yaoundé became the capital of Cameroon under the French mandate, the colony previously being administered from the "hill station" of Buea and the present primate city of Douala. This shifting of administration from one city to another explains in part the lack of absolute primacy in the Congo Republic, Zambia, and Zaire.

South Africa differs from all the other states in that it has three capitals: Cape Town is the legislative capital; Pretoria the administrative capital; and Bloemfontein the judicial capital. Before the establishment of the state of South Africa, each of these was a locally important administrative and commercial center. Today they are all overshadowed in size and industrial importance by Johannesburg.

Institutions and Governments

The mosaic of arbitrary and illogical boundaries, the diversity of African cultures and environments, and the superimposition of several alien value systems and institutions have combined to create a very complex political map of Africa that defies simple analysis and generalization. Nevertheless, a number of common issues and problems concerning the forms of government, nationalist movements, political stability (or instability as the case may be), and interstate relations can be identified that help explain some of the spatial patterns of development considered in subsequent chapters.

When the African territories gained their independence, each attempted to devise means to promote internal unity, foster a greater sense of nationalism, and provide the machinery for social and political modernization and economic development. This, of necessity, meant the abandonment of many traditional values and behavior patterns, and the adoption of constitutions and attitudes that were more European than African. Most states adopted constitutions that provided for democratic elections and multiparty systems of government that were based on the European experience. Both unitary and federal states were created. All the former French territories except the Cameroon became unitary states, while the ex-British territories of Nigeria, Tanzania, and Uganda became federal states. A preindependence federal constitution was superimposed on Northern Rhodesia, Southern Rhodesia, and Nyasaland in 1953, but terminated a decade later. Ethiopia has been joined in a federation with Eritrea; and South Africa, while exhibiting certain federal characteristics, is a highly centralized unitary state under the control of a white minority.

In theory, unitary states have a high degree of internal homogeneity and cohesiveness among their populations and institutions: there is a uniformity of language, culture, history, and national ideals. The central authority controls all local governments and determines how much power they shall have, and under certain circumstances may exercise the functions of local governments. The ideal unitary state would be compact in shape, not unduly large in area, have an even distribution of similar peoples, and have only one centrally located core region focused on the state capital and primate city. Few unitary states in the world display such characteristics, and many in Africa lack ethnic homogeneity and centrally located core regions and capitals. Many, however, have a highly centralized form of government for the purpose of reducing dissention among the different peoples that might otherwise threaten to disrupt the state system. One-party systems are common. Here the ruling party is absolute and power is concentrated in the hands of the party, and especially the party leader who is generally president and head of government. The one-party system has been adopted to centralize the state's efforts in economic development, the argument being that opposition works against the interest of the people, and opposition fosters tribalism and secessionist tendencies since

political parties are usually identified with certain regional interests. Commonly when dissatisfaction with the ruling party has intensified, the government has been toppled by a revolution or military *coup*. During the 1960s, for example, military *coups* occurred in 15 African states, because there was no other way in which the ruling clique could be removed.

Events in independent Ghana illustrate the shift toward increasing centralization within a unitary state. Ghana inherited a constitution and governmental apparatus that was based on the Westminster model. There were regional and tribal problems (in parts of northern Ghana the majority of people favored a delay in the granting of independence) and the Opposition Party in the Ghana Parliament was essentially a regional phenomenon. As government plans and projects were thwarted, and the power of tribal chiefs continued to influence Ghanaian politics, the ruling party sought ways to diminish the effectiveness of the Opposition. The main object was to gain greater control over the recalcitrant north and to silence the chiefs. This eventually led to the elimination of the Opposition, the proclamation of a republic, the establishment of a one-party state, and the assumption of virtual dictatorial powers by former President Nkrumah. In one way or another, this basic pattern has been repeated in Uganda, Zambia, the Central African Republic, the Congo Republic, and elsewhere.

Federal states, in contrast to unitary states, permit a central government to represent the various entities within the state where they happen to have common interests—defense, foreign affairs, communications, and so on—while allowing the various units to retain their identities and to have their own laws, policies, and customs in certain fields. Federation thus does not create unity out of diversity but enables the two to coexist. The federal arrangement is often the most suitable where there is a diversity of peoples, languages, religions, cultures, and historical backgrounds, and where these differences have regional expression in that various peoples see individual parts of their country as a homeland. In theory, therefore, conditions conducive to federalism are likely to exist in relatively large states where the diverse populations are organized around several core regions separated from each other by sparsely populated and relatively unproductive regions.

While many of these conditions exist in Africa, federal states are not common. This is due primarily to the absence of a federal *raison d'être*, and the excessive cultural diversities of the peoples (Fig. 6-2). The primary factor necessary to ensure the survival of a viable federation is the commitment of both the political leaders and the populations at large to federation for its own sake, and not an ideological commitment to federation as a means of achieving some secondary objective. The population as a whole must feel federal, thinking themselves as one people with an overriding federal identity so that the federal value becomes the most important fact in the federation. The durability and viability of federation are determined by the degree of symmetry or level of conformity in the relations of each separate political unit of the system to both the system as a whole and to the other component units. The higher the level of symmetry at both the national and regional levels (measured in terms of language, cultural heritage, economic welfare, political awareness, and so forth) the greater the likelihood that federation will endure. A state encompassing many diversities in its peoples, attitudes, values, and other essential characteristics, that form distinct regional patterns, may in fact not possess sufficient uniformity or symmetry for successful federation. Strong regional interests constitute asymmetry. These principles are evident in the federation of Nigeria.

The initial federal framework for Nigeria was developed by British and Nigerian political leaders prior to independence in 1960. When independence was granted, Nigeria had an estimated population of 50 million and three major core regions that formed the nucleus for three of the dominant peoples of the country: the Yoruba in the southwest, the Ibo in the southeast, and the Hausa in the north. However, Nigeria contains literally hundreds of ethnic groups (Fig. 6-2) and more than 200 languages are spoken, so that additional political divisions were deemed desirable. In 1963 the decision was reached to establish a Midwest Region, carved out of the territory's Western Region and populated mainly by Edos. Additional subdivisions were thought necessary so that no single region would be in a position to dominate the rest. The federation, however, had been so divided that the Northern Region, by far the most populous unit within the state, was able to dominate the others. Counterbalancing this was the north's landlocked situation, which rendered it dependent on southern ports for its external trade; but exacerbating the situation was the vast chasm of contrast in religion, political expertise, and economy between the northern and southern states.

Following independence, there were outbreaks of violence against the Ibo people living in the north, and an exodus of survivors resulted. Eventually the southeastern section of the federation (the original Eastern Region and Ibo homeland) declared its secession from Nigeria and pronounced itself the sovereign state of Biafra. Nigeria was plunged into a costly and bitter civil war and the failure of the federal framework was a factor. In 1968, while the war still raged, the Nigerian government decided to redivide the country into 12 political regions in the hope that such an arrangement would preclude future Biafra-style conflicts. At the same time, a military administration came to power, so that Nigeria had moved first from a position of superimposed federation and later of compromise to centralization.

The Central African Federation is a

good example of an imposed federation in which the desires of a minority were imposed involuntarily on the majority so as to perpetuate the privileged white position. There was much economic justification for federation: Nyasaland was dependent primarily on agriculture, Northern Rhodesia on mining, while Southern Rhodesia had a more diversified economy. Federation, however, was imposed on the region by the white minority (350,000 whites and 10 million Africans), most of whom lived in Southern Rhodesia. The economic benefits promised as a political lure, failed to materialize except in the white strongholds, so that the African majorities in Nyasaland and Northern Rhodesia called for the federation's dissolution, which came about in 1963.

African Nationalisms

In Europe and the New World, "nationalism" is commonly defined in terms of an ideology, and is a movement striving to unite into a single sovereign state all peoples who speak a single language, and who share in the cultural characteristics articulated by that language. Sovereignty means that the state has complete autonomy on internal matters, legal equality, and inviolability within the international context, and some precise delimitation of territory. Within the European context, the term "nation" refers to a people who regard themselves as sharing common values, goals, and institutions, as sharing a common history, and who consider themselves different from other peoples who have their own values, institutions, and history. Thus it is the combination of language, culture, economic organization, political system, religion, and the people's identity with a specific territory that defines a nation, and where this emotional nation corresponds with the legal nation, a nation-state exists.

In Africa, nationalism is a very different matter. Almost every colony incorporated many distinct ethnic groups and several languages or mutually unintelligible dialects that greatly impeded communications among the peoples and the development of common cultures. Interest groups were local rather than national and there was traditionally little sharing of values and institutions in the artificially prescribed colonial boundaries. Nevertheless, African nationalisms have emerged, and their movements have differed considerably in their causes and expressions from place to place. In Kenya, for instance, there was strong resentment against the white settlers who appropriated the most fertile lands and forced the Africans into less desirable regions. In Ghana, Nigeria, Guinea, and Zaire, there was widespread frustration at not being able to control the economy, wages, employment, and living standards. In all areas, nationalism was a reaction to poverty, deprivation, and of an inferior status, the consequences of colonial and racist ideologies; and everywhere, nationalism was an attempt to remove the indignities of colonial rule and a search for local (African) identity and participation in the political affairs by the mass of the people. Thus nationalisms have been directed at receding objects (colonialism and racism) for which replacements must be found. A number of replacements have already been devised, some imagined and some real.

In most African states, nationalist movements first emerged during the early years of colonial conquest. The Ashanti Wars (1899) and the Fulani Battle at Burmi, Nigeria (1903) were resistance movements against British rule. The Maji-Maji Rebellion (1905) and the Bambata Rebellion (1906) were unsuccessful attempts to oust the Germans from Tanganyika and the British from Natal respectively. As the colonial economies developed, and Africans were drawn into urban regions, a number of urban-based political organizations emerged aimed at in-

FRELIMO (Mozambique Liberation Front) forces on the move (1971) in their armed struggle against Portuguese colonial rule. Mozambique gained its independence in June, 1975. (UN/Van Lierop)

creasing African participation in the civil service, administration, and the economy. World War II brought more Africans more directly into the white realm, which quickened the process of acculturation, and reinforced rising expectations. An African elite emerged in most colonies that was educated in Europe, but not immediately able to participate as equals with the colonizer in the social, economic, and political spheres.

There was much debate during this preindependence nationalist period as to what should be the ultimate boundaries of the nation-states-in-the-making, some spokesmen favoring smaller units respecting ethnic groupings, others preferring political groupings of several of the existing colonial units. But nationalism within the existing boundaries was needed first; there had to be a bond between a people and a specific territory, and once independence was won, there was great reluctance to give up one's sovereignty and become part of some larger territory. A number of Pan-African movements developed that called for continental solidarity or nationhood.

President Leopold Senghor of Senegal believed the state was the expression of the nation, and was primarily a means of realizing the nation. He based his concept of African nationhood on the assumption there is a commonality of values characteristic of traditional Black Africa. Known as *Negritude*, this form of African nationalism asserted that all black people throughout the world share an unconscious experience that distinguishes them from all others, and that blackness in itself is a positive thing. This racial criterion of nationhood has been rejected by some African nationalists (many of them Muslims) and denounced by Pan-Africanists who seek a continental rather than a specifically racial basis for unity. Former President Nkrumah of Ghana was one of the most outstanding spokesmen for Pan-Africanism. For Nkrumah, Africa comprised three major civilizations—traditional Africa, Islamic Africa, and the Euro-Christian Africa—and these were to blend and form a new and uniquely African civilization. The common denominator was Africa, not race. In Tanzania nationalism combines traditional values of familyhood (*ujamaa*) with contemporary socialist thought. Under the leadership of President Nyerere, Tanzania is committed to egalitarianism and greater self-reliance.

In South Africa, African Nationalist movements, which were instrumental in exposing the inequities of the white oligarchy, were banned in 1960, and Afrikaner nationalism prevails. It is expressed in the landscape in many forms such as the reservation of specific regions for whites and others for Africans—the Bantustans—and the division of cities into group areas that lessen interracial contact and thus supports the white *raison d'être*, white supremacy.

Supranational and Regional Organizations

A number of supranational and regional organizations exist in Africa to further the economic and political aims of several states collectively. Some organizations, such as the British Commonwealth and the European Economic Community, have preserved and strengthened long-standing economic ties between Africa and Europe. Others such as the Organization of African Unity, the East African Community, and the Southern African Customs Union (whose memberships are entirely African) have addressed themselves almost exclusively to political and economic issues based in Africa.

In the immediate preindependence period as African nationalisms intensified, Britain attempted to reorganize some of its colonies into larger political units. It tried to create an East African Federation of Kenya, Uganda, Tanganyika, and Zanzibar, but this never materialized for lack of local support, although the Common Services Organization survived. The Central African Federation collapsed for reasons already stated. However, most former British colonies joined the Commonwealth, which meant preferential trade agreements, aid of a financial nature, loans, and other benefits. South Africa withdrew in 1960 after member states voiced strong criticism of its racial policies, and because the precepts of Afrikaner nationalism differed so strongly to those held elsewhere in the Commonwealth.

Similarly, French-speaking Africa has economic and financial ties with Europe, especially with France and the European Economic Community (EEC). At one time most French-speaking states belonged to the monetary union known as the Communauté Financière Africaine (CFA). This linked their currency with the French franc at a fixed rate of exchange and thus kept these countries in the French sphere of influence. France's ties with the African Franc Zone countries involve not only monetary arrangements, but also comprehensive French assistance in the forms of budget support, foreign aid, technical assistance, and subsidies on commodity exports. Several French-speaking states belong to a series of regional organizations such as L'Organisation Commune Africaine et Mauricienne (OCAM) and Union Douanière et Économique de l'Afrique Centrale (UDEAC), the purposes of which are to accelerate political, economic, social, and technical development of their members.

One of the oldest supranational organizations in Africa is the *Arab League*. Founded in 1945, the League is based on the cultural unity of the states that subscribe to it. The peoples of the Arab world are united by several things: the Arabic language, the Islamic religion, and the history of colonial subjugation. But there are also many things that continue to divide the Arab peoples. Feudalism still rears its head, and there is disapproval in certain Arab states of the government that rules in others, for example, Egypt and Jordan. The greatest unifying element of all 18 member states is the hostility to the state of Israel and the forces of Zionism in the Arab midst. Arab nationalism arose after World War I first in the Middle East, but by the end of World War II it had spread across North Africa and there was a move for the establishment of a great Arab state. The reality has been different however. Hopes were destroyed by the many divisive forces that still prevail: tribalism, poverty, illiteracy, and vested interests. The Arab League has been a loose and rather ineffective organization whose only apparent unifying factor remains the common opposition to Israel. In the economic sphere, attempts have been made to coordinate the policies of oil-producing members toward the major concessionaires, and steps were taken in the 1960s to create an Arab common market, but competitive economies and conflicting policies of the members prevented that from materializing. Nevertheless, since the formation of the League, much has changed in the Arab world: Egypt attained representative government, Algeria rid itself of French control, the Suez invasion was warded off, and Sudan became independent. These Arab states, together with Nigeria and Gabon, are also members of the powerful *Organization of Petroleum Export Countries* (OPEC).

The largest of the exclusively African supranational organizations is the *Organization of African Unity* (OAU). Established in 1963, and headquartered in Addis Ababa, the OAU, like the Arab League, is viewed optimistically as the embryo out of which an eventual all-African government may grow. Its charter defines its aims as seeking to promote the unity of Africa, to defend the independence and sovereignty of African states, and to coordinate and harmonize policies between member states on a strictly nonalignment basis. A United States of Africa is the ideal of a number of spokes-

men, among whom Nkrumah of Ghana was especially vocal. While some wish to see the rapid implementation of such a political body, others desire to maintain their total sovereignty and are reluctant to enter new political unions. The whole argument is not entirely dissimilar from that which attended the birth of the Council of Europe and ultimately it goes back to the basic question of whether political unification should precede or follow collaboration in other spheres.

The OAU's major practical achievements have included mediation in the Moroccan-Algerian dispute (1964–1965), and the Kenya-Somali border disputes (1965–1967). It failed, however, to settle the Upper Volta-Mali boundary disputes of 1975, and to end the Angolan civil war in 1976. It took almost no action to stop the genocide in Rwanda and Burundi in 1972 (hundreds of thousands of Tutsi and Hutu were slaughtered) or to condemn those responsible. It also failed to condemn President Amin for expelling an estimated 75,000 Asians from Uganda in 1972, and for systematically exterminating his opposition. The OAU has concerned itself with such persistent crises as the turmoils in Zaire, joint sanctions against South Africa, the Nigerian civil war, and liberation movements in the former Portuguese possessions. The OAU is committed to the struggle of national liberation movements in those parts of Africa that are not considered to be free of colonialism. It also is committed to the spread of education, the elimination of illiteracy, improvement of health standards, cultural exchange programs, and to economic regionalization.

All of Africa's independent states belong to the United Nations, and thus to several affiliated organizations. These include the United Nations Economic Commission for Africa (UNECA), the United Nations Development Program (UNDP), the International Bank for Reconstruction and Development (IBRD), the International

Africa House, Addis Ababa, Ethiopia. This is the headquarters of the Organization of African Unity (OAU), and the U.N.'s Economic Commission for Africa. (Alan C. G. Best)

Development Association (IDA), and the International Finance Corporation (IFC). All the independent states also belong to the African Development Bank (AFDB) established in 1964 under the aegis of UNECA. While this list is not complete, it illustrates the nature of supranational and regional organizations in Africa today, and these and others are discussed in the regional chapters that follow.

The contemporary map of Africa thus differs dramatically with that of the colonial era. While the state boundaries are essentially the same, the internal political organizations, *raisons d'être*, and approaches to both national and international issues are very different. Today the African bloc commands a powerful position in the United Nations, and is a force that should not be underestimated in world affairs.

Bibliography

Cervenka, Z. (ed.). *Land-Locked Countries of Africa*. Uppsala: The Scandinavian Institute of African Studies, 1973.

Dale, E. H. "Some Geographical Aspects of African Land-Locked States," *Annals, A.A.G.*, Vol. 58, No. 3 (September, 1968), pp. 485–505.

de Blij, H. J. *Systematic Political Geography*. Second Edition. New York: John Wiley and Sons, Inc., 1973.

Harris, P. B. *Studies in African Politics*. London: Hutchinson University Library, 1970.

Hamdan, G. "Capitals of the New Africa,"

Economic Geography, Vol. 40, No. 3 (July, 1964), pp. 239–53.

Hodgson, R. D. and E. A. Stoneman. *The Changing Map of Africa*. Princeton: D. Van Nostrand Co., Inc., 1968.

Paden, J. N. and E. W. Soja (eds.). *The African Experience*. Vol. 1. Evanston: Northwestern University Press, 1970.

Rivkin, A. *Nation-Building in Africa: Problems and Prospects*. New Brunswick: Rutgers University Press, 1969.

SEVEN

Almost 450 million people lived in Africa in mid-1977, which represents one-tenth of the world's total (Table 7-1). The distribution is very uneven: extensive areas of the Sahara, Kalahari, and the Horn are uninhabited while major concentrations occur along the Guinea Coast, the Mediterranean, and around Lake Victoria where rural densities exceed 3000 persons per square mile (1155 per sq km). In most areas, annual growth rates are high, averaging 2.6 percent for the continent as a whole with the crude birth rates and crude death rates being 46.4 per 1000 and 19.8 per 1000, respectively. All indications are that in most countries the death rates are falling more rapidly than birth rates so that growth rates will increase, and soon approximate those of Central America, where they have been the highest on earth (3.3 percent) for the past decade. In most countries this essentially uncontrolled growth has not been accompanied by an

equal or faster growth in food supply, social services, housing, employment opportunities, industry, investment, and general well-being, so that the poor and hungry have remained poor and hungry, and have little likelihood of improving their situation.

This chapter describes and interprets several important aspects of Africa's populations: the distribution and density patterns, population pressure, growth rates, migration, urban concentrations, and language, and the problems that these factors pose to the individual governments in their search for economic development and political stability. Caution is advised in interpreting the data since they are in most cases estimates based on incomplete, erroneous, and often highly suspect censuses and surveys. The Nigerian censuses serve as an illustration. The 1952 census showed a population of 30.7 million, and the 1963 census reported 55.7 million. If these figures are correct, it

THE
POPULATION
OF
AFRICA

means Nigeria's population grew at 6.1 percent per annum (Caldwell, 1968). Most demographers feel the 1963 figures are too high, and were inflated for political purposes. In 1969, the United Nations estimated the population to be 65.8 million, and the 1973 census placed the population at 79.8 million. Assuming that both the 1963 and 1973 figures are correct, Nigeria's population has grown at 4.0 percent per annum, which gives Nigeria the highest growth rate in the world and portends serious consequences in the immediate future.

Census returns are commonly erroneous for several reasons: accurate base maps necessary for the delineation of enumeration areas are lacking; there is a shortage of trained personnel; rural populations are frequently dispersed and far from transport routes and are migratory in nature; there is a belief that censuses are taken to provide a basis for increased taxation, conscription, relinquishing of wives of polygamous marriages, or suppression of a political nature; the costs are prohibitive; census boundaries are changed and poorly delimited making comparison difficult; and there is an inability to read and understand the census forms. Few countries take censuses at regular intervals, and Ethiopia has never taken one. Nevertheless, its population is estimated to be 30 million, making it the third largest in Africa after Nigeria (86 million) and Egypt (41 million) (Table 7-1).

Table 7-1 MID-1977 POPULATION ESTIMATES

North Africa	86,110,000	Rank	East Africa	51,400,000	Rank
Algeria	17,930,000	8	Burundi	4,100,000	29
Egypt	40,800,000	2	Kenya	14,500,000	10
Libya	2,480,000	32	Rwanda	4,400,000	27
Morocco	18,700,000	7	Tanzania	16,250,000	9
Tunisia	6,200,000	19	Uganda	12,150,000	11
West Africa	146,850,000				
Benin	3,200,000	33	The Horn and Sudan	52,410,000	
Cape Verde Islands	360,000	46	Afars and Issas	210,000	48
Chad	4,380,000	28	Ethiopia	30,000,000	3
Gambia	580,000	44	Somalia	3,700,000	30
Guinea	4,610,000	26	Sudan	19,500,000	6
Ghana	10,500,000	12			
Guinea-Bissau	650,000	43	Southern Africa	74,490,000	
Ivory Coast	5,550,000	21	Angola	6,770,000	16
Liberia	1,960,000	35	Botswana	800,000	42
Mali	5,960,000	20	Lesotho	1,230,000	39
Mauritania	1,800,000	37	Malagasy	8,450,000	14
Niger	4,800,000	24	Malawi	5,350,000	23
Nigeria	85,940,000	1	Mozambique	9,920,000	13
Senegal	4,710,000	25	Namibia	900,000	40
Sierra Leone	3,100,000	31	Rhodesia (Zimbabwe)	6,900,000	15
Togo	2,350,000	34	South Africa	26,600,000	4
Upper Volta	6,400,000	18	Swaziland	570,000	45
Equatorial Africa	37,325,000		Zambia	5,500,000	22
Cameroon	6,700,000	17	Island Groups (Mauritius, Seychelles Comoro, Reunion)	1,500,000	
Central African Republic	1,920,000	36			
Congo Republic	1,300,000	38			
Equatorial Guinea	330,000	47	Africa Total	447,585,000	
Gabon	900,000	41			
Zaire	26,100,000	5			
São Tomé e Principe	75,000	49			

SOURCE. *Based on data from Population Reference Bureau, and Government censuses.*

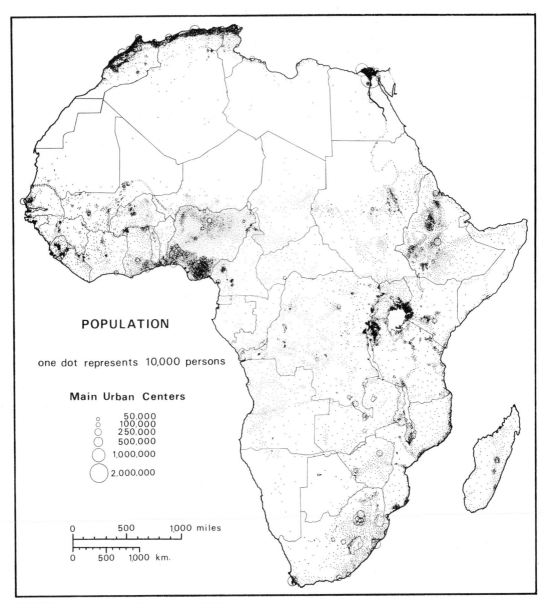

FIGURE 7-1 *Population distribution of Africa.*
Reprinted by permission of Geography
Department, University of Stellenbosch.

Distributions and Densities

The uneven distributions and densities across Africa reflect an unequal geographic distribution of resources and opportunities, differences in man's abilities to adapt to his environment, and various historical events and situations. Figure 7-1 shows that the major concentrations are situated along the coast of the Maghreb states, in the lower Nile, the highlands of Ethiopia and East Africa (especially around the lakes), along the Guinea Coast and in the interior savanna zones, along coastal and in northern interior regions of Southern Africa, and in the Malagasy highlands. Elsewhere there are smaller zones of high concentration, especially around active mineral resources (Zaire and Rhodesia), and successful agricultural schemes (Malawi, Sudan, Angola, and Tanzania).

In the northern desert states, populations are concentrated around water and tend to occupy only a small proportion of the total land areas. In Algeria, for instance, approximately 95 percent of the 18 million lives on only 15 percent of the land, and half the population is crowded into only three percent of the land, especially the coastal lowlands and the fertile valleys of the Atlas. Almost all of Egypt's 41 million are crowded into less than 5 percent of the area, and rural densities in the lower Nile exceed 3700 persons per square mile (1425 per sq km). These are some of the most fertile farm lands in the world, where the exceptionally rich alluvial soils, controlled irrigation, and a long tradition of relatively sophisticated farm practices have contributed to these high densities.

In West Africa there are two distinct belts of high population concentration, separated by a belt of lower density. The northern high-density belt coincides with the savanna and Sahel zones and includes the concentrations around the emirate cities (Kano, Zaria, and Sokoto), the nodes of Mossi country in Upper Volta, and around Bamako, Mali. Densities drop sharply to the north as rainfall decreases and grazing lands become poorer. This northern belt, it will be recalled, supported extensive and powerful kingdoms in the past, and while these have long disappeared there remain important commercial and administrative centers surrounded by both agricultural and pastoral peoples who are concentrated in places where soils are fertile, water tables are high, and disease has been controlled. During the early 1970s the region lost an estimated

300,000 persons because of drought-related problems. This interior belt is separated from the coastal concentrations by a zone of lighter density where populations are less because of the presence of the tsetse fly, the high incidence of sleeping sickness and malaria, the low intensity of a cash economy, the attraction of jobs in the cities and plantations to the south, and because the region was for centuries raided by slavers from both the north and south. This systematic depopulation would have caused abandoned farms to revert to bush, which would have increased the prevalence of tsetse and contributed to further emigration (Hance, 1970, p. 86).

The coastal belt from Senegal to Cameroon is one of Africa's most densely settled regions. It includes Iboland, the large Yoruba towns and agrovillages of southwestern Nigeria, all the state capitals and their associated core regions, and numerous smaller but important resource nodes as in Ghana, Liberia, Guinea, Ivory Coast, Togo, and Benin. Among the reasons for this high concentration are the political stability of the former kingdoms (Ashanti, Abomey, Yoruba) that permitted the development of large population concentrations; technological advances including disease control and the introduction of high-yielding subsistence crops, and the concentration of peoples in the modern consumer-oriented cities that resulted from the long history of contact with the developed world; the attractiveness and suitability of the natural environment for important cash crops such as cocoa, coffee, and palm, and subsistence crops such as manioc, yams, and corn and the development of mineral deposits and agricultural schemes that have attracted migrants from the interior regions.

In East Africa and the Horn, population densities differ sharply short distances from one another, and the overall pattern is one of "islands" of high density surrounded by seas of lower density. The major "islands" include the Kenya Highlands, the mountain states of Rwanda and Burundi, the northeast shores of Lake Victoria, the central Ethiopian Highlands, and the lower slopes of Mounts Kilimanjaro and Meru, all of which have rich soils, support intensive cultivation, and are high-rainfall regions. They contain some of Africa's most fertile farm lands and are locally important economic nodes. In contrast, the sparsely populated areas of northern Kenya, much of Somalia, and west central Tanzania are low rainfall regions and hence are unsuited to intensive cultivation. Tsetse fly and other diseases are further controls. Game reserves—the largest of which in Africa is Selousi (Tanzania)—and national parks (Serengeti, Tsavo, and others) separate population centers and help create the "island" pattern. Over 80 percent of the Kenya population of 14.5 million lives on only 10 percent of the land, and two-thirds of the Tanzanian population (16.3 million) is concentrated on less than a fifth of the land.

The countries of Equatorial Africa have a combined population of 37 million in an area the size of India and Pakistan. The region is one of the least populous in Africa where the distributions and densities are not well correlated with any particular set of environmental factors. In the past, abundant space and small numbers permitted an almost unrestricted use of the land that saw shifting cultivation and cyclical movements of settlement, especially within the rain-forest areas. A delicate balance was maintained between man and his environment, and while much of the region could support increased rural and urban populations, the

ecological balance could easily be disturbed. Given the natural environment and realistic changes in technology, it is not likely the region will ever support a large and high-density population, or be an important exporter of food to the surrounding areas. Zaire is the most populous state (26.1 million) and its population is widely distributed; the major concentrations are centered on Kinshasa, Lubumbashi, and Kananga.

Environmental factors have clearly influenced the distribution and density of population in Southern Africa: the drier and disease-prone regions in general support fewer people than the more humid and temperate zones, and there is a strong correlation between high density and rich soils and mineral workings. In South Africa there are sharp contrasts in population density and ethnic homogeneity as a result of the government's policy of separate development, and the pattern is repeated in certain ways in Rhodesia (Zimbabwe). In both countries the reserves are overpopulated, predominantly rural, lacking in development resources, and are labor reservoirs for the European-controlled regions. The European freehold areas in contrast are frequently sparsely populated. Furthermore, both South Afirca and Rhodesia (Zimbabwe) have large urban concentrations, the largest in South Africa being the Witwatersrand. Malawi has "islands" of high density similar to East Africa, and in Malagasy there are also sharp contrasts, the greatest concentration being on the agriculturally superior massif around Tananarive, center of the once powerful Merina kingdom.

Population Pressure

Since the combination of disease, climate, broken topography, poor soils, and other environmental factors may severely reduce the amount of land suitable for human occupation, and because man must frequently compete with his livestock for

space and food, arithmetic and arable densities are not very satisfactory indicators of overpopulation, underpopulation, and population pressure. Numbers must be assessed not only with reference to the physical environment, but also with respect to culture, technology, population growth, man's attitudes towards his environment, and his wants. Two areas may have the same number of people and the same natural environment, but one may be overpopulated, the other underpopulated. Similarly, a region (such as the Kalahari) having a low arithmetic density may have a greater population pressure than another where the density is high. All too frequently, population pressure has been equated with high arithmetic and arable densities, and consequently Africa has been portrayed as an essentially underpopulated continent capable of supporting an almost unlimited number of people. However, there is ample evidence to the contrary, and the time to assess the problems and formulate corrective measures is the present.

The technological component of population pressure is of prime importance because it means that population pressure is not static, and a region that is considered to be suffering from excessive populations today, may one day be underpopulated. This is implied in the concept of *critical density of population* (CDP), which is defined as

"the human carrying capacity of an area in relation to a given land use system, expressed by population per square mile; it is the maximum population density which a system is capable of supporting permanently in that environment without damage to the land" (Allan, 1965). The CDP is a function of the population (its numbers, quality, distribution, and rate of change), the methods and systems of land use, and technology employed, the crops grown, and the physical conditions of the areas. It is dependent on a combination of these factors rather than on any one of them individually.

Most discussions of population density are concerned solely with man and his environment, and omit his cattle and other livestock from the calculations. However, in predominantly agricultural and pastoral economies, livestock frequently compete with man for space and food and thus are part of the population pressure and overpopulation equations. If Africa's livestock are reduced to *population equivalents* (measured in nutritional requirements), and are added to the human populations, we have a more accurate estimate of the *biomass* that

Table 7-2 POPULATION EQUIVALENTS, 1977 (EST.) (in thousands) [a]

	POPULATION EQUIVALENTS		HUMAN POPULATION		TOTAL POPULATION		RATIO HUMANS/P.E.
	Number	Rank	Number	Rank	Number	Rank	
Ethiopia	348,600	1	30,000	3	378,600	1	1:12
Sudan	201,000	2	19,500	6	220,500	3	1:11
South Africa	172,260	3	26,600	4	198,860	4	1:7
Nigeria	165,050	4	85,940	1	250,990	2	1:2
Tanzania	144,606	5	16,250	9	160,856	5	1:10
Kenya	103,775	6	14,500	10	118,275	6	1:7
Malagasy	98,013	7	8,450	14	106,463	7	1:13
Morocco	78,532	8	18,700	7	97,232	9	1:5
Mali	68,131	9	5,960	20	74,091	10	1:13
Somalia	64,343	10	3,700	30	68,043	11	1:17
Egypt	60,625	11	40,800	2	101,425	8	1:2
Chad	56,120	12	4,380	28	60,500	13	1:14
Niger	55,658	13	4,800	24	60,458	14	1:12
Uganda	50,192	14	12,150	11	62,342	12	1:4
Rhodesia (Zimbabwe)	44,226	15	6,900	15	51,126	15	1:7

[a] *Calculated from data in U.N. Production Yearbooks, Demographic Yearbooks, Censuses, National Reports, and Government Surveys.*

must be fed from a region's agricultural base (Borgstrom, 1965). In the mid-1970s Africa's population equivalents exceeded 2.2 billion, with Ethiopia, Sudan, South Africa, and Nigeria heading the list (Table 7-2). Most countries with large population equivalents also have large human populations, but there are several whose human populations are small that support many population equivalents. The ratio of population equivalents to humans in Mali, Chad, Niger, and Somalia is over 12:1, and in these same countries there is severe overstocking, population pressure, human malnutrition, and a general deterioration in the environment.

Because almost 85 percent of the population is agricultural, population pressure is most obvious and common in the rural regions. There it expresses itself in several ways, the most common of which are soil deterioration, degradation, or outright destruction; the use of excessively steep slopes and other marginal lands; declining crop yields; a change in crop emphasis, especially to soil-tolerant crops; reduction in the fallow period and the lengthening of the cropping period without measures to retain soil fertility; food shortages, hunger, and malnutrition; land fragmentation, land disputes, and landlessness; rural indebtedness and the breakdown of indigenous farming systems; unemployment and underemployment; and outmigration (Hance, 1970, pp. 417–418). These conditions, however, may indicate problems besides population pressure. In the late 1960s, approximately half of Africa was considered overpopulated. Areas with high population density and obvious population pressure include the South African Bantustans and the Rhodesian reserves; the uplands of Rwanda, Burundi, and Kenya; the coastal areas from Nigeria to the Ivory Coast; parts of the Sahel; and much of the Maghreb.

Pounding corn, the staple food in this Upper Volta village. There is little variety in the diet, and the children here show signs of malnutrition. (World Bank)

THE POPULATION OF AFRICA

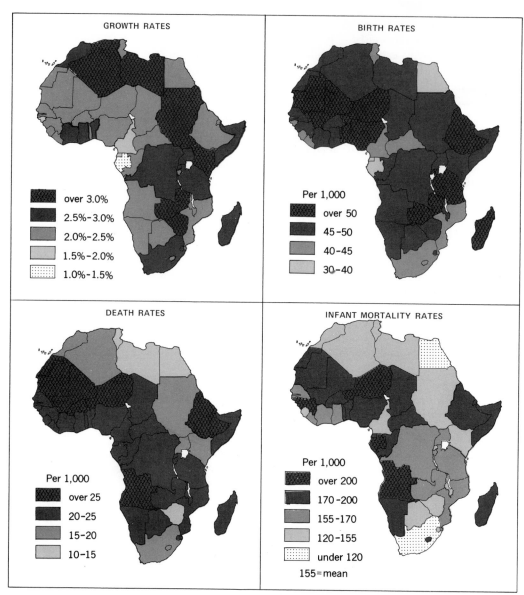

FIGURE 7-2 *Population, 1975 (est).*

Growth Rates and Population Policies

Africa's population will double in 27 years if the current growth rate (2.6 percent) is sustained. If the growth rate rises to 3 percent within the next decade, which is possible, the population could exceed 900 million by the end of the century. Figure 7-2 shows the pattern of growth in 1975. Several states, among them Kenya, Sudan, and Algeria, had an annual growth rate of about 3 percent, and it is certain the rate of increase will soon reach similar levels elsewhere. Kenya and Egypt have initiated family-planning programs, while Algeria, Zaire, and others desire larger populations and oppose any form of population control.

Africa's population growth rate has been increasing over the past several decades; at the turn of this century it was less than 1 percent per annum; from 1930–1950 it was 1.3 percent per annum; and from 1950–1970 about 2.3 percent per annum. The accelerating growth is due to falling death rates combined with consistently high, and in some cases rising, birth rates. As recently as the 1940s and 1950s, death rates were generally between 30 per 1000 and 40 per 1000, while birth rates were about 48 per 1000. For example, in the Ivory Coast, birth and death rates in 1940 were 55 per 1000 and 38 per 1000, respectively. In 1975 they were 45.6 per 1000 and 20.6 per 1000.

The theory of the demographic transition supposes that over a period of time, birth and death rates change because of changing social, economic, and political forces, and that we can see a number of distinct stages. In low-income economies where health facilities and schools are generally lacking, and the level of technology is low, crude birth rates and death rates are high and fluctuate widely from year to year, so that on occasion death rates may even exceed birth rates. However, the overall effect is a low growth rate, generally less than 1 percent. As the economy changes and improved health facilities and technology are introduced, death rates begin to fall but birth rates remain high, the net result being a high growth rate, generally between 2 and 4 percent. If the awareness of population growth increases, and population control measures are adopted, birth rates may then decline and stabilize slightly higher than the mortality rates and result in a small but stable population growth. This is the pattern of the industrialized world. In Africa, however, most countries belong to the second stage, having left the first during the colonial era with the assault on infectious diseases, and as technological changes were introduced. This was accomplished without a major transformation in the traditional social and economic lives of the people, and within an extremely short period when compared with Europe and the United States. In spite of disease control, Africa has the world's highest crude mortality rate (20 per 1000), and while this is falling, birth rates remain very high, so that most African countries are in an early period of accelerating growth (Table 7-3). Attitudes toward birth have not changed significantly on a broad front so that Africa's fertility rates remain the highest in the world.

Of the various death rates, infant mortality rates have shown the most dramatic declines. Only two decades ago they were commonly over 200 per 1000 while in the mid-1970s they averaged 156 per 1000, and ranged from a low of 103 per 1000 in Egypt to 229 per 1000 in Gabon (Table 7-3). The widespread reduction of infant mortality combined with the sustained high birth rates have resulted in a large proportion (40–50 percent) of the total population being under 15 years of age. The population pyramid for Uganda illustrates this (Fig. 7-3). As birth control measures are followed, and the length of life is extended as a result of improved health standards, the population pyramids will narrow at the base and broaden at the apex. South Africa's white population displays these characteristics and approaches more closely than any other group the model of the industrialized world.

There are important regional differences in Africa's birth rates, death rates, and growth rates. The lowest birth rates (Fig. 7-2) occur in Southern Africa, Egypt and Gabon, while the highest are in West Africa, Ethiopia, Tanzania, and Zambia. Some of the most populous countries have the highest birth rates. Birth rates vary considerably within countries according to race, socioeconomic achievement, and rural-urban residence. In South Africa, for instance, where there are extremes in life-styles, opportunities, value systems, and other factors that affect birth rates, the birth rates for the

Table 7-3 SELECTED POPULATION DATA, 1975 (EST)

Country	Growth Rate (%)	Crude Birth Rate (per 1000)	Crude Death Rate (per 1000)	Number of Years for Population to Double	Population under 15 (%)	Infant Mortality (per 1000)	Life Expectancy at Birth
Algeria	3.2	48.7	15.4	22	48	128	53
Angola	2.3	47.3	24.5	30	42	203	38
Egypt	2.4	37.8	14.0	29	41	103	52
Ethiopia	2.4	50.0	25.8	29	44	181	38
Gabon	1.0	32.2	22.2	69	32	229	41
Ghana	2.7	48.8	21.9	26	48	156	44
Guinea	2.4	46.6	22.9	29	43	216	41
Ivory Coast	2.5	45.6	20.6	28	43	164	44
Kenya	3.3	48.7	16.0	21	46	135	50
Lesotho	2.0	40.0	19.7	35	38	181	46
Liberia	2.3	43.6	20.7	30	41	159	44
Malagasy	2.9	50.2	21.1	24	45	170	44
Mali	2.4	50.1	25.9	29	49	188	38
Niger	2.7	52.2	25.5	26	46	200	38
Nigeria	2.7	50.0	22.7	26	45	180	41
Rhodesia (Zimbabwe)	3.4	47.9	14.4	20	48	122	52
Rwanda	2.6	50.0	23.6	27	44	133	41
South Africa	2.7	42.9	15.5	26	41	117	52
Sudan	3.0	47.8	17.5	23	45	141	49
Zaire	2.5	45.2	20.5	28	44	160	44
Africa	2.6	46.4	19.8	27	44	156	45
World	1.9	31.5	12.8	36	36	98	55

SOURCE. *Population Reference Bureau, Government Surveys.*

FIGURE 7-3 *Population pyramids—Uganda and South Africa.*

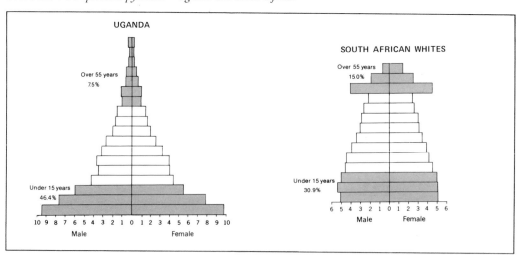

four races are as follows: Africans 43 per 1000, Coloureds 36 per 1000, Asians 33 per 1000, and whites 24 per 1000. The whites are predominantly urban, enjoy a high standard of living, are conscious of the consequences of uncontrolled population growth, and are part of the industrialized world; the Africans, however, are divided equally between rural and urban areas, are part of the "developing" world, and have not adopted birth control measures as readily as whites.

Figure 7-2 shows that death rates are generally lowest in the northern tier of states plus South Africa and Rhodesia (Zimbabwe), and are highest in tropical Africa. In Angola and Guinea-Bissau (where the Portuguese were not known for their social welfare programs), crude death rates are among the highest in the world (25 per 1000). The spatial pattern of infant mortality rates (Fig. 7-2) is very similar to that of crude death rates. In the Sahelian states, Ethiopia and Somalia, infant mortality rates possibly exceeded 300 per 1000 during the droughts and famines of 1968–1974. Death rates vary considerably within countries according to nutritional standards, access to clinics and doctors, population density, and the quality of housing and sanitary facilities present. For example, the death rate among the whites of South Africa is 9 per 1000 and that of the rural blacks is possibly 20 per 1000.

Some African countries are already feeling the strains of increasing population, which involve, among other problems, low levels of subsistence in rural areas, rising rural and urban unemployment, an increasing drift to urban areas, the spread of slums and shanty towns, and increasing claims on government resources for social services in education and health. The connection between economic backwardness and overpopulation, which is often the chief cause of that backwardness, all too often is not recognized or is ignored. Few governments view rapid population growth as a problem to be solved through the adoption of official population policies such as fertility control and family planning. The notion that rapid population growth jeopardizes national development objectives is only slowly gaining acceptability, and nowhere is fertility control assigned high priority. Official emphasis is placed almost wholly on increasing the pace of national economic growth to achieve higher standards of living, and subordinately on taking care of a growing population.

Kenya, feeling the strains of rising numbers, is one country that has initiated a program of population control. It received a $12 million credit from the International Development Association (IDA), an affiliate of the World Bank, to assist in its Five-Year Family-Planning Program, 1975–1979, and is the first country in Africa south of the Sahara to receive World Bank aid for population control (Mafukidze, 1974). The project focuses on training field personnel to extend existing family planning and maternal and child health services, strengthening the rural health system, and developing an appropriate institution to support family planning services.

Most African governments do not share Kenya's views and are unenthusiastic about family planning. The Congo, Gabon, Zaire, and Algeria, to name only a few, want additional populations, reasoning that economies of scale can best be achieved through higher population densities, and that larger labor forces mean larger domestic markets that are essential productive elements in national development. Moreover, restrictive and eugenic population policies have been denounced as imperialistic. Among the most outspoken critics of birth control programs have been the Zimbabwe Nationalists who consider birth control efforts as part of the white minority's conspiracy to retain control of the country's resources and political power. The Rhodesian government has created a special ministerial post to deal with African birth control, while at the same time white immigration is encouraged. The Nationalists argue that if overpopulation is a

While family planning services are available in many African states, there is little evidence of effective population control. If the current growth rate (2.6 percent) is sustained, Africa's population will double in 27 years. (UN/FAO)

real issue (as the government claims), the solution lies in a more equitable distribution of land and resources, not in birth control, and white immigration cannot be justified.

Family planning services are becoming more widely available through private and government programs, but the problems of instituting birth control plans are many and vary from society to society. In the franco-phone countries where Roman Catholicism is strong, birth control lacks government support. Traditional family planning practices are breaking down in the urban areas so the demand for modern contraceptives is growing with rapid urbanization and modernization. In rural areas, however, the use of contraceptives is not widespread. Ghana is considering liberalizing its abortion

A West African family of nine, the mother being in her late twenties. Almost half of Africa's people are 15 years of age and under. Death rates are dropping, but birth rates remain high so that growth rates are increasing. (UN/FAO).

laws, while in Ethiopia, Nigeria, and the francophone countries there are strong religious and cultural biases against the liberalization of abortion laws and its practice as a birth control measure.

Urban Growth

By whatever definition, Africa is the least urbanized of the continents, yet its urban growth rate is the highest. Poor census data and the multiplicity of definitions and measurements of "urban population," "town," "city," and "metropolitan area" make meaningful comparisons almost impossible. The UN defines "urban population" as the population in towns with 20,000 and more inhabitants, but the problem then becomes one of defining "town." Are the large agrovillages of Botswana and Nigeria towns—some with populations well above 20,000? And what of the forced resettlement centers and townships of South Africa, and the refugee camps that are proliferating across the continent? Their size and densities are impressive, but their functions suggest they are not towns. Nevertheless, the UN estimates that approximately one-fifth of the African population was urban in 1975, compared with 13 percent in 1960, and only 10 percent in 1950.

South Africa is the most urban country with 48 percent of its population in towns and cities. It is also the most industrial. In North Africa, where each state has its own distinct urban clusters, the urban populations range from 29 percent in Libya to 43 percent in Egypt. While there are several large cities in West Africa, and especially in Nigeria, the population is still predominantly rural, with no state having more than a third of its population classified urban. The highest urban ratios occur in the coastal states (Ghana 29 percent, Senegal 26 percent, Liberia 28 percent) and the lowest occur in the interior (Upper Volta 8 percent and Chad 13 percent). Other representative figures include Ethiopia 10 percent, Uganda 8 percent, and Zaire 24 percent.

Africa's urban population could be growing at 7 percent per annum, but the growth is not evenly distributed. In the North African countries and South Africa, where the history of urbanization has been long and the urban systems are the most developed, urban growth rates are almost twice the natural growth rates. The highest urban growth rates occur in the least urbanized states such as Upper Volta, Malawi, Niger, and Zaire. There, urban growth rates are the highest on earth—11–17 percent per annum. These figures can be misleading and should be treated with caution; the growth is

being measured from a small base, so while the rates may be high, the towns and cities are small. Natural growth rates, that is, births less deaths, are generally higher in urban than rural areas due to the control over death, especially the death of infants and children, and to the lack of control over births. However, most urban growth is accounted for by in-migration, the migrants themselves contributing to the natural increase.

While there are obvious differences in the size and growth of urban centers, in the wealth and occupations of the urban population, and in the quality of housing and social services available, there are important similarities in the urban patterns from one state to another. First, most growth occurs in the respective primate cities. Table 7-4 shows this phenomenal growth in absolute terms over the last four decades. Cairo's population, for instance, has doubled in the last 20 years, and almost all primates have doubled their populations in the last decade. Second, migration is a major contributing factor to this growth. Populations from the surrounding rural areas and smaller towns are at-

Table 7-4 GROWTH OF SELECTED PRIMATE CITIES (Estimates, in Thousands)

City	1930s Year	1930s Pop.	1950s Year	1950s Pop.	1960s Year	1960s Pop.	1970s Year	1970s Pop.
Abidjan	30	10	50	69	68	500	70	650
Addis Ababa	38	300	58	400	68	620	74	1046
Brazzaville	36	24	50	84	68	200	74	311
Cairo	37	1312	54	2603	66	4220	75	6600
Casablanca	36	257	52	682	66	1120	71	1506
Conakry	31	7	50	39	67	197	72	526
Dakar	31	54	55	300	68	600	74	714
Dar es Salaam	31	34	52	99	67	273	73	415
Johannesburg	36	519	51	919	60	1153	74	1433
Kinshasa	30	33	50	191	66	508	74	1799
Lagos	31	127	52	267	63	665	75	1400
Lusaka	—	—	56	58	63	119	74	415
Monrovia	34	10	53	27	67	100	74	180
Nairobi	36	50	57	222	62	315	75	700
N'Djamena	36	8	51	21	67	150	73	195
Salisbury	31	32	58	233	68	380	75	555
Tripoli	—	—	54	130	68	330	73	552

SOURCE. *Hance, 1975, pp. 241–42; Various National Surveys.*

tracted by the economic opportunities (real or perceived) of their country's major industrial-commercial-political center. Third, much of the economic growth, capital investment, and politicoeconomic foundation is concentrated in the primates, largely a carry-over from colonial times. The primates are at the meeting ground between the national and international economies, and are situated in strategic and convenient locations. Fourth, in all but a handful of states, the primate cities account for more than half the total urban populations: Addis Ababa has 59 percent, Conakry 59 percent, Tripoli 63 percent, Kampala 68 percent, and Banjul 100 percent. The important exceptions are Lagos 14 percent, Johannesburg 14 percent, Algiers 29 percent, and Kinshasa 34 percent. Fifth, a high percentage of the urban population is located in cities of 100,000 and more, and there is a large disparity between the primate cities and the smaller towns. The rank–size rule applies very poorly, which means the hierarchical arrangement of towns and cities associated with developed countries is generally absent and the spatial distribution of wealth and development is highly concentrated. Sixth, the major urban areas are witnessing acute shortages of housing and rising unemployment as migration adds to the local population increase.

The problems associated with this growth and the regional disparities of wealth and development are known to most governments, but few are being rectified. Most governments wish to control urban growth by making the rural areas more attractive places in which to live, with jobs and adequate social services. Commonly adopted strategies include decentralizing industry by encouraging high-manpower industry to locate at prescribed rurally based "growth centers"; introducing large-scale high-manpower agricultural projects; improving agricultural techniques, and revising land tenure; and providing improved medical, educational, and social facilities in rural areas. Specific examples are taken up in the regional chapters that follow.

Part of Adjamey, a slum area of Abidjan, Ivory Coast. Inadequate housing and social services, and high unemployment are common ailments of Africa's burgeoning cities. (UN)

THE POPULATION OF AFRICA

Migrations can be both the causes and consequences of population growth. In Africa they play an especially important role in urban growth, the circulation of income, the diffusion of ideas and values, and have contributed to the concentration of industry, economic growth, and political power in relatively small areas at the expense of the surrounding regions. While important in the development process of contemporary Africa, migrations have occurred throughout history and have contributed to the contemporary patterns of distributions, densities, and economies. They can be voluntary or involuntary, permanent or temporary, within or between states, rural–urban, urban–rural, rural–rural, urban–urban, involving individuals or groups. They are the response to changes (either real or perceived) in the natural environment, and social, political, and economic systems in either the migrant's place of origin or place of destination, or both.

Among the major precolonial migrations have been the Arab invasions across the Sahara into the Sudanic belt; the pilgrimages to Mecca; Bantu movements from the Cameroon Highlands to East and Southern Africa; the southward migration of Nilotic and Hamitic groups in eastern Africa, and the wave effect of Bushmen, Hottentots, and Khoisan peoples into the less hospitable areas of Southern Africa; the trans-Indian Ocean movements from Southeast Asia that account for the Asian names, rice culture, and other distinctly Asian influences in Mal-

A Mauritanian family facing famine and disease from persistent drought, migrating in search of food and security. (UN/AID)

agasy; the migrations and countermigrations of pastoral nomads throughout the savanna zones and certain highland regions; and the wholesale removal of slaves to the New World, North Africa, and Asia. From West Africa alone, between 8 and 12 million slaves were removed, and possibly a further 4 million were shipped from East Africa.

Migrations during the colonial era differed markedly in their scale, orientation, incentives, and consequences although of course many basic patterns of local migrations by pastoralists and traders persisted, as they do in postcolonial Africa. Tens of thousands of colonial administrators, settlers, and entrepreneurs poured into the continent from the metropoles and other colonial possessions. The British, for instance, brought with them indentured laborers from India and Mauritius to clear the land for crops and to build railways and cities in Kenya, Uganda, and South Africa. Syrians, Lebanese, and West Indians migrated to West Africa to become traders, bankers, and builders. French settlers occupied valuable farm lands in Algeria and Morocco, and the Portuguese opened up parts of Mozambique and Angola. This colonial input set in motion countless migrations by individuals in search of economic gain and by groups to meet the requirements of the colonial systems. Thousands migrated to the new cities, plantations, and mines, and entire tribes adjusted to the new administrative boundaries. At first the labor migrations were frequently involuntary. Africans were forced to build roads, railways and dams and to work on other public projects. Compensation was either lacking or inadequate, and thousands died of malnutrition, disease, and unsafe work conditions. Government-controlled recruiting organizations supplied labor to the mines of Katanga (Shaba), Rhodesia, and South Africa and to the peanut and coffee plantations of Senegal and the Ivory Coast, respectively. All colonial governments introduced some form of head tax that had to be paid in cash, forcing the African into new

regions and into new life-styles. As these and other injustices were exposed by private and government enquiries, and even by the International Court of Justice, labor laws were relaxed and migrations became more voluntary and individual.

In West Africa, where the general flow of migratory labor was and is from the interior to the coast, the French instituted a system of forced labor to ensure the success of their plantations in Senegal and the Ivory Coast, and the construction of the Kayes and Abidjan-Bobo Dioulasso railways. In the middle 1930s French-owned coffee and cocoa plantations in the Ivory Coast employed about 20,000 Upper Voltans, half of whom were forced laborers. Between 1936 and 1939 forced labor was formally abolished, but during World War II compulsory recruitment was reintroduced. Between 1940 and 1944, some 277,000 migrants entered the Ivory Coast from Upper Volta, 171,000 under this program. With the abolition of forced labor in 1946 and the movement of labor becoming unpredictable, the Ivory Coast planters formed a labor-recruiting agency in Upper Volta, which recruited 163,000 workers between 1952 and 1959. The program was carried out in such a ruthless manner that in 1960 the government of Upper Volta prohibited all further operations. While migrations continue—less than half of the Ivory Coast's unskilled work force in the private sector are Ivorians—work conditions have improved, and the Ivory Coast helps cover the costs of recruitment. Nevertheless, Upper Volta claims that payments to its treasury for each recruit are too low, that wages paid in the Ivory Coast are discriminatory, and that recruitment regulations are violated (Amin, 1974). An equal number of Malians and almost as many Guineans migrate each year to the Ivory Coast.

In adjoining Ghana, the cocoa industry has long depended on migrants from Northern Ghana, Togo, Upper Volta, the Ivory Coast, and even parts of Nigeria. Forty percent of the work force in southern Ghana comes from these regions. Migrants do most of the menial work such as clearing the forest and harvesting the cocoa. In 1969 the Ghanaian government decreed that aliens without valid residence permits would be expelled, since over 600,000 Ghanaians were unemployed, and the balance of payment deficit was worsened by immigrant workers and traders who sent home some of their earnings. Most migrants leave the north during the dry season when local labor requirements are low.

In South Africa, the mining economy is based on the exploitation of migrant workers from the Bantustans and the adjoining countries where employment opportunities are low and populations are burgeoning. Most migrants are contracted to work for periods of nine months or a year, after which they must return to their homelands until qualified for additional recruitment (Wilson, 1972). Others seek seasonal work on neighboring white-owned farms, while over the last century hundreds of thousands have left permanently for the cities. At least 500,000 migrants are recruited each year by government agencies in Lesotho, Swaziland, Botswana, Mozambique, and Malawi, and an additional 700,000 are temporarily absent from the Bantustans. In South Africa as elsewhere in the continent, the migrant is usually male, unskilled, and a temporary participant in the modern exchange economy who must support a family in his home area. If he succeeds in breaking the circulatory system, and becomes a permanent resident in the city, his family will follow.

Independence brought migrations of a different nature: the exodus of colonial settlers, and the return of African exiles. Over a million Europeans left Algeria following the Franco-Algerian War to be replaced by an even greater number of Muslims who had earlier fled to Morocco and Tunisia. Some 330,000 Portuguese left Angola, and 150,000 others left Mozambique in the months immediately before these territories gained their independence. Thousands of British settlers moved from East Africa (especially Kenya) during and after the Mau Mau uprisings and following independence, and settled in Rhodesia, the Republic of South Africa, and Canada. An estimated 75,000 Asians were expelled from Uganda in 1972, and still others were forced out of Kenya and Tanzania. Thousands of Syrian and Lebanese traders lost their licenses (and hence their livelihoods) in Ghana, Liberia, Ivory Coast, and Nigeria as these countries moved toward localizing their economies.

While these movements and the continuous drift toward urban areas have received much international attention, refugee movements have not (Brooks and El-Ayouty, 1970). Literally millions of Africans in the last two decades have fled their homelands to escape repression and discrimination. The largest of these refugee movements have been from Sudan, Angola, Mozambique, Rwanda, Burundi, Ethiopia, and Zaire, and the motivations have been primarily political and ethnic.

An estimated 300,000 Sudanese fled to Uganda and Zaire during the 1960s to escape political, social, and religious persecutions in the southern regions. An additional half-million Sudanese fled to the security of their respective ethnic homelands within the Sudan. In 1963, about 145,000 Tutsi left Rwanda following a decision by the Hutu-dominated government to sequester some of their traditional pastoral lands (Hance, 1970, p. 184). Most fled to neighboring Tanzania and Zaire. The Tanzanian government attempted to settle these and other refugees (from Mozambique and Uganda) in rural villages similar to those being established under the *ujamaa* system. During the wars of independence in the former Portuguese colonies, an estimated 80,000 refugees fled from Guinea-Bissau to neighboring Senegal; over 60,000 fled annually to Tanzania, Malawi, and Zambia from Mozambique; and perhaps as many as 700,000 Angolans, mainly Bakongo, crossed over into Zaire.

About one million drought-striken Somalis sought food, water, and medical supplies in relief camps such as this in 1975. Even greater numbers were affected in West Africa's Sahelian zone. (UN/Kennedy/Lapidoth)

Besides these international migrations, there is much movement within national boundaries to escape persecution and even annihilation: a half million Ibos returned to their homeland in the Eastern Region of Nigeria from the Northern and Western Regions prior to and during the early stages of the Biafran war. While it is impossible to state with any accuracy the magnitude of the refugee problem in Africa, the U. N. High Commissioner for Refugees estimated there to be over 1 million refugees in 1970, and possibly 1.4 million in the mid-1970s.

The 1970s have also witnessed mass migrations of unprecedented proportions in the drought-stricken regions of West Africa, Ethiopia, Kenya, and Somalia. There soil exhaustion, inadequate grazing, and crop failures have forced thousands of starving families into temporary relief centers and cities quite unprepared to accommodate them. Many will undoubtedly remain once the droughts break to become part of Africa's ever-increasing urban scene. Finally, postcolonial Africa has witnessed a substantial increase in the international movement of elites to and from Africa, while the independent governments have placed restrictions on foreign Africans and expatriates from seeking employment within their boundaries.

Language

There are more than 800 languages in Africa, some spoken by only a few hundred persons, while others are widespread and spoken by millions including both native speakers, and those for whom the languages function as a supplementary means of communication. Languages spoken beyond their region of origin have been introduced as a result of migration, trade, political domination, and the modernization process: Hausa, spoken by at least 30 million people, is the *lingua franca* from western Niger to southern Cameroon; Bambara and Dyuka are the vehicular tongues from Senegal to the Ivory

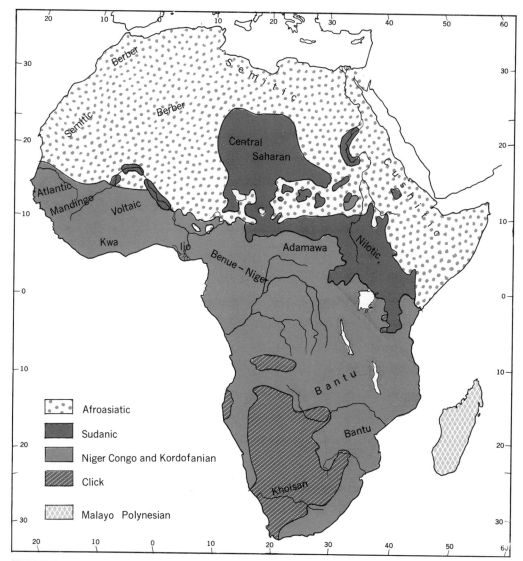

FIGURE 7-4 *Major language regions (after Greenberg).*

Coast; a pidgin English called Wes Kos is the coastal *lingua franca* from Gambia to Port Harcourt, Nigeria; Kiswahili is the most widely spoken language, especially in the towns, from southern Sudan to central Mozambique and inland to the great lakes; Arabic is the principal language of communication and religion throughout the Islamic realm; and European languages, once the languages of the elite and the colonial governments, are now recognized instruments of scientific progress and modernization throughout Africa.

Language classification is difficult in view of the still incomplete research by linguists, but four major stocks are generally recognized: Afro-Asiatic, Click, Niger-Congo, and Sudanic (Fig. 7-4). (Greenberg, 1966). The Afro-Asiatic languages, which are exclusively predominant in North Africa and much of the Horn, include Berber, Kushitic, Semitic, Chad, and Ancient Egyptian (Coptic) languages. The Click languages, so named because of the characteristic implosive "click" sounds, include Khoisan, which is spoken by the Bushman and Hottentots of Southern Africa, and Sandawe and Hatsa of interior Tanzania. The Niger-Congo languages, which form the largest group in Africa, are composed of eight substocks: Atlantic, Mandingo, Kwa, Ijo, Benue-Niger, Voltaic, Adamawa, and Kordofanian, which extend across the continent from Senegal to Tanzania and south to the Cape. In West Africa, where the language map is the most diverse, 10 languages—Hausa, Yoruba, Peul, Akan, Ibo, Malinke-Bambara, Wollof, Zarma, More, and Ewe—are used by 90 percent of the population; similarly in East Africa, Kiswahili and Nyaruanda, both Bantu languages, are spoken by millions. The Sudanic languages occupy a discontinuous belt north and east of the Niger-Congo group, and include Kanuri—language of the ancient kingdom of Bornu near Lake Chad—and the Nilotic languages Nyer, Dinka, Masai, and Turkana. There are a few outliers such as Songhai along the Niger River, and Wadai and Furian in the Darfurs of Sudan. The languages of Madagascar are Malayo-Polynesian, and are distinct from those of the African mainland having been introduced from southeast Asia 2000 years ago. Superimposed on this mosaic are English, French, Portuguese, and Italian, and in South Africa an African language of Dutch origin—Afrikaans—is widely spoken. Finally, in scattered locations in Kenya, Tanzania, and more especially in Natal, South Africa, there are pockets of Hindu, Gujarati, Urdu, and other languages of the Indian subcontinent introduced over the last century.

This mosaic of languages, unparalleled elsewhere in the world, is important in itself, but it is of fundamental importance to the geographer concerned with understanding modernization processes since language diversity prohibits easy communication, the diffusion of ideas and values, and inhibits nationalism while perpetuating tribalism. In Nigeria, for instance, where at least 30 distinct languages and 200 dialects exist, making Nigeria the most linguistically diverse of the African states, language has inhibited the Nigerians from developing a true national identity and a strong sense of nationalism. The Biafran war clearly demonstrated that the Ibo considered themselves different (if not superior) from the Hausa, Fulani, Yoruba, and others according to language and everything their language represented. In South Africa, the ruling Nationalist Government has used linguistic and ethnic criteria to distinguish and delimit the Bantustans. Language preserves and fosters one's identity, distinguishes one group from another, and is jealously guarded by its speakers.

In general, Africans—especially traders and towns dwellers—are multilingual, most having learned to speak (if not read and write) at least one other indigenous language plus a European language. Multilingualism is partly a product of colonialism (Alexandre, 1973). The pursuit of wealth and the transformation of the social, political, economic, and religious institutions could not be accomplished without a common language. The British and Germans tended to use local languages more frequently than the French, Portuguese, and Belgians. French was the only language officially recognized in the schools, courts, and administration of the French colonies, and it flourished because it promised social prestige and profitable jobs. English was used in conjunction with local languages in the British colonies, and it too afforded distinct social and economic advantages. Consequently there arose in each colony a linguistic elite or "language capitalists": the businessmen and government leaders who thought and planned in European languages but frequently failed to translate their ideas to the majority. Communications gaps were created.

Table 7-5 OFFICIAL LANGUAGES IN AFRICA

STATE	OFFICIAL LANGUAGE(S)	STATE	OFFICIAL LANGUAGE(S)
Algeria	Arabic	Libya	Arabic
Angola	Portuguese	Malagasy	Malagasy
Benin	French	Malawi	English, Chewa
Botswana	English, Setswana	Mauritania	Arabic
Burundi	French, Kirundi	Mozambique	Portuguese
Cameroon	French, English	Namibia (South	
Central African		West Africa)	English, Afrikaans
Republic	French, Sango	Niger	French
Chad	French	Nigeria	English
Congo	French, Lingala	Rhodesia (Zimbabwe)	English
Egypt	Arabic	Rwanda	French, Kinyarwanda
Equatorial Guinea	Spanish	Senegal	French, Wolof
Ethiopia	Amharic	Sierra Leone	English
French Territory of		Somalia	Somali
the Afars and Issas	French	South Africa	Afrikaans, English
Gambia	English, Wolof	Sudan	Arabic, English
Gabon	French	Swaziland	English, Siswati
Ghana	English	Tanzania	Kiswahili
Guinea	French	Togo	French, Ewe
Guinea Bissau	Portuguese	Tunisia	Arabic
Ivory Coast	French	Uganda	English
Kenya	English, Kiswahili	Upper Volta	French
Lesotho	English, Sesotho	Zaire	French
Liberia	English	Zambia	English

All governments have realized the importance of national communication in forging new values and a sense of national identity. The problem has been one of selecting and implementing national or official languages. The language of the colonizers is prestigious, being that of the modern ruling elite and being ethnically neutral. French and English are international languages that provide Africans access to scientific and technical knowledge so necessary for social and economic development. French is the official language of most former French possessions south of the Sahara, and one of two official languages in Senegal, Togo, Cameroon, Rwanda, Burundi, the Congo, and the Central African Republic (Table 7-5). Similarly, English is the official language, or one of two official languages, in all ex-British colonies excluding Tanzania where Kiswahili has been adopted. Arabic is the official language of seven Saharan states.

Five states—Rwanda, Burundi, Botswana, Lesotho, and Somalia have a single indigenous language spoken by almost the entire population and in each case that national language is also the official language. Tanzania, Kenya, Congo, and the Central African Republic have selected a *lingua franca* as an official language. In Nigeria there are several major regional languages including Yoruba, Hausa, Fulani, and Ibo, but English is the official language. As nationalism develops, more indigenous languages will probably achieve official status alongside the colonial languages, and many small languages may all but disappear. Official languages may not necessarily be the language of the numerically predominant ethnic group, as in the case of Senegal where the Wolofs do not constitute more than 30 percent of the population, but 85 percent of the population speaks the Wolof language.

Bibliography

Alexandre, P. "The Politics of Language," *Africa Report*, Vol. 18, No. 4 (July–August, 1973), pp. 16–19.

Allan, W. *The African Husbandman*. Edinburgh: Oliver and Boyd, 1965.

Amin, S. (ed.). *Modern Migrations in Western Africa*. London: Oxford University Press, 1974.

Barbour, K. M. *Population in Africa*. Ibadan: Ibadan University Press, 1963.

Barbour, K. M. and R. M. Prothero (eds.). *Essays on African Population*. London: Routledge and Kegan Paul, 1961.

Brooks, H. C. and Y. El-Ayouty (eds.). *Refugees South of the Sahara: An African Dilemma*. Westport: Negro Universities Press, 1970.

Caldwell, J. C. and C. Okonjo (eds.). *The Population of Tropical Africa*. New York: Columbia University Press, 1968.

Greenberg, J. H. *The Languages of Africa*. Second Edition. Bloomington: Indiana University Press, 1966.

Hance, W. A. *Population, Migration, and Urbanization in Africa*. New York: Columbia University Press, 1970.

Hanna, W. J. and J. L. Hanna. *Urban Dynamics in Black Africa*. Chicago: Aldine-Atherton, 1971.

In Search of Population Policy: Views from the Developing World. Washington, D.C.: National Academy of Sciences, 1974.

Kuper, H. (ed.). *Urbanization and Migration in West Africa*. Berkeley: University of California Press, 1965.

Mafukidze, T. S. "Africa's Need for Planning: Conspiracy or Myth?" *Africa Report*, Vol. 20, No. 4 (July–August, 1974), pp. 38–41.

Newman, J. L. (ed.). *Drought, Famine and Population Movements in Africa*. Syracuse: Syracuse University Press, 1975.

Ominde, S. H. and C. N. Ejiogu (eds.). *Population Growth and Economic Development in Africa*. London: Heinemann, 1974.

Paden, J. N. and E. W. Soja (eds.). *The African Experience*. Vol. I, Evanston: Northwestern University Press, 1970.

Prothero, R. M. *Migrants and Malaria in Africa*. London: Longmans, Green and Co., 1965.

Prothero, R. M. "Nigeria Loses Count," *Geographical Magazine*, Vol. XLVII (October, 1974), pp. 24–28.

Skinner, E. P. (ed.). *Peoples and Cultures of Africa*. Garden City: The Natural History Press, 1973.

Wilson, F. *Migrant Labour in South Africa*. Johannesburg: Christian Institute of Southern Africa, 1972.

PART TWO

WEST AFRICA

EIGHT

The Federal Republic of Nigeria is Africa's most populous state (85 million in 1977), and its thirteenth largest in area (about the combined area of California, Oregon, and Nevada). It is a country of great cultural and environmental diversity, and one of enormous economic potential. There are some 250 ethnic groups, although only four (Hausa, Fulani, Yoruba, and Ibo) account for over 60 percent of the total population. A federal constitution was adopted in partial recognition of the country's human and environmental diversities and, in this respect, Nigeria differs from most African states.

Despite its theoretical advantages, fed-eration has not been an unqualified success and periodically, Nigeria has been beset by regionally based crises, the most devastating and most publicized being the Biafran War of 1967–1970. A major politicogeographic issue to be resolved is the establishment of meaningful administrative units or states. In the past 20 years, Nigeria's internal political boundaries and administrative organization have undergone considerable adjustment in response to both regional and national interests. This chapter focuses on these specific issues and the general questions of regionalism and the federal experiment.

Diversity

Nigeria is a country of immense geographic diversity. Its climates are more varied than any other West African state, its vast area encompassing many distinct and varied landscapes, and over 250 different ethnic groups. The pivotal physiographic feature is the Niger River, which, with its major tributary, the Benue, forms a Y-shaped

FROM COLONY TO REPUBLIC: EXPERIMENT IN FEDERATION IN NIGERIA

system that divides the country into three regions. Below Onitsha, the Niger is navigable year round by shallow craft, and during high-water periods the Niger and Benue are navigable as far as Jebba and Yola, respectively. Both rivers have figured prominently in the historicogeographical development of Nigeria. When the *Jihad* (Holy War), waged by the Moslem Fulani of the north, brought Fulani emirates to the Niger's banks, the river became the natural boundary between the Yoruba and Fulani empires, but it did not stop the spread of Islam, which was adopted by many Yorubas to the south.

Nigeria possesses a number of distinct physiographic regions (Fig. 8-1). The highest elevations (6700 ft—2040m), occur in the deeply incised volcanic Adamawa Highlands along the Cameroon boundary. The most extensive elevated region is the Jos Plateau and its surroundings, and the high plains of Hausaland, which lie north of the Niger-Benue confluence. Together, these old crystalline plateaus make up the core of northern Nigeria from which several important rivers flow: The Komadugu and Hadeijia into Lake Chad, the Gongola and Mada into the Benue, and the Sokoto and Kaduna into the Niger. Toward the northeast, the land drops gradually into the Chad Basin, and in the northwest lies the Sokoto-Rima Basin. The Niger-Benue Lowland is separated from the coastal areas, including the extensive Niger Delta, by the Oyo-Yoruba Upland in the west and the Udi Plateau in the east, both regions lying mainly between 1000 and 2000

FIGURE 8-1 *Nigeria. Physiographic regions.*

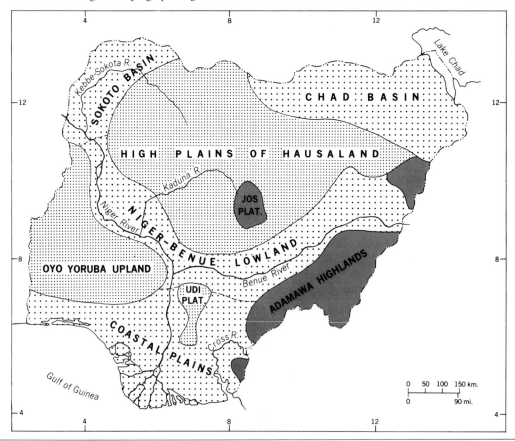

ft (300–600m). In the south, the coastal plains decline gently toward a shoreline of spits and bars and lagoons and luxuriant mangroves, where the Niger has built an extensive delta.

Nigeria possesses a wider range of climates than any other West African state. Isohyets trend generally east-west across the country, and the extreme south receives over 140 in. (3550 mm) annually, while the northern margins record less than 20 in. (508 mm). In central Nigeria, including the southern portion of the high plains of Hausaland and the northern sections of the Oyo-Yoruba and Udi uplands, rainfall is between 45 and 60 in. (1140–1525 mm). The northern periphery is steppe and thorn forest and, toward the north, rainfall variability in-

creases as the length of the rainy season decreases. Thus a series of vegetation zones lie parallel to those of rainfall, reflecting the increasing dryness from south to north (Fig. 8-2). Inland from the coastal mangrove and freshwater swamps lie areas of rainforest (better developed in the central and eastern parts than in the west), which were formerly more extensive than they are today. As a result of human activity, this inner margin of rain forest has become a zone of forest and savanna, sometimes referred to as "derived savanna." North of this belt the country becomes more open, the bulk of it being covered by a savanna that is characterized by increasing dryness.

Nigeria's physiographic variety is paralleled by the diversity of its population

FIGURE 8-2 *Nigeria. Vegetation zones and rainfall.*

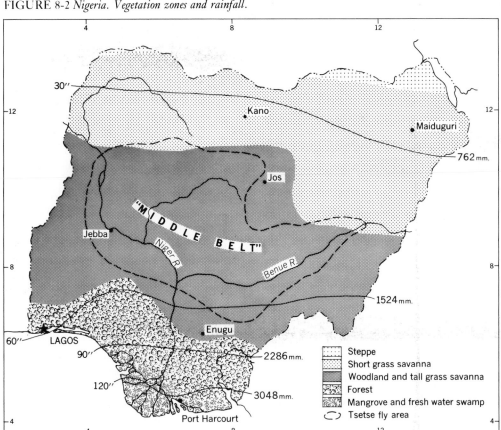

groups, and their religions, languages, and modes of living. South of the Niger and Benue rivers, two peoples dominate numerically: the Yoruba in the west, and the Ibo in the east. To the north, the majority peoples are the Hausa and Fulani. Depending on the bases employed for dividing Nigeria's population into ethnic groups, however, perhaps 250 distinct units might be recognized, numbering from a few thousand individuals to several million. The region's history, like that of other parts of West Africa, includes alternate periods of local consolidation and tribal fragmentation; both the plains of the north and the forests of the south were the scene of efforts to create lasting empires. Some of these, like Benin, became powerful entities, surviving several turbulent centuries, leaving their mark on the country to this day. Others failed in the feudal rivalries and were absorbed by more successful contemporaries. From the north came the impact of Islam, as the Fulani, living in the land of the numerous Hausa farmers and traders, rose to power and established strong emirates. From the south came the impact of Europe, and slavery gave way to legitimate trade and to territorial control.

Nigeria, then, incorporates a more complete range of conditions—climatic, vegetative, pedologic, historical, demographic—than any other West African country. Some features are shared by several parts of the country, others are confined to one area. Sections of the south to the east of the Niger River, for instance, possess soils and vegetation, as well as climatic conditions, that are similar to those found to the west of the river. But in terms of their development, these two areas are quite different. And both differ greatly from the area lying to the north of the Niger and Benue.

Emergence of Regional Individualism

Although political entities existed in the area today occupied by Nigeria prior to the spread of effective European control, there never was a unified state covering all of the territory. Nigeria, then, is a European creation, a piece of West Africa's physiographic and ethnic diversity around which boundaries were drawn and within which the course of progress has been one of constant adjustment.

The basic elements of Nigeria's internal division were already there before conquest and consolidation took place. Those divisions were not unique to the Nigerian part of West Africa; they relate to the environmental and locational aspects of the region. The peoples of the northern savanna plains traded with the far north and felt the spread of ideas from that direction. Their terrain permitted movement to a far greater extent than in the densely forested south, and their empires grew larger. They adopted Islam and propagated it vigorously, and they penetrated the lands of the southern peoples in search of slaves and tribute. The exposure of the northern peoples to Caucasoid, trans-Saharan elements also widened the gap in the somatic sense, and friction was frequent between them and their southern neighbors. It was the upheaval involving the Fulani, as well as the desire to terminate the slave trade, that contributed much to the British decision to intervene in the interior late in the nineteenth century.

The involvement of Europe in Nigeria as in other parts of West Africa, changed the whole economic and social orientation of the area. Both the north and south had achieved political organization, both had engaged in the slave trade, but the north had long experienced more of the effects of circulation and contact with an outside world. In a sense, the south was a hinterland, separated from the north by a middle belt comprised of many ethnic groups sharing only a fear of domination by their more populous and powerful neighbors. British posts of trade and administration along the southern coast (which in Nigeria presented major obstacles to permanent settlement), began to develop in earnest toward the middle of the nineteenth century, and in 1861 the site of Lagos was ceded to the crown by King Dosunmu. But in the early years, Lagos Colony remained only a minor part of the British West African Settlements, administered from Sierra Leone; in 1874 it became a part of the Gold Coast Colony, and only in 1886 did it cease to be administered from another British post.

The decade from 1880 to 1890 saw important changes initiated. The British, desiring to end the hostilities prevailing in the interior, now intervened, and in the south, a rudimentary protectorate administration was established. Also founded were several chartered companies, of which the most important, the Royal Niger Company, did much to extend British influence northward. The process of penetration was completed by Frederick Lugard, who repelled French encroachment while subjugating northern Nigerian chieftains with the aid of locally drafted forces. The result was a British-controlled territory consisting of three parts: the Lagos Colony, a Southern Protectorate, and the Northern Protectorate. Actually, the two major parts remained practically separate, each under its own administration; in 1906, Lagos and the Southern Protectorate were merged. Soon after his conquest, Lugard advised the British government to unite the country, but only in 1914 did this step take place, at which time the Nigeria Colony and Protectorate was officially established. Even then, the south and north remained under different forms of administration. Southern Nigeria was governed with the aid of a partially elected legislative council, but the protectorate to the north remained under the jurisdiction of a governor. Thus, "the North and the South . . . re-mained almost complete strangers to each other. The . . . South was looking towards England and Western Europe. The Islamic North fixed its gaze on distant Mecca. . . ." (Davies, p. 92).

The political entity now consolidated, internal differences began to become increasingly well defined. The most obvious were those between the north and south; the Southern Provinces were not divided into an eastern and western section until 1939. The exposure of the south to European influence brought change there, from which the north remained shielded. Most significant perhaps was the contrast in modes of administration. In the north, the Fulani emirates were left intact, and indirect rule prevailed. Traditional authorities and ways of life were little disturbed. Slavery was prohibited, but because the settling of Christian missionaries could take place only with the consent of the emirs, few mission schools—common in the south—operated there. In the south, on the other hand, colonial administration quickly led to African participation in government: as early as 1923, the legislative council included African members. Nigeria was the first British African territory to include African representatives in its governing body, but the important point is that this step was taken in southern Nigeria; little had changed in the north. The difference was to become even greater, for political activity rapidly grew more intense in the south, which began to produce modern political leaders. These leaders came to demand changes in Nigeria's political situation, with which the northern traditionalists did not always associate themselves.

Southern political sophistication and northern traditionalism inevitably emerged as a major centrifugal force in Nigeria's political geography. Now, the north was the distant hinterland, and the south had contact with the outside world; surrounded by other colonial territories, the north to a large extent lost its access to the sources of its cultural and religious heritage. Having once propagated Islam to the south of the Niger and Benue, the Moslems saw Christianity gain in the lands of the coast, and with Christianity came a spread of education to which the north had no access. The difference, as reflected by literacy rates, became ever larger; as late as 1931, it was less than 3 percent in the northern part of the country.

The developing transport network made the consolidation of the area possible, and it is one unifying element in the divided country. Prior to the arrival of the British, there had been trade across the Niger River between the Fulani emirates and the Yoruba kingdoms, and after the area had been brought under colonial rule, the importance of economic links in forging the whole was immediately recognized, as was the usefulness of good communications in effective control and administration. Hence, the railroad from Lagos to Kano was completed as early as 1912, with an additional link from that northern city to the navigable Niger River. Other railroads were built subsequently, from Port Harcourt to the coal fields of Enugu (1916), and on to the Lagos–Kano line at Kaduna (1932). Several branch railroads were constructed in the north, and the effect there was to stimulate enormously the production of peanuts, cotton, hides, and skins, and to promote interregional trade and contact. However, improving communications links did not eliminate the regional differences in the country's economy. In the Oyo-Yoruba southwest, cocoa became and remained the leading cash crop, while in the north and southeast, groundnuts and oil palm predominated, respectively.

The areas of productive capacity in Nigeria lie in two rather distinct belts, one to the south of the Niger-Benue Lowland, the other to the north. The southern belt, corresponding approximately to the forest zone, extends from the cocoa-growing west to the palm-supported east. North of the lowland, the most productive zone lies east-west in the Kano-Zaria latitude, extending to the margins of the Sokoto and Chad basins. The two zones are divided by the comparatively unproductive "Middle Belt," characterized previously as having been a buffer between the north and the south. The Middle Belt is an area of tsetse fly, precluding the raising of livestock (except on the high Jos Plateau and in the Adamawa Highlands), and although its transitional location permits the cultivation of both the grain crops of the north and the root crops of the south, no important cash crops have been added to these staples.

The separation of the major areas of productive capacity, resulting from a combination of topographic and climatic factors and coinciding with a historicogeographical separation of the region's major peoples, has promoted regionalism. The road and railroad networks of Nigeria are best developed within the three major producing regions (the south, east and west of the Niger River, and the north), but connecting links have long been tenuous. Kaduna is 561 and 569 mi (903 and 916 km), from the two seaports by the western and eastern lines, respectively, and the lines cross the unprofitable Middle Belt. In the mid-1970s there was still no railway connecting the eastern and western parts of the south across the Niger River, although a line is planned from Lagos to Calabar through Benin City, and only in 1966 was a bridge constructed across the Niger at Onitsha replacing a ferry (Fig. 8-3). Bridge connections to the north were those of Jebba and Makurdi; all other cross-Benue and Niger traffic used ferries. Thus the Niger and Benue rivers formed major obstacles to effective interregional contact. In the south, the Niger became an internal political boundary when, in 1939, the Southern Provinces were divided into an Eastern and Western Province. Although the boundary between northern and southern Nigeria never ran along the Niger and Benue rivers (above their confluence), but somewhat to the south, the divisive effect of

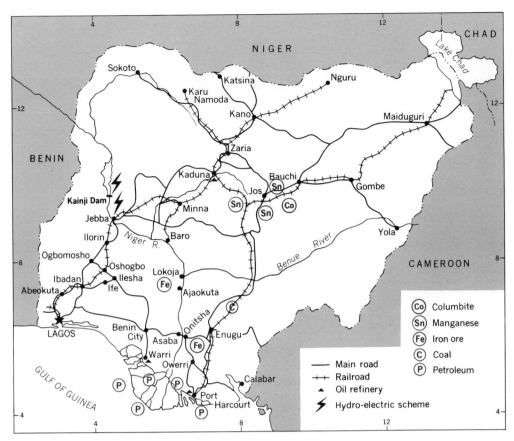

FIGURE 8-3 *Nigeria. Towns, communications, and minerals.*

these valleys remained. The core region of the north lies in the high plains of Hausaland, and it has always been separated from the Southern regions by the lagging Middle Belt, including the river lowlands.

As Nigeria developed economically and politically, the centrifugal forces of regionalism asserted themselves: they were sufficiently strong to play a major role during the time that produced unity in most colonial territories, the preindependence period. It is a measure of the intensity of regional differences, notably between north and south, that there were northern requests for delays in the attainment of sovereignty, which in the south was viewed as a national aim. In 1946 and 1947, the first real steps were taken in the creation of the modern political framework. A legislative council was established to deal with the whole of Nigeria rather than with the south alone, and regional legislatures were formed for the Northern, Western, and Eastern regions, as the former provinces were then called. The internal diversity of the country clearly called for a politicogeographical arrangement permitting a considerable amount of local autonomy; without it, the cooperation of most of the people of the north, and minority groups elsewhere, would have been lost. In 1954, a federal structure was put into effect, and after repeated adjustments, the country became independent in 1960.

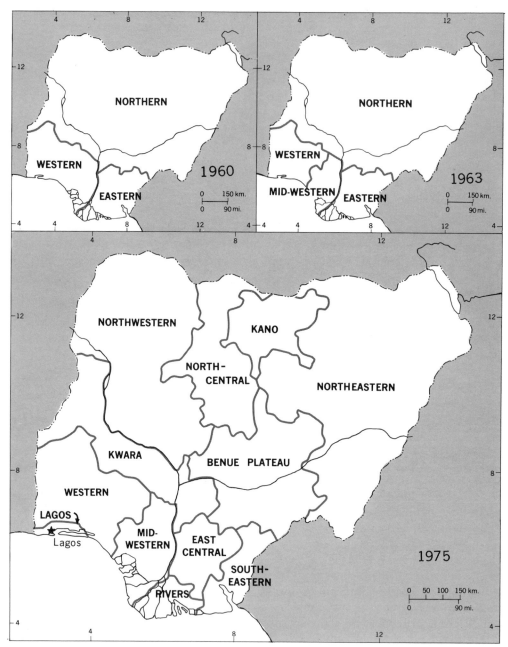

FIGURE 8-4 *The States of Nigeria—1960, 1963, and 1975.*

Federal Readjustments

When independence was granted, Nigeria was composed of three political regions: the Northern, Eastern, and Western (Fig. 8-4). Each had the ingredients of a via-ble political entity: a sizeable economic base, a strong sense of nationhood, and political parties with strong leadership that stood for the preservation of self-identity against political domination by neighboring states, and for the rapid modernization in the social and economic spheres. The Northern Region represented 79 percent of the area, and contained 53.6 percent of the total population, while the Eastern and Western Regions had 22.3 and 24.1 percent of the population, respectively. Because representation in parliament was based on population, and because political parties were organized on ethnic and state lines, the Northern Region was in a position to dominate the country politically. It meant keen competition between the Regions for increased populations that led to charges and countercharges of falsification of population data. The 1962 census, which showed the Northern Region to be the most populous, was rejected by southern politicians. The recount of 1963 confirmed the 1962 results and similarly came under much criticism from those seeking increased representation in Parliament and a greater share of the revenues (Table 8-1). The census controversy contributed much to the worsening relationships between the north and south, and especially between the Hausa-Fulani group and the Ibos. The 1964 elections were won by the government party in the Northern Region.

The Ibos in the Eastern Region and the Yorubas in the Western Region, fearing the power of the Hausa-Fulani dominated Northern Region, wanted Nigeria reorganized into smaller states. Minority groups

The 1973 census being taken in Nigeria, Africa's most populous state. The federal government does not plan to publish the results. Complete and accurate demographic data are required for development planning and proper representation in the federal government. (UN/Macauley)

FROM COLONY TO REPUBLIC: EXPERIMENT IN FEDERATION IN NIGERIA

Table 8-1 NIGERIAN POPULATIONS

	State	Area (sq mi)	1952–1953 (adjusted)	1963	1973 (provisional)	State Capitals
A	Lagos	1,381	500,000	1,443,567	2,470,000	Lagos
	Western	29,100	4,360,000	9,487,525	8,920,000	Ibadan
B	Mid-Western	14,922	1,490,000	2,535,839	3,240,000	Benin City
C	East-Central	11,922	4,570,000	7,227,559	8,060,000	Enugu
	South-Eastern	11,166	1,900,000	3,622,589	3,460,000	Calabar
	Rivers	7,008	750,000	1,544,314	2,230,000	Port Harcourt
D	Kano	16,630	3,400,000	5,774,842	10,900,000	Kano
	North-Central	27,108	2,350,000	4,098,305	6,790,000	Kaduna
	North-Western	65,143	3,400,000	5,733,296	8,500,000	Sokoto
	North-Eastern	103,639	4,200,000	7,793,443	15,380,000	Maiduguri
	Benue Plateau	40,590	2,300,000	4,009,408	5,170,000	Jos
	Kwara	28,672	1,190,000	2,399,365	4,640,000	Ilorin
	Totals	356,669	30,410,000	55,670,052	79,758,969	

A = former Western Region; B = former Midwest Region; C = former Eastern Region; D = former Northern Region.

throughout the country, which together were numerically superior to the three majority groups combined, supported this notion. In 1963, the Edo (Bini), Ika, Western Ijaw, and Ibo, who comprised the opposition minorities in the Western Region, took advantage of a political crisis there, and following a referendum, created for themselves a new state, the Midwest Region (Fig. 8-4). Following the October 1965 elections in the Western Region that were manipulated in favor of the government party, the country was reduced to a state of anarchy and widespread disorder that resulted in a military coup in January, 1966. The Yoruba and Fulani premiers of the Western and Northern Regions, respectively, were killed, as was the federal prime minister who was Hausa, while the two Ibo premiers of the Eastern and Midwestern Regions were spared. The leaders of the coup were mainly Ibos, who established a military regime under Major General Ironsi, also an Ibo. Most Nigerians saw the coup as a bid for Ibo domination, especially since Ironsi suspended the federal constitution and the elected governments of all four Regions, and attempted to establish a unitary rather than a federal form of government.

In July, 1966, a second military coup took place, dominated this time by Northerners who killed Ironsi and many of his officers and established General Gowon (a Northerner though not a Moslem), as head of state. The atrocities against Ibos, which began soon after the Ironsi coup, intensified. An estimated 30,000 Ibos, who had long dominated the civil service and the commercial and industrial life in the Northern Region, were slaughtered; over 600,000 others fled to their homeland. Not only were the immigrant Ibos the wealthiest community and political elites in the North, but they were arrogantly self-conscious of their superiority, and were leaders of progressive politics aimed at destroying the Northern Region's feudal structure. They looked down on their Hausa hosts as "unenterprising, lazy, backward, and feudal," while Northern peasants had long complained of Ibo exploitation, and educated northerners spoke of the Ibos as "vermin, criminals, money grabbers, and subhumans without genuine culture" (Legum, 1966). As reprisals against Ibo civilians in the Northern Region continued, and as Ibo military officers serving outside of the Eastern Region were slaughtered, the numbers of Ibo refugees from the Western and Midwest Regions increased, and the Ibo governor or-

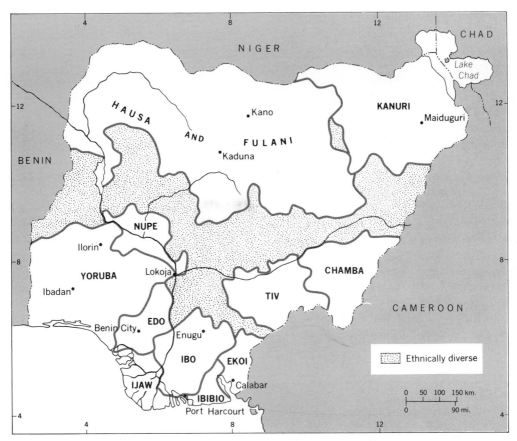

FIGURE 8-5 *Major ethnic groups in Nigeria.*

dered all Northerners and Westerners out of his Region. Reprisal brought reprisal with thousands of killings and widespread destruction of property in both the Eastern and Northern Regions.

By late 1966, the Ibo-controlled government of the Eastern Region was contemplating secession from the Federation under Gowon, and there followed six months of open defiance of the federal government which spurred minority groups throughout Nigeria to become more vocal in their demands for separate states. In May, 1967, the federal government divided the country into 12 states in place of the four Regions (Fig. 8-4). The Ibos rejected this plan and proceeded to proclaim Eastern Nigeria as the independent Republic of Biafra, which

plunged the Nigerians into 30 months of civil war. In January, 1970, the rebel state of Biafra capitulated, and Nigeria embarked on a program of reconstruction and redevelopment.

The 1967 redistricting plan divided the Eastern Region into three states: the South-Eastern, Rivers, and East-Central, the latter being the core of Iboland. The Northern Region was divided into six states: North-Eastern, Kano, North-Central, North-Western, Benue Plateau, and Kwara (West-Central). The Midwest Region retained its boundaries (established in 1963), and became the Mid-West State, while the Western Region, which contains the federal capital (Lagos), was divided into the Western and Lagos States. These states varied considerably in area and population (Table 8-1).

Changes in state boundaries were accompanied by changes in the constitution. The power of the federal government was increased, while that of the state governments was decreased. A new Federal Executive Council, the principal organ of government, was established. Its composition of 11 military officers and nine civilians reflected a power balance within and among the military establishment, the regional ethnic alliances, and the elite in the modern sector of the economy. Political parties were banned. The government's decision to revert to civilian rule in 1976 was revoked as a safeguard against the reemergence of social strife resulting from a premature withdrawal of military involvement in the political process (Nigeria, 1975).

In 1976, a new federal redistricting plan was announced and subsequently imple-mented that divided the country into 19 states and authorized the building of a new federal capital at Abuja. Abuja lies approximately 100 miles (160 km) north of the Niger-Benue confluence, and has the advantage over the present capital, Lagos, of being centrally located and within a region free from control by any major ethnic group (Fig. 8-5). It lies in a sparsely populated section of the Middle Belt where the federal government plans major agricultural and industrial development.

The following treatment of the Nigerian federation must necessarily be selective rather than exhaustive, and focuses primarily on economic and politicogeographic dimensions rather than on legal and constitutional issues. Each major region is treated separately within the 12-state federal framework.

Lagos and the Western State

The Western and Lagos states, together with the Lagos Federal District, constitute Nigeria's primary core area. Although the region comprises less than 10 percent of the total area, it has about 15 percent of the population, receives almost one-fifth of the national budget, and it accounts for 40 percent of the nation's industrial labor force and for half the country's industrial establishments. Stretching northeast from the federal capital (and primate-city), along the line-of-rail is the largest concentration of towns and cities in tropical Africa: Ibadan, Ile-Ife, Oshogbo, Ogbomosho, Iwo, and others, all Yoruba towns dating back in some instances several centuries. Historically these Yoruba towns performed the special function of affording protection in times of war. Consequently most are walled and contain land within their boundaries devoted to food crops, although today the principal cultivated areas are some distance from the towns themselves.

Many towns have two distinct parts: an old and highly congested section made up of traditional compounds and wards and a newer quarter with some vertical development, modern buildings, and wider streets. In the older sections, the population is engaged primarily in agriculture or farm-related activities such as marketing, food processing, and the crafts. Marketing is dominated by women. The newer quarters, begun during colonial times and generally situated on the outskirts of the traditional city, contain larger businesses and industries and house the more affluent and more educated Nigerians. The largest Yoruba town is Ibadan, founded as a military camp during the early nineteenth century by refugees from Old Oyo and other parts of Yorubaland laid waste by Fulani peoples from the north. When it came under British influence in 1893, its population was already over 100,000; now it is almost one million. Today Ibadan is an administrative capital, and an important light manufacturing and educational center.

Cocoa, which was brought to Nigeria from Macias Nguema Biyogo (formerly Fernando Po) in 1874, came to occupy first place among the cash crops of the region and country. Before the development of the petroleum industry, which made great strides following the conclusion of the Biafran War, cocoa frequently produced a quarter of all Nigerian export revenues. Grown by peasant farmers whose plots average only three or four acres, (1.2–1.6 *ha*) cocoa has long been the basis of the comparative wealth of the west, especially in the years after World War II. Although the total production has never challenged that of Ghana, Nigeria began exporting cocoa earlier (1895), and

Nigeria has generally been the world's second largest producer, most of the crop coming from the belt that centers on Ife (Fig. 8-6). During the early 1970s the average annual production of raw cocoa was some 230,000 metric tons, up appreciably from the 1960s despite adverse weather conditions, widespread losses from capsid and black pod diseases, and low producer prices.

Over 300,000 farmers in the Western State are directly engaged in cocoa production, and a third of the State's population is dependent in some way on the cocoa industry. The introduction of cocoa into the region involved not just a few plantation owners but a large cross section of the farming population. Standards of living rose, communication lines were extended, long-

FIGURE 8-6 *Nigeria. Commercial agriculture.*

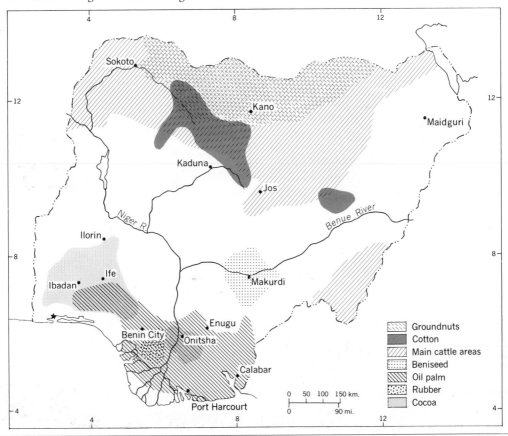

Legend:
- Groundnuts
- Cotton
- Main cattle areas
- Beniseed
- Oil palm
- Rubber
- Cocoa

isolated areas were drawn into the exhange economy, cooperative and other organizations were formed, and internal trade was stimulated. Furthermore, the cocoa industry provided both seasonal and permanent employment for thousands of workers from the northern states.

Lagos, the federal capital, occupies a strategic position and plays an important role in the region and federation. Founded more than 300 years ago by a Yoruba subgroup, Lagos became one of the leading slave ports of West Africa. It depended on the adjoining Yoruba towns for its slaves, and following the termination of the slave trade, and with the British occupation in 1861, it became a refuge for freed slaves from Brazil and the immediate interior. Under the British, Lagos became an administrative center and port, although its port functions were initially handicapped by offshore bars and a shallow harbor approach. The turning point in its development came when the British selected it in preference to Warri or Sepele as the coastal terminal of the railway to the northern regions (Udo, 1970a). Modern port facilities were completed in the 1920s and have since been improved to handle the ever-increasing exports including cocoa, cotton, groundnuts, palm kernels, animal products, tin, and columbite, many of which originate in distant areas. Lagos is Nigeria's major port and industrial city. Its industries include automobile assembly, floor milling, metal fabricating, cement, textiles, and chemicals.

The selection of Lagos as the federal capital in 1954 did not meet with universal approval, for the relative strengths of the regional party representation in the federal

The Apapa wharves, part of the port of Lagos. Lagos handles about half of Nigeria's international trade, and is the Republic's federal capital and primate city. A new federal capital is to be built at Abuja. (World Bank)

parliament were related to the numerical strength of the population in each state. By separating densely populated territory from the former Western Region, the Region's leading party lost a sizable number of voters. Several grounds were put forward to justify the action, however: first, Nigeria's administration had long been headquartered in Lagos, so that it was by far the best-equipped city for the continuation of government. Second, the inclusion of the port facilities in the federal territory constituted an assurance for the former Northern Region, which thus came to depend for its natural outlet on a federal rather than a Western Region harbor. Third, the selection of another western city would have had political consequences similar to those involved in the choice of Lagos, and the selection of any other city would have required the construction of new facilities there. Finally, Nigeria could ill afford the building of a new capital. In 1976, the decision was made to build a new federal capital at Abuja.

The Mid-West State

The creation in 1963 of the Mid-West State (then the Mid-West Region), did not receive universal support in that area. Ibos living in the region were divided on the matter: the educated class favored the proposition because they saw themselves taking a leading role in government and administration, while the uneducated Ibos preferred union with the-then Eastern Region. The majority Edo (Bini) and the smaller Ijaw and Itsekiri minorities supported the new state. The state's ethnic diversity had been considered an important ingredient in the Mid-West's political stability, since no single

Aerial view of Sapele, Mid-West State, situated in dense tropical rainforests of the Niger delta. In the middleground ocean-going vessels are loading plywood and lumber. (UAC International)

group is sufficiently large to dominate the rest. Its administrative divisions were increased from 8 to 14 after 1963 to respect the ethnic diversity, each receiving the same amount of government revenues for roads and social services.

The Mid-West focuses on Benin City (150,000), capital of the once-powerful Benin kingdom. The city lies in the forest zone, which forms the central part of the region and, besides being the administrative capital, it is a rubber processing and timber center. To the north, the forest thins out, and the oil palm no longer sustains the local economy; there, root crops and rice are staples, and cotton can be cultivated. The majority of the state's 3.3 million people, however, live in the forested belt itself, where rural densities may exceed 1000 persons per square mile. Unlike the Yoruba, the Edo do not live in large agrotowns, but in small villages that rarely have more than 2000 inhabitants.

Until the discovery of petroleum near Burutu in 1964, the region's cash economy was based almost entirely on rubber and timber; the state still produces 85 percent of the nation's rubber and two-thirds of its timber. Rubber has long been an important Nigerian export and, with the rapid pace of local industrialization and rising per capita income, domestic demands are increasing and the industry appears to have a secure future. Unlike production in Liberia, where large-scale plantations predominate, approximately 90 percent of the rubber comes from small farms (1–25 acres; 4–10 ha), under peasant management. Petroleum, however, has become the state's major natural resource and revenue producer, and this will become even more important with the completion of Nigeria's second oil refinery at Warri in 1978.

The Eastern States

The three eastern states (Rivers, East-Central, and Southeast) once comprised the Eastern Region and the breakaway state of Biafra. The region comprises only 7.7 percent of the total area of Nigeria, but contains almost one-fifth of the population and contributes more than half of the republic's exports. Some 14 million persons are crowded into only 30,096 sq mi (77,950 sq km) of territory, the southern parts being forested and swampy, the northern regions being savanna. The population is overwhelmingly rural, and around Owerri, Aba, and other parts of Iboland, rural densities are among the highest in Africa. There, population pressure is high, soil erosion is a serious problem, and farming practices need to be improved if malnutrition is to be reduced.

For many years the region's economy was based on the oil palm, the region once producing half the world's output of palm kernels. Since the Biafran War, production has declined, largely because the plantations and processing equipment were either damaged or destroyed. Other important cash crops are cocoa, rubber, cashew nuts, and rice, all of which form the basis of small processing industries. Despite these resources, the region has lagged behind the west in development, but the pace of progress has accelerated sharply during the past few years with the exploitation of petroleum in the Rivers State, and with the growth and diversification of the economy in the northern states.

Eastern Nigeria is the only major region in the country not to have experienced a lengthy period of indigenous urbanization; there is no Ibadan, Abeokuta, Kano, or Zaria. Even today, the major towns have fewer than 250,000 inhabitants. Enugu (200,000), for instance, was founded as recently as 1915 following the discovery of coal in the Udi Plateau, and it owes much of its growth to the coal industry and to its administrative functions. From 1915 to 1959, coal production increased gradually, but during the 1960s production declined and ceased entirely during the Biafran civil war. Today small quantities are railed south to Port Harcourt for shipment to Lagos, and occasionally some is exported to Ghana and other west African states.

While coal became the first mineral resource of any economic consequence in the region, petroleum now leads the field, and is by far the greatest source of Nigeria's foreign revenues. The search for oil began as long ago as 1937, but was interrupted during World War II. In 1947, the exploratory efforts were resumed, initially through shallow drilling, until the geologic mapping of the delta area was completed in 1953. Then deep wells were sunk, and in 1956, wells near Oloibiri and Afam, within the delta proper, showed commerical oil accumula-

tions. Several new deposits were subsequently located, and activity increased greatly in the whole region. Petroleum production in 1959 amounted to 4 million barrels, in 1962 it exceeded 25 million, and early in 1970, production reached one million barrels *per day*. During 1973 it exceeded the two-million-barrels-per-day mark, although in 1974 and 1975, following the world oil crisis, daily output was deliberately kept at two-million barrels. Daily production after 1976 is expected to be between three and four million barrels, and the reserves are believed to be sufficient to last another 25 years.

In 1958 petroleum formed less than one percent of total receivable Nigerian export earnings; by 1965 it accounted for almost 26 percent; and in 1974 some 95.6 million metric tons were exported, which earned

Seismic party in the mangrove swamps of the Niger Delta. Petroleum is Nigeria's leading export. (Shell/BP)

FROM COLONY TO REPUBLIC: EXPERIMENT IN FEDERATION IN NIGERIA

N5,317.6 million or 92 percent of all export earnings (Nigeria, 1975). The third Development Plan (1975–80), aims at a 10 percent annual growth rate in oil production over the five-year period, and oil is expected to account for an ever-increasing proportion of all exports.

Until 1964, all of Nigeria's crude petroleum was exported, but with the completion in 1965 of an oil refinery at Port Harcourt, a small amount started to be refined for domestic use. Nigeria has to import 20 percent of its refined fuel requirements (the Port Harcourt refinery has a capacity of 2.5 million metric tons per year), so two additional refineries are to be built: one at Warri (Mid-West State) and the other at Kaduna (North-Central State). This could give Nigeria the overall capacity to be an exporter of refined petroleum. Exploration and production is carried out in several places in each of the three eastern states and offshore. Shell-BP is responsible for two-thirds of total production, while fourteen other companies, including three Nigerian companies, are also involved.

Production costs for Nigerian petroleum are from three to seven times higher than in Middle East countries, but the oil has an exceptionally low sulphur content. Nigeria is currently the world's eighth largest producer of crude oil (3.5 percent of total), and is second in Africa after Libya. More than one-quarter of Nigeria's petroleum exports are purchased by the United States, while Britain, France, and the Netherlands, collectively, take about half. In 1972, Nigeria became a member of the Organization of Petroleum Exporting Countries (OPEC), but it has adopted a less militant stand than many OPEC states in its relations with consumer countries. Nevertheless, it followed the general trend towards higher royalties, and raised the price of oil from $4.287 a barrel to $8.310 in October, 1973, and then to $14.691 a barrel for the first quarter of 1974.

This new-found wealth and all that it promised, along with other equally important factors, plunged Nigeria into civil war in May, 1967. The then Eastern Region had a population of 12.6 million of whom Ibos constituted 64 percent, Efik and Ibibio 17 percent, Annang 5.5 percent, Ijaw and Ogoni 7.5 percent, and Ekoi, Yalla, and others the balance (Nixon, 1972). The Ibos dominated the economy in most parts of the region including the petroleum industry centered on Port Harcourt. Ibos provided most of Port Harcourt's labor force, and owned 95 percent of the city's private property and business establishments. Throughout the delta and to the east, Ibos were traders, teachers, and civil servants in almost every town and village. They also dominated government-owned plantations.

Ibo domination beyond Iboland came about gradually as more and more Ibos were forced off the land in search of new opportunities. They were prepared to do work others would not, and because of their generally higher education, they acquired both skilled and responsible jobs. They saw in petroleum a solution to their otherwise precarious and stagnating rural economy. Under the constitutional arrangements, control of petroleum rested with the federal government rather than with the Regions, and the major share of the public revenue derived from this source went to the nation as a whole rather than to the region of origin. Those immediately responsible for the production of oil thought otherwise, and wanted greater if not absolute control of the revenues. Since the petroleum fields, the refinery, and port facilities all lay south of Iboland, and the two subareas were economically and politically interdependent, it was essential that the region remain one. Indeed, so important was Port Harcourt to the changing Ibo economy that, at a time when secessionist leaders still had the option for a negotiated peace settlement, the question of making the port a part of the East-Central State came up repeatedly (Udo, 1970b).

The Biafran war brought widespread

devastation to crops and property, and completely disrupted the production of petroleum and related industries. There followed an intensive period of reconstruction and rehabilitation within a three states system, rather than within a single Biafra. For the Rivers people the creation of their own state and control over their new capital, Port Harcourt, were overwhelmingly important, but Port Harcourt was to all the Ibos an Ibo city and not easily surrendered. While many properties were abandoned, others remained in Ibo hands, and Ibos had great difficulty collecting rent and raising capital that were desperately needed to rehabilitate the East-Central State's economy. In the South-East State, Ibos experienced similar difficulties and resentment from Ibibios and Ekoi. In both the Rivers and South-East States, there are fewer Ibos in civil service and government corporations than before, while the Mid-West was the first state following the war to seek Ibo skills and capital. Indeed, postwar anti-Ibo feeling has periodically been greater in the Rivers and South-East States than elsewhere in Nigeria.

Reconstruction focused first on the resettlement of displaced farmers whose land had been destroyed. Then roads and bridges were rebuilt and paid for with revenues derived from oil. While the north-south flow of goods through Enugu has resumed and increased, Enugu and the East-Central State in general is becoming oriented more toward the ports of the Mid-West and South-West States and less toward Port Harcourt. Separate state identities have not emerged.

The Northern States

Most of Nigeria's land and people are in the northern states that extend from the northern boundary to south of the Niger and Benue rivers. At the time of the 1973 census 51.4 million persons (almost two-thirds of the Nigerian total) were counted in this 281,782 sq mi area (729,815 sq km). It has always been the most populous region, and as such has dominated the federal scheme. In theory however, the new federal arrangement should lessen this monolithic dominance.

The major peoples of the North are the Hausa and Fulani (Fig. 8-5) who have formed an alliance in which the urban-based Hausa are numerically superior, and the more rural and traditionally cattle-raising Fulani supply the ruling element. The Fulani are more ardent Muslims than their aristocratic urban counterparts who control the administration of the Hausa towns such as Kano and Kaduna. The Hausa, in contrast, are primarily settled cultivators and traders, who, before the Fulani conquest of the early nineteenth century, were organized into large states, the most prominent being Zaria, Kano, and Gabir. Today, both peoples are widely distributed but are especially numerous in and around Kano, Katsina, Sokoto, and Kaduna. Other peoples are also present, including the Kanuris, Jukun, Tiv, Igbira, Nupe, Gwari, and Bariba (Fig. 8-5). The North has been described as a world apart from the rest of Nigeria, and with much justification: this is Moslem Nigeria, where the legacy of a feudal social system, conservative traditionalism, and resistance to change hang heavily on the country. Literacy is lower than elsewhere, and per capita incomes are generally little more than half the national average. Proportionally fewer people have been drawn into the modern sector of the economy than elsewhere in the country.

The possibilities for development in the north are considerable. Rainfall is less than in the south, and it is more seasonal and quite variable along the northern border. In the Sokoto and Chad basins the lack of water has restricted settlement, but north of the

Cattle being off-loaded for slaughter at the Kano abattoir. Pastoralism is an important economy in the northern savanna lands. (World Bank)

tsetse area that covers much of the Middle Belt, the country affords opportunities for cattle-raising. The absence of fodder in southern Nigeria and the presence of diseases in the Middle Belt, make the northern savanna zone even more important from a cattle-raising point of view.

The agricultural opportunities of the north are not restricted to cattle raising (Fig. 8-6). Groundnuts, cotton, tobacco, and beniseed are important cash crops, while guinea corn, millet, and cassava are common staples. Nigeria is usually the world's largest exporter of groundnuts, accounting for about a third of the world's commercial production and, since 1961, groundnuts have been Nigeria's leading agricultural export. In 1973–74, however, sales fell to record low levels partly because of drought conditions, but also because of low prices paid to farmers, which induced them to smuggle their harvest into neighboring states such as Niger where higher prices were obtainable.

Northern Nigeria's major agricultural areas lie in close proximity to transport routes and the larger urban centers. The urban tradition in this region is very old. Kano (400,000) for instance, has been a trading center and capital of a Fulani emirate for more than a dozen centuries. Its commercial importance reached great heights during the fifteenth century when European goods reached it across the Sahara, and today it is an industrial town producing textiles, leather goods, food products, and other items based on local resources. In its immediate surroundings, population densities exceed 1000 per square mile, and up to 40 mi (64 km) away, densities frequently exceed 500 persons per square mile. Thus, well over a million people are concentrated in Kano's immediate environs, cultivating every available patch of land, which is constantly fertilized with night soil brought from the city. Still it is a food-deficit area. Although densities are less and the extent of settlement is smaller, the basic pattern is repeated at Katsina, Zaria, and Sokoto. These and other towns

The walled city of Kano is the largest commercial center in northern Nigeria. Shown here is a section of the mud-constructed town with its dense agglomeration of small dwellings. (BOAC)

serve the surrounding areas, and in the Kaura Namoda-Zaria-Kano-Nguru region, they are part of an expanding core area. But the North is vast and has several state capitals, each of which is a locally important growth center. Only short distances away, subsistence patch agriculture still prevails, the people are out of touch, and change is yet to come.

One of the changes to have affected formerly unproductive regions has been the spread of cotton as a cash crop. Cotton has been grown in Nigeria for centuries, but the strain which forms the basis of the present industry was introduced from Uganda in 1912. Cotton is a popular crop because of its economic returns, the ease of its cultivation, and its adaptability to soils that cannot be used for groundnuts and other would-be competitors. It is grown on small peasant farms and requires little capital outlay (Udo, 1970a). More than a million acres (405,000

ha) are currently under cultivation, with Zaria being the center of production. In recent years, exports have declined as domestic consumption has risen, while textile factories such as those at Kaduna, Kano, Aba, and Ikeja have increased production. The cotton growing industry is expected to spread to Sokoto with the completion of the new railway from Gusau, and possibly also into Bornu, another basically poor and peripheral region. Both these latter areas suffered widespread livestock losses and crop failures in the droughts of the early 1970s. In the North-Western State, for instance, some 300,000 cattle and 875,000 sheep and goats (20 percent of the herd) perished, and more than two million people in Kano State alone were affected by drought.

In addition to the North's agricultural possibilities, the region produces some minerals that have both local and national importance. Significantly the minerals and mineral-related industries occur in the Middle Belt, where commercial agriculture and industry based on agriculture are less common than to its north and south. Tin and columbite from the Jos Plateau have long been the region's most important minerals, and prior to the extraction of petroleum, tin was Nigeria's leading mineral export. Almost all of it is smelted locally at Jos and then railed to Port Harcourt or Lagos. Production has fluctuated enormously because of changing foreign demands, and if present production levels are maintained, reserves could be depleted by 1980.

Still further south, near the confluence of the Niger and Benue rivers, but within the Middle Belt, there are low-grade iron-ore deposits that are to be mined and converted to steel at Nigeria's first iron and steel mill at Ajaokuta. This 1.5 million-metric-ton-capacity mill was designed by the Soviet Union and will use coal from Enugu besides local ores, limestone, and water (Nigeria, 1975). It is centrally situated with respect to

the nation's major population centers, but at present has inadequate transport facilities other than the Niger itself. Ajaokuta is one of several growth centers scheduled to receive considerable federal support under the Third National Development Plan, 1975–1980. Kaduna, once the administrative capital of the Northern Region, is another. There, Nigeria's third oil refinery is scheduled to be in production by 1981. A new nitrogen fertilizer plank that uses phosphate rock from Togo and Benin is now in operation, and an automobile assembly plant was scheduled to open in 1976.

The Niger is one of Nigeria's greatest resources: it provides hydroelectric power, irrigation waters, and localized transport. The single most important multipurpose dam in Nigeria is that of Kainji (Kwara State), which has a planned generating capacity of 880 MW. A 500 MW dam is to be built downstream at Jebba, and a third will be built in the Shiroro Gorge on the Kaduna River. These will provide full flood control

The Kainji Dam across the Niger River provides hydro-electric power and controlled irrigation. (UN)

in the Niger valley as far as the Kaduna confluence, and partial flood control to the Benue confluence, and permit the expansion of agriculture (sugar, rice, and guinea corn) on the fertile alluvial flood plains. In the 1975–1980 Development Plan, agriculture receives high priority (after industry and transport), and much of the planned development is in the Middle Belt and the Sokoto-Rima and Chad Basins. At present, agriculture accounts for almost half of the G.D.P. and provides employment for about 70 percent of the working population (Nigeria, 1975).

The northern states have considerable economic potential, but their needs are several: the improvement of communications, the eradication of disease, the replacement of traditionalism in politics, education, and agriculture by a more modern outlook, and the elimination of the bases of separatist feelings among the non-Hausa, non-Fulani, non-Moslem peoples in the Middle Belt. The diversity marking Nigeria is especially characteristic of the North, where economic development and modernization are essentially confined to islands near towns and communication lines lying in a vastness of very slowly changing interior West Africa. While the northern states are seeing a transformation and diversification of their respective economies, they depend on the southern states for handling their overseas exports and for marketing their domestic products.

Politicogeographical Forces

The basic geographic premise of federalism is the existence of regionally grouped diversities; the units, while desiring to preserve their autonomy, prosper by a union. A diversity of resources and peoples does not of itself constitute an asset, nor does it guarantee the possibility of federation, but it may be useful in its attainment. What is necessary is for people to have a common *raison d'être* that can be supported by these resources. A viable federation exists where there is a strong sense of national purpose and where local interests are secondary to national ones. Ideally, the federation should have a high degree of symmetry at both the national and regional levels measured (*inter alia*) in terms of language, cultural heritage, economic well-being, and political awareness. If the system is highly asymmetrical in its component parts, and the common national ideals and interests are weak, a durable and harmonious federation is unlikely.

The politicogeographical forces that played a role in the evolution of the federal state in Nigeria continue to influence the state today, although some now exert more influence than they did previously and others have declined in importance. The centrifugal forces that were strong enough to delay the coming of independence remain, and include the separatist feelings of those living in the peripheral zones around the major regional cores. The fear of domination by the majority is strong among many of the smaller groups in all regions. The creation of new states is an attempt to reduce this domination, but ethnically based states could rekindle tribalism and run counter to Nigerian nationalism. There is also the problem of revenue allocation. The distribution of federal revenues to the various states is a compromise among many demands. Before the 1976 redistricting, half the available funds were disbursed in 12 equal parts, and half in proportion to population. Rivers State, then the smallest according to population, generated a disproportionately large amount of the federal funds (from petroleum) while the most populous state (North-Eastern) has few economic resources and is heavily dependent on its richer partners for its much needed development monies.

In recent years, especially in the post-

Biafran era, the centripetal forces that bind together Nigeria's diversities have become stronger. Nationalism is emerging, as more and more Nigerians break with tradition and identify more with the modernization processes. As the circulation of people, goods, and ideas increases, regional political and economic disparities should lessen. The interdependence of the states is constantly increasing, and interregional economic transactions are growing. Indeed, these interregional bonds reduce the likelihood of Nigeria's politicogeographic fragmentation, and strengthen the federal ideal.

Bibliography

Adejuyigbe, O. "The Problems of Unity and the Creation of States in Nigeria," *Nigerian Geographical Journal*, Vol. 11, No. 1 (June, 1968), pp. 39–60.

———. "The Case for a New Federal Capital in Nigeria," *Journal of Modern African Studies*, Vol. 8, No. 2 (July, 1970), pp. 301–06.

———. "The Size of States and Political Stability in Nigeria," *African Studies Review*, Vol. 16 (1973), pp. 157–82.

Carol, H. "The Making of Nigeria's Political Regions," *Journal of Asian and African Studies*, Vol. 3, Nos. 3–4 (July–October, 1968), pp. 271–86.

Church, R. J. Harrison. *Environment and Policies in West Africa*. Princeton: Van Nostrand, 1963.

Davies, H. O. *Nigeria: The Prospects for Democracy*. London: Weidenfeld and Nicholson, 1961.

Floyd, B. *Eastern Nigeria: A Geographical Review*. London: Macmillan, 1969.

Herskovits, J. "One Nigeria," *Foreign Affairs*, Vol. 51, No. 2 (January, 1973), pp. 392–407.

Lyons, C. H. "Nigeria," *Focus*. Vol. 21, No. 4 (December, 1970).

Legum, C. "The Tragedy in Nigeria," *Africa Report*, Vol. 11, No. 8 (November, 1966), pp. 23–24.

Mabogunje, A. L. *Urbanization in Nigeria*. London: London University Press, 1968.

Nafziger, E. W. "The Economic Impact of the Nigerian Civil War," *Journal of Modern African Studies*, Vol. 10, No. 2 (July, 1972), pp. 223–45.

Nixon, C. R. "Self-Determination: The Nigeria/Biafra Case," *World Politics*, Vol. 24, No. 4 (July, 1972), pp. 473–97.

Prothero, R. M. "Nigeria Loses Count," *Geographical Magazine*, Vol. 47, No. 1 (October, 1974), pp. 24–28.

Sada, P. O. "The Nigerian Twelve-State Political Structure," *Nigerian Geographical Journal*, Vol. 14, No. 1 (June, 1971), pp. 17–30.

Schatzl, L. *Industrialization in Nigeria: A Spatial Analysis*. Munchen: Weltforum Verlag, 1973.

Scott, E. P. "The Spatial Structure of Rural Northern Nigeria," *Economic Geography*. Vol. 48, No. 3 (July, 1972), pp. 316–332.

Udo, R. K. *Geographical Regions of Nigeria*. Berkeley: University of California Press, 1970. (a)

———. "Reconstruction in the War-Affected Areas of Nigeria," *Area*, No. 3 (1970), pp. 9–12. (b)

Nigeria. *Guidelines for the Third National Development Plan, 1975–80*. Lagos: Government Printer, 1975.

NINE

When the Gold Coast achieved its independence under Kwame Nkrumah on March 6, 1957 and took the name Ghana, a decisive new era of African history began. True, Egypt, Libya, Morocco, Tunisia, and the Sudan had gained their independence earlier, but Ghana was the first of many colonies in Africa south of the Sahara to be liberated. As a black-African state, its socioeconomic policies and performances, and its international relations and domestic politics would be critically monitored and appraised both in Africa and overseas.

Would Ghana become the model to be emulated or avoided by other territories scheduled for independence? Would political independence bring economic independence or at least greater economic self-sufficiency? Would economic ties with Britain be retained, or would Ghana seek new partners in the West, in Africa, or possibly the East? Would Nkrumah's new welfare state, which aimed at transforming an essentially agricultural, traditional society into a modern semi-industrial state, be guided by democratic principles? Would Nkrumah establish "fraternal relations with, and offer guidance and support to all nationalist, democratic, and socialist movements in Africa and elsewhere which were fighting for national independence and self-determination on the one hand and whose programmes were opposed to imperialism, colonialism, racialism, tribalism, and religious chauvinism and oppression, on the other" (Nkrumah, 1961). Would it be possible to reject tribalism and sectionalism, and cultivate in their stead Pan-Africanism?

These and similar questions were raised by numerous governments and individuals alike, and many have now been answered. Certainly Ghana's economy has diversified and reoriented itself somewhat; there has been substantial progress in education and

GHANA: AN AFRICAN EPITOME

social welfare; and there have been several changes in government both by popular election and military coup. Indeed, in its political and economic spheres, Ghana epitomizes the African scene, and is very much a "typical" African state.

The Political Kingdom

Centuries before Portuguese merchants established a fort and trading post at Elmina on the Guinea Coast in 1482, gold, ivory, slaves, and other commodities had been shipped northward across the Sahara from parts of what is today central Ghana. Within a century the so-called "Gold Coast" became the hub of European activity where several dozen forts and trading posts had been built by the English, Dutch, Danes, Swedes, and Brandenburgers besides the Portuguese, and keen international competition for the trade of the interior had developed. The success of the Portuguese in diverting southwards this trans-Saharan trade was due largely to the proximity of their Elmina trading station to this important supply area. Eventually that area became consolidated politically as the Ashanti Union of Akan States. The people on the coast, the Fante, brought goods from the interior to the coastal trading posts, and thus a north-south flow of exports was initiated which has become a permanent feature of the coastal states of West Africa. The Fante middlemen jealously guarded their role in this trade pattern and resisted efforts by the Europeans to penetrate the interior themselves. Meanwhile, they bartered with the interior producers at one end of their route and with the Europeans at the other.

Consolidation in the interior began when a number of the Akan states in the northern margins of the forest formed the Ashanti Union. The first steps were taken in the 1600s, but during the eighteenth century the union became the most powerful political and economic unit in the region. Ashanti began to encroach upon the middlemen of the south. Eventually, this led to contact with the Europeans, who failed to protect the peoples of the coastal states and tried to come to terms with Ashanti without success. The abolition of the slave trade and British efforts to eradicate its remnants brought economic ruin and strife to the region. Legitimate trade repeatedly was brought to a virtual standstill by intermittent hostilities. The Fante peoples tried to resist Ashanti encroachment by forming a Fante Confederation, but only in 1874, when the Ashanti army again crossed the Pra River—the traditional boundary—did the British retaliate. The Ashanti capital, Kumasi, was burned, and a treaty was forced upon the empire.

The events of 1874 did not end Ashanti imperialism in this area. Resentful of their defeat and the consequent liberation of the southern Fante states, the Ashanti rulers once again prepared for war, but the British in 1896 expelled the king and forestalled the outbreak of war by a show of force. At that time, Ashanti was made a protectorate, but in 1901 a new revolt erupted. When this outbreak was quelled, the British established a colony over the Ashanti Empire, and included the areas beyond the Volta River, the Northern Territories, in their possession as a protectorate.

Thus, the heart of African organization and power long was in Ashanti, and Ashanti expansionism was contained by the British, just as friction in Nigeria between the northern Moslems and southern peoples was terminated by British intervention. But in Ashanti, indirect rule did not work, and thus a colony was established there, while the Nigerian north became a protectorate. The definition and delimitation of the Gold Coast's boundaries (with the French in the west and north, and with the Germans in the east) took place mainly between 1896 and 1901; as elsewhere in Africa, there was little regard for ethnic units. In the southeast, the Ewe people were divided; in the west, the Nzima, among other peoples, were fragmented by the new political order. These divisions were to create future problems, but the incorporated area itself included many diverse African units which suddenly found themselves within a political boundary and part of a larger political entity. The Gold Coast thus faced the problems common to most modern political entities in Africa: there were perhaps over 100 distinct African states and chieftaincies, each with its own traditions. The British faced a formidable task in helping the inhabitants of the country forge a nation.

In this effort, the latent enmity between Ashanti, whose expansionism had been halted, and the peoples of the south formed an ever-present obstacle. The south increasingly became the focus of activity in the Gold Coast, both administratively and economically. Like Nigeria, Ghana has a coastal capital, Accra. As in Nigeria, much of the development that took place as a result of colonial control occurred in the south, where education made most progress, communications were most rapidly improved, and the introduction of new crops proved most successful. Eventually, the country achieved sovereignty under mainly southern leadership and as a result of pressures exerted by southern politicians and citizenry.

In many ways, Ghana repeats on a smaller scale the regional differences of Nigeria. Like its larger neighbor, Ghana has a Moslem north and a dominantly non-Moslem south. As in Nigeria, where Fulani expansionism was halted by British intervention, Ashanti imperialism was contained by British control. Both states have a highly productive southern belt, which felt most strongly the impact of colonial administration. Political sophistication came to the south at a comparatively early stage, and pressures for independence rose there, while the far north remained little changed and under indirect, protectorate administration.

Suspicions of southern designs on the part of inhabitants of northern Ghana were reflected by their desire for prolonged British involvement in their local administration. But there are important differences: unlike Nigeria, Ghana's northern regions do not have a majority population, and northern Ghana does not have a core region that is economically as significant as that of northern Nigeria. Southern Ghana leads economically and politically, which is reflected in the high degree of concentration of all types of communications in the southern third of the country; in the mid 1970s there still was no railroad link anywhere north of Kumasi.

These differences are reflected also in Ghana's politicoterritorial organization. Unlike Nigeria, which in response to its internal diversity adopted a federal constitution, Ghana became a unitary state with a highly centralized government. Tribalism has been attacked, the power of chiefs reduced, education promoted vigorously, and tight control rigorously maintained. The effort is one of eradication of divisive politicogeographical characteristics within the country rather than adjustment to them. From a geographical point of view, Ghana clearly lends itself better to this attempt than does Nigeria. The country and its population are much smaller; it has, for all practical purposes, one region where the main productive capacity, major administrative center, and best amenities for education and communication are all located. In other words, it has one rather than several core areas of activity. This is not to underestimate the country's internal variety, which is almost as great as that of Nigeria. But all of Ghana focuses on the productive south, the source of many of the political ideas being applied throughout the country, its main outlet, and area of contact with the outside world.

While Ghana adopted a unitary form of government, most Ashanti leaders preferred a federal system that they believed would protect Ashanti custom, tradition, and the chieftainship system, and provide balance between themselves and the coastal Colony. Nkrumah and his party drew their support mainly from the Colony, which contained the greater part of the population, possessed the higher education standards, and was strategically positioned to control the interior. The federal-unitary debate in the immediate preindependence period was further aggravated by the inclusion of British Togoland into Ghana. A plebiscite was held under U.N. supervision in that British-administered former German territory in 1956, to determine the peoples' wishes concerning their political future, the choice being union with an independent Ghana or the continuation as a British trusteeship pending an alternative arrangement. A majority (58 percent) of the registered voters favored union with Ghana (Coleman, 1956).

The inclusion of British Togoland in Ghana profoundly affected the Ewe people who live in the south. Colonial penetration and subsequent division of the land in this area left the majority of the Ewe in the Gold Coast, but significant numbers in both British Togoland and French Togoland. In the vote concerning British Togoland's merger with Ghana, the Ewes voted two to one in favor of continued trusteeship by Britain, implying a desire for a future merger with French Togoland. But the overall majority of British Togoland's voters favored union with Ghana, so that the Ewes were reluctantly joined with that state. Irredentist problems have arisen since the implementation of the merger, and relations between Ghana and Togo have not always been good.

When Ghana attained its independence (1957), it was initially divided into five ad-

FIGURE 9-1 *Ghana. Administrative regions.*

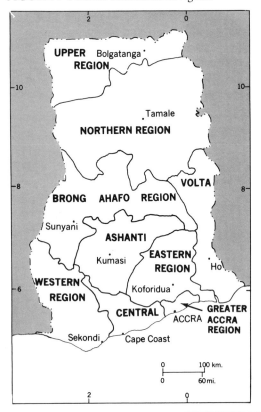

FIGURE 9-2 *Ghana. Major ethnic groups.*

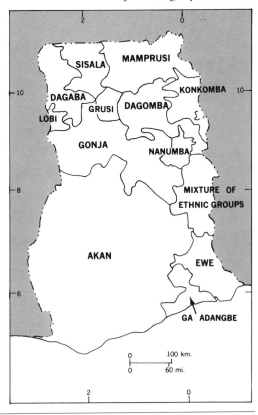

ministrative regions: the Western, Eastern, Ashanti, Northern, and Trans-Volta Togo. Since then several changes have been made in the interests of more efficient government and with a view of historical and political realities. Today there are nine Regions, and with the exception of Ashanti, they do not coincide with tribal areas. (Figs. 9-1 and 9-2). The three northern Regions (Upper, Northern, and Brong-Ahafo) have the greatest ethnic and linguistic diversity with the Gonja, Mamprusi, and Dagaba being the largest groups. The Volta Region, formerly part of British Togoland, is similarly ethnically heterogeneous, with the south being densely settled by Ewes. Various Akan groups are dispersed through the Western, Central, Ashanti, and Eastern Regions; and the Greater Accra Region, once the homeland of the Ga-Adangbe is, because of considerable migration to the capital and to Tema, its industrial satellite town, one of the most ethnically diverse regions today.

Environmental Contrasts

Ghana, like its neighbors in coastal West Africa, lies across several of the region's east-west climatic and vegetative belts. The country does not extend as far into the interior as does Nigeria, so that the total range of its environmental variety is somewhat less; indeed, the northern productive regions of Nigeria largely lie beyond 11° north latitude, which happens to be the line marking Ghana's northern border. Ghana receives most rainfall in the southwest, where its forest zone is best developed; in the southeast lies the anomalous dry zone (Fig. 9-3). In the southwestern lowlands the rainfall exceeds 80 in. (2032 mm) annually, and most of the rest of the southwest receives over 50 in. (1270 mm) The forest that has developed, lies in a triangular area that is broadest in the west and narrows eastward; its northern boundary corresponds generally to the Mampong Escarpment. This escarpment is the south-facing edge of a narrow plateau that separates the productive and densely populated south from the more empty, savanna-covered north. Along the coast is a stretch of scrub and, at the water's edge, a narrow zone of mangroves.

In the extensive savanna lands, the rainfall, although mostly exceeding 40 in. (1016 mm), is rather variable and often comes in severe storms, leading to excessive runoff and problems of erosion. As elsewhere in West Africa, a relatively unproductive "middle belt" lies to the north of the forest zone, its character reflected by the nature of its transport routes. In the south, a dense network of such routes has developed, but in the "middle belt" there are mainly north-south linking roads with very few feeders. Beyond, there is a cluster of dense population around Tamale and Bolgatanga in the Upper Region, and the northern half of the country is suited to cattle raising as well as the cultivation of peanuts and grain crops. No extensive northern areas approach the productivity of the south, however.

The pivotal physiographic feature of Ghana is the Black Volta River, which traverses the length of the country from northwest to southeast. It forms the boundary with the Republic of Upper Volta and the Ivory Coast before turning east and being joined by its major tributary, the White Volta. The entire northeastern region consists of the basin of this river system, and is underlain by near-horizontal sandstones, which have produced generally infertile lateritic soils. Some 60 mi. (97 km) from the coast, the Volta breaks through the Akwapim-Togo Ranges and then flows across the gently undulating Accra Plain before fanning out into a small delta. In the 1960s the Volta was dammed at Akosombo to provide hydroelectric power and water for the

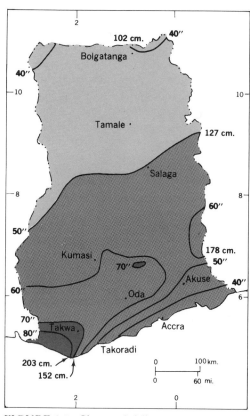

FIGURE 9-3a *Ghana, rainfall.*

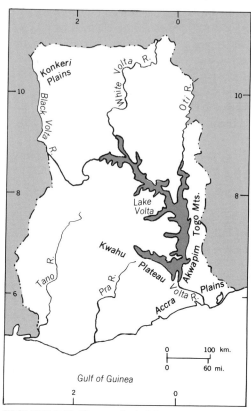

FIGURE 9-3b *Ghana, physical features.*

Accra-Tema core region, and to irrigate the adjoining Accra Plain. Impounded behind the dam is Lake Volta, one of the world's largest artificial lakes that extends some 250 mi (400 km) inland. Flowing out of the

Kwahu Plateau and Ashanti Uplands to the west, and across the densely settled Akan lowlands and coastal plains are several small but important rivers including the Tano, Ankobra, and Pra.

Transport and Development

The outstanding geographical aspect of Ghana is the concentration of its productive capacity in the south and southwest, corresponding largely to the area under forest cover. Most of the agricultural exports come from this zone, and the majority of the important mineral deposits also lie there. In fact, the area around Dunkwa (about half-way between Takoradi and Kumasi) is one of Africa's most important mineralized zones

(Fig. 9-4). Several factors have favored Ghana's relatively rapid economic development, among which the juxtaposition of its mineral and agricultural resources is a major one; transport routes served both industries at once. The productive area is located near the coast, and although Ghana has not enjoyed the benefits of a really good natural harbor, the volume of exports has risen steadily. Palm products, gold, and rubber

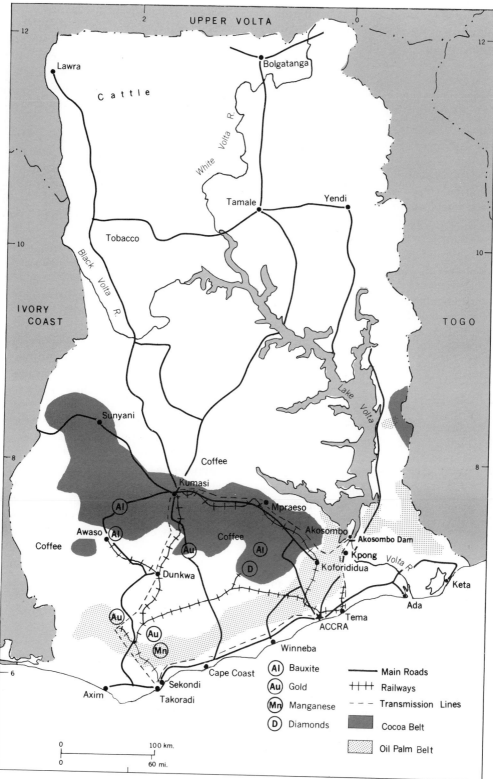

FIGURE 9-4 *Economic map of Ghana.*

were important substitutes for slaves during the latter half of the nineteenth century, but the strongest impact was made by cocoa, introduced in 1879. By 1891, it had begun to figure among the exports, and currently Ghana exports as much as one-third of the world's total production. This production is, and has always been, almost exclusively in African hands.

These developments could not have taken place without the establishment of a transport network. Having been contained at the coast for a long time, and succeeding in finally subduing all the peoples of Ghana only after the turn of the century, the British could turn to the problem of communications only at a late stage, by which time the absence of good roads and railroads was impeding the development of mining and was affecting the export quantities of rubber, timber, and palm oil. Between 1890 and 1900, mining companies exerted pressure upon the government for the provision of bulk transport facilities, and the first surveys for projected lines were made during that decade. In 1898, the Sekondi-Tarkwa line was begun, and it was completed in 1901, connecting the goldfields at Tarkwa to the coast. Immediately, heavy use was made of the line, and its extension toward Kumasi, hastened by the need for rapid transport to the rebellious Ashanti capital, was finished by late 1903.

In the east, agricultural and forest production benefited greatly from the railroad begun in 1907 at Accra. By 1915 it had reached Koforidua, and carried no less than 40,000 tons of cocoa. The process of railway construction was interrupted by World War I, but soon after 1918, it began again and Kumasi and Accra were linked in 1923. Another line was started eastward from the Sekondi-Kumasi railroad, through the Central Region, reaching its terminal, Kade, in 1927. A later phase of construction completed the triangle (1953–1956), during which period the new, important port of Tema was linked to the system at Achimota.

Throughout this period of railroad construction and operation, and with the exception only of wartime periods of gasoline rationing, railroad transportation faced the competition of roads. Furthermore, both road and rail had to compete with riverboats, especially on the Volta, and even with headload transport.

The ports of Sekondi and Accra both were roadsteads where surf boats operated between ship and shore, and for some time vied for the lead in handling the country's external trade. Originally, due to its position at the coastal terminal of the country's only railroad, Sekondi was the first port, until in the 1920s the Accra–Kumasi connection was completed. Soon afterward the more modern port of Takoradi, near Sekondi, became operative, and the western terminal began to forge ahead of its competitors (Dickson, 1969). Takoradi and Sekondi have since become virtually a single metropolitan area with a population of 200,000, and support several large industrial establishments including an automobile assembly plant and plywood and paper mills. About 75 percent of the total export tonnage, mainly minerals and timber, is shipped from Takoradi.

The effect of the transportation network in stimulating Ghana's economic development has been spectacular. In addition to gold, which until 1910 was the only significant mineral export, Ghana possesses mineable quantities of bauxite, manganese ore, and diamonds. Of these, all but the diamonds are found near the Takoradi-Kumasi railway; manganese near Takoradi and Tarkwa, bauxite near the terminal of the Awaso extension and in larger quantities not far from Kumasi itself, and gold near Tarkwa. Only the railroads could have provided the means to carry the heavy equipment required by the mining operations, and without them, the ores could not have been exported easily. When the Kibi bauxite deposits are brought into full production, a new railway spur will be needed from the Kumasi-Tema line (Fig. 9-4).

Raking cocoa beans drying in the sun, Ghana. Ghana's economy is still heavily dependent upon cocoa exports. Almost all the cocoa is grown by African peasants in the southern regions. (UN)

this belt and the concentration of other economic activities there, population has moved into Ashanti from the north and even from adjoining countries. With the rise of population pressure has come the destruction of large parts of the forest, soil erosion in serious measure, and the loss of the vegetative protection against the drying effect of the Harmattan.

Toward the northern fringe of the forest belt is Kumasi (220,000), Ghana's largest city of the interior and the northernmost point of the national core region. Founded some 300 years ago, it became the political, economic, and cultural center and capital of the Ashanti Kingdom. All major north-south trading routes across Ashanti converge on the capital, and despite British efforts to divert trade from the town following the wars of 1874, Kumasi quickly regained its commercial importance and became not only the heart of Ghana's cocoa belt, but also a light manufacturing center. From the surrounding forest came the country's initial exports—palm oil, rubber, and timber. But with the introduction of cocoa, much of the land was eventually taken up by this cash crop, and so lucrative was the trade that food staples had to be imported.

Ghana's capital, Accra (600,000), has not grown as rapidly as other African capitals or become the country's leading industrial city, largely because of its unfavorable transport system and limited water supplies. It lacks a natural deep-water harbor, in fact it has no harbor facilities to speak of at all. Cargo vessels had to anchor offshore and load their goods onto small surf boats, which was costly, time consuming, and risky. Nevertheless, Accra is an important transport node and, until the growth of Tema, it was Ghana's largest industrial city specializing in light industries such as textiles, food processing, leather goods, and printing.

Twenty miles (32 km) east of Accra is the port of Tema, opened in 1962 and originally built as a requirement of the Volta River Project. It serves the whole country

Equally impressive has been the effect of improved communications on the agricultural industries, especially cocoa cultivation. Cocoa dominates the agricultural export list to the exclusion of practically all else, and contributes between one-half and two-thirds of the annual export revenue. Although sometimes cocoa cultivation existed before adequate roads were pushed into a certain area, the actual road-building process was immediately accompanied by the staking out of farms, while elsewhere the knowledge of plans for future road construction led to the preparation of such farms in advance.

In Ghana, the forest belt is the most densely populated area, economically the most important, and in terms of communications, by far the best endowed. Lying between the narrow coastal region of scrub in the south and the savanna region of the north, it covers most of the Western and Central Regions, virtually all of Ashanti (although the forest thins out to the north), and extends into the northern part of the Eastern Region. As a result of the success of cocoa in

The Central Business District of Accra, Ghana's capital and primate city. (Alan C. G. Best)

and handles about 83 percent of all imports, and the bulk of Ghana's cocoa exports. It has become Ghana's principal manufacturing center utilizing both imported and natural resources. Its products are geared not only to local markets but those of Upper Volta, Mali, and Togo. Indeed, Tema is now the largest industrial town on the Guinea Coast west of Lagos. VALCO's (Volta Aluminium Company) aluminum smelter processes imported alumina, and is the single largest processing industry in Ghana. A steel mill, using scrap iron from Ghana's urban centers and mines, and chemicals and ferroalloys imported from Britain and Sweden, was built in 1962 in response to the expanding demands for iron and steel products, and like VALCO, it depends on relatively cheap hydroelectric power from the Akosombo Dam. Tema's third capital intensive industry is the oil refinery, built and maintained by Ghanaian and Italian concerns. It produces fuel oil, kerosene, and petrol from crude oil imported from Nigeria, Libya, and the Soviet Union. Also manufactured in the city are chemicals, paints, textiles, aluminum products, beverages, cigarettes, cement, and pesticides. The combination of Tema's close proximity to markets and to Accra, the city's special tax structures, the modern harbor facilities, and good rail connections with the interior, and the availability of cheap power have made Tema Ghana's most diversified and largest industrial city.

The Akosombo Dam of the Volta River Project, Ghana. The dam provides low-cost energy for aluminum smelting in Tema and urban-industrial needs in Accra. (Alan C. G. Best)

The VALCO alumina storage dome, Tema, Ghana. VALCO consumes almost three-fourths of the electricity produced at the Akosombo power plant. (World Bank)

The Volta River Project

Ghana's single most important development project undertaken since independence is the multi-purpose Volta River Project that was financed by long-term loans from the International Bank for Reconstruction and Development, the U.S. Agency for International Development (AID), the U.S. Export-Import Bank, and British banking institutions. Conceived as early as 1925 but abandoned for economic reasons, the idea was revived in the late 1950s, and following four years of political maneuvering, construction began in 1962. The project has four major components: The Akosombo Dam and hydroelectric plant whose ultimate generating capacity is 883,000 kilowatts; a 145,000 ton capacity aluminum smelter at Tema, which places Ghana among the world's top ten producers of aluminum; an extensive transmission system to relay electricity to Accra, Tema, Kumasi, Sekondi-Takoradi, the mining areas, and even Upper Volta, Togo, and Benin; and a modern deepwater port at Tema and related road and railway improvements. Additional but secondary benefits of the project include increased water supplies for the Accra-Tema area, development of an inland fishing industry, low-cost water transport between northern and southern Ghana, and irrigation of the Accra Plain.

Generation of electricity began in 1966, and the project currently accounts for 98 percent of Ghana's total electricity; VALCO's alumina smelter is the single largest consumer (70 percent of the total). Additional dams and electrical generating facilities may be built if markets can be found. Some 80,000 persons were removed from the land now flooded by the lake and resettled in 52 villages in the same general area. Each family that opted for resettlement into agricultural villages was promised six acres (2.4 ha) of cleared farm land; some 10,000 individuals chose a cash payment instead. Traditional shifting cultivation is prohibited in the resettlement areas, and the plots are intended for subsistence farming only (Lumsden, 1973).

Development Constraints and Strategies

When Ghana gained its independence, it was the envy of many developing countries. It had a strong agricultural and light industrial base, the highest per capita income of any tropical African country, better than average education and medical services, an efficient transport system, substantial foreign currency reserves from cocoa earnings, a dynamic political leadership, and other assets normally taken as requisite ingredients of national viability. However, these were no guarantee of economic prosperity and political stability. Indeed, Ghana has experienced considerable difficulty in meeting its national objectives.

Between 1957 and 1966, President Kwame Nkrumah and his Convention People's Party (CPP) adopted a policy of "African socialism" at home and nonalignment and Pan-Africanism abroad. Nkrumah tightened his control over the party and country, and by 1964 Ghana was a legalized single-party state that was characterized by graft and corruption within the party and civil

Black Star Memorial, Accra built by Ghana's first president Kwame Nkrumah commemorating Ghana's independence. (Harm J. deBlij)

service, economic mismanagement, a rapidly deteriorating balance of payments position, huge losses of external reserves, and the flight of foreign investment. Considerable money was spent on prestige projects such as government buildings, the national airways, superhighways, and national edifices, bringing the country to the verge of economic collapse (Guyer, 1970). The seven-year development plan announced in 1964 was designed to revolutionize agriculture, industry, and education. The aim was to build a socialist state in which there would be state industry, state farms, a state-sponsored work force, while investment by foreigners would be encouraged to obtain foreign exchange and to increase productive efficiency. Indeed, the regime emphasized total dependence on foreign capital to industrialize the country. The Volta River Project was the largest and most successful of these commitments, undertaken at a time when world cocoa prices were falling, severely curtailing government revenues.

On February 24, 1966, while Nkrumah was en route to Peking, the Ghanaian army and police staged a successful *coup*. The constitution was suspended, the CCP and all other political parties were outlawed, the national legislature was dissolved, and the army established a National Liberation Council (NLC) of four army and four police officers under the chairmanship of General Ankrah. The NLC inherited a national debt of more than £400 million compared with £20 million when independence was granted, and by 1968, this had risen to £652 million. During the last three years of Nkrumah's office, there was a 66 percent rise in the cost of living. Ankrah reduced government spending and cut imports of luxury goods, transferred several state corporations to private enterprise, and moved toward "constructive partnership" between the public and private sectors. Former Commonwealth ties were reaffirmed and a more pro-West foreign policy was adopted, while the NLC maintained its support of Pan-African aims. Many of the old regime's links with East Europe and the People's Republic of China were severed, and Ghana's relations with its immediate neighbors improved.

In 1969, Ghana was returned to civilian rule under the leadership of President Busia. But the country still suffered from foreign indebtedness, low cocoa prices, and rising imports. The government decided to deport aliens without residency permits in an effort to reduce the outflow of remittances, and to provide jobs for Ghanaians. At the time there were two million aliens including 700,000 Nigerians, 500,000 Upper Voltans, and others from Benin, Niger, Togo, and Liberia of whom 800,000 had no residency rights. Most were engaged in petty trading, or held seasonal jobs in the cocoa industry. In 1971, Busia ordered a 44 percent devaluation of the cedi, which brought huge rises in the cost of living, general public discontent and, eventually (January, 1972), his downfall in a second military *coup* lead by Colonel Acheampong.

Acheampong established a National Redemption Council of army, navy, air force, and police officers that was ethnically balanced. The cedi was revalued by 42 percent, and an austerity program was introduced. The NRC's main economic policy has been "self-reliance," which has aimed at increasing domestic food production and local raw materials for industry. However, the government has failed to provide new roads and other services for their realization, and the cocoa industry has continued to suf-

fer despite enormous rises in world cocoa prices.

The military regime revived trade with East European and other socialist countries and secured their assistance in the reactivation of numerous state manufacturing and processing projects abandoned in 1966. Trade and aid agreements have been signed with the Soviet Union, and the People's Republic of China has agreed to assist in large-scale agricultural projects. The government has also assumed a 55 percent participation in the country's mining enterprises, and 55 percent interest in foreign timber, oil, and fertilizer companies. The military is well entrenched in the machinery of administration at all levels, and a return to civilian rule seems unlikely.

Thus Ghana's economy has operated, and continues to operate, under a set of sociopolitical constraints not entirely conducive to growth and diversification. Investors both local and foreign, have lacked confidence in Ghana's political leadership and economic climate. The economy has several structural and spatial weaknesses, the principal being the high emphasis on agricultural and mineral exports, the growing balance of payments problem because of heavy reliance on imported consumer goods and equipment, the lack of basic capital goods industries, the monopolistic control of production and marketing, the high degree of industrial concentration (50 percent of the labor and 40 percent of the establishments) in the metropolitan centers of Accra-Tema, Sekondi-Takoradi, and Kumasi, and the weak interregional and intersectoral linkages.

Not only must the economy diversify, it should disperse (Darkoh, 1973). But industrial decentralization, while desirable, is rarely easy to promote, Vast areas of northern Ghana, where grains and cattle have considerable potential, need to be integrated with the more populous and prosperous south. But the northern regions are handicapped by rudimentary techniques of food production, deep-rooted cultural values and preferences, and a sparse transport network, all of which have defeated various government efforts to promote the region's economy and to integrate it more with the south. (Dickson, 1968). Poverty and underemployment prevail in the Volta Region where discontent has reappeared in various guises and secessionist aspirations are not dead. But disparities between rich and poor are not confined to these broad regions; they also exist at the local level and within metropolitan areas.

Ghana, once the model state of development in Africa, is now beset with internal difficulties that seem almost impossible to control. Indeed, Ghana epitomizes the problems of political instability, social organization, and economic development so common in Africa.

Bibliography

Boateng, E.A. *A Geography of Ghana*. Second Edition. London: Cambridge University Press, 1967.

Chambers, R. (ed.). *The Volta Resettlement Experience*. New York: Praeger Publishers, 1970.

Coleman, J.S. "Togoland," *International Conciliation*. No. 509 (September, 1956), pp. 3–91.

Darkoh, M.B.K. "Industrial Strategy and Rural Development in Africa with Special Reference to Ghana," *Geoforum*. No. 16 (1973), pp. 7–23.

Dickson, K.B. "Background to the Problem of Economic Development in Northern Ghana," *Annals*, A.A.G., Vol. 58, No. 4 (December, 1968), pp. 686–96.

———. *A Historical Geography of Ghana*. London: Cambridge University Press, 1969.

Dickson, K.B. and G. Benneh. *A New Geography of Ghana*. London: Longman Group Ltd., 1970.

Goldsworthy, D. "Ghana's Second Republic: A Post-Mortem," *African Affairs*. Vol. 72, No. 286 (January, 1973), pp. 8–25.

Grayson, L.E. "Decentralization in Planning and Economic Decision-Making in Ghana," *Journal of Modern African Studies*, Vol. 13, No. 1 (March, 1975), pp. 126–33.

Guyer, D. *Ghana and the Ivory Coast*. Jericho, New York: Exposition Press, 1970.

Hance, W. A. *African Economic Development*. Revised Edition. New York: Columbia University Press, 1967.

Hilton, T.E. "Ghana," *Focus*. Vol. 21, No. 2 (October, 1970).

Lumsden, D.P. "The Volta River Project: Village Resettlement and Attempted Rural Animation," *Canadian Journal of African Studies*, Vol. 7, No. 1 (1973), pp. 115–32.

Nkrumah, K. *I Speak of Freedom*. New York: Praeger Publishers, 1961.

TEN

Sierra Leone, once the center of administration for British West African possessions, became a sovereign state later (1961) than either Ghana or Nigeria. Although it possessed the oldest British-founded municipality in Africa (Freetown), the first modern institution of higher learning in tropical Africa (Fourah Bay College, 1827), and a long history of political activity on the part of local people, Sierra Leone was less prepared for independence than either Ghana or Nigeria. Illiteracy was in the vicinity of 95 percent, the per capita income about one-third that of Ghana, and the political difficulties involving the imposition of proportional representation on a long-privileged elite were unsolved. And, like most colonies, Sierra Leone possessed a dual economy that was regionally imbalanced. Since independence, the dual economy has persisted and growth has not been accompanied by development.

Sierra Leone, named by Portuguese navigators exploring the monsoon coast of West Africa in the sixteenth century, occupies the zone between the southern divide of the Futa Jallon Mountains and the coast. The descent, from over 6000 ft (1830m) to the embayed coastline, is accomplished by a series of steps representing, in the upper regions, cyclic erosion surfaces and, in the lower areas, raised marine terraces. Between the southern boundary of Senegal and the western border of Ivory Coast, the West African coast line trends northwest to southeast, thus lying directly in the path of the moisture-bearing air masses. The resultant rainfall is high (Freetown receives 157 in.–3988 mm), but is concentrated during the marked wet season. During the dry season the dusty Harmattan is very much in evidence. This, then, is the prime example of the monsoon coast of West Africa.

Considering its small size (27,700 sq mi

SIERRA LEONE: PROGRESS IN POVERTY

184

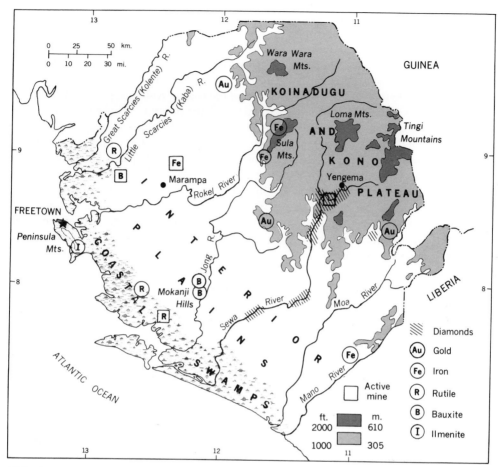

FIGURE 10-1 *Sierra Leone. Natural environments and minerals.*

or 71,740 sq km) and compact shape, the environmental diversification and the range of raw materials found in Sierra Leone are remarkable. In some cases, their exploitation has yet to begin. The fishing grounds off the country's shores may be the best of West Africa. The coastal regions, with their swampy lowlands, carry rice and could produce much more of this commodity than they do. Cocoa can be grown in the southeast, ginger in the south-central region, and peanuts in the north. While the small remnant of hot, wet forest in the southwest is suitable mainly for extractive activities, the north can sustain a cattle industry. Cassava and kola nuts are grown, and coffee (robusta)

has joined the list of exports. There are large reserves of medium-grade iron ore at Marampa and in the Sula Mountains, and many river gravels of the east are richly laden with diamonds. Extensive bauxite deposits exist in the Mokanji Hills and at Port Loko, while rutile is found in the swamplands and estuaries along the south coast (Fig. 10-1).

Yet Sierra Leone is a poor country. The per capita income is under $150, only 5 percent of the work force is in manufacturing, and the majority of Sierra Leoneans have not been drawn into the modern sector of the economy. About three-quarters of the population is engaged in agriculture, using largely traditional methods, but agriculture accounts for less than a third of the GDP. Three-fifths of the value placed on agricultural output is in subsistence production, and despite the emphasis placed on rice, Sierra Leone has a shortage of this staple food and spends more on food imports than it receives from the export of coffee, cocoa beans, palm kernels, and kola nuts, which comprise the leading agricultural exports. Before the Marampa iron ore mine closed in late 1975 mining accounted for 85 percent by value of the country's total exports, yet for only 16 percent of the GDP, and employed an even smaller percentage of the work force. The economy depends heavily on foreign trade with diamonds the main commodity, dictating not only the level of government revenue but the availability of foreign exchange for importing capital goods for development. Manufacturing is poorly represented and emphasizes the processing of local agricultural and forestry resources.

There are, and have long been, marked disparities in the levels of economic, social, and political-administrative development between the coastal region, especially Freetown, and the interior. Southern Sierra Leone is somewhat more developed than the latosol-covered, repeatedly drought-stricken interior north. This is partly due to the pedological and climatic factors, but the south has also benefited from the magnificent Freetown harbor and its contact with Europe. These differences long found expression in their respective political status: the small colony of Sierra Leone was on the coast, the large protectorate was the almost untouched, traditional interior. This separation has its roots in historicogeographical developments that go far to explain the socioeconomic condition of the present-day state.

The People: Kings and Creoles

The oldest numerically important residents of Sierra Leone appear to be the Temne people, who had settled the coastal regions of the country by the fifteenth century and with whom the Europeans made contact soon afterward. Calling for fresh water and other needs, the Portuguese and other Europeans found in Freetown West Africa's best natural harbor, and it soon became a trading center for slaves and ivory as well as a revictualling station. No continuous white rule was set up, however, and the resident traders came under the local African rulers. Meanwhile, the Mende people were settling in the north, and Sierra Leone did not escape the effects of the Fulani and Mandingo holy war, which spread Islam from the north, beginning in the early eighteenth century.

At various times there have been between 100 and 150 chiefdoms in the area of Sierra Leone. When Granville Sharp, the British opponent of slavery, succeeded in establishing in Sierra Leone a small settlement for freed slaves in 1787, one of these kings gave his permission for the use of a section of his land for this purpose. "Province of Freedom," as the settlement was called, did not survive long, for the king's successor wiped it out. But in 1791, it was revived under the auspices of the Sierra Leone Company, sponsored by British abolitionists, and this time the effort had permanent success. The settlement was rebuilt and named Freetown, and freed slaves were brought there, not only from captured slave vessels, but also from the Americas, where some had gained their liberty by joining the British forces during the American Revolution and others had been emancipated in the West Indies.

Britain outlawed the slave trade in 1807, and in the following year the government took charge of the settlement as a colony, continuing the policy of making it a homeland for emancipated slaves. Freetown became an important base from which operations against the slave trade were carried out. During the half-century after 1808, an estimated 50,000 freed slaves were thus brought to Sierra Leone.

The first groups of slaves, who had come from the Americas, had in common some knowledge of the English language, and many were Christians. Those who arrived after 1807, however, never having made the Atlantic crossing, not having been exposed to Anglo-America, and coming from various parts of Africa, had little or nothing in common. As a result, an extremely heterogeneous community developed in Freetown and its immediate vicinity. The government now embarked upon a policy designed to provide these people with a common language, religion, and culture. Schools were built, missionaries sent to the colony, and much was achieved in a remarkably short time. It was during this period that Fourah Bay College was established (1827). The new immigrants responded well, were active and very successful as traders, and began to settle in other parts of the general area of Sierra Leone.

These people came to be known as "Creoles," and they soon attained a privileged position in the embryo country, carrying on most of the trade, enjoying educational opportunities not available to the vast majority of the people in the hinterland of Freetown, sharing a common language which has come to be known as "Krio," and enjoying a position of influence in the administration of their part of the region. Indeed, they were responsible for the first efforts to expand the colony's influence into the interior, although they failed initially to interest the British in accepting the responsibilities inherent in this move. Eventually, however, this development did come about.

Colony and Protectorate

What led to the extension of British power into the hinterland was not the Creoles' desires, but French activities in West Africa and the realization that Freetown's strategic qualities would be endangered if French encroachment went unchecked. Hence, between 1890 and 1896, treaties were signed with chiefs in the interior, and in the latter year, boundaries were defined as agreed upon by the French and Liberian governments. While the coastal region remained a colony, the interior became a protectorate and the administrative division of Sierra Leone had become a fact.

In Sierra Leone as elsewhere, the protectorate status of the bulk of the country required the introduction of the principle of indirect rule, and so the chiefs remained in power, traditional ways were encouraged, and few modern amenities were introduced. But the Creoles, who had been involved in government in Sierra Leone ever since the colony obtained a legislative council in 1863, found their influence waning rather than increasing after the protectorate had been established. British district commissioners and administrators governed both the protectorate and the colony, and Creoles were gradually removed from those offices they held.

In 1924, when a new constitution was drawn up, the legislative council consisted of a few elected Creoles and, for the first time, protectorate representation in the persons of nominated chiefs. It foreshadowed independence and eventual proportional representation for all citizens of Sierra Leone, which inevitably meant the loss of privileges and the end of cultural isolation for conservative Creoles. A unitary constitution was introduced in 1951 giving political power to those who won a majority of votes. A decade later independence was granted, and a predominantly protectorate party won the elections and formed the government of the new state. In 1975 Sierra Leone became a one-party state.

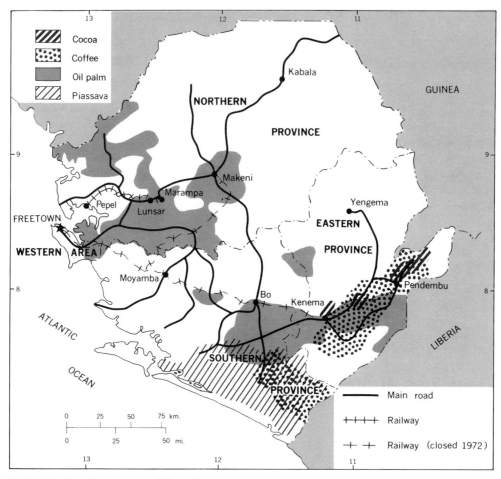

FIGURE 10-2 *Economic map of Sierra Leone.*

Throughout the colonial era, British policies toward the development of Sierra Leone were unimaginative and largely un-coordinated. Little money was spent on basic education, improving staple food production, large-scale development projects and communications, and the Western Area (the former Colony) usually received a disproportionate share of the limited development funds. While cash crops such as palm kernels, cocoa, piassava (a fiber obtained from the raphia palm), and coffee became important exports, little effort was made to ensure efficient production, marketing and distribution. A narrow-gauge railway was built from Freetown east through Bo (the

protectorate's former capital), and Kenema to Pendembu by 1908, and a branch line reached the northern trading center of Makeni by 1916 (Fig. 10-2). These cut across traditional sea-bound porterage routes and diverted much of the trade, especially palm produce, to Freetown. Roads complemented the railway until the late 1920s when feeder roads were linked. But the line was poorly maintained, costly to operate, and unsuitable for transporting modern consumer goods, and so was phased out between 1971 and 1974. Its closure is of limited significance since the railway served few areas for which adequate road transport alternatives are not now available (Williams and Hayward,

Alluvial diamonds are an important source of income to Sierra Leone. Here workers are panning the gravels into baskets. (UN)

1973). In 1933, a special-purpose private railway was built from Pepel to the iron ore mine at Marampa.

The lack of commitment that characterized Britain's administration of Sierra Leone is well illustrated by the diamond industry. In 1935, a British company was granted a 99-year concession over the entire country for diamond mining, mainly alluvial operations. A wave of illicit diamond digging and smuggling took place, especially during and immediately after the lean years of the Second World War. Sierra Leone's diamonds are over 50 percent gem stones, and the country lost perhaps one-half of the returns for its most valuable product. Eventually the government stepped in (1955), limiting the company to 450 sq mi in the Yengema area, and established a monopoly on the purchase of gems. But incalculable losses had already been sustained. Not only had revenues been lost, but much of the land's agricultural potential had been destroyed, and farm outputs declined as labor was diverted to mining areas (Forde, 1974).

Development in the Seventies

When Sierra Leone achieved independence, it inherited a markedly dualistic economy in which diamonds dominated the export sector and subsistence agriculture the domestic. The economy was largely in the hands of Lebanese, the Creole minority, and a few British expatriates. The Lebanese controlled a disproportionate amount of the country's wholesale trade, most of the retail trade, and were closely associated with much of the country's agricultural exports and diamond marketing (Stanley, 1970). Furthermore, there existed a strong regional imbalance in the economy; primacy prevailed in Freetown, while social and economic backwardness persisted in the Provinces, especially the Northern Province (Riddell, 1970). The country also inherited a politically inexperienced people and a paternal system of government that supported the authority of the chiefs. These difficulties contributed to a decade of political instabil-

Periodic Markets

A phenomenon common to much of tropical Africa is the rural periodic market. As the term implies, this is a market that operates at intervals, commonly either in or between villages. These intervals vary from place to place according to the amount of goods produced for sale, the size of the consumer population, tradition (perhaps influenced by religious principles), the density and nature of transport facilities, distance from other markets (especially urban centers), and other factors. In much of northern Nigeria, southern Ghana, Ivory Coast, Liberia, Guinea, and the interior states of West Africa, these markets are held every seventh day. Elsewhere they may meet every second, third, fourth, or eighth day or at another interval. In Sierra Leone, periodic markets are not as common as elsewhere in West Africa, and they are relatively recent phenomena. In southern Nigeria a four-day cycle is common among the Yoruba, but there is no clear spatial pattern of market frequency for Africa as a whole.

Periodic markets form a sort of interlocking network of exchange places that serves even areas where there are no roads; as each market in the network or "ring" gets its turn, it will be near enough to one section of the area so that people who live in the vicinity can walk to it carrying whatever they have to sell or trade. In this way, small amounts of produce filter through the market chain to a larger regional market, where shipments are collected for interregional or perhaps even international trade. Itinerant traders travel from one market to another in a market "ring" taking goods and customers to different markets each day. What is traded depends on where the market is located. In the savanna zone, sorghum, millet, groundnuts, and shea-butter (an edible oil drawn from the shea-nut) are common food items; in the forest zone, yams, cassava, and palm oil are commonly sold. In general, the quantities traded are small, and their values are low: a bowl of sorghum, a bundle of firewood, a gallon drum of kerosene, a few canned goods, a packet of cigarettes, cooking utensils, and clothing. The marketplaces are arenas not only of trade, but also for social and cultural exchange. Here the latest news can be heard, professional letter writers attend to important business, clothing is fashioned, marriage contracts can be made, and the people barter, discuss, argue, gossip, eat, and drink. At the end of the day, the marketplace is deserted; three, four, seven days later the market reopens.

ity that witnessed military coups, counter-coups, the presence of Guinean troops to support the government, and the introduction of a one-party legislature in 1973.

In 1974 the government introduced a five-year plan (1974–1975 to 1978–1979), whose major objectives were to raise the standards of living of the masses who lived in the isolated rural communities, to provide greater economic and financial self-sufficiency, to reduce the regional economic imbalances, and to diversify the economy (Sierra Leone, 1974). Agriculture and mining were allocated the greatest share of the

A periodic market at Po, Upper Volta. This is a four-day market. Note the small quantities of food and merchandise offered for sale. (World Bank)

planned investment. In the agricultural sector, the primary objective is self-sufficiency in rice, the country's staple food, which can be grown in both swamplands and upland areas. Over half the total agriculture allocation is for the Northern Province where large-scale sugar cane and rice projects are planned, and the pastoral economy is to be improved. Mineral projects scheduled for development or expansion include the Port Loko bauxite-alumina complex north-east of Freetown, bauxite mining in the Mokanje Hills, rutile mining near Gbangbama, and ilmenite mining near Freetown (Fig. 10-1). These assume additional importance following the closure of the Marampa iron ore mine in 1975 (due to high energy costs), and the uncertain future of diamond mining in the east.

Like many development plans, that of Sierra Leone calls for new processing industries in the smaller towns and rural areas. These include the processing of sugar, lumber, fruit, and cotton, the objectives being to promote local growth, contain the primacy of Freetown, and to reduce the migration of labor to Freetown. But Sierra Leone does not offer a promising field for major modern industries because its market is small and the population's purchasing power extremely limited. Emphasis is placed not on import substitution, but on industries based on local raw materials for which adequate labor is available. Foreign investment is encouraged. The government promises assistance for establishment of industries in the form of cheap credit, export incentives, arrangements for repatriating capital and profits, and measures for encouraging reinvestment of profits. The government is also committed to creating a wider regional market for industry through the Mano River Union with Liberia and the West African Economic Community (ECOWAS), which was founded in May, 1975.

While these plans are ambitious and take cognizance of existing spatial and structural attributes of the economy, they do not materially alter the fundamental patterns and problems. Sierra Leone retains its dual economy and regional imbalances, becoming increasingly dependent on exports for development revenues, and progress in the social and economic spheres is slow and costly.

Bibliography

Clarke, J. I. (ed.). *Sierra Leone in Maps*. London: London University Press, 1966.

Due, J. M. and G. L. Karr. "Strategies for Increasing Rice Production in Sierra Leone," *African Studies Review*, Vol. 16 (April, 1973), pp. 23–72.

Forde, Enid R. A. "State Policy and Land Use in Sierra Leone," *Rural Africana*, No. 23 (Winter, 1974), pp. 15–38.

Harvey, Milton E. and P. Greenberg. "Development Dichotomies, Growth Poles and Diffusion Process in Sierra Leone," *African Urban Notes*, Vol. 6, No. 3 (Fall, 1972), pp. 117–136.

Riddell, J. B. *The Spatial Dynamics of Modernization in Sierra Leone*. Evanston: Northwestern University Press, 1970.

Riddell, J. B. "Periodic Markets in Sierra Leone," *Annals*, A. A. G., Vol. 64 (December, 1974), pp. 541–48.

Sierra Leone, Ministry of Development and Economic Planning. *National Development Plan, 1974/75–1978/79*. Freetown: Government Printer, 1974.

Stanley, W. R. "The Lebanese in Sierra Leone: Entrepreneurs Extraordinary," *African Urban Notes*, Vol. 5, No. 2 (Summer, 1970), pp. 159–74.

Williams, G. J. and D. F. Hayward. "The Changing Land Transportation Patterns of Sierra Leone," *Scottish Geographical Magazine*, Vol. 89 (1973), pp. 107–118.

ELEVEN

Liberia is the only African state that has never been colonized or overrun by a European power. Like Sierra Leone, coastal parts of this country served as a haven for freed slaves, in this case from the New World, but, unlike its western neighbor, Liberia has existed as an independent political entity for well over a century. Its status as an independent country, however, was no guarantee of economic prosperity. Indeed, until relatively recent times (since World War II), Liberia's economy lagged behind its neighbors, and most of the development infrastructures provided for by colonial administrations elsewhere in Africa, were absent in Liberia. Only short distances from Monrovia and other coastal settlements there was little evidence of a modern society: a subsistence economy prevailed, hospitals and schools were few and far between, roads were almost nonexistent, and the indigenous peoples (Kpelle, Bassa, Kru, Gio, Krahn, and others) were poorly represented in government. However, since World War II, Liberia's economy has diversified and assumed many of the structural attributes of colonial Africa, and the interior regions are now integrated more efficiently with the rest of the country. Liberia could be on the verge of considerable economic growth and development, financed substantially by external sources of capital.

LIBERIA: THE PRICE OF SELF-GOVERNMENT

Liberia owes its origins to the movements aimed at the abolition of slavery and slave trade prevailing in America around the turn of the nineteenth century. In 1818, representatives of the American Colonization Society crossed the Atlantic in search of African land to which freed slaves could be repatriated. Gradually, by purchase and conquest, settlement expanded under the guidance of white governors and with aid from American organizations and individuals. The burden of administration and financial support became too much for the American Colonization Society, which in the 1840s indicated a desire to withdraw its administrative assistance. In response to these developments and to pressure from within what essentially was the colony of a private society, President J. J. Roberts in 1847 proclaimed the settlement independent. Thus began the fight for survival of the tiny state in turbulent Africa.

Liberia did not solve many problems by attaining sovereignty. Indeed, from several points of view the situation deteriorated. The support from the American Colonization Society was terminated, and efforts to collect duties on goods exported had little success. In addition, European interest in the African west coast was on the increase, and frontier disputes with the French in the Ivory Coast and the British in Sierra Leone were frequent. The "Independent African State of Maryland" in the east was absorbed by Liberia in 1857, but the problem of effective national control remained. The African peoples of the interior retained their traditional ways of life and religion and did not pay allegiance to the new rulers on the coast. This induced Britain and France to bring pressure to bear upon the Liberian government to cede certain areas, and boundary treaties were signed with Britain in 1885 and with France in 1892. These treaties notwithstanding, Liberia lost still more territory as recently as 1910, when the French, claiming

Liberian failure to exercise control over certain peoples, took 2000 sq mi (3220 sq km) of the nominally Liberian interior.

The cultural, linguistic, religious, and economic differences between the Americo-Liberians (who, by 1867 probably numbered about 19,000) and the indigenous peoples led to the establishment of two individual politicogeographical regions in the state of Liberia. The coastal belt was delimited to a distance about 40 mi (64 km) inland and fragmented, for administrative purposes, into five counties (one of which was Maryland County, the former "independent state"). The interior was divided into three provinces and nine districts, but for a century after the arrival of the first colonists, there was little local participation other than by those who had come under the immediate influence of the new settlement, within which they resided.

The Americo-Liberian (or Afro-American) element became an important force in the politicoeconomic growth of Liberia. Having long lived in America, these people were often almost as foreign to Africa as were the European colonists elsewhere. They may have adapted more quickly, but they separated themselves from the local inhabitants, who were slow to cooperate in the development of the Liberian state. The division between the settlers and the local people came to be expressed politicogeographically, the Liberian government ruling a coastal strip to about 40 mi (64 km) inland, but being ignored—and unable to have much impact—in the interior. Meanwhile, some of the repatriates gave expression to their feeling of superiority over the local people (who are called "aborigines" in the constitution), which was not calculated to enhance the prospects for unity. Although these mutually hostile sentiments are still not completely eradicated, the differences are now, after more than a century of independence, growing less. It was not until the 1920s that the Liberian government attempted to unify the two regions and to change the attitude of indifference towards the indigenous populations.

For the first 80 years of Liberia's existence as an independent state, the Liberian economy was almost totally subsistent. Only limited amounts of coffee, palm oil, and camwood were exported to the United States and Europe. The piassava industry faced the competition of easily accessible supplies in Sierra Leone (notably Sherbro Island), and coffee exporters could not compete with the rapidly expanding industry of Brazil. By the end of the nineteenth century, Liberia was debt ridden, and had few prospects of emerging from this condition.

In the years prior to World War I, the country appeared on the verge of losing its sovereignty. American loans were provided, but under conditions that Americans should be in charge of customs duty collections, Americans should train a frontier police force, and an American should "advise" the Liberian government on all monetary matters. Meanwhile, the government was exploring the possibility of granting concessions of land to foreign companies, as was happening elsewhere in Africa. Thus, from 1904, foreign companies inspected Liberian possibilities, and in 1906 a British company established a sizable rubber plantation near

Monrovia, capital of Liberia. Although the city has changed much during the past few years, Monrovia remains one of Africa's least well-appointed urban centers. (Harm J. deBlij)

LIBERIA: THE PRICE OF SELF-GOVERNMENT

Monrovia. Britain, the first nation to recognize the Republic of Liberia in 1848, was then the leading supplier of Liberia's imports, and soon after World War I, Germany and the Netherlands became the leading trade partners.

The major breakthrough did not come until 1926, when one million acres was leased to the Firestone Company for a 99-year period. Previous investigations had proved Liberia to be very suitable for rubber cultivation and the American company laid out extensive plantations, began to employ thousands of Liberian workers, and spent much money within the country. By the mid-1930s, rubber occupied a place of importance in the list of Liberian exports, and from 1940 to 1961, rubber was the country's leading export. Firestone put Liberia under American financial supervision and provided a regular income to both Liberians and the government. Its system of labor recruitment, while approved by the Liberian government, was frequently criticized overseas.

American involvement in Liberia's development increased during World War II. Pan American Airways opened up Roberts Field east of Monrovia, and the U.S. Army Air Corps began to use it to stage American assistance to the Mideastern and North African theaters. The U.S. Navy built the country's first modern harbor at Monrovia, which enabled iron ore development to follow. In 1944, the Liberian dollar was raised to parity with the U.S. dollar, and American models were introduced in government and business. Natural resource surveys were undertaken for the first time and the value of iron ore deposits was recognized.

The Era of Change

Liberia's first century of independence was a "century of survival" and near isolation, not one of spectacular economic accomplishment or social and political enlightenment. Indeed, Liberia was in many ways less prepared to deal with a changing world than most African countries of similar size at the close of World War II. In 1939, Monrovia, Liberia's capital and largest urban center, had no telephone system, piped water, or sewage disposal. In 1950, the country had only eight hospitals (426 beds) and 15 physicians, of whom only two were Liberians. For a population of 750,000 there were only 253 schools with a total enrollment less than 21,000 of whom 96 percent were in elementary school (Von Gnielinski, 1972). And there were only 220 mi (354 km) of public roads—mainly around Monrovia and the Firestone plantations—but no public railway. The interior was isolated politically, economically, and geographically from the coastal areas, and there was a need to unify and assimilate the various population groups. Other than Firestone there was no large-scale foreign investment in the country.

To launch Liberia into an era of change, President Tubman initiated two important policies in 1944 (Clower, 1966). First, a policy of "unification" that aimed at the assimilation and unification of the Liberian people. This required constitutional changes that gave the right of suffrage to all Liberians and revised the regulations for governing the interior. And then came an "open door policy," which encouraged the investment of foreign capital in the development of Liberia. The pace of development thus picked up markedly, especially in mining iron ore, railway construction, the expansion of forestry resources, and the improvement of agriculture in the interior.

As in Sierra Leone, the interior hills of Liberia contain substantial iron ore deposits (Fig. 11-1). Since 1951, four of these have been tapped by foreign companies, and since 1961 iron ore has been Liberia's leading ex-

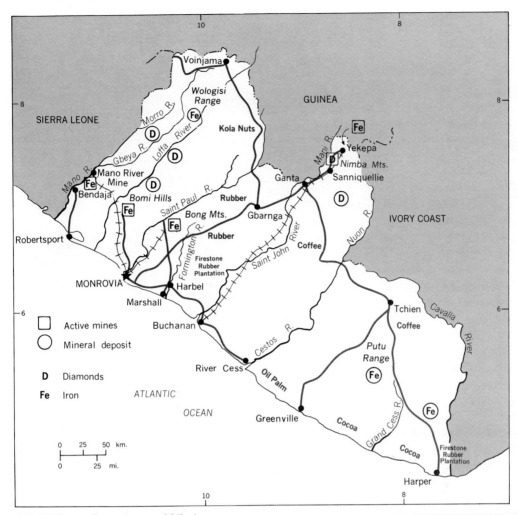

FIGURE 11-1 *Economic map of Liberia.*

port with earnings above $200 million in 1975. The Bomi Hills deposit 50 mi (80 km) northwest of Monrovia was the first to be developed. Reserves exceed 20 million tons of magnetite and hematite containing 66 percent pure iron. A decade later (1961), the Mano River deposit located 20 mi (32 km) further inland from the Bomi Hills and close to the Sierra Leone border, was opened with the assistance of the Liberia Mining Company (LMC) in which the Republic Steel Corporation holds a 60 percent interest. Both mines required railways to be built and special loading facilities at Monrovia. Most

of their ores are shipped to Holland, Britain, West Germany, and the United States.

The largest deposits—probably over 3000 million tons, including at least 235 million tons of high grade ore of 65 to 70 percent iron content—are being exploited by the Liberian American-Swedish Minerals Company (LAMCO) in the Nimba Mountains close to the Guinea border. The ore has almost no overburden and is low in impurities. The Nimba project, which includes not only the mining operations, but a pelletizing plant at the new port of Buchanan, and a 170 mi (270 km) standard gauge railway

Aerial view of iron ore operations, Bong, Liberia. Behind the pelletizing and concentrator plants is an open-pit mine. (Bong Mining Company)

from the mine to the coast, is the largest single private enterprise in tropical Africa. Its main shareholders are Swedish companies and the U.S. Bethlehem Steel Corporation. The fourth open-cast mine is operated by the Bong Mining Company (DELIMCO) in the Bong Ranges a short distance inland from Monrovia. The ores, while extensive (250 million tons), are poorer, having an average iron content of only 38 percent. The mine is connected with Monrovia by a 50-mi (80 km) standard gauge railway, and is operated by German and Italian interests.

Collectively these four mines produce over 23 million tons of ore annually, making Liberia the leading producer and exporter in Africa, and the fifth largest producer in the world. Several additional iron ore deposits (Mount Beeton and Mount Tokadeh) are being brought into production near the Nimba Mountains, while untapped reserves remain in the Wologisi Range in the far northwest, and the Putu Range in the east. Japan has shown interest in the Wologisi ores, which may lead to its production, the construction of new railways, the expansion of harbor facilities at Robertsport, and the provision of new employment.

Despite all these changes, Liberia in the middle 1970s still remained a dominantly subsistence agricultural country (Beleky, 1973). Per capita income is less than $300, and 80 percent of the population depends on agriculture for its livelihood. Some people

Tappers taking rubber latex to a collecting station on a Firestone rubber plantation, Harbel, Liberia. (Firestone)

are engaged in diamond mining and a few in the winning of alluvial gold. There is virtually no manufacturing other than the production of chemicals and explosives required by the mines, a petroleum refinery that uses imported fuel, a cement factory, and a handful of smaller and privately owned concerns producing shoes, beverages, plastics, confectioneries, furniture, and building materials. Some 95 percent of the raw materials required by these industries must be imported. Manufacturing contributes only 5 percent to the G.D.P. and employs only 5 percent of the total labor force in the monetary sector.

Rubber remains an important industry ranking after iron ore and diamonds in the export market. Firestone is still the country's main producer (52 percent of the total), but in recent years it has lost its prominence in acreage and the number of employees. Firestone's estates, which total some 80,000 acres (32,400 ha) or one-third of the country's total, are located at Harbel and Cavalla (near the Ivory Coast border), and employ over 14,000 workers most of whom are tappers. Six other foreign companies (including B. F. Goodrich) control 17 percent of the acreage, while some 5000 Liberian farmers account for the balance. The small producer is disadvantaged by poor management, a shortage of efficient tappers, low yields, and high transport costs (Stanley, 1968). Since 1965, overall production has risen 10 percent per annum, but prices have declined appreciably.

The focus of economic activity in the postwar period has shifted from the coast toward the interior. A network of roads and railways has emerged linking these activities with the coast and especially Monrovia, which has grown in the last 30 years from an insignificant town to an important city with a population exceeding 200,000. Along these arteries commercial crops, especially coffee, rice, oil palm, and rubber, are grown and the forestry industry is being expanded (Fig. 11-1). But Liberia needs transport routes connecting more parts of the country with the emerging core region. The present transport network is sparse and is oriented to the coast with only rudimentary internal connections (Stanley, 1970). As recently as 1968, there was no road connection between Monrovia and Robertsport, Greenville, and Harper, three of the five county headquarters along the coast but surface communications have since improved. Thousands of square miles of the interior, especially in the east, do not enjoy the benefits of even a passable road, and Liberia has limited connections with the neighboring states. Liberia's rivers do not serve as countrywide communications, for they are obstructed by rapids: the St. Paul River is navigable from its mouth at Monrovia to White Plains about 15 mi (24 km) inland; in the east, the Cavalla River is navigable for 50 mi (80 km) from its mouth. In any event, the rivers run directly from the interior to the coast and thus parallel any existing transport routes.

Another post-World War II phenomenon has been Liberia's growth as a nation of registry for foreign-owned oceangoing vessels. Attractive rates and laws made the Liberian flag a "flag of convenience," and, in the middle 1970s, Liberia had the largest registered tonnage in the world.

Whatever the political indignities of colonial rule, it cannot be denied that colonialism did bring certain material assets to many African territories that are lacking, or were for a long time, in Liberia. The Afro-American settlers and their descendants have in many respects remained as divided and separated from their indigenous countrymen as did the whites elsewhere, but without bringing to Liberia the techniques, capital, and experience of the Europeans. The pattern of the country's development, political and economic, in many respects resembles that of, say, Angola. Economic activity is aimed at the exploitation of raw materials. Involvement of the majority of the local people in government has been minimal, and the internal economy has not had much of a chance. Many other amenities colonial rule helped bring, such as agricultural research stations, schools, hospitals, and communications, were lacking until fairly recently.

When development came to Liberia, it came on terms more or less dictated by those desiring to exploit the country's raw materials; the Liberians had little choice but to welcome whatever benefits accrued. Unlike much of the remainder of Subsaharan Africa, Liberia did not experience the salutary efforts of a colonial power attempting to "prepare" the country for independence while instituting development plans and building dams, roads, and airfields. There was not the centripetal effect of a rising anti-colonial nationalism releasing energies which elsewhere, with independence, have been put to excellent use. In many ways, Liberia suffered many of the negative, divisive effects of colonial rule, although not by Europeans, without receiving a share of its benefits. Such, for the majority of the country's inhabitants, has been the legacy of Liberia's particular brand of independence.

Bibliography

Beleky, L. P. "The Development of Liberia," *Journal of Modern African Studies*. Vol. 11, No. 1 (March, 1973), pp. 43–60.

Clower, R. W. et al. *Growth Without Development: An Economic Survey of Liberia*. Evanston: Northwestern Univeristy Press, 1966.

Liebenow, J. G. *Liberia: The Evolution of Privilege*. Ithaca: Cornell University Press, 1969.

Miller, R. E. "The Modern Dual Economy: A Cost Benefit Analysis of Liberia," *Journal of Modern African Studies*. Vol. 10, No. 1 (May, 1972), pp. 113–21.

Schulze, W. *A New Geography of Liberia*. New York: Longmans Inc., 1974.

Stanley, W. R. "The Cost of Road Transport in Liberia: A Case Study of the Independent Rubber Farmers," *Journal of Developing Areas*. Vol. 2, No. 4 (July, 1968), pp. 495–510.

Stanley, W. R. "Transport Expansion in Liberia," *Geographical Review*. Vol. 60, No. 4 (October, 1970), pp. 529–47.

Stanley, W. R. "Rural Transport Development in Liberia," *Rural Africana*. No. 15 (Summer, 1971), pp. 89–95.

Von Gnielinski, S. (ed.). *Liberia in Maps*. New York: Africana Publishing Corporation, 1972.

TWELVE

The geography of former French West Africa may be treated in several ways. For our purposes, this vast francophone realm is divided into two separate units: an interior tier of contiguous and sparsely populated states that border the Sahara; and four smaller states (Guinea, Ivory Coast, Togo, and Benin) that are part of the humid Guinea Coast where French interests first focused, and strong economic dualism prevails. The two regions are linked by history (both colonial and indigenous), and their economies are, to some extent, interdependent.

Although perhaps only 10 percent of the population speaks French in these regions, few would deny that the intensity of the cultural and political impact made by France justifies the continued application of the term "francophone," even after independence. The governing elite is French speaking, the political machinery is based on French example, and virtually every modern institution in each country is based on French models. French feeling prevails because the territories participate with France in several supranational organizations. France's role in West African development differed markedly from place to place, and its role in contemporary francophone West Africa is changing. This chapter examines the French legacy of Ivory Coast, Guinea, Togo, and Benin (formerly Dahomey).

A FRENCH LEGACY: IVORY COAST, GUINEA, TOGO, AND BENIN

French lines of penetration into the interior of West Africa were to some extent controlled by the consolidation of British, German, and other interests along the coast. Eventually, the French obtained five corridors between the coast and the inland areas: Dahomey between German Togoland and British Nigeria, Ivory Coast between British Gold Coast and independent Liberia, Guinea between Liberia and Portuguese Guinea, and the stretches on either side of British-held Gambia, now combined in the Republic of Senegal.

The first decree with the aim of establishing a central government for French West African possessions was issued in 1895. At this time, Senegal, Guinea, Sudan, and Ivory Coast were placed under the jurisdiction of the Governor of Senegal, where France's oldest West African colonial settlement was located. Dahomey was added in 1899, but there was much competition between the administrations of the various individual colonies, preventing the introduction of an all-encompassing budget, a step that Paris regarded as an essential element in French West African unity. The system of administration that was to survive until the late 1950s was established by a new decree issued in 1904, by which time central control had become more effective. Dakar became the seat of the governor general of the federation, and as such the capital of the vast French West African realm.

The 1904 decree by no means ended the French campaign for the consolidation of its West African empire. Effective occupation was not complete in Niger until 1906, in Mauritania until 1910, and Ivory Coast until 1914. Even after World War I, several changes took place. Upper Volta was not created until 1920 when it was excised from parts of Niger, Ivory Coast, and Sudan; it was dismembered in 1932 and recreated in 1947. And in 1922, although not actually a part of the federation, Togo became a League of Nations mandate, the eastern part of which was under French administration.

France's main interest in West Africa was the exploitation of the federation's resources, not the welfare of its people. Exploitation first focused on the coast, but later extended into the drier interior as roads and railways were built and new opportunities were foreseen. While imports and exports were in the hands of a few large French corporate monopolies like SCOA (Société commerciale de l'ouest africain) and CFAO (Compagnie française de l'Afrique occidentale), the administration stimulated economic activity for its own profit in various ways. Taxation was undoubtedly the most important for it encouraged the production of cash crops for export, and provided some revenues for extending the infrastructure (Hopkins, 1973).

Coffee, cocoa, and palm oil became the products of the forest belt, while cotton and groundnuts predominated in the interior. A program of compulsory crop cultivation was introduced, and where cash crops could not be grown, the local peasants were forced to migrate to areas where they could. Thus, thousands of Mossi and Bobo from Upper Volta migrated south to the Ivory Coast's coffee and cocoa plantations, while the Bambara and others went west to the groundnut plantations of Senegal. Forced labor was also introduced, whereby Africans worked on public works projects like roads and railways, and, if required, on European plantations.

African ownership in the money economy was minimal, and almost no African entrepreneurs existed before World War II. In precolonial days, Africans controlled the middleman trade between European exporter and African peasant producer, but during the colonial era, Lebanese merchandisers, content with lower profit margins, took control. It was not until 1946 that France made much effort in developing the basic infrastructure for the federation. Then, considerable expenditures were made on roads, railways, ports, agricultural schemes, water supplies, schools, and hospitals. Even so, it was France, not the federation, that benefited most. Roads and railways linked the ports with their export-oriented hinterlands such as the Sansanding Project of central Mali, and the Richard-Toll Scheme on the lower Senegal River. And the majority of schools and hospitals were situated either in or close to these islands of French exploitation.

France controlled the federation's external economy. It provided its territories with manufactured goods, technical assistance, and financial aid in exchange for raw materials and semi-processed goods. Very little intraterritorial trade was conducted other than the distribution of consumer goods from Dakar and, to a lesser extent, from Abidjan. Trade between the federation and other African territories was almost nonexistent.

Economic policy was dovetailed with various social and political policies, first those of "assimilation," and later "association." Association in turn led to the establishment of autonomous states within the French Community (1958), and in 1960 to complete political independence (see Chapter Five). Only Guinea, whose anti-French sentiment was strongest, chose independence outside the Community in 1958. The other territories chose autonomy buttressed by continuing French economic aid. They gained their independence in 1960.

Supranational Organizations

In contemporary West Africa, several supranational organizations exist to strengthen the economic, political, and ideological ties between the francophone states and Europe (especially France), and to promote stronger ties within Africa. The most important of these are the Communauté Financière Africaine (CFA), the West African Economic Community (CEAO), l'Organisation Commune Africaine et Mauricienne (OCAM), and the Lomé Convention (Table 12-1).

The Communauté Financière Africaine, also known as the Franc Zone, embraces all countries whose currencies are linked with the French franc at a fixed rate of exchange, and who agree to hold their reserves mainly in the form of French francs and to effect their exchange on the Paris market. Each country has its own central issuing bank, and its currency is freely convertible into French francs. All the former French West African territories except Guinea and Mauritania are members. France's ties with CFA countries involve not only monetary arrangements, but also comprehensive French assistance in the form of budget support, foreign aid, technical assistance, and subsidies on commodity exports.

In 1973, six West African francophone states (Table 12-1) formed the West African Economic Community (CEAO), which came into effect the following year and replaced the now defunct West African Customs Union (UDEAO). This coordinates not only customs and trade measures, but also develops policies regarding transport, communications, energy, and tourism, and is designed to develop trade between member states in agricultural and industrial products. Nonmanufactured crude products may be imported and exported by CEAO members without internal taxes. OCAM has similar objectives, but it is more continental in scope and membership and operates within the framework of the OAU.

The most far-reaching trade and aid agreement to have been ratified by the West African states is the Lomé Convention. Named after the Togolese capital where it was signed in February, 1975, the Lomé Convention is a cooperative effort between

Table 12-1 REGIONAL ORGANIZATIONS

	CFA Zone	UMOA	Entente	OCAM	CEAO	Lomé Convention ACP	ECOWAS
Benin	X	X	X	X	OS [a]	X	X
Chad	X					X	
Guinea						X	X
Ivory Coast	X	X	X	X	X	X	X
Mali	X				X	X	X
Mauritania					X	X	X
Niger	X	X	X	X	X	X	X
Senegal	X	X		X	X	X	X
Togo	X	X	X	X	OS [a]	X	X
Upper Volta	X	X	X	X	X	X	X

CFA: Communauté Financière Africaine—(Franc Zone).
UMOA: West African Monetary Union.
OCAM: L'Organisation Commune Africaine et Mauricienne.
CEAO: West African Economic Community.
ACP: African, Caribbean, and Pacific States.
ECOWAS: Economic Community of West African States.
[a] OS: Observer status only.

46 African, Caribbean, and Pacific states (ACP) and the nine countries of the European Economic Community (EEC). Among other things, the Lomé Convention provides for the transfer of industrial technology and financial aid from the EEC to the ACP countries. There is promise of help with industrial programs, multistate rural development projects, and promotion of their products in foreign markets. It gives the developing nations privileged access to the EEC for their exports, whether raw materials or manufactured goods. Thus, separately and collectively, these and other agreements bind together the francophone states and provide them with greater economic opportunity than would otherwise be possible.

Ivory Coast: Progress Through Cooperation

The Ivory Coast is by far the richest and economically the most diversified territory in former French West Africa. It produces a wide range of crops and forestry products, the most important being coffee, cocoa, palm oil, and lumber (Fig. 12-1). The Ivory Coast is the leading coffee producer in Africa (closely followed by Angola), and is generally the world's third largest after Brazil and Colombia. First grown in 1891, coffee now covers more than 1.7 million acres (700,000 ha) of the southern forest zone, and almost all the acreage is African-owned.

Most of the coffee (robusta) is marketed in the United States and Europe as instant coffee. The second most important food export is cocoa. Over a million acres (405,000 ha) are cultivated in the southeast where the plant was first introduced from the Gold Coast in 1895.

Together these crops provide almost half the annual export revenues, but for many years, coffee was by far the dominant export accounting for up to 70 percent of the total. By the early 1970s however, both coffee and cocoa had declined in importance,

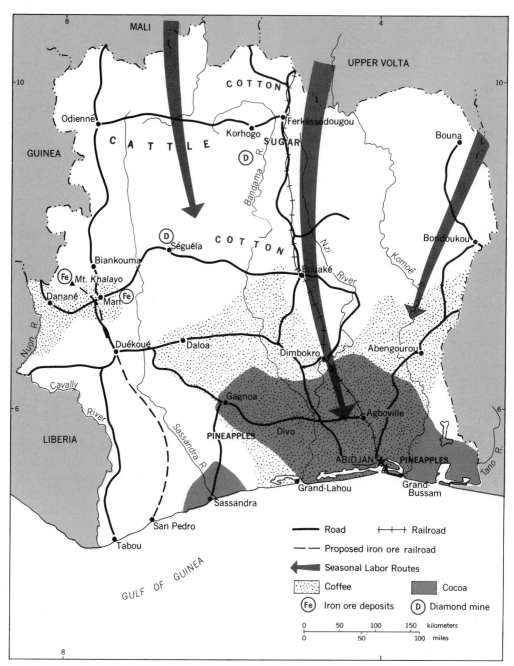

FIGURE 12-1 *Economic map of Ivory Coast.*

and timber and timber products headed the export list. The country, however, depends on a system of price supports for coffee instituted by France and Ivorian farmers frequently receive twice the world market price. This was the situation that led the leaders of the Ivory Coast to desire continued close association with France when the question of independence was under discussion.

In recognition of the vulnerability of the country's economy, depending as it does on crops whose world price varies greatly, agricultural diversification has been encouraged. Pineapples, bananas, and cotton have shown considerable promise and are now the principal exports after wood, coffee, and cocoa. Sugar production is being expanded in the northern regions around Ferkessédougou to meet domestic requirements. Livestock production is foremost among the agricultural priorities with the aim of reducing the country's dependence on the highly irregular flow of cattle from Upper Volta, Mali, and Niger. New areas are being opened up in the north as trypanosomiasis and other diseases are brought under control.

Ivory Coast has benefited from its coastal location, although access was initially difficult because of the straight coastline, many offshore sandbars, and constant silting of river mouths and artificial harbors by longshore currents. For many years the largest port was Port Bouet located on a sandbar across the Ebrie Lagoon from Abidjan. In 1950, the Vidri canal was cut through this bar, and the large sheltered port of Abidjan was developed. The canal was widened in 1975, and new deep-water quays were opened to make Abidjan the largest and busiest port in West Africa.

Abidjan is a thriving modern city whose population has grown from a mere 46,000 in 1945, to a modest 185,000 in 1959, to over 700,000 in 1976. It has replaced Dakar as the largest manufacturing city in francophone West Africa, and its industries include textiles, chemicals, oil refining, auto assembly,

engineering, and food processing. Its markets are expanding both locally and nationally, and its economic hinterland includes the interior states of Upper Volta and Mali. Abidjan is the coastal terminus of the nation's only railway, a line that runs north through Bouaké and Ferkessédougou to Ouagadougou, capital of Upper Volta. While crossing several agroeconomic regions and passing through some densely settled areas, the line operates well below capacity and suffers from increasing competition from truck traffic. It lacks good feeder roads and branch lines, and other than Bouaké it serves no industrial town.

Communications have always posed problems for the Ivorians, yet transport development has never been a high government priority. The southern forests, which today provide the main exports, long formed serious obstacles to the development of an adequate road system. Poor harbors retarded development of the southwest, and even today only two small ports serve this vast area. Sassandra handles most of the region's timber, pineapple, and banana exports, although producers prefer to truck their produce to Abidjan where facilities are better. The second port is San Pedro, recently enlarged to handle the ever-increasing exports of timber and wood products and iron ore, which is being mined at Mount Khalayo close to the Liberian border. This one-billion-ton medium-grade iron body is being developed by Mitsubishi of Japan, the British Steel Corporation, Usinor of France, and Hoogoners of Holland. The ore will be transported by a new 200-mi (322 km) railway to San Pedro for pelletizing before shipment overseas. A second iron ore deposit may be opened at Mount Tia, some 15 mi (24 km) from Khalayo. The project marks a revitalization of the mining industry, once dominated by bauxite, but since 1970 only a minor contributor to the national economy. Considerable reserves of manganese and copper are known to exist.

Ivory Coast needs to overcome regional

Logs from Ivory Coast's southern forests awaiting shipment from the port of Abidjan. (UN)

differences in development and attitudes. The cash crops have always come mainly from the south. In most aspects of development—education, social services, political consciousness, and escape from subsistence agriculture—the northern savanna has lagged behind the forest south. Bouaké (100,000), a market center benefiting from its location on the railroad, on a main motor road to Abidjan, and near the forest-savanna transition zone, is the most important urban agglomeration in the interior, but its small size, in spite of its advantageous position, reflects the limited needs of its region. There is some hope that the cultivation of cotton will improve the position of the north.

At the time of independence, Ivory Coast chose to rely on free enterprise and foreign investment to accelerate economic growth, and it adopted a monetary system in common with other francophone territories, which ruled out inflationary policies. The result has been a phenomenal record of economic growth and development. Since independence the G.D.P. has grown, in real terms, at an annual rate of 8 to 10 percent

(O'Connor, 1972). Growth has been recorded in all sectors of the economy, but especially manufacturing, which has emphasized import substitution. One-fifth of the G.D.P. is accounted for by manufacturing, the highest in the former French West African realm. In the 1960s, light manufacturing and agricultural processing grew by more than 20 percent per annum, and foreign private investors, mainly French, provided most of the capital and technological know-how, with small-scale, rather than large-scale, prestigious projects receiving priority.

Export earnings have increased on average about 12 percent per annum since independence. Exports have diversified, mainly in the agricultural sector, and the country enjoys a favorable balance of trade, with the main markets being France, the United States, and the EEC countries. Trade with adjoining francophone states is small but expanding.

French presence in Ivory Coast is obvious. There were twice as many Frenchmen in the country in 1975 than when independence was granted, and Europeans still hold key positions in industry, and provide technical, administrative, and economic expertise. President Houphouet-Boigny wants greater Ivorianization, but is reluctant to force the issue. Abidjan has been called an "island of prosperity" created for the comfort of Europeans, and critics claim that the country is trading its future prosperity and independence for rapid growth in the short term (O'Connor, 1972). Rapid industrialization has also brought thousands of Ivorians from rural areas in search of employment in Abidjan, Bouaké, Gagnoa, Abengourou, and other urban centers, but nonagricultural jobs are not increasing as fast as urban demands.

Unlike Guinea, which severed its ties with France in 1958, Ivory Coast has cultivated its French connections and has succeeded in attracting much new investment to the country. The country's political stability has, to a large extent, been due to the economic growth that has resulted from this strategy. President Houphouet-Boigny has not only advocated strong links with France, continued support of the Entente, OCAM, and the CEAO, but he has also proposed dialogue between black African states and South Africa. He is vehemently anticommunist, and abhors radical governments such as that of neighboring Guinea, and he has chosen to keep Ivory Coast a passive member of the OAU. Given its economic performance to date, and the strong economic ties with France and the West in general, Ivory Coast appears to have a brighter future than most West African states if the gulf between the "haves" and "have-nots" can be closed.

Guinea: The Distant Relative

Having been a part of the French West African Federation for over a half century, Guinea, in 1958, was the only prospective Community state to refuse further participation in the French framework. This was the result of a variety of political and economic, as well as historical, factors and caused the immediate cessation of French aid (then amounting to some $17 million annually), the removal of many essential facilities, and the immediate departure of over half the white population, numbering more than 7000.

Guinea withdrew from the Franc Zone and declined membership in all major monetary, trade, and cultural agreements with the francophone group, and turned first to the Soviet Union, and later to the People's Republic of China for technical assistance and models of social and economic reform. It has remained ideologically and economically distant from its francophone neighbors and has adopted a socialist economy with direct state control of production and consumption in every sector except mining. Mining is the most prosperous sector, and is being developed by American, Russian, Yugoslav, and Swiss concerns.

Guinea is a land of variety, physiographically, ethnically, and economically, and it is a country of considerable potential. Its physiography is dominated by the highland mass of the Futa Jallon, rising several thousand feet and consisting of a dissected plateau with prominent peaks and deep valleys. The Futa Jallon forms the central backbone of the country, beyond which the land begins its gentle decline into the Niger Basin. In the north, elevations of over 5000 ft (1525 m) are sustained, and southward, the mountains (here referred to as the Guinea Highlands and mainly crystalline), are shared by Sierra Leone and Liberia, and so are the iron ores they contain as, for instance, in Mount Nimba on the Liberian border (Fig. 12-2).

The highlands support cattle rearing and plantation agriculture of coffee and ba-

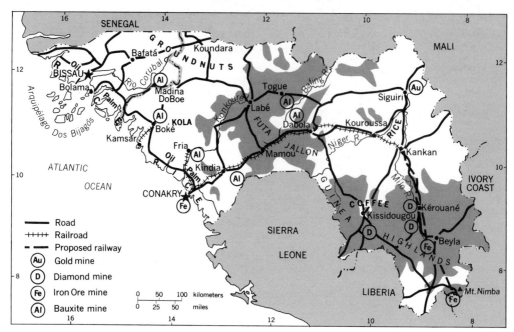

FIGURE 12-2 *Economic map of Guinea and Guinea Bissau.*

nanas. They draw a large amount of precipitation from the air rising along their slopes, concentrated especially during the months of July and August but lasting from March to December; soil erosion is a major problem. Conakry receives some 170 in. (4318 mm) annually, but in the lee of the mountains the totals drop rapidly, and savanna conditions prevail. The coastal plain, less than 50 mi (80 km) in width, is hot and humid, being low in elevation and wedged between the swampy coast and the sudden slopes of the Futa Jallon. In spite of its character, the plain is densely populated and supports the cultivation of a variety of subsistence crops, including rice, corn, palm, and kola nuts. In the vicinity of Conakry, the coastal plain narrows on account of the jutting ridge upon which the town is located, and there some banana cultivation is carried on.

Prior to independence, bananas were the leading export, but the industry received a serious blow when France refused to purchase the harvest after the negative vote of 1958 and when many European planters withdrew. Pineapples, coffee, citrus, and palm kernels are all grown commercially, but Guinea has experienced difficulty finding markets, and controlling distribution. Some Guinean farmers find it more profitable to smuggle their produce over the borders into Sierra Leone and Liberia than to market it through state channels. One-third the coffee crop is brought out of the country illicitly. The 1973–1978 development plan places great emphasis on the reorganization of agriculture to control this loss of revenue, and to make Guinea more self-sufficient in foods.

While agriculture remains the principal occupation for the 4.6 million Guineans, mining has become the country's most important foreign currency earner and the principal contributor to the G.D.P. (Table 12-2). Bauxite and iron ore are the principal mineral resources, and they could provide the revenues needed to transform the national economy. It is most unlikely that the mining centers themselves will become industrial growth points; that is a rarity in

Table 12-2 COMPARATIVE DATA (latest estimates)

	Benin	Guinea	Ivory Coast	Togo
Area (sq mi)	43,383	94,926	124,500	21,622
Population (1000s)	3200	4610	5550	2350
Crude birth rate	50.9	46.6	45.6	50.9
Crude death rate	25.5	22.9	22.7	25.5
Infant mortality	149	216	164	163
Percent urban	18.0	19.5	20.4	13.5
Percent labor force in agriculture	84	86	86	78
Literacy rate	24	5–10	22	8–12
GNP per capita ($)	100	125	320	135
Major exports	Oil palm Cotton	Bauxite Aluminum Coffee	Wood Coffee Cocoa	Phosphate Cocoa

SOURCES. *Population Reference Bureau (1975), USAID, and Government Reports.*

Africa. Instead, they will remain spatially small specialized units of production linked by rail to Conakry and their overseas markets. Few benefits are likely to be diffused from the mines into the local regions.

Gold has long been mined from the Siguiri region in the northeast (Fig. 12-2), although production is now negligible. Diamonds, mainly of industrial quality, are mined in the valleys of the southeast; but considerable revenues are lost because of illicit traffic into Sierra Leone and Liberia. Neither gold nor diamonds has had much regional impact. Iron ore was mined just 5 mi (8 km) from Conakry between 1953 and 1967, but when operating costs soared, and richer and more profitable ores in Liberia and Mauritania came into production, the mine was closed.

In the southeastern interior, high-grade iron ores have been exploited since 1974. The Nimba deposit, an extension of that in Liberia and with reserves estimated at 600 million tons, is being mined by companies from Japan, Spain, Yugoslavia, and Belgium. By 1980, annual production is scheduled to exceed 30 million tons. An even larger deposit is being mined 80 mi (130 km) further north in the mountains near Beyla. Relative isolation from the coast, and the proliferation of iron mining in West

Africa during the 1960s delayed their exploitation. Until railways are laid to connect with the Conakry-Kankan line, the Nimba ores will be exported through Buchanan, Liberia, the closest outlet to the mines.

Guinea possesses 30 percent of the world's known bauxite reserves, and since 1952 has been exporting bauxite to France and the United States. Production in 1973 approached 3 million tons, and if current projections are realized, Guinea may become one of the largest producers in Africa. The Friguia (Fria) deposit, 90 mi (145 km) north of Conakry, was the first to be mined on a large scale, and its aluminum processing plant was producing almost a million tons each year by the mid-1970s. Following several years of negotiations involving the World Bank, USAID, the Guinean government and American companies, a new mine came into production at Boké in 1973. When fully operational, it will have an annual production of 9 million tons, and Guinea will receive 65 percent of net profits. Several Arab states have financed an aluminum smelter at Boké, which will handle half the mine's output, the rest being exported in its raw state.

A smaller, but nevertheless substantial deposit (44 million tons) is being mined at Debele (Kinia) by the Soviet Union. A short railway was built, and harbor facilities were extended in Conakry to handle the output estimated at one million tons per year. Agreements have also been signed with Yugoslav and Swiss companies for the exploitation of the Dabola and Togue deposits respectively, located high in the Futa Jallon north of the Conakry-Kankan railway (Fig. 12-2).

This mineral activity required Guinea to improve its grossly inadequate and poorly maintained transport system. The 375-mi (603 km) narrow-gauge railway from Conakry to Kankan, whose principal freight was once bananas, is being upgraded at an estimated cost of $555 million to handle the bauxite concerns in the Futa Jallon. It may later be extended across the border to Bamako, capital of Mali, and become that landlocked state's principal outlet to the sea. A new line from the remote southeastern iron ore workings of Nimba may be built to Conakry, while the Boké mine north of the capital required new roads and a railway to the port of Kamsar (Fig. 12-2). Since much of the country is mountainous, transport is difficult and both maintenance and construction costs are high. On the other hand, the combination of broken terrain and heavy rainfall has given Guinea tremendous hydroelectric potential. This is being realized, largely with Soviet and Arab aid, and ties into the mining sector.

This spectacular investment in minerals, which should make Guinea one of the richest West African states, was not accomplished without difficulty. Having withdrawn from the French fold, Guinea had the task of seeking foreign support without prior experience. Aid has come from several sources, including the communist bloc, the United States, and Canada. Most investment

has been in mineral-related activities, although Guinea has attracted some foreign investment to its manufacturing sector that is presently limited to processing local raw materials and import substitution.

Guinea has enjoyed neither economic nor ideological support from its neighbors. Indeed, following the break with France and the francophone group, Guinea followed an almost isolationist course. In 1970, a force of Guinean dissidents and Portuguese troops lead a commando raid from Guinea-Bissau, which at the time was fighting its own liberation wars against Portugal. Most neighboring states were accused by President Sekou Touré of aiding and abetting anti-Guinean sentiment, which resulted in Guinea's withdrawal from the Organization of Senegal River States—an organization composed of Senegal, Mali, Mauritania, and Guinea for the development of the Senegal Basin—and further retreat into isolation. While rapprochement with Senegal and Ivory Coast has failed, Guinea has improved its relationships with Sierra Leone, Liberia, and Mali. Furthermore, Guinea has enthusiastically supported the independent government of Guinea Bissau.

Guinea has demonstrated that it is possible to sever the umbilical cord, yet survive in a competitive world. It has broadened its technical assistance base, diversified its economy, improved its infrastructure, and achieved a favorable balance of trade. On the other hand, the vast majority of its people (85 percent) live at the subsistence level; per capita food production is declining; its infant mortality rate is the highest in West Africa; the per capita income is only $125; and its literacy rate is among the lowest in Africa (Table 12-2). Material benefits from this investment have yet to reach most Guineans.

Togo and Benin: Partners in Poverty

The two small elongated states of Togo (21,622 sq mi or 56,000 sq km) and Benin

(43,484 sq mi or 112,624 sq km), wedged between Ghana and Nigeria, have essentially

Guinea-Bissau

After 500 years of Portuguese rule, and ten years of guerrilla warfare, Guinea-Bissau (13,948 sq mi) gained its freedom in September, 1974. Under the leadership of Amilcar Cabral, the PAIGC (African Party for the Independence of Guinea and Cape Verde) instilled a sense of nationalism among Bissauans and led a successful but costly war of liberation against oppressive Portuguese colonialism. The low-lying terrain, forests, swamps, meandering rivers, and wide estuaries that prevail in all but the eastern interior, were assets for the liberation forces.

Under Portuguese rule, few advances were made in the social, economic and political spheres. Education and manufacturing were not encouraged, and few roads and no railways were built. A settler population did not exist, and almost no Portuguese remain. Since independence, 90,000 refugees have returned from Guinea and Senegal, increasing the population to about 650,000. The main ethnic groups are the Balante (30 percent), Fulani (20 percent), Mandingo (13 percent), and Mandayiko (14 percent). Non-indigenous groups include Syrian and Lebanese traders, and Cape Verdian *mesticos*.

All land is now nationalized, and every effort is to be made to revitalize the agricultural economy, devastated by war. Rice, maize, cassava, beans, and sweet potatoes are the staple crops, and small quantities of groundnuts and palm oil are exported. There is no mineral production (large bauxite reserves exist in the Boe area), and industry is negligible. Bissau (70,000), the capital, is the only town of any size.

similar physical environments. Sandbars and coastal lagoons give way to low-lying plains and plateaus, and eventually to the southwest-northeast trending Togo-Atakora Ranges, which reach their highest peaks (3250ft–990m) in western Togo (Fig. 12-3). Although deeply dissected and well-forested in the south, they are densely populated and produce almost all of Togo's coffee and cocoa. Climatically, the coastal belt falls into the anomolous dry zone that extends west to Accra, yet is sufficiently moist to support the all-important oil palm. Most of the region has a savanna climate, but north of the Atakora Range, rainfall diminishes sharply and becomes highly variable in the vicinity of the Niger River.

Togo and Benin were carved out of West Africa to suit French, German, and British interests. In the 1890s, France conquered the Adja kingdom of Port Novo and established the colony of Dahomey (which remained the name until 1975), while Germany occupied Togoland, a smaller sliver of land of diverse peoples to its west. Following World War I, Togoland became a League of Nations mandate, divided for administrative purposes between France and Britain. British Togo was administered as though it were a part of the Gold Coast. French Togo was established as a Class C mandate, and, except for a brief period of incorporation into Dahomey during the period between the two world wars, remained a separate political entity.

In 1946, the mandate system was superseded by the trusteeship system of the United Nations, and France and Britain continued their administration. In 1956, the inhabitants of French Togo voted in a plebi-

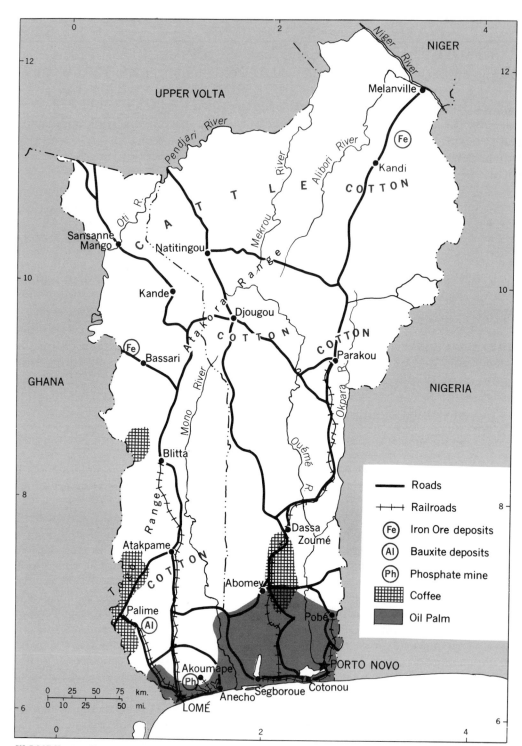

FIGURE 12-3 *Economic map of Togo and Benin.*

scite to become an autonomous republic within the French Union, and France attempted to tie the Trust Territory more closely to Paris than the Trusteeship Agreement appeared to permit. However, the United Nations refused to end the trusteeship status. At the same time, the inhabitants of British Togo voted in favor of union with the Gold Coast. Both Togo and Dahomey received independence from France in 1960.

It is important to recognize the individual contributions made by both Germany and France in the development of the present-day Republic of Togo. During its brief period of rule, Germany established a good railway and road system, focusing on Lomé and its harbor. The Germans introduced crops and developed the economy, founded an educational, judicial, and administrative system, and made considerable progress in the unification of the country. Togo became Germany's model colony (Darkoh, 1968). The French, however, did not continue the rapid pace of development initiated by Germany, and for several decades the country floated on what the Germans had founded. It was not until the immediate preindependence period that Togo's infrastructure was expanded and its exports, especially cocoa, were increased. (See Table 12-2 for basic data.)

In Dahomey (now Benin), France's performance was equally poor, except in the field of education. Large numbers of Dahomeyans received a secondary education, and later they held government positions in several parts of the Federation. Following independence, however, this educated elite was replaced by local civil servants and was forced to return to Dahomey where jobs were not to be found. As in Ivory Coast, France favored the southern region, but less was achieved in commercial agriculture, forestry, and communications. Today, both countries are troubled by political instability, economic stagnation, and strong regional economic imbalances, due in large measure to this colonial experience.

Benin has suffered from extreme political instability since independence, there being five military coups in the first nine years. Benin's ethnic diversity and unhealthy economy, reflected in the chronic inability to balance the budget, largely explains this instability. The Fon, Adja, and Yoruba form the largest ethnic groups in the south, and dominate most branches of government and the cash economy, while the less numerous Baribas, Peuls, and Sombas of the north claim they have been discriminated against. Most southerners are subsistence farmers, and a small minority participates in the export economy, producing oil palm products and some cocoa. Oil palm supplies 60 percent of the country's annual exports, although cotton from the northern region is reducing this dominance.

Manufacturing is limited to small-scale processing of primary products for export, or import substitution of consumer goods and is concentrated in the capital Porto Novo (110,000), and the major port, Cotonou (185,000). There are still only about 40,000 wage and salary earners in a population of more than 3 million, and half of these work for the government, not in manufacturing and commerce. Cotonou has a modern deep-water harbor, and is connected by the main line rail to Parakou, the largest northern town, and by two shorter lines to Pobe and Segboroue. It handles a fourth of Niger's foreign trade, and if the railway is extended from Parakou to Dosso (Niger), and on to the Arlit uranium deposits, which seems likely, Cotonou may well experience further, but not substantial growth. It is unlikely that the northern region—where cattle, cotton and groundnuts are the major sources of income—would benefit from this extension unless feeder roads were built, and marketing systems improved.

The spatial pattern of Togo's development is very similar to that in Benin. Most

Small subsistence farms in cleared patches of forest in the Massif Cabrais of southern Togo. Note terraces to reduce erosion. (UN)

of the exports, capital accumulation, wealth, urban populations, and political decision makers are concentrated in the south and form the core, while the majority of the country comprises the periphery. The country's three short railways converge on Lomé (230,000), the capital and primate city (Fig. 12-3). They draw the resources and peoples to the south, and play little role in dispersing goods, ideas, and technology from the core to the periphery.

Lomé's manufacturing, like that of Porto Novo and Cotonou, is dominated by import substitution and agricultural processing. A large cement plant was completed in 1975 to serve the five Entente countries and Ghana, and the oil refinery, opened in 1976, is supplied by Nigeria and Gabon. A few miles northeast, phosphate is mined at Akoumape and railed to the coast for export. Phosphate provides almost half of Togo's foreign revenues, and, since coming into production, it has substantially corrected the balance of payments problem.

Togo lacks industrial towns and cities away from the coast. A few small commercial centers and agricultural collection depots are located along the railways, but none is a real growth point. Palimé (35,000) is a railhead for the cocoa farmers of the southwest, and Blitta serves cotton interests north of Lomé. The northern half of Togo lacks railways, good roads, and much profitable commercial farming other than groundnut production, and it is poorly integrated into the national economy. The country is seeking a market for its vast (1000 million tons) high grade iron ores, which, if developed, will require an extension of the railway from Blitta. As in Benin, the population is predominantly rural (86 percent), and farms are generally small, intensively cultivated, and devoted primarily to subsistence crops.

As members of the Franc Zone and other francophone organizations, both Togo and Benin receive technical and financial aid from France. Togo has purposely kept this to a minimum, and has participated only peripherally in the Entente and OCAM. It chose not to join the West African Economic Community (CEAO), an exclusively francophone organization, but is now a member of ECOWAS along with Ghana, Nigeria, and other nonfrancophone states. It already receives power from Akosombo (Ghana), and almost 100,000 of its citizens are seasonal workers in Ghana each year.

Similarly, Benin has shown an increasing tendency to loosen its ties with the institutions that are a legacy of French rule. Its trade, like Togo's, is still primarily with France, but that may lessen since the Lomé Convention presents new possibilities. It is seeking to increase its economic links with both Nigeria and Togo after several years of almost no interchange. The problems of development in Togo and Benin are shared by many other small African states seeking higher standards of living for their citizens.

Bibliography

Ajayi, J. F. A. and M. Crowder (eds.). *History of West Africa*. Vol. 2. New York: Longmans, 1974.

Barbour, K. M. "Industrialization in West Africa," *Journal of Modern African Studies*, Vol. 10, No. 3 (October, 1972), pp. 357–82.

Church, R. J. H. *West Africa*. 7th edition. London: Longmans, 1974.

Darkoh, M. "Togoland Under the Germans," *Nigerian Geographical Journal*, Vol. 11 (1968), pp. 153–68.

Davidson, B. "Guinea-Bissau and the Cape Verde Islands: The Transition from War to Independence," *Africa Today*, Vol. 21, No. 4 (1974), pp. 5–20.

Hopkins, A. G. *An Economic History of West Africa*. New York: Columbia University Press, 1973.

Hoyle, B. S. and D. Hilling (eds.). *Seaports and Development in Tropical Africa*. London: MacMillan and Co., Ltd., 1970.

O'Connor, M. "Guinea and the Ivory Coast: Contrasts in Economic Development," *Journal of Modern African Studies*, Vol. 10, No. 3 (October, 1972), pp. 409–26.

Ogundana, B. "Seaport Development: Multi-National Cooperation in West Africa," *Journal of Modern African Studies*, Vol. 12, No. 3 (September, 1974), pp. 395–407.

Peterec, R. J. *Dakar and West African Economic Development*. New York: Columbia University Press, 1967.

Sigal, E. "Ivory Coast: Booming Economy, Political Calm," *Africa Report*, Vol. 15, (April, 1970), pp. 18–21.

Swindell, K. "Industrialization in Guinea," *Geography*. Vol. 54 (November, 1969), pp. 456–58.

Tice, R. D. "Administrative Structure, Ethnicity, and Nation-Building in the Ivory Coast," *Journal of Modern African Studies*, Vol. 12, No. 2 (June, 1974), pp. 211–29.

White, H. P. "Dahomey: The Geographical Basis of an African State," *Tijdscrift voor Economische en Sociale Geografie*. Vol. 57 (1966), pp. 61–68.

THIRTEEN

From Senegal to Chad lies France's legacy across interior West Africa, including Mauritania, Mali, Niger, and Upper Volta. Once territorial divisions of France's West and Equatorial African empire, these states form a continuous block stretching 2800 miles (4500 km) from Dakar in the west to the Darfur Plateau in eastern Chad (Fig. 13-1). They extend over 20 degrees of latitude from southern Chad to northern Mauritania, mostly across the Sahara Desert and West Africa's troubled *Sahel*. Their combined area of over 2 million sq mi (5.2 million sq km) is equal to two-thirds the continental United States, Chad alone being almost twice the size of Texas. Their combined population, however, is only 28 million, or one-third the Nigerian total, but in view of the low and variable rainfall, the limited agricultural and pasture land, the enormous livestock population (280 million population equivalents), and the sparsity of development resources

and industry, it is doubtful whether the land can and should support any more.

The six states form a distinct region with similar ecological characteristics, development problems and prospects, and colonial histories. From 1968 to 1973 they shared in the worst drought in living memory, a drought that devasted the local economies and brought widespread hunger, disease and death to man and beast alike. Recurrent drought is a characteristic, and the drought of the early 1970s was unusual only in its severity and the attention it received beyond Africa. Since drought figures so prominently in the behavior of millions of nomads and sedentary farmers, and plays a central role in the economic policies and development prospects of all six states, it receives special attention in this chapter.

Physiographically, the region has considerable diversity, but given the vastness of the area this is not readily apparent. Much

THE DESERT TIER: PROBLEMS IN THE INTERIOR

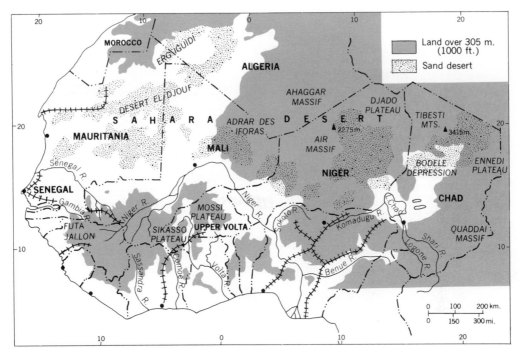

FIGURE 13-1 *West Africa. Physical features.*

of the region is a rocky and sandy plateau, lower in the west and south, and higher in the north and east (Fig. 13-1). In west-central Chad the land rises from 800 ft (250 m) in the Lake Chad Basin to over 11,000 ft (3300 m) in the volcanic Tibesti Mountains in the north, and to over 5000 ft in the Quaddai Massif along the eastern border. In northern Niger, the Air Massif rises abruptly from the surrounding desert plains to heights of 6200 ft (1900 m), while in adjacent Mali, the Adrar des Iforas reach some 2300 feet (700 m) above sea level. Elsewhere, the land is gently undulating to flat, broken only occasionally by isolated hills, dry river courses, and a few steep escarpments. The Niger River system dominates the region from western Mali to western Niger, while the Senegal flows west from the Futa Jallon to the Atlantic, and the Volta drains south across Upper Volta to the Guinea Coast. Much of Chad, Niger, Mali, and Mauritania has only interior drainage.

Climatically, this West African sub-region falls into three distinct latitudinal belts (Fig. 13-2). North of the 4-in. (100 mm) isohyet, which runs from central Mauritania eastwards to central Chad, lies true desert where temperatures and evapo-transpiration rates are high, rainfall is low and irregular, and the vegetation cover too meager to support permanent grazing. To its south lies the Sahel, or "border" region, where the average annual rainfall increases southward to the 24 in. (600 mm) isohyet, but where rainfall is highly variable, yet generally sufficient to support short grasses, acacias, and thorn scrub. Along the southern border of the six-state region lies the savanna.

While three separate climatic regions exist, each with its distinct agropastoral potentials and population densities, the basis of survival in the Sahel is the interdependence between desert and savanna, pastoral and arable economies, and herder and farmer. It

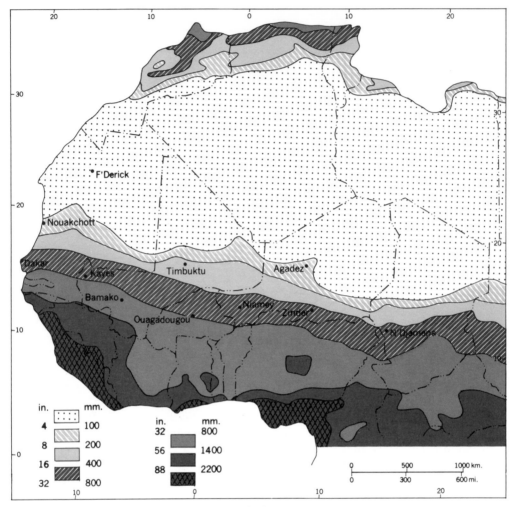

FIGURE 13-2 *West Africa. Average annual precipitation.*

is this interdependence of peoples and economies, so critical for the survival of the region's ecology and people, that is currently being put to the test.

Disaster in the Sahel

The Sahel became almost a household word in the Western World in 1974 following reports of five years of unusually light rain, widespread crop failure, the starvation of possibly 20 million cattle, 12 million sheep, goats, and camels, and the starvation of 200,000 people from disease, thirst, and malnutrition. Television programs, and newspaper and magazine articles portrayed emaciated children suffering from malnutrition standing pitifully before their desert shelters or refugee camps, surrounded by dying cattle and parched landscapes. Fields and pastures lay bare except for helpless herds of emaciated cattle and carcasses, and in the dry river beds or wadis, women and

This lean-to represents home to this nomadic Peul family, camped on the outskirts of Tahoua, Niger along with hundreds of other families displaced by years of drought in the Sahel. (UN)

children dug deep into the sands to retrieve those precious buckets of water. At the refugee centers, some with 60,000 and more displaced persons, trucks and vans belonging to the International Red Cross, UNFAO, USAID, OXFAM, and other relief agencies, unloaded bags of powdered milk, sorghum, millet, rice, and medicines. Such were the scenes, but how common were they? While the tragedy will never be fully documented, there is ample evidence to suggest the drought extended across Sahelian West Africa and into the Sudan, Ethiopia, Somalia, and Kenya, and that perhaps in all, more than 25 million persons were directly affected. In the six West African Sahelian states, possibly half the population was afflicted.

Drought conditions varied from place to place, and generally were at their worst in 1972 and 1973 (Dalby and Church, 1973). After an unusually wet period from 1962–1967, when rainfall often averaged 20–30 percent above the mean, a mild drought occurred in 1968, followed by five years of abnormally low precipitation. The following rainfall data from Niger illustrate the conditions. Tillabery, a river town north of Niamey, reports a 30-year (1940–1970) mean annual rainfall of 19.2 in. (488 mm). Rainfall in 1971 and 1972 were 10.2 in. (259 mm) and 14.3 in. (364 mm), respectively. Miradi, Niger's third largest town just north of the Nigerian border, has a 30-year mean of 24.8 in. (630 mm), but its rainfall in 1971 and 1972 was 12.5 in. (318 mm) and 11.3 in.

(288 mm), respectively. For Agadez, an oasis town toward the northern edge of the Sahel, the corresponding figures are 6.3 in. (160 mm), 3.7 in. (93 mm), and 3.0 in. (72 mm). Four or five years of below average rainfall and frequent high winds, combined with overgrazing, means a reduced vegetation cover, destruction of the root system, and finally widespread soil erosion.

The severity of the drought can be seen from the following stock losses: Chad 70 percent, Mali 55 percent, Mauritania 70 percent, and Niger 80 percent. The cattle population in Chad totaled 4.7 million in 1972, and under 3 million a year later. In northern Mali and Chad up to 90 percent of the livestock were lost, and it will take from 5 to 10 years for the herds to regain their original size. The loss of livestock is not only a personal catastrophe to the nomad whose whole life is geared to the raising of animals, but a national disaster to those states whose economy is dependent on the sale of animals and animal products. Such products figure prominently in each of the Sahelian states.

Agricultural output also showed drastic declines. In Senegal, where groundnuts (peanuts) normally supply 80 percent of the foreign exchange, the 1972 output totaled only 540,000 tons as compared with 920,000 tons in the previous year. The drop was even more dramatic in Niger where it was reported the drought reduced 1973's output to under 20,000 tons while in 1972 some 204,000 tons were produced, and in 1967, the peak year, almost 300,000 tons were harvested. Mali's grain production dropped by 50 percent in 1972, and the millet harvest in the St. Louis region of Senegal plummeted from 63,000 tons in 1968 to 1000 tons four years later. Similar declines were recorded for cotton, cow peas, and other crops across the Sahel.

Crop failures, livestock losses, dried-up wells and river courses forced thousands of refugees to towns and relief centers. Nouak-

Weeding a field of Guinea corn in the Sahelian zone of Niger. (UN/FAO)

chott, capital of Mauritania, whose population in 1971 was 45,000, had over 120,000 within the next year. At Mopti, central Mali, the population swelled from 55,000 to 110,000, and in neither town was there adequate housing and water. In Niger, at the height of the drought some 300,000 refugees out of a total population of 4.3 million were registered at official relief centers, and probably twice that number sought refuge elsewhere.

Death rates, especially infant mortality and child mortality rates, which normally are among the highest in the world, rose as a result of the aggravated conditions. Reliable data are not available, but during "normal" years, infant mortality rates range from 159 per 1000 in Senegal to 204 per 1000 in Upper Volta and, on the average, half the children die before their tenth year (Table 13-1). Disease and malnutrition accompanied the drought.

The extent and seriousness of the drought were not formally acknowledged by the six governments concerned until the middle of 1973, partly because of insufficient verifiable evidence, but primarily because the governments were reluctant to admit their inabilities to handle the crises. Once the disaster had been officially proclaimed, overseas relief efforts intensified. The United States contribution for the fiscal years 1973, 1974, 1975 totaled $214.7 million, of which $120.4 million were for grains and the balance for technical assistance, equipment, airlifts, and medical supplies. U.S. contributions by state for 1973 are shown in Table 13-2. Grain contributions in 1973 included the United States (256,000 tons), EEC (110,000), France (70,000), People's Republic of China (50,000), Federal Republic of Germany (32,000), Canada (26,000), and the USSR (10,000). Many countries (including Nigeria and Zaire) made cash contributions (Sheets and Morris, pp. 129–30).

Relief efforts were hampered by poor communications, inadequate local distribu-

Table 13-1 SELECTED DATA: SAHELIAN STATES (latest available data)

	Chad	Mali	Mauritania	Niger	Senegal	Upper Volta
Area (000s sq mi)	496	479	398	489	76	106
Population (1977 est. in millions)	4.3	5.9	1.8	4.8	4.7	6.4
Population growth rate percent	2.4	2.4	2.3	2.7	2.4	2.2
Infant mortality rate	175	188	169	200	159	204
Life expectancy in years	40	38	46	38	44	36
Percent pop. urban	8	13	8	4	29	4
Percent pop. engaged in agriculture	85–90	83–87	85–90	85–90	70	88
People per doctor	63,900	37,100	25,900	54,100	14,500	92,800
GNP per capita in U.S. $	85	70	175	110	285	70
Literacy (%)	5–10	5	1–5	5	5–10	6
Primary school enrollment as percent of 5–14 age group	18	15	12	8	26	7
Secondary school enrollment as percent of 15–19 age group	3	2	4	1	17	2
Electricity production (KWH per capita per year)	13	9	65	12	89	6
Miles improved road per 1000 sq mi	1	10	2	5	37	26
Mile of railway per 1000 sq mi	—	1	1	—	8	5
Population equivalents (in millions)	56.1	68.1	37.0	55.6	30.2	31.8

SOURCE. *Data from Population Reference Bureau, AID, and U.N. documents.*

Table 13-2 SAHEL DROUGHT ASSISTANCE, 1973 (U.S. Government Assistance only)

	FOOD		NONFOOD	TOTAL
	Metric Tons	$	$	$
Chad	8,000	1,027,000	195,000	1,222,000
Mali	55,000	8,095,000	2,494,000	10,589,000
Mauritania	33,000	4,187,000	300,500	4,487,500
Niger	61,000	9,866,000	580,000	10,446,000
Senegal	45,000	4,748,000	244,491	4,992,491
Upper Volta	35,000	5,742,000	318,000	6,060,000
Regional	19,000	3,466,000	127,664	3,593,664
U.N. Contribution			300,000	300,000
Reserve			137,345	137,345
Total	256,000	37,131,000	4,697,000	41,828,000

SOURCE. *Sheets and Morris, 1974, p. 130.*

tion systems, corruption, and the high cost of transport. More money was spent on airlifting fuel and equipment required by the relief operations, than on airlifting grains and medicines. Grain rotted on the docks in Dakar, Abidjan, and Lagos, and at transshipment centers such as Maiduguri, Ouagadougou, Rosso, Niamey, and Koulikoro (Rosenthal, 1974). Grains unloaded in interior railheads could not be transported by truck over district roads made impassable by summer rains. Rains, badly needed by the farmer, were a curse to relief agencies.

Climatic Change or Human Error?

The evidence of distress in the Sahel is easier to perceive than the underlying causes of the disaster. Social scientists and climatologists may not agree on these causes, but most recognize they are both naturally and man induced. Reid Bryson has suggested that changes in weather patterns in the Sahel may be part of a more permanent southward shift of the monsoon belt in the northern hemisphere (Bryson, 1973). This implies recurrent failures of the summer rains and possibly more permanent aridity. It is theorized that climatic change is instigated by increased amounts in carbon dioxide in the atmosphere that increase the surface-to-upper atmosphere temperature gradient. An increase in particulate matter in the atmosphere decreases this gradient, but more so at the poles than along the equator, hence increasing the equator-to-pole temperature gradient at the surface. The increase in these

two temperature gradients provides the basis for a southward drift of the monsoon belt, and consequently less rainfall along the northern fringe of this belt. The level of particulate matter in the atmosphere depends not only on the amount of volcanic activity, industrial pollutants, and dust from mechanized agricultural practices, but also on dust and ash emitted from slash-and-burn agricultural practices and cattle movements, both of which are common in the Sahel and adjoining regions.

There is ample evidence in written records and archaeological sites that rainfall amounts have varied dramatically in the past (Baier and Lovejoy, 1976). During the fifteenth and sixteenth centuries, when the Songhai Empire was at its height, more humid conditions prevailed that permitted higher densities of man and cattle in the Niger valley. An eleven-year drought oc-

Grain from the United States being off-loaded and bagged at Dakar, Senegal. The U.S. was one of several states sending food and medical supplies to drought-torn interior West Africa during the 1970's. Poor road and rail links between the coast and the interior hindered relief efforts. (World Bank)

curred in the middle of the sixteenth century, and another at the turn of the seventeenth. A seven-year drought occurred sometime between 1690 and 1720, and there were severe famines in either the 1740s or 1750s, and again in the 1790s.

According to local chronicles and travelers' accounts, much of the Sudano-Sahel region recorded favorable rains throughout the nineteenth century. Lake Chad was at its highest recorded level in 1874, but 40 years later it was at its lowest. Then the mean depth was only one to two meters, the greatest depth being only four meters, and people on the eastern side of the lake migrated west to find fresh grazing and drinkable water (Grove, 1974). Heavy rains in 1916 restored Lake Chad to its mean level for the first half of the twentieth century, but with the onset of the last drought the lake level once again

dropped, and the fishing village of Bol, which once stood on the lake shore, was 18 mi (29 km) from water by 1973. The Sahel suffered a serious drought from 1912 to 1914, when in northern Nigeria the isohyets were from 125 to 220 mi (200–350 km) south of their mean position (Grove, 1974). Similar conditions prevailed in 1941 and 1942. Unusually heavy rains fell in the 1950s and early 1960s when most regions also recorded dramatic increases in their human and livestock populations, so that when drought conditions returned there was insufficient pasturage, and consequently exceptionally high stock losses.

The drying up of lakes and rivers, the reduction of vegetation cover, and increased soil exposure and soil erosion along the desert edge, have been labeled incorrectly "desert encroachment." The United States

Dry, sandy soil being ploughed prior to planting, Senegal. (AID)

AID Office of Science and Technology has estimated that about 250,000 sq mi (647,500 sq km) of arable land in the Sahel have been forfeited to the Sahara in the past 50 years (Rosenthal, 1973). Elsewhere it has been said that the desert is "advancing" at about 20 to 30 mi (32–48 km) each year. But this so-called "desertification" of the Sahel is probably not so much a natural expansion of the Sahara because of climatic change, as it is a deterioration of the environment *in situ* under the impact of human and animal activity. After centuries of use and misuse, the delicate balance between man and environment is once again threatened, and because of high population and livestock numbers it is most serious. The major differences between the recent drought and previous ones are that more people are involved making recovery difficult, and that it is assumed modern technology can somehow correct the problems.

Before West Africa was arbitrarily divided by France and other colonial governments, and boundaries were superimposed on the landscape, pastoralists regularly migrated across the savanna, Sahel, and desert zones in search of new grazing lands and food. They followed the rains north to the desert edge and then back to the southern savanna, but not into the more southern tsetse fly belt. Their timing was carefully calculated so as to provide feed and water with the least dangers from disease and conflict. The nomadic Tauregs purchased manufactured goods from the southern cultivators, and for manure left on the fields they received both grazing rights and grain. Thus there was a strong symbiotic relationship between pastoralist and sedentary farmer, a relationship between savanna and Sahel. Migration to the south was the Tauregs' principal survival mechanism.

But colonialism changed the system. Boundaries prevented free pastoral migrations; land once grazed or sown to staple foods was sown to cash crops needed to earn foreign exchange; taxes were imposed on cattle, and the nomads were encouraged to become sedentary. The introduction of cash crops, especially cotton and peanuts, meant that more marginal lands had to be brought under cultivation to produce the basic staples. In many cases these ecologically fragile

Taureg herdsmen in Niger feeding their goats with relief supplies from the UN/FAO World Food Program. Possibly 12 million sheep, goats and camels, and 20 million cattle perished during the five year drought of the Sahel beginning in 1968. (UN/FAO)

zones could not take the strain of intensive cultivation, and because of increased demands, fallow periods of 15 to 20 years were reduced to 5 years or even less. Output declined with fertility until the land was eventually abandoned to lie exposed to the sun and wind. As cultivators spread further out from their towns and villages, the pastoralists were squeezed further into the desert. Annual firing of the grasslands, and excessive woodcutting for fuel, livestock enclosures, and food for camels and goats, also contributed to the deterioration of the natural environment (Grove, 1974).

Western technology has inadvertently contributed to the deteriorating conditions in several other ways. First, the inoculation of livestock against disease has cut fatalities and helped swell the ranks of cattle now in search of limited grazing. The FAO es-

timates the cattle population rose from 18 million in 1960 to 25 million in 1971, and the World Bank believes the optimum population is 15 million (Wade, 1974). Second, each state has dug hundreds of deep wells, some between 1000 and 2000 ft (300–600 m) and costing more than $20,000 each, which have concentrated the cattle in areas too small to be supported by the natural veld. Around each well the grass is soon eaten and trampled, but beyond the cattle's reach lie grazing lands, so that during the recent droughts, most cattle died from lack of forage, not water. There is much controversy concerning the merits and demerits of water holes, especially deep wells. Third, modern medicines have reduced human mortality rates while fertility rates have remained high, so that natural growth rates have steadily increased. Food production,

THE DESERT TIER: PROBLEMS IN THE INTERIOR

Village women using a common well in Koaltinquin, Upper Volta. Water is one of the critical problems for the people of Upper Volta and the Sahel.

however, has increased at far slower rates. Thus the deterioration of the Sahel is due to the combined and cumulative effects of over-population, short-term changes in climate, traditional agropastoral practices and, above all, the impact of western economic and so-cial systems.

Strategies for Change

Any strategy devised to control the de-teriorating situation in the Sahel and Sahara Desert, and to provide for a more stable fu-ture, must rest on a number of assumptions. If planners accept the thesis of climatic change with an intensification of desert con-ditions, one type of strategy must be devised and implemented. The abandonment or at least strict control of cattle raising might be one strategy. However, if planners reject cli-matic change as the principal cause for the present plight, but see some cyclical pattern of periodic drought, then a different strategy should be adopted. This should include the reestablishment, with modifications, of pre-drought economies. If however, planners recognize the fact there is no predictable variation in the rainfall regime, but accept variability to be normal, and accept the fact that environmental mismanagement and mis-use are primarily responsible for the disas-ters, then a third strategy needs to be devised. Whatever plan is adopted, it should not ignore traditional behavior, values, and systems.

Each state has devised both short-term and long-term plans, the latter being more regional in scope and coordination, the former being geared to specific immediate needs of the individual countries (Shear and Stacey, 1975). At the height of the last drought, most short-term strategies, other than emergency relief measures coordinated by overseas agencies, were self-help projects. In Niger, for instance, government workers donated between two and 25 percent of their salaries to a relief fund to buy food. In Mauritania, businesses were asked to contribute 10 percent of their profits, and employees one day's salary, to a fund to provide more boreholes and relief vehicles. These merely supplemented relief efforts, and were not directed at the broader issues of providing more food and controlling the environment. The overall long-term goals are the prevention of food shortages and the conservation of land and water resources, or ecological reclamation. In a region where the per capita production of food crops has declined between 1 and 2 percent per year for the last decade, and where most of the population now lives at or below the subsistence level within a precarious environment, these are major objectives.

Several factors restrict food and crop production. These include low work productivity (inefficient tools and methods), the use of unimproved seeds and fertilizers, insufficient exploitation of available surface and ground water resources (irrigation), and decreasing soil fertility from years of monocropping. Disease, such as onchocerciasis, has foreclosed settlement and farming in otherwise fertile river valleys such as the Red, Black, and White Voltas in Upper Volta. And the pricing and marketing systems are not conducive to farming.

In the livestock sector, problems vary from country to country, and from one climatic zone to another. The most common are destocking, disease control, effective range management, greater efficiency in marketing meat and livestock produce, and the development of new rangelands in areas currently either too distant from markets or limited by tsetse fly. If pastoralism is to be viable and an important contributor to the national economies, greater interstate cooperation is required. Traditional interzonal and interstate migrations should be preserved, although modified. Ideally, Taureg pastoralists should be permitted access to north-south corridors through sparsely populated regions, and fields and pastures should not be permanently enclosed. Trypanosomiasis should be controlled in the middle belts of the Guinea Coast states that would open new pasture not only to local herds but to those of the north.

The southern states, especially Nigeria, Ghana, and Ivory Coast are already important markets for beef from Mali, Niger, and Upper Volta, and as their per capita incomes rise, the demands for beef are likely to rise too. Mali and Niger in particular have a comparative advantage in cattle so that more and more cattle owners will be tempted to breed cattle. This could mean a more sedentary husbandry around feeding stations, and the introduction of forage cultivation and a greater use of agricultural by-products such as cottonseed. This, it has been argued, would increasingly involve farmers as well as nomadic herders and traders, extend the linkage of the cattle sector to the rest of the economy, and reduce the pressure of overgrazing on the open range (Stryker, 1974). In theory, increased exports derived from these new activities, mean additional tax revenues for public investment. However, because of the openness of the boundaries, governments are unable to collect their taxes, and any further increases in the rates at which exports are taxed would encourage greater illegal interstate movements. During the early 1970s in Mali for instance, with taxes on cattle exports equal to nearly 10 percent of the value per head of those exports, only about one-half paid the tax (Stryker, ibid).

Fortunately, government leaders see the major issues in a regional rather than national context, although—not unexpectedly—national interests sometimes take precedence. To deal specifically with problems directly caused by the last serious drought and related ecological problems, the six Sahelian states have established the Permanent Interstate Committee for Drought Control in the Sahel (CILSS), headquartered in Ouagadougou. Among its objectives are the creation of green belts around villages, improved marketing storage and distribution facilities, and the creation of a climate monitoring system. The Lake Chad Basin Commission, composed of the four states sharing Lake Chad, is examining the irrigation potentials of the rivers leading to the lake.

Mali, Mauritania, and Senegal are members of the Organization for the Development of the Senegal River (OMVS)—the successor to l'Organisation des états riveraines du Senegal (OERS), of which Guinea was once a member. In 1974, OMVS negotiated a 800,000 million CFA francs multiproject scheme that includes a hydroelectric dam and irrigation scheme at Manantali (Mali), an irrigation dam on the Senegal delta at Diama, a river-maritime port at St. Louis (Senegal), and expansions to the present river port at Kayes (Mali). Subsequently bauxite and iron ore may be mined, an aluminum smelter constructed, and factories developed. Saudi Arabia, Iran, Kuwait, France, and Canada, together with the World Bank, UNDP, and the African Development Bank have made commitments.

The World Bank has programs addressed to regional transport problems, and with USAID is dealing with onchocerciasis control in the Volta River Basin. Other regional organizations operating in West Africa dealing in one way or another with development issues are the Niger River Commission, the Economic Community of West Africa (CEAO), the African Development Bank, and the Economic Community of West African States (ECOWAS).

Contrasting Problems and Prospects

While the six Sahelian states share many environmental and institutional characteristics and problems (the most pressing being poverty within a harsh environment), each state has its individual development priorities, problems, and prospects. Each desires a more balanced economy, greater control over its resources and environment, and additional industry not merely import substitution manufacturing, but heavy industry that is believed to bring prestige, wealth, and greater economic viability. Several desire steel mills, petroleum refineries, aluminum smelters, and automobile factories. But one large integrated iron and steel mill, and only two or three petroleum refineries, for instance, could meet the combined needs of all 16 West African states. Ideally, what is required are a number of integrated economic organizations operating on a regional basis (Adedeji, 1970). A few exist in the form of CEAO, OCAM, OMVS, and ECOWAS, but they do not concern themselves with the real issues of manufacturing specialization, marketing, and distribution on an effective regional basis.

SENEGAL

Of the six Sahelian states, Senegal has the most diversified economy, mainly because of its privileged status during the colonial era, its resource endowment, coastal location, and political stability. Dakar became the primate city and federal capital of French West Africa, and thus the most influential, the most prestigious, and the most

Aerial view of Dakar, capital of Senegal, and former capital of French West Africa. (Georg Gerster)

cosmopolitan. Its economies were geared to and dependent upon a vast hinterland that extended east to Upper Volta and Niger, but when this interior was divided into separate independent states, Dakar lost this pre-eminence. This was underscored in 1960 when Mali broke diplomatic relations with Senegal and closed down its rail links from Bamako to Dakar until 1963. In an effort to revitalize industry, a free-trade zone was established in Dakar in 1974. Manufacturing, which accounts for more than a third of the GDP, emphasizes the processing of locally produced groundnuts, cotton, rice, and phosphate ores. However, Senegal also has a diversified chemicals industry that utilizes imported raw materials, several metal fabricating and truck assembly plants, and the largest textile industry in French-speaking Africa. Most industries are located in metropolitan Dakar (700,000), Thies, Kaolack,

and towns along the railway to St. Louis (the former capital) and along the main line into the interior (Fig. 13-3 and Table 13-1).

While Senegal's economy is more balanced than others in the region, agriculture accounts for a third of the GDP, and provides employment for 70 percent of the economically active population. Its agriculture is essentially monocultural, the overwhelmingly important cash crop being groundnuts that provide 75 percent of all export earnings and almost a third of budget revenues. Since independence, and with the abolition in 1968 of the *surprix* for groundnuts and groundnut oil at French ports, production has declined, almost to disastrous levels in the early 1970s. Consequently the government is attempting to diversify its rural economy by expanding the production of cotton, rice, sugar, and market garden produce especially along the Senegal River

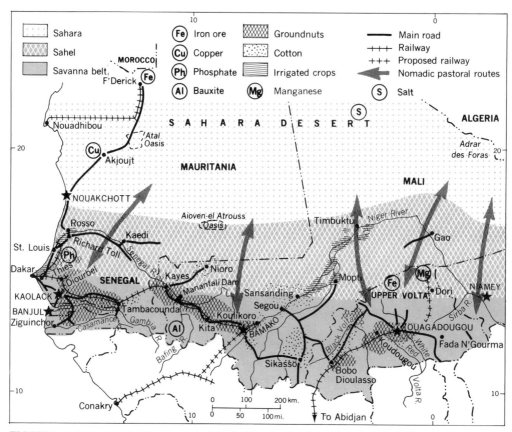

FIGURE 13-3 *General identification map of Mali, Mauritania, Senegal, and Upper Volta.*

(Richard Toll Scheme), and along the Casamance River in the south. Development in this southern region is hindered by the Republic of Gambia, which separates it from the national core.

Since independence, President Senghor has pursued a policy of "African Socialism" and increased Senegalization of the economy, while maintaining close economic relations with France and encouraging other Western investment. To ensure a more prosperous future, Senegal must not only cultivate these ties and reduce its chronically unfavorable balance of trade, but it should attempt to regain some of its markets and influence in West Africa. But individual nationalisms, both political and economic, in the adjoining states will not make this easy.

MAURITANIA

In the neighboring Islamic Republic of Mauritania, a vast compact territory of scanty vegetation, barren surfaces, poor communications, and negligible internal commerce, the pattern of recent development has focused on minerals. The Miferma iron ore mine at F'Derick (Fig. 13-3) came into production in 1963 and now produces over 10 million tons of high grade ore each year. Until December, 1974, when all holdings were nationalized, the reserves—estimated at over 100 million tons—were controlled by French, British, Italian, German, and local interests. A railway, connects the mine with Nouadhibou (formerly Port Etienne) where the Government is building an integrated iron and steel mill funded by

Gambia, Africa's smallest independent state (4261 sq mi 11,036 sq km) is virtually an enclave within Senegal, and is Senegal's natural outlet to the Atlantic Ocean. Indeed, Gambia, which comprises a narrow strip of land on either side of the River Gambia, and whose boundaries correspond to no natural or demographic boundaries, was the object of French interests in the eighteenth century before being reserved for Great Britain by the 1783 Treaty of Versailles. In 1807, the British established a military post at Bathurst (now Banjul, the capital), to control slavery, and acquired additional territory up river by concluding treaties with local chiefs establishing British protection over their lands. For administrative purposes, the territory was divided into a coastal colony and an interior protectorate, and from 1821 to 1843 Gambia was administered from Sierra Leone. In the 1860s and the 1870s Gambia was used as a pawn in negotiations with France with the aim of exchanging it for more desirable territory elsewhere. But British merchants convinced London of Gambia's commercial and strategic worth, and final boundaries were drawn in 1889.

The artificiality of Gambia has been detrimental to both Gambia and Senegal in that its boundaries cut ethnic units and restrict the natural flow of goods and ideas. In May 1973, following a visit to Senegal, President Jawara said he saw the proposed unification of Gambia and Senegal as "an inevitable and necessary development," but rejected the idea of immediate political integration. He saw the future union developing through economic integration and cooperation. Gambia is a smuggling base for manufactured imports into Senegal, and an illegal recipient of Senegalese cattle and groundnuts. Groundnuts and groundnut products normally contribute about 96 percent of total exports, with Britain and the EEC countries being the principal markets.

Its size, shape, and location combined with its small population (580,000), sparsity of resources, and rural economy that is subject to the vagaries of unreliable rainfall and prolonged droughts, make Gambia one of Africa's poorest countries with extremely limited development opportunities.

Kuwait, Saudi Arabia, Qatar, and Abu Dhabi. Further south the government controls a rich copper mine at Akjoujt, which is linked by road with the state's new capital Nouakchott (80,000). There the People's Republic of China is building a new harbor and giving technical assistance in the construction of a cement works and sugar refinery. By 1974, minerals accounted for 80 percent of all exports, and two-thirds of all salaries in the modern sector of the economy.

By the late 1960s, Mauritania had reduced its economic, military, and technical ties with France, and had loosened its ties with other former French West African territories. In 1973 it left the Franc Zone and the West African Monetary Union to join the Maghreb Economic Union. Its bank is supported by several Arab states including Kuwait and Saudi Arabia. This increased

Iron ore storage and loading facilities, Nouadhibou, Mauritania. Nouadhibou is connected by rail with the Miferma iron ore mine at F'Derick, and will have an integrated iron and steel mill funded by Saudi Arabia, Kuwait and other oil-rich Arab states. (World Bank)

identification with the Arab world is not un-expected since three-fourths of its population is Arab, and almost 95 percent of the people are Muslim. But transport links with its neighboring Arab states are limited, and the population that resides in the extreme south-west is separated from the major population centers of Algeria and Morocco by thou-sands of square miles of unuseable desert land. The small non-Arab population, mainly sedentary Soninke, Wolof, Toucou-leur, and Bambara, has strongly but unsuc-cessfully opposed Arab domination, yet re-mains an important centrifugal force in the south. Northern Arabs favor union with Morocco.

In 1976, Mauritania gained the southern part of the former Spanish Sahara including the as-yet-untouched iron ore deposits ad-joining the Miferma mine, while the phos-phate-rich northern sector of the former Spanish colony was annexed to Morocco. (see Chapter thirty-three). Mauritania and Morocco, long distrustful of each other, now share a common border.

MALI

Mali, like Mauritania and Guinea, has attempted to reduce its dependence on French aid, technical assistance, and trade, and become more self-sufficient. But unlike its western neighbors, Mali lacks known mineral resources, has a less favorable geo-graphic location as a landlocked state, and has suffered a series of economic and political crises that were aggravated by the droughts of the early 1970s. Under President Keita, the government developed a socialist economic policy that saw the nationalization of most enterprises, the creation of a network of rural cooperatives, and close economic ties with both the Soviet Union and the People's Republic of China. But increasing economic problems, especially with the state corporations, led to a rapprochement with France, culminating in Mali rejoining the Franc Zone. However, the economic situation did not improve, and political antagonisms developed between those preferring closer ties with China and those who preferred greater rapprochement. A military coup followed in 1968, and although civilian government is provided for in the new constitution, which was approved by referendum in June 1974, the military intends to remain in power until at least 1980.

Despite cutbacks in infrastructure and social investment, the dismantling of cooperatives, and the closing of some state industries, Mali's economy has not prospered.

The vast majority of Malians are engaged in subsistence agriculture, the per capita income is still less than $100, there is a serious balance of payments problem, and the country is one of the poorest in Africa (Table 13-1). Cropland is limited to the southern half of the country where rainfall is between 25 and 55 in. (635–1400 mm), irrigation is possible, and where small-scale traditional farming accounts for 90 percent of the land under cultivation. It is in this already densely populated region that tens of thousands of northern Taureg and Djerma refugees have been settled. The government is encouraging the planting of cash crops, especially rice in the Sansanding irrigation scheme, and cotton further south in the Sikasso region (Fig. 13-3). On the Bafing River, a tributary of the Senegal, near Kayes, the Chinese are helping the Malians build the Manantali Dam which will provide 771 million kilowatt-hours (kwh) and almost a million acres (405,000 ha) of irrigated land. They have also agreed to help the Malians build a new railway from Bamako to the railhead in Guinea that will serve the coun-

Covered market in Bamako, capital of Mali.

try's major population centers, and reduce Mali's dependence on Dakar and Abidjan. Thus, Chinese participation is firm, and Mali has not achieved the economic independence it sought as early as 1960.

UPPER VOLTA

Many of the same development problems that beleaguer Mali exist in Upper Volta, also a primarily agricultural country and possibly the poorest in Africa. Most of Upper Volta lies in the Savanna-Sudan belt south of the Sahel proper (Fig. 13-3) so that it receives higher and more dependable rainfalls than other Sahelian states. However, much of the land has thin and infertile soils, and over a third the area is uninhabited because of the presence of river blindness and sleeping sickness. Although the river valleys are flat and contain some of the most fertile soil, and usually dependable supplies of water, they are generally uninhabited because of the as-yet uncontrolled *simulium* fly. Consequently, the population is concentrated in the Mossi Plateau around the capital city and Mossi headquarters, Ouagadougou (140,000), and in the higher ground around the country's chief market center and Bobo headquarters, Bobo Dioulasso (95,000). In these regions, population densities sometimes exceed 400 persons per sq mi (160 per sq km), and pressure on the land is great.

This population pressure, combined with a general lack of employment opportunities in mining and manufacturing, and the proximity of jobs in the plantations and mines in Ivory Coast and Ghana, results in an annual out-migration of almost a half million Voltaians. Some 100,000 stay away for the length of the dry season when there is little work to be done at home; almost 300,000 remain for one to five years; and a further 100,000, stay permanently. Out of a total population of 6.4 million (Table 13-1), the largest for the Sahelian states, this is an appreciable number. As Ghana and Ivory Coast reserve more and more of the jobs for their own nationals, it means population pressure will increase in Upper Volta, and there will be less money in circulation unless the government can provide alternative employment. At present the government is concentrating its development efforts on the rural sector, and secondarily upon infrastructure and manufacturing, but with 85 percent of the population at the subsistence level, tax revenues are small, and the country must depend heavily on subsidies from France.

If the manganese reserves at Tambao are developed, they would supply the country with much needed revenues, but the manganese itself cannot be developed without a new railway, additional power, a new cement plant, and general improvements to the country's physical infrastructure. The mining project is under review by Japanese and French interests, and entails a 220-mi (354 km) extension of the Abidjan-Ouagadougou line to Tambao with a further extension to Gao, Mali, or even a line from Ouagadougou to Niamey with a branch line to the mine. These interdependent projects also require the joint efforts of Upper Volta, Mali, and Niger, but there are serious interstate rifts such as the border dispute between Mali and Upper Volta that could prevent, or at least delay, their realization.

NIGER

The large landlocked state of Niger was hardest hit by the drought of the early 1970s with cattle losses of 60 percent and sheep losses of 28 percent; possibly as much as one-quarter of its population either perished or emigrated to neighboring states. Its major cash crop and principal export, groundnuts, dropped from a peak of 298,000 tons in 1967 to only 20,000 tons in 1973. Millet and corn, the two staple food crops, were also severely affected, so that starvation and malnutrition were widespread, and the economy devastated. President Diori, who had been in power since independence (1960), was blamed for mishandling the economy and emergency re-

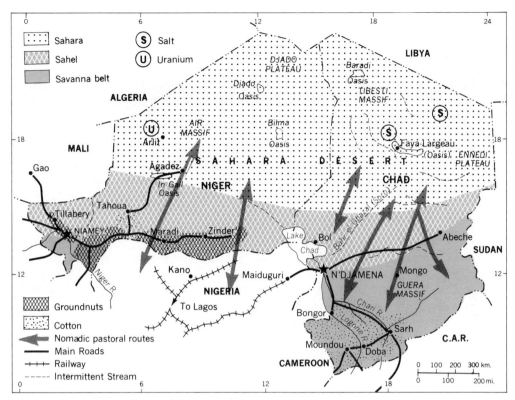

FIGURE 13-4 *General identification map of Chad and Niger.*

lief measures, and for failing to attract foreign capital. He was deposed by a military coup in April 1974, and succeeded by Lt. Col. Kountche who has encouraged economic relations with states other than France.

The northern two-thirds of Niger is desert and uninhabited except for scattered oases and mining camps. Agadez, the largest settlement in the Air Massif, receives only 6.3 in. (160 mm) of rain on the average, yet Tauregs and other nomads keep considerable livestock in its vicinity. Only in the extreme south, along the Niger River and in the Maradi District, is there permanent settlement. About 96 percent of the population is rural (Table 13-1), but only 3 percent of the land is cultivated. Niamey, the capital, is the largest town (115,000), and only three others—Zinder, Maradi, and Tahoua—all in

the south, have populations over 30,000 (Fig. 13-4).

Niger's external economic orientation is toward France and the coastal states, especially Nigeria and Benin. Nigeria takes 85 percent of Niger's animal exports, is now the principal transit route for Niger's foreign trade, and is an important recipient of seasonal labor. Taureg migrants depend on Nigeria's pastures, and during the last prolonged drought, thousands made Nigeria their permanent home. France has long been Niger's principal source of financial, technical, and military aid, and in the late 1960s France was responsible for developing the uranium ores at Arlit, the largest known deposits in Africa. Production started in 1971, and by 1974 uranium had become Niger's principal export. While this prominence was due in part to the poor showing of groundnuts and cattle, uranium is expected to remain the country's major source of foreign revenues. Two additional uranium mining companies have since been established involving French, German, and Japanese interests, and a fourth involving United States interests is planned. Oil prospecting is in progress and if all these mining concerns prove successful, Niger could have considerable much-needed financial resources to invest in its unprofitable agricultural sector that supports the bulk of Nigeriens.

CHAD

The largest and least accessible of the West African Sahelian states is Chad (Fig. 13-4). It has few natural resources, no railway, poor roads, a per capita income less than $100, and a divided people (Table 13-1). While its physical environment is not conducive to general economic prosperity, especially prosperity based on agriculture, its institutional resources, size, and location are even less so.

For decades Chad has suffered from regionally based political and economic disorders. The arid north is Muslim, nomadic, sparsely populated, lacking in known mineral resources, and is isolated from the rest of the country. It has traditionally opposed political domination from the south, and until 1965 (five years after independence), it remained under French military administration. It has periodically received weapons and technical assistance from Libya in its struggles against the south. Traditionally northerners have been excluded from government.

Southern Chad is wealthier, more populous, better educated, sedentary in its way of life, and largely animist or Christian. Here lies the capital, N'Djamena, and the densely populated and relatively fertile Longone and Chari valleys where cotton is by far the dominant cash crop, and same areas are subject to seasonal flooding. The region is normally self-supporting in foodstuffs, and exports large quantities of meat to Nigeria, Cameroon, and Zaire. The major livestock belt coincides with the Sahel, extending east from Lake Chad to the Darfur Plateau. Economically, southern Chad is geared more to its neighbors than to the north, and this will become stronger should the Cameroon railway be extended, as planned, from N'Gaoundéré to Sarh (formerly Fort Archambault).

In 1973, Chad embarked on a unique program of social change to produce cohesion among its various ethnic groups and regions. The president ordered all French names to be replaced by Chad names (Fort Lamy, the capital, was renamed N'Djamena), and pagan initiation rites were reintroduced and made compulsory for high government officials. This "Chaditude" or "authenticity" policy was, by definition, anticolonial, and so certain cooperative agreements with France were terminated, and relations with France deteriorated. Nevertheless, Chad remains dependent on France for some technical, military, and economic aid. Like the other Sahelian states, Chad has a poor record in education, health services, and industry (Table 13-1).

Conclusion

While the economies of each of the six Sahelian states have diversified since independence, primarily through the introduction of mining and the expansion of manufacturing, they remain predominantly agricultural. The majority of peoples are still subsistence farmers and pastoralists who have benefited little from this recent input of foreign capital and technology. They remain poor, under- and malnourished, close to the survival level, and have few options to improve their well-being. Institutional constraints hold them to this way of life more than the natural environment. What is required to provide them with adequate food and housing, higher incomes and greater economic opportunity, is a change in attitude towards the environment, widespread rural reform, and a change in the means of production.

Agricultural development should be of top priority in all national development plans. This does not necessarily mean large-scale irrigation schemes to produce cash crops, but rather improved farming techniques, marketing and storage facilities, new strains of seed and breeding cattle, and the use of small storage dams and irrigation works. Cooperative efforts, proved successful in Tanzania and elsewhere, could be adopted. Many such changes could be implemented without great financial strain, social disorder, and technological expertise. However, without immediate and effective management of population growth, the success of these development programs can only be marginal.

Bibliography

Adedeji, A. "Prospects of Regional Economic Co-operation in West Africa," *Journal of Modern African Studies*, Vol. 8, No. 2, (July, 1970), pp. 213–31.

Baier, S. and P. Lovejoy. "The Desert-Side Economy of the Central Sudan," *International Journal of African Historical Studies*, Vol. 8, No. 4 (1975), pp. 551–81.

Barbour, K. M. "Industrialization in West Africa: The Need For Sub-Regional Groupings Within an Integrated Economic Community," *Journal of Modern African Studies*, Vol. 10, No. 3 (October, 1972), pp. 357–82.

Bornstein, R. "The Organisation of Senegal River States," *Journal of Modern African Studies*, Vol. 10, No. 2 (July, 1972), pp. 267–83.

Bryson, R. A. "Climatic Modification by Air Pollution, II: The Sahelian Effect," Institute for Environmental Studies, Report, Madison, 1973.

Church, R. J. H. *West Africa: A Study of the Environment and of Man's Use of It*. 7th Edition. London: Longman Group Ltd., 1974.

Dalby, D. and R. J. H. Church (eds.).

Drought in Africa. London: University of London, 1973.

Esseks, J. D. "The Food Outlook for the Sahel," *Africa Today*. Vol. 22, No. 2 (April–June, 1975), pp. 45–56.

Glantz, M. H. *Politics of Natural Disaster: The Case of the Sahel Drought*. New York: Praeger, 1975.

Grove, A. T. "Desertification in the African Environment," *African Affairs*, Vol. 73, No. 291 (April, 1974), pp. 137–51.

Hopkins, A. G. *An Economic History of West Africa*. New York: Columbia University Press, 1973.

Rosenthal, J. E. "The Creeping Catastrophe," *Africa Report*. Vol. 18, No. 4 (July–August, 1973), pp. 7–13.

Rosenthal, J. E. "Survival in the Sahel," *War on Hunger*, Vol. 8, No. 8 (August, 1974), pp. 1–40.

Shear, D. and R. Stacy. "The Sahel: An Approach to the Future," *War on Hunger*, Vol. 9, No. 5 (May, 1975), pp. 7–14.

Sheets, H. and R. Morris. *Disaster in the Desert: Failures of International Relief in the West African Drought*. Washington:

Carnegie Endowment for International Peace, 1974.

Stryker, J. D. "The Malian Cattle Industry: Opportunity and Dilemma," *Journal of Modern African Studies*, Vol. 12, No. 3 (September, 1974), pp. 441–57.

UNESCO. *Sahel: Ecological Approaches to Land-Use*. New York: UNESCO, 1975.

United States, House of Representatives, Committee on Foreign Affairs, *The Drought Crisis in the African Sahel*. Washington: Government Printer, 1973.

Wade, N. "Sahelian Drought: No Victory for Western Aid," *Science*, Vol. 185 (1974), pp. 24–37.

PART THREE

EQUATORIAL AFRICA

FOURTEEN

Equatorial Africa is one of the continent's most distinct geographic regions. Composed of six states—Zaire, Cameroon, the Central African Republic, Congo, Gabon, and Equatorial Guinea—the region is dominated physiographically by Africa's greatest river, the Zaire (Fig. 14-1). Much of the region, especially central Zaire is plateaulike and lies below 3000 feet (900 m). In the periphery there is great topographical variety. The Ruwenzori Mountains adjoining the state of Uganda rise above 13,000 feet (3900 m), while the Mitumba Mountains which form the eastern flank together with the lakes of the western rift valley (Mobutu, Amin, Kivu, and Tanganyika), generally stand above 5000 feet (1500 m). In Cameroon, beyond the Zaire Basin proper, the Adamawa Massif and Manengouba Mountains rise to similar heights. The central lowlands of Zaire, once one of Africa's great interior lakes, are flat, forested, and often swampy.

Lakes Mai-Ndombe and Tumba are remnants of this ancient feature.

Zaire is Equatorial Africa's giant. With an area of 905,365 sq mi (2,345,000 sq km), the Republic of Zaire is a land of great distances, difficult communications and severe environmental obstacles to progress. The rich copper fields and economic core of Shaba lie some 1700 miles (2700 km) from Boma, Zaire's coastal port in the narrow proruption west of Kinshasa. Coffee grown in the foothills of the Ruwenzori Mountains adjoining the state of Uganda, must travel some 1800 miles (2900 km) by road, rail, and riverboat to the Atlantic Ocean prior to export. The Zaire River, Africa's largest, loops through the country, plunging over numerous rapids and falls making uninterrupted navigation impossible. Between Kinshasa and its mouth, in a distance of only 215 mi (345 km), the Zaire drops almost 900 ft (270 m), as it traverses the Crystal Moun-

SPATIAL INFLUENCES IN THE GROWTH OF ZAIRE

243

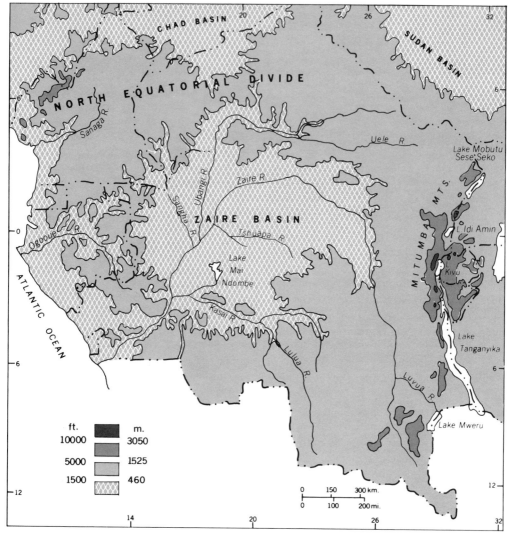

FIGURE 14-1 *Equatorial Africa. Physical features.*

tains, and goods from the interior must be transferred to trains for the journey to the coast. From Kinshasa to Kisangani, however, and from Kinshasa to Ilebo, the Zaire and its major tributary the Kasai are navigable for 1085 mi (1740 km) and 513 mi (820 km) respectively. The Ubangi can be used by modern riverboats as far as Bangui, capital of the Central African Republic.

Whatever the interior produces must be priced high enough to permit several trans-

shipments. The non-navigable sections of the Zaire have been circumvented by railroads, but each break of bulk increases the cost of the product. It was Henry Morton Stanley, the first white man to know the area well, who observed that without railroads the territory was not worth a penny. Many parts of the country remain isolated from modern transportation, in spite of the fact the Belgians built over 80,000 mi (128,000 km) of roads. During the rainy season, roads may be impassable for weeks; a very small mileage, mostly near the urban centers, is asphalted and usable throughout the year. The country's vastness and the huge costs of building communications between the various areas of population concentration scattered around the "empty heart" have perpetuated a high degree of internal fragmentation and have delayed the evolution of a Zairian people that might be referred to as a nation.

Yet Zaire has tremendous economic potential. Its mineral wealth, hydroelectric potential, and forestry resources are among the greatest in Africa, if not the world, and certainly greater development would have occurred had the country not been bedevilled by a series of political crises. Three distinct phases can be recognized from the early 1880s to the present, and each produced obstacles to progress above and beyond those of physiography and environment. During each phase, the country had a different name. From 1885, it was the Congo Free State; from 1908 to independence in 1960, it was the Belgian Congo; and since 1973 it has been the Republic of Zaire.

In the immediate postcolonial period, the country was known as the Democratic Republic of the Congo, but this was changed as part of the government's "Africanization" or "authenticity" drive. Also changed were the names of cities, regions, geographical features, streets, and buildings. In this chapter, Congo refers to the Belgian Congo and is used only in the colonial context. Otherwise current names are used. Thus Kinshasa, and not Leopoldville, is used even for the colonial era. The most important name changes are given in Table 14-1.

Table 14-1 ZAIRIAN NAME CHANGES

Towns	
Colonial Name	Current Name
Albertville	Kalemi
Baningville	Bandundu
Coquilhatville	Mbandaka
Costermansville	Bukavu
Elisabethville	Lubumbashi
Jadotville	Likasi
Leopoldville	Kinshasa
Luluabourg	Kananga
Paulis	Isiro
Ponthierville	Ubundu
Port Francqui	Ilebo
Stanleyville	Kisangani
Thysville	Mbanza Ngungu
Natural Features	
Congo River	Zaire
Lake Leopold II	Mai-Ndombe
Lake Rete	Ishangelélé
Lake Delcommune	N'Zilo
Stanley Falls	NgaKéma
Stanley Pool	Malebo
Districts	
Katanga	Shaba
Leopoldville	Bandundu
Orientale	Upper Zaire

Congo Free State

The explorer whose name became closely connected with the Congo was Henry M. Stanley, a British-born, American journalist. Having succeeded in his earlier search for Livingstone (whom he had found at Ujiji on November 10, 1871), Stanley for the first time penetrated the Zaire Basin. After his initial contact with the unknown interior, he went to Europe, trying first to interest the British in establishing their influence in this part of Africa. The "Scramble for Africa" began to gain momentum, and Stanley's work became known to King Leopold II of Belgium. Leopold, who had visions of an empire for Belgium, saw his country without colonies at a time when Britain, France, Portugal, and the Netherlands already possessed vast overseas realms. In 1876, the king convened the Brussels Geographic Conference, with the purpose of supporting exploration and research in equatorial Africa. In 1878, Leopold and Stanley met and established an organization which aided Stanley on a number of subsequent journeys through the Congo. In effect, the explorer was now working for the Belgian king, founding settlements and signing treaties on behalf of Leopold with Congolese chiefs.

Thus Belgium entered the colonial scene in Africa and became involved in the disputes which marked that period of expansion. In 1884, Bismarck called the Berlin Conference where an attempt was to be made to settle these colonial conflicts by agreement on arbitrarily defined boundaries. Belgium, relative latecomer in Africa, found itself backed by Germany in its claims to rights in the Congo region, because Germany wished to impede the expansionist efforts of its chief rivals, Britain and France. Hence, the International Congo Association, an outgrowth of the original committee supporting Stanley's explorations, achieved recognition in Berlin, and a Congo Treaty was signed. The sovereign state thus created was named the Congo Free State, and later in 1885 the Belgian Parliament authorized King Leopold II to become king of this country also. In this manner, the Congo Free State initially became the personal possession of King Leopold rather than a Belgian colony.

The Congo Treaty gave Leopold the tasks of suppressing the slave trade in this area, creating effective control over the country, and improving living conditions for the Africans who had become his wards. Leopold was very wealthy, but he visualized the Congo experiment as a money-making venture, and he expected quick returns for his initial investments. He sent a large number of agents into the Congo whose duty it was to gather specified quantities of ivory and rubber. While the agents forced the local population into collecting these products, the empty lands were parcelled out to concessionaires who paid levies on their profits.

During this early phase, therefore, the products of the Congo came from the low-lying basin rather than the rim of the northern, eastern, and southern periphery. Barges were floated on the rivers, and produce-collecting stations were established at various points along their courses. Wild rubber was by far the most important product, and since labor costs were low and the demand great, profits were considerable.

The Congo itself, however, benefited but little from this arrangement. In fact, the change in the producing areas was largely detrimental: the king's agents used barbaric methods to enforce the gathering of quotas, and African opposition was met with devastating force. Entire villages were burned and their inhabitants decimated. It has been estimated that the African population during Leopold's reign was reduced by between three million to eight million. The African's fear of the slaver was replaced by a fear of the white man. Meanwhile, Leopold long failed to adhere to one of the major conditions of his assumption of control over the Congo Free State: slavery remained rampant in the east until near the turn of the century, and the long-awaited campaign against it came only after the most powerful of the slavers began to pose an economic threat to the king.

An effect of Leopold's acquisition of unoccupied land was that in a region where shifting, "patch" agriculture, hunting, and gathering are necessary adjustments to environmental conditions, the peoples were confined to lands that at the moment he acquired them, were only temporarily occupied, and that were too small and unfit for permanent habitation. Thus, the local economies, such as they were, were totally disrupted. Forced labor destroyed the traditional social organization and broke up families. Local famines resulted.

A country's development involves more than the extraction and sale of minerals and the gathering and exporting of forest products. It involves, also, the betterment of the

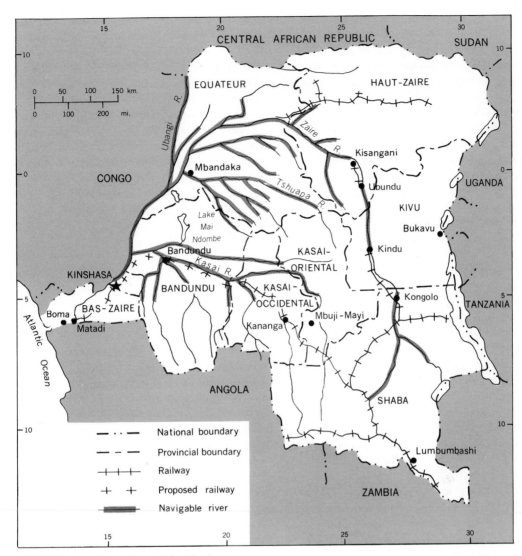

FIGURE 14-2 *Zaire. General identification map.*

people through the improvement of farming methods; the provision of social amenities, education, and health facilities; research on the eradication of local diseases; the introduction of better types of crops; and so forth. During its Free State period, the Congo produced a revenue that dwarfed the profits made in many other African territories. But the improvement of local conditions—one of the prime requirements stated in Berlin in 1885—was minimal, except

where the export-oriented communication system was concerned. For instance, from 1898 to 1903, the value of exports was $46 million, while imports totalled a mere $20 million.

The major contributions of Leopold and Stanley were the expansion of the area of the Congo, especially in the southeast, and the organization of a transport system that could efficiently handle the products of the interior. Leopold realized that the plateau surrounding the Zaire Basin proper might contain valuable resources, and he managed to appropriate the area today known as Shaba at a time when the African chiefs there were planning to request protection from the British.

Considerable headway was also made in linking the rubber- and ivory-producing interior to Matadi. A railroad connecting Matadi and Kinshasa was begun in 1890 and completed in 1898. Construction of the line between Kisangani and Ubundu did not commence until 1903, and was completed as late as 1906. Thus the Ngakema Falls had been bypassed, but another rail link was needed to connect Kindu and Kongolo (Fig. 14-2). It was built immediately afterward so that Shaba was linked to Matadi, but no less than five transshipments were necessary. Shaba did not assume real significance in the economic sense until after the end of the Congo Free State. By 1904, the international outcry regarding the "Congo atrocities" had forced Leopold to appoint an official commission of inquiry. The King was forced to abandon his Free State, and in 1908 the Belgian Parliament assumed responsibility for the territory.

Belgian Congo

From 1908 until 1960, Belgium administered the Congo as a colony, and it was early in this period that the first real steps were taken in development toward the modern state. Among the legacies of Leopold was a number of concession companies, to which the king had granted long-term rights prior to the termination of the Free State. As early as 1891, such concessions had been granted to the Comité Spécial du Katanga, and in 1906 to the Union Minière du Haut Katanga. The Belgian government continued to recognize these concessions, and, as a result, these big companies exerted considerable influence over Belgian decisions concerning the colony. Shortly before 1960, the Union Minière's assets stood at just under $2 billion, when it was contributing almost half of the Congo's annual tax revenue.

Great changes came to the economy of the Congo between 1910 and 1920. In 1913, the export of rubber, long the major product, fell by 50 percent. The full impact of the mineral wealth of Shaba began to be felt, and whereas the economic heart of the Congo had long been in the forests, the minerals of Shaba now came to form the country's backbone.

The whole history of the Congo during the colonial period was one of increasing economic dependence upon the wealth of Shaba; transportation routes were built to serve it, investments were made to accelerate development there, internal communications, hydroelectric projects, housing for the labor force, schools, and many other public works and facilities were constructed. Taxes collected from the products of other provinces were used to improve conditions in Shaba. During the colonial years, Belgium's investment in Shaba was considerable, but the returns were less than desired.

Four transport routes converged on Shaba during the colonial era. Mention has been made of the route via Kongolo, Kindu, Kisangani, and Kinshashi requiring five transshipments. A second route lay southward, and, by 1909, the Rhodesian railroad had reached Sakania on the Shaba-Copperbelt boundary. The Belgians immediately began the construction of a link to Bukama, but after reaching Lubumbashi, construction was interrupted by World War I and was not completed until 1918. During the prewar period, while the Rhodesian connection was still under construction, Dar es Salaam handled some of the copper traffic (via Kigoma on Lake Tanganyika), but after 1918 much of the traffic went southward via Victoria Falls to Beira, itself still a lengthy and expensive journey.

Between 1923 and 1928, the route was built that has since carried a large share of Shaba's produce, linking Bukama to Ilebo. Requiring only two transshipments, this 1724-mi route (2758 km) carried almost half of the Union Minière's copper shipments before the upheaval of independence. Very soon after this route was completed, the shortest link to the coast was constructed, namely, the Benguela Railroad through Angola, directly westward over a distance of 1312 mi (2100 km). Finished in 1931, the Benguela Railroad was built partly with Belgian capital, and of course, no transshipments were required. Its terminal is the ocean port of Lobito, and its initial effect was the almost complete diversion of Shaba's copper traffic from the east coast (Beira) route. Later, however, development within Angola and rising production in Shaba put strain upon the west coast routes, and Beira, 1624 mi (2600 km) from Lubumbashi by rail, again began to handle Shaba's exports.

The last railroad to be constructed to handle Shaba and Copperbelt products was that linking Maputo (formerly Lourenço Marques) to the Rhodesian system, but it was never of major importance to Shaba. Just before independence 48 percent of Union Minière's copper production traveled via Matadi, 30 percent went through Beira, and 22 percent via Lobito.

What Shaba produced, therefore, was

Copper ingots awaiting shipment to the coast from Shaba, Zaire. Most copper is sent to Matadi by rail/river barge combination; some is sent to Lobito, Angola, via the Benguela Railway. (Gécamines, Zaire)

SPATIAL INFLUENCES IN THE GROWTH OF ZAIRE

sufficiently valuable to overcome the region's unfavorable location. This very factor led to some industrial development in the towns of Lubumbashi, Likasi, and Kolwezi. The mining industry required supporting undertakings such as chemicals, explosives, cement, coal, and food processing. The copper ore itself, although among the richest in the world (5 to 6 percent purity) had to be reduced to copper matte (99 percent metal) before shipment to the coast, and this required large quantities of power. At first, coking coal was supplied from Europe, Rhodesia, South Africa, and even the United States. But the cost was high, the railways often congested, and the supply not always guaranteed, so the Congo's own deposits at Kalemi and Luena were brought into production. However, this low-grade coal proved unsatisfactory in the smelting operations, but was used by the railways and Shaba's industry. The problem was eventually met by developing several hydroelectric facilities in the region, and by Belgium investing in Rhodesia's Kariba Dam, one of Africa's biggest hydroelectric schemes.

The mines were developed initially with labor intensive methods, but from the end of the 1920s they became increasingly capital intensive. Migrant workers came not only from Shaba itself, but from Zambia, Angola, Ruanda, Burundi, and distant parts of the Congo. In 1927, Union Minière instituted a recruitment program that was designed to improve productivity by providing a more permanent work force than had previously existed. Mine workers were recruited for a minimum of three years, housing and social amenities were provided, and miners were permitted to bring their families. To some extent the ethnic units intermixed, and in Shaba the process of acculturation was more complete than elsewhere.

Mining was not confined to copper and to Shaba. Uranium was mined until 1961 at Shinkolobwe just west of Likasi, while lead and manganese mines opened along the line-of-rail near Lubumbashi. Five hundred miles

(800 km) to the northwest around Tshikapa, Kananga, and Bakwena, industrial and gem diamonds were found in large quantitities, and, by World War II, the Congo had become the world's leading exporter of the industrial variety. Gold was found in the Kilo-Moto region in the remote northeast, while tin mines opened at Manono (Fig. 14-3). The mining concessionaires grew into major financial empires that exerted tremendous influence in the Congo's administration.

While the Belgian Congo's economic core developed in the extreme southeast, its administrative core emerged in the west. The estuary port of Boma was the colony's first capital, but in 1927 Belgium moved the colony's administration to Kinshasa, then a small river town of only 23,000 inhabitants located across the Zaire River from Brazzaville. It quickly became the Congo's largest city (400,000 at the time of independence) and Africa's most important river port. Light industry was introduced, but Kinshasa remained first and foremost an administrative center and the headquarters of the colony's major extractive industries and financial institutions. Thousands of Congolese came to Kinshasa in search of work and new opportunities, and from this immigrant group grew a small but important class of *évolués* who eventually formed the vanguard of the nationalist movement.

Between the economic and administrative cores lay the vast and sparsely populated Zaire Basin whose contribution to the export economy was limited to the production of rubber, palm products, coffee, cotton, and timber (Fig. 14-4), most of which was derived from European-owned plantations that enjoyed strong government backing. These large-scale operations were not concentrated in any one area, but were widely scattered, making collection and shipment to Boma and Matadi both costly and time consuming. Most products, and especially palm oil and kernels from the lower Kasai, Kwilu, and Zaire rivers, and rubber from the Kisangani and Mbandaka areas, relied heav-

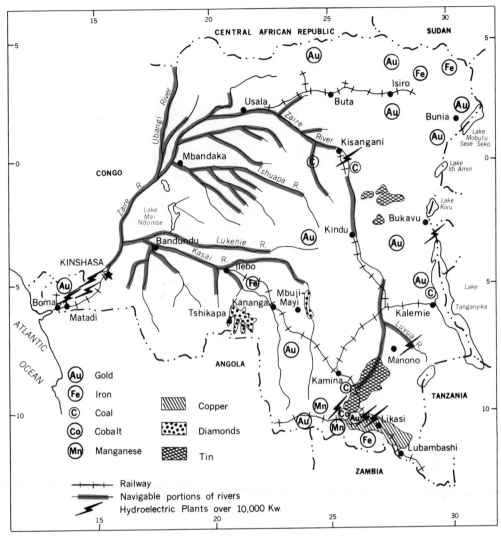

FIGURE 14-3 *Zaire. Minerals.*

ily on river transport. In contrast, cotton, grown primarily in the drier regions along the northern border and in the southcentral regions of Kasai, was more dependent on road and rail service. Most of the timber cut for export came from the Mayumbe forests between Kinshasa and Boma, while the forests of the Lake Mai-Ndombe region were cut primarily for domestic needs. High transport costs incurred by road, rail, and riverboat kept the timber industry depressed.

In the remote highland areas of the east, where the climate was more attractive for European settlement than other parts of the territory, a different type of agriculture emerged. There, privately owned and operated estates were established by European settlers who emphasized high-value low-bulk export crops that could withstand high transport costs. Arabica coffee was the principal commodity, but tea, pyrethrum, tobacco, and livestock were also important. Agricultural colonization also occurred in

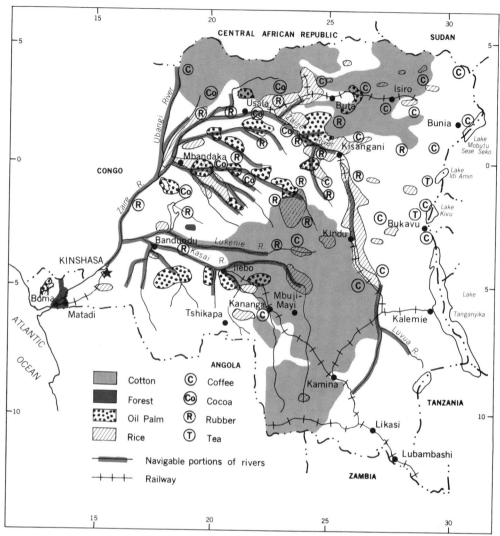

FIGURE 14-4 *Zaire. Commercial agriculture and forestry.*

Shaba, but there emphasis was placed on producing cattle, hogs, and grains for local rather than export markets. Taxes from plantation and estate agriculture were applied more to mining and industrial expansion than to further agricultural development.

From the days of Leopold until the end of the colonial era, the course of development and change was controlled by the Belgian government, the Roman Catholic Church, and big business. Little attempt was made to draw the colony's various regions and peoples together under the flag of a single and unified state. The Belgian government was naturally the major force, and it saw its colonial task as a paternal one. Almost all important decisions were made in Brussels—not in the colony where none of the Congolese, European representatives of the Belgian government, or white settlers possessed any political rights or voice in the fate of the territory. The Roman Catholic Church, while accomplishing much in pri-

Rubber latex, one of the Zaire Basin's principal forestry products. (Sabena)

mary education, strengthened the image of the Belgian as the father of the Congolese masses. Big business, part-owned by the Belgian state, did little to advance the average African peasant, although it pro-

vided both employment and revenues that accelerated the transition from a subsistence to an exchange economy. Out of this triumvirate arose the mutual-interest policy of paternalism to the detriment of national unity. The Belgians failed totally to give the Congolese a sense of belonging to their own country.

Never having participated, in the Western sense, in the political decision-making affecting the Congo as a political entity, the Congolese were not ready to accept a Western-type of state when independence was granted. They had not only been deprived of the chance to negotiate with the white leadership, but more importantly they had done little negotiating with each other. Political parties really did not have a united Congo as their major goal, and centered on peoples and regions. Of the few leaders who were able to see beyond ethnic limits, several also saw that Belgian administrative fragmentation of the Congo provided opportunities for the secession of areas in which they dominated. As the colonial period ended, the Congo teetered on the brink of feudalism, the provinces of Oriental, Kasai, and Katanga each attempting to go its own way independently of any central government in Kinshasa.

Independent Zaire and Zairization

The political crises that beset the newly independent state in 1960 were symptomatic of several spatial and structural imbalances in the economy, and in the control of political power and the state's resources. Since independence, various governments have attempted to change these imbalances through specific economic and political policies. Of the various changes instituted to provide political stability and socioeconomic development, the most important have been the restructuring of the national, provincial, and local governments, nationalization of most sectors of the economy, a reordering of

priorities in mining, agriculture, and industry, and the development of the transport system.

In 1963, the 6 provinces of the former colony were fragmented into 21 units, each of which became a province with substantially greater powers. In addition, the city of Kinshasa and its immediate surroundings became a Federal District. Two major factors played a role in this experiment: pronounced ethno-regionalist sentiments in some areas (like that of the Bakongo people in Kinshasa Province), and dissatisfaction with the status quo in areas located far from the provincial capitals (Young, 1963). The former Katanga was divided into 3 provinces, and Kasai into 4. The scheme was decried as a reversal to tribalism, but actual ethnic homogeneity existed in only 6 of the 21 provinces. Rebellions in 1964 and 1965 showed weaknesses in the system and the failure of both parliamentary institutions and federal government. General Mobutu seized power in a bloodless coup in November 1965, and found general support for the restoration of a unitary state, and the end of parliamentary government.

In 1967 a new constitution establishing centralized presidential rule was ratified, and all federal elements of the earlier constitutions were eliminated. The 21 provinces were reduced to 8, the old colonial boundaries being adopted except that Leopoldville (Kinshasa) Province was divided into 2. Elected assemblies at the provincial level were abolished. For administrative purposes, each region was divided into subregions and territories. At the local level, authority is held by chiefs and village headmen appointed by the government. At the regional level, governors are appointed by the president and they are rotated from one region to another to assure better control.

This redistricting was the prelude to Mobutu's "authenticity" drive, a movement designed to create greater national identity. Basic to this was the replacement of European names with traditional names. Thus the Republic of the Congo became the Republic of Zaire; President Joseph Mobutu changed his name to Mobutu Sese Seko Kubu Ngbendu Waza Banga; and the capital Leopoldville was renamed Kinshasa (see Table 14-1). All Zairians were ordered to adopt traditional names, which brought Mobutu into direct conflict with the Catholic Church. This new philosophy brought changes to foreign policy and national economic planning: Zaire sought closer ties with neighboring Congo and Guinea, formerly considered too radical, and it has given ideological support to Tanzania and Zambia in their stance against white-dominated Southern Africa.

"Authenticity" has also meant increased "Zairization" of the economy. On the eighth anniversary of his accession to power, Mobutu ordered the immediate nationalization of all plantation companies and the Belgian mining company MIBA. Later the state took control of all large enterprises in the import-export business, services, agriculture, transport, industry, and construction. Union Minière, Zaire's largest mining company, was nationalized in 1966 and renamed Gécamines. "Zairization" was introduced not only to add "authenticity" but to revitalize the economy which had suffered numerous setbacks since independence. It was not until 1966 that the GDP reached its 1958 level, and agricultural output in 1972 was below that of 1959. Total mineral production in 1973 was only slightly above the 1958 level, while the volume of zinc, tin, coal, and diamonds was lower (Tables 14-2 and 14-3).

Table 14-2 AGRICULTURAL PRODUCTION, 1959–1972 (1000 tons)

	1959	1964	1968	1972
Palm oil	244	177	206	168
Palm kernels	61	47	48	37
Cotton fibers	63	15	12	21
Timber (000 cum)[a]	228	180	137	80
Rubber	40	35	41	40
Coffee	62	38	55	79

[a] *Cubic meters*

Table 14-3 MINERAL PRODUCTION, 1958–1973 (1000 tons)

	1958	1964	1970	1973
Copper	237	276	387	500
Zinc	114	105	109	82
Cobalt	6	7	15	15
Manganese	319	—	329	334
Tin	11	5	1	1
Coal	294	106	n.a.	n.a.
Industrial diamonds (000 carats)	16	15	12	12

SOURCES. *Peemans (1975)*, Rapports Banque du Zaire *(various issues)*, *and* Quarterly Economic Review *(various issues)*.

N.A.: not available.

Market scene in Kisantu, lower Zaire. (Sabena)

Subsistence agriculture supplies 70 percent of the population with a living, but accounts for only half of agriculture's total contribution to the GDP. In the wage sector, agriculture accounts for 30 percent of all employment, as against 16 percent in mining and 24 percent in manufacturing (Peemans, 1975). Agriculture has suffered more than any other sector of the economy since 1960. Export crops, especially oil palm products, cotton and timber have declined sharply (Table 14-2). Many peasant farmers, unable to control prices, have reverted to subsistence farming or have turned to growing foodstuffs for the burgeoning urban markets. Domestic food production is declining: in 1973 Zaire imported 42 percent of its food requirements as against only one percent in 1958. Only about 1 percent of Zaire's land area is planted to field and tree crops, and another 1 percent is used as permanent pasture. The most intensively cultivated areas adjoin the towns, but even there land has been abandoned because of poor transport, and because imported foods may be purchased at lower prices in the urban centers.

In 1974, following the nationalization of most agricultural schemes, Mobutu unfolded a plan aimed to make Zaire self-sufficient in food by 1980. He promised to give massive support for the improvement of roads in rural areas, for the development of cooperative and credit facilities, and for the establishment of a national fertilizer industry. In Shaba, the mining companies were instructed to create 12,350 acre farms (5000 ha) to reduce the region's dependence on maize imports from Zambia and Tanzania. Unemployed town dwellers are being diverted to these and other rural projects. Rice production is being expanded under Chinese supervision, and is expected to become Zaire's third most important staple after manioc and maize.

Mining is the real source of Zaire's wealth, accounting for 80 percent of all exports, and contributing between 20 and 25 percent to the GDP. Copper alone generally accounts for 60 percent of all exports, and is followed by cobalt, diamonds, zinc, manganese, and tin. Zaire is the world's leading producer of cobalt, and the fifth largest pro-

Copper mine at Lubumbashi, Shaba, heart of Zaire's copper producing region. (Gécamines, Zaire)

ducer of copper. A half million metric tons of copper were produced in 1974, and the state-owned copper complex Gécamines, has investment plans for the period 1975–1980 costing about $500 million with a view of expanding productive capacity to 600,000 tons. When the new mines in the Tenke-Fungurume area commence production in 1977, an additional 130,000 metric tons of copper will be produced, along with 3000 metric tons of cobalt. Other major mineral projects under development include a uranium enrichment plant at the Inga hydroelectric scheme on the Zaire River west of Kinshasa, and offshore oil production near the Cabinda border.

Mining in Shaba was almost unaffected by the disturbances that followed independence, and production has remained relatively stable since. However, during the international economic recession of the early 1970s, the price of copper and consumer demands fell, placing great strains on the Zairian economy. With the decline in agricultural exports, Zaire is even more dependent on its minerals; hence the renewed interest in revitalizing the ailing agricultural sector.

Mineral production and industrial output should rise with the completion of several new transport and hydroelectric schemes, and the upgrading of railways in Shaba and Kivu. The new railway from the port of Banana through Boma to Matadi, which will link with the line to Kinshasa, may be connected by the longer and urgently needed line to Ilebo (Fig. 14-2). This would provide Shaba with a direct rail link to its own coast, and reduce Zaire's dependence upon the route through Angola. The Mungbere-Aketi line in the north was extended to the river port of Bumba in 1975, and there are plans to build a railway from Kinshasa to Kisangani. Should the Trans-African Highway from Mombasa to Lagos be built as planned, new agricultural regions could be opened up in the north, and the cotton and coffee interests better served.

Zaire has the greatest hydroelectric potential in Africa (103 million kw), and 13 percent of the world's potential. However, less than 10 percent of the gross potential

Inga hydro-electric dam on the lower Zaire River, between Kinshasa and the coast. Zaire has the world's largest hydro-electric potential. (Georg Gerster)

was installed in 1976, with three-fourths of the power being generated in Shaba, and 14 percent in the Kinshasa region. Energy development has been closely linked with the development of mining and metallurgical industries that consume about 80 percent of the country's total electricity output. The largest scheme is on the lower Zaire at Inga, where the theoretical potential (40 million kw) is equivalent to all the power presently used in the United Kingdom, or to the U.S. hydroelectric capacity in 1960. Phase I of the Inga project was opened in 1972. Phase II added a further 1000 MW in 1976, and Phase III could add another 1700 MW. Much of the power will be transmitted to Shaba over 1000 mi (1600 km) away, while some will be used by the new Maluka metallurgical complex near Kinshasa, and the chemical-metallurgical complex near the port of Banana. To support industrial growth in the northeast, two hydroelectric stations are to be built at Wagenia and Wanialukula, providing one million kwh per year.

The Inga-Shaba power line, the Ilebo-Kinshasa railway, and the Inga hydroelectric plant, will absorb about 25 percent of Zaire's investment until 1980 (Peemans, 1975). They emphasize the importance of Zaire's two core regions, and the problems of distance between them. Kinshasa and Shaba represent about 90 percent of national employment, and 77 percent of wages distributed. While industry is still concentrated in Shaba, the government is encouraging decentralization to the provincial capitals and lower-order towns.

Ten cities have populations over 100,000 but most are not industrially diversified: Kananga (597,000) specializes in palm oil products; Lubumbashi's (410,000) major industries are mine-related; Mbuji-Mayi (340,000) produces little but diamonds; Kisangani (300,000) is the country's major textile center; and Likasi (150,000) specializes in chemicals and copper refining. Kinshasa (2 million) is the most diversified industrial city (engineering, auto assembly, clothing, chemicals, foods, and others), but, like all other Zairian cities, it is short of qualified personnel and has a serious unemployment problem. With the exception of Lubumbashi, the provincial capitals are not supported by lower-order towns and cities, and their trade areas are small. Interprovincial economic linkages are weak, and are restricted by inadequate communications and a generally poor population. Vast areas of unproductive land still separate these towns and resource regions.

Size has always been both an asset and a liability to Zaire. Its almost 1 million sq mi (2.3 million sq km) encompasses great mineral wealth, about 10,000 mi (16,000 km) of navigable waterways, and sufficient topographical variety to provide it with unrivaled hydroelectric potential. On the other hand, this vastness encompasses great ethnic and linguistic diversity that has made political unity difficult from the days of King Leopold, through the colonial era, to the present. It has also made transport both costly and time consuming, and, if problems of distance are to be overcome, it will require great expenditures on the road and rail networks. But in a developing country where the population is predominantly rural and widely distributed, and in need of improved health and education facilities, higher incomes, and better housing, and where development funds are limited and dependent on exports whose prices are subject to severe fluctuations, it will not be easy to overcome the problems of size.

Bibliography

Boute, J. "Demographic Trends in the Republic of Zaire," *Africana Library Notes*, No. 21 (December 1973), pp. 15–24.

Duignam, P. and L. H. Gann (eds.). *Colonialism in Africa*. Vol. 4, London: Cambridge University Press, 1974.

Hoskyns, C. *The Congo Since Independence*. London: Oxford University Press, 1965.

Huybrechts, A. *Transports et structures de développement au Congo*. Paris: Mouton, 1970.

Legum, C. *Congo Disaster*. Magnolia, Mass.: Smith, 1969.

Miracle, M. P. *Agriculture in the Congo Basin*. Madison: University of Wisconsin Press, 1967.

Peemans, J. Ph. "The Social and Economic Development of Zaire Since Independence: An Historical Outline," *African Affairs*, Vol. 74, No. 295 (April, 1975), pp. 148–79.

Young, M. C. "The Congo's Six Provinces Become 21," *Africa Report*, Vol. 8, No. 9 (October, 1963), pp. 12–13.

———. *Politics in the Congo: Decolonization and Independence*. Princeton: Princeton University Press, 1965.

Quarterly Economic Review.

Rapports Banque du Zaire.

FIFTEEN

The smaller and northern portion of Equatorial lowland Africa (Zaire being the larger), forms a corridor from the Bight of Biafra and the mouth of the Zaire River as far east as the Sudan, and as far north as the margins of the Sahara (Fig. 15-1). It comprises three republics derived from former French Equatorial Africa: the Central African Republic, Congo, and Gabon; Equatorial Guinea, once a Spanish colony; and the United Republic of Cameroon, consisting of the former French Trusteeship and part of the former British Trusteeship. This sparsely populated region (only 11 million inhabitants in an area four times the size of California) is predominantly forested, rich in minerals, but lacking in many of the requisites for quick and widespread economic development. While several natural and institutional constraints to economic progress and political stability are shared by them all, each state has its own particular development prospects and priorities. These are reviewed against the background of the territories' colonial heritages, and within the context of change in contemporary Africa.

Problems of the Past

French Equatorial Africa before the Second World War possessed many of the characteristics of the Congo Free State prior to World War I, but the abuses continued much longer. From the early 1500s, the major product of the region had been the slave, taken westward from the coasts to the Americas and eastward across the Sudan to the Arab world. As many as 150,000 slaves may have been taken annually as late as 1840

DEVELOPMENT CONTRASTS IN EQUATORIAL LOWLAND AFRICA

259

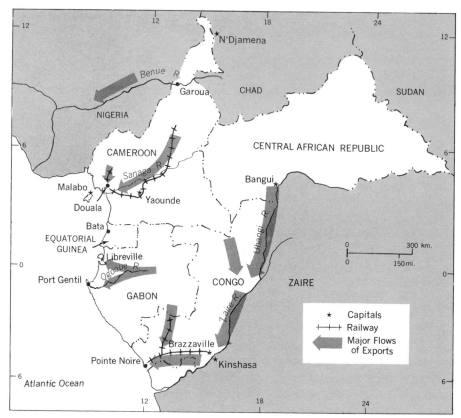

FIGURE 15-1 *General identification map of Equatorial Africa.*

The period of exploration, starting in earnest in the 1820s saw Britons such as Dixon Denham, and Germans like Heinrich Bath and Robert Flegel travel across the region in the interests of their respective homelands. French interests were stimulated primarily by De Brazza, who founded the city of Brazzaville (1880) and explored parts of present-day Congo and Gabon.

French exploration continued between 1880 and 1890, when the upper reaches of the Ubangi River were penetrated and treaties signed. The object of France's push into this interior region was the establishment of an axis across Africa as far as the borders of what was then Abyssinia, and French flags were eventually planted that far east. But British power forced the French to withdraw from the entire Nile Basin. German influ-

ence, meanwhile, was established in Cameroon, and the British had also taken most of present-day Nigeria, while the Congo Free State had been created to the south. French penetration was thus confined to a northerly path, and hence Chad became a part of the corridor of France's realm in equatorial Africa.

After the period of exploration and consolidation came the first attempts at administration. The Berlin Conference had adopted a resolution which affected the Belgian as well as the French sphere of influence in the Zaire Basin: a free-trade zone was to be recognized there. Thus, it was felt that direct French government efforts to administer the region might lead to international protests, and, moreover, the system of permitting private companies to exploit the Congo Free

State was deemed successful. A similar solution was used in the French areas, and thus the period of exploration was followed by a phase during which concession companies, which possessed a monopoly of trade and a measure of sovereignty, literally ruled the region. The consequences resembled those that led to the outcry over the "Congo atrocities".

Initially, it was thought that boundless wealth lay in this part of Africa, but after the early rush of exploitation of wild rubber and ivory by the concession companies, the reality of the situation began to penetrate. This part of Africa was, and still is, hot, humid, and disease ridden. The tsetse fly eliminates the use of oxen or horses for transportation of goods overland, road-building materials are scarce, the forest dense, the population sparse, and the labor supply limited at best. Thus, human portage, with its tremendous cost, along tedious and narrow pathways was the only way of carrying supplies to the interior settlements and exports to the coast. This was true until as late as the mid-1930s, when the railway between Brazzaville and Pointe Noire, begun in 1922, was finally completed.

Just as Stanley had emphasized the need for railroads in the Congo (Zaire), so De Brazza had envisaged a railroad system for French Equatorial Africa, of which the Pointe Noire-Brazzaville line was the priority project. But De Brazza wanted the line to lie entirely in French territory, not, as Leopold suggested, partly in Belgian and partly in French territory as a joint enterprise. Thus, the Matadi-Leopoldville line was built by the Belgians alone, and materials too heavy for human portage sometimes reached

the interior of French Equatorial Africa via that connection. However, French Africa benefited but little from the Belgian link: the port of Matadi was congested, and the railroad operated near saturation point, so that there was little space for French freight.

Further north (Fig. 15-1), a railroad was built from the port of Douala in Cameroon for the export of bananas, cocoa, and palm oil from plantations established during the German colonial era. In Gabon, the Ogooué and N'Gounie rivers were virtually the only communications links until after World War II. No railroad was built there during the colonial era, and very few roads connected Libreville, the capital, with its forested interior.

When, after the end of World War II, France was confronted with a need for stimulating development in this grossly underdeveloped part of its colonial realm, it faced several major obstacles, not the least of which was the detrimental effect of decades of neglect. Distances are great—as great, indeed, as those in Zaire. The known mineral resources were few, agricultural diversification had barely begun, and communications were rudimentary. As in the case of Belgium, France initiated a Ten-Year Plan with an emphasis on transportation, both external and internal. Begun in 1946, the program bogged down in several areas simply because local conditions were not sufficiently well known or understood. Ultimately, however, its effect was at least to create a structure upon which further development could be based when the year of independence (1960) came to French Equatorial Africa.

Gabon: Richness in Resources

Gabon is a small compact country rich in mineral and forest resources: dense tropical forests extend from the coast to the Congo border and into the interior highlands

where there are rich deposits of uranium, manganese, and iron ore (Fig. 15-2). The climate is moist and hot, the soils heavily leached, and malaria and other tropical dis-

Trucks transporting okoumé *and mahogany logs to N'djole on the Ogooué River. The forestry industry is shifting into the interior as the coastal reserves are nearing depletion.* (UN)

eases are endemic. Gabon's population is about 1 million, and its growth is one of the lowest in Africa (below 1 percent), primarily because of high death rates and a high incidence of infertility caused by disease and malnutrition.

If Equatorial Africa has one resource in abundance, it is the forest, but timber industries there have suffered from a series of conditions detrimental to their growth. First, industries based on the exploitation of certain tree varieties are hampered by the fact that a multitude of trees make up the rainforest, and any specific type is likely to be widely dispersed. Thus, trees may have to be moved over considerable distances, even to the waterways along which they can be floated down to the coast, and this presents

its own problems. Second, the labor supply is limited, and, of course, the internal consumption of lumber is small, so that most of it must be exported. Third, loading facilities at the small coastal ports are inadequate, and wood is a bulky, heavy, and expensive product to ship over long distances. Thus, only the most valuable woods, commanding a high enough price on the world market to withstand the cost of production and transportation, can form the basis for a successful timber industry.

Gabon is fortunate in that its forests contain some of the most valuable woods produced anywhere. Indeed, the development of this country has not taken place in spite of the forest but because of it, and because of the fact that a system of navigable

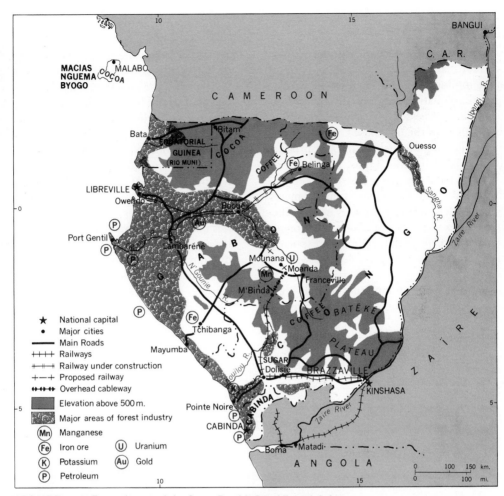

FIGURE 15-2 *Economic map of the Congo People's Republic and Gabon.*

waterways, focusing upon the Ogooué River, traverses it. What has limited the timber industry (in addition, of course, to flunctuations in the world prices) has been the perennial shortage of lumberers and skilled rowers more than the scarcity or wide dispersion of tree types. Gabon, along with Congo and Equatorial Guinea, has the world monopoly on the production of *okoumé*, a light wood used in the manufacture of plywood. The forest also yields ebony and mahogany, and for many years these woods yielded 90 percent of Gabon's export revenues.

Inevitably some of the mismanagement

characteristic of the rubber- and ivory-exploiting concession companies also has marked the timber industry. The coastal belt is almost worked out, and reforestation and other conservation practices have become imperative. Cutting has moved inland to what is known as Zone II where highly capitalized French firms dominate the industry. Here there is great potential, although river transport is less practical because of the more broken nature of the land than along the coast and in Zone I.

Whereas forestry dominated Gabon's money economy for more than six decades, minerals have accounted for most of the country's economic growth since the mid-1960s. They now provide 75 percent of foreign revenues and should dominate exports for many years to come. Rapid growth in the mining sector has been led by petroleum. Exploitation began in 1957 near Port Gentil and witnessed spectacular growth in the 1970s with the opening of the Gamba-Ivinga and Anguille fields. In 1975, production exceeded 10 million tons, two-thirds of it coming from the newly discovered offshore fields. The Port Gentil refinery meets domestic demands and supplies most of the new requirements of Cameroon and Congo. Over 85 percent of the crude oil is exported, mainly to France, Curacao, Senegal, and Ivory Coast.

Gabon's other important minerals are manganese, uranium, and iron ore. Over 200 million tons of manganese ore are known to exist in the highlands near Moanda (Fig. 15-2), and Gabon is the world's fourth largest producer after the USSR, South Africa, and India. Until the new trans-Gabon railway is completed, production is limited to 2 million tons per year, the ores being transported by overhead cableway to M'Binda and thence by rail to Point Noire, Congo. A few miles north of Moanda, uranium is mined at Mounana. Annual production has fluctuated widely since 1970 as a result of changing demands and prices, and technical difficulties encountered now that the ores are no longer extracted by open-cast methods. Production is expected to stabilize at 1500 tons per year, despite Gabon's intentions to limit supplies and raise prices in anticipation of an improved world market for uranium in the

The Ogooué River, Gabon, is navigable for 155 miles (248 km). Logs from the surrounding forests are floated down river to Owendo for shipment overseas. (UN)

1980s. All uranium is exported as concentrates to the French Atomic Energy Commission.

In the remote northeast near Belinga (Fig. 15-2), there is a 1000 million-ton deposit of high-grade iron ore. Exploitation will begin only with the completion of the trans-Gabon railway, which will not be ready until 1980. Inferior-quality iron ore is located closer to the coast and port of Tchibanga, but there are no plans to develop them. Finally, small quantities of gold are mined at Lastoursville on the upper Ogooué, and lead, zinc, and phosphate are known to exist in profitable amounts.

For decades, Gabon's export economy has been hampered by poor transport and restricted geographically to the lower reaches of the Ogooué River. The new trans-Gabon railway should alter that. Work started on the 350-mi, line (560 km) in 1974 and is scheduled for completion by 1980. It is being built not only to serve the mining interests and the once all-important forest industry but also to stimulate the rural economy. Roads are to be built linking the railway with the small and widely dispersed agricultural regions such as the Woleu and N'Tem valleys in the extreme north, where cocoa is an important cash crop. Gabon does not meet its own food requirements, and the government has never placed much emphasis on agricultural development: only 1 percent of total investment in the second Five-Year Plan (1971–1975) was directed to the rural sector. Farming is difficult in the rainforest areas, and agricultural output is hampered further by the fact that more money can be made in the mines and lumber camps.

Congo: The Assets of Location

One of Congo's major assets is its geographical location (Fig. 15-1). It has been a gateway to the interior ever since the French began their administration of Equatorial Africa. Stretching as it does from the narrow Atlantic coastline south of the equator along the Zaire and Ubangi rivers to nearly 4 degrees north latitude, this became France's principal access route to the Central African Republic (then Ubangi-Shari). Brazzaville became the major city, administrative capital, and dominant service center for the French equatorial realm, while Pointe Noire became the region's busiest and best-equipped port.

The transit of goods to and from the interior became the major source of revenue for Congo. Brazzaville itself developed into a modern city, thanks to considerable French investment in government infrastructure, cultural centers, and, to a lesser extent, in industry. Its hinterland, however, could not compete with that of Kinshasa, but it performed a break-in-bulk function between the coastal railroad and the Ubangi River. The region surrounding it saw little development. Brazzaville's *raison d'être* was its governmental functions, and with the dissolution of the federation, it was faced with stagnation and decay. Pointe Noire, more favorably situated for future development, retains the monopoly over the external trade of much of interior Equatorial Africa and has developed into a large (150,000) industrial port with a petroleum refinery, chemical plants, sawmills, ship repair yards, and numerous import substitute industries.

Congo's great liability is the paucity of its resources. Although it has much variety in its mineral and agricultural production, there is very little quantity. There is an overdependence on forestry products, but there is nothing like Gabon's bright prospect of future diversification. Forests cover 50 percent of the area, and timber and wood products generally constitute almost half the exports. Exploitation began at the coast and penetrated inland following the Congo-

Ocean railway (from Pointe Noire to Brazzaville), while more recent activity has focused on the Sangha Valley of the northern interior (Fig. 15-2). There, stands of *okoumé*, limba, and mahogany are being cut, and vast areas are being replanted. At present, much of the lumber is floated downriver to Brazzaville and then railed to Pointe Noire, but this should decrease once the new arterial highway is completed from the river-port/lumbertown of Ouesso to the coast.

Like the majority of African countries, Congo is not self-sufficient in staple foods, yet it produces a number of export crops. The long list of crops actually harvested might give the impression that this is an area with great possibilities: bananas, manioc, sugar, rice, coffee, cocoa, peanuts, and citrus fruits are but a sample. Indeed, this may be a country with real potential, but at present the rural population is simply too small and poor to produce any of these crops in quantity. What can be done was indicated after World War II, when a group of Frenchmen settled in the Niari Valley (Fig. 15-2) and began to cultivate rice, peanuts, and tobacco for export, in addition to market-garden produce for Brazzaville, Pointe Noire, and Dolisie. The region supplies the entire country with its sugar needs, and sugar is now the leading food export. The scheme has been an example for other similar ones, but they are still experimental and make only a small contribution to the export economy. A small group of individual farmers producing locally cultivable crops is one thing, but the development of a stable, growing peasantry is another. It is worth noting that in the 1975–1977 development plan, agriculture received one of the smallest shares (7.2 percent) of the development funds. Reform is being launched through the formation of cooperatives, and emphasis is placed on increasing cocoa, palm, manioc, and livestock production.

Agriculture is severly handicapped by unfavorable natural conditions. The soils are sandy and deeply leached, and dense forest extends over much of the north, reducing the cultivable land to pockets scattered

Petroleum terminal at Cap Lopez, Gabon. Gabon is an associate member of OPEC. The Port Gentil refinery meets domestic needs and supplies Cameroon and Congo with their oil requirements. (Elf Gabon)

across the country's southern half. Temperatures and humidity are perpetually high, and rainfall is heavy except along the coast. All but the higher areas around Brazzaville and the extreme southwest are plagued by tsetse flies, which preclude most forms of animal husbandry.

In the area of mineral exploitation, also, Congo can boast wide variety but little quantity. As recently as 1969, mineral exports accounted for less than 5 percent of total exports. Copper, lead, gold, zinc, and diamonds have been produced, but only lead has regularly ranked among the exports largely because of its proximity to the Congo-Ocean railway. A rich potassium chloride deposit near Pointe Noire came into production in 1969, but the project has been beset by technical and marketing difficulties, and production in 1974 was less than 500,000 tons as against the targetted 800,000 tons. Petroleum production has increased steadily since 1962 but is not expected to be a major source of foreign revenue.

Almost as bleak is the industrial situation, which of course is related to the smallness of the local market, the poverty of the population, the backwardness of agriculture, and the limited mineral production. Industrial output is concerned mainly with the processing of agricultural and forest products and is concentrated in the capital, the Niari Valley, and Pointe Noire. The inflow of foreign capital into manufacturing virtually ceased following the government's announcements to further nationalize industry. The country's larger industrial concerns, such as the cement, textile, and printing plants, are state-owned. Despite a Marxist orientation, Congo does most of its trading with the West (especially France), but its economic ties with the Soviet Union, China, and Cuba are increasing. China, for example, has provided technical and financial assistance for hydroeletric installations near Brazzaville, a textile complex at Kinsoundi, and a shipyard at Pointe Noire.

Central African Republic: Problems of the Past

The Central African Republic lies across an upland that forms the transition zone between the forested Zaire Basin and the steppe-and-desert basin of Chad, and it occupies part of the Sudan-Chad divide as well. Thus, it partakes of several climatic and vegetation belts. The southwest is covered by dense forests, but northward an increasingly dry savanna replaces this growth. Since the country lies higher than either Gabon or Congo, the climate is somewhat cooler in the central parts, and perhaps the best evidence for this amelioration is the cattle population of nearly a half million (against a mere 35,000 in Congo). The most important consequence of the republic's location with reference to the major physiographic features of equatorial Africa, however, is that a certain variety is brought to the economic picture. While there is not the exchange of goods which takes place in West Africa between the peoples of the dry north and the forested south, the resource base is more diversified, for instance, than that of its southern neighbor, Congo.

Although favorable in some respects, the location of the republic also has some disadvantages. Its capital and major river port, Bangui, is more than 900 mi (1440 km) from the sea. Toward the east and northeast, the country gets very dry, and there is a rainfall deficiency over much of the non-forest zone. Soil erosion is rampant in some parts of the country due to careless cutting for plantation development. As elsewhere in equatorial Africa, there are labor problems, and the country shares with Gabon and Congo an excessive movement of rural people to the towns, especially to Bangui (350,000).

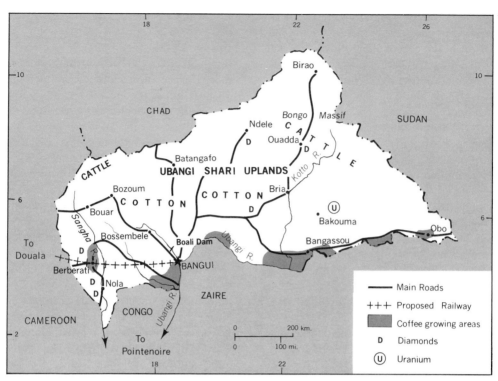

FIGURE 15-3 *Economic map of the Central African Republic.*

To some extent, the human problems of the Central African Republic are the result of the abuses of the recent past. There, the rule by concession companies led to the worst conditions in all of French Equatorial Africa, and the Africans' opposition was bitter and desperate. When the period of exploitation came to an end, there remained an enmity between black and white which continues to delay progress today. The past hangs heavily over the Central African Republic for in a sense the forced labor on the land, imposed by the companies, alienated the African from the soil and led to the exodus to the cities after World War II. The government's major effort to stimulate the cotton industry has been impeded by these factors, even though a number of areas in the central and southern part of the country are suitable for the cultivation of this crop.

Involved also has been the fact that some two-thirds of the acreage under coffee, the republic's second export after diamonds, was in European hands. Coffee does well along the edge of the forests in the Upper Sangha Valley and the Upper Ubangi Valley, and it is an easier crop to grow than cotton. Africans accused Europeans of attempting to divert African coffee growers' efforts toward cotton, leaving the easier, more profitable crop to the Europeans. Such difficulties have beset the country throughout the period of contact with Europe, and they are continuing after independence. Nevertheless, time may solve the human problem, while the economic opportunities remain. In addition to cotton and coffee, such crops as sisal, tobacco, cocoa, and rice can be cultivated. In general, the areas offering the best opportunities lie in the southwest (Fig. 15-3), in the region of the Upper Sangha, and in the southeast, along the northern slopes of the Upper Ubangi, broadly in the vicinity of Bangassou.

In recent years, agricultural production has declined following a brief period of general prosperity in the late 1960s which was attributed to the successful implementation of "Operation Bokassa." Under this program, supported by the European Development Fund and various French agencies, increased production in cotton, coffee, livestock, and staple foods was achieved. Insecticides, fungicides, and fertilizers were made available; villages were regrouped to provide poles of development; and rural electrification was introduced to help small farm-based industries located away from major towns. However, inefficient administration, domestic politics, a deterioration of relations with France, and prolonged unfavorable weather conditions, brought this short period of economic growth to a close.

The availability of road materials and the presence of an intensive river system have produced a network of communications which, for equatorial Africa, is good, although it does little to reduce the high cost of the lengthy journey of all exports to the sea and their overseas markets. At present, 90 percent of the Central African Republic's exports travel 700 mi (1120 km) of the Ubangi and Zaire rivers to Brazzaville, and another 300 mi (480 km) of rail to Pointe Noire. Although the mineral exports (diamonds and some gold) are not bulky, the heavy freight charges on the agricultural exports and almost all imports have led to a search for alternative routes to the sea. Several railway proposals are under consideration, the most feasible route being from Bangui via Berberati to the new Trans-Cameroon railway that terminates in Douala (Fig. 15-3). The port of Douala is not only nearer to the Central African Republic but the journey would also be much faster than the river-rail route to Pointe Noire and would require no transshipment. Such a link could stimulate development in the western region but would, of course, be detrimental to the interests of Congo. Less feasible routes, but nevertheless under consideration, are from Bangui to the Sudan, and from Bangui to the new trans-Gabon line.

Industrial development has barely begun. Less than 50 manufacturing establishments were in operation in 1975, most of them in and around Bangui, with the majority processing locally derived primary materials. The textile and leather industries constitute the chief industrial sector, while major projects planned include a plywood and chipboard factory, an additional textile complex, and a cement factory. A major asset is the Boali hydroelectric scheme about 50 mi (80 km) from the capital, which provides power for these enterprises. French influence is still dominant, despite a series of moves to reduce it in 1974 following France's unwillingness to develop the Bakouma uranium deposits (north of Bangassou), from which the government hopes eventually to earn substantial revenues that could lift the country from its present state of economic backwardness.

Despite some advances, the Central African Republic remains a poor and underdeveloped country whose major constraints to development may be traced back to the unfortunate legacy of colonial maladministration. France did little to provide its colony with the essentials for political stability and economic progress. If economic growth is to be achieved, there must be both sustained foreign technical and financial assistance and domestic economic and administrative reforms.

Cameroon: Progress and Cooperation

The wedge-shaped state of Cameroon, extending from Lake Chad in the north and the Sangha River in the east to a narrow but important coast line in the west, never was a

Equatorial Guinea (10,820 sq mi or 28,025 sq km), one of Africa's ministates, is divided for administrative purposes into two provinces: Macias Nguema Byogo (formerly Fernando Po) and Rio Muni. The former is a small volcanic island 30 mi (50 km) off the Cameroon coast whose soils are rich, and rainfall is high. Rio Muni, the larger of the two provinces, is bordered by Cameroon on the north and by Gabon on the east and south. Its narrow and densely forested coastal plain, cut by the fast flowing and unnavigable Woleu River, gives way to a succession of valleys and spurs of the Crystal Mountains.

After almost 200 years of Spanish rule, independence was granted in 1968. A year later, following internal political disorders and antiwhite riots in Rio Muni, most Spanish residents fled the country, and the fragile economy—based on cocoa, coffee, and timber—almost collapsed. Cocoa is the major export crop, 90 percent of which is grown on African-owned plantations on Macias Nguema Byogo and worked by Nigerian contract labor. The rest is grown by small farmers organized into cooperative groupings in both provinces. Coffee is grown chiefly by Fangs in northern Rio Muni, while the timber industry is dominated by highly capitalized European-owned companies operating on the mainland. *Okoumé* is the chief wood. Other less important exports are bananas and palm oil. Industry is virtually nonexistent, no minerals are produced, but offshore oil prospecting is in progress. Spain is the principal trading partner and source of financial and technical assistance.

Almost one-third of the approximately 330,000 Guineans live on Macias Nguema Byogo, 40,000 of whom live in Malabo (formerly Santa Isabel), the republic's capital and main economic, educational, and religious center. Despite its size, Equatorial Guinea has great ethnic variety, with the Fang being the largest and most influential group in Rio Muni and immigrant and refugee Nigerians being dominant on Macias Nguema Byogo. Although some Nigerian groups have advocated the island's annexation or purchase, the Nigerian government has never espoused this claim. In 1975–1976 the Nigerian government evacuated its nationals, charging maltreatment and inhuman employment conditions. Likewise, the governments of both Cameroon and Gabon have refrained from seeking the annexation of Rio Muni, despite strong regional ethnic affinities, territorial contiguity, and potential economic gain.

part of French Equatorial Africa. Influenced in turn by the British (until 1884), the Germans (until World War I), and the French (who held a Mandate over the bulk of the territory from 1922 to 1946 and a Trusteeship until 1960), Cameroon forged ahead of the remainder of equatorial Africa at an early stage and has remained in the lead ever since. Reunited with part of the British sector of the original Mandates, this is the most populous country in former French-administered equatorial Africa (6.5 million people), though it is by no means the largest (179,558 sq mi, or 465,054 sq km).

Cameroon's internal physiographic variety is considerable, and as a result a wide range of crops can be cultivated. Its north-south extent is no less than 10 degrees of latitude, so that in the south and along the rather narrow coastal belt, conditions are those of the tropical rainforest, whereas in the north, dry savanna and steppe lands occur. Topographically, the country rises in a series of escarpments toward an interior plateau covering the bulk of its area, but a number of prominent features mark the landscape: Mount Cameroon (13,354 ft or 4006 m) in the extreme west, and the Adamawa Highlands farther north rise from the coastal belt and the interior plateau, respectively. In the extreme north, Cameroon partakes of the central part of the Chad Basin, Lake Chad, and the land also drops in the extreme southeast, where the rivers are tributaries of the Zaire.

Most of the development has taken place to the west of a line drawn north-south, slightly east of Yaoundé (Fig. 15-4). Included in this western region are the important highlands of the former British section of Cameroon, which are among the more densely populated parts of the country and the scene of early settlement by Europeans, as well as most of the major towns and communications. There also lie the major port, Douala (380,000) with a capacity of the same order as that of Pointe Noire, the agricultural region of the Sanaga Valley, the capital, Yaoundé (260,000) and the growing industrial center of Edéa, near a major hydroelectric project on the Sanaga River. Two railroad arteries lead to Douala: one connects the port to N'Kongsamba, the railhead for the highlands, and the other leads to Ngaoundéré, serving the northern areas, Yaoundé, the Sanaga Valley, and Edéa.

Cameroon's potential for development is by no means limited to this western area, however. The initial extraction of the usual products from the coastal and southern rainforest, the proximity to the coast and a good harbor, and the western location of the highlands, where much of the early development took place, have led to the early and continuing pre-eminence of the west in terms of economic geography. But in the absence of major mineral deposits (except possibly bauxite, of which local deposits may replace the imported variety smelted at Edéa's plant), the country's major asset lies in the variety of crops that can be grown, a variety that is as large as it is because of the internal environmental diversification of the republic.

Apart from the usual unfortunate consequences of military conquest, the peoples of Cameroon were more fortunate than many others in Africa as far as the nature of their colonial administration was concerned, and this has much to do with the present potential for progress. The German administration at a very early stage embarked upon a program of crop research and drew up an economic blueprint calling for an embryo transportation system, limitations to land alienation, the perpetuation of certain facets of African traditional authority, and the participation of Africans in agricultural development. Despite the brevity of their period of tenure, the Germans had made some notable progress by the time the French took over the responsibility for Cameroon. Although certain aspects of French administration in the Mandate were not designed to reap the maximum possible harvest from the base that had been laid, Cameroon was and remained ahead of French Equatorial Africa proper.

Especially important in Cameroon's economic development was the early introduction of cash crops and the encouragement given to African farmers at an early time. Thus cocoa made its appearance among the country's exports before 1914, and by World War II, African producers were exporting all the cotton, cocoa, peanuts, and corn and the bulk of oil palm products. The pattern persists today, with peasant farmers dominating agricultural ex-

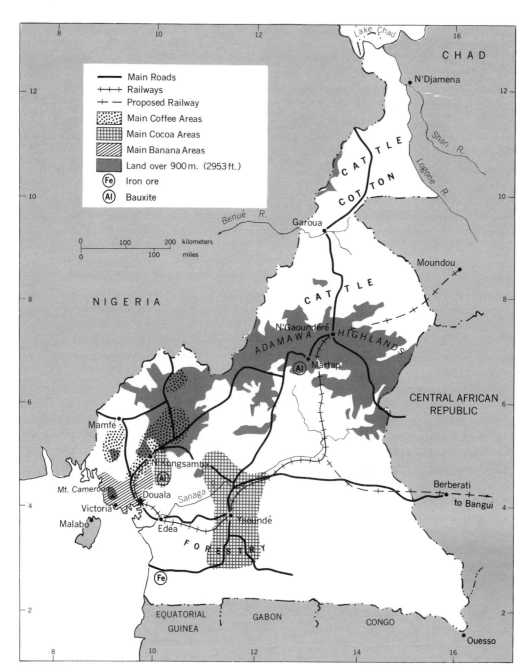

FIGURE 15-4 *Economic map of Cameroon.*

port production with the exception of rubber, bananas, and coffee (which collectively represent 30 percent of all exports and which are still produced on large plantations begun during the German era).

This early participation of African growers greatly facilitated the introduction of other crops found suitable for the region. Tea is grown along the highland slopes, and rice, cotton, and groundnuts are cultivated in the far north. The Adamawa Highlands and the high grassland areas in the former British Cameroon territory support a sizeable cattle population (Fig. 15-4), although the region is subject to severe stock losses associated with recurrent droughts. Domestic consumption of meat is low, so that surplus cattle are exported to Nigeria, and meat is shipped to Equatorial Guinea, Congo, and Zaire. The government has launched a major effort to increase food crops to eliminate the need for food imports, to give employment around the major towns and cities, and to check rural-urban migrations, which are especially pronounced in the north and west.

The years since independence have seen important growth in the Cameroon economy, but relatively little structural change. Cameroon remains heavily dependent on primary exports and on overseas investment and technology to sustain growth. Its considerable resource diversity, past performances in agricultural and manufacturing production, and the relatively centrist and experimentalist political economic policy (compared with other francophone states) have helped create a measure of economic viability and potential for expansion uncommon in tropical Africa. Having cultivated a diversified and viable rural economy, the government is now promoting the manufacturing sector.

Herdsmen trekking their cattle from northern Cameroon to Yaoundé. Cameroon exports cattle and livestock products to Nigeria, Gabon and Zaire. (UN)

DEVELOPMENT CONTRASTS IN EQUATORIAL LOWLAND AFRICA

Cameroon's manufacturing output ranks third in francophone Africa after Ivory Coast and Senegal; however, only 2 percent of the labor force is engaged in manufacturing, and industrial products account for one-fourth of all exports. To date, industry has not been integrated into the economic structure and has provided only limited spread effects. The Third Development Plan (1971–1976) gave priority to industries such as paper and pulp, textiles, cement, fertilizer, sugar, and aluminum that utilized locally produced raw materials. Industry is dominated by the Edéa aluminum smelting complex which utilizes imported ores and locally generated hydroelectric power. Mining is not currently significant, although great effort is being made in offshore oil exploration close to the Nigerian border.

Cameroon is actively seeking to strengthen its regional economic links through membership of the Central African Customs and Economic Union (UDEAC) and through developing routes to the sea and sources of manufactures for its landlocked neighbors, especially Chad. Still, less than 10 percent of its trade is with UDEAC members (Gabon, Congo, and the Central African Republic), while almost 30 percent of its exports goes to France, which provides most of the technical assistance and financial loans. The rail extension from Yaoundé to Ngaoundéré, completed in 1974, and funded by the United States and the EEC countries, could open up the northern regions, and provide southern Chad with a new outlet. The line makes exploitation of the northern bauxite deposits near Martap more feasible (Fig. 15-4), but greater power and alumina extraction capacity are also required before these could be fed into the Edéa complex.

Plans to extend the railway to Moundou (Chad) and to build a branch line to Berberati (Central African Republic) are under consideration.

The modest success in the development of Cameroon's predominantly agrarian economy must be measured against the results of similar efforts in other parts of lowland Equatorial Africa. Major problems still confront the country, whose political geography has always been complex. The extreme northern region suffers from remoteness from the country's capital and southern core area, and its natural outlet is still through Nigeria with which there are also strong social and cultural affinities. The long-term division of the country into British and French territories has presented problems upon the reunion of the southernmost British section with the French zone. Lying across the Bantu-Negro transition zone in the southwest, and penetrating the Moslem African world in the north, Cameroon's internal ethnic variety is as great as that of its physiography, and this has been an obstacle in the struggle for national unity.

Under the federal constitution adopted in 1961, Cameroon moved to increasing political, economic, and social integration, while pronounced regional variations in the economy, dating back to earlier administrations, persisted. In 1972, Cameroonians overwhelmingly approved a new constitution creating a unitary state. Since then, a completely centralized administrative system has prevailed, and Cameroon has lessened its dependence on France, withdrawn from OCAM, and sought new ties with China and the Soviet Union, while remaining committed to the West.

Bibliography

Bederman, S. H. "Plantation Agriculture in Victoria Division, West Cameroon: An Historical Introduction," *Geography*, Vol. 51 (1966), pp. 349–360.

Bederman, S. H. "The Demise of the Commercial Banana Industry in West Cameroon," *Journal of Geography*. Vol. 70 (1971), pp. 230–234.

Davies, W. J. "Politics, Perception, and Development Strategy in Tropical Africa," *Journal of Modern African Studies*. Vol. 13, No. 1 (March, 1975), pp. 35–53.

"Gabon: Railways and Rivalries," *Africa Confidential*. Vol. 14 (May, 1973), pp. 2–4.

"Gabon Growth," *Africa Digest*. Vol. 21 (August, 1974), pp. 75–76.

LeVine, V. T. "The Central African Republic: Insular Problems of an Island State," *Africa Report*. Vol. 10 (November, 1965), pp. 17–23.

LeVine, V. T. *The Cameroon Federal Republic*. Ithaca: Cornell University Press, 1970.

Pelissier, R. "Equatorial Guinea: A New Republic," *Geographical Magazine*, Vol. 41 (November, 1968), pp. 91–96.

Surveys of African Economies: Cameroon, Central African Republic, Chad, Congo (Brazzaville), and Gabon. Washington: International Monetary Fund, 1968.

Thompson, V., and R. Adloff. *The Emerging States of French Equatorial Africa*. Stanford: Stanford University Press, 1960.

Vennetier, P. "Problems of Port Development in Gabon and Congo-Brazzaville," in B. S. Hoyle and D. Hilling (eds.). *Seaports and Development in Tropical Africa*. London: MacMillan and Co., Ltd., 1970.

PART FOUR

SOUTHERN AFRICA

SIXTEEN

More than 74 million persons live south of the Zaire-Tanzania border in a region of immense environmental and institutional contrasts. Included are about 4.7 million whites, mainly of British, Dutch, and Portuguese ancestry. Before the mass exodus of Portuguese settlers from Angola and Mozambique in 1974–1975, the whites may have numbered 5.4 million. Politically Southern Africa has long been dominated by this resident minority and by Europe: Portuguese presence in Angola and Mozambique dates back to the 1480s; Dutch merchants and farmers settled the Cape over 350 years ago; the French established trading posts on the Madagascar coast in the late seventeenth century; and British settlement, which began in South Africa in the early 1800s, had crossed the Zambezi by the beginning of the twentieth century. From these early beginnings and coastal strongholds, the white sphere of influence spread across the sub-continent bringing to Southern Africa a unique set of politico-economic conditions and problems.

Physically, much of Southern Africa is a high plateau, bounded by narrow coastal plains and the Great Escarpment, and drained by some of Africa's largest rivers: the Zambezi, Limpopo, and Orange among others (Fig. 16-1). Nowhere did these provide Europe's colonial settlers easy access to the interior; in fact, they were major obstacles to colonial expansion. Out of this 2.5 million-sq mi area (6.5 million sq km), six landlocked territories (all once British) and five coastal states have been carved.

Independence came late to Southern Africa; five British territories gained theirs between 1964 and 1968, and the Portuguese did not withdraw until 1975. It has yet to be recognized in Rhodesia or granted to Namibia (South West Africa). Although Europe has played the dominant role in the politico-

ON THE TIGHTROPE: LANDLOCKED ZAMBIA AND MALAWI

279

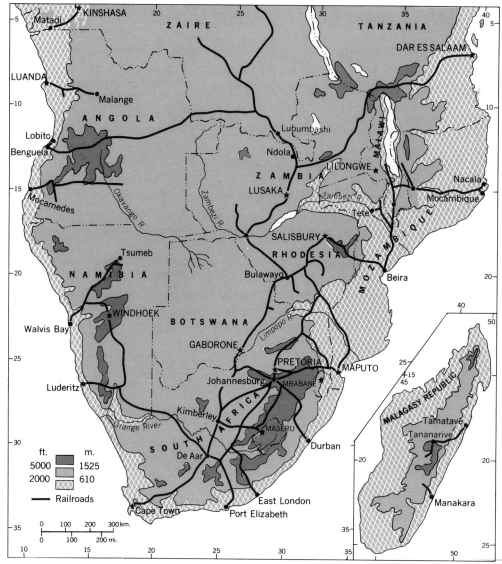

FIGURE 16-1 *Southern Africa. General identification map.*

economic development of Southern Africa, the South African influence has been strong in all territories other than Angola and Malagasy.

Included in this realm are Zambia and Malawi, two landlocked states that once were part of the Central African Federation, together with Rhodesia (then Southern Rho-desia). While having very different natural environments, resources, economies, and po-litical leaderships, Zambia and Malawi share similar problems in view of their landlocked position north of the Zambezi, and their former politico-economic orientations to-wards Britain and the south.

Colonial Beginnings and Orientation

The areas now known as Zambia and Malawi were originally settled by Bantu-speaking peoples from the north, the major wave occurring in the fifteenth century when the Moravi pushed east to Lake Malawi, and the Luba-Lunda kingdoms extended south to the Kafue River and east to Lake Bangwelu. The greatest influx took place between the late seventeenth and early nineteenth centuries. Later, Nguni peoples arrived from the south. By the mid-nineteenth century the various peoples of Zambia and Malawi were largely established in the areas they occupy today, the dominant groups being the Bemba, Kaonde, Chewa, and Nyanja. A rich diversity of agricultural and pastoral practices prevailed alongside highly competitive political systems and long-distance trade, especially in slaves.

As the region was plundered by slavers, and the delicately balanced subsistence economies were destroyed, Christian missionaries, traders, and explorers penetrated from the south and east. David Livingstone reached the Victoria Falls in 1855 and spent the next 18 years mapping out the terrain, spreading the gospel, and promoting legitimate trade. His travels took him up and down the Zambezi and Shiré rivers, the length of Lake Malawi, and into northern Zambia. His vivid descriptions of the land and peoples provided the impetus for further missionary work, and whetted the appetites of those with colonial ambitions, among them Cecil Rhodes.

Cecil Rhodes, who had made his fortune from diamonds and gold in South Africa (between 1870 and 1890), wished to see the highveld of central and eastern Africa under British rule and settlement. He also wanted to annex to his personal mining empire the copper deposits of present-day Shaba (formerly the Katanga). The British government, concerned at the time with maintaining British supremacy at the Cape and anxious to prevent German, Portuguese, and Boer settlement north of the Limpopo, granted a charter to Rhodes' newly formed British South Africa Company in 1889, giving it powers to make treaties and conduct administration north of this river. Thus, in 1890, his Pioneer Column, a group of about 190 whites, left Rhodes' farm near Kimberley and trekked north through eastern Botswana and onto the highveld of what is now Rhodesia. There the company concentrated its activities, subjugated the Africans, and expropriated their land.

Rhodes' personal ambitions north of the Zambezi were never fully realized (the rich copper deposits of Shaba falling to King Leopold II of Belgium) but, through treaty and coercion, most of what became Northern Rhodesia came firmly within the British sphere of influence. The company accepted administrative responsibility for the territory in return for the mineral rights, but its profits were few. Ores were discovered at Kansanshi, Broken Hill (Kabwe), and in the area of the present Copperbelt, but transport costs inhibited small-scale operations, while large investments went to the Congo (Zaire) and elsewhere. However, by 1909 the British South Africa Company had built a railway across the territory to Shaba, and copper began to move south to the Indian Ocean port of Beira. Coal moved north from Wankie, Rhodesia, and the small settler community along the line-of-rail provided the mines with maize and cattle. Further east, following successful Church of Scotland missionary activity and opposition to the slave trade, the British established the Nyasaland Protectorate in 1891.

Colonial rule meant a new economic order. In both territories European settlers obtained land at nominal prices and, with the introduction of hut and poll taxes, thousands of Africans were forced to work several months of each year on European estates growing coffee and tobacco in Nyasaland and tobacco and maize in Northern Rhodesia. Still others were forced to meet their needs by working in the mines and on the farms of Southern Rhodesia and South Africa. By 1903, some 6000 migrants left Nyasaland for work in the south. Land alienation meant that many Africans were made tenants-at-will with little or no legal right to the land they cultivated, and it produced a typically colonial dual economy.

But real economic progress was slow in coming. Distances were great, communications inadequate, and markets small. The whites of Northern Rhodesia resented the British South Africa Company's restrictive policies on land and mineral rights, and the imposition of an income tax in 1920. The company itself was in financial difficulty, so in 1924 it transferred its administrative responsibilities for Northern Rhodesia to the Colonial Office, and the territory became a protectorate.

In the late 1920s, huge deposits of copper ore were discovered south of Zaire's border, and the Copperbelt was born. By 1930 there were nearly 30,000 Africans employed in the region, and the white population for the territory as a whole reached almost 14,000, up from 3600 a decade earlier. But the Depression delayed development: thousands of employees were dismissed, and many whites left the territory. With economic recovery, however, the mines were brought into full production; mining-related industries were started in Mufilira,

Aerial view of Mufilira, Zambia, one of the Copperbelt's largest mining towns. (Roan Consolidated Mines Ltd.)

Nchanga, and Ndola; and the region became the protectorate's economic heart (Fig. 16-2). European immigration accelerated, many of the new arrivals settling not only in the Copperbelt but also in towns and on farms along the line-of-rail. Most rural areas suffered impoverishment through the absence of able-bodied men in the mines.

In neighboring Nyasaland, events took a different course. The railway from Nsaje to Blantyre-Limbe was built between 1903 and 1908 and was extended north to Salima in 1935. Between 1900 and 1920 the number of whites increased as tea and coffee plantations and other agricultural enterprises were developed in the Shiré Highlands. Few white settlers went to the northern areas. In Nyasaland, too, economic dualism prevailed, and the Africans became increasingly dependent on work opportunities in Southern Rhodesia and South Africa. Contact with the south meant rising expectations, firsthand experience in social discrimination, and peasant discontent.

Following World War II, Britain proposed that Northern Rhodesia, Nyasaland, and Southern Rhodesia be united in a federation, and in 1953 this became a reality. Most Africans opposed closer links with Southern Rhodesia, fearing stronger settler control north of the Zambezi. In particular, they feared land alienation like that in the south, and they feared an erosion of their political rights guaranteed under the protectorate system. Despite their protests, federation was imposed and the Central African Federation was born.

Britain argued that federation would benefit each component from an economic point of view, providing a better balance, greater diversification, and a wider resource base for the economic efforts of the new state. Federation, however, worked primarily to the advantage of whites in Southern Rhodesia who dominated the mainly white Federal Parliament, seated in Salisbury. Southern Rhodesia diversified and prospered under the arrangement, but the northern partners did not. Much of the revenue generated in the Copperbelt and along the line-of-rail was used to fund development projects south of the Zambezi, not in Northern Rhodesia where the needs were greater. More importantly, federation meant an increased dependence of the northern partners on Southern Rhodesia for jobs, manufactures, and technicians. Consequently, development outside the mining sector in Northern Rhodesia, and agriculture in Nyasaland, was extremely limited.

Federation produced closer economic ties between the two Rhodesias than between either of the Rhodesias and Nyasaland (Sills, 1974). The railway connection over the Victoria Falls bridge strengthened these ties: coal moved freely from Wankie northward, together with manufactured goods from Southern Rhodesia and South Africa, while this became the Copperbelt's principal outlet to its overseas markets. Nyasaland, in contrast, separated from Southern Rhodesia by a wedge of Mozambique territory, was linked by rail with Beira. Road connections between the two northern partners were poor, and they had little to exchange with each other. The two Rhodesias were drawn even closer together as partners in the massive Kariba project (Chapter Seventeen).

Mounting African opposition to federation, especially from the northern members, led to a British reconsideration of it and finally to its dissolution in 1963. In July 1964, Nyasaland became independent under the name Malawi, and three months later Northern Rhodesia became Zambia. Independence meant new *raisons d'être* for each state, and in the case of Zambia, significant reorientation in its politicoeconomic alignments.

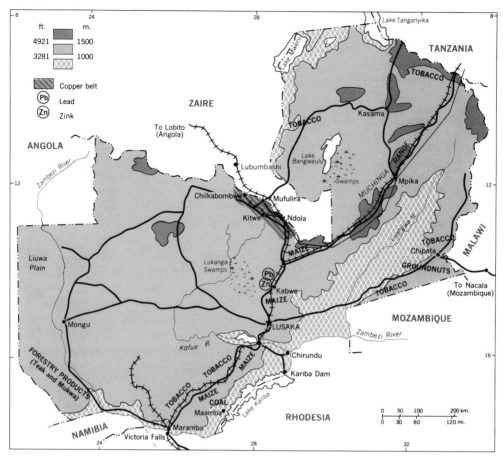

FIGURE 16.2 *Economic map of Zambia.*

Zambian Reorientations

With independence, Zambia attempted to reduce its dependence on the industrial complex of white-ruled Southern Africa, which to a large extent was responsible for Zambia's weak internal economy, an economy in which minerals contributed little to overall national development. An unexpected impetus to this was provided for in November 1965 when Rhodesia unilaterally declared its independence (UDI) of Great Britain. To force the Ian Smith regime to back down, the United Nations imposed sanctions against Rhodesia and since Zambia was so dependent on Rhodesian technology, transit, and manufactures, there was good

reason to fear economic (and political) chaos in Zambia.

The immediate problems centered on the export of copper and the import of oil and other essential goods. Britain, Canada, and the United States provided military planes to handle these materials, but not in sufficient quantity to meet both local and overseas needs. The shortage of coal and transport dislocations retarded growth of copper production, and it was not until 1969 that 1965 output levels were surpassed. Oil became a scarce commodity, and the cost of food and most imported goods soared.

Zambia met the challenge by concen-

Kafue

The Kafue River rises in the Copperbelt and joins the Zambezi near Chirundu, about 40 mi (64 km) downriver from the Kariba Dam (Fig. 16-2). In its upper reaches it provides water to the Copperbelt's towns and mines. It then flows through the tsetse-infested Lukenga swamps south to the Itezhi-Tezhi Gorge where a 900-MW capacity dam is under construction. There the river turns sharply east and flows through the Kafue Flats where cotton and maize are important cash crops, and fishing is an important industry. At the small industrial town of Kafue, water is diverted to Lusaka, Namwala, and other towns along the line-of-rail.

East of the railway the Kafue plunges some 1900 ft (580 km) in 12.5 mi (20 km) into the Zambezi Gorge. Here the river was dammed, and a 600-MW power plant was installed in 1972. The supply of water is regulated from Itezhi-Tezhi. Together with the Kariba Dam and power installations at Victoria Falls, the Kafue Project makes Zambia self-sufficient in its electricity needs. The copper industry uses about 70 percent of total output. Surplus power may be exported to Zaire and Botswana. The Kafue Project was specifically developed to reduce Zambia's dependence on Kariba, especially on output from the Rhodesian turbines.

trating its efforts (with considerable sacrifice) on developing its own industrial and energy resources, increasing its industrial output of both consumer and capital goods, and most importantly by utilizing Tanzanian and Angolan outlets for its copper. A coal mine was brought into production at Maamba to replace imported supplies from Wankie (Fig. 16-2); electrical output was increased from the Victoria Falls, while construction of a new power station on the Zambian side of the Kariba Dam was started, and a new hydroelectric project was completed on the lower Kafue (see box item); by 1971 the main road between Zambia and Tanzania was paved; a 1060 mi (1705 km) pipeline was laid between Dar es Salaam and Ndola by 1968, and a refinery opened at the latter site soon after; plans pushed ahead for the Tan-Zam Railway between Dar es Salaam and the Copperbelt; the government acquired a 51 percent holding in mining and strategic industries in an effort to control the state's industrial requirements; and Zambianization

of the economy and administration was accelerated. However, efforts to check rural-urban migration and to increase production of maize, meat, and other foods to offset Rhodesian imports were far less successful.

The situation worsened in January 1973 when Rhodesia closed its borders with Zambia, ostensibly in retaliation for guerrilla incursions from across the Zambezi. A month later, Rhodesia reopened the border to the copper traffic (since Rhodesia stood to lose valuable transit dues), but the measure backfired as Zambia decided to reroute all its exports to the north. Many states came to Zambia's aid by subsidizing copper exports by road through Tanzania and Kenya, while essential mining supplies and oil were airlifted from South Africa and Beira, respectively.

The original rerouting plan placed most of the burden on Dar es Salaam and Lobito. They were the best equipped to handle the 61 percent of imports and 50 percent of exports which previously had traveled via Rhodesian Railways. Dar was to take 43,000 tons of imports and 20,000 tons of exports each month, while Lobito's monthly quotas were 35,000 tons and 30,000 tons, respectively. Zambia's projected monthly imports and exports were 117,000 and 67,000 tons. However, because of fluctuating copper prices, the flow of copper was irregular, and so too was the inflow of merchandise.

Five ports handled most of Zambia's foreign trade: Lobito, Dar es Salaam, Nacala, Beira, and Mombasa (Fig. 16-1). Each has its particular assets and problems. Zambia's natural outlet to the west is Lobito, a port equipped to handle 80,000 tons of imports and exports each month, and thus theoretically capable of taking all of Zambia's exports. However, because of increasing port surcharges, port inefficiencies, a shortage of rolling stock, and political uncertainties in Angola (and even Zaire), Lobito is far from ideal. In 1975, for example, the Benguela Railway was closed by the upheavals of the Angolan Civil War, and Zambia was forced to seek alternative routes. Just prior to that closure, Lobito was handling 40 percent of Zambia's imports and 30,000 tons of copper each month. The Benguela Railway normally operates at capacity, serving both Zambia and Zaire, but it needs realigning and upgrading. A new, shorter route bypassing Zaire is under review.

Dar es Salaam, Tanzania's principal port and former capital, is expected to become the main outlet for Zambia's copper and the country's major port of entry for manufactures. Following UDI, copper was hauled to Dar over the Great North Road—once known as the "Hell Run" because of its deplorable conditions. Before being upgraded in 1971, sections were impassable during the rainy seasons, others in the mountains were too narrow for the large

trucks, and maintenance facilities en route were grossly inadequate. Costs were high, the service unreliable, and Dar itself had insufficient ore-loading and storage facilities. By mid-1976 the new Tan-Zam Railway (or Tazara) was operating near to capacity, but Dar was unable to adequately handle the higher volume of traffic.

The Kapiri-Mposhi station on the Tan-Zam Railway, Zambia. Built by the People's Republic of China, and opened in 1975, the Tan-Zam Railway links Zambia's Copperbelt with Dar es Salaam, Tanzania. (Zambia Information Services)

The three remaining ports—Nacala, Beira, and Mombasa—handled between them almost 45 percent of Zambia's total overseas trade in 1975. Mombasa was used during the emergencies of 1973–1974, but it is not a viable outlet on a permanent basis because of its location. On the other hand, Nacala and Beira are important to Zambia although neither is connected directly by rail with the Copperbelt. Zambia and Malawi have agreed in principle to a rail connection to feed into the Nacala system, and there is also the possibility that Mozambique may extend the Beira line beyond Tete and into Zambia.

Malawi's relationships with its neighbors are, and have always been, different than Zambia's. This is because Malawi is bounded by three rather than eight other territories (Fig. 16-1), geographically it is dominated by Mozambique (and not Rhodesia), and its political leadership has adopted and adhered to a "southward-looking" policy of economic and political alignment. South Africa, and not Rhodesia, has been its principal southern ally and trading partner.

When independence was granted (1964), it was generally assumed Malawi would seek closer politicoeconomic ties with its independent colleagues to the north. This included support of the OAU in its determination to liberate the white-controlled southern territories, condemnation of Rhodesia's UDI, and membership in the East African Community. However, Malawi's president, Kamuzu Banda, has steadfastly resisted such

measures, and Malawi has continued to rely heavily upon South Africa for its economic needs, and upon Mozambique for access to the sea. Banda has warned other African states of the dangers of accepting aid from Communist countries, supported dialogue and détente with South Africa, resisted FRELIMO "freedom fighters" from using Malawian territory, and has established diplomatic relations with South Africa. He has repeatedly stated that if Africa's leaders are genuinely interested in promoting the welfare of blacks in white-ruled Southern Africa, they must talk with, and not fight the political leadership in South Africa and Rhodesia (Reitsma, 1974). Such a position led some states to call for Malawi's expulsion from the OAU.

Banda's policy is based on realism. More than 100,000 Malawians have been employed each year in South Africa's mines,

Women carrying bundles of tobacco grown in the vicinity of Lilongwe, Malawi's new capital. (World Bank)

ON THE TIGHTROPE: LANDLOCKED ZAMBIA AND MALAWI

Malawi's first capital was established toward the end of the last century at Zomba, about 40 mi (64 km) north of the country's twin cities, Blantyre-Limbe. It never shared in the development of the south and was almost destroyed by storm in 1946. A commission was established to select a new site, but interest waned during the years of federation with the Rhodesias. In 1964, however, Prime Minister Banda proposed to Parliament that the capital be moved to Lilongwe, and this was agreed to in 1968.

Lilongwe was selected partly because of its central location within Malawi, and partly to encourage economic development north of the economically dominant southern region. The city sits in the largest and one of the most productive agricultural plains in the country where tobacco is the principal cash crop. Approximately 520,000 acres (210,000 ha) of rich arable land and pasture are being reorganized to increase crop and animal production, partly to meet local demands and partly for export.

The new capital has been built onto old Lilongwe, historically the chief service center for much of the north. The city itself has four major areas: old Lilongwe, Capital Hill where the government buildings and main shopping areas are situated, and two industrial zones and their associated residential areas. Population in 1975 was estimated at 55,000, and by the end of the century it could reach 500,000. Built with South African assistance, Lilongwe is joined by modern highway with Chapala (in Zambia), Blantyre-Limbe, and Zomba, and there are plans to extend the railway to it from Salima. Special concessions have been offered to entrepreneurs wishing to establish industry there.

and an additional 200,000 have worked in Rhodesia. More than twice as many Malawians work outside Malawi than in paid employment in it. Following a plane crash in 1974 in which 70 Malawian workers were killed, Banda suspended Malawi's labor agreements with South Africa and recalled all 106,000 workers home. A permanent repatriation of these migrant workers would not only aggravate an already high unemployment rate but it would also mean the loss of Malawi's third most important source of foreign revenue.

Dependency on South Africa extends into other fields. South Africa helped Malawi build a new capital city at Lilongwe and an international airport to serve it. It provided both technical assistance and financial

aid for the national highway between Lilongwe and Zomba (the old capital), and the rail extension east of the Vila Cabral-Nacala line in Mozambique.

Malawi is totally dependent on Mozambique for access to the sea. Beria is its natural outlet, with which it has been linked by rail since 1908. Until the opening of the Liwonde-Cuamba-Nacala line in 1970, this route carried almost 100 percent of Malawi's tea, tobacco, cotton, and coffee exports, together with most of its imports. Since then, much of the traffic originating in central and northern Malawi (along with Zambian copper) has been exported through Nacala. Both routes faced disruption during Mozambique's anticolonial wars of the late 1960s and early 1970s, but Banda's skillful handling of both FRELIMO and Portuguese forces prevented closure. Closure of either or both lines would have dealt a crippling blow to the Malawian economy since there are no alternate routes to the sea.

Malawi's transport links with Rhodesia have never been good, and thus the amount of interstate traffic has been small. While Mozambique was still Portuguese, and Malawi was part of the Central African Federation, a limited amount of traffic passed between the two territories. But during Mozambique's anticolonial wars, this was severed completely as FRELIMO units mounted their attacks on the Cabora Bassa dam and the town of Tete—midway between Rhodesia and Malawi.

Malawi's transport links with Tanzania are almost nonexistent. This is because Malawi's core region lies in the south (Fig. 16-3), while its essentially underdeveloped northern areas adjoin equally underdeveloped areas in Tanzania. When the line is extended from Salima through Lilongwe and Chapala to the Tan-Zam Railway, Malawi will, in fact, have a route (albeit circuitous) through Tanzania.

Some Similarities and Contrasts

Besides being land-locked and situated directly north of white-dominated Southern Africa, Zambia and Malawi share a number of important geographical characteristics. They also have their differences. Malawi is a small but environmentally diverse elongated state less than one-sixth the size of Zambia, an essentially compact state with much greater environmental uniformity. Their populations are similar (about 5.5 million in mid-1977), although growth rates are higher in Zambia (3.5 percent versus 2.6 percent), and Zambia has a larger expatriate element (50,000 versus 7000).

Malawi's considerable variations in altitude and location within the rift valley system, produces a wider range of climatic, soil, and vegetation conditions than in Zambia. It possesses some of the most fertile soils in Africa: in the lake-shore plains, the Lake Chilwa-Palombe Plain, the lower Shiré valley, the Lilongwe-Kasungu high plains, and in the tea-producing areas of Chole, Mulanje, and Nkhata Bay. Good soils and humid conditions mean that half the country is cultivable, but only one-third is currently in use, with the greatest intensity of land-use and the highest population densities occurring in the south (Fig. 16-4).

In contrast, Zambia is essentially a vast gently undulating plateau with wide shallow basins, lakes, swamps, and grassy plains. It forms the divide between the Zambezi and Zaire drainage systems, and its major topographical features are the Zambezi River and the Muchinga Mountains (Fig. 16-2). Its soils are widely infertile, being overmature on much of the plateau and badly eroded and immature in the escarpment zones. Population densities vary considerably but are heaviest along the line-of-rail and around the provincial and district capitals such as Chipata, Kasama, and Mongu.

Good environmental conditions in Malawi have contributed to the country's diverse agricultural economy. Tea, cotton, groundnuts, and some tobacco are grown around Blantyre, Mulanje, and Chiromo, while the major tobacco area centers on Lilongwe (Fig. 16-3). Small pockets of cash cropping occur in the northern highlands and along the lake shore. Agriculture supports 90 percent of the population and accounts for about 94 percent of domestic exports. In Zambia, however, agriculture plays a negligible role in the export economy. Productivity is low, surpluses are few, and the main crops are maize, groundnuts, sorghum, and millet. Agricultural development is one of Zambia's top priorities, where

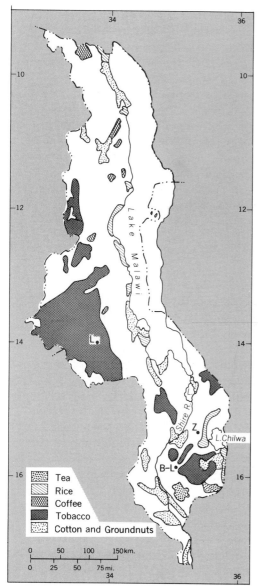

FIGURE 16-3 *Economic map of Malawi.*

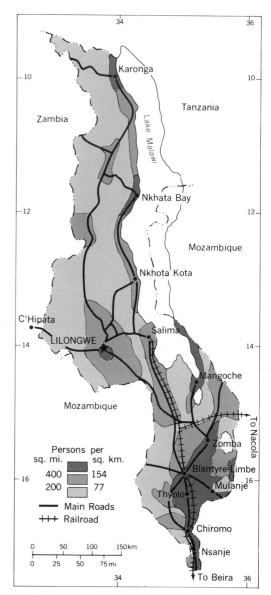

FIGURE 16-4 *Malawi. Population density.*

the aims are to improve income and nutritional standards, and lower imports. Both countries have allocated substantial financial resources to the rural sector in the form of cooperatives, extension services, resettlement schemes, and feeder roads.

In both countries there are regional and structural imbalances in the economy. Economic dualism is greatest in Zambia. Large

disparities of income and living conditions exist between mining and other workers, between Zambians and expatriates, and between persons on the line-of-rail and those in the periphery. Minerals dominate domestic exports (97 percent in 1974), with copper alone accounting for about 93 percent of the total. Copper has financed much of Zambia's manufacturing, most of which is centered on

A village meeting to discuss land allocation and the provision of marketing services, new roads and other facilities called for in the 520,000 acre (210,000 ha) Lilongwe Land Development Program, Malawi. (UN)

the Copperbelt, and in Lusaka, Kabwe, and Maramba (formerly Livingstone). Since the late 1960s numerous capital intensive industries (auto and truck assembly) and resource-oriented industries (explosives, chemicals, oil refining, and wire manufacturing) have been established. In contrast, industry in Malawi is primarily agro-based, although greater emphasis is being given to import substitution.

This export of bulky raw materials, and import of manufactured goods, machinery, and equipment, place severe strains on the transport systems and great reliance on the neighboring territories. Both Zambia and Malawi realize the implications and are anxious to develop and diversify their domestic

economies to lessen these dependencies. Their success or failure will largely be determined by the policies adopted by the political leadership. Malawi's Kamuzu Banda, who has spent 40 years in Britain and the United States, has adopted a cautious and nonmilitant approach to his neighbors. To date, he has welcomed both private and government investment from the West and shunned aid from Communist countries. Zambia's Kaunda has resolutely defied white-ruled Southern Africa, and has been more international in his search for aid. Both leaders are acutely aware of the problems that stem from their countries' geographic location and colonial heritage.

Agnew, S., and M. Stubbs (eds.). *Malawi in Maps*. London: University of London Press, 1972.

Arnold, G. "Changing the Communications Map," *Africa Report*, Vol. 20, No. 4 (July–August, 1975), pp. 37–41.

Chipembere, H. B. M. "Malawi's Growing Links with South Africa," *Africa Today*, Vol. 18, No. 2 (April, 1971), pp. 27–47.

Coleman, G. "Some Implications of International Labour Migration from Malawi," *East African Geographical Review*, no. 12 (April, 1974), pp. 87–101.

Connell, J. "Lilongwe: Another New Capital for Africa," *East African Geographical Review*, no. 10 (April, 1972), pp. 89–110.

Davies, D. H. (ed.). *Zambia in Maps: Graphic Perspectives of a Developing Country*. New York: Africana Publishing Corp., 1972.

Durand, L. *et al.* "Malawi," *Focks*. Vol. 19, No. 3 (December, 1968), pp. 1–11.

Hall, R. S. *Zambia*. London: Praeger, 1965.

Kay, G. *A Social Geography of Zambia*. London: University of London Press, 1967.

Kay, G. "A Regional Framework for Rural Development in Zambia," *African Affairs*, Vol. 67 (1968), pp. 29–43.

Mercer, A. "Rural Development in Malawi," *Optima*. Vol. 23 (March, 1973), pp. 7–13.

Mihalyi, L. J. "Legacies of Colonialism: Zambia," *Focus*. Vol. 24, No. 10 (June, 1974), pp. 1–8.

Pettman, J. "Zambia's Second Republic," *Journal of Modern African Studies*, Vol. 12, No. 2 (June, 1974), pp. 231–44.

Pike, J. G. et al. *Malawi: A Geographical Study*. London: Oxford University Press, 1965.

Reitsma, H. J. "Malawi's Problems of Allegiance," *Tijdschrift voor economische en sociale geografie*, Vol. 65, No. 6 (1974), pp. 421–29.

Sills, H. D. "The Break-Up of the Central African Federation," *African Affairs*, Vol. 73, No. 290 (January, 1974), pp. 50–62.

SEVENTEEN

Rhodesia, or Zimbabwe as it is known to most African nationalist groups, is one of two remaining strongholds of white supremacy in Africa and a theater of bitter racial conflict. It occupies a pivotal location where white supremacy comes face to face with militant African nationalisms. In many ways it is a natural fortress, bounded on the north and south respectively by the Zambezi and Limpopo rivers, and on the east by the Great Escarpment and the Inyanga Mountains. To the west lie the semiarid plains and desert wastelands of Botswana, themselves separated from the Atlantic by the tablelands and deserts of Namibia. Within this compact and landlocked plateau country of 150,783 sq mi (390,759 km), the various races have failed to produce an integrated society where there is parity in government and equality in the social and economic spheres.

The Zambezi has played an important role in the settlement and development of Rhodesia. The river itself has dangerous rapids and waterfalls, and its steep valley sides are hot, disease ridden, and densely vegetated. In the precolonial past, it hindered the southward expansion of the Mashona, Matabele, and Sotho peoples, and it marked the southern limit to the slave trade. During the colonial era it was the boundary between British protectorate administration and limited alien settlement in Zambia and Malawi and more direct colonial rule and extensive settler colonialism in the south. It was also a divisive factor in the former Central African Federation. Today, the Zambezi divides white-ruled southern Africa from independent black Africa. It is bridged in only three places along the Zambian-Rhodesian boundary (Victoria Falls, Kariba, and Chirundu). Since 1973 these border posts have been closed, thus effectively isolating Rhodesia from the north. Partly because of the Zambezi's barrier effect, colonial Rhodesia looked toward the south and east.

RHODESIA (ZIMBABWE): FAILURE IN PARTNERSHIP

Ever since the arrival of the first white settlers in 1890, whites have controlled Rhodesia's export economy and strategic resources, dominated the parliament, and devised ways to protect their privileged way of life. At no time has there been a genuine sharing of the wealth and power between the white minority and the African majority, and the present impasse climaxes this near century of failure in partnership.

During the precolonial days, the high Rhodesian plateau was occupied by numerous African groups, the dominant being the Mashona and Matabele. The Shona-speaking peoples comprised a loose federation, each tribe occupying a geographically distinct homeland. In the second half of the last century they were dominated by the more powerful Nguni-speaking peoples, known as the Matabele, and led by Chief Lobengula. In 1859 the Matabele permitted the London Missionary Society to open a mission station at Inyati, and soon afterwards European adventures and hunters entered the region. Following Lobengula's accession to the throne in 1868, European activity was discouraged in Matabeleland, although it continued further north and east in Mashonaland. Gold was discovered in the vicinity of Gwelo, and by the 1880s the belief was held by many Europeans in South Africa that the area north of the Limpopo was rich in precious minerals and that it was possibly a "Second Witwatersrand."

International interest in the region quickened as the scramble by European powers for African territory gained momentum. German imperialists competed with the Portuguese in their search for a continuous band of territory across southern Africa, while the British government was persuaded to maintain and extend its hold on Bechuanaland (now Botswana) to provide a corridor north between the South African Boers and the Germans. Cecil Rhodes saw in the region its strategic qualities and persuaded

the British High Commissioner for South Africa to obtain Lobengula's promise that the Matabele would not enter into agreement with any foreign power without British approval. Lobengula agreed, and by placing his territory in British hands, he prepared the way for British expansion. The treaty of 1888 granted the British complete and exclusive charge of all metals and minerals in Lobengula's kingdom, but not the right to land. In the years that followed, however, land was expropriated and its division between colonizer and colonized became one of Rhodesia's major political issues.

Given the Royal Charter to the newly formed British South Africa Company, Rhodes made preparations to occupy the territory north of the Limpopo, and in particular Mashonaland. His Pioneer Column pushed through the Bechuanaland Protectorate and onto the Rhodesian highveld east of the Matabele stronghold. By September 1890 the Column had established Fort Salisbury where the pioneers disbanded and each was free to select 3000 acres (1210 ha) of farmland promised under the charter. Additional land was later secured by treaty between Rhodes and Lobengula and, following the chief's defeat in battle (1893), European settlement spread into Matabeleland, especially around Bulawayo—Lobengula's abandoned capital.

By the turn of the century, Bulawayo had become Rhodesia's largest town and chief railway center. The line from South Africa through Bechuanaland had reached it by 1897, and five years later the line reached Salisbury, already linked by rail with Beira in Portuguese Mozambique. The line was extended north from Bulawayo to Wankie in 1903 and crossed the Zambezi at the Victoria Falls early the following year (Fig. 17-1). Thus the basic physical infrastructure was completed within 15 years of the pioneers' arrival, and the stage was set for both colonial consolidation and expansion.

The Zambezi River below the Kariba Dam, with Zambia on the left, Rhodesia on the right. This rugged and thickly forested region is a staging ground for guerrilla attacks against white-ruled Rhodesia. (World Bank)

But economic prosperity and progress were slow to materialize as droughts, rinderpest, and East-Coast fever brought havoc to ranching and other enterprises. Recurrent uprisings and rebellions by both the Matabele and Mashona brought death and destruction to many areas, and it was not until the Mashona were suppressed in 1897 that widespread white occupation was assured. Discontent with the Company's power and administration was common, and the Company itself soon realized that Rhodesia's gold resources were not nearly as extensive as had been supposed. Knowing that gold would not fill its coffers, the Company decided to protect and improve its assets by trying to build up a larger European population through the encouragement of land settle-

ment and farming, especially along the line-of-rail. It also relaxed the law requiring that only enterprises in which it had an interest could undertake mining operations. The result was a surge in prospecting, and the opening of many mines and mineral-related industries.

In 1923, a referendum was held among the white electorate on whether to seek responsible government as a self-governing colony of Britain or to ask for union with South Africa. By a vote of 8774 to 5989 Rhodesia became a self-governing colony under whose constitution Britain retained a right of veto on discriminatory and constitutional matters (Bowman, 1973). Although this prevented the removal from Africans of their largely theoretical right to the fran-

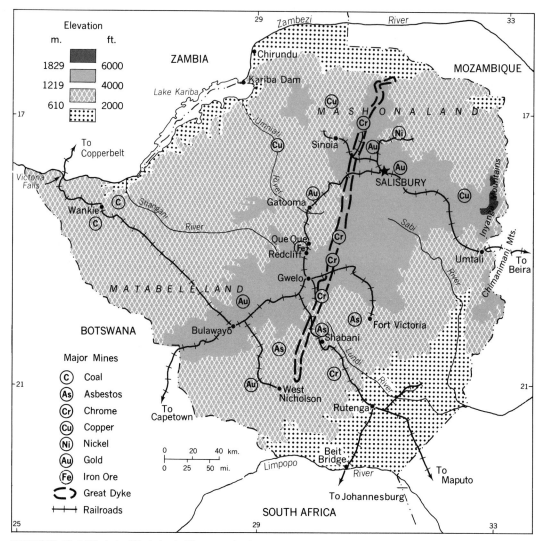

FIGURE 17-1 *Rhodesia (Zimbabwe). Towns and mines.*

chise, it did not prevent the establishment of a racially stratified and segregated society.

The next great surge of Rhodesian history flowed from World War II. It was initially economic and financial as minerals were exploited and industry developed, but it also led to political and social changes and culminated in the Central African Federation (1953–1963)—a federation between the two Rhodesias and Nyasaland (Malawi). This political union brought great economic benefits to Rhodesia, especially to its white population. The demand for textiles, automobiles, and other consumer goods greatly expanded; tobacco production surged; the communications network around the national core developed; and major undertakings, such as the Kariba hydroelectric project, were begun. Rhodesia profited from the copper revenues of Zambia, the labor from Malawi, and markets throughout the federation. Its contributions to the development of Zambia, Malawi, and its own African peoples, however, were far less evident. But federation produced a politically conscious African working class in the urban areas, and African nationalist movements gained momentum spurred on by independence elsewhere in the continent.

Yet federation failed. The reasons were many, but especially important were the lack of effective spatial and economic integration and the refusal by Rhodesia's whites to share with their African countrymen the profits of their labor and the power of government. Following the dissolution of federation, the Rhodesian government resumed the powers that had been transferred to the federal government in 1953, and the colony fully expected to achieve independence like Zambia and Malawi. But Britain was not prepared to give independence before guarantees were incorporated in the constitution for majority rule, for immediate improvement in the political status of the African peoples, and for the elimination of racial discrimination. Rhodesia's ruling white minority refused to accept these conditions, and on November 11, 1965, Ian Smith's government declared its independence unilaterally. A new phase of Rhodesian history was born.

Land Apportionment and Agriculture

Land ownership and land apportionment have been crucial issues in Rhodesia since the end of the nineteenth century. Prior to alien occupation, land was owned and occupied according to customary law, which generally meant communal ownership and grazing rights and the production of basic crops such as maize, sorghum, and beans. There was adequate land for all, man-land ratios were low, and once the soil became exhausted it was simply abandoned for some other. The major natural limitations to man and his livestock were the broken terrain and excessive rainfall in the Chimanimani and Inyanga mountains, high temperatures, and low annual rainfall (under 30 in. or 762 mm) in the Zambezi Valley, even lower rainfall (below 16 in. or 406 mm) in the southeast lowveld, and recurrent and widespread disease such as East-Coast fever and sleeping sickness. The most productive soils, reliable rainfall, and nutritious grasslands occurred in a broad belt stretching along the highveld northeast to southwest through the central regions.

These customary practices and areas of production were dramatically altered by Rhodes' Pioneer Column and the British South Africa Company. Each pioneer claimed for himself up to 3000 acres (1210 ha), while the Company both sold and leased large areas of land to incoming settlers and companies, and rewarded each member of the victorious columns of the Matabele Campaigns (1894) with 6000 acres (2420 ha) of land (Kay, 1970). Such actions prompted additional African uprisings and eventually led to the establishment of Native Reserves which were supposed to give the African some security and protection from the settlers. Beyond these reserves, land was held by the Company or designated for European use, although a small amount was available for African purchase.

In 1930, Rhodesia passed the Land Apportionment Act, which, with its various amendments, has been the cornerstone of Rhodesia's residential segregational policy. The original act reserved one-half of the colony for whites, one-third for African occupation, and the balance went unassigned. The white lands in general occupied the core of the plateau around the major cities where soils are fertile, rainfall generally reliable, and mineral wealth exceptional. The fringing African lands were of poorer quality, less accessible to urban centers, and spatially more fragmented. The act also prohibited Africans from growing certain cash crops, most notably tobacco. During the 1950s and

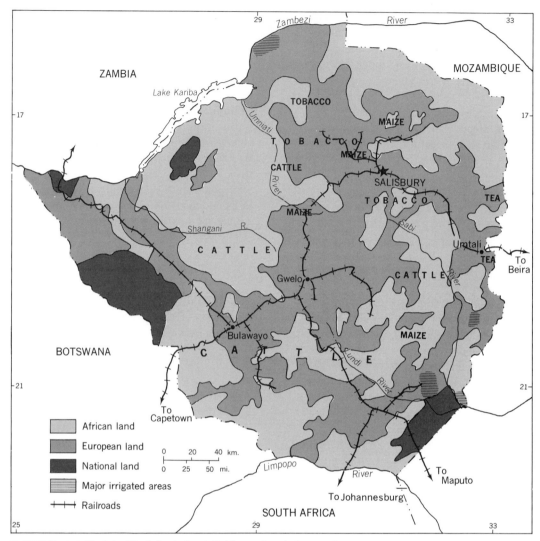

FIGURE 17-2 *Rhodesia (Zimbabwe). Land division and agriculture, 1976.*

1960s the amount of African land was increased to 46 percent, while white-owned areas were reduced accordingly. In 1969 the Land Apportionment Act was replaced by the Land Tenure Act which gave equal areas (45 million acres or 18.2 million ha) to Africans and whites, while approximately 8 percent of the total area was designated "national land," to be used as game reserves, national parks, and special purpose areas. This had the effect of consolidating the smaller fragments into more viable units while retaining the basic pattern of a white core and African periphery (Fig. 17-2).

Land apportionment reserved for the white minority the most suitable farmlands where tobacco, sugar, cotton, and other cash crops could be grown with adequate space for expansion. In contrast the Africans faced overcrowding and mounting population pressure, and their opportunities for commercial production were limited. These conditions were aggravated still further by the Native Land Husbandry Act of 1951. This

Table 17-1 RHODESIA: SELECTED COMPARATIVE DATA, 1973

	Africans	Non-Africans [a]
Employment by Industry		
Agriculture and forestry	349,000	4,800
Mining and quarrying	54,400	3,560
Manufacturing	121,100	22,050
Construction	58,200	8,070
Transport and communications	20,500	10,880
Services	216,800	34,010
Total employment	890,000	116,340
Annual Average Earnings (R$)		
Agriculture and forestry	142	3,160
Mining and quarrying	397	5,335
Manufacturing	566	4,511
Construction	506	4,342
Transport and communications	817	4,474
Services	540	3,480
Agricultural Output (R$million)		
Gross output	64.1	247.3
Sales of principal crops and livestock	16.2	195.2
Number of cattle owned (thousands)	3,037	2,573
Education		
Secondary schools	150	49
Secondary school pupils	35,876	29,465
Secondary school teachers	1,699	1,721

SOURCE. Africa South of the Sahara, *1975*. London: Europa Publications Ltd., *1975*.

[a] *Non-Africans include whites, Asians, and persons of mixed racial parentage.*

act attempted to change communal landowning in the reserves to permanent individual title and to destock the African herds. The aim was to improve agricultural productivity, but it was seen by many as the white man's way of destroying the tribal system and keeping a permanent work force of landless Africans in the cities, since farmers who violated the conservation measures were deprived of all rights to land. So strong was African reaction to the Land Husbandry Act that the government was forced to suspend it, but not before local nationalist movements had capitalized on its injustices.

Agriculture has always figured prominently in Rhodesia's economy. In 1974 it accounted for 18 percent of the GDP, second only to manufacturing (23 percent). Although its percentage contribution is declining, the value of farm output continues to increase. As Table 17-1 indicates, Africans account for a disproportionately small share of the output and have much lower average annual earnings than the other races. Their agriculture is largely traditional and primarily concerned with subsistence. Almost two-thirds of their land is unsuitable for cropping, much is overgrazed, and about 10 percent has been denuded of its soil. Maize is the dominant crop, but millet and groundnuts are also important. Africans are still prohibited from growing flue-cured tobacco, but they may grow burley and Turkish tobacco. Small areas of irrigated wheat, cotton, and sugar adjoin large white-owned projects, especially in the southeast.

European agriculture is highly developed, regionally specialized, and very de-

Tobacco estate, Salisbury. Before UDI (November, 1965), tobacco was Rhodesia's major export, but UN sanctions cut sales by half. Almost the entire crop is grown on white-owned farms. (Rhodesian Ministry of Information)

pendent on cheap African labor and overseas markets. More than half the farms have between 1000 and 5000 acres (400–2000 ha).

As Table 17-1 indicates, less than 5000 non-Africans (whites, Asians, and others) are employed in agriculture and forestry, yet more than 90 percent of the sales of crops and livestock comes from their land. Tobacco is by far the most important revenue earner, and before UDI it was Rhodesia's major export. The major producing areas are on the northern highveld around Salisbury (Fig. 17-2). As a result of sanctions, tobacco production was cut by half so that farmers were forced to diversify into cotton, cattle, and other commodities. Tea is grown on large estates in the eastern highlands around Umtali and Inyanga, most of which is marketed domestically. Cotton, produced primarily in northern, western, and southwestern parts of Mashonaland in both African and white-owned areas, has shown remarkable expansion since the early 1960s. The bulk is exported, but

Aerial view of the Mazoe citrus estates near Salisbury, a good example of white-owned commercial agriculture in the Rhodesian core region. (Rhodesian Ministry of Information)

increasing amounts will supply local textile operations. Other important commodities include sugar, wheat, citrus, maize, and livestock.

Since 1965, Rhodesia has attempted to become more self-sufficient in agriculture and has encouraged agricultural diversification. Important gains have been made in the production of wheat, soybeans, sugar, and cotton. Large-scale irrigation projects are located along the Sabi and Lundi rivers in the southeast, while considerable potential exists around Chirundu on the Zambezi.

Mineral Resources and Industry

Rhodesia is richly endowed with minerals. The greatest concentration occurs in and adjoining a narrow geological feature known as the Great Dyke, which extends from north of Salisbury south to West Nicholson (Fig. 17-1). Gold, chrome, asbestos, nickel, and iron ore are all found in this zone. Mining's share of the GDP is gradually declining, but minerals figure prominently in the list of exports. For more than 50 years, gold was Rhodesia's leading mineral export and the main reason why Europeans first occupied the territory. Many of the smaller and older workings closed after World War II when gold still accounted for more than a fourth of all mineral revenues. Sanctions imposed following UDI provided an incentive to increase gold output to improve the balance of payments as did recent increases in the sale price of gold.

Today's major revenue-producing minerals are copper, asbestos, and chrome.

Processing plant and tailing dumps of the Pangani asbestos mine, Rhodesia. Rhodesia is the world's major producer of top-grade crysotile asbestos, and asbestos is the country's leading mineral export. (Rhodesian Ministry of Information)

RHODESIA (ZIMBABWE): FAILURE IN PARTNERSHIP

Kariba Dam

Kariba Dam was built across the Zambezi River when Rhodesia was federated with Zambia and Malawi, and was then a major centripetal force in the union. Located midway between the Zambian Cobberbelt and Rhodesia's Great Dyke, it supplied both with power (starting in 1960) from generators located on the south bank. This 420-ft high (128 m) dam, 1900 ft (579 m) across the top, was an economic necessity, not merely an object of national prestige. Its power supplemented that derived from the Wankie collieries and contributed to the rapid expansion of mining and industry in both Zambia and Rhodesia. Today it provides approximately 80 percent of Rhodesia's total consumed electricity.

The south bank generators that served both Rhodesia and Zambia until the completion of the 900-mw plant on the Zambian bank, have an established capacity of more than 700 mw. A two-lane highway across the dam wall was opened once the project was completed, which lessened considerably the road distance between Salisbury and Lusaka. That route was closed during the political upsets of the early 1970s. Behind the dam wall spreads Lake Kariba, the world's largest artificial lake encompassing about 2000 sq mi (5180 sq km). The lake was stocked with fish to provide the basis for a fishing industry in a region low in protein consumption, and it also became an important international tourist attraction. About 50,000 persons had to be evacuated to make way for the lake.

Rhodesia is the world's leading producer of top-grade chrysotile asbestos, the major workings being at Shabani and Pangani. Both are well situated for export through South Africa. Before UDI, Britain and the United States were the major markets for Rhodesian minerals. Britain has adhered to UN sanctions while the United States violated them between 1971 and 1973 when it imported much-needed chrome, nickel, and asbestos. The most important post-UDI mineral development has been the opening of a nickel mine at Bindura (north of Salisbury) which could double the total value of Rhodesian mining exports.

Rhodesia is fortunate in possessing large coal deposits at Wankie. This coal alone supplied power for the mines and industries before hydroelectric power was harnessed. Production fell following the border closure with Zambia and as Kariba and smaller hydroelectric projects came into operation. Coal supplies the country's iron and steel works at Que Que and Redcliff where local iron ores and limestones are also mined. Given the necessary investment, Rhodesia could, like South Africa, produce oil from coal, a factor likely to receive serious attention if sanctions persist and local oil is not found.

Industrial development in Rhodesia accelerated after World War II, and especially during the period of federation and immediately after UDI. Federation provided Rhodesian industry with an expanded market for metal goods, textiles, building materials, chemicals, and other commodities. When federation failed, Rhodesia attempted to secure South African markets but with limited success. Today the emphasis is placed on developing local markets, but low African wages and a relatively small (275,000), afflu-

Salisbury, capital of Rhodesia. Formerly the capital of the ill-fated federation, Salisbury remains the seat of government, financial headquarters, and primate city of Rhodesia. Shown here are the central business district with its impressive vertical development, and the main railway yards and associated industry. (Rhodesian Ministry of Information)

Kariba Dam on the Zambezi River. Completed in 1960, the south-bank (Rhodesian) generators provide 80 percent of Rhodesia's electricity needs. The dam and Lake Kariba were once important tourist attractions. (UN)

RHODESIA (ZIMBABWE): FAILURE IN PARTNERSHIP
303

ent white population are important constraints. UDI had a net positive effect on industrial development. Rhodesia intensified its efforts to become self-sufficient in many basic industrial requirements, including textiles and clothing, foodstuffs, paper and printing, wood and furniture, fertilizers and chemicals, and many metal products. Import controls, introduced shortly before UDI in order to protect the balance of payments, protected manufacturers seeking to alter the quality and range of their output. Total manufacturing output has more than doubled since 1965.

Most industry is concentrated along the line-of-rail between Salisbury and Bulawayo, and virtually all of it lies in white-owned areas (Fig. 17-1). Salisbury (590,000) and Bulawayo (380,000) account for more than three-fourths of all manufacturing establishments, of the net output of manufacturing, and of the total labor force in manufacturing industries. Like most primate cities, Salisbury has the greatest variety of industry, it is the seat of government, and it has almost half of Rhodesia's white population. Bulawayo is the chief regional center and manufacturing city in the south. Its industries include metal refining, food processing, textiles and clothing, auto assembly, and tobacco processing. It is also an important railway junction.

Rhodesia's heavy industry is located in Que Que and Redcliff where steel tubes, rails, and other metal products are manufactured. Other important industrial towns in-

Part of the Bata shoe factory, Gwelo. Manufacturing employs about 14 percent of Rhodesia's gainfully employed blacks. (Rhodesian Ministry of Information)

clude Umtali, the chief regional center on the border with Mozambique and site of a strategic oil refinery; Gwelo, home of Rhodesia's largest ferroalloy plant and footware industry; and Gatooma, Rhodesia's largest textile town, which is centrally situated within the cotton belt. Compared with most African states, the development of manufacturing in Rhodesia is far advanced. But, as Table 17-1 shows, there are vast income differentials between the races in manufacturing and related industrial activities. The gap has widened since UDI.

The material benefits of Rhodesia's rapid economic growth have not been equally shared by the races. Minimum wages for African workers in industry are below the poverty level, and poverty among Africans is increasing not only absolutely but relatively to the white population. There are inadequate schools (Table 17-1) and housing, a shortage of trained manpower, and a rapidly growing (3.6 percent per annum) but workless African population. The rural-urban drift continues despite government attempts to halt it. The government prefers to rely on new immigrants to fill skilled jobs rather than train its African people. In the decade following UDI, over 108,000 new white immigrants entered the territory and over 76,000 left, but many skilled jobs remained vacant.

External Linkages and Pressures

Rhodesia's position as one of Africa's most industrial states results from several factors: a rich diversity of readily accessible mineral and agricultural resources; more than half a century of close politico-economic relationships with Britain and South Africa; a good working relationship with Mozambique, which provided Rhodesia access to markets and materials through Maputo and Beira; a brief but nevertheless profitable union with Zambia and Malawi; economic support from the United States and Western Europe in the form of markets for its minerals and tobacco; a small but skilled and capitalized white resident population that exploited its fellow countrymen; and the power to legislate and enforce programs of development irrespective of the consequences to the African majority. However, conditions are constantly changing, and the Rhodesian *raison d'être* faces many obstacles of both internal and external origin.

When Rhodesia had legitimate government under the British crown, and when Mozambique was Portuguese, Rhodesia experienced few difficulties in gaining access to its overseas markets. Most of its exports and imports passed through Beira and Maputo, while lesser amounts traversed eastern Botswana and exited or entered South African ports, most notably Port Elizabeth. Britain supplied much of the development capital and technical expertise, and South Africa was a reliable source of mining equipment, general merchandise, and moral support for the minority regime. However, UDI dramatically changed much of that. Britain immediately imposed economic sanctions with the expectation Rhodesia would be brought to its knees in a matter of weeks or months. A ban was imposed on Rhodesian tobacco, copper, asbestos, sugar, and animal products which collectively accounted for over 90 percent of all exports. An oil embargo was imposed, and the United Nations called on Britain to take all necessary action to end the rebellion.

Britain ruled out the possibility of military force and chose instead economic strangulation with full international support. South Africa and Portuguese Mozambique, however, opposed such sanctions, and Rhodesia's other neighbor, Zambia, was both too weak and too dependent on its white-ruled neighbors to enforce them. Thus oil

Zimbabwe Nationalist Movements

Black nationalism has operated under several banners. It originated in the 1950s in opposition to land appropriation and discrimination in industry, housing, and education. The African National Congress was formed in 1957 to articulate African grievances but was banned two years later as African nationalisms were making their mark elsewhere in the continent. Many of its leaders were detained without trial, while others regrouped to form the National Democratic Party whose aim was "one-man–one-vote" which it sought to achieve through a combination of moral pressure, civil disobedience, and propaganda abroad. It too was banned, as was its successor, the Zimbabwe African Peoples' Union (ZAPU). ZAPU drew its hard-core support from Matabeleland, while a splinter group, the Zimbabwe African National Union (ZANU) drew its strength more from the Shona. ZANU was banned in 1963 and its leaders detained, but the organization moved into exile to mount guerrilla campaigns against the Smith regime.

It was not until 1971 that African opinion was once again formally expressed, this time through the African National Council (ANC), a legal political organization tolerated by the Rhodesian government and led by Bishop Muzorewa. It resolutely opposed all government settlement proposals and managed to unite ZAPU and ZANU forces into a reconstituted ANC at a meeting in Lusaka in December 1974.

continued to enter through Beira and Maputo, machinery and manufactures through South Africa, and Rhodesian exports continued to leave through established outlets. Portugal opposed sanctions because it stood to lose valuable revenue from transit traffic, and because it sympathized with the white regime, Portugal itself maintaining white elitist systems in Angola and Mozambique. South Africa's involvement was far more complex. While careful not to recognize the Smith regime, South Africa clearly supported many of Rhodesia's domestic policies, several of which were modeled after its own. It supplied Rhodesia with strategic manufactures and materials; of equal importance, it supplied paramilitary units to combat guerrilla movements and freedom fighters who had entered from Zambia and Mozambique.

Independent black Africa militantly opposed UDI but was unable to bring about the collapse of the illegal regime. Through the OAU and United Nations, it sought to extend sanctions to Portugal and South Africa and to encourage Britain to take military action, but it failed on both accounts. It has, however, lent moral support to the black nationalist movements within Rhodesia and has supported freedom fighters based in Mozambique and Zambia. Following Portugal's withdrawal from Mozambique in 1975, this activity intensified, and in March 1976 Soviet-backed Cuban forces and Zimbabwe Liberation Army units engaged with Rhodesian troops along the eastern border. Mozambique closed its border, announced a state of war, and seized a considerable amount of Rhodesian rolling stock and tons of tobacco, chrome, copper, and asbestos awaiting shipment to Mozambiquan ports. Mozambique's leaders have said the ports will not be reopened to Rhodesian traffic so long as minority rule prevails in the rebel colony and as long as it (Mozambique) receives compensatory international financial support.

Before the eastern border was closed, nearly 40 percent of Rhodesia's exports and imports passed through Maputo and Beira. Rhodesia's newly completed (1974) and only direct railway link with South Africa across the Limpopo at Beit Bridge cannot compensate for this loss primarily because the South African ports and railway system are already seriously congested and cannot cope with the additional traffic diverted from Mozambique.

Independence in Mozambique and Angola caused South Africa to reassess its Rhodesian interests. In 1974, it withdrew its paramilitary aid and took an active role, out of self-interest, in behind-the-scenes diplomatic moves with Zambia, Tanzania, and Botswana to help create an atmosphere in

which constitutional settlement might be achieved. In August 1975, South Africa sent observers and advisors to a meeting between Rhodesian officials and representatives of the African National Council (ANC) which was held in a South African railway coach parked on the Victoria Falls bridge astride the international boundary. The white representatives sat in Rhodesia and faced their counterparts across the table in Zambia.

Internal politicoeconomic structures are of equal importance to external forces, and in the long run may play the decisive role in Rhodesia's future. Since UDI the mood of white Rhodesians has hardened. The policies of partnership were abandoned in 1962 and replaced by more rigid systems designed to entrench white supremacy. Pass laws were reinforced, and opposition leaders frequently detained. By mid-1976, black op-

In August 1975, Rhodesia's Prime Minister Ian Smith discussed the future of Rhodesia with representatives of the African National Council (ANC). They met in this South African railway coach parked on the Victoria Falls bridge, the whites sitting in Rhodesia and the blacks in Zambia. (Rhodesian Ministry of Information)

position to the white-supremacist government had become more violent as Chinese-trained guerrillas aided by Russian and Cuban advisors, engaged Rhodesian troops in battle along the Mozambique and Zambian borders, and attacked the vital road and rail corridors to Botswana and South Africa. The mobilization of white reservists put additional strains on Rhodesia's overburdened economy, while thousands of whites, anticipating defeat, fled the country leaving behind most of their assets.

If Rhodesia is to survive as a viable entity and to develop its human and natural resources to their maxima, there must be true partnership in government and management of the state's resources. The question is no longer how to perpetuate white supremacy, but how to create conditions for meaningful partnership.

Bibliography

Bowman, L. N. *Politics in Rhodesia: White Power in an African State.* Cambridge: Harvard University Press, 1973.

Clarke, D. G. "Land Inequality and Income Distribution in Rhodesia," *African Studies Review*, Vol. 18, (April, 1975), pp. 1–7.

Dunlop, H. "Land and Economic Opportunity in Rhodesia," *Rhodesian Journal of Economics*, Vol. 6, (March 1972), pp. 1–19.

Good, K. "Settler Colonialism in Rhodesia," *African Affairs*, Vol. 73, No. 290 (January, 1974), pp. 10–36.

Kay, G. *Rhodesia: A Human Geography.* New York: Africana Publishing Corporation, 1970.

———. *Distribution and Density of Population in Rhodesia.* Hull: University of Hull, Geography Department, Series No. 12, 1971.

Kubiak, T. J. "Rhodesia," *Focus*, Vol. 20, No. 10 (June, 1970), pp. 1–11.

Mlambo, E. *Rhodesia: The Struggle for a Birthright.* London: C. Hurst, 1972.

O'Meara, P. *Rhodesia: Racial Conflict or Coexistence?* Ithaca: Cornell University Press, 1975.

Roder, W. "The Division of Land Resources in Southern Rhodesia," *Annals, A.A.G.*, Vol. 54 (March, 1964), pp. 41–52.

Stephenson, G. V. "The Impact of International Economic Sanctions on the Internal Viability of Rhodesia," *Geographical Review*, Vol. 65, No. 3 (July, 1975), pp. 377–87.

Williams, E. L. "Perspectives on Rhodesia," *Optima*, Vol. 25, No. 1 (1975), pp. 2–23.

Zelniker, S. "Settlers and Settlement: The Rhodesian Crisis, 1974–75," *Africa Today*, Vol. 22, No. 2 (April–June, 1975), pp. 23–44.

EIGHTEEN

From the southern boundary of Tanzania, along 1700 mi (2700 km) of southeast African coastline to the borders of South Africa, lies newly independent Mozambique. In 1975, following a decade of war between FRELIMO (the Front for the Liberation of Mozambique) and Portuguese armed forces, nearly five centuries of Portuguese influence and control in the region came to an end. Independence also brought major changes in the relationships between Mozambique and its neighbors, as economic ties forged during the colonial period were broken.

Mozambique is a large, but not a populous or very productive country. Its 303,073 sq mi (784,961 sq km) extend, elongated and Y-shaped, along the eastern flank of the Southern African plateau (Fig. 18-1). In 1977 the population was estimated to approach 10 million, and some 60 percent of Mozambique's inhabitants reside in the area lying to the north of the country's great natural dividing line, the Zambezi River. But it was the southern part of the territory that generated the bulk of the revenues during the colonial period. The country's capital and leading port, Lourenço Marques (renamed Maputo at independence), served as a transit for the rich South African mining-industrial complex centered on Johannesburg; the city was also a focus for Mozambique's tourist industry. Labor from southern Mozambique was employed in South Africa's mines, and the colonial government stood to benefit. By comparison, the more densely populated northern regions were always more remote and, despite the Portuguese imposition of forced cropping of cotton, much less productive.

Mozambique's spatial morphology is complex. In the south, the country is only 55 mi (88 km) wide; in the middle, about 200 mi (320 km), and in the north, some 500 mi (800 km). A wide wedge of territory extends

MOZAMBIQUE: INDEPENDENCE AND INSECURITY

westward along the Zambezi River, separating Rhodesia (Zimbabwe) and Zambia. Malawi, in turn, penetrates deeply into northern Mozambique. The country's pronounced territorial attenuation has always had political, economic, and social significance. During the decade of insurgency, the populous north proved fertile ground for the Tanzania-based FRELIMO forces. Today, southern Mozambique thrusts deeply into white-dominated Southern Africa, fracturing the buffer zone that long protected the south against the march of African nationalism.

Physical Environments

Most of Mozambique lies on the seaward side of southern Africa's Great Escarpment, occupying the region's most extensive coastal plain. Nearly half the country's total area lies below 750 ft (229 m) above sea level. This coastal lowland is widest in southern Mozambique, where it covers virtually the entire territory, but northward it becomes narrower, and higher country approaches closer to the coast. In interior central and northern Mozambique, elevations rise to a plateau level ranging from 500 to 2000 ft (150 to 600 m), and near the western boundaries with Malawi, Zambia, and Rhodesia (Zimbabwe), there is mountainous terrain reaching as high as 7000 ft (2100 m). Hence Mozambique's topography generally declines from west to east so that, from the Rovuma River in the north to the Limpopo in the south, streams have an eastward orientation.

The pivotal geographical feature of the country is the Zambezi River. The Zambezi is a physiographic as well as an historical divide: almost all of Mozambique's higher ad more rugged terrain lies to the north, while most of the south is gently undulating, coastal lowland. The country's colonial imprint was stronger to the south of the river: both the capital and the second city, Beira, and all the really effective communications with the African interior, developed in southern Mozambique. The Zambezi Valley itself is the scene of the huge Cabora Bassa hydroelectric project (Fig. 18-1), but there was little modernization in northern Mozambique. But it was the savanna-clad, village-dotted, subsistence-crop north that was most directly exposed to the impact of African liberation forces, and there the insurgents achieved their first major successes against Portuguese power. For a time there was talk of partition in Mozambique, and the only feasible dividing line seemed to be the Zambezi. Events in Portugal overtook such designs.

Most of Mozambique is tropical savanna country, and heat and high humidity prevail over all but the high-elevation sectors. Although the coastline lies in the path of the southeast trade winds, and the warm Mozambique current flows southward offshore, Mozambique receives rather low annual rainfall, totals averaging 30 in. (76 cm) along the coast and increasing significantly only against the high slopes of the far western interior. Low elevation interior areas share the marginal rainfall that is characteristic of coastal stations: Tete, far up the Zambezi, records only 23 in. (58 cm). The rainfall comes mainly during the high-sun season (October or November to April), a rainy season that is accompanied by such high temperatures that much of the country is permanently moisture deficient. Only north-central and northwestern Mozambique and the high slopes along the Rhodesian (Zimbabwean) border generally maintain favorable moisture balances. This condition is reflected in the natural vegetation, for large areas of the savanna are sparse and erosion prone, and bush country covers much of the gently rolling south. In common with much of savanna Africa, soils are generally rather infertile, with the exception of more productive alluvial soils in sections of the river valleys and the *machongas*, the humus-rich, moist patches of lowland between interior dunes of the coastal plain.

Precolonial Spatial Patterns

The major events that shaped the historical geography of Mozambique had their origins and foci beyond the country's present borders. The great majority of the present population's ancestors arrived here during the great Bantu migration from the north and west during the first millennium A.D., but later a major readjustment occurred resulting from the emergence of the Zulu Empire in South Africa. The peoples of Mozambique are part of the Central Bantu cluster, but the Zambezi River again performs its divisive function as descent rules to the north are in accordance with the matrilinear principle, while patrilinear societies prevail to the south. The peoples south of the Zambezi are related to those in Zimbabwe, including the Thonga and Shona; northern Mozambique is occupied principally by the Makua, Makonde, and Yao peoples, whose domains extend into adjacent Tanzania and Malawi.

The first non-Africans to arrive on Mozambique's coasts were not the Europeans, but the Persians and Arabs who had created a Moslem sphere of influence along the East African coast that extended as far south as Sofala. Eastern Africa's most powerful Moslem city states were Malindi, Mombasa, and Kilwa, but along the coast of what is today Mozambique the Moslem traders had also established themselves in substantial settlements at Mozambique Island and Sofala. These coastal towns were the foci for a trading hinterland where Swahili (Islamized Africans) were the middlemen. When the Portuguese first arrived in the area, Sofala and Mozambique Island were under the sway of more powerful Kilwa, and Mozambique was part of the Indian Ocean trading region. From India and the Middle East came metal tools, cotton textiles, and leather goods; in return, the Swahili traders were able to send ivory and, importantly, gold from the plateau interior. Sofala was known for its gold export. And, of course, Mozambique provided the Arab traders with a steady supply of slaves bound for Middle Eastern markets.

The European Intrusion

Portuguese ships first reached Mozambique during the last years of the fifteenth century, and almost immediately Portugal was embroiled in disputes and conflicts with the Arabs. But Lisbon's principal interest was in the Far East, and colonization of East Africa was not a high priority. Portuguese efforts to secure footholds along the East African coast were designed to protect and reinforce the Indian Ocean trade routes.

Even when Mozambique's boundaries were defined, in the 1890s, Portugal still did not control its colonial domain effectively. In terms of spatial organization and territorial integration, Mozambique in 1890 was little different from Portuguese East Africa three centuries earlier. As late as 1894 Lourenço Marques (now Maputo) was attacked and partially destroyed by a powerful African force. Not until 1902 was control finally established over the long-dissident Barué region. North of the Zambezi River, colonial consolidation came still later. Indeed, the Portuguese pacification campaign in Yao country was not over even when World War I commenced and German East African troops entered northern Mozambique.

The colonial spatial system of Mozambique, therefore, was substantially the product of the twentieth century. During the 1890s various colonial administrators wrote treatises proposing new systems of organization. One significant product of this period was the *circumscription*, a civil administrative unit designed to entrench colonial control over the territory's indigenous peoples and to facilitate their exploitation in the economic interest of both colonial Mozambique and metropolitan portugal. But ultimately the developments that were occurring in Southern Africa's highveld interior—in the Transvaal and in Rhodesia (Zimbabwe)— had greater impact on Mozambique than the new Portuguese policies had. While Portugal's administrators were directing the pacification campaign and reorganizing Mozambique's provinces and circumscriptions, the full dimensions of the Witwatersrand gold fields were being realized, Johannesburg was growing into a major mining center, white settlement in Rhodesia (Zimbabwe) was expanding, the inevitable Anglo-Boer War took place, and the Union was established in South Africa (1910). The opening of the present century signalled the start of unprecedented economic and urban development in Southern Africa, whose shock waves strongly affected the course of events in Mozambique.

Colonial Legacies

South of the Zambezi River, Mozambique lies interposed between ocean and highveld, astride the most direct routes from the plateau to the outside world. North of the river, Mozambique was never in that position. Communication lines to colonial Northern Rhodesia (Zambia) were always oriented south and westward; the eastern route did not materialize until the construction of the Tan-Zam railroad—which traverses Tanzania, not Mozambique. And while Mozambique forms the obvious outlet for Malawi, development in colonial Nyasaland never matched that of South Africa and the Rhodesias, so that Mozambique gained little advantage from its monopoly.

Portugal's colonial presence, therefore, focused strongly on southern Mozambique, for the economic geography south of the Zambezi River soon revealed its potentials and opportunities. Lourenço Marques, the territory's southernmost town, had been made the capital of Mozambique in 1898; before the first decade of the twentieth century was over, its port had been connected by rail to the Southern Transvaal (Fig. 18-1). The shortest overland distance from Johannesburg to the coast was through Lourenço Marques, and the port facilities required expansion to handle the growing tonnage there. At about the same time the locational advantages of Beira, opposite Southern Rhodesia, led to the construction of a railroad to link its port to Salisbury and other areas of that developing colony's heartland.

Mozambique would have benefited from its break-of-bulk situation even under normal circumstances, but in Southern Africa during the early decades of the twentieth century, things were far from normal. The feverish growth of the Rand generated not only an expanding volume of trade, but also a demand for a commodity Mozambique could supply: labor. The Portuguese consolidated their locational advantages by negotiating the Mozambique Convention with South Africa. According to the terms of this convention, Mozambique would supply to South Africa a certain number of laborers annually, in return for which South Africa would guarantee the passage through Lourenço Marques of at least 40 percent of the trade (by volume) generated in the Southern Transvaal. This unique arrangement secured Lourenço Marques' competi-

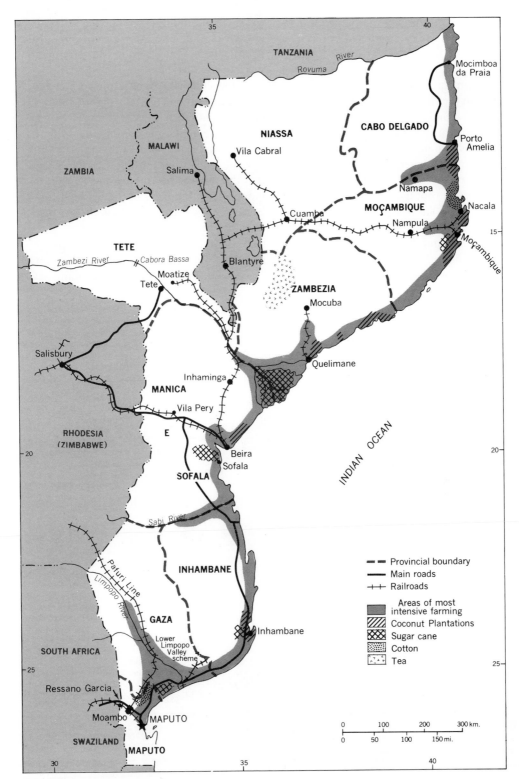

FIGURE 18-1 *Mozambique.*

tive position against Durban, the South African port most favorably positioned to serve the Witwatersrand.

The impact of these circumstances upon urban development in Mozambique can still be observed in the townscapes of the country's first and second cities. Anglo-Portuguese investment transformed these long-dormant towns into modern, spacious, skyscrapered urban centers whose central business districts and suburbs alike reflect three-quarters of a century of primacy. As recently as 1955, Lourenço Marques was linked via the new Pafuri line to Rhodesia, so that both Beira and the capital could serve the Rhodesian hinterland. As the map of communication lines indicates, the major roads of Mozambique parallel the railroads in their orientation to the interior (Fig. 18-1). Internal communications in Mozambique were never adequate.

The colonial spatial framework of Mozambique as it emerged during the first half of the twentieth century was insular and linear: insular in that the largest cities and towns were islands of wealth and growth in a sea of stagnation, and linear in the sense that the modern transport lines, in Mozambique as in other parts of the world, stimulated some growth poles along their routes. In southern Mozambique, only 55 mi (88 km) separate Lourenço Marques (Maputo) from the South African border at Ressano Garcia, but this short corridor contains sev-

The central business district of Maputo, capital and primate city of Mozambique. Maputo is a favorite holiday resort of South Africans, and the single most important outlet for the Witwatersrand, South Africa. (Mozambique Information Center)

eral substantial towns (including Moamba) and extensive farms serving the nearby urban market (Fig. 18-1). Lourenço Marques in 1970 had a population of over 200,000 and, shortly before the European exodus, perhaps as many as 50,000 whites—the largest and wealthiest domestic market. A second corridor developed from Beira to the Rhodesian border at Vila de Manica, and still another linear area of development extended along the Zambezi River with Tete as its focus. That region received a major boost when the decision was made to proceed with the Cabora Bassa hydroelectric project above Tete on the Zambezi, but the Portuguese never enjoyed the benefits to be derived from this scheme. A fourth, incipient corridor of development emerged during colonial times in the hinterland of Mozambique Town, from where an internal railroad was constructed via Nampula to Vila Cabral. In the comparatively densely populated triangle between Mozambique Town, Vila Cabral, and Quelimane, there developed the territory's most effective internal transport network.

In southern Mozambique, the subdivision of the territory's districts into circumscriptions paid off handsomely. Combined with a very severe labor law that was tantamount to involuntary servitude to the state, the administrative arrangement of the

The Cabora Bassa Dam on the Zambezi in November, 1974. Located in remote Tete province, and once a target of anti-Portuguese FRELIMO forces, the Cabora Bassa Dam is scheduled to supply most of its power to South Africa. (Mozambique Information Center)

MOZAMBIQUE: INDEPENDENCE AND INSECURITY

circumscription in the rural areas produced a steady stream of "volunteer" labor for the South African mines, men who recognized such work as the only alternative to serfdom. In each circumscription, the South African mining companies had their recruitment centers, and they were aided in their search for manpower by the Portuguese administration at local as well as provincial levels, for the rewards lay in the terms of the Mozambique Convention. This system became a cornerstone in the economic policy of the Salazar regime, when the demands placed by Lisbon upon the overseas empire grew markedly. And long before the attention of the world in general was turned to the excesses of colonial oppression, there was widespread criticism of the practices prevailing in Mozambique.

Southern Mozambique had the twin advantages of location and saleable labor; Mozambique north of the Zambezi had neither. Northern Mozambique's large peasant population was brought forcibly into the modern economic sphere through the practice of compulsory cropping, mainly of cotton. During Salazar's *Estado Novo*, villagers were compelled to plant acreages of cash crops in proportion to their numbers and their subsistence acreages. To add more than 1 acre per person each year to the already marginal food crops spelled disaster for many villagers, for the cotton fields came to replace, not supplement, the subsistence acreages. Local famines occurred, but the colonial administration used force to sustain the cotton production. The cultivators did not fare well when they sold their meager production on markets at prices controlled by the Portuguese buyers. In 1956, when the system was in full operation, over 500,000 sellers received an average of $11.17 per person for their year's labor in the cotton fields (Harris, 1958, p. 31).

In addition to the revenues gained from its transit functions, labor provision, and forced cropping, Mozambique during the middle of the twentieth century also witnessed the expansion of European agriculture in favored areas of the territory. This development is reflected by the rapid increase in the European population of the country. As recently as 1930, the white population of Mozambique was only 16,000, and during the decade of the 1930s it grew by only about 10,000. But during the 1940s, more than 20,000 whites, mostly Portuguese, arrived in Mozambique to settle, and during the 1950s, Mozambique's white population nearly doubled, from under 48,000 to over 90,000. Notwithstanding the accelerating pace of change in Africa during the 1960s, Portuguese continued to arrive in large numbers in Mozambique even after the first songs of the coming African rebellion had occurred. In part this was the result of farm settlement programs set in motion before the political problems engulfed Mozambique (and then Portugal itself); until 1970 Lisbon believed that its centuries-old presence in the African empire would be sustained and that accommodation with the insurgents (if not their outright defeat) would take place. Thus even while the war was waged, work on the Cabora Bassa hydroelectric project continued, farmlands were laid out, and farm settlements were built. One of the earlier and larger farm projects was the

Picking cotton in northern Mozambique. During the colonial era, Mozambique's peasant farmers were required to grow cotton or some other cash crop for the Portuguese authorities. (Mozambique Information Center)

Lower Limpopo Valley Scheme, where a quarter of a million acres were designated for irrigation and occupation by 10,000 farm families. In the hinterland of Beira another major scheme, involving 75,000 acres, was laid out. By allocating land to African as well as European families, the colonial administration hoped to create the sort of nonracial community that would prove multiracialism possible in Portuguese Africa—while white immigration was encouraged and the white sector strengthened.

The agricultural development program eventually fell victim to the rising tide of African nationalism in Mozambique. The Lower Limpopo Valley Scheme reached only about one-quarter of its projected dimensions; thousands of farmers left for Portugal as independence approached. Other schemes were similarly abrogated. Nevertheless, Mozambique's agricultural potentials were substantially proved by what was achieved. In the hinterland of Maputo approximately to the latitude of Inhambane, sugar grows in exportable quantities, as does rice; a variety of fruits including citrus, pineapples, and bananas also do well in the southern part of the country. Sugar estates also developed along the Zambezi River and in the hinterland of Quelimane, and remnants of the cotton plantings still exist in many areas of the country, especially in the north (Fig. 18-1). Along the coast, especially between 17° and 20° south, the coconut palm abounds, and copra, coconut oil, and related products in recent decades have accounted for over 15 percent by value of Mozambique's exports. The coconut plantation at Quelimane, with 50,000 acres (202 sq km) and about 4 million palms, is often identified as the largest of its kind in the world. Cashew nuts, sisal, tea, tobacco, and groundnuts are also produced in relatively small quantities in various areas of Mozambique (sisal and groundnuts in drier upland areas, tea and tobacco along better-watered slopes). In recent years timber exports, mainly from Manica e Sofala District, generated about 3 percent by value of annual exports.

Mozambique's agricultural industry, of course, was oriented during colonial times toward Portugal: cotton, sugar, tea, and other farm produce went to Portuguese markets. The African peasants' subsistence crop, as elsewhere in Southern and East Africa, is maize (corn), which is not part of the overseas trade. Livestock holdings have always been limited because of the prevailing diseases. The new political situation in Mozambique requires a reorientation of agricultural priorities, as is noted later.

The mining industry has never been a major contributor to Mozambique's economy, for reasons enumerated previously. The coal mine at Moatize, near Tete, has long been the only major operation of its kind in the country; other minerals have been mined at small workings elsewhere, including the tantalite mine at Murrua (reputedly the largest deposit of this rare mineral in the world) and the gold mine at Brangança. Before 1970, some potentially significant discoveries were made. Near Namapa, an iron ore deposit was located with sufficient promise to attract Japanese capital for development; and deposits of manganese and asbestos were found near the Swaziland border. The natural gas discovery near Maamba, northwest of Maputo, stimulated hopes that a search for oil on the coastal plain or on the adjacent continental shelf might succeed. But at the time of independence, no major mining development had yet been achieved on any of these new finds.

During the 1960s hopes were expressed by the colonial administration that the Beira-Zambezi Valley region might become Mozambique's mining-industrial heartland. The coalfields near Tete, connected by rail to Beira's port, served the Beira-Rhodesia railroad (some coal was also shipped coastwise to local power stations). The Cabora Bassa hydroelectric project would stimulate industrial as well as agricultural development, and among new mineral finds was

Tea estate in Zambezia Province, Mozambique. (Mozambique Information Center)

some gold in Manica e Sofala District. Jute and cotton mills at Vila Pery, sawmills along the rail link to Malawi, and the discovery of additional iron ore in the Zambezi Valley all contributed to the anticipation that the long-divisive Zambezi might become the country's center of gravity. Whether these hopes will become reality depends in large measure on the country's new political and economic directions.

Mozambique did not, during colonial times, develop a major industrial base. Industries were oriented either to the small local market or to distant Portugal: at Maputo the oil refinery, small steel plant, fertilizer and chemical factories supplied local demands, while other industries processed raw materials (cotton, sisal, tea etc.) prior to their shipment to Portugal. Some Mozambiquan products found their way to South African and Rhodesian markets, but the role of these countries as trading partners was always far overshadowed by their transportation requirements.

As the wealth of the interior grew, Mozambique sustained yet another external impact: a rapidly expanding flow of tourists visiting the cities, beaches, and the Gorongosa Game Reserve. Hotels and holiday camps did a growing (if strongly seasonal) business; in the peak years of the late 1960s the tourist industry brought Mozambique over $5 million in revenues. In considerable measure the tourist industry was a spinoff from the investments made in the territory's two major cities, for spacious, "Continental" Maputo and Beira were the prime attractions for South African and Rhodesian visitors.

What Mozambique might have been

without its transport functions lies revealed in coastal towns such as Inhambane, Quelimane, and Mozambique Town. With populations between 10,000 and 30,000, small ports that participate mainly in coastal shipping, limited communications with mainly agricultural hinterlands, and industries restricted to the processing of agricultural products, these small urban places reflect the modest development of the colonial interior—and in their contrast against Maputo and Beira, they reveal the magnitude of the impact made by Mozambique's transit function.

During the colonial period, Mozambique's balance of trade normally showed a large deficit. In the late 1960s the value of exports averaged approximately $104 million, and of imports, $156 million. A large part of the deficit was made up by earnings derived from the transit trade to and from South Africa and Rhodesia (Zimbabwe), and from revenues produced by the labor from Mozambique employed in South Africa (this income declined during the decade as the flow of labor decreased). Still Mozambique showed an overall deficit of about $12 million, in contrast to more profitable Angola. The country's exports are mainly the agricultural products identified earlier; principal imports include various kinds of machinery and finished textiles.

Problems of Development

The former "province" of Mozambique became independent on June 25, 1975, its new government announcing intentions to follow Marxist principles of national organization while indicating, simultaneously, a sense of realism concerning the country's relationships with neighboring states. Mozambique is a classic example of the emergence and success of the insurgent state, and the country faces the problems always confronted by states that have undergone radical, revolutionary change.

SPATIAL MORPHOLOGY

Mozambique's territorial dimensions remain as much a source of problems for the new administration as they were for the old. The country's attenuation places the capital about 1200 mi (1920 km) from the northern boundary, which is farther than Jonannesburg, South Africa, lies from Lubumbashi, Zaire. Malawi's penetration and the Zambezi proruption present problems to the new administration that differ from those they posed for the Portuguese, but they remain problems nevertheless. Potential irredentist issues exist along the Tanzanian and Malawian borders. The contrasts between north and south in Mozambique were not wiped out by FRELIMO's success: southern Mozambique now adjoins ideological foes in South Africa and Rhodesia, as northern Mozambique did during the period of insurgency. Southern Mozambique is patently vulnerable to South Africa, and it is here, in the south, where the country is territorially narrowest and least defensible. A strong case can be made for the removal of the capital functions from Maputo to a more northerly, central location: to Beira, if not to Quelimane. Maputo, under the new politicoterritorial circumstances, has taken on the qualities of a forward capital. Given the country's need to reorganize and redirect its priorities, this is hardly desirable.

DEMOGRAPHY

Mozambique's population distribution is characterized by a concentration along the coast; a strong rural agglomeration, especially in the Mozambique and Zambezia Districts and in the Maputo–Inhambane region; and very low densities in the upper Limpopo, upper Zambezi, and upper Rovuma-Lugenda areas (each of these areas adjoins the national boundary). The period of insurgency caused considerable dislocation in the north; some 10,000 Makonde fled to Tanzania to avoid Portuguese reprisals, and many Lomwe (a Yao subgroup) moved into Malawi. In southern Mozambique, the population pyramid was for many decades markedly asymmetrical as a result of the labor migration to the South African mines and the departure of tens of thousands of adult males to seek other employment in South Africa or Rhodesia (Zimbabwe) and thus to escape the hardships of Portugal's *shibalo* system. It will take decades, perhaps generations, to redress the resulting imbalances. The great majority of the people, of course, live in dispersed homesteads, small hamlets, or villages characteristic of the eastern and southern African rural scene, with their surrounding, communally worked fields of maize (corn), the principal subsistence crop.

Mozambique's white population was always most strongly concentrated in the major cities and in the better agricultural areas, but independence was attended by a substantial exodus that reversed decades of European expansion and productivity. Although some white residents of the territory returned after independence was achieved, it was difficult to gauge the impact of these movements upon the country's economic development.

The other substantial minority sectors in Mozambique are the "*assimilados*" (persons of mixed African-white ancestry), who number about 40,000, as well as several thousand Pakistani, Goans, and Indians, and a smaller number of Chinese. The Asian minorities acquired leading roles in local trade and commerce during the colonial period, but their role in the new Mozambique and its changed economic order is also uncertain. Just before independence, Mozambique's various commercial associations numbered just over 4000 members, of whom more than 1000 were Pakistani, Goans, Indians, and Chinese.

The tasks that lie ahead in the fields of education and health are enormous. At independence, perhaps 6 percent of Mozambique's nearly 10 million inhabitants were literate. Reliable birth and death rates have never been available, but various estimates suggest that births average 43 per thousand annually and deaths 23 per thousand. Officially, infant mortality was given as between 90 and 100 per 1000, but some observers believe it was double that. Whole regions of Mozambique never had medical facilities to speak of; tens of thousands of children never saw a school. It is not surprising that, shortly before independence, President-designate Samora Machel appealed to Portugal for $150 million in aid to survive the first six months of independence. Economic uncertainties and staggering postwar needs rendered Mozambique's future problematic.

Reorganization and Recovery

Mozambique in 1975 faced a future of uncertainty—not only because its internal reorganization had just begun but also because developments in the South African Republic and in Rhodesia (Zimbabwe) would have strong impact in the young state. Whatever the political future of Rhodesia (Zimbabwe) and South Africa, the spatial economic geography of the region will remain the same: Mozambique's locational assets will be sustained. No matter what the final disposition of Rhodesia's political conflicts will be, Zimbabwe's most efficient outlet will still be through Maputo and via Beira. And whatever the nature of social change in South Africa, Maputo would continue to be in a strong competitive position along the southeast coast for the trade of the Witwatersrand. Recent developments in Swaziland (the entire country is situated in Maputo's hinterland) confirm Mozambique's locational advantage. Built with Portuguese as well as British and South African money, the Swaziland Railroad carries iron ore exploited through Japanese investment. Mozambique should reap long-term benefits.

To pay for what Mozambique must do within its boundaries, the country has the option to apply some political (and economic) realism and to preserve the salient elements of its economic relationships with the interior. If it is possible for the United States to trade with China, then surely Mozambique can support UN sanctions against Rhodesia while handling South African trade. Mozambique would receive revenues from about 10 million tons of goods handled for South Africa at Maputo each year; taxes and other income from approximately 100,000 Mozambique workers still laboring in South African mines; and payments for Cabora Bassa electricity should the projected sale of power to South Africa be implemented upon the project's completion. Clearly the most sensitive problem facing the new government relates to the labor force working in South Africa. Cooperation with the Republic to sustain as egregious a system as the Mozambique Convention designed would risk the credibility of the avowed Marxist administration, but the return of 100,000 unemployed workers and the loss of the revenues they generate would produce serious problems as well. In mid-1976 the Mozambique government had made no decision public on this matter, but South African goods continued to pass through Maputo's docks.

The long-term advantages of such a posture are immediately evident. Transport routes are often redirected by political conditions that prove to be temporary (the Tan-Zam Railway was built to provide Zambia a free Indian Ocean outlet, and its completion may predate majority rule in Zimbabwe by only a few years). Once the trade has been diverted, often on the basis of long-term agreements, much time is involved in its reallocation, and docks lie idle. By sustaining its connections with the interior, Mozambique may avoid eventual outflanking. Already, it has lost its railroad primacy through the completion of the direct Bulawayo-Johannesburg link (also the result of political conditions in the region).

A short-term opportunity lies in Mozambique's demands for support and reparations from Portugal. Mozambique's products were sold to Portuguese buyers at very low prices (sugar fetched only half the price it might have secured on the world market), and Portugal obtained from South Africa in gold the payments for labor forces Mozambique sent to the mines. Portugal's new political posture would be put to the test by Mozambique's claim to these balances due; certainly such a claim would have validity.

These externally oriented efforts would confirm and perhaps entrench the spatial development pattern Mozambique acquired during the colonial period, but internally sweeping changes are required. These involve a reorganization and reorientation of agriculture; an intensification of exploration and mining; the reorientation of transport systems to promote national integration; the allocation of development funds to diminish the regional disparity between the deprived north and the far more developed south; and the stimulation of Mozambique's meager industrial base.

Colonial practices and the ravages of war left agriculture in Mozambique in disarray, and in mid-1975 the country was forced to appeal to other countries for relief as local famines threatened. Rumania, Sweden, and South Africa (a long-time supplier of Mozambique) sent initial shipments, but it was evident that the symptoms were those of extended difficulty in agriculture. These problems appeared most acute in populous northern Mozambique, where both subsistence and cash agriculture had suffered from the decade of conflict and its aftermath of dislocation and involuntary population movement. Tens of thousands of Africans had left the region for Tanzania and Malawi and were returning; many white estate owners abandoned their plantations. Reorganization on the Tanzanian pattern might be the solution for a region that has known little but exploitation and war.

The cash crops of Mozambique never produced revenues comparable to those derived from the transport industry, but their relative importance may now grow substantially. The Machel government has given indications that it wishes to continue the development of the agricultural projects laid out during the colonial period and has published incentives to persuade Portuguese farmers who left for Portugal to return to the country. Not only are the farms frequently unattended, but also old markets either have disappeared or must be renegotiated. Portugal bought the great majority of Mozam-

bique's farm products, but at abysmally low prices; if the Portuguese buyers cannot pay world prices, then Mozambique's exporters must seek new markets—at a time when the world economy is unfavorable.

The extractive industries of Mozambique generally have shown little growth in recent years. The 1961 production was actually greater than that of 1970. There is hope that the country may contain hitherto undiscovered mineral ores, notably in the poorly mapped crystallines of the interior; the coastal plain and continental shelf may yield oil. The fuller exploration of Mozambique is a matter of urgency, but it also poses a problem for the Machel regime in the context of its determination to avoid involvement with capitalist enterprises except where absolutely necessary.

The transportation routes of Mozambique, as noted earlier, have served prin-

The central business district of Beira, Mozambique. The growth of Beira has depended primarily on transit traffic to and from Rhodesia and Malawi. (Mozambique Information Center)

cipally the external and exploitative interests of the country prior to independence. A good all-weather road from Maputo to Beira was not completed until shortly before the Portuguese withdrew; much of the most recent road building was related to the war effort. It was always easier to travel from Maputo to Johannesburg, or from Beira to Salisbury, than, say, from Beira to Mozambique Town. Thus, Mozambique developed as a series of corridors and more or less isolated pockets. To go from port to port was easier by sea than by land; to travel from north to south in the interior is still a difficult journey.

Mozambique's internal communications are not as poor as are those of some other African countries, but they are nevertheless in urgent need of improvement and integration. A major all-weather north-south surface link is a major objective in a country where self-reliance and internal sufficiency must improve. Mozambique shares with other African countries a great degree of cultural diversity; it shares with other morphologically elongated countries the problem of inhibited internal circulation. Without improved transport facilities, the task of national consolidation will be greatly hampered.

Reference has been made previously to the regional, north-south disparaties that have marked Mozambique throughout its modern development as a colonial dependency. The population's center of gravity lies to the north of the Zambezi River, but southern Mozambique has been the most developed sector of the country. The north, where the war of liberation succeeded first, must be given priority now as the infrastructure of independent Mozambique is built. Obviously the reorganization of agriculture (especially the subsistence sector) must begin in the north; the most urgent transport needs are also in the north. It is likely that the north will prove to be the most underexplored region of Mozambique, for here lie the largest areas of crystalline rocks similar to those producing the minerals of Rhodesia and Zambia. And Nacala, connected now by rail to Malawi as well as Vila Cabral in Niassa District, has the best natural harbor north of Maputo (Fig. 18-1). The north has opportunities in agriculture, mining, and transportation; it needs attention from a government determined to end its remoteness from the center of activity.

Mozambique achieved independence with a foreign debt of nearly $850 million. Its proximity to South Africa and Rhodesia has discouraged industrial development; if political motivations lead to an end in the transit functions of the ports and railroads, the country will lose about 40 percent of its annual revenues. Obviously there is a need for change in industry as well as agriculture: the domestic market is small and poor, but Mozambique must begin to reduce its dependence upon the manufactures of its neighbors and Portugal. In the kind of planned economy the new government envisages, such industrial redirection can also serve to enhance the position of the north in the country's regional economic geography. Future development in Mozambique will be the product of pragmatism as well as idealism: the pragmatism applied to the revenues to be won from abroad, the idealism to govern their investment at home.

Bibliography

Abshire, D. M., and M. A. Samuels (eds.). *Portuguese Africa: A Handbook* New York: Praeger, 1969.

Alpers, E. A. "Ethnicity, Politics and History in Mozambique," *Africa Today*, Vol. 21, No. 4 (1974), pp. 39–52.

Arrighi, G., and J. Saul. *Essays on the Political Economy of Africa*. New York: Monthly Review Press, 1973.

de Blij, H. J. "The Functional Structure and Central Business District of Lourenço Marques, Moçambique," *Economic Geography*, Vol. 38, (1962), pp. 56–77.

Duffy, J. *Portugal in Africa*. Penguin African Library, 1962.

Ferreira, E. de S. *Portuguese Colonialism in Africa: The End of An Era*. Paris: UNESCO, 1974.

Harris, M. *Portugal's African Wards*. New York: American Committee on Africa, 1958.

Geshekter, C. L. "Independent Mozambique and Its Neighbors," *Africa Today*, Vol. 22, No. 3 (July–Sept., 1975), pp. 21–36.

Moreira, A. *Portugal's Stand in Africa*. New York: University Publishers, 1962.

Newitt, M. D. D. *Portuguese Settlement on the Zambezi*. New York: Africana Publishing Co., 1973.

Potholm, C. P., and R. Dale (eds.). *Southern Africa in Perspective: Essays in Regional Politics*. New York: The Free Press, 1972.

Williams, E. L. "African Giant: The Saga of Cabora Bassa," *Optima*, Vol. 24, No. 3 (1974), pp. 94–105.

NINETEEN

Five hundred years of Portuguese rule in Africa came to a convulsive end in November 1975 when Angola, Lisbon's most profitable colonial possession, achieved independence amid chaos and civil war. The conflict among rival nationalist movements, each with its cultural and regional core areas, ravaged Angola for months; it bitterly divided the Organization of African Unity, damaged U.S.–Soviet détente, brought yet another foreign army to Africa, and opened a new chapter in the breakdown of the buffer zone that has for two decades separated South Africa from its strongest African adversaries.

Angola is one of those creations of European colonial competition that threw together peoples of diverse cultures and histories and separated others with strong common traditions and other bonds. The vast country (481,000 sq mi or 1,247,000 sq km) extends from the forests of the Zaire Basin to the margins of the Kalahari Desert, and from a lengthy Atlantic coastline to the heart of south-central Africa. Among its 6.7 million people, the Bakongo in the north have ties with the Bakongo of western Zaire; in the south the Ovambo are part of a greater nation that extends into Namibia. Angola's core area, including the capital, Luanda, and its hinterland, is the domain of the Mbundu. In the early 1970s the white population of Angola reached nearly 500,000, strongly concentrated in Luanda, the other urban centers, and on the better agricultural lands.

ANGOLA: THE RISE OF THE INSURGENT STATE

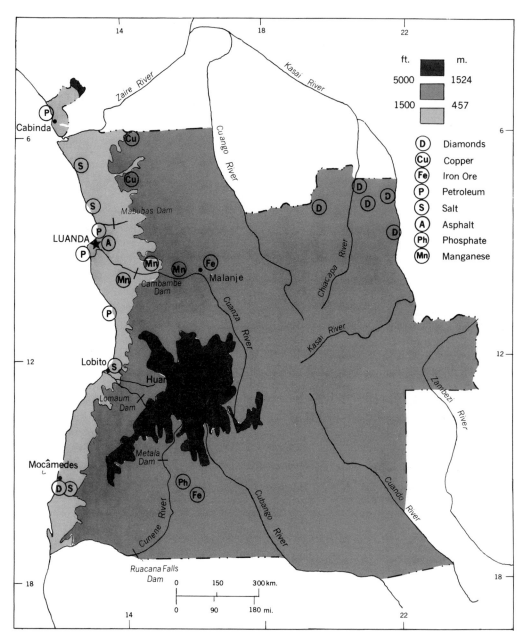

FIGURE 19-1 *Angola. Physical features and resources.*

Physical Environments

Angola is a large and essentially rectangular country (with minor proruptions) lying wholly within the tropics. A narrow coastal plain, arid in the south and becoming gradu- ally more humid and broader in the north, gives way in a series of steps to a highland interior between 3000 and 5000 ft (1000 and 1500 m). Central Angola, source area of the Cunene, Cubango (Okavango), Cuando, Cuanza, Cuango, and other major rivers, rises to heights above 8500 ft (2600 m) in the Bihé Plateau (Fig. 19-1). Because the plateau drops precipitously to the coast in a series of large escarpments, none of the rivers (other than the Cuanza) is navigable for any great distance, and none figured prominently in Portugal's early penetration into the interior. Only small valley stretches, most notably along the Cunene (which forms the southwestern boundary with Namibia) are irrigated, but most have great and largely untapped hydroelectric potential. Several northeastern rivers, among them the Chicapa, Kasai, and Cuango, all of which flow into Zaire, have cut deep valleys into the hard African tableland, exposing rich diamondiferous gravels. In its northwestern corner, Angola shares with Zaire the wide and navigable estuary of the Zaire River, beyond which lies the oil-rich enclave of Cabinda.

Angola has tropical climates tempered by altitude and cool maritime breezes. Along the coast, the northward-flowing Benguela Current and prevailing atmospheric conditions of high pressure combine to inhibit precipitation, so that much of the Atlantic lowland is either arid or semiarid. Moçamedes, for example, has an average annual rainfall less than 2 in. (51 mm), Lobito 9 in. (229 mm), and Luanda only 16 in. (405 mm). This littoral is noted for its frequent fogs and relative coolness as cold water from the ocean bottom wells up close to shore. Over 70 in. (1780 mm) of rain fall in the maombe forests of Cabinda, in the northern plateau around Uige (formerly Carmona), and along the eastern border with Zaire. There precipitation is decidedly seasonal with one or two peak periods, the heaviest rains coming being between September and April. In general, average annual temperatures decrease latitudinally and altitudinally, so that on the Bihé Plateau almost temperate conditions prevail, and winter frosts are not unknown.

Northern Angola has patches of tropical rain forest, and in many valleys and sheltered slopes of the northern subplateau zone, a rain-and-cloud forest thrives because of the condensation of moisture brought in by the westerly sea breezes. There the agricultural potential is similar to most humid tropical areas, and coffee and oil palm have proven successful. Central and eastern Angola's natural vegetation is woodland savanna, patches of which have been cleared to make way for maize, coffee, and a host of other crops. The Bihé Plateau supports the densest human populations. Southern and coastal Angola are the least favorably endowed regions in terms of soil, rainfall, and vegetative cover for human settlement. Dry savanna and steppeland conditions prevail in the southern interior, and in the more humid parts, pastoralism is possible.

Colonial Beginnings and Policies

Portuguese presence in Angola dates back to 1482 when Diogo Cao landed at the mouth of the Zaire River and established contact with the Manikongo people. Initial contacts were brief and cordial but led to the establishment of a slave-trading port at Mpinda. Permanent Portuguese settlement was delayed until 1575 when Paulo Dias de Novais, the newly appointed governor, founded the garrison of Luanda. For the next 250 years, Portuguese interests were confined to the profitable slave trade, and the establishment of military garrisons and religious missions in the immediate vicinity of Luanda, Benguela, and other coastal ports. Loose administration was organized through these points, but Angola itself was economically controlled from Brazil (Duffy, 1962). An estimated 3 million Angolan slaves were taken to Brazil's plantations.

Angola derived virtually no social or political gains from this administrative arrangement, while food crops including maize, cassava, and rice were introduced to the region from the New World and elsewhere.

The abolition of slavery in 1836 undermined the colonial economy of Angola, for slaves had been the greatest source of revenues. Thus, in the second quarter of the nineteenth century, Portuguese policy was motivated by the need for new revenues and new sources of production. Between 1836 and 1861 the area of Portuguese control doubled, and by the late 1870s military garrisons and mission stations were firmly implanted on the Bihé Plateau and as far east as the Cuango River. Expansion met with fierce resistance, but the Angolan peoples were no match for the militarily superior Portuguese.

Portuguese expansionism was eventually thwarted by British, Belgian, French, and German interests in central Africa. Portugal had hoped to link its territorial claims in Mozambique with those in Angola in a cross-African axis, but Stanley had begun acquiring land in the name of the International Association of the Congo, and both German and Belgians had staked claims in the Lunda and Cassange areas. Portuguese aspirations were further negated at the Berlin Conference, and after much diplomatic maneuvering between Portugal and London following Cecil Rhodes' treaties with Lobengula in Matabeleland, Portugal and Britain negotiated a treaty (1891) that set the present boundaries between Mozambique, Malawi, Zambia, Rhodesia, and Angola. But the implied colonial "right of occupation" far from guaranteed effective control with the newly defined boundaries. This was achieved only after 30 years of military "pacification" and the introduction of an administrative system. Portuguese colonial rule did not begin in any systematic way until the second decade of the twentieth century.

The course of Angolan development was determined primarily by politico-economic conditions in, and government policy eminating from, Portugal. Throughout its tenure in Africa, Portugal was a poor country: its per capita income and literacy rates were the lowest in Western Europe; a considerable proportion of its people lived at the subsistence level; infant mortality rates were among the highest in Europe, while birth rates were among the highest in the world; the majority of Portugal's inhabitants made their living from agriculture, while manufacturing contributed little to the national economy; freedom of thought and action were not tolerated by dictatorships; and the Portuguese remained largely uninformed about changing world conditions and very conservative in their attitudes. Little wonder that "development" was so painfully slow in Angola (and Mozambique).

Portugal looked upon its colonies (officially referred to as "provinces" after 1951) as reservoirs of human labor and natural resources to be exploited for the benefit of the metropole first, Portuguese settlers second, and the Africans last (see Chapter Five). Angola was to finance its own development, produce financially profitable development schemes, but not compete with Lisbon. Policy was paternalistic, the African being treated as a child with little or no culture or civilization worthy of recognition. Beginning in 1890, Portuguese policy toward the Angolans was one of "tendential assimilation," officially respecting local institutions and customs while gradually attempting to bring the Africans into contemporary life (Abshire and Samuels, 1969). From this developed the *assimilado* system, an *assimilado* being an African who fulfilled certain educational, financial, and social requirements that entitled the individual to equal "citizenship" alongside the Portuguese. Only the *assimilado* had the right of unrestricted movement within Angola (and Mozambique), all others requiring permission of the local administrator to leave their *circumscricao* (district). The *assimilado* represented Angola's elite, and before the system was abandoned (1961), they numbered only 40,000, under 1 percent of the total population.

Such investments as were made in Angola went mainly to impressive visible projects including dams, port facilities, railway improvement, and settlement schemes, from which black Angolans derived little material benefit. Until the 1960s, funds were not generally available for African schools, hospitals, clinics, housing, and farm improvement. As in Mozambique, a steady supply of cheap labor had to be assured for the plantations, mines, and other economic projects. Every African male had to show he was productively employed six months of the year or face conscription as a laborer for the government or private employer. Contract labor became the most obvious form of human injustice and provided the focus abroad for the condemnation of Portuguese rule (Duffy, 1962).

Following World War II, Angola was seen as a place to relieve population pressure in the Portuguese metropole, and from which resources should be extracted to bolster Portugal's faltering economy. In 1940, Angola's white population numbered only 44,083 (1.2 percent of the total), but by 1960 it numbered 172,529, and before independence it reached nearly a half million. Most of this phenomenal increase resulted from the settlement of Portuguese peasants in government-sponsored *colonatos* or settlement schemes such as Cela (north of Huambo), and the far more successful Matala scheme on the Cunene River (Fig. 19-2). Migrant

families were usually provided with free transportation, a house, farm holding and basic farm tools, seed, and a cash subsidy for two years. These schemes, first established exclusively for whites but later extended to Africans, provided Portugal with a means to control possible discontent in selected rural areas, besides stimulating the local economy and producing foods for Portuguese markets. Economic costs were generally high, but the schemes were justified politically.

Colonial Angola had the second largest white population in Africa (after South Africa), but its whites never had high educational standards. In 1950, for example, half the whites had no education at all, while 17 percent attended school for five or more years. Fewer than 2 percent of the immigrants arriving between 1953 and 1964 had more than four years of education (Bender and Yoder, 1974). In Angola whites were the elite; in Portugal they represented the poor majority. Although Portugal gave great emphasis to its settlement projects, the overwhelming majority of the Portuguese were employed in commerce, not farming. Whites monopolized positions as waiters, bus drivers, bank clerks, and taxi drivers, jobs commonly held by Africans elsewhere in colonial Africa. Two-thirds of the professionals in 1968 lived in only 3 of the 16 districts—Luanda, Benguela, and Huambo—and 42.4 percent lived in Luanda, the capital, alone. Thus, spatially, the white presence was very concentrated.

Economic Resources and "Development" Regions

As long ago as 1893 a Portuguese government official remarked of Angola: "We have good land and labor to work it; we lack only capital and initiative." Such an observation could have been made in the mid-1970s. Although it is true bush has been cleared and pre-empted for export crops (coffee, cotton, sisal, and others) and mines have

opened and processing plants have arisen, much of Angola's vast agricultural potential and mineral wealth still await the input of capital, the development of domestic markets and transport systems, and a political system conducive to economic investment. The first half of the twentieth century saw virtually no development of Angola's mineral resources other than alluvial diamonds and gold from Dundo and environs, and manganese ore from the highlands east of Luanda (Fig. 19-1). Exports were dominated by coffee and cotton grown by peasant farmers under strict colonial supervision, and for which sub-free market prices were paid.

In the period 1970–1975, Angola's economy showed buoyancy and confidence. The GDP (held at constant prices) grew at approximately 11 percent per annum. Most of the stimulus was derived from price and quantity increases in exports that flowed in part from Portugal's revised and more liberal economic policies. Exports and manufacturing diversified, while cotton and coffee producers received higher prices than ever before. Coffee has been the major crop in terms of export sales, and during the 1950s Angola was the largest coffee producer in Africa. It now ranks second to Ivory Coast, although during the severe droughts of 1974 that affected northern coffee growers, Angola temporarily regained its primacy. Cotton has customarily been Angola's second agricultural export, and for decades it was grown by peasant farmers supervised by European concessionaires who were given a buying monopoly at fixed prices. As in Mozambique, the system was abolished in 1961 in favor of free cultivation and sales. Output did not materially change as a result: yields per acre increased, while the area under cultivation decreased. Other important cash crops include sisal, sugar, maize, and oil palm products, most of which in the colonial era were produced on large corporate plantations and *colonatos* rather than on traditional African holdings. Agriculture has regularly contributed from 20 to 25 percent of GNP, engaged about 88 percent of the population and is regionally specialized and highly localized (Fig. 19-2). Only 2 percent of the land area is cultivated.

Angola has a rich and diversified mineral base, possibly one of the richest in Africa. Until the 1950s however, little was known of this mineral potential, and mining was confined to diamonds and manganese, both in the northern region. By the mid-1970s mineral production also included petroleum, iron ore, copper, manganese, and sulphur. Petroleum has headed the list of exports since 1973 and promises to be Angola's principal source of foreign revenues for years to come. The Cabinda field is the most productive (see box item), but production from the vicinity of Luanda is not insignificant.

During the colonial era, manufacturing never received high priority in the scheme of development. But increased economic autonomy during Portugal's final years of rule resulted in expansion of Angola's raw material processing industries, and growth in import substitution industries. Food processing industries, led by sugar refining, fish product preparation, and vegetable-oil extraction, are the most developed. Beverages, tobacco, and textiles are important growth industries with slowly expanding domestic markets. Angola faces many of the difficulties encountered elsewhere in Africa in its struggle towards industrial self-sufficiency. The two major handicaps are scarcity of skilled labor and limited purchasing power, both consequences of a colonial system that very strongly favored the metropole.

Viewed spatially, Angola's nonsubsistence economy is linear and insular. Primary development has occurred in and around the major towns and resource regions that are linked together by three railway arteries running parallel to each other and perpendicular to the coast (Fig. 19-2). Secondary development has occurred along the coast and highways that connect these arteries. Between these development axes and associated growth centers lies the periphery: subsistence farming, empty but potentially productive agricultural lands, and untapped mineral resources. Little attempt has been made to integrate the various regions into viable units. Luanda, the capital, for example, has poor communications with all but the northern region, and its degree of

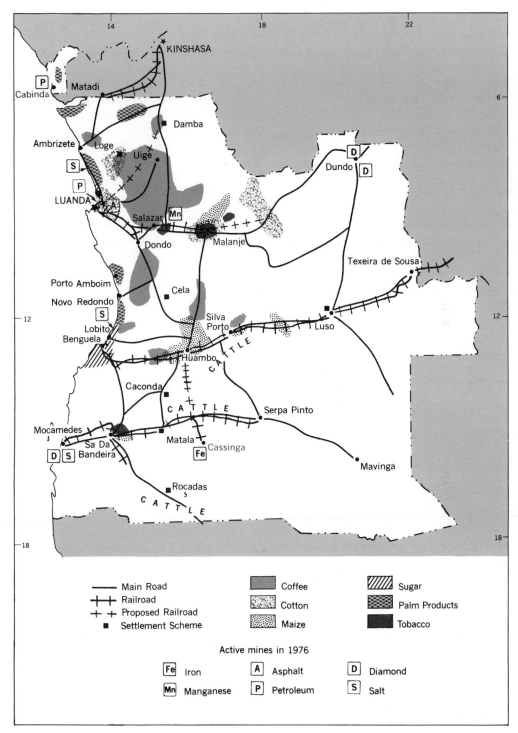

FIGURE 19-2 *Angola. Economic map.*

primacy is even less than that of Maputo, which also has poor national communications. Like Mozambique, Angola has several distinct development corridors, but unlike Mozambique, only one is dependent on the transit traffic from the minerally rich interior beyond its borders.

Northern Angola contains the greatest diversity of natural resources and economic activities in the state. Its principal city and port is Luanda (500,000), on which the northern transport network focuses. The Luanda railway is Angola's oldest, dating back to the 1880s and originally intended as a trans-Africa line. It terminates 264 mi (423 km) inland at Malanje (45,000), an important agricultural, transshipment, and administrative center on the plateau (Fig. 19-2). In the Malanje area, cotton, tobacco, sugar, and maize are grown, and to its east are the profitable cotton areas of the Cuango Valley; a rail line has been projected to extend into this area. West of Malanje are the once-productive manganese mines. The region's economic mainstay, however, is coffee, almost all of it being *robusta*. The major coffee-producing area centers on the Uige Plateau. Prior to the uprisings of 1961, one-third of the regional harvest came from peasant farms. The insurrection of March 1961, marking the onset of organized opposition to Portugal's rule, in one night took the lives of

about 1000 coffee growers and threatened to set aflame all of northern Angola. It caused only moderate damage to the coffee plantations. Equipment was destroyed but the plants were left untouched since the rebels hoped to inherit the abandoned European holdings—which they did (Abshire and Samuels, 1969).

Along the moister coastal plains north of Luanda, sugar and cotton are grown on large estates, and in the lower Cuanza Valley southeast of Luanda, market gardening is being extended using waters diverted from the Cambambe Dam. This is to meet the food requirements of the capital, which previously was heavily dependent on Malanje and other areas. Luanda itself remains Angola's largest port and chief manufacturing city. It experienced a phenomenal rate of industrial and urban growth in the 1960s and early 1970s following the discovery of oil both locally and in Cabinda. Its population doubled during the 1960s, and the whole townscape was changed by a building boom producing modern avenues, skyscrapers, theaters, schools, and hospitals. Its industries include oil refining, chemicals, textiles, food processing, car and truck assembly, and a host of others, many of which were geared to the relatively affluent white population concentrated in the city prior to

Modern apartments stand in contrast to a muceque *(slum) in Luanda, Angola's capital (U.N. photo by J. P. Laffont).*

Coffee beans being turned over to dry. Coffee is Angola's leading agricultural export (U.N. photo by J. P. Laffont).

independence. Luanda drew to it countless thousands of Angolans in search of jobs and a better way of life, only to find disappointment and deplorable living conditions in the *muceques* (slums) that ring the city proper and contain one-fourth of Luanda's metropolitan population. Total Portuguese withdrawal in late 1975 brought industry to a halt, fighting near the city, and even greater economic hardship to its people.

Central Angola focuses on the Bihé Plateau, and the Benguela Railway which traverses it from the port of Lobito to connect with the interior rail system at the Zairian border (Fig. 19-2). The Benguela Railway, which follows an old slave route across Angola, was started in 1903 from the port of Benguela just south of Lobito to connect with the then recently discovered copper riches of Katanga (Shaba). The original concession was held by a British company headed by a personal acquaintance of Cecil Rhodes. The company experienced numerous setbacks in building the line, which reached the eastern border only in 1929, and the copper mines three years later. Since then the line has been beset by several difficulties stemming from the control of alternative transport routes from Zambia and Zaire to the coast: at times Zaire has preferred to ship its copper and manganese through Kinshasa and Matadi; Zambian exports during and after the Rhodesian blockade and prior to completion of the Tan-Zam Railway, put severe strains on the already overly used route; and during the Angolan civil war, Zambian and local traffic was again disrupted.

The two major economic nodes along this central route are Huambo (formerly

The Benguela Railway, Angola. The main west-bound traffic to the port of Lobito is copper from Zambia and Zaire. (Gécamines, Zaire)

Novo Lisboa) and Lobito-Benguela. Huambo (100,000) is the primary regional center for the rich and agriculturally productive Bihé Plateau, which, because of its temperate climate, attracted large numbers of Portuguese settlers. This densely settled region produces much of Angola's maize and important quantities of *arabica* coffee (Fig. 19-2). Between Huambo and the coast, in the lower and drier areas around Cubal, there are vast sisal plantations, sisal often being Angola's third most valuable agricultural export. Lobito (75,000), which handles a more specialized cargo than Luanda, but approximately an equal volume of traffic, has one of the finest natural harbors in Africa. Protected by a 3-mi-long (5 km) sandspit parallel to the shore, the harbor is deep and modern, and has undergone repeated expansion to handle the mineral traffic generated in Zaire and Zambia. When the Benguela Railway was extended to it from the port city of Benguela in 1920, Lobito developed into Angola's second most important industrial city. Today its main industries include cement works, food processing, and general metal fabricating.

Southern Angola has lagged behind all but the remote eastern regions in economic prosperity. The main foci have been the Rocadas and Matala settlement schemes along the Cunene River, the rail terminus and fishing port of Moçamedes, and more recently the Cassinga iron ore mines, which are connected by rail to the Moçamedes lines east of Matala (Fig. 19-1). The mines came into operation in 1957, and by 1970 were producing over 6 million tons of high-grade hematite ore each year. Iron ore is Angola's fourth ranking export by value. The southern region is less favorably endowed with rain than the rest of the country so that its agriculture is extensive rather than intensive, and cattle are the mainstay of the rural economy beyond the settlement schemes. A joint effort of Portugal and South Africa to develop the region and Ovamboland in adjoining Namibia focused on regulating the flow of the Cunene and harnessing hydroelectric power from the Calueque Dam. The projects, however, came under repeated guerrilla attacks, and South Africa's direct military presence in southern Angola during the post-independence Angolan civil war emphasized their importance to South Africa.

Independence and Civil War

Angolan independence was preceded by over a decade of local rebellion and urban violence, and the rise and fall of aspiring African nationalist groups whose only apparent common objective was the end of colonialism. Regional and not necessarily national interests frequently took precedence in the struggles against Portugal. Three major divergent movements emerged in the anticolonial struggle: the Angola National Liberation Front (FNLA) headed by Holden Roberto and backed by Zaire, France, and the United States; the Soviet-backed Popular Movement for the Liberation of Angola (MPLA) headed by Agostinho Neto; and the moderate socialist National Union for the Total Independence of Angola (UNITA) headed by Jonas Savimbi and backed by certain Portuguese business interests, the People's Republic of China, and South Africa. Ideological, personal, ethnic, and regional differences split the groups and kept them feuding to the advantage of Portugal. The MPLA's strongest and most consistent support came from the Mbundu people situated in the general vicinity of Luanda and its hinterland. The FNLA's strongest support came from the Bakongo people further north, especially around Uige. UNITA's support was probably the broadest, includ-

Amidst the chaos of civil war (late 1975), Portuguese families await transportation for themselves and their possessions from Luanda back to Portugal (U.N. photo by J. P. Laffont).

ing all areas south of the Benguela Railway, and focused upon the Ovimbundu on the Bihé Plateau.

Competition between these groups intensified following a series of events in Portugal. In April 1974, the Portuguese dictatorship was overthrown in a bloodless coup led by army officers disenchanted with the slow rate of decolonization in Africa and convinced the revolutionary wars could only be settled by a political solution. Years of fighting had strained the Portuguese economy and demoralized its people. Thus facing military defeat in the colonies and civil war at home, war-exhausted Portugal decided to grant Angola and Mozambique their independence in 1975. When the Portuguese finally withdrew from Angola on November 11, 1975, they conferred independence and sovereignty on the "Angolan people" without recognizing any particular movement as representing Angola's legitimate government. All three nationalist movements held independence ceremonies in the areas they controlled.

What followed was one of the bloodiest and costliest civil wars ever fought in Africa. The MPLA, whose strategic position at the

Cabinda

Cabinda is a 2800 sq mi (7,252 sq km) territory on the Atlantic coast sandwiched between the People's Republic of the Congo and Zaire and separated from Angola proper by Zaire's only outlet to the sea (Fig. 19-1). Until the discovery of oil in 1966, the Angolan enclave was neither a major asset nor a liability to Angola or to the Portuguese. Timber, coffee, and cocoa were its major exports. In the weeks immediately preceding Angolan independence, however, Gulf Oil was pumping 160,000 barrels of oil per day from what is possibly one of the largest oil fields in Africa. That yielded the Angolan treasury about $40 million a month and represented 85 percent of Angola's oil production. Since 1973, oil has been Angola's leading export.

Cabinda's oil and location were critical geopolitical issues in the postindependence Angolan civil war. Each of the major liberation movements (MPLA, UNITA, and FNLA) was committed to keeping Cabinda a part of the Angolan state because of its assets. However, a separatist movement—the Front for the Liberation of Cabinda, formed in 1963—seeks sovereign status for the enclave and declared its independence in 1975. The pronouncement went unheeded, and Cabinda remains a part of Angola, although President Mobutu of Zaire has actively supported the separatist movement with funds and weapons. Mobutu's ultimate objective appears to be Cabinda's annexation. During the civil war, Cabinda was occupied and controlled by the Soviet-backed MPLA. About half of the territory's 80,000 inhabitants reside in the city of Cabinda.

heart of the country and in control of Luanda gave it an advantage that overcame its numerical inferiority, expanded its sphere of domination with the aid of Soviet arms and, later, with the support of southern Africa's new centurions, the Cuban forces, which eventually numbered between 12,000 and 15,000. A northward thrust drove the FNLA forces back toward the Zaire border, and a group of white mercenaries hastily recruited in Europe in support of FNLA suffered heavy casualties without having any real effect upon the course of the conflict. As the FNLA retreated and the northern front failed, the MPLA, now bolstered by Cuban troops, accelerated its southward push on the divided armies of UNITA. The headquarters of UNITA, Huambo, fell to the MPLA-Cuban forces in January 1976, shortly after the withdrawal of South African forces began. South African troops had entered Angola in order to protect installations along the Cunene River that were deemed vital to irrigation projects in Namibia. The MPLA's southward push stopped short of a confrontation with remaining South African forces, and there were reports that the MPLA's leaders had allayed South African fears concerning the Cunene dams. As the Movement's military successes increased, the Organization of African Unity, its member states, and a growing number of countries around the world recognized its leaders as the legitimate government of Angola.

Angola's brief but brutal civil war closed one chapter in south-central Africa's political geography, but it opened another. The presence of Cuban forces in Southern Africa gave a new dimension to Soviet influence on the continent, and it altered the balance of strength in the rapidly disintegrating buffer zone north of the South African Republic. Most immediately, Rhodesia (Zimbabwe) felt the impact of its new, greater vulnerability: Mozambique, Angola's ideological ally, in March 1976 closed its Rhodesian border and announced a state of war. Salisbury's white minority regime faced greater isolation than ever before, as its troops fought battles against insurgents along its borders, negotiations with black leaders failed, and South Africa remained aloof. Pretoria faces its own challenge in Namibia, where the course of events appears also to be overtaking the slow and unproductive negotiations whose objective is social and political reform acceptable to the South African government. The South West African Peoples Organization (SWAPO), viewed by many as a legitimate representative of Namibian African aspirations, has been excluded from the talks: the pattern is familiar.

Meanwhile, as the ultimate confrontation between South Africa and black Africa approaches, Angola faces the reality of independence amid a staggering array of problems and obstacles. Apart from the lack of preparedness so familiar upon colonial withdrawal from African countries, Angola's bridges, railroads, and other facilities lie heavily damaged; population has been severely dislocated and regional animosities intensified; a reported 40,000 Cuban immigrants have entered the country in addition to Havana's army and technical advisors, perhaps signaling a new colonial era; and to the south lies the unresolved issue of Namibia, whose final disposition cannot occur without Angolan involvement. Angola is a country of considerable potential, but it will be some years before its peoples can fully reap its benefits.

Bibliography

Abshire, D. M., and M. A. Samuels (eds.). *Portuguese Africa: A Handbook*. New York: Praeger, 1969.

Bender, G. J. and P. S. Yoder, "Whites in Angola on the Eve of Independence," *Africa Today*, Vol. 21, No. 4 (Fall, 1974), pp. 23–37.

Davidson, B. *In the Eye of the Storm*. London: Longmans, 1972.

Duffy, J. *Portuguese Africa*. Cambridge: Harvard University Press, 1962.

El-Khawas, M. A. "Foreign Economic Involvement in Angola and Mozambique," *Issue*, Vol. 4, No. 2 (Summer, 1974), pp. 21–28.

Henriksen, T. H. "End of an Empire: Portugal's Collapse in Africa," *Current History*, Vol. 68, No. 405 (May, 1975), pp. 211–215 and 229.

Marcum, J. *The Angolan Revolution*. Cambridge: M.I.T. Press, 1969.

Miller, J. C. "The Politics of Decolonization in Portuguese Africa," *African Affairs*, Vol. 74, No. 295 (April, 1975), pp. 135–147.

Minter, W. *Portuguese Africa and the West*. New York: Monthly Review Press, 1974.

Niddrie, D. L. "The Cunene River: Angola's River of Life," *Journal of the American Portuguese Cultural Society*, Vol. 4 (1970), pp. 1–17.

Niddrie, D. L. "Changing Settlement Patterns in Angola," *Rural Africana*, No. 23 (Winter, 1974), pp. 47–77.

de Spinola, A. *Portugal and the Future*. Lisbon: Arcadia, 1974.

Wheeler, D. and R. Pelissier, *Angola*. London: Pall Mall, 1971.

TWENTY

In terms of resources, South Africa is the richest country in Africa. The diversified resource base includes gold and diamonds, iron ore and good quality coal, alloys and copper, as well as fertile soils and adequate water supplies in several regions. South Africa is the continent's most developed country in economic terms, possessing a sizeable iron and steel industry, plants for the conversion of coal into oil, and more than half the industrial establishments in Africa. It supplies a higher percentage of its own needs for manufactured goods than any other African country, while it leads the continent in the production of gold, platinum, coal, chrome, sugar cane, and corn. With only 6 percent of the continent's population, South Africa's GNP is about one-fifth of the African total. It accounts for over half of Africa's energy consumption and output of electricity, and has almost 40 percent of the continent's registered motor vehicles.

An integrated road, rail, and airways system has been developed linking the cities which are among the largest in Africa.

South Africa's human resources, too, are varied. Every continent has contributed to the complex demography of this large (472,500 sq mi or 1.2 million sq km) country. The arrival of the various component groups was not simultaneous, but each has made its specific contribution to the development of the state. Today, the country displays an incredible patchwork of races, languages, religions, customs, and modes of living. The spectacular progress made in the economic sphere in certain regions is in sharp contrast to the social backwardness in others.

South Africa today is engaged in a unique experiment in multiracial development—an experiment that is being imposed upon the African majority together with the Asian and Coloured communities, by the

SOUTH AFRICA:
THE CHALLENGE
OF
SEPARATE
DEVELOPMENT

white minority. Officially termed "separate development" or "multinational development" by the ruling Nationalist Party, but more commonly known as *apartheid*, the program envisages a number of independent racial states being carved out of the existing colonial metropole. The decolonization process is thus unique: territorially, it is internal and not external. Anthropogeographic boundaries are being superimposed on a pre-existing cultural landscape in an effort to create ten independent African states and one white-controlled state. To achieve this, economic conditions must be changed, industries relocated, new towns built, populations resettled (often involuntarily), political institutions developed, and new legal systems devised. The costs, human and economic, are incalculable.

South Africa has become a laboratory for the political and economic geographer seeking to predict the consequences of this singular attempt to solve the local version of a worldwide problem. In this chapter, an effort is made to present these developments in a geographical perspective without losing sight of the fact they have their roots in a combination of unusual historical circumstances. Whatever the consequences, the changes will have far-reaching significance for Africa and the world at large.

The Physical Setting

South Africa is a land of diverse natural landscapes that have both helped and hindered human settlement and economic development. Adverse relief and rainfall conditions have seriously restricted the extent and nature of agriculture, while the rich and diverse mineral resources have provided the basis for Africa's most important mining economy and mining-related industries. The 1800-mi (2900-km) coastline from Mozambique to Namibia has few natural harbors, and the adjoining coastal lowlands are narrow, varying from desert in Namaqualand to marshland in northern Natal and Kwa Zulu. In the southwestern Cape, the east-west trending Cape Ranges rise to heights of 6000 to 7500 ft (1800–2250 m), and were effective barriers to early colonial expansion into the interior (Fig. 20-1). Behind them lies the vast Karoo, a sparsely settled dryland region that merges with the Kalahari and Namib deserts of Botswana and Namibia, respectively. Behind the dissected coastal perimeter further east rise the spectacular Drakensberg Mountains, reaching to 11,000 ft (3300 m) near the Lesotho border, and stretching from the eastern Transvaal southwest into the Cape Province. The Drakensberg Escarpment rises, in places, almost 6000 ft (1800 m) above the adjoining lowlands where it forms a major barrier to communications between the coast and the interior plateau.

The interior plateau, or Highveld, stands between 3000 and 6000 ft (900–1800 m) and centers on the Transvaal and Orange Free State. Here lies South Africa's mineral wealth—its gold, coal, copper, diamonds, platinum, asbestos, and others. The Witwatersrand, for example, is Africa's richest gold-producing zone. In general the landscape is gently undulating, broken in places by isolated hills and highland areas such as the Soutpansberg and Waterberg mountains. Flowing westward across the Highveld from its headwaters in Lesotho, is South Africa's major river, the Orange, and its principal tributary, the Vaal. Both provide the basis of irrigated agriculture and supply the interior urban centers with their industrial water requirements, while water from the Orange River is also being diverted southward to the Cape Midlands and several south coast towns. The Limpopo forms South Africa's northern boundary and drains much of the Transvaal before emptying into the Indian Ocean. Hundreds of smaller rivers such as

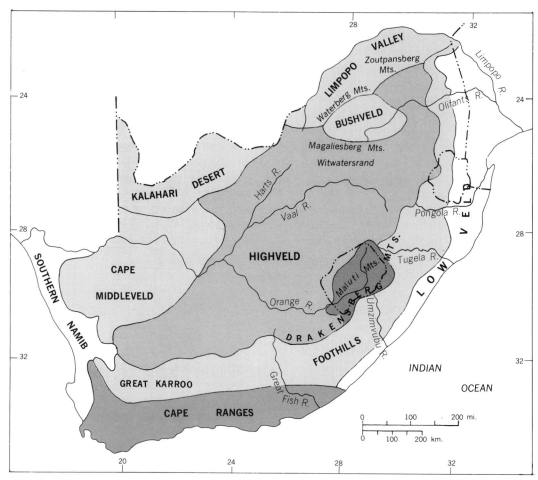

FIGURE 20-1 *South Africa. Physiographic regions.*

the Tugela, Umzimvubu, and Great Fish pour out of the Drakensberg, cutting deep valleys across Natal, the Transkei, and the eastern Cape. Few have been dammed to control erosion or to provide much-needed irrigation water and hydroelectric power.

South Africa has great climatic diversity tempered predominantly by elevation and latitude: a summer-dry "Mediterranean" climate prevails around Cape Town; a humid subtropic climate occurs along the Natal coast; highland savanna and steppe characterize much of the Highveld; and semidesert and desert conditions cover much of the Cape interior. Rainfall is highest in the Drakensberg and decreases in general from east

to west (Fig. 20-2). Namaqualand and Bushmanland receive less than 8 in. (200 mm), while coastal Natal, the Drakensberg, and parts of the Cape Ranges receive over 56 in. (1400 mm) annually. Only 10 percent of the area receives over 30 in. (760 mm), the amount generally required for grain farming. Both evaporation rates and rainfall variability are high, and in the interior droughts are common and occasionally prolonged. Winter snowfalls are common in the Drakensberg and are not unknown in Johannesburg, while overnight frosts occur from June through August in the higher elevations.

The diversity of climates, soils, and topography makes possible a diversity of agri-

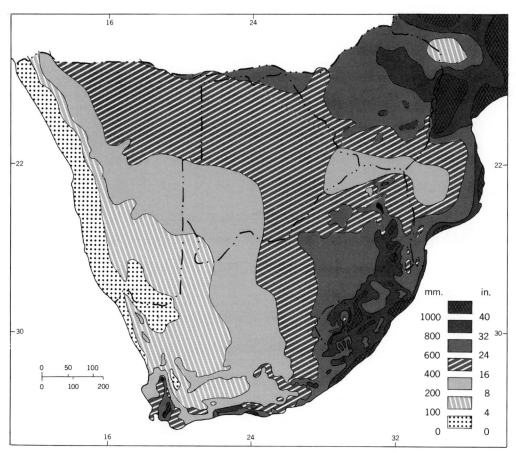

FIGURE 20-2 *Mean annual rainfall of Southern Africa.*

culture. However, it is unfortunate that the heaviest rainfall occurs either in the higher elevations or on land too steep and broken for cultivation. The combination of steep slopes and high rainfall—especially in the Drakensberg foothills of Natal, Kwa Zulu, and the Transkei—has produced much soil erosion and reduced the amount of land available for farming despite serious attempts to promote conservation practices. Since the majority of South Africa's black peoples are farmers, this is a serious constraint to local development.

Peoples and Regions: The Search for Nationhood

South Africa's population (26.6 million) consists of four major groups: Africans, Whites, Coloureds, and Asians (Table 20-1). Almost three-fourths (19 million) are Africans, the vast majority of whom are Bantu-speaking peoples. They are culturally and ethnically diverse and comprise four major language groups and several "national" units. The largest linguistic group is the Nguni (11.0 million) which includes the Zulu, Xhosa, Ndebele, and Swazi. The Sotho-speaking South Africans (6.2 million) include the Tswanas, Pedi, and South Sotho or Basuto, while the two smallest linguistic

Table 20-1 POPULATION GROWTH, 1911–1977 (in thousands)

Year	AFRICANS '000	%	WHITES '000	%	COLOUREDS '000	%	ASIANS '000	%	TOTAL
1911	4,019	67.3	1,276	21.4	523	8.8	152	2.5	5,973
1921	4,697	67.8	1,276	22.0	545	7.9	164	2.3	6,927
1936	6,597	68.8	2,003	20.9	769	8.0	220	2.3	9,588
1946	7,830	68.6	2,372	20.8	928	8.1	285	2.5	11,416
1960	10,908	68.2	3,088	19.3	1,509	9.4	477	3.0	15,983
1970	15,058	70.2	3,751	17.5	2,018	9.4	620	2.9	21,448
1977 (est)	19,000	71.5	4,350	16.3	2,470	9.3	762	2.9	26,582

SOURCE. *Republic of South Africa*, South Africa 1974, *p. 68, and official census reports (various years).*

groups are the Venda (700,000) and the Shangana-Tsonga (1.1 million).

Although the various populations mingle in the urban areas and on the fringes of their traditional homelands, each ethnic group is associated with a specific area (Fig. 20-3). Thus the Zulu (4.5 million) are concentrated in the heart of Natal east of the Drakensberg Escarpment; the Xhosa (4.4 million) are concentrated in the Transkei of the eastern Cape; and the Venda are in the northern Transvaal. The Xhosa were the first to confront the advancing Europeans in the eastern Cape during the eighteenth century, and the Great Fish River became the scene of a series of wars between these two

FIGURE 20-3 *South Africa. Racial dominance and ethnic "nations."*

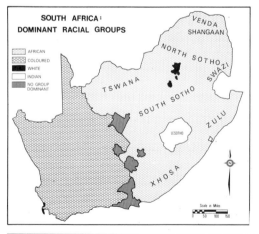

pastoralist groups. The Zulu rose to power when they found strong leadership in Natal, and the distribution pattern results largely from their influence. The Zulu might was broken by the white invaders a century ago, but the Zulu nation survives today.

Since the African groups entered what is contemporary South Africa from the northeast, it is not surprising that their highest concentrations are in the north and along the east coast. On the plateau itself, the Bantu-speaking peoples first encountered the Bushman (Sarwa) and Hottentots, and later the Boers, and by the seventeenth century had reached the Orange River. Their distribution was general, but highest densities occurred in the disease-free uplands and the more humid regions. Along the foot of the Great Escarpment, the coastal belt afforded easier migration routes, and there the Xhosa and Zulu made the greatest penetrations to the south. The present distribution is very similar, except for the urban centers which have drawn hundreds of thousands of Africans from their homelands. The 1970 census recorded that only 46.5 percent of the Africans resided in areas reserved exclusively for them, and that 35 percent were urban dwellers.

The Whites form the second largest racial group (4.4 million), and like the Africans they are culturally and ethnically diverse. Although comprising only 16.3 percent of the population (Table 20-1), Whites dominate virtually every aspect of life in South Africa. Permanent white settlement dates back to 1652 when Jan van Riebeeck established a revictualing station at Table Bay for ships of the Dutch East India Company sailing between Holland and Southeast Asia. Large-scale settlement was officially discouraged, but the population grew and was augmented by French Huguenot and German immigrants, and slaves imported from Malaya, Mozambique, and East and West Africa (Wilson and Thompson, 1969). The immigrant groups brought with them their languages, values, and essentials of life, including their staple crops (wheat, vines and citrus) and technology. Gradually they spread eastward in search of new land beyond official Dutch control, and by the eighteenth century had clashed with the southward migrating Xhosas. In 1806 Britain gained control of the Cape, and for the first time colonialism was followed in earnest: English was declared the sole official language, the courts and education systems were anglicized, British settlement was encouraged, and slavery was abolished in 1834. British colonialism spread to Natal in the 1840s, while the Afrikaners, descendants of the original Dutch immigrants pushed into the interior (1836), followed soon after by the British and other European groups.

Among the white immigrants, the Afrikaners have separated themselves most completely from their European heritage. They identify themselves as intensely with Africa as do black Africans; they are fiercely proud of their language, which has evolved from Dutch and has a unique flavor today, and do not think of any part of Europe as their racial or cultural homeland. The English-speaking South Africans, on the other hand, have not relinquished their ties with Britain,

Cape Town and Table Mountain. This was the site of the first permanent South African white settlement. Today, Cape Town is South Africa's second largest city and its legislative capital. (Satour)

SOUTH AFRICA: THE CHALLENGE OF SEPARATE DEVELOPMENT

do not display the undivided allegiance to South Africa of the Afrikaners, and consider themselves Europeans first and foremost. There are exceptions, naturally, but the sentiments among whites are mostly divided along these lines. An appreciation of this is indispensable to the analysis of the Afrikaners' efforts to consolidate their position in this outpost.

Ironically, it was not the Afrikaners who brought to the interior of South Africa the modern ways of life which they view with such pride today. The nineteenth-century Dutch wished to escape from British overlordship at the Cape, and they entered the interior with the intent of establishing pastoral republics, ranching cattle and sheep. Thus, they became known as *Boers* (a Dutch word literally meaning "farmer"), and their economic mode of life resembled more the Africans' than that which was developing in Europe. The discovery of diamonds near the confluence of the Orange and the Vaal rivers (1867), and the subsequent discovery of gold along the Witwatersrand (1886) drew thousands of white immigrants who brought with them capital, technical skills, and the knowledge of Europe's progress in the Industrial Revolution. Opposed bitterly by the Boers, these people infiltrated the interior republics and founded cities such as Kimberley and Johannesburg, exploiting resources which could not have been exploited by pastoralists. Against the Boers' will, the isolation of the interior came to an end, as railroads penetrated the highlands,

roads were built, and urbanization gained momentum.

After their defeat in the Anglo-Boer War, the Afrikaners were to participate in the economic progress of their country —progress that was initiated by recent immigrants from Europe. The level of their participation rose constantly, and Afrikaners in due course began to attain positions of power. The ratio of rural to urban dwellers among Afrikaners changed continuously in favor of the latter. In the early days of the Union, the majority of Afrikaners still lived on the land, and the bulk of the English-speaking people and other immigrants resided in the growing cities. Today, the Afrikaner is as much an urban dweller as is his English-speaking contemporary.

Over 86 percent of the South African Whites are urban dwellers (Table 20-2). They enjoy the highest standard of living of any racial group; they control the vast majority of the country's wealth, industrial resources, and land; and they have absolute political power. Each year their numbers are augmented by about 30,000 new immigrants from Western Europe, but this increase, together with the low natural growth rate (1.4 percent), will not ensure the continued politico-economic domination, a situation viewed with alarm by the ruling Nationalist Government.

The Coloured population numbers 2.5 million (Table 20-1) and constitutes the majority sector in the western Cape (Fig. 20-3). They form the largest component in Cape

Table 20-2 URBAN POPULATION (Percentage) 1911–1970

Year	Africans	Whites	Coloureds	Asians	Total
1911	13.0	53.0	50.4	52.8	24.7
1921	14.0	59.7	52.4	60.4	27.9
1936	19.0	68.2	58.0	69.5	32.4
1946	24.3	75.6	62.5	72.8	36.4
1960	31.8	83.6	68.3	83.2	47.2
1970	35.0	86.7	74.3	86.2	48.0

SOURCE. *Republic of South Africa*, South Africa 1974, *p. 75, and official census reports (various years)*.

Table 20-3 POPULATION OF PRINCIPAL METROPOLITAN AREAS (white urban areas), 1970

Urban Areas	Total	Africans	Whites	Coloureds	Asians
Johannesburg	1,432,643	809,595	501,061	82,639	39,348
Cape Town	1,096,597	107,877	378,505	598,952	11,263
East Rand	895,527	541,823	323,187	19,243	11,274
Durban	843,327	224,819	257,780	43,699	317,029
Pretoria	561,703	234,695	304,618	11,343	11,047
Port Elizabeth	468,577	201,574	149,569	112,154	5,280
West Rand/Vanderbijlpark/ Vereeniging	421,018	259,139	148,350	11,583	1,946
Sasolburg	304,371	188,746	111,136	2,288	2,201
OFS Gold-fields	208,891	157,271	50,098	1,522	0
Bloemfontein	180,179	95,510	74,516	10,152	1
Pietermaritzburg	158,921	68,262	45,503	8,756	36,400
East London	123,294	51,244	56,807	13,249	1,994
Kimberley	103,789	48,797	29,397	24,657	938

SOURCE. *Republic of South Africa*, South Africa 1974, *p.* 76.

Town (60 percent of the total) and in almost all other towns in the Cape Province (Table 20-3). The Coloureds include not only persons of mixed white and African blood, but also Malay people who have remained remarkably distinct racially for many generations. Intermarriage with the early slaves began to produce these mulattoes, who in addition to white blood might have Hottentot, black slave, or perhaps Asian blood. The Hottentots also intermarried with the slaves so that the numbers of the new Coloured community soon attained significance. All this took place, however, while the western Cape was the only region of Southern Africa that was permanently settled and organized by whites. Cape Town was the only real town, and the Coloureds worked there and on the surrounding farms.

When the white man finally invaded other parts of Southern Africa, the Coloured did not participate. That element in the white population which desired to trek onto the plateau was opposed to what it considered miscegenation. The racist elitism that was developing among these Afrikaners belied the fact that mixed marriages at the Cape had been producing Coloured offspring for generations, and that people of Dutch extraction—who were now the core of the Afrikaner group—had participated actively in this process.

Throughout the 1960s the Coloured community grew at 3 percent per annum, but since 1970 the growth rate has dropped to about 2.4 percent as birth rates declined more rapidly than death rates. Like their white contemporaries, the Coloured peoples speak either Afrikaans or English, but Afrikaans predominates (90 percent in 1970). This fact attests to their early association with the Cape Dutch settlers, even though the Dutch community never integrated the Coloured community with its own. About one-third of the Coloured church-going population attends the Dutch Reform churches, another third attends English churches, and 5 percent practices the Islamic faith. In view of the segregationist philosophies of the Dutch churches, the number of Coloureds adhering to them is remarkable. Islam is most prevalent in Cape Town, where it is practiced by the Malay peoples as it has been for centuries.

Like other nonwhites, the Coloureds face discrimination in jobs, wages, housing, and general amenities, and they are denied representation in the national parliament. Various avenues of employment are closed to them by law, and a sizeable portion of the community has always lived in poverty in both the urban and rural areas. The Coloured cannot compete successfully with the skilled European (if he is not barred from such competition by law), and he loses jobs in the unskilled field to Africans who work for lower wages. In Cape Town (1.1 million) they have maintained themselves in only a few industries including stevedoring, textile work, building, and food processing. Still, there are more Coloureds in manufacturing occupations (mostly general labor) than in agriculture and other primary industries, and the difference is growing despite the problems they face in the cities.

The smallest of the racial groups is the Asian (Table 20-1). In 1860 the first group of indentured Indian laborers were brought by the British to work the newly founded sugar estates of Natal. The practice was to continue for a half century, until the South African government became alarmed at their numbers and stopped the process in 1913. By this date, the Asian population was about 155,000. Most Indians, whose period of indentured labor had expired, declined the free passage back to India and remained to develop market gardening near the cities and to enter the general urban labor pool. Wealthy merchants immigrated at the turn of the century and established successful commercial enterprises in competition with the Whites, especially in Durban. Today their stamp is unmistakable there, and over one-third of this city's population is Asian (Table 20-3).

The great majority of South Africa's Asians are Indians and about 70 percent of these are Hindu. They speak a variety of Indian languages (although English is the *lingua franca*), and separate themselves from the 20 percent who are Moslems, many of

Mosque and shopping area of Grey Street, Durban, Natal. This is the heart of Natal's Indian community, and part of Durban's central business district. (Alan C. G. Best)

whom have moved to the Transvaal. Since 1913 the Asian population has increased between 2 and 3 percent per year; in 1970 the birth rate was 32.7 per 1000, and the death rate 6.8 per 1000—the lowest of any racial group. While most of the economically active Asians were employed almost exclusively in agriculture before the turn of the century, today about two-thirds of the employed are in manufacturing, commerce, and finance. Large numbers, especially in metropolitan Durban, are in textile work, general manufacturing, retail trade, construction, and the transport business. Some have achieved considerable wealth and property and a university education; a growing number is entering the professions.

Over 83 percent of the Asians live in Natal, the greatest concentration being metropolitan Durban (Fig. 20-3 and Table 20-3). They are not permitted to live in the Orange Free State, nor can they move freely from one province to another. Under the Group Areas Act, which reserves for each race a specific and separate residential area, tens of thousands of Asians are being removed from city centers to more peripheral locations where business opportunities are reduced and major changes in life-styles must be made. From central Durban, for example, more than 230,000 are being moved to Chatsworth and other new towns some 10 to 15 mi (16–24 km) away. An even greater number of Coloureds from Cape Town's District Six were removed under the Group Areas Act during the 1960s.

A Nation Divided: The Policy of Separate Development

This, then, is the South African nation, although few would assert that South Africa's peoples are indeed a nation in any sense of the word. The question is how a nation thus fragmented can evolve along desirable lines. The Brazilian answer has been integration, and although not completely successful, this example is often quoted as one where failure has been averted. The South African response has been along completely opposite lines. Asserting that integration leads to cultural and moral decay as well as to racial pollution, the white ruling minority has produced a blueprint of separate living for the sectors of the South African population which is at present being implemented. It is a plan which has no rival anywhere in the world and is considered a unique solution to a unique problem. Although admittedly intensifying the divisive factors between South Africa's peoples, it will, according to its architects, lead to political independence for each sector while leading toward economic interdependence. The South African state, therefore, is envisaged

as developing along lines similar to that of the British Commonwealth. There will not be a federation and therefore no central government, but a group of adjacent, racially based units, each internally independent politically.

The goal of the blueprint for separate development is the preservation of Western culture in the South African outpost. The mingling of white, African, and Asian cultures is deemed undesirable, and thus each must be provided with his own "homeland" in which cultural development may take place without a threat to its purity. Obviously, this involves the relocation of hundreds of thousands of people who have for centuries been thrown together by the forces of economic development, urbanization, and mutual need. A complete reorientation of the South African economy, massive relocation of industry, and alterations to the transport network are among the major problems facing the state in consequence of the regional form of *apartheid*.

The policy of separate development has

Apartheid

Apartheid is an Afrikaans word meaning "apartness" or "separateness." South Africa's white minority government is committed to the separation of the four races politically, socially, and territorially. Integration it maintains would result in the loss of cultural identity. Only the Whites are represented in the national parliament. The Asians and Coloureds have separate representative councils with limited legislative and administrative powers, while the African majority is being reorganized politically and spatially into quasi-independent homelands or bantustans.

Although the white government recognizes four separate races, the South Africans are more commonly labelled either "White" or "Nonwhite," and much of the legislation reflects these designations. Entrances to all public facilities such as railway stations, post offices, and libraries are marked "Whites Only" and "Nonwhites." Park benches, elevators, beaches, hotels, and sports facilities are similarly marked, while each race has its own schools, universities, and residential areas. There are several white universities, some being Afrikaans-speaking (e.g., Stellenbosch), some English-speaking (e.g., Durban), others bilingual (e.g., Port Elizabeth). The university for the Coloureds is in Cape Town and that for the Asians is in Durban-Westville. The Africans have three universities, and if the policy of separate development is fully implemented, each bantustan will have its own.

In South Africa, mixed marriages and sex across the color line are criminal offenses. The Group Areas Act reserves for each race a separate residential area in the urban regions. Often these areas are separated from each other by buffer zones such as cemeteries, highways, and vacant land. The influx of rural Africans to the cities is restricted by law to the number of jobs available, and certain skilled jobs (e.g., mine engineering) are reserved for Whites.

Every South African is issued an identity card that gives the holder's race and legal address. Africans are required to carry them at all times, and failure to produce one upon police demand may mean a fine, imprisonment, or even banishment to the bantustans. Each day almost 4000 Africans are arrested for pass violations. Africans must regularly prove to the municipal authorities and police that they are gainfully employed and legally resident in designated urban areas. At Sharpeville in May 1960, the police shot indiscriminately with automatic weapons into an unarmed crowd of women and children demonstrating against the pass laws, killing 67 and wounding 186. The riots of June 1976, in Soweto and other African townships, are further examples of black opposition to South Africa's race laws.

Many of *apartheid's* more vocal and influential opponents have been detained without trial, often for months. Intellectuals may be put under house arrest and "banned." All "Nonwhite" opposition is considered illegal.

been articulated by various Nationalist governments since coming to power in 1948. Separation, the Nationalists argue, must be effected between the races in all spheres of life. Thus a mass of legislation affecting labor, housing, rural-urban migration, and other important matters has been introduced. One of the government's first undertakings within this framework, was an inventory of the human and environmental resources of the African reserves, and the Tomlinson Commission presented its findings in 1955. The report contained not only inventories of the natural resources and the socioeconomic conditions of the widely diverse and highly fragmented reserves, but it also made recommendations for their improvement. The Tomlinson Report became the government's blueprint for territorial separation, and since then an abundance of legislation has reinforced the basic premise.

The Nationalist government sees South Africa not as one nation with a common citizenship and rights, but as composed of many "nations" that are entitled to self-determination within their own prescribed geographical areas. These "nations" are defined in terms of language, culture, and tradition, and each, according to the government, should retain its identity and determine its own future. Territorial separation makes that possible. Those areas set aside for the 19 million Africans are called "homelands" or "bantustans." They may eventually become fully independent sovereign states free to apply for membership in the United Nations and other international organizations. The Transkei receives its independence in October 1976.

Ten homelands have been designated: Transkei, Ciskei, Kwa Zulu, Bophuthatswana, Lebowa, Venda, Gazankulu, Basotho Qwa Qwa, South Ndebele, and the Swazi Territory. They vary considerably in area, resources, *de jure* and *de facto* populations, and territorial makeup (Table 20-4). All but Basotho Qwa Qwa and South Ndebele are at present territorially fragmented. Extreme fragmentation occurs in Kwa Zulu, homeland of the Zulu nation. Collectively the homelands comprise only 13 percent of the Republic's total land area, and they form a discontinuous arc from the Great Fish River of the eastern Cape, north through Natal and the Transvaal, and west to the Botswana border (Fig. 20-4). The bulk of South Africa (87 percent of the area) is reserved for the Whites, an area in which the Coloureds and Asians will continue to reside in segregated locations.

Table 20-4 HOMELANDS: AREAS AND POPULATIONS

Homeland	National Group	Designated Capital	Area sq. Miles	Number of Blocks		1970 Population	
				1975	Proposed	de Facto	de Jure
Basotho Qwa Qwa	S. Sotho	Phuthaditjhaba	198	1	1	24,000	1,254,000
Bophuthatswana	Tswana	Heystekrand	12,589	19	6	884,000	1,658,000
Ciskei	Xhosa	Debe Nek	3,000	19	1	524,000	924,000
Gazankulu	Shangaan	Giyani	3,395	4	3	267,000	650,000
Kwa Zulu	Zulu	Ulundi	12,119	29	10	2,097,000	4,026,000
Lebowa	N. Sotho	Leboakgomo	6,753	9	4	1,083,000	2,019,000
Swazi Territory	Swazi	Schoemansdal	1,235	2	1	118,000	460,000
Transkei	Xhosa	Umtata	18,000	2	2	1,734,000	3,005,000
Venda	Venda	Makwarela	3,062	3	1	264,000	358,000
South Ndebele	Ndebele		580	1	1	178,000	234,000

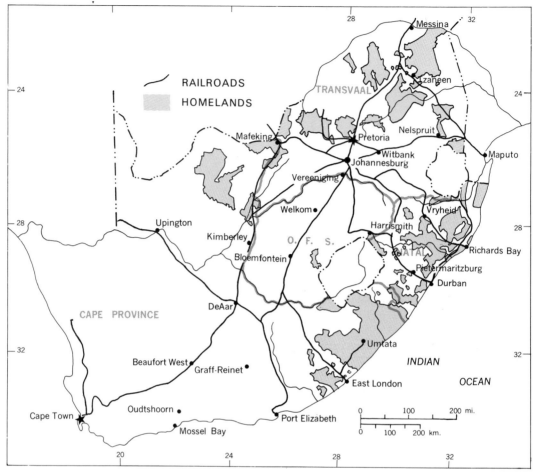

FIGURE 20-4 *South Africa. General identification map.*

Reversals in Prevalent Trends

Among the most significant trends to accompany South Africa's path toward leadership of the African economic scene have been the growth of urban centers and the expansion of the manufacturing sector of the economy. Urbanization was first stimulated by mining, but the contribution of mining to the national income has declined in favor of manufacturing and even agriculture. Yet the cities continued to grow, and Johannesburg, once based entirely on mining, now has over 60 per cent of its white employed population engaged in professional, administrative, and commercial activities. After an early phase dominated by agriculture, the South African economy between 1929 and 1943 was sustained mainly by mining as the most important single contributor. Since 1943, however, manufacturing has taken the lead, now contributing almost three times as much as mining and agriculture combined. These manufacturing industries have not relied only upon overseas markets; indeed, their success is largely a reflection of the incrdased capacity of the South African market. Even though their respective shares were disproportionate, Africans, Coloureds, and Asians benefited from the economic progress of the country as well as the Whites. Thus, a multiracial market with constantly increasing purchasing power developed, and any interference with this trend is likely to have severe negative consequences for South Africa's thriving economy.

Urbanization in South Africa has advanced further than in any other part of Africa, and Johannesburg, Cape Town, and Durban have no rivals in terms of industrial output on the subcontinent. As break-in-bulk places, the cities on the coasts benefited by the progress of mining and industry on the plateau, and Port Elizabeth and East London vie with Cape Town and Durban for the trade of the interior. On the Highveld, the Witwatersrand became the core of the entire country. Further gold discoveries were made and towns sprang up east and west from Johannesburg, so that a lengthy urbanized belt developed. North of Johannesburg, Pretoria prospered as the country's administrative center, and southward, Vereeniging on the Vaal River benefited from ample water supply and the proximity of coal deposits. The southern Transvaal thus became the hub of all South Africa, with an east-west manufacturing and mining axis and a north-south administrative and transportation axis. Johannesburg alone has over 1,500,000 inhabitants today, but the two axes of the southern Transvaal include over one-quarter of the population of the entire country. A megalopolis is developing there (Table 20-3).

In the urban centers of South Africa, and especially on the Witwatersrand, the representatives of the racial sectors of the population have long been thrown together in the common economic effort. In spite of residential segregation and job restrictions based on race, the fortunes of black and white in South Africa have become inextricably mixed. The urban centers, from Cape Town (the first city) and Kimberley (the first mining town) to Johannesburg and Durban, have attracted the capital investment and skills of foreigners and the muscle of the African. Together, they achieved South Africa's economic progress, most dramatically reflected in the urban sprawl and high-rise core of the Golden City. Johannesburg became the continent's financial capital, overseas investors displayed much confidence in South Africa's future, and every sector of the economy blossomed. In 1912, total employment in industry is estimated to have been under 100,000; in 1975 it exceeded 1 million.

The four industrialized regions of South Africa are the Witwatersrand, the Durban-Pinetown area, the region around Cape Town, and the area of Port Elizabeth. Mining stimulated these industries in large measure. The manufacture of explosives became a major industry on the Witwatersrand, and the need for mining boots stimulated the footwear manufacuring of Port Elizabeth and Durban. The need for coal and electricity increased constantly. An iron and steel industry was established at Pretoria, with a subsidiary plant near Vereeniging. A further step toward self-sufficiency was taken with the construction of the world's largest oil-from-coal plant at Sasolburg in the northern Orange Free State.

As the urban centers grew, so did the market for agricultural products. No longer a subsistence pastoralism, South African agriculture produced a vast variety of specialized fruits and vegetables, a higher corn yield per acre than anywhere else on the continent, wheat, a variety of other cereals, and sugar. Near the cities, market gardening and intensive agriculture developed. But whether around the cities or in the vast interior, the bulk of the labor was carried on by Africans under the direction of white landowners.

Thus, the African for decades was leaving his homeland for city, mine, and farm. As elsewhere in Africa, detribalization was proceeding apace, and in the cities could be found a permanently settled African population which was as solidly urban—though poorer—as its white counterpart. Nevertheless, there remained parts of South Africa which were recognizably tribal in nature. Zululand, in Natal, and the Transkei, in the eastern Cape, although affected by the steady stream of emigrants, changed but little as South Africa progressed. Subsistence agriculture, poor soil management, and diseased cattle characterized these and other reserves, and the exodus was the result of local conditions as much as of the attraction of the cities and mines of the white man.

The degree to which the races are spatially integrated and economically interdependent can be seen from Tables 20-3 and 20-5. All cities, other than Pretoria, have more Nonwhites than Whites, and in most cases Africans form the majority. The 1970 census showed that some 4.4 million of the 15 million Africans resided in white urban areas, and a further 3.7 million lived on white farms. Thus 8.1 million Africans, or 53.5 percent of the total, lived in white areas where they outnumbered the Whites by more than two to one. Table 20-5 shows that in the same year, 70 percent of the economically active persons in South Africa were Africans, excluding the subsistence farmers in the homelands. Should separate development be implemented to its fullest, and territorial racial purity be achieved, the white areas would be deprived of virtually the en-

tire labor force in the case of agriculture and mining, and nearly half in the case of manufacturing. Clearly this is unrealistic and impracticable. Nevertheless, separate development does call for some fundamental changes in the spatial and structural organization of the South African economy.

The policy of *apartheid* calls for the resettlement of thousands of Africans in the homelands, and the strict control of migration to the cities. White industrialists are being encouraged to decentralize their operations to the homelands and peripheral regions to relieve some of the congestion of the metropolitan areas and to stimulate the homeland economies. Towns are being built in the homelands, but few have industry and a diversified economic base, and most are merely residential appendages of the richer and economically more productive white areas. Agriculture, still the mainstay of the homeland economies, is being reorganized. In varying degrees the physical infrastructures and educational facilities are being improved, and each homeland has been provided with rudimentary political and administrative systems, albeit closely controlled by Pretoria.

Reorientation toward separate development is, of necessity, proceeding only slowly. The question is whether separation

Table 20-5. ECONOMICALLY ACTIVE POPULATION BY INDUSTRY, 1970 (thousands)

	Africans	Whites	Coloureds	Asians	Totals
Agriculture, forestry, and fishing	2,014	99	119	7	2,239
Mining and quarrying	605	63	7	1	676
Manufacturing	512	280	169	63	1,024
Services	1,064	325	161	23	1,574
Commerce and finance	349	419	85	54	907
Construction	265	96	77	10	446
Electricity, gas, water	32	14	3	—	50
Transport and communications	140	164	28	8	339
Unemployed and unspecified	624	38	55	15	732
Economically Active	*5,604*	*1,498*	*704*	*181*	*7,987*
Total population	15,058	3,751	2,018	620	21,448
% Economically active population	70.2	18.8	8.8	2.2	100.0

SOURCE. *Republic of South Africa*, South Africa, *1974, p. 500.*

of the races will be permitted at all by the economy, or whether markets, resource distribution, and entrepreneurship will be so inhibited by fragmentation, that the favorable trends of the past will be reversed. Much will depend on developments within the homelands where for centuries little change has taken place. The sudden increase in population that these areas are experiencing as a result of resettlement requires rapid economic growth (Maasdorp, 1974). The carrying capacity of the land must be improved, there must be scope for labor in industry, and vast quantities of capital are required. South Africa is prepared to pay the price of racial separation, but what is required may be too much for the state to carry.

Agriculture and Mining

Although environmental conditions are problematic and only 15 percent of the total land area is arable, South Africa has a strong and diversified agricultural and pastoral economy. Sharp contrasts in farming techniques, types of farming, and yields occur from place to place but especially between the white and African areas. In the former, specialized commercial agriculture is emphasized, while subsistence production prevails in the latter. White farms produce over 90 percent of the country's agricultural output in the monetary sector, including much of the corn and sorghum consumed in the adjoining homelands. Cattle and sheep have traditionally had higher earnings than crops and are raised extensively in both white and African areas. Wool, most of which is produced in the Karoo and the Orange Free State, is the most important pastoral product and is South Africa's second export after gold. Livestock is the principal source of cash in most homelands.

Several agricultural regions may be defined (Fig. 20-5). Intensive agriculture occurs in the southwestern Cape where viticulture, horticulture, and deciduous fruit growing predominates and where Coloureds provide much of the farm labor. Sugar cane is grown on large white-owned estates along the Natal coastal plains, and in a few of the adjoining African areas. There sharp contrasts in land use are accentuated by the fragmented nature of the Kwa Zulu homeland. On the Highveld, maize and wheat are the major crops, while citrus, tobacco, dairying and ranching are locally important. Africans provide most of the farm labor, sometimes on a seasonal and contractual basis.

Agriculture is being revitalized and industry expanded in the Karoo with water and hydroelectric power from the massive Orange River Project. Agricultural production is to be increased by $200 million per year. The Hendrik Verwoerd Dam, opened in 1972, provides industrial water and power to Bloemfontein and Kimberley and irrigation water to the Sundays River and Great Fish River via many canals and a 51-mi (82 km) tunnel through the Drakensberg. When completed, the 20 hydroelectric stations will generate a peak supply of 229 MW, and the 15 dams and their canals will irrigate an additional 760,000 acres (300,000 ha) at an estimated cost of $1.3 billion. Smaller but significant irrigation schemes exist on the Vaal-Harts, Pongola, and Crocodile rivers (Fig. 20-5).

The African homelands are not part of South Africa's generally prosperous agricultural economy. They form the overcrowded, economically depressed periphery within the South African space economy. East of the Drakensberg the homelands are predominantly mountainous, broken or hilly, and have only small areas of flat or gently undulating land where cultivation is possible. In all, one-third of the total land area is moun-

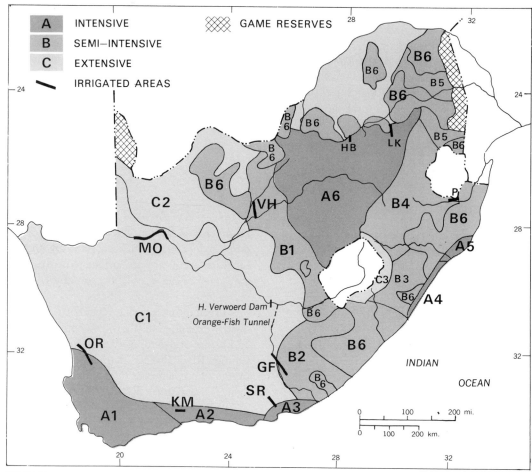

FIGURE 20-5 *South Africa. Agricultural regions.*

A. *Intensive*

1. Southwestern Cape: *deciduous and citrus fruit, vines, wheat, other cereals, sheep, dairying, timber (pine).*
2. Southern Cape Coastlands: *citrus and deciduous fruit, dairying, lucerne, ostriches, timber (pine).*
3. Eastern Cape Coastlands: *citrus fruit, pineapples, chicory, maize, dairying.*
4. South Natal Coast: *dominantly sugar, subtropical fruits.*
5. Zululand Coast: *sugar and timber (gum).*
6. Northern Orange Free State and Southern Transvaal: *maize, dairying, cattle, sheep.*

B. *Semiintensive*

1. Western Orange Free State: *maize, wheat, sheep, cattle.*
2. Eastern Cape Interior: *sheep, cattle, dairying, citrus fruit.*
3. Natal Midlands and East Griqualand: *timber (wattle and pine), dairying.*
4. Northern Natal, Eastern Orange Free State, Southeastern Transvaal: *maize, cattle, dairying, sheep, timber (mainly wattle).*
5. Eastern Transvaal: *subtropical fruits, citrus fruits, vegetables, timber (wattle, gum, pine).*
6. Homelands (Bantustans): *cattle, maize, subsistence crops.*

FIGURE 20-5 (continued)

C. Extensive
1. Karroo: sheep, goats.
2. Northern Cape: cattle ranching.
3. Drakensberg Foothills: sheep, cattle.
4. Northern Transvaal: cattle ranching.

D. Irrigated areas
OR—Olifants River: Lucerne, winter cereals, citrus fruits, vines.
MO—Middle Orange: cotton, lucerne, wheat.
KM—Kamanassie: Lucerne, tobacco, wheat, vines.
GF—Great Fish: Lucerne, citrus fruit.
VH—Vaal-Harts: Lucerne, groundnuts, cotton, tobacco.
LK—Loskop: wheat, tobacco, citrus fruit.
SR—Sundays River: citrus fruit, lucerne.
HB—Hartebeestpoort: tobacco, vegetables, citrus fruit, wheat, fodder crops.
P—Pongola: sugar, cotton.

tainous, 20 percent is hilly to broken, and 46 percent is gently rolling or flat. Much of the latter occurs in Bophuthatswana and Lebowa where rainfall is light and variable, and the soils are thin. About 79 percent of the total areas is used for grazing, and only 15 percent is cultivated.

In 1955 the Tomlinson Commission reported that if the homelands were properly planned, they could support a farming population of about 2.1 million, while an additional 258,000 could earn a living in forestry and mining (South Africa, 1955). Today there are about 8 million Africans in the homelands, and several million more may be resettled there from white areas. This requires rural planning, resettlement, and general development on a scale not seen before.

The homelands have been divided into economic farm units that vary in size according to the environment and prevailing agricultural practices. Dams, irrigation canals, and contour banks have been constructed, and the farms divided into grazing camps, arable plots, and residential units. Despite these efforts, overgrazing is common, yields are low, and soil erosion is widespread. Less than 10 percent of those engaged in subsistence farming earn more than $80 per year,

and over 40 percent earn less than $30. Only small gains have been made in cash-crop farming and irrigation, except under close European supervision. Small acreages of sisal and cotton are grown in the northern regions, while tea, sugar, and subtropical fruits are produced on a small scale in Kwa Zulu and the Transkei.

To reduce the rural poverty and malnutrition that are endemic to the homelands, not only must the land be increased and consolidated but also traditional farm practices must be changed and nonagricultural jobs created. Yields are kept low by archaic tenurial systems, overstocking, backward techniques, and an excessive dependency on the work of women, children, and aged people. Furthermore, the homelands are kept poor by their proximity to the more prosperous white areas.

If economic development in the homelands is to be accelerated, these regions must be provided with a greater share of the South African resource base. Their location is such that most mineralized regions lie beyond their borders (Fig. 20-6). The absence of large mineral deposits within the homelands is a natural consequence of the White's exploitation of the country's resources. Indeed, the homelands are regions

A white-owned farm in the productive Paarl Valley, Cape Province. The architectural style of the farm houses is "Cape Dutch" and relates to the 17th and 18th centuries when the Cape frontier was penetrated. The southwestern Cape is one of the world's major wine districts (Satour)

The Hendrik Verwoerd Dam, part of the Orange River Project. Water is being diverted to both agricultural and industrial projects in the Orange Free State and Cape Province. (S.A. Information Service)

A Transkei village. Like other homelands (Bantustans), the Transkei is overpopulated, economically underdeveloped, territorially fragmented, and dependent upon the white areas for jobs and manufactured goods. (Alan C. G. Best)

in which the Whites, mainly from their point of view, had little or no interest. Lebowa and Bophuthatswana are most favorably endowed: both have active asbestos and chrome mines and untapped deposits of manganese, platinum, and iron ore. In contrast, the Transkei Ciskei, and Kwa Zulu have no significant mining activities and few known minerals. Ironically, the Tswanas do not like to work in the mines and so Bophuthatswana's mines employ migrants from the Transkei, Kwa Zulu, and other less fortunate homelands. In 1974, when South Africa's mineral production exceeded $6 billion, only $60 million was for minerals produced in the homelands.

Most of South Africa's known mineral resources and active mines are located in the white areas, especially on the Highveld (Fig. 20-6). Johannesburg's gold mines are still active and profitable after almost a century of working, although most of the Republic's gold now comes from fields of the Western Rand, and from Welkom in the Orange Free State. Diamonds, the first mineral to be mined on a considerable scale, are mined in Kimberley, Pretoria, and at Jagersfontein in the southern Free State. East and south of the Witwatersrand are Africa's largest known reserves of bituminous coal, a particularly valuable asset since South Africa has no known petroleum reserves but a high energy-consumptive economy. Elsewhere there is copper (Phalaborwa), iron ore (Thabazimbi, Sishen, and Postmasburg), manganese, chromium nickel, and many more that have contributed to the country's mining-industrial economy. Gold is by far the most valuable mineral produced; when the price of gold rose sharply in 1974, output was valued at over $3 billion, but actual production was lower than in the four previous years.

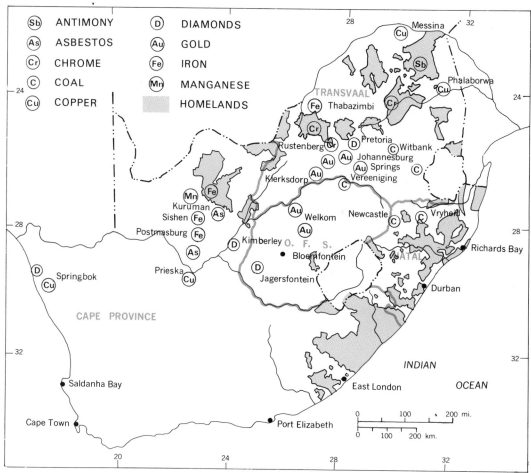

FIGURE 20-6 *South Africa. Minerals.*

Mining accounts for about two-thirds of all exports and 12 percent of the GDP. Its importance, however, is much greater than these figures suggest. Mining provided the catalyst for industrial development, railway construction to the interior, the migration of African labor to the cities, and it permitted the subsidization of a large part of South African agriculture. It provides work for about 700,000 persons, 90 percent of them being Africans recruited not only from the homelands but also from Botswana, Lesotho, Swaziland, Mozambique, and Malawi. These migrants work long hours for low wages and live separated from their families in the mine compounds for the length of their contract, normally nine months to a year.

Industrial Growth

In South Africa, industrial development has taken place at a rate that may be described as phenomenal. Until after 1930, the country depended mainly on the export of gold, diamonds, wool, and corn, and purchased the bulk of her manufactured goods.

New mine recruits from Malawi waiting to be assigned sleeping quarters at the Bafokeng mine, Bophuthatswana. (Alan C. G. Best)

Then, government action, tariff protection, the emergence of a home market, and isolation during the war all combined to stimulate industrial development. The establishment of an iron and steel industry and the development of engineering and metal-working industries created South Africa's largest and most important industrial block. More persons are employed in this type of industry than in any other and the value of the output is highest (South Africa, 1974). Foods are next in importance, followed by textiles and clothing manufacture and the chemical industries. Initially, these industries specialized heavily to supply a local demand, the chemical industry depending on its sales of explosives to the mining industry, and the engineering industries being likewise tied to mining.

The location of the South African industries has depended on the presence of raw materials, the existence of markets, and availability of power and water supplies as well as labor. Since the economic core of the country has long been the Witwatersrand, the development of an impressive industrial complex in association with the mines is no surprise. Markets appear to have been the dominating factor, and thus the highly diversified Witwatersrand complex dwarfs that of Durban, Cape Town, and Port Elizabeth. The industrial heart of the country is far from the homelands, which for their economic well-being must share the industrial development of the rest of South Africa.

To correct the spatial imbalances of the country's industrial activities, and to provide much needed development in the homelands, the government introduced an industrial decentralization program. It designated two types of areas where industrial growth is encouraged: areas immediately outside the

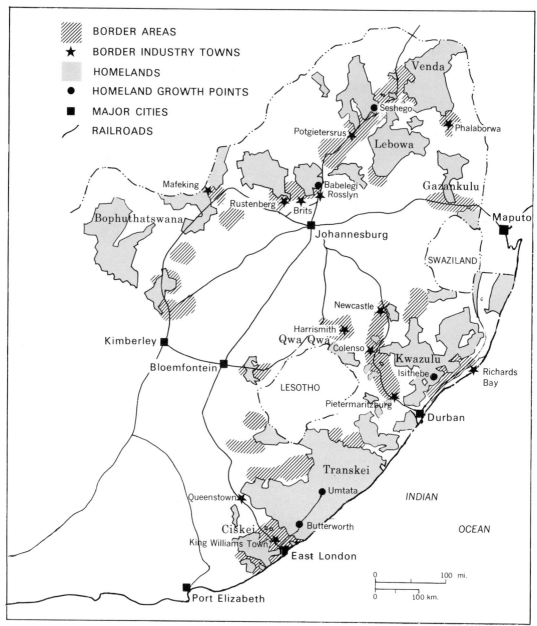

FIGURE 20-7 *South Africa. Border industries and growth points.*

homelands ("border areas"), where white capital and skills can combine with black labor in an economic effort theoretically beneficial to both, and certain areas within the homelands themselves, where these industries are needed to relieve pressure on the land.

Under the border industries program, white entrepreneurs are offered a number of incentives to relocate their businesses or to establish new factories in certain prescribed white towns within 30 mi (48 km) of the homelands (Fig. 20-7). In theory these industries are labor intensive and are designed to halt migration at the homeland borders and provide beneficial spillover effects into the homelands (Best, 1971). Most border industries are located near Pretoria, Durban, Pietermaritzburg, and King Williams Town, rather than in the smaller and more peripheral towns where the need is greatest. Benefits to the homelands have been marginal since wages are generally lower than in the major industrial centers, job reservation is enforced, and wages are spent in the white areas. The number of jobs provided by the scheme has fallen far behind population increases and demands.

The second phase of industrial decentralization, that is to places within the homelands, was begun in 1970. The scheme encourages white industrialists (including foreign investors) to locate their factories in government-appointed growth centers such as Butterworth in the Transkei, Isithebe in Kwa Zulu, and Babelegi in Bophuthatswana. Tax holidays and subsidized transport and housing are offered in return for which local labor must be trained to assume skilled and managerial positions. Eventually the business must be sold either directly to an African or to the Bantu Investment Corporation which will manage the business until an appropriate buyer can be found. Despite the incentives, there were fewer than 100 small industrial establishments with a payroll of only 4500 in the mid-1970s. Neither decentralization scheme has overcome the inherently negative characteristics of the homelands, and there has been little mobilization of African capital and only marginal benefits to the homelands.

A new, and highly controversial, growth point is being developed at Richards Bay about 80 mi (130 km) north of Durban (Fig. 20-7). This government-sponsored project was designed to relieve some of the port congestion at Durban, Cape Town, and Maputo that stems in part from the ever-expanding industrial requirements of the Witwatersrand. It is to provide a new outlet for an anticipated increase in coal exports from northern Natal and the eastern Transvaal, and will provide new jobs and economic opportunities for neighboring Kwa Zulu. By 1976, Richards Bay had an aluminum smelter and several small petrochemical and food processing industries, just the beginning of what may become another Durban within two or three decades.

The recently completed railway from Richards Bay to Vryheid cuts across a portion of Kwa Zulu and passes through that homeland's newly appointed capital, Ulundi. Kwa Zulu's chief executive officer, Gatsha Buthelezi, claims Richards Bay as part of his homeland and has stated the Zulus are not prepared to accept independence unless this claim is met. Richards Bay will almost certainly remain "white."

Urbanization

Cities and towns, geographers have often said, are a response to a region's needs. As might be expected from the vigorous economic development of South Africa, there has been more urbanization there than elsewhere in Africa. All the major industrial towns and urban centers are situated in the white areas; the homelands have produced only dormitory townships that house the labor required across their borders. For example, Kwa Zulu's largest "towns," Umlazi (250,000) and Kwa Mashu (230,000) are merely residential appendages of Durban, having no manufacturing and few tertiary industries of their own because the competition in Durban is too strong.

The South African government, recognizing the need for a reduction of population pressure on the land, and desirous of reducing the number of Africans in the "white" cities, is artificially establishing towns throughout the homelands. Several dozen such "towns" are being built, some with regard for the needs for the developing region, others apparently quite arbitrarily, and with little chance of survival and growth. This is one of the unique aspects of the Tomlinson Commission's plan: it is an experiment in forced urbanization, the likes of which the world has never seen. Africans who are considered surplus in the white areas are thus "endorsed out" of the cities and sent to government-controlled "resettlement areas" in the homelands. Those resettled are generally the old, the very young, and widows who have lost their right to stay in homes they have occupied for years. Most resettlement areas lack adequate housing, sewage, clinics, and schools. Few have any industry of their own, and few are within commuting distance to places where goods, services, and employment may be obtained.

The South African government plans to build a capital city in each of the homelands to replace the present administrative centers in white South Africa (Best and Young, 1972). In selecting the sites in partnership with the homeland leaders, Pretoria sought unoccupied land central within the homelands and places having no strong historic identity. Most of the capitals are to be built on existing or potential development corridors. However, given their location within the overall South African space economy, little industrial growth can be expected, and they will remain primarily small administrative centers.

In contrast to this, South Africa's "white" cities are dynamic and viable, and places of modernization and social change. Here lie the country's major industries, financial institutions, universities, and technological might. In short, the cities represent South Africa's wealth and prosperity. Of course, this has not been accomplished by the whites alone; indeed, it has depended in large measure on the labors of all races. The "white" cities have attracted hundreds of thousands of Africans, and the urbanized African population of these places has been an ever increasing problem to city and government officials. Mines and industries drew

the Africans to the cities, where they became a permanently resident sector of the population, a situation which the South African government deems undesirable since it hampers the effectiveness of control, leads to overcrowding of the black suburbs, and above all, causes racial mixing and loss of cultural identity.

South Africa's cities such as Johannesburg, Kimberley, and Durban, now contain large numbers of fourth- and fifth-generation urbanized Africans. Many of these urban dwellers have never seen their homelands with which they are supposed to have some identity. The results of a survey in Soweto (800,000), the country's largest African township about 15 mi (24 km) southwest of Johannesburg, may well represent the attitude of the urban African and emphasize the dangers and dilemmas of the homeland policy. Seventy percent of the respondents showed they would prefer to live in South Africa under multiracial government than in South Africa under a white government or in the homelands under tribal government; 61 percent said they would not accept a good job in the homelands if it were offered them, and 88 percent would prefer black South Africans to form one nation irrespective of tribal origins. It is the urban black who presents the greatest challenge to the government in its implementation of multinational development, for he is more aware of social, political, and economic inequalities in South Africa than the rural black.

Johannesburg is South Africa's largest city, and its problems are symptomatic if not entirely representative of the country's multiracial centers (Table 20-3). Its African population (like that of Pretoria, Germiston, and other cities) has long increased faster than housing can be provided, and conditions in the city's "shantytowns" have been among the worst forms of urban squalor in the world. To be sure, the cities have their share of lowerclass white suburbs, but the major solution for the prevalent urban decay was considered to lie in the removal of Africans.

Pimville shantytown, Johannesburg. Each dwelling place has on average 20 occupants while sewage and sanitary facilities are non-existent. Influx control measures have been introduced to control migration to the cities. (Alan C. G. Best)

Part of Soweto, Johannesburg's largest African township. It is very difficult for Africans to qualify for single-family housing (lower right); Bachelors and married men without their families live in dormitory-like quarters (center). Townships such as this became battlegrounds of racial riots in 1976. (Alan C. G. Best)

SOUTH AFRICA: THE CHALLENGE OF SEPARATE DEVELOPMENT

Hence the construction of peri-urban townships such as Soweto (800,000) and Tembisa (100,000), and the homelands' resettlement schemes (Fig. 20-8).

Johannesburg exemplifies several other characteristics of the South African urban scene. Its areal extent is vast, covering perhaps four times as much territory as a European city of comparable size. Its core and central business district are congested and small compared to the entire urban region. Vertical development is considerable and comparable to that of any American city of similar population. The city's functional zones, as a result of the decline of mining and the growth of industry, are interdigitated, although the residential areas are strictly segregated according to race. Unlike the cities of former French and Portuguese Africa, the civic and administrative buildings of South Africa's cities are dispersed throughout the central city. This is one of the points of contrast between the urban places of British-influenced Africa and those of the remainder of the continent.

In many ways, Johannesburg is unique, being not only the largest South African city but also the heart of the country's most intensely industrialized area and the financial capital. East and west of Johannesburg, along the outcrop of the gold-bearing reefs of the Witwatersrand, a string of mining towns

Johannesburg—"City of Gold." Located at the heart of the Witwatersrand, South Africa's primary core region, Johannesburg is the Republic's largest city. Note the vertical development in the downtown area, and the gold mine dumps in the distance. (S.A. Information Service)

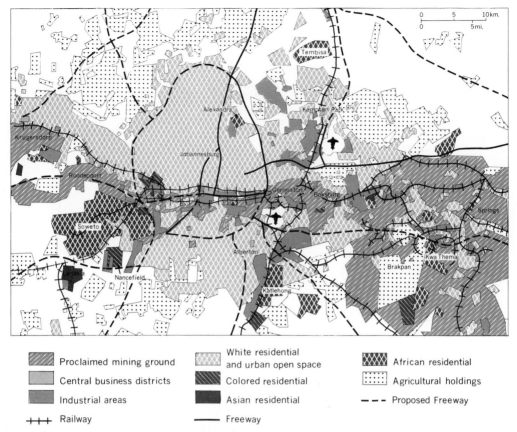

FIGURE 20-8 *South Africa. Land-use on the Witwatersrand, 1973.*

has sprung up, and their urban areas are merging into a South African megalopolis. Racial segregation is strictly enforced under the Group Areas Act. Buffer zones such as expressways, railways, cemeteries, mining and industrial areas separate the various residential group areas (Fig. 20-8). Johannesburg's northern boundary is within sight of expanding Pretoria, the country's administrative capital and most rapidly growing city. Southward lies the lifeblood of the industrialized Southern Transvaal—the Vaal

River and the water supplies of Vaal Dam. There also lie Vereeniging, the new iron and steel plants, and, in the Orange Free State, the newly developing mines and industries. The Johannesburg area, therefore, has been the focal point of mining, industry, communications, commerce, financial affairs, and administration in South Africa. The city has received a succession of stimuli that have kept it in the forefront of rapidly urbanizing South Africa.

Homeland Consolidation

Before the homelands can achieve meaningful independence, and before there can be either widespread regional develop-

ment or any credibility to separate development, the homelands must be consolidated and enlarged. Pretoria is not prepared to re-

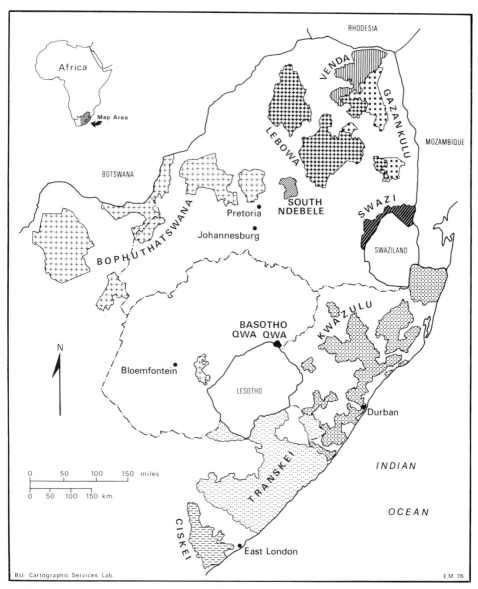

FIGURE 20-9 *South Africa. Homeland consolidation proposals, 1975.*

lease any land above and beyond that provided for in the 1936 Native Trust and Land Act, but is prepared to consolidate the fragmented areas into more viable units (Fig. 20-9). If the consolidation proposals are approved, Kwa Zulu will be reduced from 29 blocks to 10, Bophuthatswana from 19 to 6, and Lebowa from 9 to 4 (Table 20-4). Only the smaller homelands—Basotho Qwa Qwa,

Venda, South Ndebele, the Ciskei, and the Swazi Territory—will be single-block states.

The proposals suggest that Pretoria is not anxious to alter the status quo, for complete consolidation could threaten the South African *raison d'être* and weaken existing economic linkages. Pretoria is essentially "tidying up" the jigsaw puzzle, not creating viable states, so that the homelands will remain deprived of essential growth points, resources, transport routes and other essentials. If the proposals are accepted and implemented, thousands of persons of all races will be forced to resettle at enormous human and economic cost. In Natal alone, approximately 250,000 Zulu will be uprooted, and over 8000 Asians, 4000 Whites, and 1500 Coloureds will be removed from land scheduled to become part of Kwa Zulu.

The logistical and financial problems of consolidation are staggering. The government faces the problems of moving tribes to places where they can adapt without intertribal conflict and utilize their new surroundings efficiently. Given the ethnic diversity within short distances, this will be difficult and could lead to disorder within the new homelands. Some Africans will lose good farms, such as the sugar estates in southern Natal, and they may not be compensated with similar land elsewhere. Most white farmers have objected strongly to consolidation since they also fear unfair compensation, including land denuded of soil for land they have improved for generations.

The consolidation proposals have been rigorously contested by the white opposition parties, the homeland leaders, white farmers, and others directly concerned with this wholesale movement of people. Both white farmers and African leaders claim their has not been adequate consultation and that Africans, in particular, are powerless to oppose the government. The homeland leaders argue correctly that the proposals do not substantially improve the homelands' well-being, but are designed to satisfy government interests.

Problems and Prospects

The policy of separate development is a sophisticated strategy for the preservation of white political domination of the black. The separate-states approach is an attempt to consolidate white domination through the strategy of divide and rule, while appeasing both local and international critics of South Africa's racial injustices. Although South Africa maintains that the basic principle of separate development consists of conceding to the various African groups the same rights to self-determination which the whites have claimed for themselves, it does not mean the Republic is creating African states that will be equally powerful. Even should the new black states form some sort of federation or confederation, they will not match the political, economic, and military strength of the Republic.

The future states of Southern Africa will continue to be economically interdependent, but as the experience of Botswana, Lesotho, and Swaziland has shown, this need not undermine their political sovereignty.

Economic self-sufficiency, though desirable, is not an essential precondition for acceptable separation of the homelands. Having provided the political machinery for self-government, South Africa must now provide for modernization. For although the bantustans lack most of the elements necessary for rapid modernization and economic independence, they possess (through recent constitutional changes) greater political consciousness and power than ever before.

The homeland leaders now have the means, through the legislative assemblies, to expose the dangers, contradictions, and uncertainties inherent in Pretoria's pseudo-decolonization program, and they can be heard more effectively both within and beyond South Africa's borders. Chiefs Buthelezi (Kwa Zulu), Matanzima (Transkei), and Mangope (Bophuthatswana) are the most vocal leaders although all homeland leaders have rejected Pretoria's land-consolidation proposals, and all are now emphasizing their common problems and aspirations rather than their differences. Chiefs Buthelezi and Matanzima are leading a movement calling for a federation of black African states in southern Africa as an alternative to Pretoria's bantustans, which they reject as fraudulent. The federal concept has been accepted in principle by other homeland leaders while generally rejected or ignored by Whites. A federation offers many attractions to South Africa's blacks, but remains only a dream as long as its member states are territorially fragmented and economically dominated by the Republic, a pattern Pretoria intends to preserve.

The reorganization of the South African state is one of the unique aspects of present-day Africa, meriting attention no less than does the success of the wind of change elsewhere. Whatever the moral implications of this form of *apartheid*, it cannot be denied that South Africa has become a laboratory for geographic study. The future of the new Republic will be mirrored in this effort, now in its second decade of execution. The political framework, the economic structure, human relations, and even the survival of the very state are in the balance. For South Africa, this is a period of transition. Both the process and the results are of absorbing interest, as some trends are intensified and others are fundamentally reversed. Should it be permitted to run its full course, the process of racial separation will create a state which will be unique. But even if the scheme is not carried to completion, the impact already made is ineradicable; indeed, it is the salient aspect of the political, social, and economic geography of South Africa today.

Bibliography

Best, Alan C. G. "The Republic of South Africa: White Supremacy," *Focus*, Vol. 25, No. 6 (March–April, 1975), pp. 1–13.

———. "South Africa's Border Industries: The Tswana Example," *Annals, A.A.G.*, Vol. 61, No. 2 (June, 1971), pp. 329–343.

Best, Alan C. G., and Bruce S. Young. "Capitals for the Homelands," *Journal for Geography (Tydskrif vir Aardrykskunde)*, Vol. 3, No. 10 (April, 1972), pp. 1043–1054.

Board, C., R. J. Davies, and T. J. D. Fair. "The Structure of the South African Space Economy: An Integrated Approach." *Regional Studies*, Vol. 4, No. 3 (October, 1970), pp. 357–392.

Carter, Gwendolen M. *The Politics of Inequality: South Africa Since 1948*. New York: Praeger, 1959.

Cole, Monica M. *South Africa*, Second Edition. London: Methuen, 1966.

Desmond, Cosmos. *The Discarded People: Account of African Resettlement in South Africa*. Harmondsworth, Middlesex: Penguin, 1971.

Fair, T. J. D. "Southern Africa," in R. M. Prothero (ed.), *A Geography of Africa*, Second Edition, London: Routledge & Kegan Paul, 1973, pp. 327–379.

Hill, Christopher. *Bantustans: The Fragmentation of South Africa*. London: Oxford University Press, 1964.

Houghton, Hobart. *The South African Economy*. New York: Oxford University Press, 1967.

Maasdorp, G. *Economic Development in the African Homelands*. Johannesburg: South Africa Institute of Race Relations, 1974.

Marquard, Leopold. *The Peoples and Policies of South Africa*, Fifth Edition, London: Oxford University Press, 1971.

Niddrie, David I. *South Africa: Nation or Nations?* Princeton, N.J.: D. Van Nostrand, 1968.

Rhoodie, N. (ed.). *South African Dialogue*. Johannesburg: McGraw-Hill, 1972.

Schmidt, C. F. "A Spatial Model of Authority-Dependency Relations in South Africa," *The Journal of Modern African Studies*, Vol. 13, No. 3 (September, 1975), pp. 483–90.

South Africa, Republic of. *South Africa, 1974*. Johannesburg: Perskor Printers, 1974.

South Africa, Republic of. *Summary of the Report of the Commission for the Socio-Economic Development of the Bantu Areas Within the Union of South Africa*. (The Tomlinson Report.) Pretoria: Government Printer, 1955.

Thompson, L., and J. Butler (eds.). *Change in Contemporary South Africa*. Berkeley: University of California Press, 1975.

Wilson, Monica, and Leonard Thompson (eds.). *The Oxford History of South Africa*. New York: Oxford University Press, 1969, 1971 (2 vols).

TWENTY-ONE

Namibia, once known as South West Africa, occupies a unique position in the annals of African colonial history. Once a German colony, then a mandate of the League of Nations, Namibia has, since World War II, lacked a clearly defined and universally recognized legal administration. For over 30 years, it has been the subject of heated debate within the United Nations and at the International Court of Justice and a coveted prize of South Africa since 1919. Confusion over its legal status has resulted in the imposition of South African laws and institutions, and the material advancement of the colonial minority at the expense of the African majority.

From Colony to Mandate

European exploration of the Namibian coast dates back to the fifteenth century when Portuguese navigators landed at Cape Cross (1484) and Walvis Bay (1487). Like the Dutch who followed them in the seventeenth and eighteenth centuries, the Portuguese made no attempt to colonize or even establish permanent settlements along the desert coast. That phase of Namibian history was left to Germany and Britain in the late nineteenth century following a brief period of missionary activity by Cape Dutch, British, and German church organizations. In 1878 Britain annexed Walvis Bay on behalf of Cape Colony, and the area was incorporated into the Cape of Good Hope in 1884. Germany laid claim to the remainder of the coast from the Orange River to the

NAMIBIA: POLITICAL GEOGRAPHY OF A COVETED PRIZE

FIGURE 21-1 *Namibia. Physical features.*

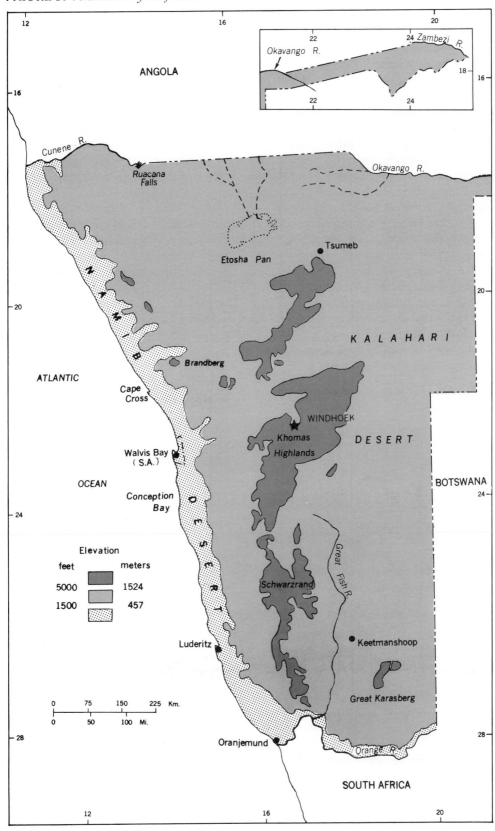

Cunene and inland to the twentieth degree of longitude, while a corridor was claimed northeast to the Zambezi (Fig. 21-1).

German occupation first focused on Lüderitz on the coast and then on Windhoek on the interior highland. There the settler community confiscated land and cattle from the Nama (Hottentots) and Herero and forced the local peoples into labor units to work their newly acquired farms. In 1903 the Bondelswarts Hottentots revolted against German rule but were quickly suppressed along with the Herero, whose numbers, on the extermination orders of General von Trotha, were reduced from 80,000 to 15,000. Following these and other uprisings, European settlement spread to Otjiwarongo, Tsumeb, and Keetmanshoop aided by railway construction and government-sponsored land schemes. Diamond discoveries near Lüderitz in 1908 brought more German and white South African settlers to the colony, and by 1914 the European population totaled 15,000.

When World War I began, South African troops occupied the German colony in the name of the Allied cause, and the territory was placed under South African military rule. Following the war, as provided for by the Treaty of Versailles, Germany ceded its colonies to the principal allied and associated powers. The former colony became a Class C Mandate of the League of Nations, and according to the mandate, the territory was officially transferred to "His Britannic Majesty" to be governed on his behalf by the Union of South Africa which then paid allegiance to the British crown. Under the mandate, South Africa was given full powers of administration and legislation over Namibia as an integral part of the Union, and the Union was obliged to "promote to the utmost the material and moral well-being and the social progress of the inhabitants of the territory." For South Africa's General Smuts, this relationship amounted to annexation in all but name.

In the interwar years, the economic and administrative links between Namibia and South Africa were continuously strengthened: European settlement was encouraged; South African mining companies acquired all diamond rights from German-owned operations; a European Legislative Assembly was established in Windhoek, the capital; communications were expanded and linked with the Cape; German settlers were encouraged to become British citizens; and the African reserve system was introduced and modeled after that in South Africa. In 1933, following several years of severe drought and worldwide economic depression that brought near disaster to Namibia's farming and mining sectors, the South African government pressed for the incorporation of Namibia into the Union. But this was disallowed by the Mandates Commission and opposed by the remaining German settlers who preferred a return to German rule, or at least closer association with their former metropole.

The United Nations Controversy

With the demise of the League of Nations (1946), South Africa refused to place its mandate under the United Nations trusteeship system, but immediately and unsuccessfully sought the territory's incorporation. That same year the government produced a "petition" signed by 208,850 Africans, in addition to a majority of the whites in the territory, appealing to the United Nations to permit the final inclusion of the territory in South Africa. The petition was rejected by the United Nations, where it was realized that the literacy percentage of the African population (then about 430,000) was so low that the number of signatures could not possibly reflect the desires of a people who were aware of the meaning of the document. Meanwhile, the South African government, led by the victorious Afrikaner nationalist majority of 1948, began to perpetrate in Namibia the practices of *apartheid* which were being legalized in South Africa. Hence, in 1949, the UN General Assembly placed the matter before the International Court of Justice at The Hague, requesting an opinion on several aspects of the issue.

The International Court judged that South Africa was at fault in not submitting petitions and reports on Namibia to the United Nations. In addition, it stated that South Africa was not (without permission from the United Nations) allowed to change the political status of the territory. Finally, the Court ruled by eight votes to six that South Africa was at no time legally required to place Namibia under the trusteeship system. The decision without question strengthened South Africa's hand in the debate. In the first place, no decisions of the International Court of Justice are binding, and the major question of the relations of Namibia with the United Nations had, for all intents and purposes, been decided in favor of South Africa. The Union, therefore, continued to intensify its policies of racial segregation within the territory and its political integration with the South African state as a virtual fifth province. Appeals from within the region went unreported and unheeded.

South Africa's continued implementation of *apartheid* in Namibia and its refusal to recognize UN decisions prompted Ethiopia and Liberia in 1960 to charge that South Africa had violated both the terms and spirit of the mandate and its obligations to the United Nations. After six years of deliberations the International Court of Justice rejected the claims on grounds that Ethiopia and Liberia had no standing before the Court. Despite the inconclusiveness of the Court decision, the UN General Assembly resolved that South Africa should be stripped of its mandate and that responsibility for the territory should be assumed by an 11-nation UN-appointed council. In 1969 the Security Council called on South Africa to withdraw its administration from Namibia, but the Republic ignored the injunction. By a vote of 13 to 2 the International Court of Justice upheld the UN position and found that "the continued presence of South Africa being illegal, South Africa is under obligation to withdraw its administration from Namibia immediately and thus put an end to its occupation of the Territory." The opinion was subsequently endorsed by the Security Council but was again rejected by South Africa (Dugard, 1973).

Soon after, the Republic outlined its policy of "self-determination" within an *apartheid* framework, which called for the territorial dismemberment of Namibia into one white and ten African homelands. This intensified world opinion against South Africa and provoked widespread unrest within Namibia, led by nationalistic organizations, such as the South West African People's Organization (SWAPO), which seek a territorially unified independent Namibian state.

A Coveted Prize

What South Africa acquired in 1919 appeared to be a real liability: it was vast, largely desert and steppe, sparsely populated, and expensive to organize and govern even after the attempts made by the Germans to develop it. There were those who referred to its acquisition as "Smuts's folly," and it did seem that, apart from some revenues from diamond production, it could contribute little to a fast-developing, wealthy state. The tenacity with which South Africa is defending its position in Namibia today is indicative of its potential usefulness as an integral part of the South African state.

The period since World War II has seen the evolution of a new Africa and the confrontation of ideological opposites, black and white nationalism. To the latter, fighting for a permanent place on a black continent, the possession of territory has become a matter of vital interest. South Africa's pressures on Britain for the transfer of the former High Commission Territories (now Botswana, Lesotho, and Swaziland) and its refusal to yield in the Namibian question are reflections of this situation. By continuing to rule Namibia, South African power extends from the Cape to the Zambezi River, a situation the South African government finds psychologically satisfying, politically desirable, and strategically reassuring.

Economically, also, the importance of Namibia has changed greatly since 1919. Although the existence of diamonds was known at an early stage, the real potential of the territory has only recently come to light: diamonds are the most important mineral produced and the main revenue earner. Since 1970, output has averaged between 1.6 and 2.0 million carats annually, with earnings in 1974 of about $225 million. About 98 percent of the diamonds are gemstones, most of which are extracted from raised coastal beaches between Oranjemund and Conception Bay, a region closed to the general public (Fig. 21-2). Virtually the entire production is controlled by a subsidiary of the South African-based De Beers Consolidated Mines. At present production levels, the known reserves will last another 17 years, although recent offshore investigations indicate an even longer lifetime.

The center of mining in the interior is Tsumeb, a rapidly growing town where some industrial development related to mining is taking place. There, over 800,000 tons of copper, lead, and zinc concentrates are produced each year with sales in excess of $55 million, making it Namibia's second largest revenue earner. Five new copper

mines opened between 1969 and 1975: at Otjihase (near Windhoek), Kramzberg, Oamites, Assis Ost, and Onganja. A uranium mine, the largest open-cast project in southern Africa, will come into full production at Rossing by 1977 at a cost of over $150 million, and supply uranium to the U.K. Atomic Energy Authority among others. Additional mining operations include zinc at Rosh Pinah, flourspar at Omburu, and salt at Swakopmund (Fig. 21-2). Collectively, minerals earn over $360 million (60 percent of all exports) with the United States, South Africa, the Federal Republic of Germany, Britain, and Japan being the major markets. All mineral rights are held by the South African administration. Although the governments of the United States and West Germany have announced in accordance with UN resolutions they will not supply export credits or guarantees to mining companies in Namibia, the governments of Britain, France, and Canada have not done so.

Mining is dependent on cheap migratory labor from the homelands; without it, profits would be substantially less or the mines would close. Each year approximately 40,000 laborers (of whom 70 percent are Ovambos) contract to work at a fixed rate for periods of between 6 and 18 months in the mines and mine-related industries. Prospective workers are recruited through government-run labor bureaus and, if accepted, are graded according to physical fitness and age for work in the mines, factories, and farms. Minimum wages are laid down for each class, ranging from about $17 a month for an unskilled mineworker to $8 for a farm laborer less than 18 years of age. The workers are not free to choose their employers or the type of work they are to do. The system forbids the forming of trade unions, the organization of strikes, and the right to break contracts before they expire.

Another of Namibia's highly coveted resources is the sea. The cold Benguela Current has helped produce one of the world's most bountiful fishing areas off the Namib-

FIGURE 21-2 *Namibia. Economic map.*

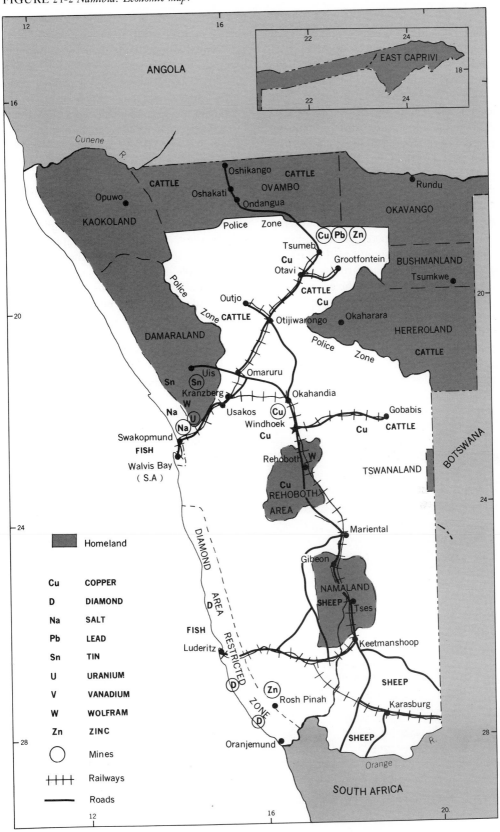

NAMIBIA: POLITICAL GEOGRAPHY OF A COVETED PRIZE

ian coast. The industry was originally based on the fishing of lobster and white fish for local consumption (although the United States was an important market for lobster), but it is now based on the large-scale processing of sardines and pilchards. Fishmeal, canning, and oil extraction account for 90 percent of the total fishing revenues, with South Africa and the United States being the principal markets. The industry is based at Walvis Bay and Lüderitz (Fig. 21-2).

Although Namibia's fishing and mineral resources are almost unrivaled in Southern Africa, its agricultural potentials are limited but nevertheless jealously guarded by its South African settlers, and farming accounts for 15 percent of the GDP. The entire coastal region at the foot of the omnipresent escarpment is desert. This, the Namib Desert, is one of the driest in the world,

Lead ingots from Tsumeb on the dockside, Walvis Bay. Walvis Bay is Namibia's major port and fishing center, and an exclave of South Africa. (Alan C. G. Best)

Karakul sheep in typical grazing lands of central Namibia. Karakul pelts (Persian lamb) are important exports to the United States and West Germany. (Alan C. G. Best)

most of it receiving less than 2 in. (50 mm) of rainfall annually. In general, rainfall decreases in a northeasterly direction, and reliability is low (Fig. 21-3). The principal areas of white-owned farms receive less than 12 in. (505 mm) of rain each year. Only the northeastern extremity, including the Caprivi Strip and the Ovambo homeland, has an annual rainfall of over 20 in. (508 mm), but given the high evapotranspiration rates, this is still subhumid. Eastern Namibia merges into the Kalahari Desert, although latosols and a thorntree-studded grassland make the term "steppe" more applicable. In general, soils are poor, and the grasslands are capable of supporting only extensive pastoralism. Irrigated agriculture is carried on in a few valleys. On a per capita basis, the white population has ten times more land than the African, and if the availability of water is taken into account, this proportion could be 50 to 1 (Wellington, 1967).

The European-owned farms are large (up to 40,000 acres or 16,200 ha) and primarily devoted to cattle ranching in the north and central plateau, and to the raising of karakul sheep in the south (Fig. 21-2). Karakul pelts (Persian lamb) earn more than $37 million in foreign revenues each year, with West Germany, France, and the United States being the major markets. Cattle, meat, and butter are sold in South Africa almost exclusively. As with mining, the agricultural sector depends on cheap and plentiful labor recruited from the homelands, especially Hereroland, Damaraland and Namaland.

The white economy is geared to and controlled by foreign interests. It is dependent on the availability of cheap labor, and provides very few benefits to the adjoining homelands. The contribution of Namibia's resources and labor to the income of foreigners is estimated at 37 percent of the GDP, one of the highest in Africa. In 1973, the GDP was $923.4 million, of which primary industries accounted for half and manufacturing one-tenth. South Africa is the

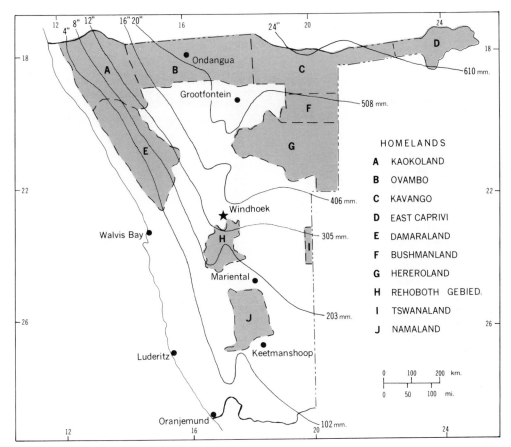

FIGURE 21-3 *Namibia. Average annual precipitation.*

HOMELANDS

A KAOKOLAND
B OVAMBO
C KAVANGO
D EAST CAPRIVI
E DAMARALAND
F BUSHMANLAND
G HEREROLAND
H REHOBOTH GEBIED.
I TSWANALAND
J NAMALAND

dominant trading partner, supplying 80 percent of the imports (mainly machinery, mining equipment, steel goods, and food), and is the principal source for the territory's technical and professional manpower and development monies.

Namibia's wealth, development, and technology lie within the southern "Police Zone" reserved for the white minority composed primarily of Afrikaners and settlers of German-descent, numbering in all about 100,000. Here per capita incomes are 20 times higher than those in the African homelands, and here the African majority has no political rights and few of the rewards of its labor. Here also the majority is restricted in its movements and denied economic opportunity and many fundamental human rights.

Although it is vulnerable to the whims of outside markets and the maintenance of communications depends on an outside power, Namibia internally faces the perpetual threat of droughts which can cripple the agricultural sector of the economy, require imports of subsistence grains from South Africa, and create serious conditions in the north. At such times, which are relatively frequent due to the high variability of precipitation, the territory's dependence on South Africa is clearly illustrated. Returns from the Karakul industry are drastically reduced, cattle die in great numbers and meat sales to the Republic dwindle, and costly imports are necessary. In the present situation, such imports obviously come from South Africa, but in the event of closure of this av-

The downtown area of Windhoek, capital of Namibia. Note the German-style architecture in this former German colony. (Alan C. G. Best)

enue, the territory would be hard put to find a source for its most urgent needs. From the politicogeographic point of view, this aspect of the dependence of Namibia upon South Africa is the most serious: when the economy prospers, it does so on the basis of South African markets. When it fails, it requires South African support. Nevertheless, unlike many other African countries, Namibia normally has a favorable trade balance, and while this is so, it remains an asset to the Republic.

South Africa covets Namibia not only because mineral and agricultural resources exist or because the white minority there seeks protection. The South African state, it is felt, has made considerable investment in the region, has organized its economy and developed its transportation network, and now deserves the fruits of these efforts. In addition, it is argued that the precarious agricultural sector of the Namibian economy will render the territory permanently dependent upon South Africa, and that political independence and economic dependence are antithetical. These factors, coupled with the desires of the resident white minority, the security requirements of the South African state, and the inability of the United Nations seriously to influence the course of events, have created in Namibia a virtual fifth province of the South African Republic.

The Odendaal Commission

As a result of UN criticism of South Africa's administration of Namibia, South Africa appointed the Odendaal Commission in 1962 to inquire into the moral and material welfare of Namibia's African population. In particular, the commission was directed to investigate the agricultural, mining, and industrial potentials of the reserves and to inquire into the need for additional health and educational facilities. The commission concluded that Namibia's black populations differed in customs, language, levels of economic development, and social and political systems, and that they "would prefer to have their own homelands and communities where they would retain residential rights, political say and their own language to the exclusion of all other groups" (South Africa, 1964). It rejected any system of one-man–one-vote, fearing the Ovambos (who comprised almost one-half the African population) would dominate all groups and lower the standards of administration and government, which in turn would hamper the Whites "to whom the Territory mainly owed its economic progress." The commission further suggested that the South Afri-

can government take over most branches of administration then in control of the territory's administration and take initiative in demarcating and developing African homelands.

Not unexpectedly the Odendaal proposals came under scathing attack from most sectors of the United Nations. They were denounced by the Special Committee on Ending Colonialism on grounds they would intensify *apartheid*, legalize racial discrimination, dismember the territory, and exacerbate tribal antagonisms. In view of this criticism, South Africa temporarily refrained from implementing its homeland policy but pushed on with selected development projects that were designed to appease public opinion as much as they were to promote the local economies. However, the homeland policy was later reactivated, and despite much opposition from those being affected, Ovambo became Namibia's first self-governing homeland in 1972.

African Homelands

South Africa's homeland policy in Namibia is very similar to that in the Republic in both rationale and execution. South Africa maintains that there are ten African groups distinct from one another in language, culture, and history, whose separate indentities must be preserved in separate geographic territories, each with its own political and social institutions.

The homelands fall into two separate regions: a northern zone composed of Kaokoland, Damaraland, Ovambo, Kavango, East Caprivi, Bushmanland, and Hereroland; and three spatially separate southern homelands—Namaland, Tswanaland, and Rehoboth Gebiet (Fig. 21-2). Collectively the ten homelands comprise 130,000 sq mi (336, 700 sq km) or 41 percent of the total land area, but as Table 21-1 shows, the homelands themselves vary considerably in area and *de jure* population. Unlike the South African homelands, each Namibian home-

land is a single territorial block, and the seven northern units form an unbroken buffer between the white-controlled south and independent Angola to the north.

These ten artificially defined landlocked areas have much in common: they are peripherally located with respect to the white exchange economy on which they depend for employment and consumer goods; they are lacking in almost all the resources, technology, capital, skills, and physical infrastructures necessary for economic prosperity; local political and administrative expertise, long suppressed under the *apartheid* system, is scarce; mining, manufacturing, and commercial agriculture are almost nonexistent; the predominantly subsistence agricultural-pastoral economies are severely restricted by light and erratic rainfall, poor groundwater resources, and poor pasture land; there are no opportunities for acquiring the skills in most occupations

Table 21-1 NAMIBIA: POPULATION AND
AREAS, 1975

Homeland	Area (sq mi)	De Jure Population (est.)
Ovambo	21,640	400,000
Damaraland	18,520	75,000
Kavango	16,092	58,000
Hereroland	22,767	58,000
Namaland	8,366	40,000
East Caprivi	4,452	30,000
Bushmanland	9,234	27,000
Tswanaland	600	21,000
Rehoboth Gebiet	5,350	20,000
Kaokoland	18,902	9,000
Totals	125,923	738,000
Police Zone		
Europeans		100,000
Coloureds		36,000
Namibian Total		874,000

in the adjoining modern sector of the economy; and there is little prospect of material progress, since there is almost no capacity for saving or for the acquisition and application of modern techniques of production. Indeed, the homelands are neither politically nor economically viable and are merely poor dependencies of white South Africa.

The northernmost tier of homelands corresponds with the old German "treaty lands," later the "native reserves," and on account of their climate and tribal histories are areas the German colonists avoided. Annual rainfall decreases from 24 in. (610 mm) in East Caprivi to only 2 in. (50 mm) in the west, averaging only 5 in. (127 mm) in Damaraland and 20 in. (508 mm) in densely populated Ovambo (Fig. 21-3). Evapotranspiration rates are high throughout the region, and the soils are generally salt. Perennial streams are absent except in northern Kavango and East Caprivi. In the more humid areas the staples include pearl millet, sorghum, and maize, while cattle and goats are widely distributed and are an important source of income. Water from the Cunene

River's Calueque Dam, some 25 mi (40 km) across the Angolan border, which South African troops defended during the post-independence Angolan civil war, is diverted south into Ovambo where 10,000 acres (4050 ha) of irrigated land are being brought into production. Rice, sorghum, groundnuts, and jute are the major cash crops, but despite these efforts, Ovambo, like all other homelands, is deficient in food.

Population densities are highest in Ovambo and along the Kavango River, where agricultural potentials are greatest, and densities are lowest in Kaokoland, Damaraland, and Hereroland. Although densities are low, population pressure is high and malnutrition is widespread. Over the centuries the populations have migrated from one grazing area to another so that most regions are ethnically diverse and not as homogeneous as the South African government would like or even maintains. As in South Africa, many thousands of Africans reside within the white area. If the Odendaal plan and subsequent homeland legislation are fully implemented in the interests of producing ethnically homogeneous units, 95 percent of the Damaras, 66 percent of the Bushman, and 74 percent of the Hereros will have to be uprooted from their present locations and resettled in areas officially designated as theirs. In contrast, about 95 percent of the 400,000 Ovambos reside in their homeland, the remainder being temporarily absent as contract workers in the mines and towns in the southern "Police Zone."

The three separate southern homelands are equally poor in resources, although Namaland and Rehoboth Gebiet are more favorably situated with respect to employment opportunities and transport facilities. Pastoralism is the chief means of livelihood, but this is restricted by brackish groundwater frequently too mineralized for livestock consumption. As in the north, involuntary resettlement is underway, with 93 percent of the Namas being affected.

Given the institutional and environmental limitations of the reserves, the homelands have little chance of being anything but poverty-stricken dependencies of white-controlled South Africa. Economic viability is the prime requirement for survival in the face of political pressure. This does not imply that such survival depends on absolute self-sufficiency; however, absolute dependence on the foreign state that is attempting to intensify its degree of control is fatal. The homeland leaders comprehend the present economic realities and the consequences of a dismembered Namibia and have resisted South Africa's intentions.

Opposition has taken various forms over the last century of colonial rule. Since World War II, the Namibians have appealed to the United Nations for redress of their grievances, greatest of which have been the alienation of their land, the contract labor system, restrictions of freedom of movement, and the state of poverty in the African areas that stems from the colonial system. For two decades these appeals went unheeded. Then guerrilla groups launched an armed struggle for liberation, especially in the remote Caprivi Strip adjoining Zambia and Botswana. The UN's ineffectiveness in the matter provoked protest actions by SWAPO, local leaders, churchmen and the public. In December 1971, for example, a prolonged and effective strike by contract workers shut down the Tsumeb mine and smelter complex, together with other mines, and brought the railways, fishing, and construction industries to a standstill. The South African government countered by extending the powers of the police force and repatriating all strikers and illegal residents to the reserves. Protest has also come in the form of noncompliance of government regulations and the boycotting of elections of government-appointed candidates in the homelands.

Toward the end of 1974, following the internal disorders in adjoining Angola which saw renewed guerrilla warfare in Ovambo and the Caprivi Strip, the South African government adopted a new strategy to appease African opposition. It proposed an independent Ovambo, free to amalgamate with the Ovambos across the border if the Angolan government would consent, and a loose confederation of the rest of the population groups dominated by the white-run economy and political system. This too was rejected, since it would not provide for an economically sound and politically stable state. Meanwhile, the Security Council called on South Africa to grant Namibia independence on the basis of territorial integrity and to withdraw its administration by May 1975. South Africa failed to comply, but in September 1975 it convened a constitutional conference in Windhoek attended by representatives of all of Namibia's population groups. The conference adopted a resolution calling for greater equity in the administration of the territory as a step toward a single independent state. Full independence is scheduled for 1978.

The Namibians are adamant on the need to preserve the territorial integrity of their country and to secure their rights to self-determination, national unity, and independence. Having long been considered part of the prize, the Namibians now want an equal share of the wealth to which they have contributed.

Bibliography

Dugard, J. *The South West Africa-Namibia Dispute.* Berkeley: University of California Press, 1973.

First, R. *South West Africa.* Harmondsworth: Penguin, 1963.

Fraenkel, P. *The Namibians of South West Af-*

rica. London: Minority Rights Group, 1974.

Goldblatt, I. *History of South West Africa.* Cape Town: Juta and Co., Ltd., 1971.

Kory, M. "The Contract Labour System and the Ovambo Crisis of 1971 in South West Africa," *African Studies Review,* Vol. 16, No. 1 (April, 1973), pp. 83–106.

Leistner, G. M. "South Africa's Economic Ties with South West Africa," *Africa Institute Bulletin*, No. 2 (April, 1971), pp. 111–121.

Merrens, A. *South West Africa and Its Indigenous Peoples.* New York: Taplinger, 1967.

Persaud, M. "Namibia and the International Court of Justice," *Current History*, Vol. 68, No. 405 (May, 1975), pp. 220–225.

South Africa, Republic of. *Report on the Commission of Enquiry into South West African Affairs, 1962–1963.* Pretoria: Government Printer, 1964.

South Africa, Republic of. *South West Africa Survey, 1967.* Pretoria: Government Printer, 1967.

United Nations. *A Trust Betrayed: Namibia.* New York: UN, 1974.

Wellington, J. H. *South West Africa and Its Human Issues.* London: Oxford University Press, 1967.

TWENTY-TWO

Although Botswana, Lesotho, and Swaziland are separate political entities, they share several important politicogeographical characteristics. First, each is landlocked and each bounds the Republic of South Africa: Lesotho lies entirely within the Republic; Swaziland, although nearly enclosed by the Transvaal and Natal, has a short but crucially important eastern boundary with Mozambique; and Botswana shares most of its borders with South Africa and Namibia but is also bounded by Rhodesia. Of the various neighboring countries, however, South Africa wields by far the most influence in each of the three independent states.

Second, traditional leadership has always been strong in these ethnically homogeneous territories: the Swazi have rallied under King Sobhuza II; the Tswana, first under Chief Tshakedi Khama of the Bamangwato and today under President Seretse Khama; and the Basotho, first under Chief Moshesh during the nineteenth century and under Chief Jonathan today. Ethnic homogeneity and strong leadership helped ensure the survival of traditional values under colonialism and have contributed to the strong sense of nationalism that currently prevails.

Third, until their independence (Botswana and Lesotho in 1966, and Swaziland in 1968), the three territories were British dependencies collectively known as the British High Commission Territories. As such, they depended on Britain for administration, services, and financial assistance for whatever development projects were contemplated. As it was, Britain's investments in their infrastructures and social services were minimal, and for more than 70 years Britain failed to meet its colonial responsibilities. This resulted in part from the belief, shared by both Britain and South Africa, that the High Commission Territories would be in-

THE HOSTAGES: BOTSWANA, LESOTHO, AND SWAZILAND

corporated someday into South Africa. It was not until that possibility was removed following World War II that Britain accepted its responsibilities and provided the means for development and modernization.

Fourth, in view of their proximity to South Africa, the three territories have been dominated by the Republic in the political and economic arenas. South Africa provides them with manufactured goods, employment for their surplus labor, markets for their resources, and technical assistance and capital for their mining and agricultural projects. Their coinage and money are tied to the South African rand. The three territories form part of the periphery to the South African core, and thus a colonial relationship exists between them and South Africa. Although politically independent sovereign states, they are integral and inseparable parts of the South African sphere of influence.

Fifth, in each territory, economic development is based on the exploitation of either agricultural or mineral resources. It has only recently approached the takeoff stage in Swaziland and Botswana and has yet to be attained in Lesotho. At present there is no appreciable industrial development or urbanization, agriculture needs reorganization, and economic dualism is increasing in Botswana and Swaziland. Land, either its own-

ership or use/misuse, has played a crucial role in the development of agriculture in each territory. All development takes place under the watchful eye of South Africa.

Finally, all are opposed to *apartheid* and all that it stands for, but none is sufficiently independent of South Africa to be an effective agent of change. Swaziland has been the most conservative in its relationships with South Africa, while Botswana has attempted to follow (within practical limits) a measure of independence, and Lesotho has oscillated between general compliance with and open opposition to South Africa's policies. Thus, in several ways, Swaziland, Lesotho, and Botswana are South Africa's hostages.

On the other hand, there are important differences between these countries, especially in their areas, natural environments, resources, and development potentials (Table 22-1). The small, mountainous kingdom of Lesotho, perched high in the Drakensburg Mountains, contrasts sharply with the large, arid, and plateaulike country of Botswana, which occupies much of the Kalahari Basin. Swaziland, the smallest and richest of the three and having the largest expatriate population, lies along the Transvaal escarpment itself and has great topographical, climatic, and pedological diversity. Its sparsely populated western highveld, where

Table 22-1 COMPARATIVE DATA: BOTSWANA, LESOTHO, SWAZILAND

	Botswana	Lesotho	Swaziland
Area (sq mi)	220,000	11,720	6,704
(sq km)	546,000	30,355	17,364
Total population (1977)	800,000	1,230,000	570,000
Non-African population	2,800	2,000	11,000
Population growth rate	2.4	2.0	2.7
Urban population (%)	38	2	5
Literacy rate (%)	20	59	36
Per capita GNP in U.S. dollars (1973)	284	99	140
Number of people per doctor	15,300	24,900	8,300
Capital city	Gaborone (28,000)	Maseru (25,000)	Mbabane (30,000)

humid temperate conditions prevail, differs significantly from the densely settled subtropical middleveld, which in turn differs from the hot, semiarid, and less populous eastern lowveld. Each of the three territories has its own distinct development problems and prospects that arise from the uniqueness of their environments and histories, and from their external relationships with Britain and South Africa. In Lesotho, the major problem is population pressure and non-development; in Botswana, it is aridity and the pastoral economy; and in Swaziland, it is land ownership and economic dualism.

Botswana: Aridity and the Pastoral Economy

Botswana, the largest of the three ex-High Commission Territories, occupies much of the Kalahari Basin, a vast and gently undulating plateau between 3000 and 4000 ft (1000–1300 m) above sea level. Although there is little topographical variation, except in the extreme east, Botswana is a land of great surface contrasts, the most striking features being the Kalahari Desert, the Okavango Delta, and the Makgadikgadi Pans (Fig. 22-1). The Okavango Delta is a 6500-sq mi (16,835 sq km) swampland on the northern edge of the Kalahari Desert, where the Okavango River terminates after flowing across southeastern Angola and the Caprivi Strip. At present, it has little economic value (other than an embryonic tourist industry based on game) because of its peripheral location with respect to the major population concentrations in the east and because of the presence of tsetse fly, malaria, and other health hazards. In unusually rainy years, waters from the delta flow into the adjoining Mbabe and Chobe depressions and occasionally into Lake Ngami and the Makgadikgadi salt pans. The only other permanent rivers are the Chobe and Limpopo, which form parts of the northern and southeastern boundaries, respectively.

Aridity is the single most important natural impediment to development. Rainfall is light and erratic and decreases from northeast (Kasane 27 in./687 mm) to southwest (Tshabong 10 in./249 mm) (Fig. 20-2). Only 20 percent of the country has an average annual rainfall above 20 in. (500 mm). Variability is high throughout, with the steepest gradient occurring in the southeast where almost one-third of the population lives. All regions experience a summer maximum, with the heaviest falls occurring during brief and highly localized thunderstorms. Because temperatures are high (especially during the summer), and strong winds sweep across the open veld, much moisture is lost through evapotranspiration. The porous sandy soils reduce still further the amount of moisture available for pastoral and agricultural use. Because of these conditions, and because of the distribution of surface water, Botswana is very dependent on groundwater for its daily water requirements. Indeed, three-fourths of the human and livestock populations depends entirely on this source, yet less than 17 percent of the boreholes yield more than 2000 gallons of water per hour. The provision of new boreholes is costly and is a major objective of the government, which, until recently, had little financial resources at its disposal (Botswana, 1973).

About three-fourths of the country is covered with porous Kalahari sands. In the extreme southwest there are small stretches of open sand dunes, but elsewhere the sands are covered with grasses and acacias typical of steppe and savanna environments. The soils are frequently highly alkaline and low in humus and thus of low agricultural value. In all regions the veld vegetation and soil are delicately balanced, and if abused by poor agricultural and pastoral practices, they quickly degenerate, and recovery is slow.

Given these environmental limitations,

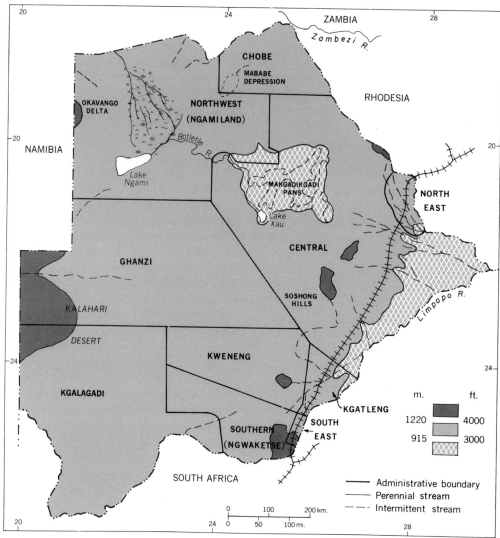

FIGURE 22-1 *Botswana. Districts and surface features.*

and generations of abuse from man and beast, the amount of land suitable for farming and pastoralism is extremely limited. Only 6 percent of the area, all of it in the east, can sustain semi-intensive mixed farming. The best areas are around Gaborone, Kanye, Francistown, and Mahalapye, and they are already farmed to capacity, and ecological overstress is evident. In the adjoining areas, and extending for about 80 mi (130 km) west of the line of rail, semi-intensive pastoralism prevails, cultivation is widely scattered, and crop yields are consistently low. Then to the west, desert conditions take over, and neither pastoralism nor agriculture is practiced. One region of possible agricultural expansion is the Okavango Delta, where preliminary soil and water surveys indicate there are about 1.4 million acres (567,000 ha) of potentially irrigable land capable of producing maize, rice, millets, and numerous industrial crops. But such development presumes great inputs of capital, the construction of roads and canals, and fundamental changes in attitude toward one's surroundings. Development there is unlikely for many years.

It is within this arid environment that the Batswana must eke out a living, mainly from the land. The population is concentrated in the eastern zone and is almost absent (except for small bands of Bushman) from the Kalahari Desert and the Okavango Delta. The population is composed of eight major Setswana-speaking tribes, and several smaller non-Batswana groups including Bushman (Sarwa), Hereros, Europeans, and Asians. According to the 1971 census, half the Batswana lived in agro-villages, the largest being the tribal headquarters such as Serowe (15,723), Kanye (10,664), and Molepolole (9448). Surrounding these administrative centers are subordinate villages and widely dispersed non-nucleated villages.

Typical kraals in Serowe, traditional headquarters of the Bamangwato people, Botswana. Note the separate enclosures for the cattle. (Alan C. G. Best)

Scattered around the villages, sometimes to a distance of 40 mi (64 km), are the communal grazing areas, agricultural "lands" and "cattle posts." With the onset of the summer rains, women and children leave their villages for the "lands," returning following the harvest. Men and boys are frequently absent tending their cattle in the more distant "cattle posts," so that up to one-third of the village propulations may be absent at any one time. Traditionally the chief authorized the commencement of ploughing and harvesting, and he allocated the "lands" and "cattle posts." Because the "lands" are scattered and often far from the village centers, valuable time and energy are lost, and the system of production is generally inefficient.

The cattle are grazed on communal lands that are rarely fenced or scientifically managed. The tenure system hinders herd improvement because grazing control is virtually impossible, and good and poor quality stock freely intermix (Smit, 1970). Most areas are overgrazed, and few cattle "posts" have sufficient water. In the more humid regions, each beast requires about 20 acres (8 ha) of veld, while in the drier areas up to 50 acres (20 ha) are required. The highest concentrations occur in the southeast, in the Shashi-Motloutse drainage areas, and along the Botletle River (Fig. 22-2). The lowest concentrations are found in the Kalahari Desert, the Makgadikgadi Pans, and the Okavango Delta where the veld is poor and tsetse fly is common.

Cattle ownership is very uneven. Approximately half the national herd of 1.5 million head is owned by 10 percent of all the population, while 30 percent owns no cattle at all, and the average herd size for about 90 percent of the owners is only 13 cattle. The largest herds belong to the chiefs, European ranchers, and those who have acquired income from working in the mines and cities of South Africa. Since livestock and livestock products have, until the mid-1970s, accounted for 75 to 95 percent of

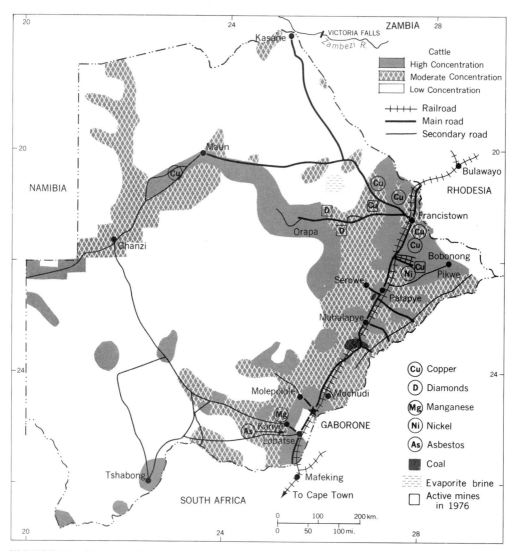

FIGURE 22-2 *Botswana. Economic map.*

Botswana's exports and have provided the principal source of cash income in the rural sector, this ownership pattern is particularly significant. During the severe droughts of 1965–1966, when the national herd was reduced by about one-third, it was the small cattle owner who suffered most.

The cattle industry suffers not only from the vagaries of climate and the adherence to traditional values but also from a variety of diseases (nagana, foot and mouth,

and anthrax), uncertain overseas markets, and a grossly inadequate transport system. Cattle must be trekked up to 400 mi (640 km) across the Kalahari to the government-owned slaughterhouse and canning factory in Lobatse—the largest in Africa. Even within the eastern zone, few cattle are railed or trucked because of high costs. Trekking is hazardous because of limited and irregular water supplies and grazing, and so many producers sell their livestock at low prices to

The Botswana Meat Commission in Lobatse, Botswana. This government-owned slaughter house is the largest in Africa. Until Botswana's copper and diamond deposits came into production in the mid-1970's, meat and livestock products were virtually the only exports. (Alan C. G. Best)

local intermediaries, who thus enjoy a monopolistic position and collaborate with big buyers. Cattle from the north were once trekked directly to Zambia and Rhodesia, but this practice was terminated in 1968 in an effort to control disease and increase the output at Lobatse. At present, chilled carcasses comprise the major livestock exports, with the United Kingdom, South Africa, and Zambia being the principal markets.

Botswana's economy entered a new phase in 1971 with the opening of the De Beers (Anglo-America Group) diamond mine at Orapa (Fig. 22-2). The kimberlite pipe (second largest in the world) is worked by open-cast methods, and annual production is expected to hold at about 4 million carats. Fifteen percent of the diamonds are of gemstone quality, and the mine has an expected life of at least 30 years. A second mine is being developed at Letlhakane.

The largest mining operation, however, centers at Pikwe-Selebi where a 44-million

ton deposit of low-grade copper-nickel ore was brought into production in 1973 (Fig. 22-2). Financed by West German banks, the Industrial Development Corporation of South Africa, Canada, the IBRD, and USAID, this multimillion dollar project has run into numerous unexpected difficulties with the smelting operations, the low-quality coal being used from near by Morupule, and water supplies from the Shashe River. The mine required a new railway spur, additional roads, a thermal power station, and has given rise to Botswana's largest township (30,000). It and the diamond mines provide the government with much needed revenues for the improvement of roads, health and education facilities, and for investment in the livestock industry. However, mining will have a negligible effect on industry and manufacturing within Botswana, and it will strengthen economic dualism and increase income differentials.

Botswana is thus a classical underdeveloped open economy, exporting primary products and importing manufactures, primarily from South Africa. The Botswana Meat Commission is the largest processing industry in the country. The only other industries include two small breweries, a taxidermist, and a handful of small plants producing furniture, leather goods and clothing. These are located in Lobatse (16,000), Francistown (24,000), and Gaborone (28,000), all situated on the line-of-rail. Gaborone was established as the capital in 1965 just before independence. Until then the administration was run from Mafeking, South Africa. Like Brazilia and Lilongwe, Gaborone is a planned, forward-looking capital whose site was selected with the hopes of stimulating growth in a frontier region (Best, 1970). To date, little industrial growth has materialized, and the economic core has shifted northward. Like most developing countries, Botswana lacks the means of integrating its space and may be unable to spread the benefits derived from its mining resources.

Lesotho: Population Pressure and Nondevelopment

Lesotho constitutes one of the very few countries in Africa that may be called a nation-state because the great majority of its people are of one nationality—the Basuto. The first Basuto leader, Moshesh (c. 1780–1870), welded the nation out of the peoples scattering before the marauding Zulu, consolidated them in the rugged mountains of the Drakensberg, and then ruled them with wisdom and cunning such as no other leader displayed. He successfully withstood the whites, both Boer and Briton, and guided his people into a position of strength that ensured their survival long after his death. He was, however, unable to prevent the isolation of his nation, and the very isolation that once ensured Basuto survival has become a great liability. One of Moshesh's aims was the establishment of a British protectorate over his country at a time when both the British Cape Colony and the Boer's Orange Free State Republic sought its annexation. He eventually succeeded, and when the Union of South Africa was created, the Basuto people were permitted to remain a separate political entity. They gained their independence from Britain in 1966.

Thus the political awakening of the Basuto came early, and British policy restricted white settlement in the territory to administration and commerce; all land remained in the hands of the Basuto. This land, however, proved inadequate for the needs of the people, and as the population increased, so did poverty and population pressure.

Basuto men began to seek work on the mines of the Witwatersrand and in the Orange Free State. A permanent system of migration developed, and with it the vulnerability of Lesotho grew. Basuto families depend on wages earned by their kin working in South Africa for the payment of taxes and the purchase of imported foods and merchandise.

This mountain kingdom may be divided into three distinct physiographic regions running northeast to southwest. Each has its own distinct climatic and pedologic characteristics and agroeconomic potentials and problems. In the far west lie the borderlands and the so-called "lowlands," really a misnomer, since much of the land is higher (5000–6000 ft or 1525–1630 m) than the bulk of the South African Highveld. Here the gently undulating plateau is studded with mesas and buttes, the sandy soils are impoverished and severely eroded, and rainfall is light (under 30 in. or 760 mm) and erratic. Despite these adversities, the region, which represents only 17 percent of the total area, supports about 40 percent of the *de facto* population. Here arable densities approximate 600 persons per sq mi (230 per sq km), and

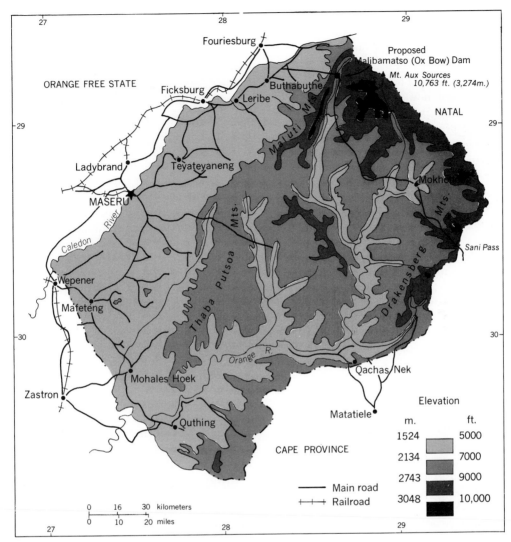

FIGURE 22-3 *Lesotho. General identification map.*

the Basuto live in both nucleated towns and villages and dispersed farmsteads.

The lowlands contain the capital, Maseru (25,000) and the country's largest villages. Here also is the densest communications network, which centers on the only paved road stretching from Leribe to Mafeteng (Fig. 22-3). A smaller but also densely populated lowland follows the Orange (Senqu) River, which cuts through the southern mountain ranges. In both regions, maize and millet form the staple crops, al-

though winter wheat is also widely grown in the Orange River Valley.

In the center of the country lies a belt of foothills whose elevations and slopes become steeper and more barren toward the east. Its soils are generally more fertile and less eroded than to the west, but agriculture is not so advanced. Communications become difficult, few roads penetrate the region, and pastoralism dominates. Finally, the eastern section of Lesotho (58 percent of the area) is composed of the scenically magnificent Maluti-Drakensberg Mountains, where slopes are steep and soils are thin and badly eroded. Here rainfall is heavy (40–70 in. or 1016–1778 mm), much of it falling as summer thundershowers. The growing season is short, and winter snows may last several weeks. Cultivation is limited but expanding as population pressure mounts elsewhere.

Pedologically, Lesotho is one of the poorest countries in Africa. Unfavorable parent material, unreliable rainfall, sparse natural vegetation, and strong relief have combined to hamper soil development. Overgrazing and mismanagement have destroyed large portions of those regions that were best endowed, and one of the characteristics of present-day Lesotho is the large number of gullies and heavily eroded fields, fast reducing the available useable soil acreage. Indeed, soil erosion is the country's greatest obstacle in the face of agricultural self sufficiency (Smit, 1967). Almost 40 percent of the total cultivated surface is really unsuitable for cultivation, with the greatest incidence of soil erosion occurring in the extreme west and in the Orange River Valley. Although the largest proportion of the fields in the mountains are on steep slopes, soil erosion is less common than in the foothills and the lowlands, because of the lower population densities, because the soil is not so exhausted after a shorter period of cultivation, and because soils here are less sandy than those in the lower lying areas.

It is recognized that if soil erosion remains unchecked and the population continues to grow at 2 percent per year, the Basuto will soon face mass starvation and irreparable damage to their land. Yet little has been achieved in controlling the problems. To be sure, terracing and grass stripping have been introduced, dams have been constructed, and trees have been planted, but little progress has been made in changing the social parameters. Stock still have great social and ritual importance so that quantity takes precedence over quality, and overgrazing and the breeding of poor strains are com-

mon (Perry, 1976). Widespread rural reform is required.

According to tradition, all land belongs to the Paramount Chief. Acting as a trustee for the Basuto, he administers the land through the local chiefs. Every Mosuto (a Basuto male) householder has a traditional right to three fields—one for maize, one for wheat, and one for kaffircorn. Usually these fields are scattered so that everyone gets both good and inferior land. However, because of population growth and the limited amount of land available, not everyone today has the full complement. Indeed, 14 percent has no land at all. When land is not used for two consecutive years, or when a Mosuto leaves the area permanently, the land can be granted to someone else. Migrant workers retain their right of possession as long as the land is cultivated for them. However, the local chief has the authority to expropriate and reassign land as he choses.

According to the communal land tenure system, land may not be enclosed because that would encourage individual occupation and prevent communal grazing following harvesting. Not all land is cultivated each year. Indeed, approximately one-fourth remains idle for the lack of a plough, seed, or the energy to work. Ploughing and harvesting begin only after authorization from the chief, and poor judgment can spell disaster. A poor harvest means not only food shortages that year but also a lack of seed to plant the following, so that the shortage is perpetuated unless money can be raised with which to buy seed. This continuous demand for food, seed, and cash forces the Basuto, especially the men, to seek work in South Africa.

Ploughing must begin as soon as the first rains fall, but if the rains are late, crops run the risk of frost damage before they mature. Traditionally, all land was cultivated with the hoe, but now the plough is widely used so that larger areas can be cultivated. However, ploughing across the contour has promoted soil erosion. Very little crop rota-

Ploughing against the contour in the Lesotho lowlands. Poor farm practices and an archaic tenurial system severely limit agricultural output. (Alan C. G. Best)

tion is practiced, and as maize is planted year after year in the same field, much of the soil is exhausted. In the past, fertilizer was rarely applied, and as the soil deteriorated it was abandoned. Today, however, shifting cultivation is no longer possible as virtually all cultivable land is used, and little manure is applied since, in the absence of firewood, cattle dung is used for fuel. Commercial fertilizer is beyond the means of most farmers. Land under cultivation is shown in Figure 22-4.

Attempts to raise agricultural output center on five large rural development schemes, all of which are pilot projects designed to find ways of reconciling agricultural progress with traditional tenure. These are heavily dependent upon aid from the United States, Britain, Sweden, and the World Bank. The $10 million Thaba Bosiu project, for example, is financed by the United States and the World Bank. The Department of Agriculture is attempting to foster new attitudes toward farming through its "Progressive Farmers" program, whereby

the participants must employ modern methods of farming in order to make a living solely from agriculture and not join the migrant worker circuit. Agricultural and marketing cooperatives have been established but without much success.

Since the early 1950s, crop yields have declined steadily, and Lesotho must now import almost one-third of its food requirements. Yet winter wheat is exported to South Africa in exchange for corn which is preferred in the diet. Animal products, primarily cattle, sheep, wool and mohair provide up to three-fourths of the exports, while diamonds make up the balance. The value of imports exceeds exports, by seven to one, with manufactured goods, foodstuffs, machinery, and transport equipment heading the list.

In reality, labor is Lesotho's principal export. Each year about 45 percent of the adult males, and between 6 and 10 percent of the female labor force (representing over 130,000 persons in all), are employed in South Africa's mines, cities, and farms. Mi-

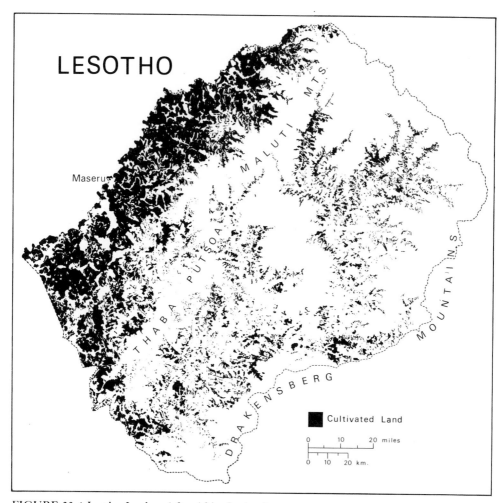

FIGURE 22-4 *Lesotho. Land use (after Africa Institute).*

grant remittances and deferred pay generally exceeds the value of exports and constitute the principal source of expendable income within Lesotho. Less than 10 percent of the Basuto are wage earners within the country, and 85 percent of the population is engaged in subsistence agriculture.

Lesotho has almost no chance of diversifying its economy and lessening its dependence on South Africa for employment, manufactured goods, and technical assistance. It has few known natural resources other than water and diamonds, and it lacks the capital, technology, markets, and communications required for manufacturing. Its most valuable natural asset is water, especially the Orange River. For years there has been discussion of diverting water from Malibamatso (Ox Bow) on the upper Orange River to the Southern Transvaal industrial complex, but the project has foundered on the Republic's unwillingness to make acceptable commitments to buy the water or invest in the proposed power station. Similarly, South Africa has been reluctant to build smaller hydroelectric and irrigation projects to meet Lesotho's own needs. In contrast, the De Beers Corporation has announced plans to develop a medium-size diamond mine at Letseng-la-Terae in which the Le-

Basutos wrapped in blankets against the cold winter winds outside a labor recruiting office in Mohaleshoek, Lesotho. Migrant labor to South Africa's mines and farms is Lesotho's major export. (Alan C. G. Best)

sotho government will hold 20 percent of the equity.

Perhaps the greatest immediate hope for growth can be achieved through tourism. Lesotho's spectacular scenery, winter sports potential, and gambling facilities (at Maseru) are all within a few hours drive from the Witwatersrand, Durban, and the Orange Free State. If tourism is to be developed to its fullest, roads within Lesotho will need upgrading and extending. At present, the most scenic region has but a few third-class roads which can be blocked by snow in winter and washed out by rain in summer.

Swaziland: Land Division and the Dual Economy

LAND DIVISION

Swaziland, smallest of the former High Commission Territories, appears to have the greatest potential for growth. It possesses a proven resource base which has been exploited for several decades, there is some industry, and there is some climatic and pedologic diversification. Moreover, the Swazi people, although not entirely homogeneous ethnically, share a common history (including successful resistance to Zulu aggression), an attachment to and identification with Swazi territory, and a rapidly growing degree of political consciousness and desire for progress. There are about 500,000 Swazi in Swaziland proper, and in addition perhaps as many as 100,000 Swazi people, paying allegiance to the Swazi paramount chief, live beyond the borders in South Africa.

The distribution of the Swazi nation over an area far in excess of Swaziland itself is a reflection of one of the major problems facing Swaziland today: the problem of land. The Swazi, although not conquered by the Zulu, were unable to prevent their powerful southern neighbors from claiming much of their territory. Subsequently, when contact was made with the first white invaders, Swazi chiefs carelessly ceded away vast tracts of land in return for trivial objects. Most guilty was Chief Mbandzeni (Umbandine), who by the time of his death in 1889 had assigned the entire land of the Swazi to whites. Thus, the Swazi by the end of the nineteenth century had lost those lands they had successfully defended against the Zulu.

Having ceded their land, the Swazi, aware of their predicament in being squatters on what was once their own territory, appealed to Britain for protection. The British, realizing the problems involved, refused to establish a protectorate over the Swazi when the appeal was made in 1893. Indeed, Britain was concerned over events on the South African Plateau at this time, and was prepared to allow Swaziland to become a part of the South African Republic. Doubtless, this would have happened had the matter not been under review at the time of the outbreak of the Boer War; when the war was over, the British agreed (in 1902) to establish a protectorate over the Swazi. Thus, the Swaziland Protectorate came into being through a succession of the sort of accidents that make history.

The establishment of the protectorate, however, did not end the land problems of the Swazi people. Whether or not under protectorate status, Swaziland had been ceded to white settlers. With the Swazi indicating their desire to remain outside a unified South Africa, it became necessary to define the international boundaries of the country. This was completed in 1907, while a specially appointed commission was attempting to unravel the complex of adjacent and overlapping concessions with the aim of returning to the Swazi people some of the land they once owned. The commission in 1907 published a plan for the partition of the territory along lines which essentially form the basis of present-day land division in Swaziland.

After the dilimitation of its international boundaries, the area of Swaziland was found to be 6704 sq mi (17,364 sq km), all under concessions. The commission proposed that exactly one-third of the total land of each concession be returned to the Swazi nation, that the pieces of land thus deducted be consolidated as much as possible, and that these stretches of territory form the home of the Swazi people. The Swazi, in return for this allotment of land, were given five years (July 1, 1909, until June 30, 1914) to leave the land remaining under concession and move to their own areas. Any Swazi able to make private arrangements with the white landowners to remain on the ceded lands could do so, however. In fact, no major migration of Swazi to their own areas resulted, most being able to stay on the ceded land. The important achievement of the commission, nevertheless, was that the Swazi nation obtained tribal lands with which the people could identify themselves, on which the chief and elders could live, and where Swazi practices of land ownership, cattle and goat herding, and so on, could be maintained.

In 1914, the population of Swaziland was perhaps somewhat over 100,000, with about 1000 white settlers, and, at that time, population pressure on the land was much less than it is today. The commission dealing with the territory's partition, in recognition of a future greater need for land, developed a mechanism by which land could be purchased from the white landowners for inclusion into the Swazi nation's areas, or for Crown land which at a later stage might be vested in the Swazi nation. The growth of the Swazi people outstripped the increase in available land, however. Today, with the population of Swaziland estimated to be 500,000, about 60 percent of the total area

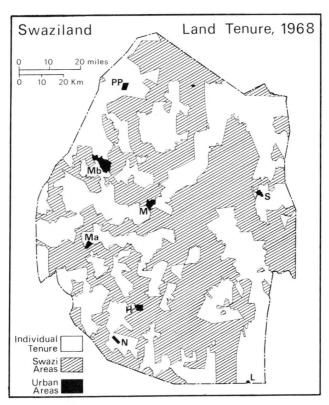

FIGURE 22-5 *Swaziland. Land Tenure, c. 1968.*

comprises Swazi nation land, the remainder being held on a freehold or leasehold basis. The patchwork quilt pattern persists, and on the Swazi nation land lives 84 percent of the total population (Fig. 22-5).

The Swazi who live on the land (as against the 10 percent who are urbanized and active in the mines) are pastoralists, and there are about 630,000 cattle in the country. This, according to experts involved in the problems of Swaziland, is 200,000 more cattle than the country can hold adequately, and the annual net increase, largely due to tribal customs and economic conditions, is over 16,000. In addition, Swazi own about 275,000 goats, which contribute to the overgrazing from which much of the territory suffers.

The Swaziland government has made considerable effort to improve the agricultural practices, but has been faced with re-luctance to adopt the proposed changes. This can be attributed to several factors, not the least important of which is similar to that experienced in Rhodesia and South Africa: while much land lies apparently unused in white landholdings, Africans are loathe to improve conditions on what they have, feeling that such improvements would not be necessary if they had the white lands. In addition, there are the tribal customs which reduce the number of cattle taken each year for slaughtering, including their use as a form of currency, the prestige associated with numbers (rather than quality), and their inclusion in the usual bride price.

Nevertheless, some Swazi have accepted such principles as contour farming, fallowing, and other forms of soil conservation, and are farming for profit rather than subsistence. There are some model farms run by Swazi which earn as much money as do many white farms. But the land initially given to the Swazi nation through the partition of the concessions was by no means Swaziland's best land, so that opportunities for this sort of progress have been few. It is considered vital that other Swazi adopt the necessary practices to prevent the degree of soil erosion from which large parts of Lesotho suffer, and local technicians are constantly working to effect these changes. The dreaded cattle disease, East Coast fever, has been virtually eliminated by the enforcement of regular dipping of all cattle.

THE DUAL ECONOMY

The division of land toward the end of the last century marked the beginnings of Swaziland's social and economic dualisms which have persisted to the present. Indeed, over the years they have intensified and their spatial manifestations are most pronounced (Maasdorp, 1976). Today there are islands of modernization and development surrounded by broader areas of traditionalism and economic backwardness. The modern economy largely represents European mining, agricultural, manufacturing, and commercial interests, while the traditional economy is characterized by subsistence cultivation and pastoralism. Real national viability can only be achieved with the complete integration of these two sectors through the structural transformation of the social and economic systems. Little attempt was made to integrate them until the 1960s.

During the colonial period, and especially in the earlier years, Swaziland was an impoverished dependency lacking both the infrastructures and government encouragement needed for development. Britain refrained from providing the necessary development capital since there was a possibility Swaziland would be incorporated in the Union of South Africa; the Union would not undertake large-scale investment without some guarantee of incorporation. The Swazi themselves were subsistence farmers and pastoralists and thus totally deficient in the skills and capital required for modernization, while the revenues derived from the small quantities of gold, tin, tobacco, cotton, and cattle produced by the few European settlers were also insufficient to transform the economy.

After World War II, Swaziland experienced considerable economic diversity and growth when Britain belatedly accepted its responsibilities for the promotion of economic development, and it became clearer that incorporation with South Africa would not materialize and independence would be achieved. The British Commonwealth Development Corporation, in partnership with private enterprise, established timber plantations of exotic softwoods and eucalyptus in the highveld, erected a pulp mill at Bhunya, and established irrigation schemes and a sugar mill in the lowveld at Mhlume (Fig. 22-6). This government initiative encouraged additional investment of private South African and British capital in the citrus, sugar, forestry, and cattle industries, and saw the improvement of roads, education, health facilities, and a greater participation of Swazi in the cash economy. In 1964 a railway was opened between the new iron ore mine (Ngwenya) and Maputo in Mozambique, which provides Swaziland with an outlet for its exports, permits easier access to petroleum products and other bulky imports, and reduces its dependence on South African transport.

Swaziland's economy is more diversified than that of Lesotho and Botswana, although mining and agriculture are still foremost, and manufacturing is mainly concerned with the processing of local raw materials. Wood pulp, timber, and wood products head the export list, but are closely followed by sugar and minerals (mainly iron ore and asbestos). Meat, fruits, rice, cotton, and tobacco are also exported. Since 1964, Japan has purchased all of the iron ore exports, while Britain and South Africa buy most of the other exports. Increasing quantities of coal from the lowveld are being ex-

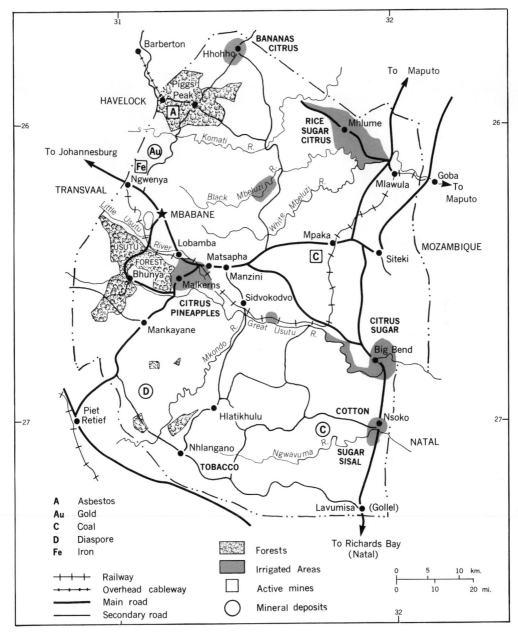

FIGURE 22-6 *Swaziland. Economic map.*

ported to Mozambique and Kenya, while markets for pulp are being developed in Chile. South Africa provides about 90 percent of all imports—mainly machinery, transport equipment, clothing, and general merchandise. Unlike either Lesotho or Bo-

tswana, Swaziland has a visible trade surplus.

The economy is concentrated in four core regions which collectively account for only 15 percent of the area but 90 percent of all primary and secondary production (Fair

The Swaziland Railway hauling iron ore from Ng-wenya in the western highveld to Maputo, Mozambique. (Alan C. G. Best)

The Big Bend sugar mill in Swaziland's lowveld. Swaziland's agricultural exports include sugar, rice, citrus and pineapples, mainly from European-owned estates. (Alan C. G. Best)

et al., 1969). The national core is the most diverse and includes the Usutu Forest, the Bhunya pulp mill, the Malkerns irrigation scheme, the Ngwenya iron-ore mine, Manzini (30,000) and its industrial satellite township Matsapa, and the administrative capital Mbabane (30,000). Matsapa has several light industries including a brewery, cotton gin, and abattoir. The national core accounts for almost half of Swaziland's primary and secondary output, and contains the new legislative capital, Lobamba, and more than half of the territory's European population (8000).

Subsidiary resource core regions are located at Big Bend and Mhlume where sugar, citrus, and rice are produced; and at Havelock, site of the world's fifth-largest asbestos mine and close to the vast private afforesta-tion scheme at Piggs Peak (Fig. 22-6). Each region has become an important source of local employment, thus reducing the amount of temporary migration to South Africa, but none has manufacturing (other than basic processing) and diversified services. Each is geared to external markets, and the inter-nodal economic linkages are weak. Surrounding these cores lies the periphery, encompassing 85 percent of the total area, possessing three-fourths of the total population, and producing only 10 percent of the primary and secondary output. Its functional linkages with the cores are minimal, and it represents the subsistence sector of the dual economy.

Thus, Swaziland has several ingredients required for national economic viability that are lacking in both Botswana and Lesotho. What is required is progressive leadership under the *Ngwenyama*, King Sobhuza II and his successors. To date, the king has epitomized Swazi traditionalism, and has been suspect of contemporary modernization. In 1973, he abrogated the constitution and dissolved all political parties on the grounds they were alien to Swazi traditions of government. Such actions reemphasize the problems and dilemmas of developing countries with strong socioeconomic dualisms.

Since the turn of the century, South Africa's economic interests in and influences upon Botswana, Lesotho, and Swaziland have been strong, and they are likely to remain so because of the combined forces of location, history, politics, and economics. Over the years the three countries have become inseparable economic dependencies within the South African sphere of influence. They depend on South Africa for manufactured goods, employment for their surplus labor, and markets for their exports produced with South African capital and technology; they are tied to the South African economy by the South African Customs Union and the South African rand.

When the three territories chose to remain outside the projected Union of South Africa in 1909, an economic arrangement (the Customs Union) was agreed upon which was to tie them almost inextricably into the South African economic framework. It meant that all goods leaving the three territories had to travel through South Africa and be transported by South African carriers. Thus transport links between South Africa and the territories developed, and South African quality control standards were introduced in marketing. Furthermore, each territory adopted South Africa's currency, and the custom's revenues were shared according to a formula that favored South Africa and prejudiced the junior members. In 1969 the agreement was renegotiated on a more equitable basis, but the same linkages remain.

In 1974 Swaziland issued its own currency, the *emalangeni*, which is at par with the South African rand. By 1977, Botswana plans to establish its own central bank and thus be independent of the rand whose devaluations have been harmful to the Botswana economy and unrelated to the latter's economic situation. Lesotho, the least independent of the three territories, plans no changes in its currency arrangements with South Africa.

Botswana is seeking closer ideological and economic ties with Zambia. A new road from Francistown now links Botswana with Zambia at Kazangula where the two countries claim a common boundary of only a few yards (Fig. 22-2). In theory this provides an indirect link with the Tan-Zam Railway and access to the sea through Dar es Salaam, Tanzania, should the southern border ever be closed or traffic be disrupted on the Rhodesian-owned railway that traverses the east. Botswana is also anxious to see an independent Namibia and a rail link west to Gobabis and Windhoek.

Swaziland, long dependent on South African ports, was linked by rail to Lourenço Marques (now Maputo) in 1964 and since then has enjoyed a greater measure of independence from South Africa. However, following Mozambique's independence (1975), the Swazis have shown concern over the new government's ability to provide adequate port facilities (at Maputo) and political stability, which are vital to Swaziland's economic survival. Thus, Swaziland has investigated the possibilities of building a branch line south from Phuzumoya to the South African railhead at Gollel (Lavumisa) which feeds into Richards Bay, Natal (Maasdorp, 1976). Thus, dependence on South Africa would be reinforced once again.

Lesotho, in almost every way is more dependent on South Africa than are Botswana and Swaziland. Poorer in resources, lacking in development potential and industry, and surrounded by the Republic, Lesotho is truly a hostage of South Africa. In many ways, it is no more independent of South Africa than are the embryonic homelands.

Bibliography

Best, Alan C. G. "Gaborone: Problems and Prospects of a New Capital," *Geographical Review*, Vol. 60, No. 1 (January, 1970), pp. 1–14.

Best, Alan C. G. "Swaziland," *Focus*, Vol. 25, No. 6 (March–April, 1975), pp. 14–16.

Botswana, Republic of. *National Development Plan, 1973–78.* Part 1, *Policies and Objectives.* Gaborone: Government Printer, 1973.

Campbell, A. C., and G. Child. "The Impact of Man on the Environment of Botswana," *Botswana Notes and Records*, Vol. 3 (1971), pp. 91–110.

Fair, T. J. D., George Murdoch, and H. W. Jones, *Development in Swaziland: A Regional Analysis.* Johannesburg: Witwatersrand University Press, 1969.

Halpern, J. *South Africa's Hostages: Basutoland, Bechuanaland and Swaziland.* Baltimore: Penguin Books, 1965.

Holm, J. "Rural Development in Botswana: Three Basic Political Trends," *Rural Africa*, No. 18 (1972), pp. 80–92.

Knight, D. B. "Botswana at the Development Threshold," *Focus*, Vol. 26, No. 2 (November–December, 1975), pp. 9–13.

Leistner, G. M. E. *Lesotho: Economic Structure and Growth.* Pretoria: Africa Institute, 1966.

Leistner, G. M. E., and P. Smit. *Swaziland: Resources and Development.* Pretoria: Africa Institute, 1969.

Maasdorp, G. "Modernization in Swaziland," in C. G. Knight and J. L. Newman (eds.), *Contemporary Africa.* Englewood Cliffs, N.J.: Prentice-Hall, 1976.

Perry, J. W. B. "Lesotho: Environment and Tradition Hamper Development," *Focus*, Vol. 26, No. 3 (January–February, 1976), pp. 8–16.

Potholm, C. P. *Swaziland: The Dynamics of Political Modernization.* Berkeley: University of California Press, 1972.

Potholm, C. P., and Richard Dale (eds.). *Southern Africa in Perspective: Essays in Regional Politics.* New York: The Free Press, 1972.

Sillery, A. *Botswana: A Short Political History.* London: Methuen and Co., 1974.

Smit, P. *Lesotho: A Geographical Study.* Pretoria: Africa Institute, 1967.

Smit, P. *Botswana: Resources and Development.* Pretoria: Africa Institute, 1970.

Stevens, R. P. *Lesotho, Botswana and Swaziland: The Former High Commission Territories in Southern Africa.* New York: Praeger, 1967.

Wallman, S. "Conditions of Non-Development: The Case of Lesotho," *Journal of Development Studies*, Vol. 8 (1972), pp. 251–261.

TWENTY-THREE

The island of Madagascar constitutes the domain of the Malagasy Republic, whose population of 8.5 million traces its history not only to Africa but also to Asia. Madagascar's African connections were forged substantially by France, the country's colonizer, for the French administered the island as part of their African possessions. But Malagasy's cultural heritage is largely Indonesian, and despite its membership in OAU and its participation in African diplomatic matters, there is very little active contact between the island and eastern Africa, its nearest neighbor. In certain spheres the links with francophone West Africa are stronger, though not as strong even as the ties with France itself. Malagasy's insular isolation is symbolic of its aloofness.

Madagascar's physiography, however, is unmistakably African. Its remarkably straight eastern coastline lies at the foot of a high escarpment that rises steeply, some-

times in a series of steps, to elevations near 10,000 ft (3000 m) that are sustained by crystalline and volcanic rocks; westward, this high plateau surface declines to lower elevations and the basement rocks are covered by sedimentaries similar to those that fill Africa's great basins. Madagascar shares with Africa its paucity of good natural harbors. The east coast has few adequate inlets, and dangerous offshore coral reefs form a hazard to navigation; the country's leading port, Tamatave, occupies one of the few harbor sites available (Fig. 23-1). Coastal communication takes place between Tamatave and Farafangana along the Pangalanes Canal, a valuable intracoastal waterway at the foot of the escarpment but behind a raised shoreline. The west coast tends to be mangrove-studded and inhospitable to port development, and only the northwestern sector of the island provides some good natural harbors, including Diego-Suarez on Madagas-

MALAGASY: ASIAN OUTPOST, AFRICAN ISLAND

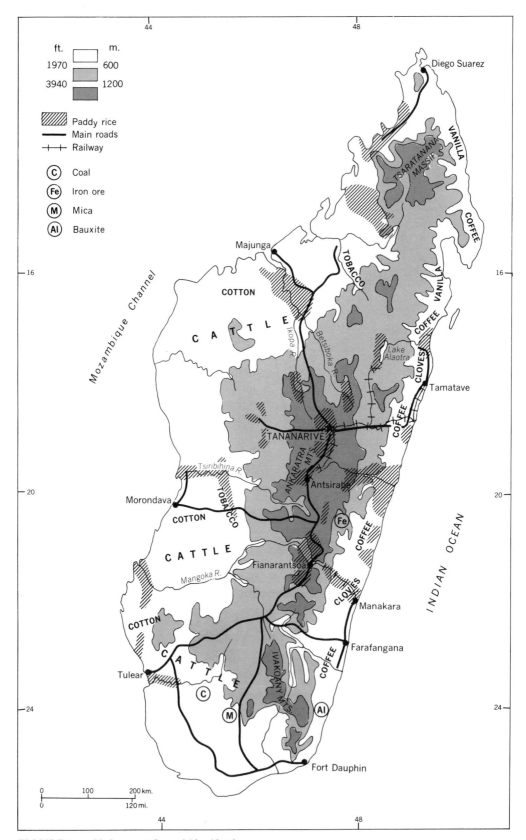

FIGURE 23-1 *Madagascar. General identification map.*

Rice terraces in the central highlands of Madagascar. Rice, introduced from Southeast Asia centuries ago, is the island's staple grain. Note the very narrow terraces, too narrow for bullocks to plough. (Malagasy Ministry of Information)

car's northern tip—not the most favorable position in relation to the country's core area. In terms of relative location, Tamatave has the greatest advantage, but the surface connection between Tamatave and the capital, Tananarive, involves negotiation of the great eastern escarpment.

Climatic conditions are as diverse as the island's physiography. They vary from tropical rainy (monsoon) conditions along the entire east coast, where rainfall exceeds 100 in. (2450 mm) and hurricanes strike each year, to low-latitude steppe conditions in the extreme southwest. Most of the highland interior and north coast areas are savanna. The island lies in the path of the moist southeast trades so that much moisture is wrung out of the atmosphere before reaching the lower west side, which suffers from high rainfall variability and strong seasonal regimes. Temperate conditions, similar to those in the highlands of Kenya and Rhodesia, prevail in

the Ankaratra Mountains near Tananarive. Here the indigenous forest has been cut, soil erosion is among the worst in Africa, and population pressure is high.

Agriculture is hampered by the latosolic soils that cover much of the island. They are very infertile, severely eroded, and require expensive treatment to enable viable cash-cropping and subsistence production. Where volcanic materials penetrate the surface, especially in the central highlands around Tananarive and Fianarantsoa, better pedologic conditions have resulted. Some of the richest soils are found in the savanna areas and along the valley floors. In most places erosion is due primarily to systematic firing of the bush and forest, and to subsequent overgrazing.

If names such as Tananarive, Fianarantsoa (the southern plateau city), and Tamatave appear to differ from those on the African mainland, the contrast confirms

Malagasy's linguistic distinctiveness. Madagascar's peoples speak a language that is basically Indonesian, with some Bantu words; just how the island came to be a Southeast Asian outpost remains a matter for debate. One theory holds that Southeast Asians first reached the African coast, mixed to some extent with the local peoples, and then emigrated to Madagascar. In coastal Kenya, some cultural phenomena, such as the use of the long-house, suggest that an early contact of this kind may have occurred. The evidence suggests that Madagascar's modern population first reached the island between 2000 and 1500 years ago.

The Colonial Period

Little is known about Madagascar's territorial organization prior to about 1500 A.D. As along the East African coast, Arabs and Persians made contact and established trading posts and slave stations in northern Madagascar during the fourteenth and fifteenth centuries. During that period the Merina (or Hova) peoples probably were settling in the plateau heartland around present-day Tananarive, and eventually a powerful kingdom arose there. Other, competing states developed elsewhere, and the Europeans arrived to exploit the conflicts, to buy slaves, and to sell firearms. The French competed with the British for a sphere of influence over Madagascar and, following the British withdrawal, France in 1885 assumed a protectorate over the Merina kingdom. From this base, France extended its control, waging a final war in 1895 when the last resistance of Merina dissidents was broken.

Madagascar never ranked high in France's order of colonial priorities (Nelson, 1973). The first decade of French control witnessed the suppression of two insurrections, but during the 1920s a movement arose in favor of assimilation and *département* status for Madagascar. France rejected this effort, and World War II temporarily defused the rising tide of Malagasy nationalism. But a major revolt erupted in 1947, evidence that while the formula of the Fourth Republic might be appropriate for conditions in West and Equatorial Africa, it was inadequate for Madagascar. Tens of thousands of lives were lost as France put down the nationalist rebellion, and the country was still recovering when De Gaulle in 1958 gave France's African dependencies the opportunity to choose independence under the terms of the Fifth Republic. Madagascar chose autonomy within the French Community, and in 1960 the independent Malagasy Republic (*République Malgache*) was proclaimed.

France's response to Madagascar's economic needs and potentials confirmed the island's lowly position in the priorities of Paris. The surface communication system developed slowly; the Tananarive-Tamatave rail line was completed in 1913 (branches now extend northward to Ambatondrazaka and southward to Antsirabé), and the Fianarantsoa-Manakara line was laid by 1935; but railway development under French occupation never went farther (Fig. 23-1). By independence only about 2000 mi (3200 km) of the country's roads were paved, and during the wet season whole regions of Madagascar are effectively isolated. Little was done to combat disease in the potentially productive northwest.

Development Problems and Prospects

During the colonial era, development was limited by Madagascar's isolation from the mainstream of economic progress, the conservatism and ethnocentricity of the Mal-

Tananarive, capital of Malagasy. The town occupies a commanding position high above the Betsimitatatra Plain in the central highlands. (Malagasy Ministry of Information)

agasy, and by an undistinguished colonial policy. Since independence this insular state has experienced a slower rate of economic growth than most African states. Its export economy, based mainly on coffee, has not paralleled that of Ivory Coast, Kenya, or Angola, and the provision of essential social services and industries has been slow. Like much of francophone Africa, Madagascar has relied heavily on French aid, technical assistance, and markets, and since 1971 has sought financial and technical assistance from China and the Arab countries (notably Libya and Kuwait). Expatriates still either run or manage most of the export oriented agricultural estates, mining operations and industries, although the Supreme Revolutionary Council—established in June 1975 following the assassination of Colonel Rat-

simandrava—has declared that the state will take active control of banking and insurance, energy, transport, minerals, and foreign trade. Ethnic rivalries, especially between the Merina and various coastal groups, or *côtiers*, have compounded the economic ills and have contributed to political strife that has prevailed since 1971.

The Revolutionary Council is committed to developing the country along socialist lines initiated by the previous regime and set out in the 1974/1977 Development Plan. This includes extensive nationalization of key areas of the economy and agricultural reform, the latter strategy being an attempt to defuse the ethnic rivalries that underlay the disorders of the early 1970s. Rural reform is based on the traditional *fokonolona* communes and distribution cooperatives.

Fokonolona

Fokonolona is the Merina name for a village or hamlet organization traditionally composed of the heads of all village households. It was once the basic unit of local government under the Merina kings, but during the colonial era it was largely suppressed. In 1962, following independence, the system was reactivated. Today, the Supreme Revolutionary Council is using the *fokonolona* to gain its assistance in plans for rural economic and social development, particularly through self-help programs. They are seen as a means of making the rural areas more democratic and narrowing the income differentials of the various sections of the population. There are about 10,000 *fokonolona* communes.

Migration from overpopulated rural areas, such as the Betsimitatatra Plain around Tananarive, the borders of Lake Alaotra, and sections of the east coast, is being encouraged to underpopulated regions with an agricultural potential. These include the Betsiboka Valley of the north, and the Morandava and Mangoky basins in the west, where there is great potential for rice, raffia, sugar, tobacco, and livestock (Fig. 23-1). A lack of transport and capital, rather than adverse environmental conditions, have limited development in these regions.

Agriculture is the mainstay of the economy, providing employment for 90 percent of the population and accounting for 90 percent of export earnings. A wide range of cash crops removes much of the instability experienced by many primary producers. Robusta coffee is the leading export (70,000 tons in 1974); it accounts for 30 percent of the foreign trade earnings, and occupies about one-fourth of the rural population. Most is produced on small east coast farms badly in need of replanting and reorganization.

Cloves are the country's second export followed by vanilla, of which Madagascar is the world's leading producer. Both are grown along the narrow east coast lowlands (Fig. 23-1). These industries periodically suffer from cyclone damage, and in recent years severe competition (from Zanzibar in particular), fluctuating prices in the world market, and competition from synthetic flavoring derived from coal tar have been major aggravations. Of the major cash crops grown mainly for domestic use, cottonseed, groundnuts, cassava, maize, and sisal are showing small increases, but self-sufficiency has yet to be achieved.

Madagascar's traditional means of livelihood have characteristics of both mainland Africa and Southeast Asia. The similarities with mainland Africa lie more with the pastoral economy than with agriculture. Over three-fourths of the island is used for grazing by the 11 million cattle and 1.5 million sheep and goats, with the southern and western regions being the most important (Fig. 32-1). There, almost every inhabitant owns some cattle, and the average per capita meat consumption is one of the highest in the Third World. Cattle are hoarded as a form of capital, a mark of prestige, and as instruments of ceremony. Selective breeding and controlled range management are rarely practiced, most of the cattle being allowed to roam and graze at will with little provision taken against the popular custom of cattle stealing. If more scientific methods were adopted, more meat could be sold within Madagascar, especially in the protein-deficient and densely settled highland areas. There, and on the eastern seaboard, cattle are used primarily for trampling the rice paddies prior to planting and for providing traction.

Comoro Islands

Between northern Madagascar and the African mainland lies a group of four volcanic islands called the *Comoros*. The total area of these islands is about 850 sq mi (2200 sq km), and the 1977 population was 350,000 (est.). In 1960, the French-administered Comoros achieved internal autonomy under the terms of De Gaulle's Fifth Republic. A political crisis arose in 1975, when the voters on one of the islands, Mayotte, indicated a preference for continued ties with France, a position that clashed with the independence-minded peoples of Grande Comore (largest and most populous island), Moheli (the smallest), and Anjouan. Mayotte's population is mainly Christian, but Islam prevails elsewhere; Mayotte became French as early as 1843, but the other islands fell under French control after 1885. France responded favorably to Mayotte's expressed intentions, but the government on Grande Comore unilaterally declared the Comoros' independence. In retaliation, France cut off its aid to the islands.

The Comoros are overpopulated and poverty-stricken. Land is excessively fragmented; spices and perfume products are exported, as well as some tropical fruits and tobacco. But there is no manufacturing to speak of, not even in the capital, Moroni (15,000), on Grande Comore. Corn in the lower areas and rice on the higher slopes are staple foods, and there is heavy dependence on the coco palm. Opportunities are severely limited, and there is a steady stream of emigration, especially to Madagascar.

In several ways, subsistence farming (especially among the Betsileo and Merina) is reminiscent of Southeast Asia: the emphasis is on paddy rice; the farms are between 2 and 3 acres (about 1 hectare), fragmented, and intensively cultivated; two rice crops are grown each year if climate permits; and terracing of the hillsides is a common feature. However, yields are generally low. On the Tananarive Plain, for example, 3- to 5-acre farms (2 ha) produce only 2 or 3 tons of rice per acre, and the average output per acre for the entire island is only 0.7 metric tons. In Japan, rice yields are between 20 and 25 metric tons per acre.

Rice is the main subsistence crop, accounting for almost half the total value of agricultural output and one-third of all cultivated land. Per capita rice consumption is one of the highest in the world. If greater applications of fertilizer were used, improved rice strains were adopted, and the fields were consolidated, Madagascar could become one of the world's leading rice exporters. East Africa is a logical market, but first Madagascar must feed its own population. Since the late 1960s the gap between supply and demand has widened, and the island is now an importer of rice. The importance of rice is acknowledged by the fact that 12 percent of the budget of the 1974/1977 Development Plan is devoted to its improvement.

Like most developing countries, Madagascar suffers from a grossly inadequate transport network, a small internal market, a shortage of labor and skills, and an uncontrollable rate of inflation. Industry is limited to the manufacture of consumer goods and the processing of agricultural/pastoral products in Tananarive (515,000), Fianarantsoa (60,000), and the three largest ports. Local-born Indians, Chinese, and Comorians control much of the industry and commerce and

Rice paddies on the east coast lowlands. Note the escarpment in the background rising up to the Ankaratra Mountains. (Malagasy Ministry of Information)

have not integrated socially with the Malagasy. Development is spatially discontinuous, there being only small isolated nodes of production separated by larger areas of subsistence, economic stagnation, and out-migration.

Years of ineffective government planning and policy implementation have discouraged private investment. This may well be discouraged still further by the Supreme Revolutionary Council's decision to nationalize vital sectors of the economy. Government priority is in infrastructural development (particularly the improvement of communications with loans from China and the Soviet Union), agriculture, and livestock. Madagascar's mineral potential is largely unknown, and current production is limited to mica, chromite, and graphite,

which collectively contribute only 5 percent of the exports. The exploitation of bauxite, nickel, and iron ore is constrained by the lack of finance, adequate transport, and guaranteed markets.

While still dependent on France and the European Economic Community (EEC) for much of its technical assistance and foreign trade, Madagascar is turning increasingly toward both China and the Soviet Union. Both countries are committed to improving the communications systems and to developing industry and agriculture. Chinese and Russian presence in Madagascar could conceivably reduce this island state's isolationism and bring to Madagascar a greater involvement in the political and economic affairs of East Africa.

Bibliography

Atlas de Madagascar. Tananarive: L'Association de Geographes de Madagascar, 1969.

Haseltine, N. *Madagascar.* London: Pall Mall Press, 1971.

Jackson, R. T. "Agricultural Development in the Malagasy Republic," *East African Geographical Review,* Vol. 9 (April, 1971), pp. 69–78.

Kent, R. K. *Early Kingdoms in Madagascar,*

1500–1700. New York: Rinehart & Winston, 1970.

Malagasy Republic. Institut National de la Statistique et de la Recherche Economique. *Population de Madagascar: situation au Ier Janvier,* 1970. Tananarive: ministere des Finances et du Commerce, 1971.

Nelson, H. D., et al. *Area Handbook for the Malagasy Republic* Washington, D.C.: U.S. Government Printing Office, 1973.

Ominde, S. H., and C. N. Ejiogu (eds.). *Population Growth and Economic Development in Africa.* London: Heinemann, 1974.

Rabemananjara, J. "A United Madagascar Looks Ahead," *Optima* Vol. 18, No. 4 (December, 1968), pp. 174–85.

Thompson, V., and R. Adloff. *The Malagasy Republic.* Stanford: Stanford Univeristy Press, 1965.

PART FIVE

EAST
AFRICA

TWENTY-FOUR

The contrasts between lowland equatorial Africa, as exemplified by the Zaire Basin, and highland East Africa, which comprises Tanzania, Kenya, Uganda, Rwanda, and Burundi are sharp and significant. For the most part, East Africa is higher, cooler, drier, and less forested. The vast majority of the people are semi-sedentary pastoralists and peasants who depend directly on the land for their livelihood, yet much of the region has only marginally useful agricultural and pastoral land. Only 4 percent of the five-state region may expect to receive more than 50 in. (1270 mm) of rainfall in four years out of five, while half the region may expect less than 30 in. (760 mm). Droughts can strike with devastating force and frequency in the northern areas and in central Tanzania.

Much of East Africa is a gently undulating plateau that lies more than 3500 ft (1050 m) above sea level (Fig. 24-1). The highest areas adjoin the rift valleys along the region's western boundary and east of Lake Victoria: the Ruwenzoris of Uganda, and the Aberdares of Kenya rise above 13,000 ft (4550 m), while several volcanoes tower even higher above the expansive savanna plains. Permanently snow-capped Mount Kilimanjaro exceeds 19,300 ft (5880 m), and on the equator, glacier-fringed Mount Kenya rises to 17,065 ft (5200 m). On the lower slopes of these and other mountain zones, where soils are rich and rainfall is generally high, population densities are among the highest in Africa, and agricultural land use is intense. Unlike Equatorial Africa to the west, highland East Africa has few known mineral resources, and mining plays only a minor role in each of the national economies.

Of the five East African states, the United Republic of Tanzania is by far the largest (364,900 sq mi or 945,087 sq km), larger in fact than the others combined. It is also the most populous (16.2 million in

TANZANIA: FROM COLONIALISM TO SOCIALISM

415

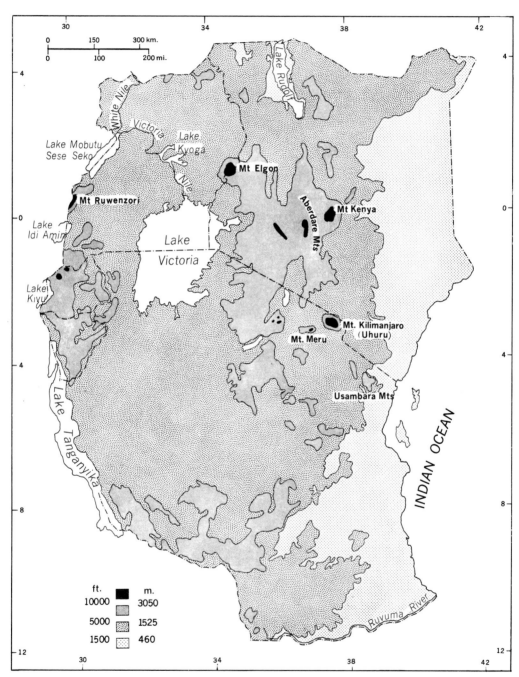

FIGURE 24-1 *East Africa. Physical features.*

1977). Tanzania comprises mainland Tanganyika, formerly a UN trust territory held by Britain, and the islands of Zanzibar and Pemba, formerly a British protectorate. In April 1964, following several months of open conflict between Zanzibar's African majority and its Arab and Asian minorities, these two independent territories merged under the name Tanzania and embarked on a unique program of social and economic development that seeks greater economic self-sufficiency. A "cooperative approach" to development has been adopted which is based in part on traditional values, in part on contemporary socialist thought, and in part on the strong intellectual and charismatic leadership of President Nyerere. Self-reliance through rural reform is the major thrust.

Resource Limitations

Although Tanzania is a tropical country, rainfall totals are remarkably low, and variability is high (Fig. 24-2). A broad belt stretching from northeast to southwest across the heart of the country has less than 20 in. (500 mm) of annual rainfall, and only on the highest topographic prominences are totals over 70 in. (1780 mm) recorded. Only one-fifth of the area can expect (with 90 percent probability) more than 30 in. (762 mm) of rainfall in a given year, and less than 5 percent can expect over 50 in. (1270 mm). Even where the annual rainfall is higher, it may come during a relatively short wet season, limiting cultivation and rendering pastoralism a very precarious business during the dry season. An associated feature of the highly concentrated rainfall is its arrival in intense storms, leading to excessive run off and erosion. The high temperatures and great amount of evaporation further limit the usefulness of the precipitation.

The best-watered areas lie spread about the dry heart of the country and include the coastal belt, the Kilimanjaro and Meru slopes and surroundings, the Lake Victoria region, the western section beyond Tabora, the Southern Highlands (around Lake Malawi), and the belt extending from there northeast to Morogoro. In total, however, perhaps about one-fifth of the country may be described as adequately watered. Tanzania, which forms part of the divide between three of Africa's greatest rivers (the Zambezi to the Indian Ocean in the south, the Nile to the Mediterranean Sea in the north, and the Zaire to the Atlantic Ocean in the west), does not itself possess any such large watercourses. Indeed, the central part of the country has two major basins of internal drainage (Lake Rukwa in the south and the Rift Valley trough in the north), so that the local drainage systems are of but minor significance on a continental scale. The eastern part is drained largely by the Rufiji River and its tributaries, and, in the west, the Malagarasi River follows a brief course ino Lake Tanganyika. Many streams are ephemeral or intermittent and are of no permanent value, so that during the dry season people often have to undertake long treks to obtain water. The Rufiji, which drains to the Indian Ocean, has major potential for irrigation and hydroelectric power development, while the Pangani to the north already supplies energy to Arusha, Moshi, Tanga, and Dar es Salaam.

Soil is another important resource, yet much remains to be learned concerning the country's pedology. Soil analysis and mapping are slow and expensive, and except in the important agricultural areas, the soils are known only in general terms. It is clear, however, that the most fertile are the reddish-brown soils derived from volcanic materials in the highlands of the north (Kilimanjaro, Meru), and the south and southwest (around the north end of Lake Malawi). Good soils, although variable in certain qualities, also are found in the alluvial valleys

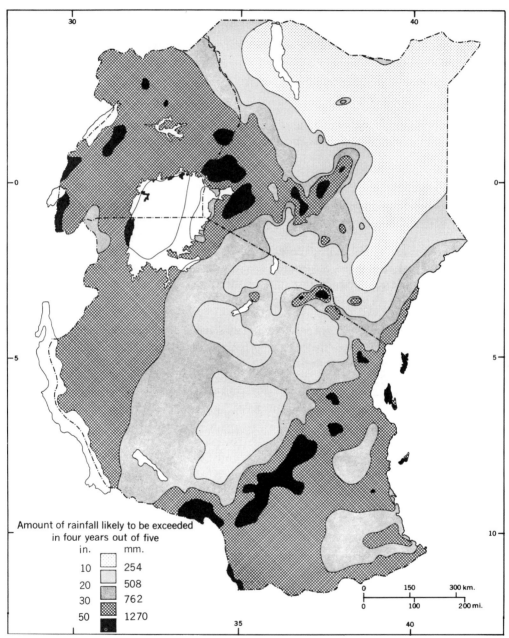

FIGURE 24-2 *East Africa. Annual rainfall probability (after E. W. Russell (ed.)*, The Natural Resources of East Africa, *1962*).

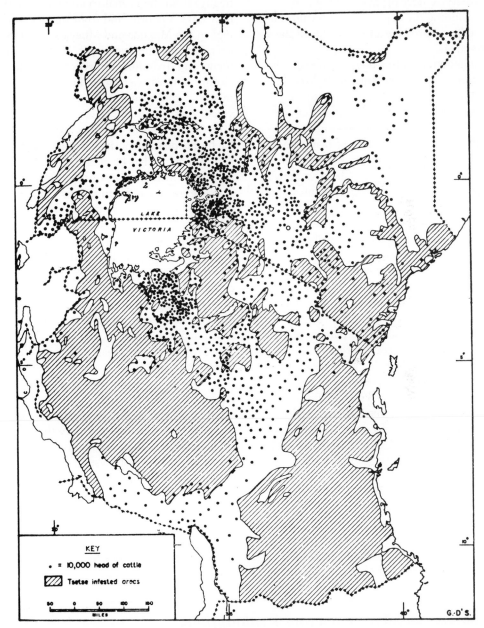

FIGURE 24-3 *East Africa. Cattle population and tsetse fly infestation.*
W. T. W. Morgan (ed.). East Africa: Its Peoples and Resources. *Nairobi: Oxford*
University Press, 1969.

where they await irrigation (Berry, 1972). The remainder of the country is largely covered by the familiar, deep-weathered, reddish soils that develop on the crystallines of the African plateau, with their limited carrying capacity. Under proper farming practices, including the application of fertilizers, these soils can produce annual yields in the moister areas.

Although Tanzania does not possess the dense forests of lowland equatorial Africa, over two-thirds of the country lies under bush, parkland savanna, and patches of denser scrub. The natural vegetation has been affected by the activities of man, the original growth having been replaced over wide areas by a tree-poor grassland savanna. Well over half the country remains infested by the dreaded tsetse fly (Fig. 24-3), which thrives under the prevalent conditions and limits human occupation; only small parts of the country are free from malaria.

Mineral deposits are widely distributed over Tanzania, but few are of economic significance. Since independence, mining has generally accounted for less than 3 percent of the GDP and about 5 to 10 percent of all exports. There is no area where minerals lie juxtaposed with a region of agricultural importance, the whole supporting an urban-industrial core; there is no Witwatersrand, Copperbelt, or Shaba, nor is there a highland core such as that of Kenya. Rather, mineral development has been isolated, with most production coming from peripheral regions (Fig. 24-4). The single most important deposit is that of diamonds from Shinyanga, where a kimberlite pipe, similar to those of South Africa and Botswana, was discovered in 1940, and production began soon after. Production reached a peak in 1967 (988,000 carats), when diamond sales comprised nearly 90 percent of total mineral sales, and diamonds were Tanzania's third most important export after coffee and sisal.

Until the mid-1960s, gold was mined in substantial quantities (up to 500,000 gm annually) from the Kiabakari and Geita fields near Lake Victoria, and from smaller workings in the Mpanda and Mbeya areas. However, high production costs, obsolete equipment, and dwindling reserves forced the closure of most operations, but with the rise in world gold prices, production may be revived. Salt is now the second most valuable mineral export, but revenues are very small. Rich phosphate deposits occur at Minjingu, and pyrochlore has been discovered at Mbeya. Substantial deposits of high grade iron ore, noncoking bituminous coal, and limestone are located in the Ruhuhu Valley and associated highlands north of Lake Malawi where there is also a great potential for hydroelectric power. Before the Tan-Zam Railway was completed, these resources were considered too remote to be exploited. Now they are being developed, and a 500,000 tons capacity integrated iron and steel plant is scheduled to be in production there by 1980. The project is being financed by an interest-free loan from China.

Overall, Tanzania's natural resources, especially those required by industry and for export markets, are limited in quality, quantity, and by accessibility. Before they can contribute more to the economy, improvements to the transport system must be made, capital and markets must be found, and certain skills and technology be developed. Of fundamental importance, given the nature of Tanzania's present agrarian economy and development program, is the paucity of its soils and water.

Colonial Achievements and Exploitations

The Tanzanian space economy has developed in several distinct phases and under different *raisons d'être*. Prior to 1884, the region's main contact with the outside world was through Arab trading and slave-raiding caravans entering from Bagamoyo, but except for the first efforts to build some coastal stations (including the settlement of Dar es Salaam), nothing was done by the Arabs to introduce any effective form of territorial organization.

The 30 years after 1884 mark the German period of occupation, and several of the tangible assets of Tanganyika were created during this time. Having initially used the settlement at Bagamoyo as the administrative headquarters, the Germans shifted the capital to Dar es Salaam and began to develop the site. Karl Peters, founder of the German Colonization Society and Governor of German East Africa, recognized the need for railway links with the interior, in the interests of both effective control over the rebellious African population and economic development. Thus, the railroad from Dar es Salaam to Kigoma was completed as early as 1914, having been begun in 1905. The line to Moshi, begun in 1893 (the first railroad to be laid in a German colony), was completed by 1911.

The first German settlements were on the coast, but the Tanga-Moshi railroad opened progressively distant areas for agriculture, and it was thought that the railroad to the great lakes would capture trade in that region. It was a miscalculation, the only sizeable volume of such trade coming during a brief period of early exploitation in Katanga.

In addition to their work on the transportation system, the Germans, as in Cameroon, did much research in the field of agriculture. Unlike Cameroon, however, there was virtually no effort to stimulate African interest in cash cropping. The Germans established European-owned plantations and introduced, among other crops, sisal (which became the country's leading export product), coffee, cotton, and tea. The plantations were situated on alienated land near the railroads in the hinterlands of Tanga and Dar es Salaam, but the period of expansion under German rule was too brief for the vol-

ume of exports to attain significance. The real contribution of the Germans was the successful introduction of several crops which in the future were to become mainstays of development.

World War I terminated German rule, and Tanganyika became British under the mandate system of the League of Nations. Britain encouraged African participation in cash-cropping despite objections from local white farmers. The Chagga people of the slopes of Mount Kilimanjaro responded to Britain's inducements, planting coffee as a cash crop where formerly only subsistence crops had grown. The Kilimanjaro Native Planters Association was formed, and crops were sold communally. As production attained significance, white planters, from whose estates the coffee trees had spread to the Chagga, expressed concern over the competition that would result and the dangers of inferior quality crops and inadequate protection from disease. Eventually, however, the region was to become an outstanding example of interracial cooperation among farmers, occasional friction notwithstanding.

By the outbreak of World War II, the colonial economic system was firmly entrenched. First, against much local resistance, administrative control had been established through the expropriation of land, imposition of taxes, maintenance of low wages, construction of roads and railways from strategic control centers on the coast, and the strict enforcement of British colonial values. Second, capitalist modes of production under the direct control of a colonial elite had been established through the introduction of plantations, essential processing industries, and monopolistic trading companies. Third, traditional economies had been reduced to dependent economies dominated by the more capital intensive, export-oriented, colonial economy. African labor had been drawn away from the production of staple subsistence crops to work in the money economies of the mines, plantations,

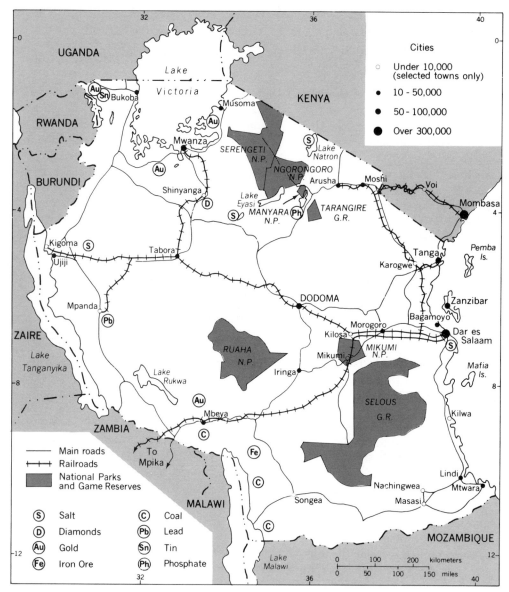

FIGURE 24-4 *Tanzania. Towns, transport, and resources.*

towns, and cities, so that food shortages occurred, indigenous values and means of production were destroyed, and the spillover effects from the cores to the peripheries were marginal.

Dar es Salaam, the capital, had developed into the primate city through the agglomeration of British capital and adminis-

trative services and needs, and the concentration of human and capital resources drained from the rest of the colony. Its railways to Kigoma, Mwanza, and Arusha carried cotton, coffee, tea, pyrethrum, tobacco, and other crops grown on European estates and African lands for foreign markets. In the immediate vicinity of Dar es

Sisal fibres drying in the sun near Tanga. The fibres are extracted from the leaves, dried, and then made into rope, gunnysack, and rough clothing. (UN)

Salaam itself, extensive sisal and coconut plantation had been established, and smaller acreages of cashew nuts, soya beans, and rice were in production (Fig. 24-5). Further north, Tanga had developed into an important port serving the richly productive slopes of Mounts Kilimanjaro and Meru, and its immediate hinterland that accounted for much of the colony's sisal output. Zanzibar, a protectorate separate from the mainland, and not united with it politically until 1964, was already the world's largest producer of cloves and an exporter of spices.

Around the shores of Lake Victoria, commercial agriculture, especially cotton production, was largely in African hands. But considerable acreages of once-productive land were destroyed through poor farming methods, lack of adequate equipment and capital, limited economic incentives, poor

managerial ability, and the practice common to so many areas of Africa, overgrazing. Cash-cropping spread southward as the lakeshore lands deteriorated, and in the process more and more Africans were drawn into the colonial economy. There, as elsewhere, the extension of roads was structured to serve external rather than internal markets, and the towns of Mwanza, Musoma, and Shinyanga became control centers in this framework.

In the extreme southeast, Mtwara became the port for the disastrous groundnuts scheme (box item) in the late 1940s, and for a while part of a secondary core region that functioned independently of Dar es Salaam. Elsewhere, the exploitative core-periphery structure focused on mining mica near Morogoro, diamonds at Shinyanga, lead and gold at Mpanda, tin at Karagwe, and salt at

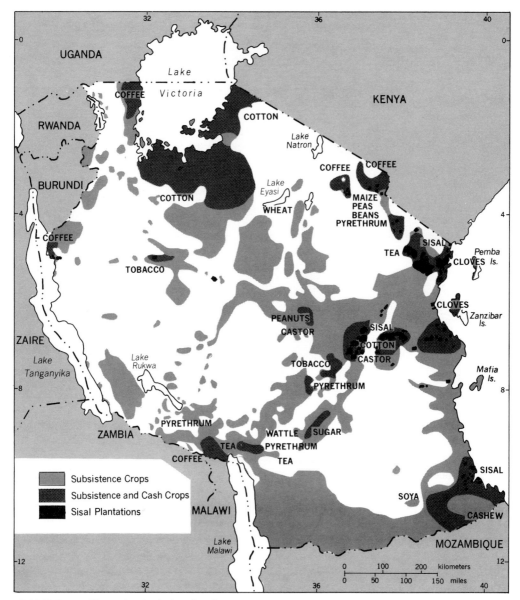

FIGURE 24-5 *Tanzania. Agricultural regions.*

Nyanza. Thus the colonial economy, in a spatial sense, was peripheral as many of these agricultural and mining areas lay on or near the boundaries of this huge, compact territory, and they presented major problems to development and administration.

Socialist Principles and Priorities

During the colonial era, the capitalist economy was geared toward the exploitation of the territory's people and resources for the profit of British investors. Very little expen-

The East African Groundnut Scheme

The ill-fated East African Groundnut Scheme illustrates the problems of attempting large-scale commercial agriculture in a tropical environment without adequate pilot testing, and proper understanding of the region's human and environmental potentials and limitations. Following World War II, Britain's margarine, food, and industrial oils were in short supply, so Britain decided to invest heavily in a vast groundnut-producing scheme in East Africa, mainly in southern Tanzania. The plan called for the eventual clearing of about 2.4 million acres (972,000 ha) in Tanzania alone, and another 810,000 acres (328,000 ha) in Kenya and Zambia. The expenditure was unlike anything ever before experienced in East Africa (estimated at $70 million), and the expectations were unrealistic: the south would be transformed into a thriving agricultural-industrial region within a matter of years, and thousands of Africans would be brought into the modern sector of the economy.

After only superficial surveys of the soil, moisture conditions, traditional farm practices, and labor conditions, British engineers cleared thousands of acres of dense bush with secondhand bulldozing machinery, including tanks made obsolete during World War II. The port of Mtwara was improved, and a railway was started toward Nachingwea. But the soils of the region soon became leached of their nutrients, packed by the heavy equipment, and baked by the overhead sun. There was widespread labor unrest, serious breakdowns of machinery, and general mismanagement of operations. The first crop was minimal compared with what had been expected, and as early as 1949 it had become clear that the region was not suited to the type of agriculture being imposed on it. The funds supporting the scheme were nearly exhausted, and the entire project had to be revised several times before being officially abandoned in 1951. Today, small quantities of cashew nuts, sisal, grains and even some groundnuts, are produced on these lands, but southern Tanzania is not the rich agricultural region it was intended to be.

diture of time, effort, and money was given to improving the welfare of the African; and little understanding of, and respect for, their traditional ways of life was shown. In reaction to these economic, social, and political realities, Tanzanian leadership and various political organizations, especially the Tanzania African National Union (TANU), has, over the years, formulated a unique program of development that is based on traditional values and contemporary socialist thought. The principal architect of this special brand of African socialism has been President Julius Nyerere.

In the years immediately following independence (1961), Nyerere issued several statements on the strengths of traditional African values, the spirit of cooperation built around the extended family as the basis of socialism, the need for greater self-reliance and egalitarianism, and the urgent need for rural reform. The most important of these ideas were stated in a document known as the Arusha Declaration (1967), later to be amplified in a series of papers authored by the president. The Declaration was a TANU party statement of intent to build socialism in Tanzania with a view to promoting self-reliance, rural development, and good leadership.

In the words of Nyerere, Tanzania is committed "to build a society in which members have equal rights and equal opportunities; in which all can live at peace with their neighbours without suffering or imposing injustice, being exploited, or exploiting; and in which all have a gradually increasing basic level of material welfare before any individual lives in luxury." (Nyerere, 1968). To create this kind of society, he advocated building upon the basic principles of *ujamaa*, literally "familyhood" (in Swahili). These are the respect of others, sharing of basic goods, and the obligation to work. To these, which characterized the way of life in Tanzania long before the colonial intrusion, must be added the instruments necessary to defeat poverty and hunger that existed in traditional African society. In other words,

shortcomings of the traditional systems had to be corrected, and new inputs from the more technologically developed societies had to be added.

In contemporary Tanzania, land and labor, not money, are considered Tanzania's major assets; foreign domination in industry, technical assistance, and employment are being replaced by Tanzanian-owned concerns; commercial banks and other financial institutions are nationalized; education is being reorganized to serve the masses not just an elite; exploitation of the countryside by the small urban sector is being checked; government spending encourages rural development rather than urban-industrialization; and rural development stems from community *ujamaa* villages not through large foreign-owned, or even large domestically owned estates and plantations.

Ujamaa Villagization and Rural Development

Once the Tanzanian government had stated its intent to reduce its dependence on external sources of development, self-reliance was an automatic corollary; and since Tanzanian society is overwhelmingly rural, self-reliance must be rurally based. Hence the Arusha Declaration's emphasis upon rural reform. But collective living, village resettlement, and rural reform predated the Arusha Declaration by several years. In the first Five-Year Development Plan (1964–1969), two approaches to rural development were outlined, and one was adopted. Development could be achieved through the gradual "improvement" of agricultural methods using existing extension services and without resettlement, or by the "transformation" of production methods through the concentration of investment and trained manpower in a few selected areas. The latter method was adopted.

The plan called for the establishment of 74 village settlements, each composed of 250

families, who were to be removed from high-density areas such as Kilimanjaro, the Pare and Usambara Mountains, and the Southern Highlands, and resettled in less-populated areas with presumed agricultural potential. Each settlement was to grow one major cash crop using new methods, fertilizers, and a high degree of mechanization. It was hoped these settlements would stimulate neighboring farmers to improve their methods of production, and industrialization would follow. By the end of 1965, 22 pilot schemes had been established, but it soon became clear that failure was inevitable. Most schemes were overcapitalized, mechanization proved to be uneconomic, planning was inadequate, and there was too much central government participation in the operations and far too little enthusiasm and involvement on the part of the peasants (Berry, 1972). Recognizing these shortcomings, the government modified its approach and gradually phased out the program.

Mount Kilimanjaro, Tanzania. The lower slopes of Africa's highest mountain are planted to coffee, bananas and other cash crops. Most of the farms belong to the Chagga who have resisted ujamaa *villagization.* (Alan C. G. Best)

Since then, the principal method to socialize agriculture and increase domestic farm production has come through the growth of *ujamaa* villages, the rationale of which was outlined in Nyerere's *Socialism and Rural Development*, (1968). Farming is done on communally owned land by those who live and work as a community. The peasants live together in a village, farm together, market together, and undertake the provisions of local services and small local requirements, such as boreholes and water storage. Farm equipment, livestock, storage sheds, and other units of production belong to the village. Strongly individualistic and competitive attitudes, fostered under colonial capitalism, and present in most rural areas, are suppressed. Decisions are reached collectively, and each village operates on the basis that it is economically independent (Omari, 1974). In theory, each village is al-lowed to develop according to the social customs and experiences of its people, and according to local environmental and economic conditions. Thus a certain degree of local autonomy prevails, which is considered essential for the program's success.

In 1976 some 3 million Tanzanians (18 percent of the total) lived in over 7000 *ujamaa* villages. Voluntary resettlement has been slow, except in the poorer, more arid regions, where wells, power, seed, and livestock, provided by the central government, were major incentives. Villagization was intended to be voluntary, for, in the words of Nyerere, "Viable socialist communities can only be established with willing members; the tasks of leadership and of government is not to try and force this kind of development, but to explain, encourage and participate." (Nyerere, 1968).

However, since 1974, resettlement has

become compulsory in several densely populated areas in Mara, Mwanza, Kigoma, and Shinyanga, and in the Ufipa, Iranga, and coastal regions. There the population has been resettled in "development villages," whose economic base is not necessarily farming. Indeed, little thought would appear to have been given to the new means of livelihood, and the system is reminiscent of the resettlement schemes in South Africa. The villages are uniformly planned, the houses being laid out in rows along roads and around schools and administrative offices, frequently, however, without adequate water, sewerage, or power facilities. The cooperative spirit is absent. Such regrouping makes the provision of schools, clinics, and other social services cheaper, but the program lacks all socialist content and may breed resistance to future government programs. Without more careful planning, forced villagization could be counterproductive. The widespread food shortages and near famine conditions in many rural areas in 1974 have been attributed to these rural upheavals. Greatest resistance to *ujamaa* villagization has come from the Chagga coffee farmers who live on the slopes of Mount Kilimanjaro. They are the most prosperous and well-educated group in Tanzania, and have threatened to destroy their lucrative estates rather than be wrested from their traditional homes and farms and placed into communal villages by outsiders.

Street scene, Zanzibar Town. Once a thriving slave market and subsequently the world's major clove producer, Zanzibar is an important port for coastal traffic in East Africa. (UN)

Industrial Potentials and Problems

Tanzania's industrial potentials and problems must be seen in the context of the country's colonial past, and the prevailing socialist philosophy. Colonialism did not lend itself to manufacturing for internal markets, nor to the creation of towns and cities, other than the capital, a few ports, and essential administrative centers. These towns were first and foremost geared to meet the needs of the metropole, not Tanzania. Resources produced were for export and shipped in their raw state, not converted into manufactured goods for internal markets. The transport network reflects this orientation; it is woefully deficient in links between regions (Fig. 24-4).

Manufacturing accounts for only 11 percent of the GDP, but has been growing consistently since 1970 at between 10 and 15 percent per year. Food processing, together with the beverage, textile, and cigarette industries, dominate the manufacturing sector. Current priorities, like those of most African states, include greater outputs of refined oil (from imported crude oil), cement, fertilizer, paper products, metal goods, and chemicals, all from industries that are capital- rather than labor-intensive. Foreign participation is

Zanzibar

Zanzibar, united with Tanganyika since April 1964 in the United Republic of Tanzania, comprises two islands—Zanzibar and Pemba. The islands are inhabited by a great variety of people of whom the Shirazis form the majority. The Arab, Asian, Somali, and European minorities (possibly 60,000 out of 430,000) have traditionally dominated commerce and trade. For centuries, Zanzibar was an Arab stronghold whose domain extended onto the African mainland. Until it became a British protectorate (1890), Zanzibar had been a center of a large and prosperous slave trade, and an entrepôt for much of East Africa. However, as the mainland economies developed under German and British rule, and the ports of Dar es Salaam, Mombasa, and Tanga prospered, Zanzibar's commercial functions and hinterland decreased. Although only 25 mi (40 km) from the mainland, Zanzibar's economic links with Tanganyika are weak.

Zanzibar's economy today is dominated by cloves, the islands accounting for about 80 percent of the world's output. Pemba has most of the clove trees, but Zanzibar Town is the chief processing, marketing, and distribution center. Two-thirds of the cloves and their extracts are exported to southeast Asia (especially Indonesia), the rest goes mainly to Europe and America. The industry has long been threatened by disease, tropical storms, fluctuating world prices, and in the last few years by synthetic substitutes for oil extracts. Coconuts, coconut oil, copra, ropes and matting are also exported, but further economic diversification is required. The islands could produce a great variety of tropical crops for both local and mainland markets.

With its mixture of peoples and cultures, fascinating history, open air markets, and its own special urban landscape, Zanzibar Town has a great tourist potential. However, the government has restricted visitors (especially since the uprisings of 1964) and has done little to promote tourism.

still important. In fact, since the government's pronouncements on self-reliance, foreign finance has actually increased, but the source has changed. Tanzania now has closer economic ties with the People's Republic of China, the Federal Republic of Germany, and Japan, and weaker ties with Britain, although Britain remains Tanzania's leading export market.

Industrial activity is concentrated in Dar es Salaam (440,000), for reasons common to most African capitals. Its main industries include oil refining, food processing, cigarette manufacturing, and others geared for local and national consumption. Most importantly, it handles Zambian copper exports. Industrial and population growth quickened there in the early 1970s as a result of real and perceived opportunities stemming from the construction of the Tan-Zam Railway. Indeed, immigration increased to alarming proportions before influx-control measures were adopted. To control this growth still further, and to lessen the regional inequalities of industrial output, the government instituted a policy of industrial decentralization. For the period 1970–1975, some 81 percent of planned industrial invest-

The central business district and harbor, Dar es Salaam, Tanzania's primate city and terminus of the Tan-Zam Railway. (Tanzania Information Services)

ment, and 76 percent of planned employment was scheduled for places other than the capital.

Industrial decentralization is a logical and necessary part of Tanzania's program of self-reliance. If fewer industrial goods are to be imported, but increasing demands are to be met without great expenditures on transport, industry should be located, wherever possible, close to markets. But much of the market is rural and inadequately served by road and rail, which present problems to the country's industrial planners. The problems are not only where to encourage industry and to concentrate investment but also what types of industry should and could be established. Industries with strong forward and backward linkages, such as petrochemicals, heavy engineering, and vehicular man-

ufacture, while theoretically desirable, are quite unrealistic except in one or two places, such as Dar es Salaam and Tanga, certainly not in the smaller and more peripheral towns. Industries more likely to appear are those utilizing local resources; but textile plants, fruit and vegetable canneries, and other such establishments, cannot provide the motive force necessary for rapid industrialization at a national level. Furthermore, industrialization should be integrated (at both the regional and national level) with the villagization program.

The principal industrial growth points in the decentralization scheme are Tanga, Arusha, and Dodoma. Tanga (70,000) is Tanzania's second largest port and an important outlet for the agriculturally prosperous Mount Kilimanjaro region including Arusha

Scene in Ngorongoro Crater, Tanzania. Tanzania has several world-famous game reserves and national parks (Serengeti, Ngorongoro, Manyara, Selous), tourism being one of the country's leading industries. (Alan C. G. Best)

(60,000). Among its industries are rope making, textiles, and food processing, but these and others have suffered from the strong competition of Mombasa located across the border in Kenya, and with which the Kilimanjaro region is linked by rail. Dodoma (30,000), Tanzania's new capital, lies about 300 mi (480 km) west of Dar es Salaam (Fig. 24-4). It is situated in a sparsely populated agricultural region and is connected by road and rail with several other designated growth points together with Dar es Salaam. The government hopes it will provide both industrial and ideological stimulus to what is now an underdeveloped region. As such, Dodoma has several parallels with Lilongwe and Gaborone. The recently completed Tan-Zam Railway could play an important role in the decentralization scheme. It provides a new development corridor across the central and western regions and serves several resource regions and towns such as Iringa, Mbeya, and the Kipengere Range, where coal and iron ore are to be developed by China.

Tourism and the Future

Among Tanzania's greatest assets are the magnificent game reserves, national parks, and scenic attractions. From Mount Kilimanjaro in the east to Lake Victoria in the west lies a zone of incomparable scenery and wildlife. The Serengeti and Selous wildlife sanctuaries, Mounts Kilimanjaro and Meru, the Ngorongoro Crater, Lake Manyara, and the coastal regions of the lakes and Indian Ocean, all rank among Africa's finest tourist attractions. The tourist trade is growing (over 100,000 overseas visitors), but Tanzania is not favorably located with reference to the main lines of communication. Nairobi

The Tan-Zam Railway

The arch-colonist Cecil Rhodes once envisaged a Cape-to-Cairo railway that would consolidate British interests throughout the length of Africa and traverse present-day Tanzania and Zambia. But for many political and economic reasons that imperial dream was never realized. In the early 1960s, however, Presidents Kaunda of Zambia and Nyerere of Tanzania, became interested in a railway link between their two countries that would provide landlocked Zambia with an alternative route to the sea that skirted then white-controlled Southern Africa: Rhodesia, South Africa, Angola, and Mozambique. Several feasibility studies were conducted and requests for financial aid were submitted to Britain, the United States, the Soviet Union, France, West Germany, Canada, the African Development Bank, and the World Bank. The project was rejected as being uneconomic. Tanzania and Zambia then turned to the People's Republic of China.

After brief studies of the Tanzanian section of the proposed line, a tripartite agreement between Tanzania, Zambia, and China was signed in Peking in 1967, under which the Chinese agreed to finance and build the railway from Dar es Salaam to the Zambian Copperbelt town of Kapiri-Mposhi. Known as the Tan-Zam Railway—or as the *Uhuru* (Freedom) Railway in East Africa—and built at an estimated cost of $400 million, the line represents China's largest aid project in the Third World, and the third most costly in Africa, after the Aswan and Volta Dams (Graham, 1974). Construction began in April 1970, and the 1100 mi (1770 km) line was completed in late 1975. Up to 15,000 Chinese and 45,000 African workers were engaged on the project during the peak construction period; at that time this represented 20 percent of Tanzania's labor force in paid employment.

The railway is being financed with an interest-free loan, repayable over a period of 30 years from 1983. Approximately 70 percent of the cost is for the Tanzanian section, mainly because of its greater length and more difficult terrain, but the two countries will share equally in the repayment. Local costs, mainly for labor and materials, are being met by a commodity credit arrangement, whereby Chinese products, such as clothing and household utensils, are purchased.

Although built primarily for political reasons, the Tan-Zam Railway will assist economic development in both Tanzania and Zambia. In Tanzania, the railway traverses rice and sugar estates in the Kilombero Valley and the Southern Highlands, where tea, coffee, pyrethrum, wheat, maize and cattle have great potential. Up to 1 million acres (405,000 ha) of wheat could be grown on the Ufipa Plateau west of Mbeya. Rail spurs are to be built by China to the rich coal and iron deposits in the Southern Highlands which will lead to a new integrated iron and steel complex. For Zambia, the railway means a securer outlet for its copper, possible new agricultural and forestry development in the northeast, and easier access to oil and other imports.

has a far more frequented airport than Dar es Salaam, and internal communications, as well as hotels and other facilities, are better elsewhere in East Africa. Many tourist trips to Tanzania's game reserves begin and end in Nairobi, hence Tanzania has not reaped the maximum possible returns from these assets. But the Tanzania Tourist Corporation, which owns most of the country's international-standard hotels, is upgrading its facilities and expects a 20 percent per year growth rate in tourism over the next five years. Tourism has become one of Tanzania's major sources of foreign revenues.

Despite efforts to industrialize, to diversify its economy, and to become more self-reliant, it would seem that Tanzania, for many years, will remain predominantly agricultural and dependent on external markets for its coffee, cotton, sisal, and other cash crops. It will differ from Zaire, Nigeria, and others in the emphasis given to industry and to the means of production. Its strong economic and ideological ties with the People's Republic of China and its commitment to the eradication of poverty and ignorance, distinguish Tanzania from other African states. Nyerere's experiment in socialism has provided the country with a measure of political and economic stability rare in Africa, and this is a major achievement.

Bibliography

Arrighi, G., and J. Saul (eds.). *Essays on the Political Economy of Africa*. New York: Monthly Review Press, 1973.

Bailey, M. "Tanzania and China," *African Affairs*, Vol. 74, No. 294 (January, 1975), pp. 39–49.

Berry, L. (ed.). *Tanzania in Maps*. New York: Africana Publishing Corporation, 1972.

Brooke, C. "Types of Food Shortages in Tanzania," *Geographical Review*. Vol. 57, (1967), pp. 333–357.

Cliffe, L., and J. Saul, *Socialism in Tanzania*. 2 vols. Dar es Salaam: East African Publishing House, 1973.

de Blij, H. J. *Dar es Salaam: A Study in Urban Geography*. Evanston: Northwestern University Press, 1963.

Graham, J. D. "The Tanzam Railway," *Africa Today*. Vol. 21, No. 3 (1974), pp. 27–41.

Hatch, J. *Tanzania: A Profile*. New York: Praeger, 1972.

Knight, G. C. *Ecology and Change: Rural Modernization in an African Community*. New York: Academic Press, 1974.

Luttrell, W. L. "Locational Planning and Regional Development in Tanzania," in *Towards Socialist Planning*. Dar es Salaam: Tanzania Publishing House, 1972.

Newman, J. L. "Hazards, Adjustments, and Innovation in Central Tanzania," *Rural Africana*, No. 19 (Winter, 1973), pp. 4–19.

Nyerere, J. K. *Socialism and Rural Development*. Dar es Salaam: Government Printer, 1967.

Nyerere, J. K. *Freedom and Socialism*. Dar es Salaam: Oxford University Press, 1968.

Nyerere, J. K. "From Uhuru to Ujamaa," *Africa Today*, Vol. 21, No. 3 (1974), pp. 3–8.

Omari, C. K. "Tanzania's Emerging Rural Development Policy," *Africa Today*, Vol. 21, No. 3 (1974), pp. 9–14.

Simko, R. A. "Tanzania: Experiment in Cooperative Effort," *Focus*, Vol. 24, No. 5 (January, 1974), pp. 1–8.

TWENTY-FIVE

South of turbulent Ethiopia, east of tense and recently aggressive Uganda, and north of war-involved Tanzania lies Kenya, East Africa's heartland. A revolution brought Kenya independence; the leader who was thrust into national prominence during that period, Jomo Kenyatta, headed a government that has been stable and conservative for more than a dozen years. That stability and conservatism brought Kenya substantial progress and comparative prosperity, but it also generated criticism among other African countries more strongly committed to socialist objectives. Throughout Kenyatta's tenure in office, the country's development issues have focused on land-ownership and land reform. Indeed, for a very long time, land has figured prominently in Kenya's domestic politics.

Territorial Definition

A geometric boundary was drawn to separate German East Africa from a territory known until 1920 as the British East Africa Protectorate. It was delimited from Lake Victoria along the northern slopes of Mount Kilimanjaro, and on to the coast. Although the product of convenient agreement rather than a carefully considered adjustment to local conditions, as is true of so many other African boundaries, this line ran through dry, relatively empty lands. The people to be affected were the nomadic Masai cattle herders of the region.

One consequence of the definition of the German-British boundary in East Africa was the channeling of British penetration toward the Lake (Victoria) Region. What remained of the British sphere of influence in

KENYA:
THE
PROBLEM
OF
LAND

East Africa included only one port, Mombasa. Like the Germans, the British recognized that effective communications with the hinterland were a prime requirement for effective government and economic progress, and railroad construction from Mombasa toward the densely populated Lake Region began in 1895. This was nearly a decade earlier than the Germans' first steps in connecting Dar es Salaam with the interior by rail.

Although the Germans and the British had agreed on the location of the border between their respective claims between Lake Victoria and the coast, the hinterland around and beyond Lake Victoria remained in dispute. In 1888, the British East Africa Company was created, which campaigned in Britain to rouse government and public interest in spreading British influence in this part of Africa. The officials of this company realized that the kingdom of the Baganda people, along the northwestern shores of Lake Victoria, was likely to play a leading role in a developing East Africa. In 1893, largely due to the efforts of the company, Uganda—of which the Baganda Kingdom forms a part—became a part of the British sphere of influence. For years, the claim made by Peters to this region for Germany had been disputed, and the abrupt termination of the role played by Emin Pasha against the spread of British influence led to German recognition of British hegemony in Buganda.

Having thus secured the entire northern Lake Region, the British, less troubled than the Germans by rebellions, began to exercise control. The railroad begun at Mombasa reached the first of several escarpments in 1900, and a number of railway workshops were built where the city of Nairobi stands today. The British East Africa Company, unlike the British South Africa Company and the Royal Niger Company, did not thrive as a result of mineral concessions and agricultural development. Burdened with administrative functions London was reluctant to take over, and hampered by a lack of direction in policy, the company was in frequent financial difficulties. Eventually, Britain assumed the responsibilities of a protectorate over the entire territory first opened by the company, including also Zanzibar and Uganda.

The Kenya Highlands

East of Lake Victoria the British East African domain included much land which could at best be described as steppe. In general terms, only the southwestern quarter of the territory could be considered an asset; the administration of the remainder was a liability.

The railroad which was under construction from Mombasa toward the Lake Region reached the steep ascent to the higher areas of the territory in 1900. The initial object was to connect Mombasa with Kisumu on Lake Victoria, an achievement which occurred in 1903. The railroad had been built in view of future potentialities rather than existing opportunities, and at the time it was completely uneconomic. Its contribution in opening up the country and eliminating slavery, disease, and poverty were among the factors leading to its construction, and British administrators sought means to reduce the drain upon the home exchequer.

Connecting Mombasa and Kisumu by the shortest possible route, the railroad crossed southwestern Kenya in its entirety, including the region which has come to be known as the Kenya Highlands (Fig. 25-1). This is Kenya's most diversified area, and tropical Africa's most extensive highland zone, as the bulk of it lies over 5000 ft (1500 m). The soils are among Africa's best, derived in large part from volcanic rocks. There are extensive areas of rather flat land, and the climate is cool and sufficiently moist

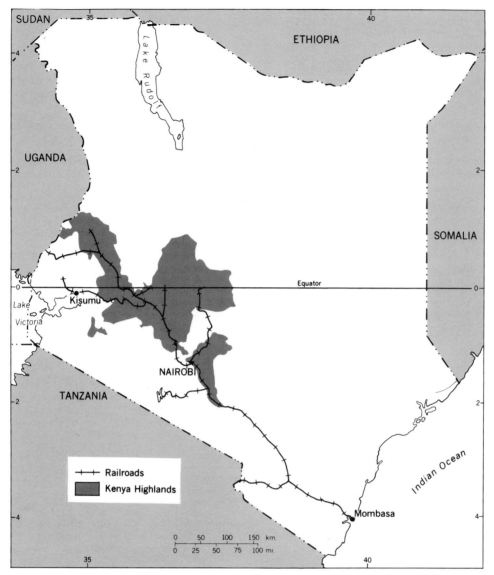

FIGURE 25-1 *The Kenya highlands.*

to permit specialized cropping. Depending somewhat upon the contour boundary selected, the Kenya Highlands cover some 60,000 sq mi (96,600 sq km). This includes several extremely high sections, such as the Aberdare Mountains and Mount Kenya, as well as the lower lands in the Eastern Rift Valley, whose floor nevertheless lies several thousand feet above sea level. Included also

are steep escarpments and dense forests, but in general the land is of excellent quality for intensive agriculture and large plantations.

None of this potential was evident when the railroad was being laid across the Highlands, which are divided into two sections by the Rift Valley. There was no dense African population on the fertile lands and, of course, there were no plantations.

The lands had been occupied by many people in the past, as subsequent research has proved, but they were vacated just at the time Charles Eliot, first Commissioner of British East Africa, saw them. Eliot envisaged a thriving European farming community in the Highlands, economic prosperity, civilization—and a paying railway. He advised the British government to encourage white immigration into the protectorate. The first few settlers arrived before the turn of the century, but white immigration into Kenya really began in 1902. Initially occupying the land around Nairobi, the white settlers soon commenced to penetrate other parts of the Highlands. With this, the seeds of friction had been sown, to reach fruition a half-century later.

Land and the Africans

In response to the concentration of Kenya's resources in the southwestern sector of the country, most of the people occupy this region. This was true in Kenya before the coming of the white settlers, as it has been true since their arrival. It was, however, not true at the exact moment in history marking the first organized penetration by Europeans, and Charles Eliot saw British East Africa in a unique condition: the majority of the African people had vacated the lands they normally occupied and cultivated.

Land was granted to the settlers under the Crown Lands Ordinance, which stipulated that land not in beneficial occupation at the time was at the disposal of the crown. Areas of sparse or haphazard cultivation might also be considered for settlement, as indeed they were. The area placed under European freehold or leasehold increased rapidly, in fact, out of all proportion to the growth of the number of whites. From the beginning, it must have been clear that the white settlers could never expect to farm the huge areas placed under their care. Eventually, no less than 16,700 sq mi (43,250 sq km) were thus alienated.

What had caused the African population to vacate the Highlands? The Kikuyu people, who occupied much of the land between the Aberdares, Mount Kenya, and the lands of the Masai to the south, had cleared much of the forest land for cultivation. Having displaced the Wanderobo hunters toward the end of the nineteenth century, the Ki-kuyu are said to have compensated the former with livestock for the lands they occupied. Prior to the arrival of the whites, the Kikuyu lived in an uneasy balance with their enemies, the raiding, cattle-herding, nomadic Masai and the Kamba (Fig. 25-2). In the south, some land may have been relatively empty because of the aggressiveness of the Masai, but these people were already declining in strength when the first whites penetrated there.

In 1898 and 1899, however, a sequence of events occurred which changed the situation drastically. In 1898, there was a great smallpox epidemic which ravaged the population, followed directly by an outbreak of rinderpest which decimated the livestock. Beginning during this period, an interminable drought persisted for many months, ruining the crops which might have saved many people, and while it was breaking, an unprecedented invasion of locusts followed. These four disasters reduced the African population of the region, and the survivors turned northward and fled back in the direction of Fort Hall. The general effect was the temporary depopulation of the eastern sector of the Highlands—and it was just at this time that the British commissioner first saw the lands as "empty."

The catastrophe also affected the Masai seriously and dealt them a series of blows from which these people never were fully to recover. It was through the lands of the Masai that the railroad was drawn before it

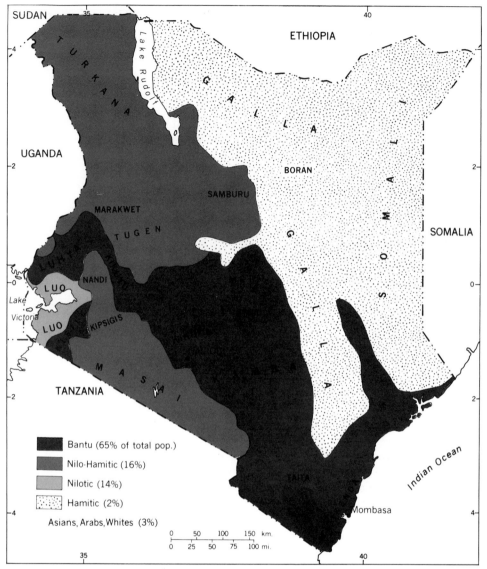

FIGURE 25-2 *Kenya. The major ethnic groups.*

reached the Highlands proper, and this was
an added problem for these beleaguered cattle herders. In 1904, the Masai were confined to two reserves, one to the south of the
line, and the other in Laikipia, which is to
the north. This move completely emptied
the Rift Valley from Naivasha to Nakuru, as
well as the lands east of Nairobi. In 1911,
the northern Masai reserve was closed, and
the people moved across the railroad to the
southern area, described as ample for their
needs in the official documents involved.
Just what the criteria were for the determination of the land requirements of a nomadic
pastoral people dependent upon the vagaries
of a variable climate never were made clear,
but the effects upon the Masai have been obvious.

Masai herders and cattle in southern Kenya. Pastoralism is the dominant economy in Kenya's sub-humid regions, and suffers from periodic drought, overgrazing, and traditional attitudes towards cattle ownership. (World Bank)

It is true, however, that the lands available to the various African peoples in the first decade of the present century were sufficient for their immediate needs, reduced as a result of their decimation. Of course, their confinement in demarcated areas did not immediately alter their methods of patch agriculture, and as time went on, the method began to reduce the capacity of the soil. Lands which were initially adequate eventually failed to provide the required yields, which the British administration ascribed to "wasteful and harmful methods" of African agriculture. Meanwhile, Africans who had left their section of the Highlands in 1899 began to return, either to overcrowd the lands set aside for African occupation or to find that the lands they left some years previous had been reserved for white occupation.

As the reserves became areas of severe population pressure, many Africans made their way to Nairobi and onto the European settlers' farms in search of wage labor. By 1912, 12,000 were thus engaged outside their home areas, in 1927, 152,000 and in 1939 as many as 200,000. As the number of settlers and their prosperity increased, Nairobi became the thriving center of a wealthy farming region. The town grew rapidly and attracted many unskilled laborers, for whom there were insufficient jobs and grossly inadequate housing. In contrast, there were less than 10,000 white settlers in the entire country in 1914, and under 30,000 in 1948. The white population of Kenya never exceeded 70,000.

Since the early 1920s, land has been the central issue in Kenya. After the end of World War I, when a number of Kikuyu returned from service in other parts of the world, political organization among the

Africans began to come about, and the oft-expressed aim was to effect a change in the government's land policies. Pressure rose, in response to which the Secretary of State for Colonies in 1932 appointed the Kenya Land Commission (Carter Commission). The task of this body was to investigate the needs of the African population in terms of land and to consider every claim made by the local inhabitants. As a result of its lengthy deliberations, some hundreds of square miles changed hands, but basic policies (such as the reservation of certain areas on the basis of skin color) were not altered.

When, after World War II, African veterans received a work permit whereas whites obtained land concessions, the land crisis entered its crucial stages. African grievances were rife. There had been restrictions upon African cultivation of certain cash crops such as coffee and tea, the argument being that good quality was to be maintained and that Africans would cause a deterioration of the level of Kenya exports. In addition, the whites did not especially want the competition of African farmers, and, finally, African land was best put to use under staple crops. These practices, and the differences between wage scales for Africans and non-Africans, unemployment in Nairobi, segregation practices, and the need (for Africans only) to carry an employment registration certificate created increasing tensions. The return to Kenya of Jomo Kenyatta late in 1946 was followed by much political and illegal activity, and the Mau Mau crisis broke in earnest in 1950. The "stolen lands" issue plunged Kenya into an abyss of division as the Africans initiated an unprecedented campaign of murder and destruction.

Underlying the entire matter was the contrast between the white and black man's approach to the ownership and use of Kenya's land. The Africans, and especially the Kikuyu, viewed land as the only real security, something sacred, eternally the possession of the people who once occupied it and depended upon it. Communally owned, the temporary abandonment of such land did not change the situation at all, and when the Kikuyu returned to find the lands of their people occupied by settlers it was, indeed, from their point of view, stolen. The whites, of course, applied European concepts of land ownership to the Highlands they found nearly empty: it was parceled out, purchased, fenced, and partly cultivated. Many African squatters were permitted to live on the unused portion of such land, but they were compelled to work 180 days a year for this right. Thus reduced to servitude by the fact of their existence on lands they considered theirs, the Africans within the Highlands reserved for white ownership had their grievance, as had those in the African reserves.

The traditional system of land tenure and land use of the Kikuyu is known as the *githaka* system. *Githaka* means land, and includes all land owned by *mbari*, an extended family or subclan, each member of which was entitled to cultivate part of the *githaka*. The plot, *ngundu*, could not be sold or leased without permission of the *mbari's* leaders, and on it the "owner" was free to grow whatever he chose, usually millet, maize, sweet potatoes, and beans. On the death of the "owner," the *ngundu* was passed from father to son. Part of each *githaka* was used for communal grazing, and the average *ngundu* was probably less than 4 acres (1.6 ha) (Taylor, 1969). Men were responsible for the raising and milking of livestock, breaking virgin land, and the care of certain crops. Women did most of the cultivating, and communal grazing of the whole *mbari* was supervised by one or two men. A strong sense of identity and belonging existed between the individual and his land.

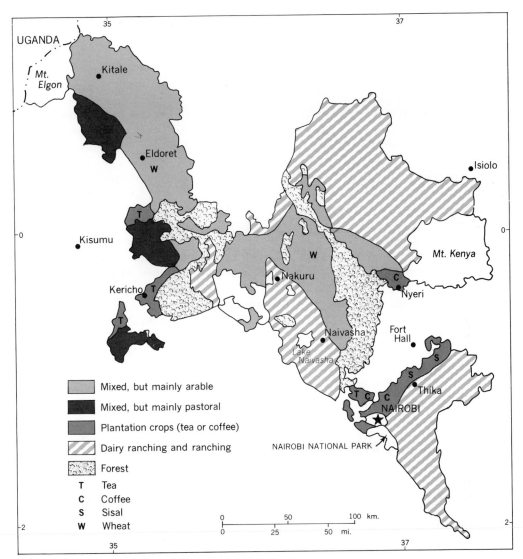

FIGURE 25-3 *Kenya. Land use in the Kenya Highlands.*

Land and the White Settler

At their maximum extent (excluding forest reserves), the Kenya Highlands comprised 11,571 sq mi (29,970 sq km), or about 5 percent of the Kenya total. Approximately 7 million acres (2.8 million ha) were divided among fewer than 4000 farms and estates which yielded more than 80 percent of Kenya's agricultural exports and much of its domestic requirements (McMaster, 1975).

Just before independence, these holdings provided employment for 6900 full- and part-time European workers and for almost 300,000 Africans (42 percent of the total wage labor force). They also contained about 1 million landless Africans. To the whites, land represented wealth, security and power, and was the personal property of those who farmed it. As the region developed through the infusion of capital and technology, the Highlands became the richest and most extensive white-controlled agricultural area in East Africa, and the economic heart of Kenya.

The white settlers introduced such crops as coffee (almost exclusively the *arabica* variety), tea, pyrethrum, sisal, and a host of cereals, vegetables, and fruits (Fig. 25-3). Whereas settlement by whites in Africa has been attracted mostly by mineral finds (Witwatersrand, Copperbelt, Shaba), Kenya's whites came to cultivate the soil, and in this respect the Kenya situation, from the large-scale point of view, was unique. The achievements of the settlers should not be underrated. Their number was never large (all of Kenya contains fewer whites than the Copperbelt), but their impact upon the country was at least as great. In the Highlands grew an agrarian economic core yielding such rich harvests that Kenya could develop in step with other parts of colonial Africa without a single mineral figuring significantly among the exports.

Although the European settlers brought progress in the spheres of education and health and built towns and a network of roads, they also planted the seeds of racial unrest. The landless majority was reduced to a state of servitude. Its population grew at an alarming rate, its geographic mobility was severely restricted, and the economic opportunities were limited. Demands for more land were made, but even had these been met, the problems of overpopulation would not have been solved. African leaders exploited the land issue, as it was bound to provoke strong reactions among the people, and the Mau Mau movement was born (1950). During the first two and a half years of the emergency, more than 10,000 people died (less than 100 were European), race relations were worse than ever before, and the economy was dealt an almost irreparable blow. But in 1953 a Royal Commission came to Kenya to study means of improvement, and in 1955 it reported that the policy of reserving land on the basis of race should be terminated.

Land Reform and Resettlement

The first phase of land reform began with the implementation of the Swynnerton Plan in 1955 (Odingo, 1971). The plan called for a change in African ownership from customary tenure to individual freehold. This meant the enclosure and registration of existing rights; the consolidation of land fragments; the introduction of lucrative cash crops, high-yielding livestock, and marketing facilities; access to agricultural credit; and the provision of rural water supplies and technical assistance. The plan aimed at providing Africans with the means to progress from subsistence agriculture to modern planned cash farming. Economic farming on a large number of fragmented parcels of land was clearly impossible, thus consolidation into freehold units was the cornerstone of the plan.

At first, many Africans treated the plan with suspicion. The Luo around the shores of Lake Victoria and the Abaluhya further north resisted all land reform efforts for six years, while soil erosion, poor farming methods, and increasing numbers impoverished them still further (Jones, 1965). However, in Kikuyuland, where land pressure was greatest, agricultural production rose by about 15 percent per year. By 1974, about 12 million acres (4.8 million ha) had been reorganized into over 650,000 individual holdings. Coffee, pyrethrum, pineapples, tea, and tobacco were introduced, and the quality of livestock was greatly improved. Vast areas of the Kenya Highlands were literally relandscaped, and new settlement patterns and areas of production emerged.

But the plan was not without its prob-

Intensive cultivation and careful terracing near Keroka, Kenya. Tea, coffee, bananas, maize, pyrethrum and other crops are grown in this area, one of the most densely settled and intensively used in western Kenya. (Commonwealth Development Corporation)

The main highway between Mombasa and Nairobi, Kenya. Note the open savanna landscape, so common in East Africa. (World Bank)

KENYA: THE PROBLEM OF LAND

lems. Even when conceived, there was insufficient land to go around in Kikuyuland, so that consolidation and resettlement into viable economic units actually intensified the problems of landlessness. In places illegal subdivision has occurred, and land once devoted to high value cash crops has reverted to staple foods. Migration to Nairobi, Nakuru, and other urban centers accelerated as the population swelled, and the number of landless increased.

The second phase of land reform was far more ambitious and initially more problematic than the first. It centered on the decision to open up the Highlands for farming by all races. The first step, beginning in 1961, was the government's purchase of a little over 1 million acres (405,000 ha) of European-owned farms and estates out of which 36,000 African-owned farms were created. Next, the government instituted a program of instruction in agricultural techniques and marketing and encouraged the formation of cooperative societies. Since commercial production was essential in order to provide cash to repay the loans, careful planning of crop types, intensity of land-use, and methods of production had to be ensured. Three types of settlement were planned: high-density smallholder settlements intended for Africans with limited capital and agricultural expertise; low-density smallholder settlements for more experienced farmers with some capital; and a scheme for large-scale and cooperative farms and ranches.

Farms in the low-density schemes were designed to yield a net income of about $500 a year, the average farm being only 37 acres (15 ha). Normally its farmers had to be members of the tribe in whose area the land was situated. Farms in the high-density schemes averaged 27 acres (11 ha) and were expected to yield a net annual income of $140. (Whetham, 1968). Because most farmers prior to being resettled were either unemployed or landless, they lacked both capital and experience and were in debt almost to the full value of their land and stock. Once selected and installed, they were supervised by government officials and offered technical assistance wherever possible. For a while, group interests threatened to jeopardize the scheme before it had a chance to get started, but by 1974 some 36,000 families had been resettled on about 1.2 million acres (486,000 ha). The average cost of establishing each small-scale farm was more than $2000, and was financed by loans and grants from the United Kingdom, West Germany, and the IBRD.

Because of serious management and production difficulties encountered by the small-scale cultivators on what were once large-scale farms, the government has decided not to subdivide any additional estates. Rather they are being kept intact and run like state farms (*shirika*). Each is run by a state-employed manager and farmed by salaried workers, who also receive about 2.5 acres (1.0 ha) of land for their personal use. Several farms have been purchased by Kenya's small African elite, but still the largest acreage remains in European hands.

Success or failure of resettlement should be assessed from the point of view of its purpose. It was politically and not economically motivated. It relieved an explosive situation and helped stabilize a moderate nationalist government by creating a new landed middle class that acted as a buffer against agitation by the rural masses. But resettlement has not solved the problem of landless Kikuyu nor the problem of urban unemployment to which landlessness contributed. The economic consequences are well documented. The government spent about $28 million over five years in buying out the European settlers (of which $25 million left the country), and another $30 million in converting the estates into African-owned farms. During the first five years of resettlement, production fell in almost every type of operation except for the low-density schemes. There, traditionally high outputs were maintained because of the intensity of supervision and technical advice, because of the large amounts of development capital, and because the settlers were selected for their farming abilities. In 1967, for the first time, Kenya's small farmers contributed more than half the total output of marketed agricultural products.

Before decolonization of the Kenya Highlands, Europeans accounted for almost all Kenya's coffee exports, and coffee was and remains the leading export. Today, almost half the output is produced by some 300,000 smallholders. Yields on the large estates (numbering about 300 in 1975) are double those on small farms, and the quality is higher. In recent years, coffee (predominantly high-grade arabica) has contributed about one-fourth of the gross farm revenues and earned Kenya more than $65 million annually in foreign revenues. The major producing areas are immediately north of Nairobi, the Western Highlands, and the slopes of Mounts Kenya and Elgon (Fig. 25-3).

Population Pressure and Policy

The 1969 census put the Kenya population at 10,942,705. In 1977, it was estimated to be 14,500,000 and increasing at 3.3 percent per year. If this rate is maintained, the population will double in only 21 years, and by the end of this century the population will reach 31 million. Given the fact that only 17 percent of the total area is suitable for cultivation and pastoralism under presently available technology and practices, and that 80 percent of the people live on less than 20 percent of the land, Kenya faces unenviable population problems. Figure 25-4 shows the geographical distribution of the population.

If to these already alarming figures are added another 103,775,000 population equivalents (the sixth largest in Africa), the situation becomes even more ominous, especially when it is realized that much of the northern and eastern cattle areas is subhumid and subject to prolonged and devastating droughts. Furthermore, almost 90 percent of the population is rural and dependent on the soil for its livelihood. Rural densities already exceed 1200 persons per square mile (460 per square kilometer) in parts of Kakamega District (Western Province), Kisii District (Nyanza Province), and several areas of Kikuyuland. Resettlement and land reform in these areas have done little if anything to alleviate the pressure, evidence of which still abounds: rural-urban migration, soil erosion, the cultivation of marginal land, malnutrition, and social distress.

In 1966, Kenya became the first country in Africa south of the Sahara to adopt an official population policy. The program is viewed as being an integral part of, rather than as an alternative to, efforts toward social and economic development. The aim is to make family planning information, education, and services available on request through free clinics in all government hospitals and health centers. The government provides 25 percent of the program costs, the remainder being shared by domestic and overseas organizations and the International Development Association, an affiliate of the World Bank. The present target is to reduce the growth rate by 1 percent in the next 10 years. That may well be too little too late.

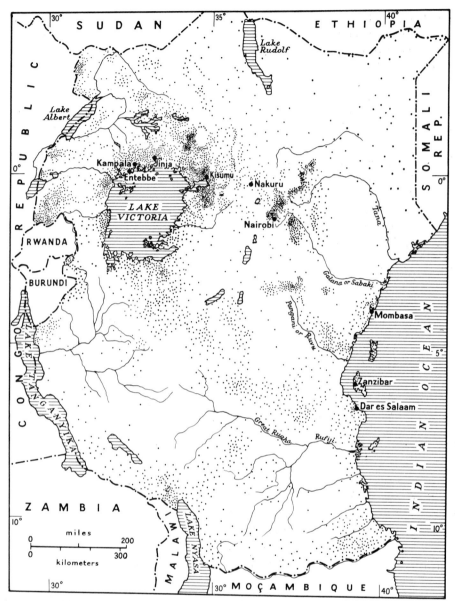

FIGURE 25-4 *Population distribution in East Africa. Each dot represents 5,000 people.*
L. D. Stamp and W. T. W. Morgan. Africa: A Study in Tropical Development.
3rd edition. New York: Wiley, 1972. After P. W. Porter and W. T. W. Morgan.
Reprinted by permission of John Wiley.

African smallholders have made spectacular inroads in Kenya's tea production, especially in the high-density settlement areas. Prior to independence, tea (Kenya's second most important export) was almost exclusively a plantation crop, with the largest concentrations being around Kericho and Limuru. In 1975, about one-third the total production came from smallholdings. As new plantings reach maturity in Kikuyuland, and along the slopes of the Aberdares and Mount Kenya, smallholdings may account for the largest share. Another crop successfully produced on small farms is pyrethrum, a daisylike plant used in the manufacture of insecticides. Over 90 percent comes from these farms, much of it from the higher altitudes of Central and Nyanza Provinces.

Small farms now produce significant and increasing quantities of sugar, tobacco, rice, fruits, and vegetables. The Mwea Irrigation Scheme (11,250 acres or 4,556 ha), for instance, provides about 70 percent of Kenya's rice supplies together with smaller amounts of cotton, maize, and other crops (Hornby, 1973). There, rice is produced on small tenant holdings, each consisting of about 4 acres (1.6 ha) of paddy. Small farms also account for the bulk of the country's principal staple, corn, while most of the sisal and wheat is grown on extensive farms and estates.

Tea estate near Kericho in the Kenya Highlands. Once owned by a white settler family, this estate is now part of an African cooperative. (UN/IDA)

Nairobi and Mombasa

Nairobi (800,000) and Mombasa (350,000) are respectively Kenya's capital and principal port. They are the two most important cities on the railway that links them (Fig. 25-5), but are separated from each other by an extensive low rainfall area of light population density (Fig. 25-4) and low economic productivity. Each city has its own distinct hinterland, but they are functionally interdependent and together form part of Kenya's emerging national core.

Nairobi started as a break-in-slope railway camp at the edge of the Kenya Highlands at the turn of this century when the Mombasa line was laid to Lake Victoria. Over the years it has developed into Kenya's principal administrative, commercial, and industrial center, and thus the country's prime generator, transformer, and distributor of the forces of change and modernization. Its growth has been part of the general economic growth that has characterized not only Kenya but also Uganda. The 1948

census put Nairobi's population at 118,976, and that of 1969 at 509,286. Its current growth is estimated at 8 percent per year, but housing, jobs, industry, and basic social services are not growing as fast, so that slums are expanding, and unemployment is rising.

Nairobi has more than half the country's industrial establishments and an equally impressive share of the industrial output and employment. Many of its processing industries depend on locally derived agricultural and forestry resources and include grain milling, clothing, tobacco, beverages, printing and publishing, and a host of construction-related industries. The government is attempting to arrest this primacy and to encourage decentralization to Kisumu, Naivasha, Nakuru, and Kitale where adequate transport, resources, markets, and labor exist. The state-owned railway yards and engineering works are the largest in East Africa, and the capital forms

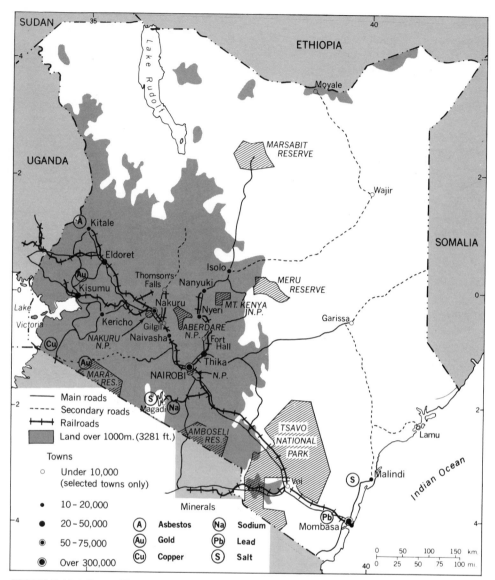

FIGURE 25-5 *Kenya. Towns, transport, and resources.*

the hub of a dense transport network that extends into Uganda and Tanzania. Nairobi is strategically located (Fig. 25-5) with respect to several of Africa's popular game reserves (Ambolseli, Tsavo and Serengeti), and its airport is the busiest in East Africa.

The city itself, once strictly planned on racial lines, is one of Africa's most attractive, with broad tree-lined streets and boulevards, modern high-rise buildings, and spacious residential areas. The parliamentary buildings, university, mosques, marketplaces, and the Nairobi National Park are all tourist attractions, which, together with the game reserves, bring almost 400,000 overseas visitors to Kenya each year.

Important to Nairobi's cultural and economic life are the Asians who face an uncertain future and much discrimination. They have always dominated Nairobi's retail

Aerial view of Nairobi, Kenya. The capital of Kenya is East Africa's largest urban center, and its bustling, high-rise business district reflects its prosperity and growth. (Kenya Information Services)

trade, and throughout the country have held skilled and semiskilled jobs, a situation the present government resents. Several hundred noncitizens have been expelled, while others have lost their licenses to trade.

The cultural impact of the Asian on East Africa is considerable. Apart from the tangible influences such as the architectural peculiarities of Nairobi and parts of Mombasa, the Asians (139,000 in 1969) brought with them and retain their home religions, languages, and living habits. Like the Africans, they were restricted in their ability to occupy land, and their representation in Kenya's governmental affairs has always been disproportionately small. Since independence, discrimination against them has intensified. This is partly due to the cultural isolation in which many Asians continue to live and partly to their envied economic status.

About 250 mi (400 km) southeast of Nairobi lies the port of Mombasa-Kilindini. Its hinterland comprises not only Kenya but also Uganda and the Moshi-Arusha region of northeastern Tanzania. It is the best equipped harbor in East Africa, and whatever development takes place in the interior will benefit the city, already the second largest in Kenya, and third in East Africa. Unlike Nairobi and Dar es Salaam, Mombasa is an old city, established by the Persians, and then occupied for centuries by Arab slave traders. It fell to Portuguese invaders in 1505, and subsequently came under the control of the Zanzibar Sultanate. Still later British overlordship sanctioned this merger by creating a Kenya Protectorate under the administration of Zanzibar. Ultimately this connection was severed, and the Kenya Protectorate (a strip of the mainland 10 mi (16 km) wide and 52 mi (84 km) in length) was formally attached to the sovereign Republic of Kenya.

Throughout its history, Mombasa developed as a part of the Indian Ocean littoral, with its Arab and Asian influences, rather than as an African settlement. It had many competitors—among them Zanzibar, Kilwa, Malindi, Mogadishu and Lamu—some overshadowing Mombasa during certain periods. Today, however, Mombasa eclipses them all. A century ago, slaves and ivory from the interior lakes region comprised Mombasa's major exports, and its orientation was oceanward toward Zanzibar, other Arab strongholds, and South Asia.

The coming of British administration (1886) was attended by many momentous changes: slavery was abolished; Africans flooded the island in search of work; Europeans came in large numbers to terminate old practices and initiate new; and Indian labor was imported to build the mainland railway. Each immigrant group left its mark in the landscape, and today Mombasa has several distinct ethnic enclaves. From 1900 to 1905 it was the capital of mainland British East Africa, until the headquarters were shifted to Nairobi. Since then, Mombasa has been the pulse of its hinterland (de Blij, 1968).

Today, Mombasa generates one-fifth of Kenya's industrial output. Its industries include refining of imported crude oil, metal fabricating, chemicals, textiles, food processing, cement, and glass manufacturing. De-

Aerial view of Mombasa. Once an Arab slave port, Mombasa is now the major outlet for the overseas traffic from Kenya and Uganda. (Quality Photo)

EAST AFRICA

spite this apparent industrial emphasis, Mombasa's specialization is in storage, assembly, packing, sorting, and distribution. Its immediate hinterland is not rich in resources other than sisal and copra, and its role in the modernization process of coastal Kenya has been small.

Mombasa and Nairobi represent two nodes in the Kenya nation, each with well-defined spheres of influence and dependence (Soja, 1968). They can play an important role in the modernization of Kenya, and in extending the effective national territory.

Currently three-fourths of the land area lies beyond Kenya's effective national territory. In the Northeastern Province especially among the Somali and Galla peoples, there is little government control or identity with the Kenya *raison d'être*. There secessionist sentiment is strong, guerrilla warfare has erupted periodically, and the land is poor and the opportunities very limited. Indeed the paucity of much of Kenya's periphery makes it all the more necessary that resettlement and land reform in the Highlands succeed.

Bibliography

de Blij, H. J. *Mombasa: An African City*. Evanston: Northwestern University Press, 1968.

Harbeson, J. W. *Nation Building in Kenya: The Role of Land Reform*. Evanston: Northwestern University Press, 1973.

Hornby, W. F. "The Mwea Irrigation Scheme," *Geography*, Vol. 58 (1973), pp. 255–59.

Jones, N. S. C. "The Decolonization of the White Highlands of Kenya," *Geographical Journal*, Vol. 131 (1965), pp. 186–201.

Kenya, *National Atlas of Kenya*, Third Edition. Nairobi: Survey Department, 1970.

Mboya, T. *The Challenge of Nationhood*. New York: Praeger Publishers, 1970.

McMaster, D. N. "Rural Development and Economic Growth: Kenya," *Focus*, Vol. 25, No. 5 (January–February, 1975), pp. 8–15.

Morgan, W. T. W. "The 'White Highlands' of Kenya," *Geographical Journal*, Vol. 129 (1963), pp. 140–55.

———, (ed.). *Nairobi: City and Region*. Nairobi: Oxford University Press, 1971.

——— (ed.). *East Africa: Its Peoples and Resources*, Revised Edition. Nairobi: Oxford University Press, 1972.

Odingo, R. S. *The Kenya Highlands: Land-Use and Development*. Nairobi: East African Publishing House, 1971.

Ojany, F. F., and R. B. Ogendo. *Kenya: A Study in Physical and Human Geography*. Nairobi: Longman, 1973.

Ominde, S. H. *Land and Population Movement in Kenya*. Evanston: Northwestern University Press, 1968.

———, (ed.). *Studies in East African Geography and Development*. Berkeley: University of California Press, 1971.

Soja, E. *The Geography of Modernization in Kenya*. Syracuse: Syracuse University Press, 1968.

Taylor, D. R. F. "Agricultural Change in Kikuyuland," in Thomas M. F. and A. W. Whittington (eds.), *Environment and Land Use in Africa*. London: Methuen and Co., Ltd., 1969.

Wasserman, G. "Continuity and Counter-Insurgency: The Role of Land Reform in Decolonizing Kenya, 1962–70," *Canadian Journal of African Studies*, Vol. 7, No. 1 (1973), pp. 133–48.

Whetham, E. "Land Reform and Resettlement in Kenya," *East African Journal of Rural Development*, Vol. 1 (1968), pp. 18–29.

TWENTY-SIX

The northwestern sector of former British East Africa is occupied by the state of Uganda, smallest (91,134 sq mi or 236,026 sq km) of the three major units and, with a population of about 12 million, by far the most densely populated. Landlocked Uganda shares the waters of Lakes Victoria, Idi Amin (formerly Edward), and Mobutu Sese Seko (formerly Albert) to the extent of about 14,000 sq mi (36,300 sq km), and in addition there is much territory under swamps and marshes. The country lies largely on a plateau just under 4000 ft (1200 m) above sea level, dropping to lower elevations toward the Sudd Basin in the north, and diversified by some great mountains west and east such as Ruwenzori and Elgon. The southern part of the country, especially, enjoys the ameliorating effects of elevation upon the tropical temperatures, and almost all of it receives over 30 in. (762 mm) of rainfall.

The compact territory of Uganda lies in a number of transition zones. By virtue of its location in the east-central part of equatorial Africa, its natural vegetation includes the savanna lands of the east and the forests of the Zaire margins in the west. The swampy lake regions of the south give way to the dryness and rain-deficient conditions that characterize the Sudan Basin northward. Uganda also is situated astride ethnic transition zones: south of Lake Kyoga it is generally Bantu country, in the north it is mainly Nilotic, and in the northeast, Nilo-Hamitic. The south is dominantly agricultural, much of the north pastoral. From the east have come the Arabs, Europeans, and Asians, all of whom have made their impact in the country. And from the north came many of the political ideas out of which the strong traditionalism of present-day Uganda emerged.

UGANDA: THE PROBLEM OF POLITICAL DISUNITY

Uganda became an independent state in 1962, after a lengthy sequence of political difficulties was in some measure resolved. In spite of its compact shape and relatively small areal extent, the internal variety of this country, in terms of ethnic groupings, traditions, and degree of economic development, is very great. This is true of many other African countries, but in Uganda the spatial arrangements so strongly favor the southern part of the country, mainly Buganda Province, that the final political unification of the territory long administered by Britain as a protectorate presented deeply rooted problems. These involved two major centrifugal forces which, even when the desire for independence was the strong centripetal force, tended to dominate the country's internal political geography.

The favored southern part of Uganda is inhabited in large part by the Baganda people, who number about one-sixth of the country's total population. These Baganda, along with about 1 million non-Baganda, live mainly in the region known as Buganda, where the traditional authority was the king or Kabaka. One major centrifugal force in Uganda's political geography was the reluctance of Buganda to lose its privileges by being merged into a larger Uganda, the modern state. A second was the reticence of many of the non-Baganda peoples of the country to support an independent state in which most of the power would lie in the favored south. In brief, the problem was how to fit Buganda into a larger Uganda, and the centrifugal forces remained sufficiently strong to prevent the evolution of the most common type of state elsewhere in Africa, the unitary state. A complicated federal arrangement was the product of centripetal forces seeking to end colonial administration while desiring to retain certain amounts of separate autonomy.

In many respects, Uganda is almost the complete opposite of Tanzania, and the comparison yields valuable insights. Uganda, although much smaller and far more densely populated, is primarily a country of peasant agriculture, plantations making a very small contribution to the export revenue. In spite of its dense population, Uganda each year has a sizeable annual surplus of farm produce, virtually the entire volume being derived from African smallholdings producing well over 80 percent of the annual export returns. Yet Uganda normally has a more favorable balance of trade than either Kenya or Tanzania. The major contrast, however, emerges when the spatial organization of the countries is considered: while Tanzania's development can still be best described as peripheral, and a core area, if recognizable at all, is in the initial stages of development in the northeast, Uganda has a core area that is as well defined as any. All factors seem to have conspired to make this so. When, after the European penetration, the modern phase of the country's development began, it naturally focused in the region which was at that time best organized. This, of course, was the Kingdom of the Baganda, lying on the shores of Lake Victoria (Fig 26-1). Had the outlet of the country been north or west, it would have been necessary to construct transportation lines in that direction, with the result that the isolation of Buganda from the rest of the country would have been reduced. But, as it happened, the natural exit was southeastward, through Mombasa, and the modern transport routes, focusing upon Buganda, came from that direction. That meant that they failed to cut through any part of the former protectorate except Buganda and the southern part of the Eastern Province. Thus, Buganda's political eminence was supplemented by several additional advantages: the British set up their administrative headquarters in Buganda, and when cash cropping began, the most suitable areas in terms of climate and pedology were also those near the lake and railroad.

UGANDA: THE PROBLEM OF POLITICAL DISUNITY

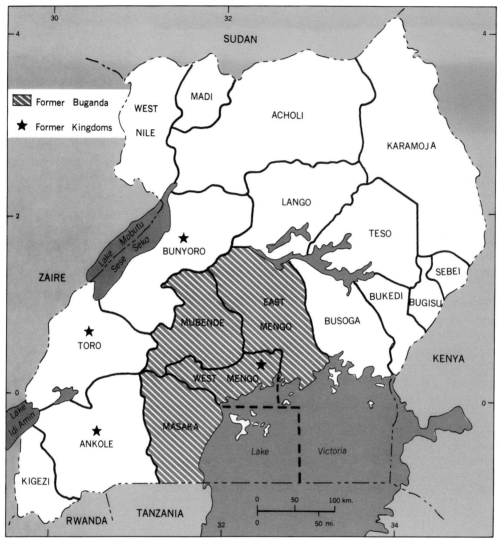

FIGURE 26-1 *Uganda. Administrative districts and former kingdoms.*

The Factor of Historical Geography

The political entity of Uganda was a creation of European colonialism, and the area prior to the first arrival of the Nyamwezi traders and the Arabs from the east in the late 1700s probably did not possess any elements of unity. Neither did it have the kind of contact with the outside world that marked the kingdoms of West Africa; for centuries no caravans reached the peoples of

Uganda, no organized exporting of products took place.

The internal heterogeneity of the area of present-day Uganda, due in large part to its character as an ethnic transition area, was expressed in political ways long before the first European explorers reached the headquarters of Buganda in 1862. Clearly, some of the political ideas from the Nile Basin had reached Uganda, for there had been considerable progress in state organization, as exemplified by the kingdom of the Baganda visited by Speke and Grant. This empire was by no means the only organized political area in the region, nor was it the first to have occupied a dominant position. The kingdoms of Bunyoro, Ankole, and Toro, whose areas also were incorporated in the Protectorate of Uganda, were similar in their organization, and had dominated the region centuries before.

Buganda was by far the most important of these politically organized units when the European invasion began, however, and in the period of colonial administration that followed, the kingdom played a leading role. But in precolonial Uganda, when there was no force binding the larger territory together, each of the kingdoms, and the tribal peoples of the more loosely organized areas elsewhere, had existed separately. Each had a physiographically rather well-demarcated territory (Fig. 26-1): Buganda between Lakes Victoria and Kyoga; Bunyoro between Lakes Kyoga and Albert (Mobutu) the Victoria Nile, and the Kafu River; Toro on the eastern slopes leading from Ruwenzori north of the Katonga River; and Ankole west of Lake Victoria and south of the Katonga. These kingdoms had their times of greatness and decline; during the course of history, they had expanded at the expense of the less well-organized peoples around them and had encroached upon each other. The frontiers between them really were frontiers in the technical sense of the word: either they were undesirable lands, with swamps or marshes, or they were areas of conflict and attempted expansion.

When, during the middle 1800s, European contact was made, the Buganda kingdom was the largest, best organized, and most powerful in the region. The early explorers saw in Buganda a fertile field for missionary and trade activities, and it was situated in the southeast of the area beyond Lake Victoria, nearest to the coast from which penetration was to take place. But in the less organized parts of the region, the slave trade was still continuing, and where the Europeans were not exercising effective power and propagating Christianity, Arab traders were converting the people to Islam. Uganda, having been a meeting place of indigenous peoples, now became an area of competition between the proponents of these religions. Egyptian influences were felt in the north, European in the south. This conflict, and a real conflict it was, became superimposed upon the regional ethnic, political, and economic contrasts that already existed. In effect, the area was in a state of instability until after the establishment of a British protectorate in 1894 over the Kingdom of Buganda and its extension in 1896 over Bunyoro, Ankole, and Toro.

Thus, there was little to warrant the incorporation of so much diversity into a single political entity. It was natural that Buganda should be selected by the British as the headquarters of administration, for in the Uganda region, Buganda was the most powerful unit, and effective control there was the prime requirement for the establishment of order. Indeed, the Baganda revolted against British overlordship not long after the establishment of the protectorate, and when the uprising had been put down, the kingdom was given special status in the Uganda Protectorate according to the Buganda Agreement of 1900. But then the British found themselves confronted by the task of forging a political whole out of the great variety within the country, in terms of the size, strength, competence, and desire to cooperate among the local authorities of nearly 30 distinct peoples, some of whom were being ruled on the basis of strong local customs and traditions, while others were still in the most rudimentary stages of tribal organization.

The evolution of the state of Uganda provides an interesting illustration of Stephen B. Jones's unified field theory of political geography. The theory places "idea" and "state" at two ends of a chain, the model being political idea-decision-movement-field-political area (Jones, 1968). In the case of Uganda, the political idea, existing first in the minds of British administrators and later developing among African residents of the region, involves the eventual independence of colonies and protectorates in general, and Uganda in particular, the specific concept being the establishment of a united Uganda out of the diversity within the protectorate's borders.

In the case of Uganda, the final decision determining the nature of the political entity was preceded by a series of earlier decisions, including the 1894 and 1896 protectorates over Buganda and the other kingdoms, and the 1900 Buganda Agreement. Although the new state emerged more than a half-century later, the decision to foster self-determination in a future national state was implied by its protectorate status during that period, and was therefore made at that early time. Subsequent decisions were adjustments to the developments taking place within Uganda as the third phase—movement—took place.

In the application of the field theory model to Uganda, movement is seen to have taken several forms. Britain ruled Uganda from Buganda territory, and the administrative headquajters was located in Entebbe (whereas the traditional seat of the Kabaka has always been within a few miles of Kampala). In those areas where only the most rudimentary form of organization existed, it was necessary virtually to create and superimpose responsible local authority. Baganda personnel were often used to staff administrative offices in such non-Buganda territories, perhaps the most striking single example of movement in the context of this model. But there were other instances. Efforts were made to imprint the Buganda pattern of administration on the other kingdoms. The nature of land ownership and occupance was changed, communal ownership being replaced by a form of individual holding by chiefs and headmen. This facilitated the introduction of a number of cash crops and accelerated the change from a subsistence to an exchange economy, an essential element of the field phase of the model.

Movement in Uganda, however, has been a slow process. It should be remembered that the initial idea was that of a united Uganda, requiring, of course, the partial submergence of tribal and local loyalties in favor of allegiance to a larger state. Movement, in the Jones model, is, among other things, the spread of a state idea. In several other countries (such as Tanzania with its Tanzania African National Union), strong national political parties have grown which have proved capable of fostering a national loyalty in addition to local and tribal attachments. This process has been less effective in Uganda, a factor which has inevitably made itself felt in the nature of the resultant political area.

The study of field phenomena in the model should be proceeded, in this particular case, by a reference to the field characteristics already clearly defined at the time of the initial (idea) phase. Uganda's territorial extent was delimited, with only minor subsequent adjustments, at about the time of the establishment of the protectorate. Hence, it is not possible here to speak of a "field" from which a defined political area eventually emerged. The character of the field changed significantly but there was no phase of territorial consolidation through war and expansion, as for instance in the case of Israel, the product of the idea of Zionism.

Furthermore, Uganda, even before it was Uganda Protectorate, possessed a core area, even though this area, Buganda, did not actually serve as such. In Buganda it possessed an area of advanced politico-territorial organization, considerable concentration of power, the beginnings of an exchange economy, and a degree of urbanization. But if a map were drawn of Uganda at that time, there would be no network of communications focusing upon this core area from the rest of the region, no integrating movement and circulation, no spread and adoption of ideas originating there. It required the initiation of the chain to forge there a functioning core area for a larger Uganda.

The special position of Buganda in Uganda was recognized by the Buganda Agreement of 1900 and was emphasized by the appointment of a resident in this province rather than a provincial commissioner. Uganda was divided administratively into four provinces of which Buganda was one; the Western Province included the kingdoms of Toro, Ankole, and Bunyoro, and the Busoga "kingdom" was the main political entity in the densely populated Eastern Province. The Northern Province included some of the least developed parts of the country, with its many small village and clan communities. Buganda Province so far outstripped the rest of the country as the decades of the protectorate wore on, and its individualism so intensified, that its function as the core area of a larger Uganda was actually impaired. The services performed by the Kabaka's government were far more complete than those of any of the other local governments in Uganda.

By independence, much of the country's productive capacity lay in Buganda. Its per capita income, level of education, and degree of urbanization were higher than anywhere else. Buganda was at the center of the country's road and rail network with virtually all roads leading to Kampala, the capital (Fig. 26-2). The railway from Kasese to the eastern border (and beyond to Mombasa) crossed the entire province.

The individualism—indeed, separatism—of Buganda has been a major centrifugal force in the political geography of this country. Uganda possesses many of the elements required for independence, the success of cash cropping has ensured economic viability, and a series of maps showing the urban centers, resources, communication grid, and core area would seem to support the assertion that the field phenomena are those of a state. But the old forces of fragmentation had not been submerged sufficiently, even in the independence year 1962, to permit the organization of the political area—the final phase of the model—as a unitary state, for which its shape, size, and communications network seem to be so suitable. While Buganda Province possessed far more cohesion than any other part of Uganda, and political sophistication and levels of education were more advanced in this region, the total population of 2 million represented only about 30 percent of that of Uganda. In an independent state with a government based on the universal franchise, therefore, Buganda could not expect to dominate politically as it dominated economically and socially. Thus, Uganda was faced with demands for secession and independence from the very core area upon which its future as a state was to depend.

The British government, in an effort to find a solution to this problem, in 1960 established an investigative body known as the Relationships Commission. In 1961, it recommended that Uganda be served by a strong central democratic government, with Buganda in a federal relationship and Toro, Ankole, and Bunyoro in a semifederal relationship with the central government. Broadly on this basis, the political area became the state of Uganda late in 1962.

It became clear, however, that Uganda's strong regional loyalties, fostered by the federal arrangement, were a hindrance to coherent development planning. Events rapidly moved to a crisis, and following a series of uprisings along the borders with Sudan and Zaire, Prime Minister Obote suspended the

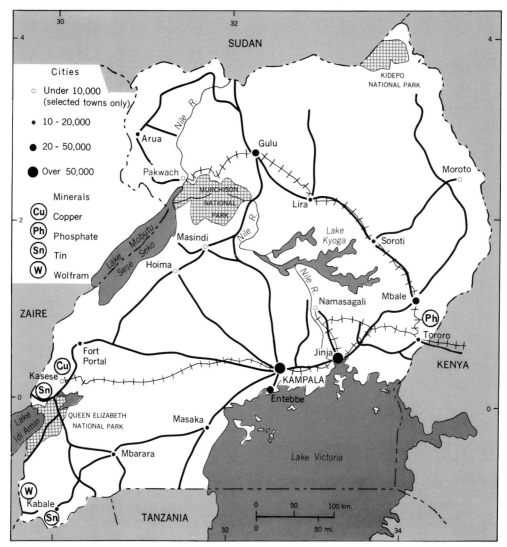

FIGURE 26-2 *Uganda. Towns, transport, and resources.*

constitution. The federal status of Buganda and the other kingdoms was abolished and a unitary state was created. Violence erupted in Buganda, the Kabaka fled to England, and Buganda was subsequently divided into four districts: Masaka, Mubende, West Mengo, and East Mengo.

The Factor of Economic Geography

Uganda has always suffered from its landlocked location, although the railroad from Mombasa reached Kisumu on Lake Victoria as early as 1901. At that time, goods were transported to the railhead by steamer, but later the railhead was extended into Uganda to eliminate the water link. Development has closely been tied to the ex-

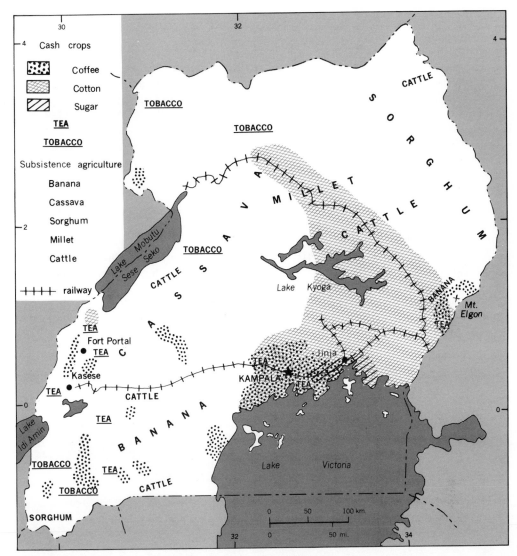

FIGURE 26-3 *Uganda. Agricultural regions.*

pansion of the transport network: and a
number of feeder roads to the central
railroad, a branch line northwards to Gulu
and Pakwach and an increase in inland water
transport have been important factors (Fig.
26-2).

Cotton was introduced during the first
decade of this century and proved to be a
success, although the industry has been severely affected by fluctuating prices on the
world market. After World War II, cotton

cultivation rose sharply, partly as a result of
the establishment of African cooperative
unions and their participation in the cotton-
ginning industry. Until then, this industry
had been largely a non-African enterprise.
Well over 2 million acres (810,000 ha) are
presently under cotton, the highest intensity
being in the Busoga, Teso, and Bukedi districts of the southeast where climatic conditions are good and distances to the railway
are not great (Fig. 26-3). Cotton is grown in

many parts of Uganda and is expanding along the southern foothills of the Ruwenzori and north of Lake Kyoga. Most commonly it is grown as a rain crop, without irrigation, on plots averaging less than one acre/hectare. Ginning, once dominated by Asians, is now under African cooperatives.

Uganda is the largest producer of coffee in the British Commonwealth. Initially, it was grown almost exclusively by the few white plantation owners and Asians; the Africans took an interest in this cash crop, however, and by the time of independence, about 30,000 acres (12,150 ha) were in plantations and some 600,000 (243,000 ha) in individual African farms. After World War II, coffee cultivation rose dramatically in Buganda, to the extent that coffee is now Uganda's leading export (70 percent in 1974). The Baganda grow mainly the ro-

busta variety, which is especially useful in the preparation of "instant" coffee, hence the ready market for this product. Arabica coffee is grown on the slopes of Mount Elgon and in Kigezi, but its acreage is far less than that of robusta, and the total coffee acreage is still less than half that of cotton. Thus coffee is economical in its land requirements and is more popular than cotton because it requires only about 80 man-days of work per acre as compared to 140 man-days for cotton.

Coffee and cotton are by far the most important cash crops and regularly yield about 80 percent of the total export earnings. Tea ranks third and is produced on both estates and small holdings, the major regions being Fort Portal in the western highlands, Jinja, and Mount Elgon (Fig. 26-3). It was once exclusively an estate crop, but since the

Tea pickers at work on a large plantation near Fort Portal, Toro District, western Uganda. About 90 percent of the tea acreage is in large estates. (UN)

The Asian Exodus

In August 1972, President Idi Amin ordered all noncitizen Asians to leave Uganda within three months. He accused them of being isolated and corrupt, of deliberately sabotaging African competition in commerce and industry, of being disloyal to the government, and of hoarding goods and money. By November, all but a few hundred of Uganda's estimated 75,000 Asians had been evacuated, leaving behind assets worth $400 million. Most held British passports, but perhaps as many as 15,000 Kenya nationals also fled rather than face persecution and possible extermination. The majority entered Britain against considerable public opposition, while others were resettled in Canada, India, and elsewhere. Tanzania, Zambia, and Malawi vociferously criticized the expulsion, while Kenya (with 140,000 Asians of its own) remained silent. Almost all the Asians' property was appropriated by government officials and the armed forces, and the economy was thrown into complete disarray. Ironically, Amin sent a delegation to Pakistan in 1974 to recruit doctors, lawyers, mechanics, and teachers to alleviate the shortage of skilled manpower he created.

The Asians (mainly of Indian origin and of diverse linguistic and religious background) first came to Uganda as indentured laborers to build the Kenya-Uganda railway. Once given their freedom, few opted to return but stayed to become traders and artisans, and gradually to occupy skilled and semiskilled jobs in industry and the civil service. By 1920, it was colonial policy that trade and commerce be reserved for Asians, but they were restricted from owning land. Because of this, most Asians were urban dwellers, and they helped monetize the peasant by buying and selling local produce and acting as a source of rural credit. They once controlled 74 percent of Uganda's wholesale trade and much of the sugar industry. Before the exodus, Uganda's largest private industrial organization (20,000 employees) was Asian owned. At no time was the economic power of the Asians convertible into political influence.

mid-1960s the government has encouraged smallholders (especially in Buganda) to produce more. Most of the estates were once owned by resident Asians and expatriate British, but they are now owned and managed by the Uganda Development Corporation. Uganda's sugar estates have likewise been expropriated from the Asians, and the production of both tea and sugar has since been unstable.

Somewhat less than one-third of Uganda's cultivated acreage is at present under cash crops, but in some parts of the country, notably the area between Lakes Victoria and Kyoga, the figure is as high as 60 percent. In the northeast (Karamoja) and southwest (Ankole and Kigezi), food crops predominate to the extent that they occupy 90 percent of the cultivated land, and in the northern regions (Acholi and Madi) 70 percent of the crop land is under food staples. Karamoja is the least productive of all regions, and its peoples, the pastoral Karamojong, have repeatedly resisted government efforts to increase food production and improve their livestock. Thus, spatially, the peripheral areas belong to the subsistence sector and are special problem areas in the space economy, while Buganda forms the economic core where the population is politically and socially dominant in national affairs.

Compared to its agricultural output, Uganda's mineral production is small and is virtually confined to copper from Kilembe (Fig. 26-2). Mining began in 1948, but production was held down until the Mombasa-Kampala railroad was extended west to Kasese (in 1956), and a smelter was completed at Jinja. The smelter is supplied with low-cost power from the Owen Falls Dam (close to where the Nile leaves Lake Victoria), and processes between 14,000 and 18,000 tons of copper concentrates each year. Copper forms about one-tenth of the exports, all of it going to Japan, but production is declining and the mine's life is in jeopardy. Jinja (65,000) has developed into Uganda's main manufacturing town whose major industries include copper smelting, grain milling, textiles, and food processing. Kampala (350,000) like most capitals and primate cities, has attracted more labor from its surroundings than can be employed. It has several light industries dependent on electricity from Jinja, but, on the whole, industry has been unable to compete with imported goods, and industrial expansion has been slower than projected.

Thus, there is a marked territorial concentration of the known wealth of Uganda, resulting in the development not only of several individual political arrangements but also of different economies, whose integration must be achieved. Similar situations have presented problems elsewhere in Africa. As a whole, Uganda's favorable balance of trade (with the United Kingdom the major trade partner) attests to the country's fortunate position among the political units of Africa. There is some danger that fluctuating world prices will at some time impede progress, and that the land will not sustain the intensive modes of agriculture to which it is being subjected. In this, however, Uganda does not stand alone, and the state has given evidence of an awareness of these dangers.

The East African Community

Uganda, Kenya, and Tanzania have for many years cooperated in a wide range of nonpolitical activities. Interterritorial cooperation was first formalized in 1948 by the East African High Commission. This provided a customs union, a common external tariff, currency and postage, and dealt with common services in transport and communications, research and education. Following independence, these integrated activities were reconstituted, and the High Commission was replaced by the East African Common Services Organization, which many observers believed would lead to the political federation of the three member states. But the new organization ran into difficulties because of (1) the lack of joint planning and fiscal policy, (2) separate political policies followed in each state, and (3) Kenya's dominant economic position. Kenya had the lion's share especially in manufacturing and was exporting more manufactured goods within the Organization than its member states. In 1964 an agreement was signed in Kampala whose aim was to reduce Kenya's industrial primacy by redistributing some of the industry to less prosperous areas But because of Nairobi's natural advantages and its access to resources, capital, and technology, Kenya's lead went unchecked.

In 1967, the East African Common Services Organization was superseded by the East African Community (EAC). The EAC aims to strengthen the ties between the member states through a common market, a common customs tariff, and a range of pub-

Kampala, capital of Uganda. This was for many generations the seat of government of the king or kabaka *of the Baganda, whose Buganda Kingdom lay on the shores of Lake Victoria. (Uganda Information Services)*

The Owen Falls Hydro-Electric Dam, Uganda. The dam is situated near Jinja where the White Nile leaves Lake Victoria and begins its northward journey. Jinja is Uganda's leading industrial town. (Uganda Information Services)

UGANDA: THE PROBLEM OF POLITICAL DISUNITY

Table 26-1 TRADE WITHIN THE EAC, 1973 (in thousands of U.S. dollars)

Imports Exports	Kenya	Tanzania	Uganda	Total
Kenya	—	47,578	62,467	110,045
Tanzania	21,557	—	2,439	23,996
Uganda	13,972	313	—	13,728
	34,972	47,891	64,906	

lic services, so as to achieve balanced economic growth, "the benefits of which shall be equitably shared." The treaty has several innovative provisions that are designed to permit greater decentralization than was previously possible. The East African Harbour Authority moved to Dar es Salaam, the post and telegraph offices moved to Kampala, and the EAC's administrative headquarters are located in Arusha, Tanzania. The monetary union that operated until 1966 no longer exists, each country now having its own currency and central bank. A transfer tax system was instituted which permits Uganda and Tanzania, under certain conditions, to tax imports of manufactures from Kenya for the purpose of protecting their own infant industries. The treaty also established an East African Development Bank to provide financial and technical assistance to promote industry. It is required to devote 77.5 percent of its funds equally to Tanzania and Uganda and the balance to Kenya. Despite these controls, Kenya's industry is growing more rapidly than either Uganda's or Tanzania's and its exports are expanding.

Trade within the EAC for 1973 is shown in Table 26-1. Kenya was by far the most important exporter ($110,045,000) and Uganda the smallest ($13,728,000). Manufactured goods provided the bulk of Kenya's exports to both Uganda and Tanzania, and these two countries now form about one-third of Kenya's export market. Uganda's trade with Tanzania (and Kenya) is very small in comparison. This is not so much a question of having so little to offer as it is of strained relations between the governments of Amin and Nyerere which date back to 1971 when Amin seized power and Obote fled to Tanzania. Since 1971, Uganda's exports to both Tanzania and Kenya have declined appreciably, while imports, especially industrial imports, from Kenya have risen.

Despite these and other setbacks, including inefficiencies and poor cooperation in rail and air services, the EAC is an example of African economic unity. Its performance has been closely monitored by Zambia, Burundi, Somalia, and Ethiopia, all of which have formally applied to join the Community. There is much merit to a broader association, especially in view of the new rail link between Tanzania and Zambia, and Burundi's reorientation away from Zaire and toward Tanzania. But there are many problems to be resolved. Both Somalia and Ethiopia have to cope first with their internal political disorders, and neither has adequate transport links with Kenya and Uganda. Within the existing Community, the lack of effective road and rail links between Tanzania and its northern partners is a major centrifugal force acting against the Community's stated objectives. Geographically Kenya and Uganda are united, but Tanzania is an outsider.

Uganda's role in the EAC depends primarily on Idi Amin. Since coming to power, Amin has undermined much of the confidence that foreign investors had in the country, which, while not a model of economic prosperity, was nevertheless relatively stable, both economically and politically. In contrast, Amin's rule has been marked by the systematic liquidation of the opposition; the expulsion of thousands of Asians and most British citizens and the confiscation without compensation of their industries and businesses; the nationalization of all British properties; the massacre of Langi and Acholi elements in the police and armed forces; the expulsion of Israeli technical advisors; and the complete disrespect for law and order. Amin has strengthened his political ties with the Arab bloc (especially Libya) and has taken a strong militant stance against South Africa and Rhodesia. The unpredictability of Amin's behavior has brought havoc to most sectors of the economy, including the once lucrative tourist industry, and his ver-

bal (sometimes military) attacks on Tanzania and Kenya seriously threaten the viability of the EAC. World attention focused on Idi Amin on July 4th 1976, when Israeli commandos rescued passengers and crew of an Air France jet skyjacked by pro-Palestinian guerrillas and held hostage at Uganda's Entebbe airport. Amin denounced the Israelis, criticized Kenya for its role in the rescue mission (the rescue planes refuelled in Nairobi), and then ordered the liquidation of many Kenya nationals living in Uganda. Uganda, long beleagured by internal political disunity and regional imbalances in its economy, now faces the problems of political disunity in a broader and more complex context.

Bibliography

Apter, D. E. *The Political Kingdom in Uganda*. London: Oxford University Press, 1961.

Bakwesegha, C. J. "Patterns and Processes of Spatial Development: The Case of Uganda," *The East African Geographical Review*, No. 12 (April, 1974), pp. 46–64.

Gukiina, P. M. *Uganda: A Case Study in African Political Development*. Notre Dame: Notre Dame University Press, 1972.

Ibingira, G. S. K. *The Forging of an African Nation*. New York: Viking Press, 1973.

Jones, S. B. "A Unified Field Theory of Political Geography," *Annals, A.A.G.*, Vol. 44 (1954), pp. 111–123.

Kabwegyere, T. "The Asian Question in Uganda," *East African Journal*, Vol. 9, No. 6 (June, 1972), pp. 10–13.

McMaster, D. N. *A Subsistence Crop Geography of Uganda*. Bude Haven: Geographical Publications, Ltd., 1962.

McMaster, D. N. "Towards a Settlement Geography of Uganda," *East African Geographical Review*, Vol. 6 (1968), pp. 23–36.

McMaster, D. N. "Political Upheavals and Economic Development: Uganda," *Focus*, Vol. 26, No. 5 (May–June, 1976), pp. 9–16.

Morgan, W. T. W. (ed.). *East Africa: Its People and Resources*. Nairobi: Oxford University Press, 1969.

O'Connor, A. M. *Railways and Development in Uganda*. Nairobi: Oxford University Press, 1965.

Parson, J. D. "Africanizing Trade in Uganda," *Africa Today*, Vol. 20, No. 1 (1973), pp. 59–72.

Rollow, J. "Uganda's Amin's Economic Revolution," *Africa Report*, Vol. 20, No. 3 (May–June, 1974), pp. 36–38.

Shaw, T. M. "Uganda Under Amin: The Costs of Confronting Independence," *Africa Today*, Vol. 20, No. 2 (1973), pp. 32–45.

Uganda. *Atlas of Uganda*, Second Edition. Entebbe: Lands and Surveys Department, 1967.

TWENTY-SEVEN

Ruanda and Urundi, prior to World War I, were among the most densely populated districts of German East Africa. When armed hostilities erupted in East Africa, Belgium participated, using Congolese troops to attack the Germans from the west. By September, 1916, Belgian forces had reached Tabora, in the central part of German territory, and one battalion actually penetrated to the Indian Ocean at Lindi. At the end of the war, the Belgians had captured not only Ruanda and Urundi, but also most of the District of Kigoma and parts beyond, and were thus in effective control of nearly a third of the people and territory of the former German sphere.

In 1919, the Supreme Council of the League of Nations, meeting at Versailles to consider the question of disposal of Germany's colonial empire, placed all of former German East Africa under British mandate. This decision aroused great resentment in Belgian circles, in view of the effort Belgium had expended in the East African war theater, and because the area captured by the Belgian forces contained land suitable for white settlement and for livestock raising, opportunities which in the adjacent Congo were rather scarce. Thus, Belgium expressed its desire to retain for occupation, at least, a section of the territory in question, and the matter was reopened for discussion. The League of Nations granted Belgium the right to solve the problem by direct negotiation with Great Britain, and an agreement was reached whereby Belgium received, under mandate, almost the entire area of the territories of Ruanda and Urundi. Boundary definition, delimitation, and demarcation (in part) took place during 1923 and 1924. In 1925, "Ruanda-Urundi" became an integral part of the Belgian Congo. As a result, Belgium came to rule the most densely populated region of former German East Africa, including over one-third of the total population of that dependency.

RWANDA AND BURUNDI: LEGACY OF DEPENDENCE AND DIVISION

Table 27-1 RWANDA AND BURUNDI

	Burundi	Rwanda
Area (square miles)	10,747	10,169
Population (1977, est)	4,100,000	4,400,000
Population density (per square mile)	360	400
Capital	Bujumbura (80,000)	Kigali (30,000)
Urban population	2%	3%
Population engaged in agriculture	96%	92%
Ethnic groups	Hutu (84%)	Hutu (88%)
	Tutsi (15%)	Tutsi (11%)
Crude birth rate	48 per 1000	50 per 1000
Crude death rate	24.7 per 1000	23.6 per 1000

Belgian Administration

A primary reason for Belgian interest in Ruanda and Urundi was the relationship of this area to Katanga, which was developing and where labor was needed—and in short supply. The Belgian government initiated large-scale transfers of the local population to the mining area, and soon found itself subjected to criticism, which also had accompanied the 1925 incorporation of Ruanda-Urundi into the Congo. Thus, the labor policy was altered somewhat, but the territories continued to provide large quantities of labor for Katanga until much later.

But in securing the administration of Ruanda-Urundi, Belgium inherited problems as well as assets. The area of the two territories combined is just under 21,000 sq mi (54,000 sq km), and their total population, which today numbers some 8.5 million (Table 27-1), already exceeded 3 million in the mid-1920s. Population pressure increased constantly, and resettlement projects became necessary, while the variability of rainfall (highest in the Zaire-Nile watershed, lowest in the western lowlands) caused periodic famines in certain areas.

The Belgians faced an especially difficult problem of administration in Ruanda-Urundi, where an effort had to be made to impose a democratic form of government upon one of the best examples of what may be called feudal Africa. In substance, these problems were not entirely different from those faced by the British in Uganda, where access was easier and more living space available, however.

The ethnic composition was such that three distinct groups occupied the territory, and the social system was based on this situation. Perhaps 13 percent of the total are Tutsi (Watutsi), the tall, proud pastoralists of Nilotic origin who arrived in the area about five centuries ago and gradually established social and political dominance over all other groups. The Hutu (Bahutu) comprise about 86 percent of the total and are a farming people of Bantu origin. The remainder of the indigenous peoples consists of some thousands of Twa, a pygmy group who became serfs of the Hutu. When the Tutsi arrived, they established hegemony over the Hutu through military conquest, possession of their cattle, and assertion of divine origin. A feudal class system known as *ubuhake* developed whereby the Hutu were permitted the use of Tutsi cattle and land, and in exchange rendered personal and military service to the Tutsi (Lemarchand, 1970). In this organization, the omnipotent ruler was the Tutsi king (*mwawmi*) who delegated power to the chiefs of his people. There was, of course, no semblance of a democracy, and without education the imposition of democracy had little meaning.

Ruanda-Urundi, therefore, was a country of vested interests (of the Tutsi) and smoldering resentment, which frequently found expression in open warfare along tribal lines. Although making some improvements in traditional agriculture and pastoralism within its mandate, Belgium found the obstacles in the path of educational, social, and political progress insuperable. When independence was granted in 1962, the territory was divided, the two new states taking the names Rwanda and Burundi.

Livelihood and Population

The republics of Rwanda and Burundi lie in one of Africa's least accessible regions. Physiographically, they form part of highland equatorial Africa: volcanic mountain masses reach over 14,000 ft (4260 m) in the Virunga Range of the north, the Western Rift Valley forms the western boundary, and the Nile rises in the east. Both countries are dominated by the north-south-trending backbone of mountains forming the eastern edge of the great rift occupied by Lakes Kivu and Tanganyika. Most areas lie between 3000 and 8000 ft (900–2400 m), and the higher elevations are the favored parts (Fig. 27-1). There, the dreaded tsetse fly is absent, soils are often volcanic and rich, and precipitation exceeds 50 in. (1270 mm) annually. By contrast, many of the valleys in the peripheral areas are low, hot, and disease-infested. Thus, although these countries possess areas whose carrying capacity in terms of human population is very great, they do not by any means cover all of Rwanda and Burundi's 21,000 sq mi (54,000 sq km).

Vertically, three main crop zones can be recognized, of which the lowest (2500 to 4500 ft or 760–1370 m) is favorable mainly to subsistence crops such as corn, beans, and bananas, although some coffee and cotton are grown (Fig. 27-3). The middle zone (4500 to 6500 ft or 1370–1980 m), covering the greatest part of both countries, is the most densely populated, and in addition to the subsistence crops normally grown at these elevations in equatorial regions, coffee and tobacco are cultivated. Finally, in the highest zone (6500 ft or 1980 m and over), cash crops such as wheat, barley, tea, to-

bacco, and pyrethrum can be grown, and there some of the European settlers, who at the time of independence numbered over 8000, established plantations. In each of the three zones, subsistence crops such as corn, beans, sweet potatoes, and a variety of cereals are grown, occupying the vast majority of the acres of cultivated land. There are two rainy seasons, a short one from October to December, and a long one from March to May.

Arabica coffee is the dominant export of each country (80 to 85 percent of the total in Burundi, and 40 to 45 percent in Rwanda), most of it grown in small stands scattered among basic food crops. Annual production averages about 20,000 tons in each country, the bulk of which is sold to the United States and the EEC, and shipped through Dar es Salaam and Mombasa. Both countries are attempting to diversify their export base by increasing production of tea, cotton, pyrethrum, forestry products, and minerals. Rwanda exports small quantities of tin concentrates and wolframite, and oil has recently been discovered in the Ruzizi Valley in Burundi.

Rwanda and Burundi are the most densely populated countries of Africa and are among the least urbanized and poorest (Table 27-1). Practically everyone lives directly off the land, of which about 40 percent is considered to be cultivable, and between 30 and 40 percent is under pasture. The remainder is in forest, a game reserve, and lakes, or is excessively steep and rocky. In Rwanda the crude population density is 400 per square mile (154 per sq km), and in Burundi 360 per square mile (140 per sq

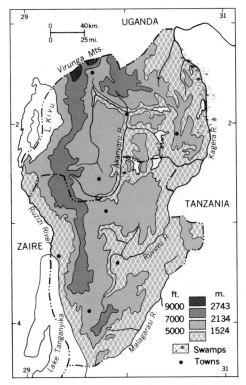

FIGURE 27-1 *Rwanda and Burundi. Relief and drainage.*

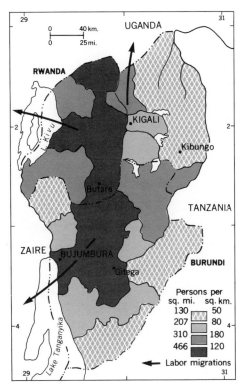

FIGURE 27-2 *Rwanda and Burundi. Population density and labor movements.*

km). Arable densities around Ruhengeri and Butare in Rwanda, and Kitegi, Burundi, exceed 1500 per sq mi (580 per sq km). Widespread poverty and overcrowding are major obstacles to development, but the need for population control has been strongly resisted by the Roman Catholic Church (du Bois, 1973). Over 96 percent of the people are rural and widely dispersed, and not concentrated in villages, thus making the provision of schools and hospitals more costly. Bujumbura (80,000), the capital of Burundi and formerly of the whole trusteeship, is the only large town. Kigali, capital and largest town in Rwanda, has a population of only 30,000. Virtually all nonagricultural activities are concentrated in these two centers.

Since most of the opportunities for farming and pastoralism lie in the higher areas, the central plateau, running north and south along the eastern side of the Nile-

Zaire divide, is by far the most densely populated part of both countries (Fig. 27-2). Toward the lower western slopes, population densities decrease considerably, and they are lowest in the disease-ridden valleys of the lower east. As part of their 10-year plan of the 1950s, the Belgians designed a program for the relocation of people, with the object of reducing the pressure where it had become most serious. But the task was a difficult one, for it meant a considerable change in habitat, crop possibilities, and climate for those who were transferred. The only empty areas in Rwanda and Burundi were the lower valleys, where tsetse and other pests had kept the population totals low. Having cleared some of these areas for resettlement, the Belgians made a start with the alleviation of population pressure on the plateau.

However, by 1960, a third of the hold-

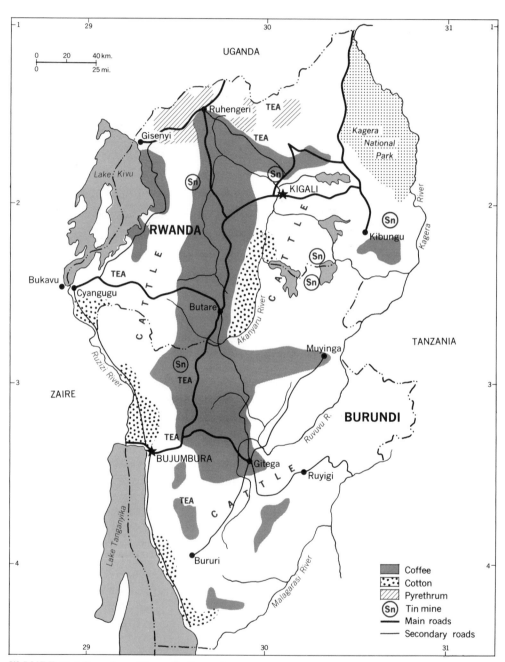

FIGURE 27-3 *Rwanda and Burundi. Economic map.*

Pyrethrum near Ruhengeri, Rwanda. One of the cash crops grown in Rwanda is pyrethrum, an insecticide base. Note the up-and-down-hill rows on the slope in the distance. (UN)

ings were abandoned because of resistance to the scheme, poor management, and flooding. In 1969 the Burundi government reinstituted the program through the *paysannat* system which had been developed in the old Belgian Congo. The *paysannat* is a large-scale farm divided into small holdings of about 4.8 acres (2.0 ha) that are contoured, have access to roads, and on which cash crops must be grown. Communal grazing land and watering points are provided, together with social services including a school, dispensary, veterinary office and nutrition center. The people are thus being grouped into villages in an attempt to bring greater social as well as economic benefits to the farmer (Baker, 1973).

All this, of course, can not be a final solution, for the population continues to grow, and the opportunities for additional land availability constantly dwindle. Per-

haps, when attitudes toward cattle change, the pastoral industry in Rwanda and Burundi could become a major source of revenue. Presently, it is still retarded by the traditionalist tribal limitations on slaughter. But modern times demand more than a subsistence economy from a state, and the resources of both Rwanda and Burundi appear very limited. Indeed, an expanded production of cash crops could find ready markets, for the range of possibilities is considerable. But any increased cash crop production requires a major increase in the acreage allotted to such crops, and that acreage, under present systems of land occupance, is not available. In a sense, Rwanda and Burundi may be indications of what the Kenya Highlands might have been had they not undergone organization into plantation agriculture.

Cattle and herdboy near Kitega, Burundi. The highland areas of Rwanda and Burundi are tsetse-free and support large numbers of cattle. Much of the country is overgrazed and overpopulated. (UN)

Contour ploughing, Rwanda. Cultivation on the steep mountain slopes of Rwanda and Burundi requires careful soil management. On the right is a conduit and small hydro-electric power station. (UN)

Since independence (1962), both countries have experienced important changes in their economic orientations and political leadership, and both have seen genocide on a scale unsurpassed in Africa. During the Belgian era they were part of the Congo Free Trade Area, which meant that goods moved freely from one Belgian territory to another, and that Ruanda-Urundi was essentially an outpost of the Belgian Congo. High tariffs virtually eliminated trade with Tanzania, Uganda, and Kenya, and most resources and labor moved westward. Adequate communications were never developed: only the poorest roads linked Ruanda-Urundi with the border town of Bukavu and the Zaire river town of Kindu, while Busumbura was served by lake steamer from Kalemi (formerly Albertville), Zaire's railhead on Lake Tanganyika. But Rwanda and Burundi are closer to the Indian Ocean and Dar es Salaam than to the Atlantic and Matadi, so that transport to the east was faster and cheaper. Thus Belgium secured extraterritorial rights from the British at the port of Dar es Salaam, but these were transit rights only and trade was kept firmly in Belgian hands.

Following the independence of Zaire and the collapse of its economic and political institutions, Rwanda and Burundi turned toward Uganda and Tanzania for their import requirements and for access to their overseas markets (Baker, 1973). But communication routes were almost nonexistent, there being only two dirt tracks from Kigali to Uganda, and none from Burundi to Tanzania. Burundi's only link with its eastern neighbor was via lake steamer to Kigoma, a route also used by the Rwandans. But when relations between Burundi and Rwanda themselves deteriorated in 1963, Rwanda found itself almost entirely dependent on its grossly inadequate northern outlet, the goods being trucked to Kasese and Kampala, and then railed to Mombasa. Transport has since been improved between Rwanda and Uganda,

and an all-weather highway is planned between Kigali and Tabora. Tanzania has joined with Rwanda in developing hydroelectric power on the Kagema River near the Rusumo Falls, and is cooperating with Burundi in mapping the water and mineral resources of the Ruvuvu River. Thus, both Rwanda and Burundi are now oriented to the east and have applied for membership in the East African Community.

While economic reorientation has been accomplished, political uncertainty prevails, and both countries have seen the massacre of literally hundreds of thousands of their people. Indeed, perhaps 300,000 have been slaughtered in tribal civil wars since independence (Lemarchand, 1974). In four months alone, in 1972, an estimated 100,000 Hutus were slaughtered in Burundi by the minority Tutsi elite. Tens of thousands of innocent women and children were dragged from their homes and schools and systematically clubbed to death, while Tutsi soldiers and civil servants murdered thousands of Hutu farmers, teachers and others with automatic weapons, machetes and spears. Approximately 3.5 percent of the country's total population was liquidated in a matter of weeks, yet the OAU and the United Nations took no action, and raised little effective protest.

In Rwanda, a Hutu revolt in 1959 overthrew the ruling Tutsi minority, and four years later the monarchy was abolished. Supporters from Burundi invaded Rwanda, but were defeated and repressive measures were taken against the Tutsi throughout the country: tens of thousands were exterminated, and possibly 100,000 fled to Zaire, Tanzania, and Uganda. Still others fled to Burundi whose government was accused of supporting the Tutsi invasions. In 1972, as genocide was being practiced in Burundi, reprisals were made against the Tutsi in Rwanda. In July 1973, the ruling Parmehutu government was overthrown by Hutu military officers discontent with the lack of economic progress and favoritism shown toward Hutu in the president's home area. Since then the new military government has taken a far more moderate stand on the Hutu-Tutsi issue than its predecessor, and has attempted to restore and strengthen its diplomatic and economic ties with its neighbors, especially Tanzania and Burundi.

The reasons underlying these atrocities are not easy to understand. It is not solely a question of the majority seeking political power and a greater share of the resources and the ruling minority demonstrating its military superiority. The two groups are involved in a conflict whose roots lie deep in the history of their relations of overlord and serf, and in the process of social transformation set in motion during and after the colonial interlude. The Rwanda revolution had a decisive psychological impact on ethnic self-perceptions in Burundi; the coming to power of Hutu politicians in Rwanda led many of their kinsmen in Burundi to share their political objectives, in turn intensifying fears of ethnic domination among the Tutsi of Burundi. Shortages of land, widespread poverty and hunger, and the exploding populations are all contributors to these disorders. Rwanda and Burundi, once dependent on and divided by Belgium, remain internally divided while age-old patterns of ethnic dependency persist.

Bibliography

Baker, R. "Reorientation in Rwanda," *African Affairs* Vol. 69, No. 275 (April, 1970), pp. 141–54.

———. "Rwanda," *Focus*, Vol. 23, No. 10 (June, 1973).

Du Bois, V. D. *Rwanda: Population Problems, Perception, and Policy*. Hanover: American Universities Field Staff, 1973.

Lemarchand, R. *Rwanda and Burundi*. New York: Praeger, 1970.

Lemarchand, R., and D. Martin. *Selective Genocide in Burundi*. London: Minority Rights Group, 1974.

Melady, T. P. *Burundi: The Tragic Years*. Maryknoll: Orbis Books, 1974.

Weinstein, W. "Conflict and Confrontation in Central Africa: The Revolt in Burundi, 1972," *Africa Today*, Vol. 19, No. 4 (Fall, 1972), pp. 17–38.

PART SIX

THE
HORN
AND
THE
SUDAN

TWENTY-EIGHT

The "Horn" of Africa, including the lands north of Uganda and Kenya and east of the White Nile, is an area of immense physiographic diversity (Fig. 28-1). Its physical core is constituted by the vast Ethiopian Plateau, rising to over 13,000 ft (3900 m) in many places, rent by great rift valleys and cut elsewhere by spectacular declivities. The plateau still effectively prevents modern communications from reaching all of the heart of the northeast. It is the source of the Blue Nile (at Lake Tana) and wrings from the air more moisture than any surrounding territory. It possesses excellent soils and good climates as well as barren wastes and inhospitable environments. Desert and steppe lands bound the plateau in all directions, separating it from the coasts of the Red Sea and Indian Ocean, from the valley of the Nile, and from the good lands of Kenya and Uganda.

The northeast is as diversified politicogeographically as it is physiographically. There, Arab and Bantu, Islam and Christianity, local and foreign empires have met. A modern political framework has been superimposed upon an area which retains many of the characteristics of its initial feudal condition. Today, this framework fragments the Horn into Ethiopia, The Territory of the Afars and Issas, and the Somali Republic (Somalia), consisting of the former Italian and British Somalilands. The present boundaries of the Horn are indeed superimposed, subsequent boundaries, and they are not, in several areas, approved by the local population.

About 34 million people inhabit the Horn of Africa, of whom the great majority (30 million) reside within Ethiopia. The Afars and Issas has a population of 200,000, and the coastal Somali Republic about 3.7 million. However, there are many more Somali people (from the ethnic, religious, and

ETHIOPIA: A LEGACY OF FEUDALISM AND IMPERIALISM

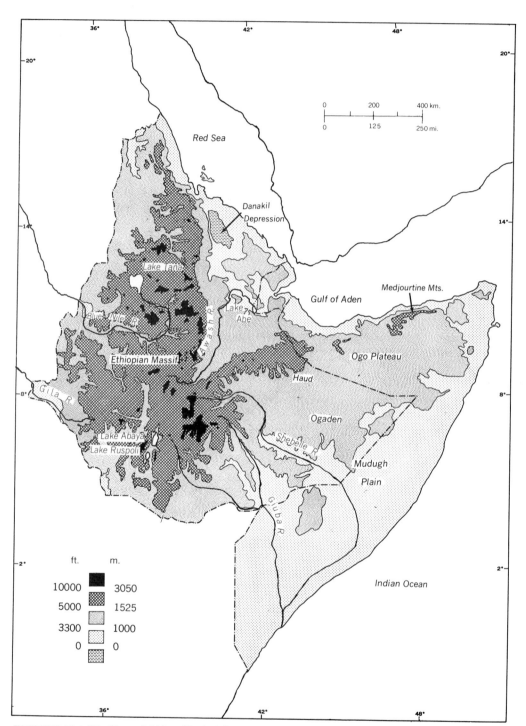

FIGURE 28-1 *The Horn of Africa: Physical features.*

other points of view) than the population of the republic might suggest. Indeed, there are Somali people under French rule, under Ethiopian rule, and also under the administration of Kenya. Formerly, the Somalis were further fragmented by the Italian and British division of Somaliland.

Neither does the population of Ethiopia justify the term "nation." Apart from the Somalis living in (mainly eastern) Ethiopia, there are numerous peoples within the confines of the state, which is itself the result of the amalgamation of a number of rival kingdoms, their consolidation under powerful leadership, and its subsequent expansionist policies. It is this expansionism which carried Ethiopian rule into Somali territory and the ensuing definition of the boundaries which created one of the major, perpetual conflicts in this part of Africa.

Feudalism and Imperialism

Ethiopia often is described as one of the oldest independent states in Africa. It is true that the territory of Ethiopia was not successfully claimed in the scramble of the 1880s by any of the colonial powers, although attempts at annexation were indeed made, and parts of the Horn that might have become Ethiopian territory did fall victim to the colonial powers. Ethiopia fell within the sphere of influence mainly of Italy, but the period of effective control over the entire country by the Italians was limited to the years preceding and during World War II, 1936–1941.

These aspects notwithstanding, to describe Ethiopia as having been a sovereign nation state since before the arrival of the European intruders is misleading. Less even than Uganda has the country progressed toward unification and internal consolidation. Being much larger and affected by severe physiographic obstacles to circulation, movement of all kinds in Ethiopa is very restricted. Until the late nineteenth century, the plateau and its periphery were occupied by a number of feudal kingdoms (whose essential structure was not very different from that of Buganda), sultanates (in the eastern margins), and tribal peoples. Only then did the first steps toward the modern state take place, with hundreds of years of almost total isolation finally coming to an end.

Several geographical factors have contributed to the evolution of present-day Ethiopia with its great complexity and heterogeneity. The area's relative location and physiography have played major roles. Mediterranean peoples made contact with the shores of the Horn when the Red Sea was the only sea route to the Indian Ocean; Greco-Egyptian and Roman excursions led to some landings and intermittent associations. The center of territorial organization in Ethiopia lay in the region of Axum, and covered a part of Eritrea, the Ethiopian Province of Tigre, and a section of the Arabian Peninsula opposite. This Axum Kingdom, itself a successor of Nile Valley empires (Nubia, Kush), was supreme from the first to the seventh centuries A.D. It was in this period that Christianity was introduced to the region, as missionaries from Egypt (the Coptic Church) settled among the people of Axum.

At this time, therefore, the main center of organization in the Horn was not as isolated from the outside world as some of the later kingdoms were to be. Axum was located against the northern extremity of the Ethiopian Massif and extended to the Red Sea coasts. Nowhere else in the region was there the organization, architecture, art, and literature of this kingdom. But as Islam rose in the east, Axum declined, and the period of contact with the Mediterranean (limited as it was) ended. However, Christianity had taken hold among the rulers of the empire, and when the remnants of Axumite power withdrew into the protective interior plateaus, it was the beginning of a permanent strife between Christian kings and the proponents of Islam.

As the Moslem religion spread into the marginal areas, the Horn went through its dark ages. Not until the twelfth century did the Zagwe (Zague) dynasty arise in the interior, whose Christian rulers engaged in ceaseless battle with the Moslems. Except for the contact between the Moslems and the center of Islam on the Arabian Peninsula, there was total isolation; the kings in the highlands were no more in touch with the outside world than were the early kings of Uganda. They waged their wars against the Moslems with varying fortunes. At times, the Islamic forces penetrated deep into the plateau, while at other times the Christian kings expanded their area of hegemony at the expense of their enemies. Like Moshesh and his Basuto, they used the military assets of the highlands to good advantage, but by the sixteenth century, the tide began to turn decisively against them. The Moslems of the peripheral areas had begun to become politically organized, and a strong sultanate had arisen centered upon Harar. Before the middle of the century, a powerful sultan crushingly defeated the Christians, and it appeared that Christianity in this region was doomed.

The apparently final defeat of the Christians in Ethiopia, however, happened to coincide with the Turkish defeat of Egypt, so that the entire Red Sea seemed likely to fall under the domination of the Moslems. At this time, however, another European power with Mediterranean interests was involved: the Portuguese, who saw one of their routes to the Indies seriously threatened, decided to take action. Portugal sent armed forces to Ethiopia, which landed at Massawa in 1541 and advanced into the interior. There, allied with the remnants of the Christian kings' armies, they defeated the Moslems not far from Lake Tana. The victory was the turning point in the Christians' fight for survival against the encroachments of Islam. Although the Moslem threat was not terminated, the war effort had taken such a toll from both sides that neither was able to deal a final blow to the other.

One side might eventually have prevailed, were it not for the invasion, at this time, of the Galla people from the southeast. Hundreds of thousands of these Hamitic people flooded onto the plateau. Their previous location appears to have been the valley of the Juba River, but pressures exerted by the Somali probably caused their exit from this region. The arrival of the Galla on the plateau gave rise to a lengthy period of upheaval, political disorganization, and wars. The center of Ethiopian power withdrew to the north, and the Galla spread as far northward as the region of Lake Tana and beyond. They were, however, not united internally, and fought among themselves as they did against common enemies. Thus, a period of chaos resulted, and eventually no less than six "kingdoms" arose, each of which was ruled by a man who considered himself to be the emperor of all Ethiopia.

Confusion also reigned in religious circles during this time, as Jesuit missionaries entered Ethiopia's kingdoms and attempted to convert the people to Roman Catholicism. Repression and bitter strife over the religious issue further divided the hard-pressed leadership, and eventually a ruler arose who expelled the troublesome missionaries (1633), and for the ensuing 150 years the country was almost entirely isolated from European contact.

Not until 1855 did change begin once more, and in this year the phase which led directly to modern Ethiopia may be said to have begun. A leader named Kassa ascended to the throne, after having defeated several of the feudal rulers on the plateau and thus having made the first step in the direction of consolidation. As emperor, Kassa assumed the name Theodore II, and he initiated a series of administrative, social, and religious

The Tisissat Falls on the Blue Nile near Lake Tana, Ethiopia. The volume of water varies greatly with the seasons. This photo shows the Falls a month after the heaviest rains. (UN)

reforms. Although he was not always successful in imposing them, his effort in this direction was the first to have been made in Ethiopia.

Meanwhile, hostilities against rebel chiefs, Moslems, and all who displeased him continued, and in addition Theodore had to deal with a new factor on the Ethiopian scene: a renewed, this time political, interest in the Horn on the part of Europe. Theodore made a fatal diplomatic error in 1867 by imprisoning the British consul in response to an alleged snub by the Foreign Office. Britain acted swiftly, sending a rescue force which landed at Massawa in 1867. The force was joined by tribesmen who had suffered the oppression of Theodore, and in

1868 the emperor's army was defeated.

Britain's first incursion was not permanent. Having achieved its objective, the force withdrew, leaving Ethiopia in renewed disarray. This coincided with the opening of the Suez Canal and unprecedented European activity along the entire east coast of Africa. Pressures upon Ethiopia increased from several sides. Egypt briefly entered the stage by taking the Eritrean coast and southeastern Ethiopia as far west as Harar, and in 1869 an Italian concern purchased the Red Sea port of Assab. The Mahdist rebellion in Sudan brought invasions into western Ethiopia.

Ethiopia's own internal division was a major factor endangering its survival. Emperor John IV emerged as the dominant fig-

ETHIOPIA: A LEGACY OF FEUDALISM AND IMPERIALISM

ure out of the feudal chaos, and he repelled the Italian advances from the port of Massawa. But he had a rival, whose power in the south and west was on the increase while John was occupied with the war in the east. This feudal king, Menelik, was encouraged by the Italians to open hostilities against John, and to this end he was given arms. In return, he was promised the throne. Before these negotiations could reach their conclusion, however, John was killed in the war against the Mahdists, and Menelik became emperor in 1889.

Menelik immediately faced the aggressive forces of colonial imperialism. During the period of his accession to the throne, Italy occupied Eritrea and proclaimed a colony in that country. Immediately after becoming emperor, Menelik signed the Treaty of Ucciali, which was to become the first serious source of conflict between his regime and the Italians. The Amharic text of the treaty, which is the only one actually signed, states that, should he so desire, Menelik could make use of Italian diplomatic channels for his business with other powers and governments. The Italian translation, on the other hand, states that Menelik *consented* to make use of such channels, and in these terms Ethiopia was virtually a protectorate of Italy. This, indeed, is what the Italians professed to believe, and the inevitable crisis arose when Menelik made direct contact with Queen Victoria. War ensued, and again the Ethiopian forces routed the Italians at the Battle of Adowa (1896) extracting from Italy a new treaty recognizing Ethiopia's sovereignty.

Menelik now embarked upon his own imperialist campaign and used the European powers to his own advantage. He expanded the territory under his sway far to the southeast, south, and west, and signed treaties with the colonial powers defining the boundaries of Ethiopia much as they are today (Fig. 28-2). He had founded the modern capital, Addis Ababa, in 1883, and followed Theodore's efforts to initiate reforms by making major efforts to modernize the country. He negotiated with the French, who had occupied the port of Djibouti for the building of a railroad from this port to the capital. He also began a road-building program, and established schools, postal services, public utilities, and other modern amenities.

The decline and death of Menelik, who had consolidated Ethiopia and withstood European intervention at a time when most of Africa was being parcelled out by the colonial powers, again deprived Ethiopia of strong central leadership at a crucial time. Even before his death, France, Britain and Italy theoretically divided the country into their own desired spheres of influence, to take effect in case of the disintegration of the Ethiopian state. Italy desired to connect her two possessions of Eritrea and Somaliland across Ethiopian territory, France wished to safeguard her interest in the Addis-Djibouti railway, and the British wanted to protect the source of the Blue Nile and the region around Lake Tana. For some time after 1913, when Menelik died, it seemed as though this division would indeed take effect, as a lengthy leadership crisis arose. Menelik's grandson and proper successor was youthful, irresponsible, and leaned toward Islam, and his reign was predictably short. Eventually, one of Menelik's daughters, Zauditu, became empress, with the young Ras Tafari (Haile Selassie) designated as heir to the throne. A struggle ensued, and the divisive forces of feudalism again were strongly felt in Ethiopia as various chiefs gained in individual power.

Naturally, the situation was extremely detrimental to Ethiopia, and when Haile Selassie was crowned in 1930, the effects of two decades of stagnation were evident everywhere. But Haile Selassie had shown signs, even before his coronation, of desiring the end of Ethiopia's isolation. He had successfully applied for the country's admission to the League of Nations in 1923, and had engaged in treaties and cooperative projects

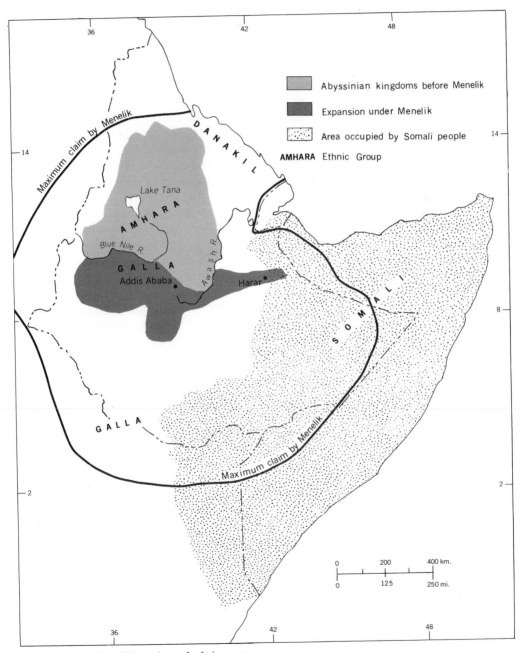

FIGURE 28-2 *Menelik's empire and ethnic groups.*

ETHIOPIA: A LEGACY OF FEUDALISM AND IMPERIALISM

483

with a number of European states. Under his rule, the country's first constitution was written, a first parliament assembled, and social reforms initiated. It is a reflection upon the Ethiopian situation that in the 1930s a new law against slavery had to be established, and that this law has not succeeded in eliminating the practice altogether.

In his attempts to unify and consolidate Ethiopia, Haile Selassie, like other rulers before him, faced an insuperable task. Ethiopia's relative location has made it a battleground between Christian and Moslem; its coastal fringes lie on one of the world's most important maritime avenues. Its high interior mountains afforded a haven for an island of Christianity amid an ocean of Islam, and its coasts attracted Moslem and European alike. But when modern times came, and boundaries were drawn around Ethiopia, the strife of ages had left a legacy of deep and fundamental division, too strong to be overcome in a matter of decades. The very physiography which once had helped ensure the survival of the Christian kings now became a major obstacle in the effort to build a nation state there in the Horn.

Viewing Ethiopia's politico-geographical characteristics of shape, the country would appear to have several assets. It is large, but compact. No lengthy proruptions extend from the country's main area (as in the case of Zaire and Namibia). The asset of its proximity to the coast is enhanced by several opportunities for port development, even though the colonial holdings of Italy, Britain, and France long prevented direct access to the sea. The capital is located in a central position, which would appear to help bind the state together.

But apart from these politico-geographical features, everything seems to conspire to effect internal division and fragmentation in Ethiopia. The same physiography that once protected the kingdoms now continues to separate the peoples, languages, and religions within the state. Having once hindered the invasion of the plateaus, it now makes communications difficult, retards the spread of ideas from the capital, isolates communities from each other, raises the cost of importing and exporting goods. True, Addis Ababa is situated in the middle of a radiating network of communications, but the network thins out rapidly, roads become tracks and eventually mere paths (if they continue at all), and the greater the distance from the capital, the less effective the contact with it (Fig. 28-3). And the less effective the contact, the less integrated are the outlying parts with the heart of the state.

If the result of these conditions was merely a limitation of movement, Ethiopia's problems would be like those of other underdeveloped countries requiring improved communications systems to stimulate development and foster a national spirit among peoples some of whom are located in remote areas. But in Ethiopia the consequences are much more serious, and their solution will require more than a better transport network. Strong actual and latent centrifugal forces exist within the state, with its Moslem and pagan majorities ruled by a Christian minority. The Islamic center of Harar and Addis Ababa seem worlds apart, but they are within 250 mi (400 km) of each other.

The period of comparative stability and progress under Haile Selassie was to be interrupted in a violent manner in 1935. In the previous year, during efforts to demarcate the boundaries in the region where Italian, British, and Ethiopian territory met, an incident had taken place at Wal Wal. Italian Somali forces had clashed with Ethiopian troops trying to control the area, and Ethiopia had taken the matter to the League of Nations. Italy massed armies on the Eritrean and Somali borders and invaded Ethiopia. The campaign ended before the middle of 1936, and Haile Selassie fled to Europe.

Italy's half-decade of rule in Ethiopia was marked by cruel repression of the local population, as Italy experienced the troubles of any authority attempting to establish effective control over the vast country. A vig-

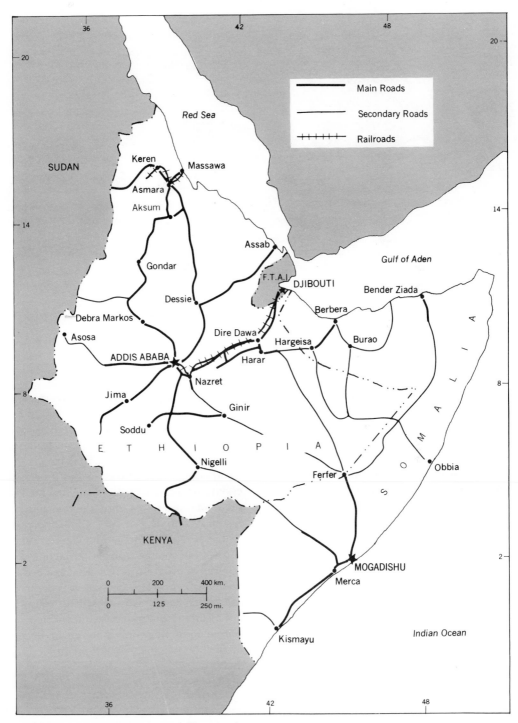

FIGURE 28-3 *The Horn of Africa: Towns and transport.*

The Bank of Ethiopia and the Lion of Judah, two landmarks in Addis Ababa of the Halie Selassie era. (World Bank)

orous program of road-building and economic development was initiated, which still has favorable effects today. Having interrupted Haile Selassie's reform program in 1936, the Italians were themselves unable to complete their plans, as British forces invaded Ethiopia in 1941 and, with the aid of patriotic forces, defeated the Italians. The emperor returned to his capital in the same year, and the sovereignty of the state was restored.

Since World War II, Ethiopia has been struggling to modernize its economy and break with the past. But little has been accomplished. The capital, Addis Ababa (950,000), has provided few impulses of change and modernization and it has grown at the expense of its surroundings. Ninety

percent of the people are still illiterate, the rural majority remains impoverished by archaic tenurial systems and methods of production, and almost half the population still lives more than 10 mi (16 km) from all-weather highways. Nowhere has it been easy to break with tradition and overcome the limitations imposed by the prevailing feudal system. But in 1974, following years of dissension in Eritrea, widespread drought and famine, and general dissatisfaction with the lack of progress in the social and economic spheres, Haile Selassie was dethroned and military rule was imposed. But this did not mean the end of feudalism, for that is engrained in the people who remain deeply divided by religious, social and ethnic prejudices.

Land and Livelihood

Ethiopia's problems in the economic sphere are as severe as those of its political geography. Once again, the initial impression is favorable: this is primarily an agricultural country, and it is comparatively well endowed with good climates and adequate soils. Estimates of the amount of arable land vary, but perhaps 10 percent of the land area (excluding Eritrea) may be so classified, and no less than 30 percent is capable of carrying livestock. But an agricultural economy, to rise above the subsistence level, requires adequate transport facilities and other forms of organization, and, again, because of the paucity of these amenities, current development falls far short of the country's potential.

The isolation of the agricultural areas is as great as that of its various peoples. It is hardly possible to describe the obstacles the topography puts in the way of communication, and the areas of arable land are for similar reasons widely scattered. Much of Ethiopia is under late youth and early maturity, and slope incidence is high. Areas of cultivable land, whether in the valleys, on gentler slopes, or on upland surfaces, often are separated by impassable declivities—and more important, they are also separated from the few routes to internal and external markets.

Three distinct environmental zones, which are actually altitudinal belts, are recognized in Ethiopia. In the hot lowlands is the kwolla, which reaches up against the valley and plateau slopes as high as about 5000 ft (1500 m). This is tropical Ethiopia, and includes also the deserts and steppe stretches around the foot of the highlands. There, bananas, dates, and other fruits thrive, as well as coffee in the higher parts. Above the kwolla lies the woina dega, or temperate belt, extending up to between 8000 and 9000 ft (2400–2700 m) Only about 7 percent of Ethiopia is forested, and most of the forest areas lie in this belt, which also sustains a wide variety of crops. Cereals, fruits such as the fig and orange, grapevines, and other Mediterranean plants thrive there. There is much pastureland, and thus a large cattle and sheep population in this zone. Highest is the dega, extending to the mountain areas of the country and including more pastureland and areas suitable for cereals such as wheat and barley.

This wide variety of conditions permits the cultivation of a large number of crops, and it has been said that Ethiopia's soils and climates make it possible to raise successfully almost any type of crop with proper care and cultivation. The limitations imposed by lack of communications, education, agricultural organization, modern implements, and incentive have retarded the development of a healthy agrarian economy. As elsewhere in plateau Africa, erosion is severe, and conservation practices are in their initial stages. Most of Ethiopia's farmers remain mired in a life of subsistence cultivation with some small local sales for cash. The main staple crop is a cereal, *teff*, but the country can produce far more than the population requires of almost every crop grown; indeed, it is often described as a future breadbasket of the north and Middle East.

Coffee is the most valuable export product of Ethiopia, often contributing half the total value of all exports. The manner in which this total is accumulated typifies much of what is problematic in Ethiopia's internal conditions. The country is extremely well suited for coffee of the arabica variety; indeed, this plant can be left untended and still produce well. There are veritable coffee forests in Ethiopia from which the beans are simply gathered, and if coffee seedlings are planted, they are often left without any form of care. The total harvest comes in large part from the wild forests, in addition to the production from the small plots of the local peasants and a relatively minor contribution from a few large plantations (Fig. 28-4). The lesson of

Market place, Harar, one of Ethiopia's historic towns in the Ahmar Mountains close to the northern Somali boundary. Note the bundles of firewood being offered for sale; they are often headloaded for more than five miles (8 km). (World Bank).

Tanzania, where the establishment of cooperatives to coordinate the production, processing, and marketing of coffee has greatly stimulated the industry, appears especially applicable in Ethiopia. In 1957, a national coffee board was established with these aims.

Some export revenue is obtained from hides and skins. There may be as many as 26 million cattle in the country, and about the same number of sheep and goats. The livestock is maldistributed in relation to the available pastureland. This is a function of the social conditions in the territory; especially large concentrations occur in the lands of the nomadic and seminomadic peoples of the lowlands. In the south, not surprisingly, a situation prevails which recurs throughout Bantu Africa: cattle are a source of wealth and are not slaughtered. Other cattle practices occur in various parts of Ethiopia, and although in much of the country they are used as animals of burden, slaughtered, and sold for meat and hide, elsewhere they are considered sacred. In the areas where precipitation totals are low, variability is great

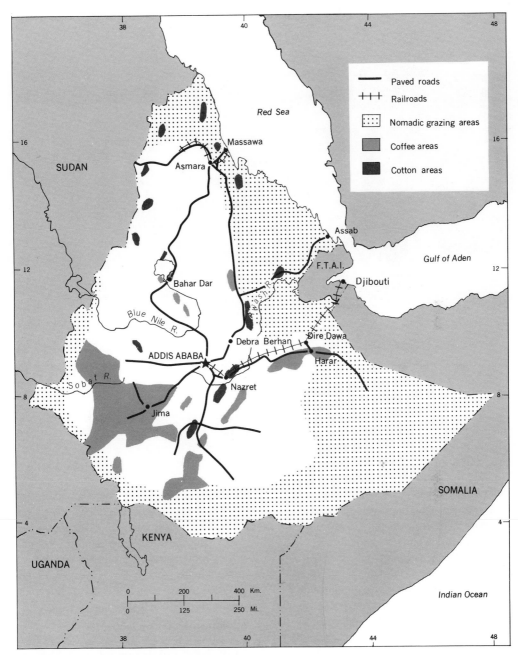

FIGURE 28-4 *Economic map of Ethiopia.*

and the dry season lengthy and intense. As a result, many cattle are underfed in these overpopulated, overgrazed regions, and disease is rampant.

Agriculture earns 99 percent of national exports, employs 88 percent of the estimated 30 million people, and contributes two-thirds to the GDP. But its potential is nowhere near fully developed: 65 percent of the land is classed as agricultural, yet less than one-fifth of this is cultivated, and agricultural output is growing at less than 2 per-

Typical thorn scrub in Eritrea and the Danakil Depression where pastoralism is the dominant economy. (*World Bank*)

cent per year. The most important element in agricultural improvement in Ethiopia, as elsewhere, is education, which must bring an appreciation of the need for reform in land tenure and ownership, soil and water conservation practices, maintenance of irrigation and other structures and equipment, and improvements in transport, communications, marketing, and credit facilities. Of these, the need for land reform is paramount.

Before the present military government deposed the emperor, about 80 percent of the land was owned by four groups: the imperial family (15 percent), the Coptic Christian Church (20 percent), the aristocracy (20 percent), and the government (25 percent). The distinction between land owned by the government and by the emperor was not always clear. The church, emperor, and the government paid no taxes, while that of large landowners was nominal. Half of Ethiopia's farmers were tenant farmers, who, on the basis of either custom or law, were

required to pay tithes to their landlords of between half and three-fourths of their total harvest, and in some cases had to provide labor and other services as required by the feudal landlord. Many different forms of land tenure and land tax existed, making reform measures difficult to conceive and even more difficult to implement (Hoben, 1973).

During the late 1960s, attempts were made to modernize the land tax system as a prerequisite to land reform. Cultivated land was taxed higher than fallow land, but in parliament it was argued the reverse should be in effect (Harris, 1974). This was to force the aristocracy to use the land more efficiently, boost production for both domestic and foreign markets, or force the aristocracy to sell to their tenants. It was also proposed that land holdings be limited to 988 acres (400 hectares)—some measured hundreds of thousands of acres in the south—and that share-cropping tithes be limited to 33 percent of the produce. But these and other

A drought-striken homestead totally devoid of vegetation. At least a half million persons perished in the droughts of 1971–74, most of them in the northeast and southeast regions. (UNICEF/Balcomb)

reform measures were successfully blocked by parliaments composed primarily of the landed aristocracy.

Hardships caused by the archaic tenurial system were aggravated by the severe droughts of 1969–1975, the worse since 1916. Drought first struck the sparsely populated northern areas of Wollo, Tigre, and Eritrea where approximately 200,000 persons died in 1971–1973 alone, and stock losses were up to 90 percent. It then spread south to Sidamo, Bale, Gemu-Goffa and Hararge (Ogaden) where an equal number of deaths were reported and an estimated 2 million persons, mainly nomads, were short of food and water. For political reasons, the military government—the Dergue—refused to allow international relief agencies to provide either food or medicine for the starving nomads in the dissident province of Eritrea. And the Eritreans accused the Dergue of using food as a military weapon against their adversaries. In the southern region, however, the Dergue publicized the drought but failed to attract the required amount of international assistance.

An estimated 300,000 persons from Wollo and Tigre, unable to pay their tithes or even harvest enough food for themselves, moved off the land and into government relief camps, or migrated to unsettled areas in Gojjam and Wollega. Commonly they resettled on vacant government-owned land and on large commercial farms and estates where food and water were available, but in most cases they were evicted and taken to refugee camps. Land they abandoned, sold, or leased was taken over by the aristocracy and consolidated into large holdings. In late 1973, Hailie Selassie decreed that all such land be redistributed to the original owners and occupants, but the emperor was deposed soon after, and the decree was not honored by the Dergue, which later nationalized all land.

Agricultural production is being aided

by several foreign-initiated and foreign-advised agencies, one of the most successful being the Swedish International Development Agency, which gives tools, fertilizers, improved seed, and technical instruction to peasant farmers. Begun in 1971, and now funded by the World Bank, the agency hopes to reach about one-fourth the farm population by 1980. Each project will have about 10,000 farm families on blocks of 185,000 acres (about 75,000 ha), and, depending on their location, will produce cotton, sugar, and staple foods. The World Bank has also played an important role in developing cash crops for export and import substitution (sugar and cotton) in the Awash Valley (Fig. 28-4). Industry has been started utilizing these resources and locally generated hydroelectricity, and in 1975 over 140,000 acres (56,700 ha) were irrigated.

Industry is still negligible in terms of its contributions to the GDP (about 5 percent), employment (55,000), and annual capital expenditure. Most factories were established with Italian, Greek, and French capital, and are concentrated in Asmara (280,000), Dire Dawa (80,000), Harar (55,000) and the Addis Ababa–Nazret development corridor along the line of rail to Djibouti. Addis Ababa (950,000) has the greatest concentration of industry, mainly light manufacturing, but it is primarily an administrative center. Described as a mask behind which the rest of the country is hidden, Addis is the headquarters of the OAU, a focal point for communications, and is centrally situated within the country and one of the most densely populated regions. The poor showing of manufacturing results from the small purchasing power of the domestic market, the lack of mineral exploitation, a shortage of skilled labor and technology, and inadequately developed hydroelectric power potential.

The Eritrean Issue

Eritrea became a politicoterritorial entity in 1890, when Italy proclaimed the country a colony. By the Treaty of Ucciali of 1889, Menelik had recognized the Italian possessions on the Red Sea, and in subsequent years the Italians used the bases in Eritrea for attacks on the emperor's lands. This, and the controversy over the terms of the treaty, resulted in the hostilities of 1896, when the Italian forces were annihilated near Adowa, and the subsequent abrogation of the treaty. Late in 1896, Menelik and the Italians defined the boundary between their respective realms. In 1935, Eritrea again became a base for Italian military activity, and in preparation for the invasion of Ethiopia, the country was the scene of feverish activity. Roads, bridges, port facilities, and airfields were built, improved, and expanded and thousands of Europeans entered the colony. The campaign was successful but short-lived, and by 1941 Eritrea, as well as Ethiopia, had been wrested from Italian control.

After World War II, Italy renounced its rights to Eritrea, and the United Nations attempted to decide upon the territory's future. Several commissions were given the task of determining the most acceptable course of action, but none managed to produce a suitable blueprint. Eventually, the General Assembly itself recommended the federation of Eritrea with Ethiopia, the former colony retaining a considerable degree of autonomy. This decision took effect in 1952, but a decade later Eritrea was unilaterally absorbed into Ethiopia as a province. A war of secession has been waged ever since, led by the Eritrean Liberation Front (ELF), a nationalist movement of Moslems and Christians, and the Marxist Eritrean Popular Liberation Front (PLF). Both have had support from Libya, Somalia, Iraq, and other Arab states, and between them they control most of the territory. Tens of thousands of persons have died in skirmishes with government troops, and the conflict could spread to Tigre and Wollo.

Eritrea is not a rich territory. It consists of two main physiographic regions, the coastal plain and the interior plateau. The former varies in width from 10 to 50 mi (16–80 km), and the latter is an extension of the Ethiopian Plateau. The descent from the highlands, which are mountainous in parts and reach 6000 to 8000 ft (1800–2400 m), is partly abrupt, as in the north, and elsewhere steplike. The lowlands are hot and dry, and in the highlands, rainfall may exceed 20 in. (500 mm) but is highly seasonal. Thus the country is much less well endowed with agricultural possibilities than Ethiopia-proper, and the latter supplies most of the food consumed in Eritrea. Overgrazing is a serious problem, irrigation a frequent necessity, and the available acreage capable of sustaining sedentary agriculture is small. Industrial development is limited to the processing of the country's small food production and the treatment of hides and skins. Asmara (280,000), located on the cooler plateau and railway to Massawa, is the capital and main manufacturing center.

Eritrea's population is as heterogeneous as the rest of Ethiopia. In the highlands live Coptic Eritreans, in the coastal plain are several nomadic Moslem peoples (possibly 55 percent of the population), and in the southwest are Negroid peasants. In addition there is an urbanized minority and a remnant of the once-large European population. Apart from the Europeans, these people generally share a low standard of living, high illiteracy, linguistic and religious diversity, and little scope for progress. Moslems and Christians alike resent the imposition of Amharic (the language of Ethiopia's politically dominant Amharic group) as the official language, and the elimination of local languages from schools. They also resent the influx of Amhara officials and the erosion of their own culture.

The loss of Eritrea would mean the loss of Ethiopia's only coastline, about 190 mi (300 km) of railroad, one-fourth of its industrial output, and the country's only oil refinery. It would mean the loss of Assab and Massawa, Ethiopia's only ports and vital contacts with the outside world. In terms of tonnage loaded and off-loaded, Assab is now Ethiopia's main port, and the principal outlet for Addis Ababa. Massawa is the port for Asmara and northern Ethiopia, although it handles some traffic from the central regions. The two ports were modernized and expanded and linked to the interior by improved roads following Eritrea's federation with Ethiopia. They are designed to handle the country's total import-export needs so that Ethiopia need not rely on Djibouti, capital of the French Territory of the Afars and Issas, once Addis Ababa's major outlet. Their loss to an uncooperative independent Eritrea would be disastrous to Ethiopia's small but vitally important foreign trade.

Eritrea is by no means the only region with secessionist leanings. In the remote southern provinces of Bale and Hararge the nomadic Somalis have never considered themselves Ethiopian but part of a greater Somalia, and for years Somalia has made irredentist claims to these regions. The strong ethnically based regional interests that weaken the Ethiopian *raison d'être* caused the Dergue to propose a confederation of east African states to include Somalia, the Territory of the Afars and Issas, Kenya, and Sudan. While theoretically attractive, it is an impracticable solution.

Ethiopia's future is hard to predict, but it is certain modernization will be slow and difficult. Centuries of feudalism, deeply entrenched social and religious patterns, widespread famine and disease, environmental limitations, and the failure to achieve effective government to fill the power vacuum caused by the emperor's dethronement, all combine to make an unusually difficult set of obstacles in the path of stability and progress. The country lacks an effective government capable of asserting its authority without coercion, and which can instill a sense of Ethiopian unity. An Ethiopian nation has yet to be born.

Bibliography

Baker, J. "Developments in Ethiopia's Road System," *Geography*, Vol. 59, Pt. 2, No. 263 (April, 1974), pp. 150–54.

Bondestam, L. "People and Capitalism in the Northeastern Lowlands of Ethiopia," *Journal of Modern African Studies*, Vol. 12, No. 3 (September, 1974), pp. 423–39.

Cliffe, L. "Capitalism or Feudalism: The Famine in Ethiopia," *Review of African Political Development*, No. 1 (1974), pp. 34–40.

Gilkes, P. *The Dying Lion: Feudalism and Modernization in Ethiopia*. London: Julian Friedmann, 1974.

Harris, J. E. (ed.). *Pillars in Ethiopian History*. Washington, D.C.: Howard University Press, 1974.

Hess, R. L. *The Modernization of Autocracy*. Ithaca: Cornell University Press, 1972.

Hoben, A. *Land Tenure Among the Amhara of Ethiopia*. Chicago: University of Chicago Press, 1973.

Last, G. C. *A Geography of Ethiopia*. Addis Ababa: Ministry of Education, 1965.

Levine, D. N. *Greater Ethiopia: The Evolution of a Multi-Ethnic Society*. Chicago: University of Chicago Press, 1974.

Mariam, M. W. *An Atlas of Ethiopia*, Second Edition, Revised. Addis Ababa, 1970.

Markakis, J. *Ethiopia: Anatomy of a Traditional Polity*. London: Oxford University Press, 1974.

Marks, T. A. "Djibouti: France's Strategic Toehold in Africa," *African Affairs*, Vol. 73, No. 290 (January, 1974), pp. 95–104.

Skurnik, W. A. E. "Revolution and Change in Ethiopia," *Current History*, Vol. 68, No. 405 (May, 1975), pp. 206–210; 230–31.

TWENTY-NINE

The Somali Democratic Republic, commonly known as Somalia, received its independence in 1960 when the British Somaliland Protectorate was united with the Italian-administered United Nations Trust Territory of Somalia. It forms the Horn of East Africa, extending along the south shore of the Gulf of Aden to Cape Gardafui, and then south to Ras Chiamboni beyond the Giuba (Juba) River. It is a poor dry land with few known mineral resources, limited grazing, thin acidic soils, and only two rivers with a regular flow of water, both in the more humid southern region. The Giuba River rises in the high Ethiopian Massif and flows south across the broad low-lying coastal plain before entering the Indian Ocean at Kismayu (Fig. 29-1).

The Shebelle or "Leopard" River also rises in the Ethiopian Massif but fails to reach the sea except during periods of exceptionally heavy rains. Otherwise, it is frequently dry during December and January and disappears in a series of sandy depressions, having paralleled the coast from Mogadishu to Giamame. Both rivers provide for irrigated agriculture, permit permanent habitation in their lower courses, and form Somalia's agricultural core. Northern Somalia, essentially the former British Protectorate, is topographically more diverse than the south and is dominated by the rugged Ogo and Mijurtein (Medjourtine) mountains.

In places rainfall is as high as 20 in. (500 mm), and perennial wells provide winter grazing. South of Hargeisa lies the Haud and Ogo plateaus, a vast wilderness of thorn bush and tall grasses but no permanent water. These are the traditional grazing lands of the Somali herdsmen, but today much of the region lies in Ethiopia. Further south still is the vast, low-lying, almost featureless plateau that comprises the bulk of the territory. Throughout rainfall is

SOMALIA: IRREDENTISM IN THE "HORN"

495

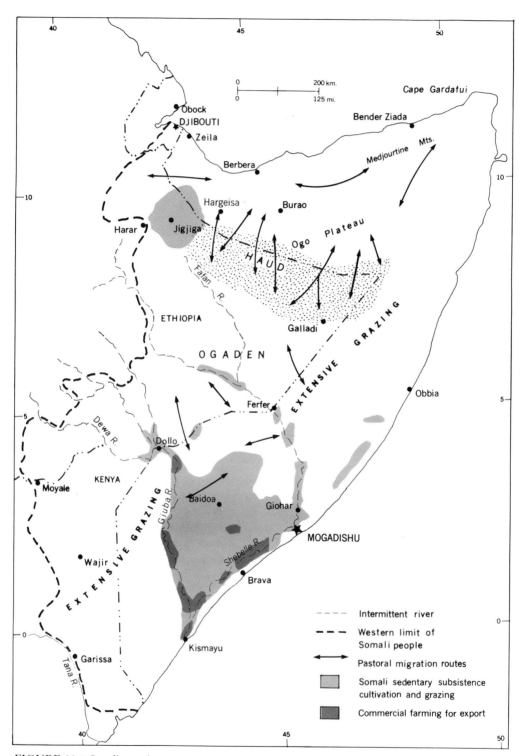

FIGURE 29-1 *Somalian regions.*

sparse and erratic, and desert conditions predominate. The heaviest rains fall between March and June and between September and December and are associated with the monsoons, but nowhere does rainfall exceed 20 in. (500 mm).

The Somali are a Hamitic-speaking people, predominantly pastoral, homogeneous in language, religion (Muslim), and culture, and they are bound together by a strong sense of nationalism. Indeed, Somali nationalism extends beyond the legal state, and for years the Somali have sought to include all their people in a single nation-state. Of the estimated 5.5 million Somali, over 1 million live in eastern Ethiopia, 300,000 in Kenya, and 70,000 in the French Territory of the Afars and the Issas. If Somalia's boundaries were extended to include all these people, its area would be increased by 63 percent to 400,000 sq mi (over 1 million sq km), and traditional migratory pastoralism could proceed unimpaired by the artificially drawn international boundaries superimposed by colonial Europe. While boundary readjustments of this magnitude are most unlikely, Somali irredentism will remain strong and a major concern of the Somali, Kenya, and Ethiopian governments.

The Somalis and Partition

The Somali were not the original inhabitants of present-day Somalia. When they first migrated from the Arabian peninsula over 1000 years ago, they displaced the ethnically related Galla peoples and small bands of Bantu, known to the early Arab geographers as the Zanj. The Zanj were concentrated along the banks of the Giuba and Shebelle and in fertile pockets between them. As the Somali swept south, pushing the Galla and Zanj before them, Yemenite Arabs set up coastal city states such as Zeila, Berbera, Mogadishu, and Brava. Like others of East Africa, they were largely dependent for their prosperity upon the entrepôt trade between the interior (in this case Ethiopia), Arabia, and the markets of Asia. By the tenth century, a ring of coastal emporia had been established through which Muslim expansion was to follow. The towns were eventually conquered by the Portuguese in the sixteenth century but recaptured by various Arab groups in the next. In turn they were replaced by the Turks, the Egyptians, the Sultan of Zanzibar, and by the end of the nineteenth century by France, Britain, and Italy.

Somali expansion, spurred by population pressure in the arid north and a desire for greener pastures and economic benefits to be gained from controlling trade routes to the interior, followed two major routes: the valley of the Shebelle and its tributaries, and the coastal plain of the Indian Ocean littoral. By the end of the seventeenth century, Somali clans occupied nearly all the land of present-day Somalia in the north and west, and they were expanding into the south beyond the Giuba River. But during the fourteenth and fifteenth centuries, Somali expansion was temporarily checked as wars broke out between the Coptic Christian kingdom of Abyssinia and the Moslem coastal states. These holy wars saw the penetration of Arab and Somali forces deep into the heart of Abyssinia but eventually their defeat in the sixteenth century. Massive Galla invasions from the southwest checked further Somali expansion and effectively divided the Somali and Abyssinian forces.

The first European contacts with the Somali coast occurred in the early sixteenth century when Portugal sacked the port of Berbera. But Portuguese occupation was short-lived and replaced in the seventeenth century by the Imam of Muscat. British, French, and Dutch merchants visited the coast en route to and from India and the Far

East, but it was not until the opening of the Suez Canal in 1869 that the Red Sea became a major avenue of European trade with Asia and the object of colonial aspirations. At the time, the Red Sea coast was subject to the nominal suzerainty of Turkey, but governed by local potentates. In 1870 an Egyptian governor was appointed over the whole coast from Suez to Cape Gardafui, and Egyptian garrisons were established at Zeila, Berbera, and later at Harrar. But in 1885, because of troubles stemming from the Mahdist revolt in the Sudan, Egypt withdrew, and the "scramble" for the Horn of East Africa began.

Britain sought additional territory to provide her garrison colony of Aden with fresh meat and cattle, Aden being considered vital for the security of British interests in the Indian Ocean. Thus the British busied themselves making treaties with the Somali east of Zeila which led in 1887 to the establishment of the British protectorate of Somaliland. French and Italian interests were consistent with traditional reasons for colonial expansion. In 1862 France had acquired from the Afars the port of Obock and the adjoining coast north of the Gulf of Tajura and present-day Djibouti. But for almost two decades Obock lay forgotten by France, and it was not until war broke out in Madagascar, and Anglo-French rivalry caused the British to close the port of Aden to French shipping, that the French government saw the necessity of establishing its own naval base and coaling station (Lewis, 1965). Thus France secured the port of Djibouti from the Issa Somali in 1885, and three years later, following regotiations with Britain, defined the boundaries of French Somaliland.

Italian entry into Somali proper began in 1889 with a concession midway along the east coast granted by the Sultan of Obbia. Soon after, Italy acquired control over the towns of Brava, Merca, Mogadishu, and Warsheikh and appointed a commercial firm as its administrative representative. Through the company, Italian interests spread into the interior until they clashed with those of Britain and Ethiopia. Britain and Italy signed treaties in 1891 and 1894, defining their respective spheres of influence, but neither the Somali or Ethiopians were partners to the negotiations. Somali herdsmen living in the interior Ogaden region became subject to Italian rule, while those in the Haud region came under the British. It was not until 1908 that the several loosely administered Italian "protectorates" were united as Italian Somaliland stretching from Bender Ziada on the Gulf of Aden south to the Kenya border (Fig. 29-2).

Somali conquest was not confined to the coast, nor was it solely at the hands of Europe. It was also effected in the interior by the Kingdom of Ethiopia, the only African state capable of contesting the Europeans and sustaining its own territorial ambitions. Menelik's expansionism had carried Ethiopian rule far eastward, beyond the limits of the massif and onto the lower sections of the Horn leading to the coastal plain. These were, and are today, the grazing areas of the nomadic Somali herdsmen, and although boundary demarcation did not take place (other than at a few fixed points great distances apart), inclusions by Ethiopian forces were common.

Menelik asserted that the Somalis had from time immemorial been the cattle-keepers of the Ethiopians and had paid annual tribute to their masters until the Moslem invasion, and that on these grounds, his assertion of hegemony over at least a part of the Somalis' lands was justified. The British, throughout the period of friction, showed an awareness of the problems facing the nomadic, pastoral people, who must practice a form of transhumance from the low plains to the foothill slopes and back in order to survive the rigors of the local environment. Menelik's actions and boundary demands prevented the migratory pattern from being followed, and the effect upon the Somalis was serious.

In 1897, further boundary definition (although very little delimitation and demarcation) took place, as Britain and Ethiopia signed an agreement which did not lead to any exchange of territory, but which terminated the nominal protection Britain had extended over certain Somali groups. Italy had likewise extended the territory nominally under her control well west of the defined boundary between Italian Somaliland and Ethiopia, and for several decades no real opposition occurred. Then the Wal Wal incident occurred (1935) when Britain finally attempted to demarcate the boundaries defined decades earlier. Haile Selassie was on the Ethiopian throne, and he recognized the encroachment of Italian rule over what Menelik had considered Ethiopian territory. The consequences are well known, for they were followed by the Italian invasion of the empire.

For some years (1942–47) the majority of the Somali people were under one administration. This was the result of war conditions, and although it was highly desirable to the Somali, the arrangement was terminated when the United Nations took charge of the fragmented Horn. Ethiopia made vigorous efforts to persuade the United Nations that the Horn should be unified under Ethiopian rule, while Somali representatives attempted to persuade the responsible bodies that the Somali people in the various sectors desired unification under Somali government. In the event, the boundaries as established previously were confirmed, and the only Somali unification that took place involved the merger of British and Italian possessions in the Horn under one flag as the Somali Republic (1960).

Somali Irredentism

The Somali people are bound together by a strong sense of nationalism and the desire for a Greater Somalia. Their ideal is symbolically represented by a five-pointed star on the Somali flag, each point representing Somali-occupied territory: eastern Ethiopia, northeastern Kenya, the French Territory of the Afars and Issas, and the former Italian and British sectors now united as the Republic. Pan-Somaliism has dominated government affairs since independence, and Somali irredentism has been strong ever since the superimposition of the colonial boundaries. At times irredentism in Kenya and Ethiopia has been accompanied by much violence.

Somalia's boundary with Kenya first followed the Giuba River, but in 1925 it was shifted west to 41 degrees east, adding about 12,000 sq mi (31,000 sq km) to Italian Somalia in accordance with the 1915 Treaty of London in which Britain promised to compensate Italy for her participation in World War I (Fig. 29-2). But it left an almost equal area within Kenya whose population was predominantly Somali. In this remote and neglected region of Kenya, then known as the Northern Frontier District (N.F.D.), British authorities set up a line beyond which the Somalis were not permitted to travel so as to prevent further intertribal warfare (Mariam, 1964). They also established administrative laws and techniques different from those applied elsewhere in Kenya, all of which reinforced the Somali sense of exclusiveness. For instance, the Somali were taxed at the rate assessed on the Arab and Indian populations rather than at the lower tax set for the Africans. As a result, entire Somali communities crossed the border into Ethiopia or Somalia where administration was lax or nonexistent. Modern progressive programs in education and pastoralism applied in the south were not developed in the N.F.D. so that the gap in development between northern and southern

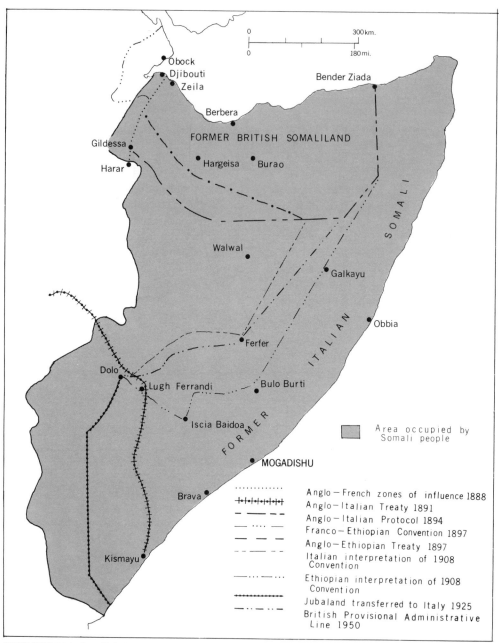

FIGURE 29-2 *Somalia's international boundaries, 1888–1960.*

regions widened with time.

As Kenya's independence approached, Somali leaders in the N.F.D. demanded separation from Kenya and union with Somalia, and a British-appointed commission confirmed this was the wish of the Somali majority. However, the British government opposed secession by the N.F.D., fearing it would encourage similar movements elsewhere in Africa, but felt Somali individualism would be protected by Kenya's federal constitution then being drafted. When

Aerial-view of Parliament House, Mogadishu. Italian-built buildings surround the square. (UN)

the Kenya African National Union (KANU) came to power, the modicum of federalism disappeared and Somali nationalists resorted to guerrilla warfare which took thousands of lives and brought suffering and repression to the Somali civilian population. Since 1967 these *shifta* wars have subsided, but the Somali still look to Mogadishu for ideological and, reportedly, material support.

Somali irredentism in Ethiopia is even more problematic since far more Somalis are involved in a much greater area, and the international boundary line is still in dispute. The cartographic agreement of 1897 is lost, and reconstruction of the line from secondary sources has led to much confusion. Italian claims put the boundary 180 mi (288 km) parallel to the east coast, while the Menelik line is much further to the east (Fig. 29-2). Similarly there are several interpretations of the 1908 Italo-Ethiopian agreement defying the boundary between the Shebelle River

and the northeast corner of Kenya (Touval, 1972). At issue are the seasonal grazing rights of the Somali in the Haud and elsewhere, now within Ethiopia. The British did not withdraw from the Haud until 1955 and stressed at the time its importance to Somalia by requiring the Ethiopians to guarantee the Somali free access to the grazing lands. The Somali government refuses to recognize any boundary treaties to which it is not a signatory and thus has not discouraged Somali nomads from entering Ethiopian-claimed pastures. However, soon after independence, border clashes became more frequent, and by 1964 had developed into military conflict extending the entire length of the disputed boundary. Although open hostilities have subsided following a ceasefire arranged under the auspices of the OAU, the Somali have not abandoned their claims.

Somali-Ethiopian issues are complicated

still further in the French Territory of the Afars and Issas. There the Issa Somali form the majority in the capital of Djibouti, and they are the largest ethnic group along the line-of-rail from Djibouti to the Ethiopian border. Thus, should France grant independence to this territory, the Somalis would be able to cut Addis Ababa off from the sea. And, if Somalia were to annex Djibouti after independence, it might give the Somali government the leverage it needs to force Ethiopia to relax its control over Somali-populated areas elsewhere.

Economic Prospects and Problems

The likelihood of Somalia ever having a diversified economy, rather than one that is overwhelmingly pastoral, is extremely low. It lacks all the requisites of a modern economy. Even its predominantly pastoral economy is handicapped by low and erratic rainfall, periodic droughts, overgrazing, inferior stock, frequent invasions of locusts, and conservative attitudes toward the marketing and ownership of livestock. Despite these limitations, livestock and livestock products earn $33 million in foreign revenue each year and contribute two-thirds of the export earnings. Live goats, sheep, and camels form the bulk of these exports, most being shipped to Saudi Arabia and Kuwait.

Three-fourths of the estimated 3.8 million Somali (in Somalia) are nomadic and seminomadic pastoralists. In the northern regions they occupy the lowlands during the winter months and trek with their livestock (predominantly sheep and goats) to the highland pastures in summer (Fig. 29-1). Further south, cattle are more numerous, and in all regions camels are highly valued, and economic transactions of the pastoralists operate on a camel standard (Lewis, 1965). The FAO has estimated that if controlled grazing were enforced, the existing range could support two or even three times the number of livestock, but most attempts to manage the pasture have failed. The total population equivalent is over 64 million, and given the paucity of the land, biomass densities are high and population pressure is among the most acute in Africa.

Agriculture is also severely restricted by the harsh environment. Less than 1 percent of the area is cultivated, and only 13 percent is cultivable, most of which is in the Giuba and Shebelle valleys. There the emphasis is on staple crops (sorghum, maize and cassava), although irrigated cash crops such as sugar and bananas are also important. Bananas were once Somalia's leading exports, the plantations being established by Italian settlers, and the industry being protected and subsidized by the Italian market. Following the closure of the Suez Canal, transport costs rose and production was cut; with the introduction in 1970 of faster and better equipped ships, the industry began to recover.

Nonagricultural and nonpastoral economic activities are of minor importance. Without capital, technology, resources, markets, and an integrated transport system, there is little likelihood of development. There are no railways, and few good roads except in the vicinity of Mogadishu (280,000), the capital and primate city (Fig. 29-1). With U.S. aid, the southern port of Kismayu (100,000) has been expanded to accommodate the projected growth in Somalia's agricultural exports from the Giuba region, and roads are being improved between it and Mogadischu. In the north, the Soviet Union has developed the port of Berbera (85,000) and has installed missile facilities as part of its military buildup in the Horn. From this vantage point the Russians have the capability of controlling the southern approach to the Suez Canal, the oil routes of the Middle East, and large

Bananas grown under irrigation in the lower Giuba valley. Italian colonists started the plantations, and prior to independence bananas generally accounted for two-thirds of Somalia's exports. Livestock now head the list. (UN)

stretches of the Indian Ocean. Indeed, Somalia's strategic location has once again been realized.

Except in 1972, Somalia has failed to receive its long-term average rainfall since 1969, and the tolls have been high: at least a third of the goats and sheep, more than a quarter of the cattle, and perhaps a tenth of the camels have perished. Vast areas of grazing in the north and northeast have been devastated and cannot be used for years to come. In mid-1975, possibly a million nomads were encamped in relief centers where they were assured food, water, and medical supplies. As in the Sahel, drought is the consequence of human improvidence, carelessness, as well as changes in atmospheric circulation. Gross overstocking of sheep was encouraged by rising prices in the

1910s which led to the installation of thousands of cement tank reservoirs. This, in turn, meant more overgrazing. Installing the tanks became a lucrative business until the government banned it.

There has been one positive side effect of the droughts: an increase in literacy and education. The government, having agreed in 1972 on a Somali script (there being no written Somali language before then), closed most schools for a year and had the teachers and students go to the nomads. Under normal conditions this would not have been feasible, but during the drought the nomads were concentrated in relief camps and around water holes. In this way the revolutionary government's official doctrine of "scientific socialism" was introduced at the grass-roots level. The mother tongue has

A literacy class being held at a relief camp established during the droughts of 1972–75. The government closed all schools for a year at the height of the drought, and sent the teachers and students to instruct the displaced nomads concentrated in these camps. (UN)

Camels and donkeys carrying wood fuel and straw along the main road (built by Mussolini) from Mogadishu to Ethiopia. (UN)

replaced Italian, English, and Arabic as the official written medium, which in time will lessen the regional differences resulting from the colonial era.

The French Territory of the Afars and Issas

The French Territory of the Afars and Issas, formerly known as French Somaliland, is the last French possession on the African mainland. French occupation dates back to 1862 when Afar (Danakil) chiefs ceded the port of Obock and its environs. As Italian and British interests in the Horn and Red Sea expanded, France acquired additional land to the south from the Issa Somali, and subsequently built a coaling station and naval base at Djibouti, today the capital and principal city.

The harbor of Djibouti (100,000) is large and well sheltered and is the obvious sea port for Ethiopia. In 1896, Menelik formally recognized French Somaliland and signed agreements with the French initiating the construction of the railroad to Addis Ababa. The first rails were laid in 1897, and the line was completed in 1917. For several decades, Djibouti was virtually the sole export harbor for Ethiopia's small external trade. However, following the incorporation of Eritrea into Ethiopia, more and more trade has passed through Massawa and Assab. Nevertheless, Djibouti still handles about half the total. The Territory itself generates few exports other than leather and skins to France, and it must import all its industrial requirements and oil. Retail trade is controlled by the Territory's 10,000 Arabs and several hundred Asians.

The Territory (8500 sq mi or 22,000 sq km) has a population of approximately 200,000 that is evenly divided between the Afar who have ties with Ethiopia, and the Issa who have ties with Somalia. Both groups are Moslem, speak related Cushitic languages, and are nomadic beyond the towns. The Issa are more urbanized than the Afar and make up two-thirds of Djibouti's population. Both Ethiopia and Somalia stand ready to assert their claims to the Territory in the event of France's withdrawal (Shilling, 1975). Somalia sees the acquisition of Djibouti as a necessity in its quest for a Greater Somalia. Ethiopia bases its claims upon an historical presence in the area and on its obvious economic interests.

In 1967, when the future of the Territory was put to a vote, nearly 60 percent of the voters opted for the continuance of French rule. The Somalis contested the outcome and many suspected agitators and illegal residents were deported. The Afar remain strongly committed to French rule as the only means to retain their ethnic independence, while the Somali are equally committed to independence and union with Somalia. Meanwhile, French rule means the continuation of aid and technology that are so desperately needed, and the Territory serves as a buffer against any Ethiopian-Somali conflict.

Bibliography

Bell, J. B. *The Horn of Africa.* New York: Crane, Russak and Co., 1974.

Box, T. W. "Nomadism and Land Use in Somalia," *Economic Development and Culture Change,* Vol. 19, (1971), pp. 222–228.

Castagno, A. A. "The Somali-Kenyan Con- *Journal of Modern African Studies,* Vol. 2, (July, 1964), pp. 165–188.

Lewis, I. M. *The Modern History of Somaliland: From Nation to State.* New York: Praeger, 1965.

Mariam, M. W. "The Background of the Ethio-Somalian Boundary Dispute," *Journal of Modern African Studies*, Vol. 2, (July, 1964), pp. 189–219.

Shilling, N. A. "Problems of Political Development in a Mini-state: The French Territory of the Afars and Issas," *Journal of Developing Areas*, Vol. 7 (July, 1973), pp. 613–634.

Shilling, N. A. "Problems of Political Development: The French Territory of the Afars and the Issas," *Focus*, Vol. 26, No. 2 (November–December, 1975), pp. 14–16.

Thompson, V., and R. Adloff. *Djibouti and the Horn of Africa*. Stanford: Stanford University Press, 1968.

Touval, S. *The Boundary Politics of Independent Africa*. Cambridge: Harvard University Press, 1972.

THIRTY

The Republic of Sudan is Africa's largest state (967,500 sq mi or 2,505,825 sq km). Sparsely populated by about 19.5 million inhabitants, the Sudan, bounding Egypt in the north and Uganda in the south, shares the peoples and cultures of Subsaharan Africa as well as the Middle East and Mediterranean Africa. Indeed, the Moslem north is the dominant region of the country in terms of size as well as population, influence in government as well as economic development. But the three southern provinces (Upper Nile, Bahr el Ghazal, and Equatoria) form a large part of the state and are of growing economic importance (Fig. 30-1). The zone of greatest transition between the Arab north and African south lies along the twelfth parallel, below which physical conditions change also: emerging from the dry heart of the central basin, the country becomes moister and the vegetation denser, as the land rises to the North Equatorial divide.

Extending latitudinally over 1200 mi (1900 km) the Sudan does constitute a geographical link between cultural regions, perhaps to a greater degree than any other African state. No other transitional state is quite as sizeable and incorporates as large a population; although Ethiopia's total number of inhabitants is greater, that country does not penetrate black Africa to the same extent. Neither can Ethiopia really be called a bridge between Arab and African from the administrative point of view; Sudan is an Islamic country, and Ethiopia is not. Furthermore, the physiographic fragmentation and ethnic, religious, and linguistic heterogeneity of Ethiopia create a far more complex picture than that of the Sudan, with its low relief, unending plains, and basic cultural-geographical division.

SUDAN: BRIDGE BETWEEN AFRICAN AND ARAB?

507

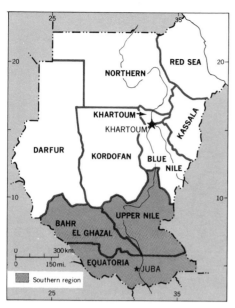

FIGURE 30-1 *Sudan. Administrative districts.*

Although a bridge in the territorial sense, the Sudan remains a divided country, with the south resisting the implementation of administrative decisions even before independence. In part, this has been the result of the tenuous communications between the government and people of the north and those of the south. Just as the Somali of eastern Ethiopia look east rather than toward Addis Ababa, many southern Sudanese look south rather than to Khartoum. The matter has been compounded by religious differences, for in the south many Africans have adopted Christianity and find themselves in a Moslem state.

The Politicogeographical Entity

The Sudan is one of Africa's large, compact political units. All of its northern and northwestern boundaries (with Egypt, Libya, and northern Chad) are geometrical, and they lie in desolate, dry terrain for the greater part. In the east, the boundary corresponds more or less to the western limit of the Ethiopian Massif. The southern border shows some adjustment to physiographic conditions, running along divide areas between major drainage lines. The Sudan has its own seaport, Port Sudan, on the Red Sea, but although the state is not landlocked, parts of it are a thousand miles (1600 km) from that exit. The southern provinces are much farther from the railroads connecting the central Sudan with Port Sudan than they are from the Uganda railhead at Gulu, which is linked to Mombasa.

The orientation of the Sudan's physiographic belts is latitudinal, and a series of climatic zones can be recognized from the desert north to the moist savanna of the extreme south (Fig. 30-2). North of the latitude of El Fasher, a vegetative cover is practically nonexistent, and the average annual rainfall is below 10 in. (254 mm). Across the Kordofan Plateau the total has reached between 25 and 30 in. (635–762 mm), and in the southwestern margins it exceeds 50 in. (1270 mm). This east-west alignment of environmental zones has not promoted contact between the north and south of the country, especially since the physiography of the south renders the building of modern transport routes difficult and expensive, and in places almost impossible. Hence, the factor of physiography is added to that of distance in the separation of the south from the northern regions.

The great longitudinal unifier, of course, is the White Nile. In the extreme south, the great river enters the Sudan via a series of rapids, all of which lie upstream from Juba. Below Juba, the Nile is navigable to Khartoum, and over considerable stretches it forms the only possible means of communication. The gradient is very low as

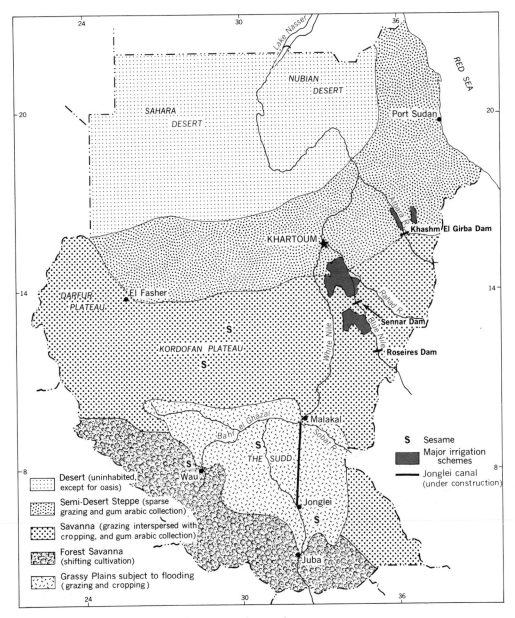

FIGURE 30-2 *Sudan. Natural environments and economies.*

the river braids its way through the Sudd, re-entering a well-defined valley in the area of Malakal. In the latitude of the Sudd, the Sudan consists of swampland and marshes, and the road from Juba to Khartoum, which traverses this region, is usable only part of the year. But the river is navigable all year round and continues to carry most of the

traffic between the province of Equatoria and the northern parts of the country.

It is along the Nile that the "bridge" character of the Sudan between black and Arab Africa can be observed to some small extent. Not only have people of the south begun to adopt modes of dress that are normal in the north, but in the settlements, the square mud huts of the desert north and the round, thatched huts of the south stand side by side. The influence and control of the Khartoum government are greater along and near the Nile than in the peripheral areas. But the river and the areas immediately adjacent to it form only a small part of the vastness of the Sudan, and interregional contact is much less evident in the distant areas.

In fact, the Sudan has also played a role in the east-west contact between African and Arab, involving peoples and ideas from beyond the boundaries of the present political entity. The savanna belt has been an avenue of penetration for Islam and a zone of transit by Africans on pilgrimages to Mecca. Some of the people involved in these movements settled in the region of the Sudan and made their impact upon local modes of living. Today, however, the modern state incorporates an area in which north-south diversification is greater than that from east to west, and if the Sudan is to form a real bridge between Arab and African, it must come through increased north-south contact and cooperation.

The republic has its origins in a turbulent past. As in the Horn, local as well as European imperialism played a part in the course of events, and the boundaries are in several places the result of the consolidation of colonial claims. The local imperialism is that of Egypt, whose interest in the lands to the south is as old as the state itself. The first exports of the Sudan included slaves, ivory, and ostrich feathers, and the Egyptians intermittently sought to extend their power over the source of these products. The invasion of Islam from the east isolated the pockets of Christianity which had formed during Roman days, and after various small Moslem states had formed and failed, a large Islamic Empire finally arose, centered upon Sennar on the Blue Nile. This empire thrived during the sixteenth century, and the region between the White and Blue Nile became a core area for the en-

tire Sudan, a position it continued to hold through the tenure of several succeeding empires. The Fung Empire held the center of the stage for well over two centuries, asserting its rule over far-flung tribal peoples, and in a sense it foreshadowed the rise of the modern Sudan.

In 1821 the empire fell as a result of an Egyptian invasion, and an Egyptian government was established at Khartoum in 1830. The entire eastern Sudan had fallen to the Egyptians, and the connection of Sudanese territory with the ports of Suakin and Massawa (the latter subsequently lost to the Italians) dates from this period. British influence was now beginning to be felt, and the slave trade was suppressed, as a result of which economic chaos developed; slavery had been one of the mainstays of the tribes in the transition zone between black and Arab Africa.

Under these conditions, the country was ripe for revolt, which came in 1881, when Muhammad Ahmad proclaimed himself the Mahdi, a messenger of Islam who was to guide the people toward freedom from Egyptian rule. It must be realized that, although there was nominal British supervision, the Egyptians were the actual administrators of the Sudan, and it was against them that the revolt which the Mahdi fomented was aimed. Support was general, and within a few years, the Mahdi's followers, the Dervishes, controlled large parts of the country.

For 13 years the Sudan was reduced to a state of disorder. Economic development was at a standstill, the livestock population was greatly reduced through the lack of care and willful destruction, disease was rampant, and general disorganization prevailed. It has been estimated that the population itself was reduced from 8.5 to 3.5 million in the period following General Charles Gordon's defeat in Khartoum (1885) until General Kitchener's victory at Omdurman in 1898.

After the successful Anglo-Egyptian war effort in the Sudan, an administration was set up whereby both Britain and Egypt had a share of the government. The Egyptian khedive would appoint a British governor general, in whom the supreme powers in the country were vested. The governor general could legislate by proclamation and was the military and civil commander. Lord Kitchener, who had led the conquering forces, was the first governor general, and he established an administrative framework in which the policy-making positions were held by British, the majority of the civil servants being Egyptian. Egypt paid a large share of the costs of administration and control, and the country became known as the Anglo-Egyptian Sudan, although in effect it remained under British control.

Egypt, however, remained nominally a part of the Turkish Ottoman Empire, and when World War I erupted, it found itself involved with both sides: with Britain in the administration of the Sudan, and with Turkey (which had joined the Axis Powers) in the war itself. Britain declared a protectorate over Egypt, solving the immediate problem but creating the basis for a new one. Egyptian nationalism arose against British overlordship, not only in Egypt, but also in the Sudan, over which the Egyptians wished to extend their sovereignty.

During the entire colonial period, the focus of activity, political as well as economic, was in the region north of 12 degrees north latitude. The southern part of the Sudan, while under British administration, remained almost completely separated and isolated from such progress as took place elsewhere, and was little involved in the continuing administrative struggle among the Egyptians, northern Sudanese, and British. To the linguistic, ethnic, physiographic, and religious individuality of the south was added a form of administrative separation which had the character of a protectorate in all but name. Thus, rather than submerging the large-scale regional differences of the Sudan, British administration actually helped foster them, leaving the problem of actual integration and adjustment to the independent state. Under British administration, therefore, the Sudan did incorporate Arab and African under a single government, but the country did not really serve as a meeting ground between the two. The British deepened the division that already existed by supporting the spread of Christianity in the south while discouraging efforts to propagate Islam.

Until the Egyptian evacuation in 1924, administration of the condominium was based on the principle of "direct rule." Then, "indirect rule" or "native administration" through tribal sheikhs and chiefs was introduced which tended to accentuate the politicogeographical contrasts between north and south. A "southern policy" was implemented to prevent the spirit of nationalism from spreading southward and to separate the three southern provinces from the rest of the country with a view of their eventual assimilation in a broader British East African Federation (with Uganda, Kenya, and Tanganyika). Some British officials saw a southern Christian Sudan as a buffer against the Arabization of East Africa (Albine, 1970). Thus Muslim and Arabic speaking people in the south were evicted while others were prevented from entering. A pass system was introduced to control interregional movement, northern merchants were replaced by Greeks and Christian Syrians, and southerners were discouraged from practicing any northern customs they had acquired. Christian missionaries (mostly Roman Catholic Italians), although excluded from the north, became responsible for education in the south.

Little effort was made to provide the requisites for widespread economic development and social betterment in either north or south, although it was decided at an early stage that the Sudan's economic future must be based on long-staple cotton from the Gezira Scheme near the confluence of the two Niles. The scheme limited the amount of funds available for development elsewhere, and once fully operative the tenants and administrative board successfully prevented the profits from being spent outside the region. Thus the regional economic inequalities were accentuated, and the south formed part of the condominium's economic backwater.

As early as 1944 an advisory council was constituted in Khartoum, with representation from and responsibilities for the six northern provinces. The Christian and pagan peoples of the south, far removed from the mainstream of Sudan development, were not identified with the Sudanese struggle for independence, and they were not represented in the council. Neither did they feel the impact of Egyptian involvement in Sudan affairs: they were far removed from Egypt itself and from the scene of much of the Anglo-Egyptian-Sudanese friction, Khartoum. The days of temporary solidarity between parts of the south and north, resulting from the Egyptian thrust southward in the early 1800s, were long forgotten. Deeper divisions, involving race and religion, and going back also to the days when the northerners were slavers and the southerners actual and potential slaves, remained. Indeed, it may be said that the southern peoples desired either British or Egyptian rule in the Sudan, but not Sudanese rule. In the decades before independence, the Egyptian crown did much to retard Sudanese nationalism and delay independence, partly because of its concern over the future use of the waters of the Nile. While the rift between the Sudanese and Egypt widened, the delay in the coming of independence was welcome in the south, where the replacement of British administrators by northern Sudanese officials was an unpleasant prospect. Thus, on the question of the attitude to Egypt, southern and northern Sudanese held entirely different opinions.

The internal fragmentation of the Sudan was long minimized by the uniform quality of British rule, even though it could do little to wipe out regional differences. In the south, the British were unquestionably quite popular, since they were seen as security against the imposition of northern rule in the form of northern Sudanese officials. When independence came, and even before the actual date of its achievement, violence accompanied the withdrawal of British government and military personnel from the south and their replacement by Sudanese (of course, northern Moslems). In August 1955, the Equatoria Corps of the Sudan Defense Force mutinied, and for some weeks held most of the south excluding the town of Juba, which remained in the hands of forces loyal to the Khartoum government. Refugees streamed over the Uganda and Congo borders, both civilians escaping from Khartoum rule and government officials seeking santuary. Belgium closed its Congo border, but among some Acholi leaders in northern Uganda there was talk of uniting the southern extreme of Sudan with Uganda. The British administration in Uganda negated these suggestions, but they were undeniably popular with a segment of the population of the southern Sudan.

Thus, Egyptian and British activities in this part of Africa have resulted in the establishment of a unique state, which is part of the Subsaharan African cultural realm as well as of the Middle East, internally divided in such a manner that people in the south consider themselves occupied by the noroh. Democratic government, predictably, has faltered, and military leadership has replaced it. Efforts to develop the south, to educate and integrate the peoples in the framework of the country are under way, but the process will be a slow and laborious one.

Sudan is primarily an agricultural country, and the rainfall limits to cultivation are offset by opportunities for irrigation that are among Africa's best. The agricultural capacity of the country is concentrated in the region which once was the heart of the Fung Empire, between the White and the Blue Nile rivers. To be sure, this is not the only region capable of development, for possibilities also exist along the Nile River north of Khartoum, along the Baraka River in the extreme east, and along the Atbara River. The south, also, can sustain sedentary cash cropping in certain areas, and there development has barely begun in the face of such major obstacles as poor communications, lack of education and incentive, civil war and traditional subsistence modes of farming.

Depending mainly upon its agricultural industries, the Sudan is thus not without bright prospects. In spite of the country's reliance upon farming, it has enjoyed financial solvency practically continuously since 1913. This was first achieved through the export of gum arabic, of which the Sudan is the world's major producer. The Kordofan Plateau has been the main source area of this product, so that the south-central Sudan initially made the major economic contribution to the country. El Obeid, chief auction center for the harvest, was connected by rail (via Sennar and Kassala) to Port Sudan (Fig. 30-3). But although this railroad was later extended to Nyala in Darfur Province, no southward line was constructed until the 1960s. Gum arabic, which is used principally in medicine, confectionery, and textile manufacture, is tapped from acacia trees. Indiscriminate tapping, resulting from the ready market and strong demand, has endangered the industry, which is now supported by the planting of trees. The region of production extends from Kassala Province through Blue Nile and Kordofan to Darfur, all "northern" provinces.

In the mid-1920s a cash crop, cotton, became the Sudan's leading export product, and has remained so ever since, annually contributing as much as three-quarters of the total export revenue. Its cultivation takes place throughout the country, under irrigation along both Niles and without it in the wetter southern provinces (Fig. 30-2). Only the northernmost Nilotic peoples (Shilluk and Dinka) produce anything other than subsistence crops, including small amounts of cotton from the Zande Scheme, so that the contribution of the south toward the annual cotton crop should not be overestimated. The south is capable of greatly increased cotton production, however, and its share in the industry is likely to increase.

The great cotton-producing area in the Sudan is the Gezira ("island") between the Blue and the White Nile. There, the crop is grown in one of the greatest irrigation projects in the world (Fig. 30-4). The Blue Nile is dammed at Sennar, a project begun in 1913, delayed by World War I, and completed in 1925. The area was connected to the coast by rail, and the plan was initially a partnership between the government, two concession companies (Sudan Plantations Syndicate and Kassala Cotton Company), and the individual tenant farmers. In 1950 the concession companies' leases expired, and the Sudan Gezira Board replaced them.

The triple partnership worked extremely well. Of the two companies, the syndicate played the dominant role, and a complete reorganization of local agriculture was achieved. The arrangement was such that the profits were divided between the tenant farmers, the government (which had provided the capital and the cost of maintaining the irrigation works), and the companies, these parties receiving 40, 40, and 20 percent, respectively.

In 1950, when the role of the private firms was taken over by the Sudan Gezira Board and the scheme was therefore in effect

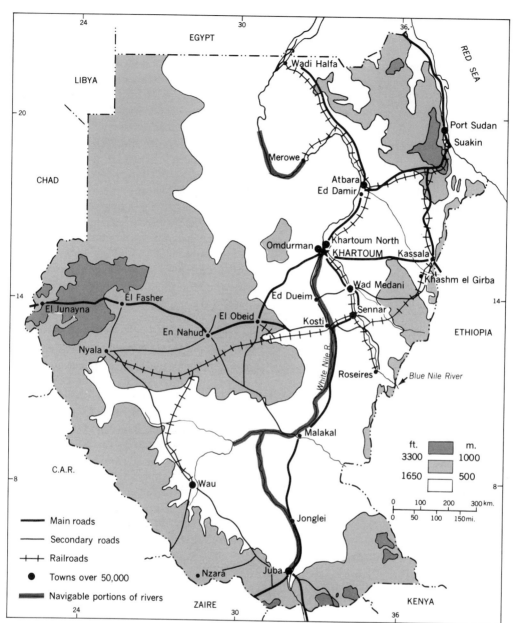

FIGURE 30-3 *Sudan. Towns and transport.*

nationalized, the profit sharing was altered somewhat. The tenant farmer now receives 42 percent of the profits directly and another 6 percent indirectly in the form of social services, while the government gets 42 percent and the Sudan Gezira Board, in charge of the entire operation, is allotted 10 percent. The project continues to function success-

fully, with nearly 80,000 tenant farmers participating, each cultivating a piece of land averaging about 40 acres (16 ha). Careful land husbandry practices have been enforced, protecting the soil. A rotation system has been developed whereby cotton is planted on a certain plot every third year. Following the cotton year, the soil carries a

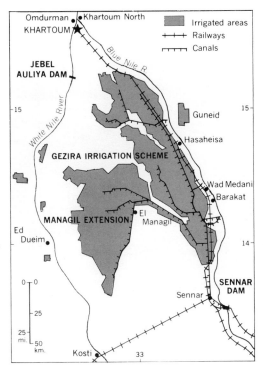

FIGURE 30-4 *Sudan. The Gezira-Managil irrigation scheme.*

crop of millet or dura, and is then left fallow the next season. Nevertheless, yields per acre are very variable, and the total harvest is great mainly because of the enormous extent of the scheme. Average yields are, for instance, substantially less than those of Egypt, although the increased use of fertilizers is expected to improve this situation.

With the completion of the Managil extension, the Gezira-Managil Scheme accounts for about 60 percent of Sudan's cotton output and covers about 1.9 million acres (770,000 ha) of cultivable land. Each year over a half million acres (202,000 ha) are devoted to cotton, but this is likely to decline because of depressed prices and the country's drive toward greater self-sufficiency in food production, partly in response to the recent droughts. Although much of the cotton is exported (to China, Japan, and India), some is used in the textile mills of Khartoum North, Wad Medani, Hasaheisa and other local towns. East of the

Blue Nile, the government is developing the 300,000-acre (121,500 ha) Rahad irrigation scheme which will utilize waters diverted from the Roseires Dam on the Blue Nile, and add substantially to Sudan's production of medium-staple cotton, groundnuts, and sorghum once it is completed in 1978.

A third major irrigation scheme is situated further east on the Atbara River below the Khashm el-Girba Dam. This scheme, completed in 1966, was for the resettlement of 53,000 Nubians from Wadi Halfa and environs displaced by the waters backed up behind the Aswan High Dam. Twenty-five villages of 250 to 300 houses each were built around Halfa (35,000), a new service center, and each displaced farmer was given two feddans (1 feddan = 1.038 acres) for each feddan he previously farmed (Fahim, 1973). Over 500,000 feddans of irrigated land are planned on which the settlers must cultivate cotton, wheat, and groundnuts in a three-crop rotation system. The tenants and management equally share the net returns from cotton, while all profits from other crops are those of the farmer. Sugar is a new and profitable crop and is processed locally.

Each of these irrigation schemes is situated in the central Northern Region which makes the greatest contribution to the country's economy, far in excess of the dry northern fringe and the dominantly subsistence south. Here lies the economic heart together with the capital, Khartoum (330,000), and its twin cities of Omdurman (310,000) and Khartoum North (165,000). This is the most densely populated area of Sudan producing by far the bulk of the exported products and consumer-oriented manufacturing. In 1975, almost 90 percent of the industrial establishments were located in Khartoum North. The region has long been the focus of administrative, religious, and educational activity, and was the core of the Fung Empire of old. It lies 490 mi (785 km) by rail from Port Sudan (130,000) to which exports are funneled, and it forms the major domestic market for the country.

The Managil Extension of the Gezira Irrigation Scheme, Sudan. The Blue Nile lies at the right, with the canal permitting irrigation in the Managil area to the left. Note the extreme flatness of the area. About 1.9 million acres (770,000 ha) of cultivable land are in the scheme. (UN)

A modern cotton textile mill at Khartoum North using cotton from the Gezira-Managil Scheme. (UN)

THE HORN AND THE SUDAN

Aerial view of Port Sudan. Port Sudan is the country's only direct exit to the sea, and practically all external trade goes through this harbor. A second port may be built at Suakin. (UN)

The South and Reconstruction

In contrast with the northern provinces, the three southern provinces (Bahr el Ghazal, Upper Nile, and Equatoria) have not received large-scale development expenditures in agricultural projects, nor have they contributed much to the national economy. Indeed, for 16 years (1955–1972) the region was embroiled in a civil war that saw over a million war-inflicted deaths and an equal number of refugees fleeing across the borders and into the bush (El-Bushira, 1975). Government forces retained control of the main towns while the rebel *Anya-nya* organization established a basic administration elsewhere, although many regions and perhaps one million persons were largely ungoverned.

The military regime that seized power in Khartoum in 1958 attempted a policy of enforced Arabization and Islamization of the south. Missionaries were expelled, the edu-

cation process collapsed, transport and communications routes were disrupted or poorly maintained, and general disorder prevailed. The population faced punitive raids by both the Sudan army and the *Anya-nya*, and was forced to supply them food and materials. Cash-cropping was replaced by basic subsistence production. Famine crops such as yams and cassava, which were easily planted and harvested, replaced the more nutritious millet. Food shortages, deteriorating diet, periodic drought, and the general absence of medical facilities and relief supplies brought a rising death toll (Roden, 1974). Survivors either drifted to refugee camps in the south or sought work in northern agricultural schemes, construction sites, and factories. By 1971, about 800,000 southerners were living in the north. The population of Juba, which dropped from 20,000 to 7000 in 1965 following a Sudan Army massacre, rose to

A kenaf estate in the Southern Region. Large areas of the "Sudd" have been planted to this fibre crop to lessen Sudan's dependence on imported jute. Southern Sudan has enormous agricultural potential. (UN)

120,000 by 1971, while Wau grew from 10,000 to 60,000 over the same period. However, little employment was available, and the population was dependent on relief supplies.

In May 1969, General Nimeiry seized power and soon after declared his government's policy of solving the age-old north-south dispute by granting regional autonomy to the three southern provinces within a so-cialist Sudan. But stability was not achieved until the Addis Ababa Agreement between the Sudanese Government and the *Anya-nya* southern rebels was signed in April 1972. Under the agreement, the south gained regional autonomy within a federal structure of government, and dropped its aim of seces-sion. It was granted a Regional People's As-sembly with a High Executive Council, and with representation in the National People's

Assembly located in Khartoum. The head of the High Executive Council is also a vice-president of the Republic. The agreement also provided for the return and rehabilitation of southern Sudanese refugees, the reintegration of *Anya-nya* rebels into the Sudanese armed forces, and the recognition of Christianity and the English language in the south, together with Islam and Arabic in the north.

The Southern Region has great economic potential, and given continued political stability and a massive infusion of capital, it could well become the main supplier of foods to the Arab world, and a source of industrial resources and food for the north. The first phase of development required the restoration of the infrastructure to prewar levels and the resettlement of refugees on the land. Roads were rebuilt, navigable tributaries of the Nile choked by weeds and obstructed by sunken vessels were cleared, and cash-cropping is gradually being reintroduced. Before the war, trypanosomiasis, rinderpest, and other diseases were largely under control, but now they are not, so that valuable farmland and pasture must be reclaimed and the population resettled. The Zande Scheme, begun in 1946 along lines similar to the Gezira Scheme, is being reactivated and modernized, together with the cotton gins and textile factories at Nzara. Likewise, coffee, tea, rice, and tobacco are once again being grown on estates established by northern entrepreneurs at the time of independence.

Several new projects are planned, the most ambitious and costly being a 175-mile-long (280 km) canal between Jonglei and Malakal that will bypass part of the Nile as it winds through the Sudd (Fig. 30-2). It will cut evaporation losses by 50 percent and provide about 3.7 million acres (1.5 million ha) of reclaimed land that could be put under irrigation. Mixed farming, pastoralism, fishing, and specialized estate cultivation are all to be encouraged. Papyrus from the swamps may be processed at Malakal to make paper and cardboard, and further south forestry is to be expanded. A road will parallel the canal reducing the distance between Juba and the north, and feeder roads will link it with the surrounding region. But all of this cannot be accomplished without the resettlement of Nuer and Dinka pastoralists and cultivators, and without an increased presence of northerners and Egyptian technicians, Egypt having agreed to finance and manage the project jointly with Sudan. Political and economic unity between north and south, however, must focus on the Nile. Already there is fear of northern domination once again.

These and other projects will not only provide the regional government with revenues so that it can be financially self-sufficient, but they will help Sudan's balance of payments and add to its national viability. However, like large-scale projects elsewhere in Africa, they may not bring benefits to the majority. There is no shortage of development funds, but bureaucratic delays and political intrigues are major problems. A $10.7 million loan from the International Development Agency became effective in October 1974 and is being used to help farmers and cultivators improve their output. Emphasis is being placed on extension services, credit facilities, marketing, and disease control.

Bridge and Barrier

Sudan's Arab element is anxious to secure Arab oil money to finance its development projects without jeopardizing the delicate truce with the Christian and pagan southerners. The Sudan could well become the breadbasket for the Near East: it has 40 percent of the potentially cultivable land of the Arab world and is strategically situated to supply the Arabs with food. Most of this potential lies along the Nile, especially in the south. The Arab countries remain vulnerable to pressure from the so-called "agro-powers" so long as they remain dependent upon imported food to any substantial extent. The Sudan, they realize, is the one country that could make them not only self-sufficient but also an "agro-power."

At present Arab oil money is financing, in part, the Rahad irrigation project, the Jonglei Canal, a petroleum products pipeline from a new refinery in Port Sudan to Khartoum, a textile mill at Sennar, and numerous smaller agricultural processing plants. The largest project under consideration is the proposed Arab/Iranian agricultural investment of up to $6000 million by 1985 to double grain production, raise meat output by 140 percent, and raise sugar output still further to provide a large proportion of the imported food requirements of the Middle East. There is also potential aid to upgrade the transport network, at present one of the greatest impediments to rapid development.

The Sudan's peculiar internal politico-geographic realities have made it difficult for President Nimeiry to adopt a single foreign policy towards the neighboring states. The policy has often attempted to be a symbolic bridge between the Arab and African worlds. While concentrating on keeping good relations with Uganda, Ethiopia, and Tanzania, there has been since 1974 increasing contact with the Arab world, in particular with the wealthier Arabian peninsular countries. Relations with Egypt and Libya have often been strained. In late 1969, Sudan concluded a tripartite agreement on military, political, and economic coordination with Egypt and Libya, but held back from joining the Federation of Arab Republics. In 1972, the governmdnt's preoccupation with its southern problem put a distance between the Sudan and its northern neighbors, and in May 1974, President Nimeiry accused Colonel Qaddafi of Libya of being

behind a plot to overthrow this government. However, rapproachement with Qaddafi was achieved in 1975, and Sudan appears to be committed to the Arab cause.

In assessing the role of the Sudan as a bridge between Arab and African, it should be remembered that the southern Nilotic peoples are themselves not representative of Bantu and Negro Africa, although linguistically they relate to central rather than northern Africa. Nor are the northern peoples racially identical to the people of Egypt. The transition from the heart of the Arab world to black Africa along the Nile River, begun in Egypt, ends in Uganda. Indeed, the most obvious zone of ethnic transition lies across the Sudan, but it would be a mistake to assume that the peoples of the northern and southern parts of the country are part of homogeneous Arab and African populations living beyond. Nevertheless, any eventual success on the part of the Sudanese in developing a nation out of the diversity of the country's population will be the result of education—and ideas in this country emanate from the north; of economic participation—and products must go to northern markets and exits; of effective administration—and the trained people in this field are the people of the north; and modes of living which are normal among the majority of the people—again the people of the north. In other words, the effort must be made by a strong central government that is aware of the regional contrasts in the country and is prepared to make certain sacrifices to promote internal unity. As was stated earlier, the period of British rule really only delayed the inevitable effort to integrate the south with the north; it was perhaps the only major British error in the modern administration of the Sudan as a dependency. Since the year of independence, 1956, the country has had but little opportunity to begin the task. In a sense, the Sudan still is two bridgeheads rather than a bridge, the first connecting beam just being laid.

Aguda, O. "The State and the Economy in the Sudan," *Journal of Developing Areas*, Vol. 7 (April, 1973), pp. 431–438.

Albine, O. *The Sudan: A Southern Viewpoint*. London: Oxford University Press, 1970.

Area Handbook for the Democratic Republic of Sudan. Washington: U.S. Government Printing Office, 1973.

Barbour, K. M. *The Republic of the Sudan: A Regional Geography*. London: University of London Press, 1961.

————. "The Nile Basin: Social and Economic Revolution," in R. M. Prothero (ed.), *A Geography of Africa*. New York: Praeger, 1969.

Beshir, M. O. *Revolution and Nationalism in the Sudan*. New York: Harper and Row, 1974.

El-Bushira, El-Sayed. "The Development of Industry in Greater Khartoum," *East African Geographical Review*, No. 10 (April, 1972), pp. 27–50.

El-Bushira, El-Sayed. "Regional Inequalities in the Sudan," *Focus*, Vol. 26, No. 1 (September-October, 1975), pp. 1–8.

Fahim, H. M. "Nubian Resettlement in the Sudan," *Ekistics*, Vol. 36, No. 212 (July 1973), pp. 42–49.

Mountjoy, A. B. "Water Policy Unites the Sudan," *Geographical Magazine*, Vol. 44 (July, 1972), pp. 705–712.

Ring, B. M. M. "Political Relationships Between Northern and Southern Blacks in the Sudan," *Africa Today*, Vol. 20, No. 3 (Summer, 1973), pp. 13–18.

Roden, D. "Sudan After the Conflict," *Geographical Magazine*, Vol. 44 (June, 1972), pp. 593–598.

————. "Regional Inequality and Rebellion in the Sudan," *Geographical Review*, Vol. 64, No. 4 (October, 1974), pp. 498–516.

Sarkesian, S. C. "The Southern Sudan: A Reassessment," *African Studies Review*, Vol. 16 (1973), pp. 1–22.

Thornton, D. S. "Agricultural Development in the Sudan Gezira Scheme," *Sudan Notes and Records*, Vol. 53 (1972), pp. 100–115.

PART SEVEN

NORTHERN AFRICA

THIRTY-ONE

Egypt occupies, quite literally, Africa's northeastern corner: geometric boundaries separate its 386,900 sq mi (just over 1 million sq km) from Libya to the west and Sudan to the south. Alone among states on the African landmass, Egypt extends into Asia through its foothold on the Sinai Peninsula—a hold that has, in modern times, proved rather tenuous. Egypt lost the entire Sinai region during the 1967 war with Israel, and then regained a toehold across the Suez Canal in the conflict of 1973. The years that followed saw intense diplomatic efforts to persuade Israel to yield more of occupied Sinai to Egypt, but by early 1976 the Jewish state had agreed only to a relatively minor withdrawal and the creation of a buffer zone between the adversaries. Most of Sinai still remained in Israeli hands.

Egypt now faces an enemy capable of striking into its very heartland in a matter of minutes, a totally new condition for a country protected for centuries (indeed, millennia) by desert and distance from its enemies. Herodotus described Egypt as the gift of the Nile, but Egypt also was a product of natural protection, The middle and lower Nile lie enclosed by inhospitable country, open to the Mediterranean Sea but otherwise rather inaccessible to overland contact. To the south, the Nile is interrupted by a series of cataracts that begin near the present boundary of Egypt and the Sudan. To the east, the Sinai Peninsula never afforded an easy crossing, and the southwestern arm of the ancient Fertile Crescent lay a considerable distance beyond. To the west, there is the endless Sahara Desert. The ancient Egyptians had themselves a natural fortress, and in their comparative isolation they converted security into progress. Internally, the Nile was then what it remains to this day— the country's highway of trade and association, its lifeline. Externally, the Egypt of the

MODERNIZATION AND CONFLICT: THE EMINENCE OF EGYPT

Pharaohs must trade, for there was little wood and metal, but most of this trade was left to Phoencians and Greeks. Egypt's cultural landscape still carries the record of an-

tiquity's accomplishments in the great pyramids and stone sculptures that bear witness to the rise of a culture hearth 5000 years ago.

The Nile

Perhaps 95 percent of Egypt's 41 million people live within a dozen miles of the Nile River or one of its distributaries. The great river is the product of headwaters that rise in two different parts of Africa: Ethiopia, where the Blue Nile originates, and the lakes region of East Africa, source of the White Nile. Before dams were constructed across the river, the Nile's dual origins assured a fairly regular natural flow of water, making the annual floods predictable both in terms of timing and intensity. The Nile normally is at its lowest level in May and June, but rises during July, August, and September to its flood stage in October, when it may be more than 20 ft (7 m) above its low stage. After a rapid fall during November and December, the river declines gradually until its May minimum. In ancient times this regime made possible the invention of irrigation, for the mud left behind by the Nile floods was manifestly cultivable and fertile. Eventually a system of cultivation known as *basin irrigation* developed, whereby fields along the low banks of the Nile were partitioned off by earth ridges into a large number of artificial basins. The mud-rich river waters would pour into these basins during flood time, and then the exits would be closed, so that the water would stand still, depositing its fertile load of alluvium. Then, after six to eight weeks, the exit sluices are opened and the water drains away, leaving the rejuvenated soil ready for sowing. This method, while revolutionary in ancient times, had disadvantages: the susceptible lands must lie near or below the flood level, only one crop can be grown annually, and if the floods were less intense (as they are in some years), some basins remain unir-

rigated because flood level did not reach them. Still, traditional basin irrigation prevailed all along the Nile River for thousands of years; not until the late nineteenth century did more modern methods develop. Even as late as 1950, as much as one-tenth of all irrigation in Egypt was basin irrigation, most of it practiced, still, in Upper Egypt (the region nearest the Sudan border).

The construction of dams, begun during the nineteenth century, made possible the *perennial irrigation* of Egypt's farmlands. By building a series of barrages (with locks for navigation) across the river, engineers were able to control the floods, raise the Nile's water level, and free the farmers from their dependence upon the seasonality of the river's natural regime. Not only did the country's cultivable area expand substantially but it also became possible to grow more than one crop per year. By the early 1980s all farmland in Egypt will be under perennial irrigation, a transformation that has taken place within one century.

The greatest of all Nile dam projects, the Aswan High Dam, was begun in 1958 and completed in 1971. The High Dam is located some 600 mi (1000 km) upstream from Cairo, in a comparatively narrow, granite-sided section of the valley. The dam wall, 364 ft (110 m) high, creates Lake Nasser, one of the largest artificial lakes in the world (Fig. 31-1). The reservoir inundates well over 300 mi (480 km) of the Nile's valley not only in Upper Egypt but in the Sudan as well, and the cooperation of Sudan was required since some 50,000 Sudanese had to be resettled. The impact of the High Dam on Egypt's cultivable area is enormous: before construction the Nile's waters could

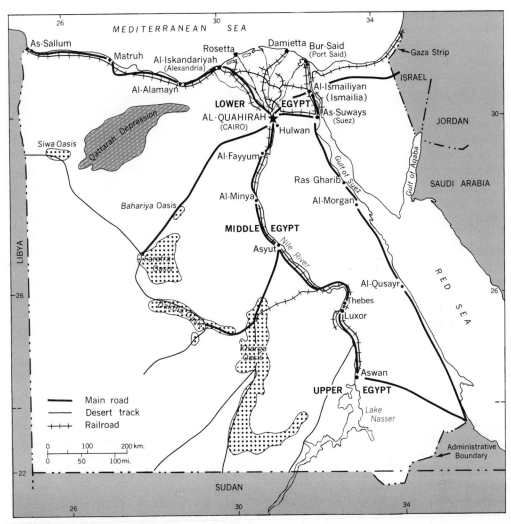

FIGURE 31-1 *Egyptian regions.*

irrigate some 6.25 million acres (2.53 million ha) of farmland. To this, the Aswan High Dam added 1.35 million acres (550,000 ha). In addition, nearly 1 million acres (400,000 ha) of farmland in Middle and Upper Egypt that were still under basin irrigation could now be converted to perennial irrigation, resulting in increased crop yields.

Egypt has often been described as one elongated oasis, and the map—almost any map of the country's human geography— confirms the appropriateness of that description. In Upper and Middle Egypt the strip of abundant, intense green, 3 to 15 mi (5 to 24 km) wide, lies in stark contrast to the barren, harsh, dry desert immediately adjacent, a reminder of what Egypt would be without its lifeline of water. But below Cairo, the great river fans out across its wide delta, 100 mi (160 km) in length and 155 mi (250 km) wide along the Mediterranean coast between Alexandria and Port Said. In ancient times the river's waters reached the sea via several channels, and the delta was flood-prone, inhospitable country; ancient Egypt was Middle and Upper Egypt, the Egypt of the Nile

Valley. But today the delta waters are diverted through two controlled channels, the Rosetta and Damietta distributaries. The delta contains twice as much cultivable land as lies in Middle and Upper Egypt, and it has some of Africa's most fertile soils. In 1977, nearly half of Egypt's population (18.5 out of 41 million) inhabited the delta region.

The increasing use of Nile waters upstream and the diminished flow of the river now pose a threat to all the progress that has been made in the delta. There is a danger that brackish water will invade the channels from the north, seep into the soil, and reduce large areas, once again, to their inhospitable and unproductive state. The consequences of such a sequence of events—a real possibility—would, of course, be calamitous.

A Pivotal Location

Egypt has changed substantially in modern times: it is a more populous, more highly urbanized country today than ever before. But Egypt's farmers, the *fellaheen*, still struggle to make their living off the land, as did the peasant in the Egypt of 5000 years ago. In a land that at one time was the source of countless innovations and the testing ground for many others, the tools of the farmer often are as old as any still in use: the hand-hoe; the wooden, buffalo-drawn plow; the sickle. Water is still drawn from wells by the wheel and bucket; the Archimedean screw can still be seen in service. The peasant still finds himself in a small, mud dwelling that would look very familiar to the farmer of many centuries ago; neither would that distant ancestor be surprised at the poverty, the diseases, the high rate of death among young children, the lack of tangible change in the countryside. Notwithstanding the Nile dams and irrigation projects, Egypt's available farmland per capita has declined steadily during the past two centuries, and population increase (2.8 percent annually in recent years) keeps nullifying gains in crop harvests. In 1820, there were slightly in excess of 1.2 acres (0.49 ha) of cultivated land per person in Egypt. By 1907 this had declined to 0.48 (0.19 ha), and in 1970 it was 0.22 acres (0.09 ha) (Beaumont et al. 1974, p. 476). The projection for 1982 is 0.18 acres (0.07 ha). In this respect Egypt resembles the crowded river lowlands of southern Asia.

And yet, of all the countries in the region loosely termed the Middle East, Egypt is not only the largest in terms of population but also, by most measures, the most influential. Its nearest rival, Turkey, has in recent decades oriented its attentions and energies principally to Europe and the West; in Africa, Egypt has no Islamic competitors to match its status. Indeed, Egypt is continental Africa's second most populous state, after Nigeria. Egypt alone is spatially, culturally, and ideologically at the heart of the Arab world. What factors have combined to place Egypt in this position?

Location is clearly a primary element in Egypt's eminence. The country's position at the southeastern corner of the Mediterranean Sea presented an early impetus as Phoenicians and Cretans linked the Nile Valley with the Levant and other parts of the Mediterranean world. Egypt lay protected but immediately opposite the Arabian Peninsula, and in the centuries of Arab power and empire, it sustained the full thrust of the new wave. The Arab victors founded Cairo in A.D. 969 and made it Egypt's capital (Alexandria, founded in 332 B.C., had functioned as the capital for centuries); they selected a fortuitous site at the junction of valley and delta.

Egypt, too, lies astride the land bridge

Rural scene in Lower Egypt. The men in the foreground are turning the ancient Archimedean screw, raising water from the canal at the left to the land at the right. Washing is being done by the women. (WHO)

A camel turns a waterwheel for irrigation and other purposes in the Nile Valley. (UN)

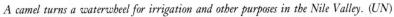

between Africa and Southwest Asia (and between the Mediterranean and the Red Sea). In modern times this has become a major asset to the country as the Suez Canal, completed in 1869, became the vital, bottleneck link in the shortest route between Europe and South and East Asia. Built by foreign interests and with foreign capital, the Suez Canal also brought a stronger foreign presence to Egypt. The Egyptian government had secured substantial shares in the Suez Canal in return for the treaty permitting construction and for the provision of cheap labor (many of whom died during the construction of the 107-mile [171 km] canal), but corruption and inefficiency compelled Cairo's debt-ridden administration to sell those shares. Britain was the chief purchaser, and in 1875 acquired Egypt's 44 percent; France held the majority 52 percent. From 1875 to 1949 Egypt received none of the enormous profits generated by the canal, but in 1949 Egypt was reinstated as a member of the canal's board of directors and awarded 7 percent of the profits. In the meantime Europe's strong presence in Egypt reflected European concern over the security of the Suez Canal; until 1922, Egypt was a British protectorate. Even when Egyptian demands for sovereignty led to the establishment of a kingdom, British influence remained paramount, and the Suez Canal remained a foreign operation.

The 1952 uprising against King Farouk and the proclamation of an Egyptian Republic in the following year presaged the showdown over the Suez Canal that was now all but inevitable. In July 1956, President Nasser announced the nationalization of the canal and the expropriation of the company that had controlled it; in October, Britain and France made a miscalculated and strategically disastrous invasion of the Sinai Peninsula. Pressured and pushed into retreat, the British and French abandoned the canal area, and Egyptian stature in the Arab world (and in the Third World generally) was immeasurably enhanced.

The pivotal location of Egypt was expressed in other ways as well. To the west, Algeria was waging a war of liberation against French colonialism, and no Arab country was in a better position to support this campaign than Egypt. To the south, the relationships between Sudan and Egypt had long been strained, but in 1953 the new Egyptian government offered Sudan the option of retaining a political tie with Cairo or full sovereignty. Sudan became fully independent in 1956. And to the east, beyond the Suez Canal and Sinai, there lay Israel, its southern flank exposed to the Arab world's strongest partner.

Egypt's prestige suffered considerably as a result of the June 1967 war, which closed the Suez Canal and made its eastern bank a truce line—a loss that was somewhat recouped during the conflict of 1973. Following international efforts, the canal was reopened in 1975.

Regions of Egypt

British and Anglo-French involvement in Egypt may not, in Arab eyes, have been a salutary experience, but it nevertheless left an enormous legacy in material assets. Apart from the implementation of the Suez Canal project, built with French capital and technicians, numerous other permanent contributions resulted, which in one century changed the face of Egypt. The country's modern regional geography reflects these imprints. The great Nile River has been harnessed, the delta's lands drained and cultivated; the city of Cairo has become the largest urban center not only in Egypt but also in all of Africa and the Middle East.

Six regions can be identified in Egypt: (1) the Nile Delta or Lower Egypt, (2) Middle Egypt, the Nile Valley from Cairo to

Thebes, (3) Upper Egypt, the Nile Valley above Thebes and including Lake Nasser, (4) the Eastern Desert and Red Sea Coast, (5) the Sinai Peninsula, and (6) the Western Deserts, including the oases.

NILE DELTA (LOWER EGYPT)

The Nile Delta covers an area of just under 10,000 sq mi (25,000 sq km). For thousands of years only the area nearest the Nile Valley was farmed, for the main part of the delta was flood-prone, sandy, lagoon-infested, and excessively salty. Seven Nile distributaries found their way to the Mediterranean Sea. Today, however, the Nile channels are controlled, as modern engineering converted the region into one of perennial irrigation, fertile farmland, and multiple cropping of rice, the staple, and the cultivation of cotton, the chief cash crop. The completion of the Aswan High Dam now makes possible the reclamation and eventual cultivation of an additional 1 million acres (400,000 ha) of delta land, and by 1990 it is likely that fully half of Egypt's population will reside in this region.

The urban focus of Lower Egypt is Alexandria, Egypt's leading seaport, containing well over 2 million residents in the mid-1970s. Founded by Alexander the Great, the city became a major center of Greek learning, with a magnificent library; it was also ancient Egypt's threshold to the Mediterranean and the country's most cosmopolitan city. During the Roman period Alexandria was second only to Rome itself as a provincial capital. Eventually the Arabs took the city in 642 A.D., and when the site of Cairo was chosen as a new regional headquarters, Alexandria went into a lengthy decline. By the early 1800s the population was a mere 13,000, but the nineteenth century saw Alexandria rise again. Railroad links to Cairo and Suez were constructed, sea traffic increased when the Suez Canal opened, harbor works were improved and expanded, and the British-induced cotton trade grew

rapidly. The foreign merchants returned, and by the end of the nineteenth century, Alexandria's population exceeded 300,000. Industrial growth accelerated especially during the period between the two World Wars (today Alexandria is Egypt's leading industrial center), and during the royal period the city served as second capital. Today Alexandria has a canal connection to the Nile, as well as road and rail connections to Egypt's heartland. The city has also become a resort, and, of course, it has shared in modern urban in-migration.

MIDDLE EGYPT

From the waterfront skyscrapers of Cairo to the monuments of Thebes, ancient capital of the Pharaohs, the Nile River gives life to the attenuated oasis that is Middle Egypt. In places the walls of the valley approach the river so closely that the farmlands are interrupted, but along most of the river's course in Middle Egypt the strip of cultivation is between 5 and 10 miles (8–16 km) wide. Occasionally it reaches 15 miles (24 km), and in a few locales the oasis extends only a few hundred yards from the river. But everywhere, the sharply outlined contrast between luxuriant green and barren desert is intense and startling. Clover (*berseem*, a fodder crop), cotton, corn, wheat, rice, millet, sugar cane, and lentils are among the crops that thrive on fields now under perennial irrigation.

The Nile valley tends to widen toward the north, and at its end lies Cairo, the country's capital. Cairo's location is quite nodal: its delta connections are good and a railroad extends along the entire length of Middle Egypt and beyond to Aswan. A string of towns lies along this route, and centrally positioned Asyut is Middle Egypt's regional focus.

The metropolitan region of Cairo in 1976 had approximately 7 million residents, and the city's rapid growth of recent decades continued unabated. Cairo is one of the 10 largest urban centers in the world, and it

Modern Cairo and the Nile. The high-rise character of this part of Cairo stands in sharp contrast to the clutter of low-level dwellings that marks much of this, the nation's primate city. (Almasy/WHO)

shares with other large cities of the underdeveloped world the problems of crowding, sanitation, health, and education of its huge numbers.

Although the Arab conquerors who made Cairo their capital in A.D. 969 selected a fortuitous and appropriate site and regional situation, settlement in the immediate area of Cairo was already quite old even then. Memphis, just 14 mi (22 km) south of Cairo, was a city in 3000 B.C., and Fustat was a river port on the site of Cairo by the middle of the seventh century A.D. The Arabs modernized that settlement and made it an impe-rial metropolis, calling it Al Quahirah, "victorious." During the early fourteenth century, Cairo had a half million inhabitants, and there was no greater city in Africa or Europe. It was a university town, a major stop in the spice trade, an architectural marvel, a center of unmatched power, the focus of Islamic learning. Its heyday was followed by centuries of decline and stagnation, beginning with a great typhoid epidemic in the middle of the fourteenth century and continuing through the country's political misfortunes, lasting into the nineteenth century. Revival began during the period of the opening of the Suez Canal and the British interventions. By 1900, its population once again was well over a half million, and the population movements during World War I and the ensuing interwar period swelled the city's numbers continuously. In the 1940s Cairo exceeded 2 million, and the growth spiral accelerated as declining death rates and sustained in-migration from the countryside prevailed. Temporary resettlements during the 1967 war with Israel, when residents of Suez, Port Said, and Ismailia came to Cairo in large numbers, also contributed to the city's growth: many of the resettled families never returned to their original abodes.

Cairo is a city of stunning contrasts. Along the Nile waterfront, elegant hotel-skyscrapers rise above surroundings that are frequently Parisian and carefully manicured in appearance. But beyond lies the maze of depressing ghettos, narrow alleys, overcrowded slums, a low skyline dominated by the mass of minarets, the towers of mosques pointing skyward. Hundreds of architectural achievements, many of them mosques, shrines, and tombs, are scattered throughout Cairo, but seemingly everywhere one encounters the mud huts and hovels of the very poor. Still, Cairo, a truly cosmopolitan center, is the cultural capital of the Middle East and the Arab world, with a great university, magnificent mosques and museums, renowned zoological and botanical gardens, a symphony orchestra, national theater, and opera. And while Cairo has always been primarily a center of government and administration, it is also an industrial city (tex-

Entrance to the Mowsky, one of Cairo's celebrated bazaars. (UN)

MODERNIZATION AND CONFLICT: THE EMINENCE OF EGYPT

533

tile manufacture, food processing, iron and steel production, assembly plants), and river port. Countless thousands of small handcraft industries exist in the traditional regions of the city, and the grand *bazaar* throbs daily with the trade in small items.

UPPER EGYPT

The Nile Valley above the Thebes Basin has been transformed by the completion of the Aswan High Dam and the filling of Lake Nasser. This is the ancient land of Nubia, where the valley's walls are steep and often close together, where scenery was picturesque but agricultural possibilities limited. Now much of the valley is submerged under Lake Nasser's waters, about 100,000 people have moved from the valley and resettled, and the whole region is transformed. Hydroelectric power, tourism, a small fishing industry, and regular lake steamer service to Wadi Halfa in the Sudan are among the ancillary assets of Lake Nasser, whose chief purpose, of course, is to enhance Egypt's agricultural output below the great dam.

Aswan, the regional center, lies at the terminus of the railroad from Cairo. A city of about 225,000, Aswan was an ancient administrative and religious center, and it has always been Egypt's point of contact with the Sudan and Ethiopia. In 1902 the first Aswan Dam was built just above the city; the Aswan High Dam lies 7 mi (11 km) upstream. The period of construction and resettlement brought Aswan an influx of population and stimulated commerce and industry.

Not all the effects of the High Dam have been positive, however. The dam contributed to the spread of schistosomiasis caused by snails living in the slow-moving and standing water in the irrigation channels. In the Nile delta the loss of the river's annual sediment load began to show in increased erosion of farmlands.

EASTERN DESERT

From the edge of the Nile valley farmlands to the Red Sea and the Gulf of Suez lies the Eastern Desert, an inhospitable, desiccated region of limestones, sandstones, and lavas, with a rugged, coral-fringed, dangerous coast. Deep ravines (*wadis*) make overland movement extremely difficult; a few small settlements exist in small basins where some agriculture is possible, and along the coast in the rare locations where anchorage is possible. The region has yielded petroleum from the fields at Al-Morgan, iron ores east of Aswan, and phosphates, but its contribution to Egypt's economy is yet minor. The population is less than 50,000, including some 10,000 at Ras Gharib and an estimated 7000 nomads.

SINAI PENINSULA

Although the Sinai Peninsula is often considered as part of the Eastern Desert region, several circumstances justify its identification as a discrete region of Egypt. Unlike the Eastern (Nubian) Desert, the Sinai Peninsula is truly a transition zone to Southwest Asia. The western part of Sinai, demarcated by the Suez Canal's east bank, looks to Egypt and has been far more strongly a part of Egypt's effective national territory than the peninsula's eastern reaches, which have long been oriented toward Arabia (and have been wrested from Egyptian control during recent conflicts with Israel). The Sinai has been the scene of several major wars and subsequent readjustments; Egypt's Palestine boundary with Palestine was delimited in 1906, but in 1947 the Gaza Strip was acquired. Gaza became an agglomeration of Palestinian refugees following the creation of Israel, and Egypt's problem-beset administration of the Gaza Strip was terminated in 1967 by the June War.

Perhaps 200,000 people live in the Sinai region, many of them in fishing villages along the coast of the Gulf of Suez and the

Red Sea, and in small basin settlements near the coast; permanent settlement also occurs along the Mediterranean coast. But as many as one-third of Sinai's inhabitants are nomadic and seminomadic, moving from one settlement to another.

The discovery of petroleum on the Sinai Peninsula, the potential for further discoveries, the economic importance of a secure Suez Canal, and the strategic vulnerability of the Sinai region have induced Egypt to accept mediation in the continuing Israeli occupation of most of the peninsula in anticipation of a staged withdrawal. Rather than a sparsely peopled, undeveloped buffer zone, Sinai has become a focal point of Egyptian concern, strategic and military as well as economic.

WESTERN DESERT

From the western margins of the inhabited Nile Valley and Delta to the Libyan boundary lies Egypt's Western Desert, an area covering fully two-thirds of the entire country. It is a region with a sparse population of under 200,000, more than one-third of it nomadic or seminomadic, but it may also be a region of potential for the future. At present, the sedentary population is concentrated in several oases (Fig. 31-1), with some substantial agglomerations (the Dakhla Oasis contains nearly 20,000 residents). These oases are sustained by well water, but the completion of the Aswan High Dam has generated optimism that it may be possible at some future time to divert Nile water into the Kharga and Dakhla oases, and perhaps

A Bedouin encampment in the Al-Alamayn area, Egypt. The Egyptian government is attempting to resettle nomads there on land reclaimed from the desert. (UN/FAO)

Al-Faiyum Oasis

A distinct geographic region within the Western Desert is the great depression of Al-Faiyum, reaching as low as 150 ft (45 m) below sea level. The depression extends about 50 mi (80 km) from east to west and some 37 mi (60 km) from north to south. By diverting Nile water into the depression a lake of about 80 sq mi (200 sq km) is sustained; the soils of the basin were deposited during an earlier period when the Nile flowed into it. Today, these fertile soils are intensively cultivated in a farming zone extending over 700 sq mi (1800 sq km), centered on the town of Al-Faiyum. The population is well over 1 million now, and the farms produce cereals, olives, cotton, and sugar cane among other crops. Since 1874 the area has been connected by rail to the Nile Valley, and some manufacturing of textiles and leather has emerged.

into other low-lying basins of the Western Desert as well, transforming these areas into breadbaskets.

The Qattarah Depression occupies an area of over 7000 sq mi (18,000 sq km) in the northern sector of the region. Under a moister climate this would be a substantial lake, but in the desert it is a region of marshes and salt flats. The surface drops to as much as 435 ft (133 m) below sea level. An area of badlands and saline surface materials, the Depression holds little promise for development, although there is intermittent talk of constructing a channel to permit inundation of the basin, with anticipated salutary effects on local climate.

The regional headquarters of the Western Desert is coastal Matruh, on the rail line to the Libyan border. Matruh's population of under 15,000 reflects the region's state of development, but recent petroleum discoveries near Al-Alamayn in the north and in the Al-Faiyum area in the northeast have stimulated activity. Still today, however, the Western Desert region is a vast expanse of empty, barren wasteland in which small islands of development are linked tenuously by the camel caravans of the nomads.

Population and Agriculture

In few parts of Africa is the reality of the modern population explosion as pervasive as it is in crowded Egypt. In 1800 the population of Egypt, according to estimates, was approximately 2.5 million (Holt, 1968, p. 174). By 1900 it exceeded 10 million, and before 1950 it reached 20 million. Successive census figures indicate that Egypt had over 26 million residents in 1960 and some 30 million in 1966, when the annual rate of increase was at an all-time high of 2.8 percent. This means that Egypt's population is now doubling every 25 years. It is now near 40 million, and would be 80 million by the beginning of the twenty-first century!

As Egypt's population has grown, its per-capita farmland has decreased, irrigation projects and Nile dams notwithstanding. Egypt may have a total area of nearly 387,000 sq mi, but its *habitable* area amounts to a mere fraction of this. When we calculate Egypt's average density of population the figure is just over 100 per square mile, but the density per square mile of productive land (its physiologic density) in 1975 was 3898—which means that Egypt was one of the most densely peopled countries in the world, despite its vast open spaces. At the same time the country's urban population has increased from about 20 percent of the total at the beginning of the twentieth century to 45 percent in 1975; by 1980 Egypt's population will be 50 percent urbanized. The projects for Cairo are startling; if present growth rates continue the city by the end of the century could have 25 million residents.

Egypt must import foodstuffs to supplement domestic production, but the country has not faced the sort of regional hunger and starvation so common in south Asia. Dietary problems do not involve quantity (the people of Egypt consume 2960 calories daily per capita) as much as nutritional balance. People can buy corn (maize), millet bread, and some vegetables, but meat or fish are scarce. Nor is Egypt sufficiently wealthy to buy such commodities: food imports consist chiefly of cereals.

In the face of the population spiral, three areas of change provide hope for the future: land reform, the further expansion of irrigated farmland, and the improvement of yields per unit area. Land reform had become an urgent necessity by the 1940s, as population growth was rapidly reducing the per-capita farmland in Egypt and increasing numbers of *fellaheen* families faced poverty and malnutrition. But in the Egyptian parliament during the royal period, the wealthy landlords were in control, and agrarian reform bills introduced in 1945 and 1950 were rejected. At the time of the 1952 revolution, 40 percent of Egypt's nearly 6 million acres (2.4 million ha) of farmland was owned by less than 1 percent of all landowners. The remainder was held, often in tiny, subdivided plots, by the mass of peasants. Thus, at this end of the scale, a mere 13 percent of the land was owned by 72 percent of all the owners, the average holding being 0.3 acres (0.12 ha). It is generally agreed that a *fellaheen* family needs two Egyptian *feddans* (just over 2 acres or 0.8 ha) to eke out a subsistence living, but in 1952 more than 2 million families owned less than 1 acre (0.4 ha).

And since Islamic law prescribed the division of land among male heirs, further fragmentation of the land was inevitable. In addition there were, in 1952, about 1.5 million families in the rural areas who owned no land at all, and who worked as tenants on the estates or as wage earners in some other sphere. Land was enormously costly, so that only the rich landowners could afford it—and the estates grew at the expense of the peasants.

In 1952, following the abdication of King Farouk, the new government implemented the first of a series of Agrarian Reform Laws that had the effect of breaking up the huge estates, dividing newly available land among *fellaheen* families, and consolidating excessively fragmented landholdings into larger, cooperatively farmed units. By the 1952 law, no landowner could hold more than slightly over 200 acres (81 ha) (plus 100 for each child); the 1961 Second Agrarian Reform Law reduced the maximum to 100-plus acres (40 ha). The impact of these measures and their implementation was enormous, both within Egypt itself and in the Arab world at large. The power of the landlords was broken without bloodshed or violence, the staged sequence of expropriation had the desired effect in the country's poorest sectors, the worst features of the tenancy system were alleviated, and the *fellaheen* had achieved a new level of recognition. In 1969 the Agrarian Reform Law was again modified to limit individual holdings to just over 50 acres (20 ha).

The redistribution of land cannot be the whole answer to Egypt's food problems, of course. If all the available farmland could instantly be divided among all the farm families in the country, the average holding would be less than 2 acres (0.8 ha)—and therefore below the poverty line. But the Agrarian Reform Laws had another effect: the creation of farm cooperatives under the aegis of the Agrarian Reform Authority. All *fellaheen* who were awarded redistributed land were required to join such cooperatives, but the Reform Authority promoted cooperative farming systems in other areas as well. These cooperatives not only provide credit, buy fertilizers, rent machinery, and offer storage and transportation facilities but they also organize the consolidation of cropping areas. In the past, small plots of cotton, corn (maize), clover, and perhaps rice would lie side by side, but subject to the same irrigation cycle; some crops would be overwatered, others inadequately supplied. Under a cooperative system, the lands surrounding a village are consolidated into three of four large blocs, each under a single crop; the farmers have responsibility for a segment of each. The effect of proper irrigation, fertilizing, and daily care (as well as overall rotation systems) is to enhance output, lower costs of production, and reduce waste of soil and manpower.

Undoubtedly Egypt's land reforms have increased annual yields. Farm families farming their own lands tend to work more carefully than tenants or hired laborers. Some considerable improvements have been recorded, and the cooperatives have made life more secure for hundreds of thousands of *fellaheen*. It will take much more time, of course, to achieve the sort of transformation of Egypt's rural areas that is envisaged by the country's planners: the most common sight still is the familiar one of old. Still, many more of Egypt's 15,000 villages now have fresh, running water and electricity, social services, and schools. The transformation *has* begun.

Reference has been made previously to the expansion of Egypt's irrigated land and the prospects for further development, perhaps in the Western Desert region as well as the delta. Some 1.35 million acres (550,000 ha) are being developed as a direct result of the Aswan High Dam. The string of oases in the Western Desert (to which Egyptians sometimes refer optimistically as the "New Valley") have possibilities as well, perhaps through the use of ground water from wells supplemented by an underground pipeline that could bring water from Lake Nasser to the Kharga Oasis. It is estimated that as many as 2 million acres (800,000 ha) could be brought into production in the oases of the Western Desert, which would add 25 percent to the present farmland of Egypt.

In addition, efforts are constantly made to increase the yields of crops on existing acreages. Better irrigation methods, successful rotation systems, careful treatment of the plants (and the effects of land reform) have indeed resulted in higher yields. United Nations (FAO) statistics indicate that the per-unit-area yield of cotton has risen by 36 percent in the two decades after 1952, corn (maize) no less than 68 percent, wheat nearly 40 percent, and rice about 62 percent. But there is a limit to these increases, and obviously Egypt cannot count on comparable figures over the coming decades.

The fact is that land reform, the expansion of farmland, and increasing yields per acre can produce a solution for Egypt's food problems only if the population problem is tackled with as much energy as was land reform after 1952. At present growth rates, the gains made through the Aswan High Dam will be cancelled by the mushrooming needs of the population in less than 20 years. Even if the "New Valley" project could be implemented by the 1990s, Egypt would face a food crisis by the turn of the century.

Industrial Alternatives

Among the priorities stated by the revolutionary government that took Egypt's helm in 1952 was the diversion of available capital from the agricultural to the industrial sector of the economy. Egypt's industries were based mainly on the treatment of agricultural products (textiles and food); there was also a pharmaceutical industry and the production of building materials. The new administration wanted to modernize these industries (the textile industry was especially inefficient), but it also planned (1) to develop heavy industries in Egypt and (2) to intensify the search for mineral resources, notably petroleum.

The exploration of Egypt has had considerable success. At midcentury the country was not known for its petroleum reserves, but today Egypt is an exporter of this commodity and there is potential for further discoveries. Both in the Eastern Desert region and in Sinai, and even under the waters of the Gulf of Suez, petroleum has been found; the Al-Morgan field in the Eastern Desert has been supplemented by discoveries west of Cairo, near Al-Faiyum, and near Al-Alamayn. These western fields may be continuations of Libya's great reserves, in which case Egypt may become a producer of world dimensions. In addition, coal reserves amounting to about 80 million tons have been found in the Sinai Peninsula near Suez, and substantial phosphate and manganese deposits in the Eastern Desert. The phosphate deposits near Al-Qusayr (on the Red Sea coast), and those near the Nile Valley in

the upper Western Desert form the basis for a fertilizer industry that satisfies the home market and exports about half its annual production.

The most impressive project in Egypt's drive toward industrial power is based on the iron deposits about 30 mi (50 km) west of Aswan, the manganese of the Eastern Desert, and local limestone and feldspar: the great steel plant at Hulwan (also Helwan), not far from Cairo. The plant began operation in 1958 with coal imported from West Germany and with Soviet technical aid and equipment; it has been steadily enlarged and now has a capacity of 1.5 million tons, so that Egypt's annual production is second only to South Africa on the continent. The hydroelectric power produced at Aswan is used at Hulwan, some 450 mi (725 km) away, which involves considerable loss during transmission. Indeed, with iron ore railed all the way from Aswan and coking coal brought in from Europe, the Hulwan steel complex is a costly operation. But it is an outgrowth of Egypt's determination, strengthened by the 1956 war over Suez, to attain a measure of self-sufficiency in this area.

Modernization and Conflict

Egypt leads the way in the Arab world in numerous spheres: in its application of socialist doctrines adapted to solve its particular problems, in its redistribution of wealth, in its drive toward industrial power, in its role as Israel's chief adversary, and in its world position relative to the great powers. Even its misadventures—the uneasy "United" Arab Republic with Syria, the disastrous 1967 June war, the closure of the Suez Canal, the flirtation with Soviet influence—have failed to significantly erode Egypt's position of leadership in the region. But Egypt has paid a substantial price. It has been forced to divert large amounts of money from its development plans to the

armed forces and defense equipment, it has lost territory to Israel and it has seen its Sinai oil refineries burn to the ground. There are large foreign debts. Relationships with some Arab states are strained over Egypt's willingness to find an accommodation with Israel that does not immediately involve the return of all occupied lands.

Egypt's 30 years of modernization and change have been attended by much strife and conflict. The creation of the state of Israel in neighboring Palestine, in 1948, generated an Egyptian attack that was crushingly repulsed by Israeli forces. This defeat was followed by political instability and rioting in the major cities, for it was seen as a matter of national disgrace; the continued British presence in the Suez Canal zone and corruption in government further fired the king's antagonists. The 1952 takeover by a group of army officers resulted.

While Egypt's national planners implemented the new administration's various reform programs, several conflicts erupted elsewhere. Britain in 1954 agreed to withdraw its troops from Egyptian soil along the Suez Canal, but following Egypt's 1955 purchase of large quantities of weaponry from Communist countries Britain and the United States withdrew their commitment to help pay for the construction of the Aswan High Dam. In response Egypt seized the Canal—and the 1956 war involving Israel, Britain, and France erupted. Ultimately the Soviet Union funded the Aswan High Dam, and President Nasser permitted the deployment in Egypt of a large Soviet army.

In 1958 Egypt and Syria engineered a political union, and the two countries were named the United Arab Republic. The arrangement proved not to be durable, and in less than four years members of the Syrian armed forces rebelled and declared Syria's secession from the Republic. Egypt made moves to subdue the rebels by sending soldiers to enforce the union, but this campaign was short-lived. Egypt retained the name United Arab Republic until 1971, when it assumed once again its old name of Arab Republic of Egypt.

If a war in Syria was averted, this was not the case in 1962 in Yemen, site of Egypt's next external adventure. A civil war in Yemen pitted royalist forces against a republican majority, and Egypt, heeding appeals for help from the latter, sent a large force to assist those in Yemen determined to establish a republic there. Saudi Arabia, Yemen's neighbor, favored—and helped—the royalists. Thousands of Egyptian soldiers lost their lives in that conflict, which cost Egypt millions of dollars. It seemed an inappropriate investment at a time when Egypt needed money at home.

The disastrous 1967 June war with Israel, and the 1973 flareup that gave Egypt its renewed foothold on the Sinai Peninsula, further punctuated three decades of intermittent war. And, as the map indicates, the Sinai question is not yet solved; Israel's limited 1975 withdrawal to new truce lines cannot be a long-term solution. As the country continues its internal war against the specter of malnutrition and hunger, its limited resources are expended on unsettled external conflicts.

Bibliography

Ayrout, H. H. *The Egyptian Peasant*. Beacon Press, Boston, 1963.

Barbour, K. M. *The Growth, Location, and Structure of Industry in Egypt*. New York: Praeger, 1972.

Beaumont, J. et. al. *The Middle East: A Geographical Study*. London: John Wiley, 1975.

Berry, L., and A. J. Whiteman. "The Nile in the Sudan," *Geographical Journal*, Vol. 134 (1968), pp. 1–37.

Clarke, J. I., and W. B. Fisher (eds.). *Populations of the Middle East and North Africa*. Cambridge: Heffer, 1972.

Collins, R. O., and R. L. Tignor. *Egypt and the Sudan*. Englewood Cliffs, N.J.: Prentice-Hall, 1967.

Gray, A. L. "The Egyptian Economy: Prospects for Economic Development," *Journal of Geography*, Vol. LXVI, No. 1 (December, 1967), pp. 510–518.

Haupert, J. S. "The United Arab Republic," *Focus*, Vol. XIX, No. 7 (March, 1969), pp. 1–8.

Haupert, J. S. "Sadd al'Ali," *Focus*, American Geographical Society, Vol. XIX, No. 7 (March, 1969), pp. 9–11.

Hopkins, H. *Egypt the Crucible*. London: Secker & Warburg, 1969.

Kanovsky, E. "The Economic Aftermath of

the Six-Day War," *Middle East Journal*, Vol. 22, 2–3 (1968), pp. 131–143, 278–296.

Mansfield, P. *Nasser's Egypt*. Penguin Books, 1965.

Mountjoy, A. B. "Egypt Cultivates Her Deserts," *Geographical Magazine*, XLIV (1972), pp. 241–250.

O'Brien, P. "The Long-term Growth of Agricultural Production in Egypt: 1821–1962," in P. M. Holt (ed.), *Political and Social Change in Modern Egypt*. London: Oxford University Press, 1968.

Platt, R. R., and M. B. Hefny. *Egypt: A Compendium*. New York: American Geographical Society, 1958.

Saab, G. S. *The Egyptian Agrarian Reform, 1952–1962*. New York: Oxford University Press, 1967.

Stevens, G. G. *Egypt—Yesterday and Today*. New York: Holt, Rinehart & Winston, 1963.

United Arab Republic, *Statistical Handbook 1952–1969*. Cairo, 1970.

Warriner, D. *Land Reform and Development in the Middle East: a Study of Egypt, Syria, and Iraq*. New York: Oxford University Press, 1962.

Wilber, D. N. (ed.). *The United Arab Republic: Its People, Its Society, Its Culture*. New Haven: Human Relations Area Files, 1969.

THIRTY-TWO

West of Egypt lies Libya, and beyond is the *Maghreb*, the western region of the Arab realm. Together, these four countries (Morocco, Algeria, Tunisia, and Libya) have a population only slightly larger than Egypt's. In 1977, Morocco's population was an estimated 18.7 million; Algeria, the largest *Maghreb* state territorially, had 18 million inhabitants; Tunisia, the smallest state in North Africa, had 6.2 million people; and Libya's population was about 2.5 million.

If Egypt is the pivot of the Arab world, Algeria is the heart of the *Maghreb*. West of Algeria lies one of the realm's remaining kingdoms, Morocco; to the east, Algeria borders relatively conservative Tunisia and militant Libya. Across the Mediterranean lies Algeria's former colonial master, France, whose hold was broken by a seven-year war of liberation that began in 1954. Algeria became an independent republic in 1962, and its successful revolution assured the new state a place of prominence in the Third World. Nonaligned, anti-imperialist, and socialist in its external and internal political orientations, Algeria has been a vigorous supporter of Arab causes. In 1967 Algeria declared war on Israel (no Algerian forces, however, reached the battlefronts); in the 1970s Algeria, a member of OPEC, fought for higher price increases on Middle Eastern oil than even some Arab countries were willing to impose on the inflation-ridden West.

ALGERIA: THE AFTERMATH OF REVOLUTION

Djezira-el-Maghreb

The states of northwest Africa are collectively called the *Maghreb*, but the Arab name for them is more elaborate than that: *Djezira-el-Maghreb*, or "Western Isle," in recognition of the great Atlas rising like a vast island from the waters of the Mediterranean and the sandy flatlands of the Sahara.

Algeria Proper

Territorially, Algeria is the second largest country in Africa, after Sudan. The great majority of Algeria's population, however, is concentrated in a comparatively small part of the country's 920,000 sq mi (2,355,000 sq km) of land. Well over 90 percent of Algeria's 18 million people inhabit northern Algeria, the region of the Atlas and the Mediterranean. This is Algeria proper, comprising little more than one-tenth of the total area but containing virtually all the good farmland, the cities and towns, transport routes, and ports.

Whereas Egypt is the gift of the Nile, it is the Atlas Mountains that form the physiographic base for settled Algeria (and, substantially, neighboring Morocco and Tunisia as well). The high ranges wrest from the air the moisture that sustains life in the valleys intervening—valleys that contain good soils and sometimes rich farmlands. From the area of Algiers eastward along the coast into Tunisia, annual rainfall averages in excess of 30 in. (750 mm), a figure more than three times as high as is recorded at Alexandria and vicinity in Egypt's delta. Even 150 mi (240 km) into the interior the slopes of the Atlas still receive over 10 in. of rainfall (250 mm), and the effect of the topography can be read on the map of precipitation. Where the Atlas terminates, desert conditions immediately begin.

The Atlas Mountains are structurally an extension of the Alpine system that forms the orogenic backbone of Europe and of which Switzerland's Alps and Italy's Apennines are also parts. In Northwest Africa these mountains trend north-northeast and commence in Morocco as the High Atlas with elevations in excess of 13,000 ft (nearly 4000 m). Eastward two major ranges appear, and these dominate the landscapes of Algeria proper: the Tell Atlas to the north, facing the Mediterranean Sea, and the Saharan Atlas to the south, overlooking the Sahara Desert (Fig. 32-1). Between these two mountains chains, each consisting of several parallel ranges and foothills, lies a series of intermontane basins rather like Andean *altiplanos* but at lower elevations, and markedly drier than the northward-facing slopes of the Tell Atlas. Here the rainshadow effect of the Tell Atlas is reflected not only in the steppelike natural vegetation but also in land-use patterns. Pastoralism replaces cultivation, and stands of esparto grass and bush cover the countryside.

Eastward the maximum elevations decline, and so does the region of intermontane basins, which eventually is pinched out as the ranges approach each other in a jumble of ridges and valleys that make eastern Algeria a distinct physiographic region. Extensions of the Atlas Mountains into Tunisia reach a maximum elevation in that country of only just over 5000 ft (1500 m). In eastern Algeria, as in the remainder of Algeria proper, the north receives significantly more rainfall than the interior, and the croplands in the coastal zone give way to pastoralism deeper inland.

Northern Algeria's climate is of the Mediterranean type, involving not only a modest annual precipitation but also a con-

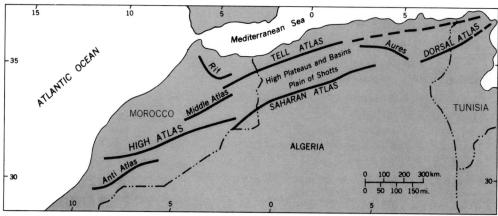

FIGURE 32-1 *Atlas ranges.*

centration of rainfall during the winter months (see Chapter Two). A summer drought of three to four months occurs when, in effect, Saharan conditions overspread the whole *Maghreb;* during the winter period the region comes under the influence of depressions common to the westerlies. This coincidence between the low-sun season and the rainfall maximum inhibits soil development, and it also gives rise to a characteristic, moisture-preserving vegetative response known locally as *maquis* (resembling California's *chaparral*). Where the rainfall is over about 25 in. (635 mm), on the foggy slopes of Morocco's High Atlas and in the well-watered mountains of eastern Algeria, the natural vegetation includes large stands of conifers and cork oaks, stands that were far more extensive in earlier years but have been reduced to second-growth maquis by centuries of overuse.

Generalizations about the *Maghreb's* climate apply hardly anywhere in Algeria proper without qualification, however, because local climate is so strongly affected by the region's varied relief. Winter snows cap the high mountains of the Atlas; steep slopes and deep valleys experience widely different degrees of warmth and moisture. An enormously complex geology further affects the development of a patchwork of soils including podzols on well-watered, well-drained slopes, latosols, sandy soils, and even somewhat saline soils in less favored areas. Alluvial accumulations in the valleys and on the plains in the coastal zone support various crops.

On several grounds, including diminishing annual precipitation and contrasts in the natural vegetation, it is possible to identify two subregions within Algeria proper. The dividing line approximately coincides with the 16 in. (400 mm) isohyet. North of this line lies "Mediterranean" Algeria or the Tell; south of it lies the steppe country. In this context the term "tell" (which means *hill* in Arabic) refers not only to the northern Atlas ranges but also to the entire zone of ridges and slopes and plains fronting the Mediterranean Sea. This is chiefly the zone of cultivation; the steppe zone to the south is an area of seminomadic pastoralism.

Algeria's intensively cultivated land lies almost exclusively in the plains of the Mediterranean zone, especially the Mitidja Plain behind Algiers and the Chelif Plain near Oran, areas that attracted the large European settler population of the colonial period (Fig. 32-2). The Europeans greatly extended cultivation on these plains and the adjacent sloping hillsides by conquering two problems the Berbers and Arabs had been unable to beat: malaria and drainage. The plains are normally separated from the Med-

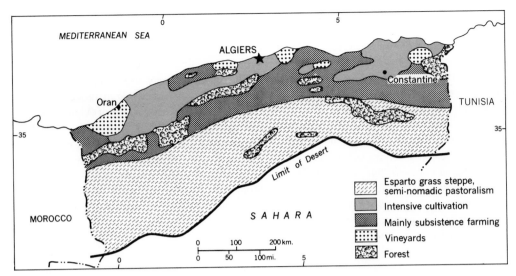

FIGURE 32-2 *Cultivated Algeria.*

iterranean Sea and without well-organized drainage systems become waterlogged. Market gardens developed around the cities and towns, cereals (wheat and barley) can be grown in the coastal zone without irrigation, and the slopes are covered with orchards of figs and olives; many thousands of acres of vineyards also cover the countryside, especially in the Mascara and Médéa areas. As France has restricted the import of Algerian wine, vines are being uprooted and replaced by other crops. Farther into the interior cereals stand on the gentler slopes and orchards cluster in the valleys, but beyond

the dryness becomes too severe and the land is given over to pasture (or esparto grass, a base for paper making and a valuable export). But Algeria's pastures are not sufficiently productive to sustain a strong ranching industry; the already low rainfall of the interior is highly variable, and the livestock must move great distances in search of adequate food. Hence Algeria has far more sheep (over 8 million) and goats (an estimated 3 million) than cattle (under 1 million). The steppe interior remained the domain of the subsistence farmer and herder even during the colonial invasion.

The Sahara

Algeria's vast Sahara region begins where the rainfall amounts to less than 4 in. (100 mm.) annually, on the south-facing slopes of the Saharan Atlas. The Sahara is mobile, expanding into Algeria's better-watered north just as it is encroaching on West African lands to the south. In 1974 the Algerian government embarked on a project designed to slow the great desert in its northward march. Some 6 billion pine and eucalyptus trees were to be planted in a

nearly continuous belt across the entire northern width of the country, eventually to cover just under 7.5 million acres (3 million ha). The project would take two decades, involve 100,000 workers, and constitute a major investment for a country that is not among the world's rich—but the desert's threat compelled it.

Nearly 90 percent, or more than 800,000 sq mi (2,072,000 sq km) of Algeria's territory is desert. There is some regional variation in the desert surface. The threat to northern Algeria is generated by the shifting sands of the Western and Eastern Great Ergs, vast expanses of dunes that extend across much of the country south of the Saharan Atlas. In the far south lie the Hoggar (Ahaggar) Mountains, made of volcanic rocks and other crystallines eroded into rugged relief that reaches as much as 9000 ft (2745 m). Elsewhere the Sahara surface consists of expanses of exposed, bare bedrock or *hamadas*, especially well developed in the far west, south of the boundary with Morocco, and surfaces of broken rock fragments or *reg*, from which the wind has removed the finest sand, leaving behind a sea of gravel, pebbles, and larger fragments. The erg, hamada, and reg regions share the desert's unyielding dryness. Countless square miles carry no vegetation at all; here and there the merest tuft of hardy vegetation manages to survive in a crack in the bedrock.

This almost endless scene of desiccation is broken by three types of human presence in the desert: the mountain-foot oases, sustained by streams that begin on mountain and plateau slopes but disappear underground to feed groundwater supplies, the growing number of petroleum installations that have made the Sahara a region of crucial importance in the Algerian economy; and the caravans of the region's nomadic inhabitants, whose camels manage to find sustenance from the meager stands of grass and bush scattered through this harsh environment.

Algeria's oases, in some instances, have developed into substantial settlements, and they form anchor-points on the trans-Saharan routes that link the Maghreb and West Africa. A number of such oases lie along the foot of the south-facing slopes of the Saharan Atlas. Touggourt has been connected by railroad to Algeria proper, and in the far west Bechar was also a railhead (the railroad now extends some distance beyond). Ghardaia, almost due south of Algiers, is linked to the coast by a good road. Almost in the geometric center of the Sahara region lies In Salah, and Algeria's southernmost settlement of consequence is Tamanrasset in the Hoggar Mountains. Regular bus service connects these distant Saharan settlements to Algeria's Mediterranean core area, and one can buy a bus ticket to cross the entire Sahara Desert from Algiers to Abidjan. Numerous smaller oases survive on sometimes precarious groundwater sources, and always they are characterized by stands of date palms shading clusters of square, flat-roofed houses, perhaps surrounding a small pond where the wellwater is brought to the surface.

Algeria's Sahara has proved to contain substantial petroleum reserves, and large-scale production began as recently as the late 1950s, when the country's war for independence was already under way. Until that time Algeria's chief exports had been the agricultural products of the Tell zone, but today two-thirds of exports by value consist of petroleum, and the areas around Hassi Messaoud and near the Libyan border have been transformed by the installations and pipelines of the new industry. Natural gas from Hassi R'Mel is used in the cities of the north and exported in liquid form, and there are possibilities that Algeria's reserves may be even more substantial than is presently known.

Historical Geography

The countries of the *Maghreb* are sometimes referred to as the Barbary states, in recognition of the region's oldest inhabitants, the Berbers. The Berbers, a Caucasian people, were in northwest Africa when the Phoenicians first reached these shores, dur-

El Oued, capital of the Souf, Algeria. A mosque dominates the skyline, and in the background sand dunes encroach upon date palms. (Georg Gerster)

Truck traffic in the Sahara Desert. In places the hard desert surface (ḥamada) requires little or no maintenance or artificial paving. Nearly 90 percent of Algeria's territory is desert. (UN)

ALGERIA: THE AFTERMATH OF REVOLUTION
547

ing the second millennium B.C. These early contacts changed Berber livelihoods (nomadic pastoralism, hunting, some farming) but little, although the Phoenicians did found some coastal settlements and introduced better methods of cultivation. One of the towns established by the Phoenicians, Carthage (in present-day Tunisia), grew to major importance during the Roman period, when the *Maghreb* became, for the first time, a realm of colonization and foreign influence. The Romans never came to the *Maghreb* in large numbers, but their impact nevertheless was enormous. They built towns and roads, aqueducts, stadiums, and monuments, laid out new farm fields, and introduced methods of cultivation that were still productive and useful 2000 years later, when the European colonizers emulated them. The region's produce, of course, was exported to Rome, and even at this early stage the *Maghreb* was a source of raw materials and grain, in the service of outsiders.

The weakening of the Roman Empire brought the Vandal tribes into the *Maghreb* (fifth century A.D.), followed just 100 years later by the Byzantine forces—but neither Vandals nor Byzantines could match the imprint made by the Arabs, who came in waves from the east beginning in the seventh century. The Berbers had lived in territorial and political accommodation with the Romans and their successors, but the Arabs were conquerors of a different sort. They demanded the allegiance of the Berber princes and the people's conversion to Islam. In the process they transformed the social structure of the region, united it politically, and changed it visually. The old Roman towns and cities acquired numerous mosques and other Arab structures; minarets towered above the urban scene. Roman buildings were often destroyed and replaced.

The Arabs and their energy also brought power to the Maghreb— unprecedented power that propelled the Arab-Berber alliance (the *Moors*) into Iberia, making that part of Europe in effect a colony of North Africa. For centuries the Moors held parts of present-day Spain, Portugal, even southern France; their imprint on the architecture of Seville and Granada, among other cities, remains visible to this day. But eventually internal as well as external pressures eroded the strength of the Moors. During the eleventh century, a new wave of Arab invaders came from the east, principally the nomadic Bedouins, including the Hillal and Suleim tribes, and their impact was disruptive and in many ways destructive. They upset the existing order, drove many Berbers into protected mountainlands, subjugated (and despised as weak) the sedentary farmers, and threatened the towns. The Maghreb became a region of uneasy standoffs and frequent local strife, and the Arab-Berber differences, submerged during the earlier period, strengthened again. Before long the Europeans succeeded in pushing their Moslem adversaries back to southern Iberia and eventually out of Europe altogether.

As Moorish fortunes lessened, the *Maghreb's* rulers called on the Moslem Turks for help against their Christian adversaries, and in so doing they brought on the next period of foreign domination. Algeria fell under Turkish control early in the sixteenth century, by which time the Spaniards also were on *Maghreb* shores. Algiers became the seat of a Turkish governor, but the Spaniards held on to a beachhead at Oran. The Algerians, Arabs, and Berbers alike, resisted these foreign rulers and the whole area was in disarray. Morocco lay more remote from Turkish power and retained a measure of independence, although the Spaniards did establish footholds along its coast as well. The *Maghreb* became a region of isolated communities, without political bond. In the mountains, Berber cultivators farmed for subsistence. Life in the towns was difficult; Moslem refugees from Spain swelled the numbers of many places. Arab peoples, some seminomadic, dominated Algeria's plainlands. Along the coast, piracy became a frequent occupation as Algerian pirate boats preyed on European traffic on the Mediterranean.

It was these pirates who focused foreign attention on Algeria once more. British, French, even American naval forces fought the Algerian pirates but were unable to eliminate them altogether. Eventually France embarked on a campaign of territorial occupation, following a diplomatic incident in Algiers in 1827, in which the Turkish governor, in a dispute over an Algerian shipment of wheat to France, struck the French representative with a fly whisk. The French first blockaded Algiers and then, in 1830, landed military forces and occupied the city.

The French occupation of Algiers did not signal the fall of Algeria as a whole. On the contrary, there now began a long and bloody colonial war in which the French first took other coastal towns and then pushed into the interior. The conflict thrust into prominence Emir of Mascara Abd-el-Kader, who led the Algerian resistance from the early 1830s until the capitulation of 1847. Ten years later there were still isolated pockets of resistance against the French, and it was not until 1871 that France finally replaced military rule in coastal Algeria with a civilian administration.

Colonial Transformation

French intentions were to make Algeria a part of France itself, and in 1871 three *départements* were established in Algeria proper; in 1875 French Algeria sent its first representatives to the parliament in Paris. The decision to integrate northern Algeria into metropolitan France was related to France's loss of territory in Alsace-Lorraine during the disastrous war with Prussia (1870–1871). Algeria afforded an opportunity to compensate both in terms of territory and prestige. The three new *départements* centered on Algeria's three major cities (Algiers, Oran, and Constantine), whose European populations were growing quite rapidly; in their hinterlands lay areas from where the Arabs and Berbers had been expelled. It was a ruthless campaign of expropriation and expulsion that not only deprived the Arabs and Berbers of their land but also drove them into areas that could not support them. But as a result Algeria's Tell lay open for European immigration.

At first, the influx of Europeans to Algeria was slower than France desired, but it was stimulated after 1878 by the destruction of French vineyards during the great phylloxera outbreak and the known suitability of northern Algeria for viticulture. The French prepared farm settlements in suitable areas to accommodate the arriving settlers, and by the beginning of the twentieth century, wine had become Algeria's most valuable export. Indeed, Algerian wine output eventually came to exceed that of France itself!

France's migration policies were not as successful as the French had wished, however. Among the immigrants there were fewer French families and more foreigners—from Italy, Spain, Greece, and elsewhere—than had been anticipated. In 1880 there were an estimated 200,000 immigrant farmers in North Africa, of whom only just over 50 percent were French. Thousands of Europeans, moreover, came to the cities of Algeria, not its rural areas. In the process, the cities witnessed still another transformation. The crowded traditional *medinas*, with their narrow, winding alleys and crowded bazaars could not accommodate the alien influx, and so the Europeans built their modern towns adjacent to the old. During the century of colonial control the cities and towns grew at unprecedented rates, not only through the arrival of so many Europeans but also because many Arabs and Berbers, driven off their lands,

The French Foreign Legion

France's colonial expansion in Africa was sustained in large measure by the Légion Etrangère, an army of foreign soldiers in the paid service of France. The Foreign Legion was founded in 1831 by King Louis-Philippe specifically to help confirm France's presence in Africa, and its first headquarters were at Sidi bel Abbès, Algeria. As its ranks grew, the Legion's arena of operations also expanded to include not only Algeria but also Morocco, Dahomey (Benin), Spain, Italy, and even Mexico and Indochina. The Legion fought for France in both World Wars. In Algeria in 1961 the Legion, always a tightly disciplined, professional fighting army, experienced a low (or high) point when one regiment, on a point of principle, threw its support to the nationalist insurgents during the anticolonial struggle. The Legion's headquarters are now in France.

impoverished, and without hope, sought in the cities their last chance for survival. Algiers under the last of the Turkish governors had perhaps 100,000 residents; at the end of the colonial period its population approached 1 million. Characteristically, the cities had their spacious, wealthy sectors, their bustling medinas and kasbahs, and their miserable, unsanitary shantytowns or *bidonvilles*, where recent arrivals lived under conditions of terrible squalor.

Terrritorial Consolidation

As European immigration into Algeria's Tell zone progressed, France continued its acquisition of Saharan Algeria and pressed its claims in adjacent Morocco and Tunisia. A protectorate over Tunisia was declared in 1881, the last of the Saharan boundaries was defined in geometric terms in 1902, and in 1912 France and Spain finally overcame the stubborn resistance of Morocco and divided that country into two protectorates, of which the larger fell to France. The boundaries thus created were to lead to conflicts among the *Maghreb* states after the colonial period ended, for they were at times defined without precision and always without concern for the interests of indigenous Moroccans, Algerians, Tunisians, or Libyans. Hence Morocco in the 1960s laid claim to western areas of Algeria's Sahara, Tunisia sought revision of its border with Algeria, and there has been friction over the Algeria-Libya boundary as oil reserves were discovered immediately adjacent to the border—on the Algerian side.

While northern Algeria's civilian administration dated from the 1870s, Saharan Algeria was under military control until the 1950s when the French, in response to the rising tide of revolution, created two *départements* in the region (Fig. 32-3). The Sahara had always presented special problems related to its vastness, its sparse, dispersed, and partly mobile population, its difficult surface transport, and (during the colonial period) its very limited productivity. The Algerian Sahara has an estimated population today of under 1 million (the 1966 census reported 502,297 people in Oasis and 210,204 in Saoura, the two Saharan *départements*). Thus the Saharan region of Algeria was not a place of high priority, and colonial policy was to control the clusters of population and

Al-Jaza'ir, "The Islands" in Arabic, is Algeria's capital, historic headquarters, and leading seaport. Founded in ancient times by the Phoenicians, Algiers became the Roman city of Icosium but was devastated during the post-Roman invasions. Algiers' site and situation, however, ensured its revival—which came in the tenth century, during the period of glory and power in the *Maghreb.* Eventually the city became a Turkish seat of government and a base for the pirates who raided European shipping on the Mediterranean during the seventeenth and eighteenth centuries. French forces in 1830 began their conquest of Algeria by attacking from the sea.

Algiers extends for nearly 20 mi (36 km) along its great Bay, crowding the slopes leading inland with tightly clustered buildings. It is positioned nearly midway between the Tunisian and Moroccan borders, and Algeria's second city, Oran (500,000), lies as far to the west as third city Constantine (400,000) lies eastward. Behind Algiers lies one of the country's richest agricultural areas.

During the colonial period, Algiers contained over one-third of all the Europeans in Algeria, then numbering nearly 1.1 million. In 1960, just before independence, there were nearly 900,000 residents in Algiers, but some 300,000 left for France and other parts of Europe. An influx of Algerians replaced this loss so that the city's growth continued; the 1977 population was an estimated 1.5 million (including the metropolitan area).

The port of Algiers, once second on the Mediterranean only to Marseilles in volume, again handles over 2 million tons of exports annually, including Algeria's wines, oranges, iron ore, and phosphates; its import volume is greater today than it was during colonial times, approaching 4 million tons per year.

to maintain the trans-Saharan routes.

In northern Algeria, work was begun in 1860 on a railroad to link Algiers and Oran, and eventually this railroad extended all the way across the *Maghreb* from Rabat and Fès in Morocco to Tunis, the capital of Tunisia. From this east-west line, feeder lines were constructed to serve the larger urban centers and major agricultural areas. Railroads also linked known mineral deposits to Mediterranean ports: the Béchar narrow-gauge line (coal), the Tebessa line (iron ore), and the Djebel Onk extension (phosphate). Until the oil and gas boom, however, Algeria never was a major producer of minerals, and the rail and road networks served principally the farmlands of the north. Only one standard-gauge rail line penetrated far into the Saharan region: the railroad to Touggourt.

Population

In common with other colonial territories, and notwithstanding French policies of land alienation and expropriation (and a nineteenth century land-clearing operation in the Tell that has been described as extermination), the population of Algeria in-

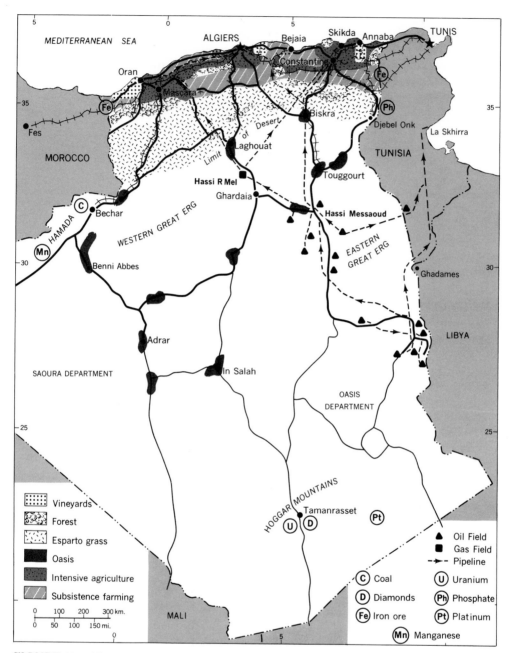

FIGURE 32-3 *Algerian regions.*

creased its rate of growth markedly during the colonial period. In 1830, the year of France's invasion at Algiers, the population of what is today Algeria probably was between 2 and 2.5 million. This had tripled just one century later; the 1936 figure was over 7.2 million (Clarke, 1973, p. 37). At independence the population was in excess of 11 million, and by 1976 it was 18 million, increasing at the rate of 3.2 percent (thus doubling in only about 20 years).

The rapid growth of population during

the past century has resulted from the introduction of modern medicine and improved sanitation; the defeat of killer diseases such as malaria, cholera, and typhus; combined with the survival of traditions that favor large families. Still, there is malnutrition and hunger in Algeria, as there always was during colonial times. Average daily calorie intake is below 2000, infant mortality still exceeds 100 per 1000 live births, and life expectancy still hovers near 50 years of age. The impact of land expropriation, forced relocation, and the rural-to-urban migration process combined to condemn millions of Algerians to incapacity resulting from deficiency diseases. More strongly perhaps in Algeria than in most places in Africa there was the contrast between the gleaming city centers, the rich villas, and the misery of the nearby *bidonvilles*—as well as the well-tended, green slopes of vines and other commercial crops juxtaposed to the poor, overgrazed, overcropped, erosion-prone drier lands where people hungered while the commercial European farmers prospered. The wind was sown, and the storm was an inevitable harvest.

Political Geography of Revolution

By the official code promulaged in 1881, Moslem inhabitants of Algeria in effect were designated to be French subjects, but not French citizens. Unlike the European settlers, the Moslems had no political rights in Paris; they were, however, subject to police regulations specifically designed to control them. Reaction to these and other discriminatory practices of the colonial regime first gained expression in the 1930s, when two movements emerged with dissimilar goals but with the joint desire to effect change. The movement led by Ferhat Abbas wanted to bring equality (as Frenchmen) to Moslem Algerians—an objective that was consistent with French theories of "assimilation." The other movement was nationalist in orientation and more militant in practice, and it issued manifestos reporting the social realities prevailing in Algeria in the 1930s: while the Europeans enjoyed a standard of living comparable to that of France, Moslem children suffered malnutrition, could find no school to attend, faced a life of deprivation. Eventually Abbas, recognizing the gap between theory and practice of "assimilation," joined the other nationalists in presenting General Charles de Gaulle with a new manifesto that summarized Algerian demands. De Gaulle stated that Algeria's loyalty during World War II had earned the territory appropriate consideration, and the change sought by the nationalists appeared within reach.

Ironically, a celebration of the Allied victory in Europe led to the first clash involving Algerian nationalists that took a substantial toll. In the town of Sétif the police fought with celebrators carrying the Algerian nationalist flag, and in the aftermath Moslem Algerians attacked Europeans, killing nearly 100. French retaliation was severe, and estimates put the toll in Moslem lives as high as 10,000. Again Abbas placed Algerian demands for autonomy before the French Parliament, but without success; rather, the French government created for Algeria a new assembly in which Moslems and Europeans would each elect 60 members. Algeria's Europeans enjoyed a universal franchise, but Moslems had to qualify to be able to vote. As it was, the assembly provided 90 percent of the population (the Moslems) the same numerical representation as 10 percent (the Europeans). It was not the sort of reform the Algerian nationalists demanded.

The period of nationalist insurgency began during the night of October 31, 1954 with coordinated attacks on police posts and other installations throughout Algeria. The nationalist movement (F.L.N., Front of National Liberation) followed these with the dissemination of a manifesto demanding Algerian independence. On August 20, 1955 another planned attack near Philippeville (now Skikda) killed a number of French settlers, and in retaliation the French executed Moslems in the city's sports stadium. Now the conflict escalated; rebel forces numbering between 20,000 and 30,000, but operating in small groups, attacked French convoys, bridges, factories, railroads, and other facilities. France responded by sending more troops, and at the height of the conflict there were a half million French soldiers in Algeria.

Another aspect of the French response had profound impact on the rural Moslem population of the country. The F.L.N. operated in the classical insurgent manner (McColl, 1969), wresting control of rural areas from the government and infiltrating villages, first in the more remote, less defensible areas of the country. The French decided to relocate as many as 1,250,000 villagers in safer areas, forcing them from their homes and sending them to what were, in effect, refugee encampments. An estimated 150,000 fled across the borders to Tunisia or Morocco. It was a massive dislocation from which Algeria is still recovering.

As the war continued, F.L.N. successes increased, and in 1958 the rebels established a provisional government with offices in Cairo and Tunis. At the same time, the Europeans in Algeria, suspicious of Paris' intentions, joined with leaders of the French army in Algeria to form a Committee of Public Safety. A political crisis was precipitated in France, which brought General de Gaulle to power. De Gaulle's administration produced a new constitution designed to redress many of the Moslems' grievances and proposing provisional self-rule for Algeria; put to the vote in a general election, the constitution was approved by a large majority of Algerians. Now De Gaulle introduced details of the plan to improve conditions in the territory, offering to discuss the proposal directly with the F.L.N. However, no meeting was arranged and the war intensified once again. During the year 1959 total casualties exceeded 75,000, and late in 1959 De Gaulle announced that, in effect, France would yield to Algerian demands after peace was restored. Now the European settlers, realizing that there would be no place of privilege for them in the Algeria of the future, started their own rebellion, first in 1960 and again in 1961. Meanwhile the war between French troops and the F.L.N. continued until, in March, 1962, a cease-fire was signed. This achievement produced a brief reign of terror by European extremists, but French voters by a huge majority approved the terms of the settlement. Algeria would be a sovereign state before the end of 1962.

Aftermaths

Algeria after 1962 has witnessed momentous changes. The success of the revolutionary war led to a massive exodus of white settlers and a major dislocation of the agricultural industry. The oil boom, first presaged in the 1950s while the war was escalating, reached a peak during the decade following independence. Economic problems of the postwar period generated several migration streams within Algeria and from Algeria to France (involving Algerian workers, not European refugees). Algeria's political posture in the world and its relationships with its neighbors proved problematic as well.

Shortly before independence, Algeria's population of somewhat over 11 million still included the great majority of the territory's more than 1 million Europeans. It is not really surprising that so many remained in Algeria even when the war of liberation appeared headed for success; Algeria's European population was overwhelmingly second or third generation, and departing for Europe, for 90 percent of this population, was not a matter of returning home—it was a matter of leaving home. As early as 1910, Algeria's European population numbered about 750,000. Actual immigration after the first decade of the twentieth century had been relatively small. But if the immigration of the late nineteenth and early twentieth century had been rapid, the European exodus of the late 1950s and early 1960s was precipitous. The Europeans did leave Algeria by the tens of thousands during the period from 1954 to 1961, but that was a trickle compared to the single year 1962, when over 650,000 Europeans left Algeria for Europe. Another 77,000 departed in 1963, and in the decade that began with the opening of the war of liberation, well over 900,000 Europeans evacuated Algeria. It was one of the great population movements of the postwar period, and its impact in Algeria was enormous.

The great majority of the Europeans in Algeria had been city dwellers—nearly 80 percent lived in the cities, one-third of the total in Algiers alone. There they were bureaucrats, bankers, merchants; they ran the country. Those who occupied 40 percent of all the cultivated land in Algeria numbered only about 20,000, and the Europeans, too, had been part of Algeria's rural-to-urban migration. The Europeans in the rural areas had the lion's share of the commercial agricultural economy, and from their fields and plantations came the country's export crops —and revenues.

The sudden and massive exodus left administrative and technical jobs unfilled and farms unattended. Jobs by the hundreds of thousands were lost, and crops went unharvested. The first task of the new Algerian government in 1962 was to ensure the country's survival, after more than seven years of fighting, over a quarter of a million casualties, and a flight of capital and technical skills. France committed financial aid to the Algerian cause, and several countries, led by the United States, sent large quantities of grain to save millions from starvation. At the same time the new government undertook a major land reform program. The European lands were taken over and remaining settler holdings were expropriated. These were then placed under the management of committees of workers in accordance with Algerian socialist principles. Each committee was made responsible to a larger state agricultural cooperative which handled the collection and transportation of produce, made available the necessary equipment, provided credit, distributed fertilizers, and awarded the appropriate shares of profit. Thus within two years, the 40 percent of Algerian farmland that had been under the control of European settlers was state owned and state run. And despite the inevitable problems attending such a drastic change the system soon worked and the state farms produced 80 percent of the country's agricultural output valued, in the early 1960s and before the height of the oil boom, at 60 percent of all exports.

But Algeria could not escape the problems of unemployment and social dislocation of the war and its convulsive aftermath, and tens of thousands of Algerians came to the cities and towns, now even less receptive than previously—and from there they left for France to seek a means of survival. Before long, this migration of Algerians to France, in the wake of the European exodus, produced its own problems: the treatment of Moslem Algerians in French cities and towns became a matter of conflict between Paris and Algiers. Many Moslem Algerians had entered France illegally and lived in urban slums under poor conditions. France was disinclined to assist these people, and French workers often mistreated the Algerians. In 1973 a wave of anti-Algerian

Aerial view of the El Hamra oil and natural gas installations, Algeria. Algeria's petroleum industry is nationalized. (World Bank)

Gas liquefaction plant at the port of Arzew, Algeria. Arzew is one of three major petrochemical centers, and will supply gas to Europe via pipeline across northern Morocco and under the Straits of Gibraltar. (World Bank)

violence in southern France led to 12 deaths and hundreds of injuries among Algerian workers, whereupon the Algerian government prohibited further emigration to France. Later, after Algeria lifted this ban, France instituted a ban against the entry of any North African migrant labor. By 1975 there were an estimated 400,000 Algerian workers in France.

Against this background of problems and difficulties, the country's emergence as a major oil producer was a key to survival and eventual progress. Oil was discovered at Hassi Messaoud in 1956, but the true dimensions of Algeria's reserves were not realized until after independence—and they may be greater even than now believed. The Sahara's largest known deposits of natural gas were found in 1956, at Hassi R'Mel, and liquid natural gas is rising rapidly toward first place among Algeria's exports. Just one decade after the first oil was brought to the surface, Algerian production was 38 million tons annually. The 1973 production was 50 million tons, and the 1975 target was 65 million tons, most of it sold to France (though by 1975 the United States was purchasing one quarter of Algeria's output). The fields along the border with Libya supplemented the production at Hassi Messaoud, but Algerian production has been inhibited by limited pipeline facilities. The Atlas forms a formidable obstacle, and part of the production from the southeast goes through the Tunisian port of La Skhirra.

Rising oil revenues enabled Algeria's government in 1975 to announce that its 1974–1977 Development Plan would entail the expenditure of more than double the original appropriation—some $26 billion. In its first decade of independence Algerian priorities have favored development of the industrial sector, and the 1974–1977 Development plan was designed to be the first stage in a 20-year transition from dependence on oil revenues to exporter of industrial products. However, Algeria's food situation was costly as the country suffered drought problems in common with many countries during the early 1970s, and it was necessary to divert oil revenues to the purchase of grain. Greater attention to organizational and practical problems in agriculture may become imperative.

Algeria's oil boom has not as yet been enough to substantially improve life for the majority—and the majority are undernourished, illiterate (over 70 percent), poor, unemployed (over 40 percent), and far removed from the foci of change and progress. Still Algeria has taken important steps in a reconstruction that, its government anticipates, will affect all its citizens before the end of the century.

Bibliography

Ashford, D. E. "Rural Mobilisation in North Africa," *Journal of Modern African Studies*, Vol. 7, No. 2 (1969), pp. 187–202.

Barbour, N. (ed.). *A Survey of North-West Africa (the Maghrib)*. London: Oxford University Press, 1962.

Bourdieu, P. *The Algerians*. Boston: Beacon, 1962.

Brace, R. M. *Morocco, Algeria, Tunisia*. Englewood Cliffs, N.J.: Prentice Hall, 1964.

Clarke, J. I. "North-West Africa Since Mid-Century," in R. M. Prothero (ed.), *A Geography of Africa*. Routledge & Kegan Paul, 1973, pp. 21–77.

Hale, G. "City and Sect in the Algerian Sahara," *The Geographical Review*, LXII, 1 (January, 1972), pp. 123–124.

Houston, J. M. *The Western Mediterranean*

World. New York: Praeger, 1964.

McColl, R. W. "The Insurgent State: Territorial Bases of Revolution," *Annals, A.A.G.*, Vol. 59 (December, 1969), pp. 613–31.

Mikesell, M. "Algeria," *Focus*, Vol. XI, No. 6, 1961.

Pawera, J. C. *Algeria's Infrastructure: An Economic Survey of Transporation, Communication, and Energy Resources*. New York: Praeger, 1964.

Waterbury, J. "Land, Man, and Development in Algeria," *North East Africa Series, American Universities Field Staff*, Vol. 17, No. 1 (1973).

Zartman, I. W. (ed). *Man, State, and Society in the Contemporary Maghreb*. London: Pall Mall, 1973.

THIRTY-THREE

Morocco is indeed *El-Maghreb-El-Aksa*, as Moroccans call their country: the farthest west. Morocco lies so far west that it has Atlantic as well as Mediterranean coasts; it fronts the Iberian Peninsula across a Strait of Gibraltar less than 12 mi (20 km) wide.

Morocco's westerly position placed it farthest (among the Maghreb countries) from the sources of the Arab invasions of the post-Roman period, but its proximity to Iberia made it the launching pad for the Moors' incursions into Europe. The western Maghreb lay relatively remote from the full thrust of Arab penetration. Three major Berber groups inhabited Morocco when the Arab influx began: the Rifian in the north (hence the *Rif* Atlas), the Amazigh in the Middle Atlas, and the Shleuh (or Chleuh) in the High Atlas and Sous region generally. Berber strength stood up to Arab imposition more effectively here than eastward, and to this day more than one-third of Morocco's population of some 18.7 million remains Berber. The association between Atlas areas and Berber peoples is no accident, of course: the mountains formed a refuge for the Berbers here as elsewhere. But the fusion of Berber and Arab traditions, the imposition of Islam, and the creation of a new order occurred in Morocco's plainlands with great success: the eighth century witnessed new regional organization under Arab rule, the formation of Berber armies led by Arab commanders, the establishment of new towns (among which Fès, founded in 808, became the headquarters of the first Moroccan Moslem state), and the beginnings of territorial expansion from a Moroccan power base.

Significantly, this territorial expansion pushed Moorish power not only into Iberia but also southward into black Africa. Moroccan armies conquered the ancient state of Ghana, and during the eleventh century the

MOROCCO: ARAB AFRICA'S WESTERN FLANK

realm of the Moors extended from southern France to the Senegal and Upper Niger rivers. More than other Maghreb states, therefore, Morocco even today reflects its old associations with black Africa—for trade connections established during the period of expansion outlasted the Moorish empire. Black Africans today inhabit many of Morocco's southern oases, and others reside in the country's traditional cities farther north, such as Fès, Meknes, and Rabat.

The majority of Morocco's varied people, however, are Arabized Berbers, the successors of those who occupied Morocco's plains and low plateaus and who sustained the changes the Arabs brought. Most of the people speak both Arabic and their traditional language, but Arabic remains the official language. The country was ruled by a succession of Arab and Berber dynasties, mainly from the ancient capital at Fès. Periods of upheaval and disarray notwithstanding, Moroccan society was always strong and quite resistant to change. When the decline of Moorish power emboldened the Spanish forces to appear on Moroccan shores to avenge the Moslem aggression, their impact was comparatively minor: the Spanish were unable to modify Moroccan society as greatly as the Moors had transformed Iberia. They did gain several footholds along the Moroccan coast (some of which they retain to this day), but Morocco managed to hold off the European colonizers until well into the twentieth century.

Neither did the Turks, who established control over much of northern Algeria, succeed in making Morocco a part of their Mediterranean empire. Moroccan pirate boats raided the Mediterranean and Atlantic shipping lanes with impunity, and when the United States engaged in an armed conflict with a pirate base elsewhere in the Mediterranean, at Tripoli (in present-day Libya), the sultan of Morocco declared war on the United States. This gesture (whose implementation never occurred) reflected both Morocco's capacity for independent action

and its rulers' concern over the potential loss of the great rewards the spoils of piracy had for centuries brought. Moroccan pirates could prey on ships that must negotiate the funnel-shaped Strait of Gibraltar, and as these vessels returned from the colonies in increasing number and loaded with riches of many kinds, their hauls multiplied. So, however, did the pressures upon Morocco's sultans to take steps not only to terminate the practice of piracy, but also to stop the enslavement of Christians captured in the process. In 1814 Morocco ceased this form of slavery, and shortly thereafter (1817) piracy was made illegal.

Still Morocco managed to negotiate the nineteenth century without falling to a colonial power, although its government weakened continuously. In large measure this resulted from various rivalries among the colonial powers; Germany had a stake because it controlled a substantial part of Moroccan external trade. Spain, of course, had residual interests in Morocco, and France had occupied adjacent Algeria. In 1902 France and Italy made an agreement whereby Italy would support French designs over Morocco in return for French backing of Italian aims in Libya. The British were willing to acquiesce to French control in Morocco as well, if the French would agree to British primacy in Egypt and the Sudan. These arrangements probably would have been formalized if Germany, the major potential (European) loser in these plans, had not objected, resolved to sustain Moroccan "independence," and insisted that Morocco remain a free trade area. In 1906, with armed conflict among the colonial powers a distinct possibility, a conference was convened at Algeçiras, Spain, to solve the Moroccan question. The German position was upheld at the Algeçiras Conference, and Morocco remained a free trade territory, but France was given wide police powers and considerable trading privileges as well.

The results of the Algeçiras agreements were short-lived. French troops landed in

Morocco in 1907, and Spanish forces arrived in 1911; German objections were neutralized through the recognition of German claims elsewhere in Africa. Again the British supported the French position, and soon the Moroccan position was hopeless. In 1912 the sultan signed the Treaty of Fès, which made most of Morocco, in effect, a French protectorate. Germany's acquiescence was secured in return for an extension of its sphere of influence in Cameroon, and Spain secured three Moroccan spheres of influence as well. These were (1) the Rif and northern strip of the country including the Spanish footholds on the Mediterranean coast, Ceuta and Melilla; (2) a smaller area centered on the Atlantic port of Ifni; and (3) the southern zone of the country, connecting to the older Spanish protectorate called Spanish Sahara. In addition, strategic Tangier, at the entrance to the Mediterranean and adjacent to the Strait of Gibraltar, was given international status by the Treaty of Fès. It retained that status, reformulated in 1923, until Tangier was made part of Morocco again at the end of the colonial era.

It was one thing to conclude the Treaty of Fès with a severely weakened sultan, but quite another to extend colonial domination over long-independent Morocco. Even during the nineteenth century the rulers at Fès did not have effective national control over all of Morocco's territory. A case in point is the attack by Berber tribesmen on the settlement at Melilla, in 1893, in which many Spanish residents were killed and for which the Sultan paid Spain extensive reparations. Fès was in no position to prevent such outbreaks, and the French found taking Morocco to be no easy task. The area of the western coastal plain including Casablanca, Fès, and Marrakech was occupied by 1912, but the foothills and ranges of the Atlas were not conquered until 1918 (Fig. 33-1). Much of eastern Morocco and the northern sector of the Atlas held out until as late as 1934. The Spanish colonizers had an equally difficult time in their Rif zone, whose coastal strip was taken during the period from 1912 to 1919 but where Berber resistance in the mountains kept troops active until the mid-1930s.

The colonial interlude in Morocco was quite brief. The Sultan Mohammed V remained in office as Morocco's traditional ruler from 1927, while the French held ultimate authority; in the 1930s a nationalist movement emerged among Moroccan intellectuals outside the country and it gathered support within Morocco as well. World War II brought France's pro-German Vichy government to Morocco, but the sultan and the nationalists were united in their opposition to Vichy and supported the Allies. In 1942 Allied forces took control of Morocco.

The postwar period soon brought matters to a head. Both the nationalists and Sultan Mohammed pushed for independence (French and Spanish administrations having been restored), and in 1953 rioting broke out in Casablanca. The French response was to force Sultan Mohammed to abdicate and to send him into exile in Corsica and later in Madagascar. A puppet ruler was placed on the Moroccan throne, but the response was a wave of resistance and terrorism. In contrast to Algeria, the French yielded to Moroccan demands and permitted Mohammed V to return in late 1955; independence was granted to French Morocco on March 2, 1956. A brief negotiation with Spain led on April 8 to the attachment of former Spanish Morocco (the northern zone except Ceuta and Melilla) to independent Morocco, and Tangier was similarly restored to Moroccan control. After initially holding its southern Moroccan territories, Spain in 1958 yielded to Moroccan demands for their return, retaining only its foothold at Ifni. The port of Ifni and its surroundings were finally turned over to Morocco in 1969, leaving Spain's Mediterranean settlements on the Moroccan coast as the only remnants of the colonial period.

Shortly after independence, Sultan Mohammed V was proclaimed king of

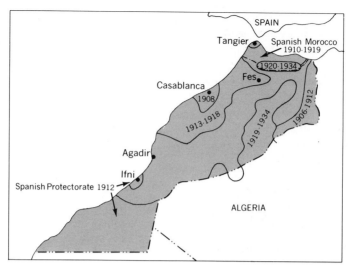

FIGURE 33-1 *Morocco. The colonial occupation.*

Morocco, in accordance with his objectives in rendering Morocco a constitutional monarchy. King Mohammed died in 1961, and his son assumed the throne as King Hassan II. In 1962, a constitution was approved that officially made Morocco a "constitutional, democratic, and social" monarchy, with Islam the state religion. The new parliament, however, rejected the royal programs of economic and administrative reforms, and a crisis developed in 1965 following which King Hassan II assumed almost total control of the country. A modified constitution and new parliament were approved in 1972.

Territorial Problems

Morocco's compact territory of just over 177,000 sq mi (nearly 459,000 sq km) includes only a small area of Sahara Desert south of the Atlas ranges. During the colonial period, France attached the Sahara directly south of Morocco to Algeria; Spain acquired a protectorate over coastal Spanish Sahara. Yet it was Morocco that was for centuries the heart of a Saharan (as well as an Iberian) empire, and upon independence Moroccan voices were raised in support of a campaign to assert historic rights over Saharan territories, including those in Algeria, Mauritania, and Spanish Sahara.

The question of the boundary with Algeria led as early as 1963 to a brief war with Morocco's newly independent neighbor, a conflict that was mediated (but perhaps not settled permanently) by member states of the Organization of African Unity. In 1958, the boundary with Spanish Sahara was redefined so that the small coastal settlement of Tarfaya was awarded to Morocco, but this proved to be a temporary accommodation. Morocco declared 1974 to be the "Year of Mobilization for the Liberation of Our Sahara," an intensification of an irredentist campaign that had been carried on in all directions for some time. Morocco declared that Spanish Sahara was not the no-man's land Spain regarded it to be, but Moroccan territory occupied by Spain. It proposed that the World Court at The Hague settle the question, but Spain also faced claims to its protectorate from neighboring Mauritania—and even from Algeria.

King Hassan's followers march on Spanish Sahara, November, 1975. Waving the Koran, the Moroccan flag, and pictures of the king, the marchers crossed the Saharan border on November 5. (Bruno Barbey/Magnum).

Spanish intentions to hold a referendum among Spanish Sahara's 70,000 residents met with objections from Morocco and Senegal; Morocco in mid-1975 massed some 25,000 troops near its southern border to confirm its position on the issue and to confront Spain's combined forces of nearly 20,000. Spanish withdrawal, however, ultimately came about when, upon King Hassan's personal, nationwide appeal, some 300,000 Moroccans gathered near Spanish Sahara's border for a dramatic, unarmed invasion.

Spain's withdrawal, however, did not produce a final settlement of Sahara's problems. Under the terms of the treaty, the territory was divided between Morocco and Mauritania, with a geometric, latitudinal boundary cutting through it at approximately 22 degrees north. Morocco named its sector Western Sahara, but integration of the region into the Moroccan sphere was impeded by Algerian action and local resistance. While sending Algerian forces into Western Sahara, Algeria in early 1976 championed the cause of the Polisario independence movement of Western Sahara before the Organization of African Unity. The issue bitterly divided the OAU (as Angola's civil war had done); many African governments favor territorial consolidation, but others are sensitive to the suppression of independence struggles. Mauritania claimed that Algerian troops had violated Mauritanian territory, and Morocco prepared for a military occupation to confirm its claim. In mid-1976 the problems of Western Sahara appeared to have the potential for a major regional upheaval.

The brief conflict between Spain and Morocco served also to focus attention on two Spanish exclaves on Morocco's north

Former Spanish Sahara has recently had several names: the Moroccans call their Saharan province the *Western Sahara;* the *Saharouis* (as the local inhabitants call themselves) refer to their country, simply, as *Sahara.* The territory extends over 100,000 sq mi (266,000 sq km) of the desert's western margins, including a 500-mi (800 km) Atlantic coastline. The population averages about 70,000, a figure that fluctuates as nomadic groups from Mauritania move across the undemarcated boundaries. Mauritania has by far the longest common border with Sahara; in the northeast there is a boundary of a few miles with Algeria and the northern border is with Morocco.

Al Aiun, in the northwest just 40 mi (65 km) from the Moroccan border, is the territory's tiny, dusty capital. The principal port is Villa Cisneros; for many years coastal residents have sold their fish catch to the Canary Islands. But Sahara's economic future lies in its large phosphate deposits, of which one, the Bu Craa field about 65 mi (100 km) south of Al Aiun, ranks among the richest in the world. Its exploitation involves several problems, but the price of phosphate has risen strongly in recent years, and the necessary investments are being made. The Bu Craa field's outlet, the port of Tarfaya, lies in Morocco.

(Mediterranean) coast. Both Ceuta (80,000) and Melilla (85,000) have overwhelmingly Spanish populations, but Morocco demanded that they be placed under Moroccan control. Spain responded by sending gunboats to the two ports and by reminding Morocco that Ceuta had been Spanish since 1668 and Melilla since 1471—before the present kingdom existed, so that there could be no question of a "return" of these places.

Morocco and Spain also have potential territorial conflicts at sea and on the continental shelf. In 1962, Morocco extended its territorial sea from 6 mi to 12, drawing Spanish protests. In the early 1970s the Moroccans began awarding offshore oil-exploration concessions to foreign companies on the continental shelf along its Atlantic coast, but no international agreement existed to delimit Moroccan and Spanish domains. This matter was still unresolved in late 1976.

Resource Problems

Alone among the Maghreb states, Morocco has failed to share in the oil boom that has boosted other Arab countries. Even Tunisia, smaller still than Morocco and similarly deprived of extensive Saharan territory, has benefited from the discovery of oil reserves under its miniscule desert area. For Morocco, then, expansionism is a practical policy based on more than historic and cultural arguments. The economic rewards could be substantial. Western Sahara remains one of Africa's least intensively explored territories.

Nevertheless, Morocco has benefited from the oil boom in an indirect way. Oil provides the base for much-needed fertilizers, and those fertilizers have become increasingly expensive as oil prices have risen. But Morocco has large quantities of a substance that constitutes an alternative: phosphates. The phosphate deposits occur on the seaward side of the Atlas, not far from the

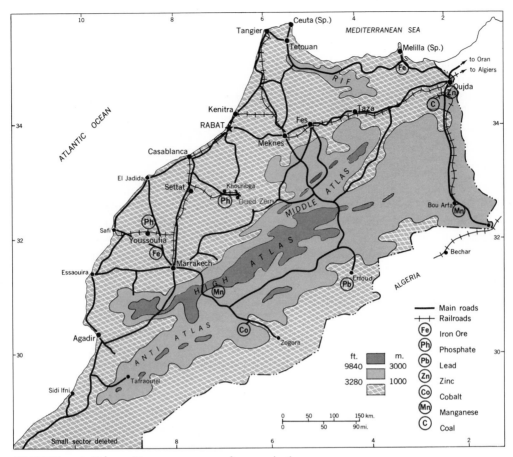

FIGURE 33-2 *Morocco. Towns, resources, and communications.*

coast, in two areas. Phosphate from the vicinity of Khouribga is exported through Casablanca, and exports from the Youssoufia area exit through Safi (Fig. 33-2). The phosphate must be concentrated prior to shipment, and both for local use and external sale the phosphate industry has attained enormous importance for Morocco.

Phosphate deposits are formed by the fossilized remains of marine animals, and they occur in layers that can be mined by underground as well as strip methods. Even after refinement of the chalky material the phosphate is a bulky product, and Morocco's 1974 production of some 20 million tons strained the country's limited port facilities. As the world's leading exporter of phosphate during the 1970s, Morocco had a special

stake in the rise in prices affecting this commodity—from under $15 to over $60 per ton in the early 1970s alone. The increased revenues were used in part to augment Casablanca and Safi as phosphate outlets through the construction of new facilities at Essaouira (for the Youssoufia deposits) and El Jadida (for the Khourbiga fields), and to construct new conversion facilities.

Phosphate deposits also figured in Morocco's claims to Spanish Sahara. Perhaps the world's richest phosphate deposits, larger even than those of Morocco, lie in Western Sahara's interior and have attracted major foreign investment aimed at their development. Spain would have been in a position to supplant Morocco as the world's top phosphate exporter (and could have had a major impact on world prices) had Madrid insisted on retaining control in its desert protectorate.

The remainder of Morocco's domestic mineral resources consist of rather small deposits of iron, coal, cobalt, lead, zinc, and some manganese, several of them positioned deep in the country's interior and expensively far from its ports (Fig. 33-2). One of the world's lengthiest cableways brings manganese up from the valley of the Draa.

Uses of the Land

Morocco, since time immemorial, has been a land of mountain pastures and trekking herds of sheep and goats, of peasant agriculture, simple plows, subsistence ways of life focused on scattered villages in the plain regions. Superimposed on this, mainly during the first half of the twentieth century, was the European practice of large-scale cash agriculture. In the rural areas, as well as in the cities, old and new Morocco now stand side by side.

Morocco's westerly position exposes the country to Atlantic influences to a far greater extent than the other Maghreb states, and coastal areas are cooled by winds blowing off the Canaries Current. The coastal areas, in common with coasts in similar relative locations, experience summer fogs and cold, damp periods. But Morocco shares with the rest of the Maghreb the essentially Mediterranean cycle of weather, so that maximum precipitation comes during the winter. As a result the high Atlas ranges are snow-capped in winter, blizzards occur, passes are blocked. Later the westward-flowing rivers swell with the meltwaters, providing their valleys in the plains with irrigation opportunities. The overall distribution of precipitation in Morocco (see Fig. 2-1, Chapter Two) reflects its orographic relationships: the Rif Atlas, most exposed to maritime influences, receives over 40 in. (1000 mm) in places, the High and Middle Atlas over 20 in. (500 mm), while the western plains between Atlas and ocean become progressively drier from north (10–20 in.) to south (0–10 in.). Beyond the Anti Atlas, south as well as east, lies the Sahara, beyond the winter lows and behind the great mountains.

Regions

To a considerable degree the traditional regions of Morocco reflect the vegetative response to the country's climatic regimes. In the north, the better-watered slopes of the *Rif* still are clothed by cork-tree forests, which over time have been cut down over much of the rest of the country; cedars and aleppo pine stands also survive, as they do on slopes of the Middle Atlas (Fig. 33-3). In the western area, between the mountains and the sea, the northern *Rharb* region, centered on the ancient cities of Meknes and Fès, has more rainfall and, in the uncultivated areas, a more luxuriant vegetation of brush and olive trees than the *Haouz* region farther south, centered on Casablanca. The vegetation becomes progressively sparser (and farming more scattered, herding more frequent) southward, until the valley of the Sous River marks the limit of cultivation with a string of irrigated lands. The heart of the country, from this valley and across the High Atlas to the esparto grass area on the Algerian border, is the country's *Sous* region, a land of steppe, drought, and bitter winter cold, of fortified, tightly clustered villages and the black tents of the nomads whose transhumance carries them seasonally up

Casablanca, Morocco's largest city and principal port. It is well situated with regard to Morocco's major agricultural areas, population centers, and phosphate mines. It is also a favorite tourist spot of the French. (UN)

Street scene, Taroudant, Morocco. In the rural areas, much of the farm produce is brought to market by donkey (UN/H. Bijur)

MOROCCO: ARAB AFRICA'S WESTERN FLANK

567

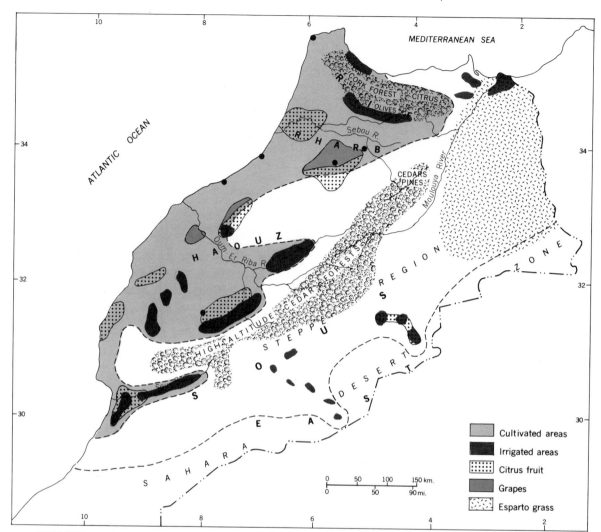

FIGURE 33-3 *Moroccan regions.*

and down the Atlas mountain slopes. Beyond the Atlas, Morocco merges into the Sahara, with its familiar pattern of isolated oases and expanses of dessication and barrenness.

Farms

Moroccan farmers always raised hardy wheat and barley where the soil and water would permit and moved their herds of sheep and goats across the steppes. Before the colonial period internal trade was irregular, depending on times of surplus; Morocco exported handcrafts, not farm products.

Then the French bequeathed Morocco not only with its modern boundaries but also with the beginnings of a transport system to tie the country together internally and to facilitate its export trade. And the French introduced their large-scale systems of agriculture on holdings as large as 2000 acres (800 ha) or more (though many were much smaller and the average French farm covered about 400 acres or 160 ha), where they used modern machinery, fertilizers, specialized seeds, crop rotation, and irrigation—and a labor force that numbered over 100,000 farm workers—to produce, for sale and export to France, a variety of crops. As elsewhere in colonial Africa, the lands occupied by the European settlers (mostly in the northwestern plains, the Rharb, and in the hinterlands of Rabat and Casablanca) were taken from their traditional owners or bought, sometimes from corruptible local rulers; soon they covered some 2.5 million acres (1 million ha) divided into more than 6000 farms. Some Moroccan landowners followed the European example and entered the cash-crop economy as well, sharing in the export trade of citrus fruits, vegetables, and cereals (wheat and some rice). At the time of independence, more than 3.5 million acres (1.4 million ha) were in Morocco's modern agricultural sector, supplying not only the export products but also wheat and other products for domestic consumption. Inevitably, the wine grape made its appearance, notably in the Rharb. For France, Morocco's farms could produce the earliest vegetables, fruits, and flowers of the season; it was the Florida of Paris.

Against this 3.5 million acres in the modern sector are nearly three times that area in the "traditional" sector of agriculture, but large-scale efforts are under way to modernize farming through the extension of irrigation in the three major river valleys (Fig. 33-2) and in the Rif and Sebou areas. Independence, here as elsewhere in Africa, led to a substantial exodus of European farmers, and the organization of state-operated farming cooperatives. In general the transfer went smoothly in Morocco, in part because Moroccans had for decades participated in the modern sector and had grown commercial crops ranging from tomatoes to tobacco and from potatoes to apricots. Citrus fruits, however, remained the leading export crop by value, followed by vegetables. Morocco's varied environments are capable of producing a wide range of crops, from olives along the Rif slopes and dates in the oases to rice in the irrigated fields and peas and beans in the better-watered northwest. From the forests comes cork; from the steppes, esparto.

Morocco's livestock herds, in which sheep (some 15 million) and goats (perhaps 9 million) outnumber cattle (3.5 million), reflect the paucity of good grazing land. The cattle herds tend to concentrate in the midsection of the western plains to the Middle Atlas' foothills; the sheep and goats are driven in constant search of pasture in the drier areas. Morocco's pastoral regions have been much less affected by change—either during the colonial period or thereafter.

Until rather recently Moroccans failed to fully exploit the profitable fishing grounds that lie just offshore in the cool Canaries Current, and fishing boats from other countries took the catch. In recent years the Moroccan fishing industry has begun to take its share, however, and Safi and Agadir have become leading fishing ports with processing and canning plants. Tonnages are still modest (the catch in recent years has been 300,000 tons, more than three-quarters of it sardines), but the industry is expanding and Morocco will benefit from current extensions of national fishing zones in offshore waters. Again Morocco's westerly position gives the country a distinction among Maghreb states.

Population Explosion

Another distinction appears unrelated to Morocco's relative location: its population is not only the Maghreb's largest but also its most rapidly growing. Its 1977 population of

Traditional farming scene near Souk-el-Arba-du-Rharb in the Rharb Plain of northern Morocco. Mechanized agriculture is still uncommon, and yields of barley and wheat (Morocco's principal crops) are generally low. (World Bank)

Irrigated agriculture, Rharb Plain, Morocco. Two-thirds of Morocco's population are engaged in agriculture, and subsistence farming occupies some 80 percent of the cultivated land. Commercial agriculture such as this is expanding. (World Bank)

18.7 million was increasing at the rate of 3.3 percent, giving a doubling time of about 20 years. The birth rate, 49.5 per thousand, is among the highest in the world; the mortality rate in recent years has been 16.5. There are the usual depressing statistics characteristic of underdeveloped countries: an infant mortality as high as 15 percent; life expectancy, barely over 50 years; population under 15 years of age, over 45 percent. United Nations figures place the average calorie intake in Morocco at 2180 daily, well under the F.A.O. minimum of 2360; medical care is still far from adequate, with about 13,000 persons for every doctor in Morocco. As elsewhere in the Maghreb, diseases of hunger and malnutrition afflict many.

The distribution of population shows a developing core of high density from Kenitra, north of Rabat, to Casablanca, along the Atlantic littoral. This is the focus of a larger zone of high density that coincides with the region of better farmlands and extends from the Rif slopes and Mediterranean coast to the coastal lowlands fronting the Atlantic. Morocco is divided administratively into two prefectures (the urban areas of Casablanca and Rabat) and 19 provinces, whose average population densities decline consistently from coast to interior. The Saharan province of Tarfaya at the 1971 census recorded only slightly over 24,000 inhabitants; the coastal province of Kenitra, only slightly over half as large, had 1,346,000. And although averages are not always meaningful, population densities in the coastal provinces are as high as 150 to 250 per square mile (60 to 95 per sq km) whereas Atlas provinces report 50 to 150 (20 to 60) and Saharan units from 10 to 50 (4 to 20). Saharan provinces are large, so that they include sections of the Atlas as well; Morocco's most sparsely peopled area is the extreme south of the country, between the Dra River and the boundary with Spanish Sahara (Tarfaya Province), with under two persons per square mile.

MOVEMENTS

Tens of thousands of Moroccans live a life of nomadism or seminomadism, but external movements affect the population picture as well. At the time of independence, there were as many as 450,000 Europeans in Morocco, over 90,000 of them in the Spanish zone and some 50,000 in Tangier. In contrast to Algeria and Tunisia, where European immigration reached a maximum early during the colonial period, Morocco's white settlers came in large numbers after World War II. It was a short-lived influx, for mass emigration attended independence and by the 1971 census, only 112,000 foreigners of all nationalities remained—many of them involved in teaching, technical aid and similar activities and, as such, replacements rather than holdovers. The French population of Morocco probably was below 70,000 in 1975, and the Jewish population, which at independence had been about 200,000 was below 30,000. Many Moroccan Jews emigrated to Israel as the Middle Eastern conflict intensified and anti-Jewish feelings in Arab countries, even as far from the scene as Morocco, grew.

A second migration stream has involved Moslem Moroccans themselves, pushed by unemployment at home and attracted by job opportunities in Europe. By conservative estimates for the early 1970s, over one-quarter of a million Moroccans were working in France, Belgium, Germany, and other European countries; some European employers even established training centers in Morocco to prepare local workers for their jobs in Europe.

URBAN GROWTH

Still another migration carries tens of thousands of Moroccans annually from the countryside to the beckoning cities. The European transformation of Morocco set in motion a process of accelerated urbanization that has not abated and which has affected ancient cities as well as new towns. One of

North Africa's most rapidly growing cities during the twentieth century is Casablanca, a small town at the turn of the century, a city of 250,000 in the mid-1930s, of 1 million in the early 1960s, and with an estimated 1976 population approaching 2 million. Of course, for centuries, Morocco had had an urban tradition, but never was the rate of urban growth as high as it has been in recent decades. As a result, the country today has a dozen cities with populations in excess of 100,000, among which, following Casablanca, the cities of Rabat (450,000), Marrakech (400,000), Fès, Meknes, and Tangier (200,000) are the largest.

Casablanca continues to outstrip its competitors, and the city now employs fully half the country's industrial labor force; it is the industrial heart of the country whose largest industry remains that of food-processing (textiles rank next). Metallurgical and chemical plants also concentrate in Casablanca, which is also Morocco's major port. Still Morocco's industries are far from fully developed, and there are plans for expansion (including an iron and steel complex at Nador, near Melilla on the Mediterranean coast, using the northeast's iron and coal) (Fig. 33-2).

The French colonial administration chose Rabat as its headquarters, and at independence the city became the modern capital of Morocco, although the king also has official residences at Fès, Marrakech, and Tangier. Rabat's port, at the entrance of a small river and favorably positioned to the Rharb, has been eclipsed by Casablanca, whose primacy strengthens with each passing year. Morocco's cities, like others of the Maghreb, have their traditional *medinas*, *bidonvilles*, and modern sectors—a structure that will mark the region's cities for many decades to come.

Morocco remains a country of unfulfilled potential. Its priority, naturally, must be some form of national population planning; but if the growth rate can be brought down, the opportunities exist for general betterment in a country where the contrasts between the advantaged and the deprived are particularly pervasive. Apart from the unsettled boundary questions that may bring ultimate benefits, Morocco has the opportunity to expand its irrigated farmlands, utilize an enormous hydroelectric potential from its Atlas valleys, diversify its industrial output, maximize its tourist advantages (which already attract by far the largest flow of visitors among Maghreb countries), and expand its range of resources (the search is far from over). It is one of Africa's countries that have the elements for a balanced economy.

Bibiography

Ashford, D. E. *Political Change in Morocco*. Princeton: Princeton University Press, 1961.

Awad, H. "Morocco's Expanding Towns," *Geographical Journal*, Vol. 130 (1964), pp. 49–64.

Beyen, J. W., and P. E. Booz. *The Economic Development of Morocco*. London: Oxford University Press, 1968.

Brace, R. M. *Morocco, Algeria, Tunisia*. Englewood Cliffs, N.J.: Prentice Hall, 1964.

Brett, M. (ed.). *Northern Africa: Islam and Modernization*. London: Cass, 1973.

Cohen, M. I., and L. Hahn. *Morocco: Old Land, New Nation*. New York: Praeger, 1964.

International Bank for Reconstruction and Development. *The Economic Development of Morocco*. Baltimore: Johns Hopkins Press, 1966.

Mikesell, M. W. *Northern Morocco: A Cultural Geography*. University of California Publications in Geography No. 14. Berkeley: University of California Press, 1961.

Monteil, V. *Morocco*. New York: Viking
Press, 1964.

Reyner, A. S. "Morocco's International
Boundaries," *Journal of Modern African
Studies*, Vol. I (1963), pp. 313–326.

Robinson, G. W. S. "Ceuta and Melilla:
Spain's Plazas de Soberania," *Geography*,
Vol. 43 (1968), pp. 226–269.

Zartman, I. W. *Morocco: Problems of New
Power*. New York: Atherton, 1964.

Zartman, I. W. "The Politics of Boundaries
in North and West Africa," *Journal of
Modern African Studies*, Vol. 3 (1965),
pp. 155–173.

Zartman, I. W. "Morocco," *Focus*, Vol. XV,
No. 6 (1965), pp. 1–6.

THIRTY-FOUR

Tunisia, the Maghreb's (and North Africa's) smallest country, has translated long-term political stability into progress against great odds. With a territory of only slightly over 63,000 sq mi (164,000 sq km), Tunisia has very little of the oil-rich Sahara lands that sustain Libya to its east or Algeria to its west. Nor does Tunisia possess the positive legacies of the colonial period on the scale of Egypt or even Algeria: there were not the major irrigation projects, large-scale commercial estates, firms and factories to take over and run. What there was had very lim-

ited promise, and for Tunisia's 4 million people (at independence in 1956) the future appeared anything but bright. But in the two decades that followed, Tunisia not only achieved regional and international political prominence out of all proportion to its dimensions but it also accomplished much in the ecomomic arena. Tunisia's success has had much to do with its long-term political stability as a one-party state under the direction of its national hero, President Habib Bourguiba.

Environmental Parameters

Tunisia's position at the eastern end of the Atlas chain endows it with an east as well as a north coast, so that marine influences affect a substantial part of the country (Fig. 34-1). The Atlas ranges, however, are much lower than they are in Morocco or much of Algeria:

the northern Tell Atlas, also known as the Kroumirie Mountains, reach elevations over 3000 ft (just over 1000 m) in only a few places. The country's mountain backbone, the High Tell and Dorsale farther to the south, enter Tunisia as the Tebessa Mountains whose

TUNISIA:
THE
FRUITS
OF
STABILITY

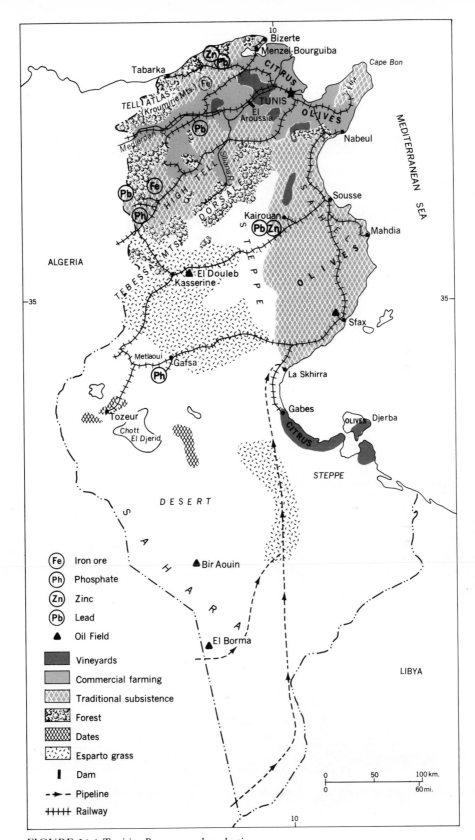

FIGURE 34-1 *Tunisia. Resources and production.*

greatest elevation is Mount Chambi (Sha'nabi) near the Algerian border at 5066 ft (1544m). The High Tell and Dorsale quickly decline in elevation and terminate in the Cape Bon peninsula. Thus Tunisia does not have a mountain barrier to separate the people of the coastal zone from those in the interior. In fact, surface communications are quite good, penetrating most of the inhabited parts of the country along networks of 1500 miles of railroads (2400 km) and 10,000 mi of roads (16,000 km).

Tunisia's north provides the greatest physiographic diversity, for this is the region that lies exposed to the rain-delivering low-pressure cells of the Mediterranean winter; here, too, the variety of relief is greatest. Northwestern Tunisia receives as much as 40 in. (1000 mm) of rainfall along the slopes of the Kroumirie Mountains, but this quickly decreases southward. The valley of the Majardah River averages about 25 in. (625 mm), and rainfall in the Tell-Dorsale highlands is only 10 to 20 in. (250–500 mm). The Dorsale forms the transition from comparatively humid northern Tunisia to dry Saharan Tunisia to the south, where rainfall declines to under 10 in. (250 mm) and, approximately where the coast bends eastward again, under 5 in. (125 mm) annually. The mountains themselves are steppe country with some stands of forest in the less accessible areas and, in common with other Atlas regions, there is much local contrast in environment as slope angles, exposures, and soil quality vary. In the higher country south of the mountains esparto grasses prevail, but then the land descends into the plains of the

Typical grazing lands in the Matmata Range of the Atlas Mountains, Tunisia. Overgrazing, thin soils and recurrent droughts are common problems in this region. (UN)

Sahara with *chotts* and some date-palm oases.

Among Tunisia's seven rather clearly defined physiographic regions, the Sahara is by far the largest (Fig. 34-2) and the steppe area ranks next in size, followed by the High and Low Tell and Dorsale region (the Low Tell of the Cape Bon peninsula is an extension of both the Tell and the Sahel regions). But the critical region of Tunisia is the basin of the Majardah River, for it contains much of the country's best agricultural lands and its best opportunities for irrigated agriculture; with the Bizerte Plain it attracted the largest number of European colonists (and it was a productive farming area even during Roman times). Flooding had been a problem in the Majardah valley as long as the region has been occupied, and the Tunisian government has implemented a major irrigation and flood control project there.

The Sahel, the coastal strip of east-central Tunisia, has long sustained a dense population because it is slightly more humid than the interior steppes and because moisture-retention in the rather sandy soils permits the cultivation of grains. The colonial period brought with it the extensive olive-

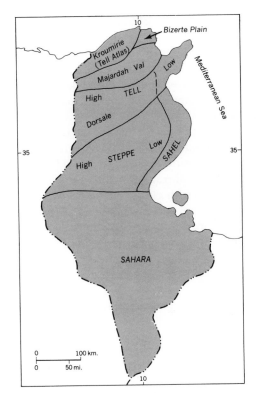

FIGURE 34-2 *Tunisian regions.*

tree plantations, and olive oil still ranks high among Tunisia's exports.

National Unity

Tunisia lay directly in the path of the Arab invasion, and the Arabization of the local Berber population was almost complete. Less than 1 percent of Tunisia's more than 6 million people still use the Berber language (and they live in the interior, remote hills); Arabic is the official language and French has come to play a dominant role in education, the daily press, and in governmental circles. This linguistic uniformity forms a strong element in Tunisia's remarkable national cohesiveness.

Tunisia's population has numerous ancestries nevertheless, and the country has a varied history. The capital, Tunis, lies near the site of Carthage, which was founded by the Phoenicians and subsequently proved a strong rival for Rome. Not only did Tunisia receive the Romans and their successors, the Vandals, as well as the Arabs but also the Moslem refugees from Sicily (who in the 11th century settled in the Sahel), hundreds of thousands of Spanish Moors who escaped Iberia as the Christians advanced on them, the Turks, and later the French. The arrival of the Spanish Moslems, beginning in the mid-thirteenth century and continuing into the sixteenth, proved a formative period for Tunisia, for these people brought with them urban traditions, agricultural skills, and irrigation techniques that transformed society in this area.

TUNISIA: THE FRUITS OF STABILITY

But it was colonial France that provided Tunisians with a common political and national objective during the period their country was a French protectorate (1881–1956). Prior to the French takeover, a Turkish *bey*, representing the Ottoman Empire, administered the area from his headquarters in the city of Tunis; as the Ottoman state weakened, the local Turkish elite achieved a considerable measure of independence that was threatened only by France's takeover in neighboring Algeria. Eventually French pressure in various spheres forced the bey to acquiesce to a French protectorate, and French colonization of the land was under way. And as early as the first decade of the twenteeth century, Tunisian nationalism found expression among Tunisian intellectuals, merchants, and professional people. The first formal movement was born in 1907 and, in the familiar sequence, it was suppressed only to rise again in a different form. Habib Bourguiba rose to national prominence in the 1930s as he founded both a nationalist political movement and a newspaper to provide it expression. Following World War II, during which the nationalists supported the Allied side, the drive for independence was renewed. It achieved success when Tunisia became independent in 1956.

Tunisia officially became a republic in 1957, and Habib Bourguiba was elected its first president. It is a measure of the country's unity of purpose that Bourguiba was re-elected every five years until, in 1974, Tunisia's ruling socialist party elected the-then 74-year-old leader president for life. Tunisia made one-party government work, and its 20-year record reflects the absence of *coups* and erosive political conflict.

France during its control of Tunisia bequeathed the country the international boundaries that have been sources of difficulty. Morocco and Tunisia were protectorates and not (as Algeria was) represented in Paris; France therefore attached its Saharan empire largely to Algeria, more se-curely a part of its overseas domain. Tunisia and Morocco have both sought revisions of their Saharan boundaries, and Tunisia still claims that its Algerian boundary should run to the west, not the east of the position of Ghadames (Libya). The situation has been complicated by the discovery of oil near El Borma, in an area to which claim has been laid by Algeria. In general terms, Tunisia frequently expresses its desire to see its Saharan realm expanded, but it has done so with moderation and no armed conflicts have been precipitated, although the oil boom has made Saharan stakes very high.

Tunisia's remarkably homogeneous culture, its common, single traditional language, its Islamic faith, its nationalism, and the leadership of Bourguiba have combined to produce a country with strong national unity. Tunis, the capital, is a prototype of the primate city, tangibly expressive of national values and aspirations and, with a population of over 800,000, more than seven times as large as the country's next ranking urban center, Sfax on the Sahel coast. Tunisia has been a melting pot whose various elements have been effectively assimilated; minorities that might not have been assimilated have come and gone. Shortly before independence the European settler population numbered over 250,000 (it had already been 200,000 in the early 1930s), half of it concentrated in Tunis alone. By 1975 fewer than 40,000 Europeans remained resident in the country, and the Jewish population, which had stayed through the independence period, was rapidly declining from its maximum of about 85,000. Nor does Tunisia face the strong regionalism that is so problematic for many other African countries. There are advantages of scale as well as content.

Under the circumstances it was surprising that Tunisia initially acceded to a Libyan proposal that the two countries unite in a confederation (Libya had secured Egyptian agreement as well, but that plan had already failed). Libya's head of state, Qaddafi, always driving for North African unity, had argued that Tunisia's partially unemployed labor force, its unfavorable trade balance and foreign debts, and its limited resources would all benefit from association with Libya, which has a shortage of labor, but is rich in capital and oil. Bourguiba's tentative agreement and proposals for a referendum produced a mild political crisis in Tunisia in 1973, and fears were expressed that Qaddafi might intend to take control of Tunisian politics after Bourguiba's departure. The referendum was at first postponed indefinitely, and subsequently Tunisia withdrew from the proposed confederation (which was to be named the Arab Islamic Republic). Shortly thereafter, reaffirming its confidence in Bourguiba, the Tunisian leader was elected president for life, and Tunisian identity as a separate state was reasserted.

Problems of Development

But Tunisia indeed is not a rich country, and until the early 1970s its debts increased and its rate of growth was very slow. Then the rise in world prices for oil, phosphates, and olive oil brought increased revenues, so that the economic growth rate rose from under 2 to over 10 percent; growth in the tourist industry also contributed markedly. But worldwide inflation consumed part of these gains, and recent good years notwithstanding, Tunisians still eat inadequately (2190 calories daily), earn insufficiently (under $250 annually per capita in 1970), live uncomfortably and briefly (infant mortality is still 120 per thousand, and life expectancy is just 52). The population is growing at the rate of about 2.5 percent per year, substantially less than Morocco or Algeria but rapidly nevertheless. Already Tunisia must spend part of its income on purchases of grain and other staple foods.

Before the oil boom in North Africa, Tunisia had modest exports of phosphate (most of it from the Gafsa area in the southwest), iron ore, lead, and zinc (Fig. 34-1), in the typical colonial-extractive pattern. Since independence a metallurgical complex has been built at Menzel-Bourguiba, where local ores are used. In the early years of independence it appeared that the course of North African history had deprived Tunisia of the opportunity to participate in the oil boom that so greatly benefited Algeria and Libya, but in 1966 oil began to flow from wells at El Borma and Bir Aouin, and another oil discovery was made at El Douleb in the country's midsection; within two years the production satisfied local demand and export could begin. A recent oil find in the hinterland of Sfax indicates that Tunisia may have even larger reserves; a refinery was constructed at Bizerte to process the crude for the local market. As recently as 1966 Tunisia's oil production was below 1 million tons; in 1971 it exceeded 4 million tons and in 1975 it was 8 million. This is not comparable, of course, to the enormous production of Libya or even the comparatively substantial output of Algeria (65 million tons), but its importance to the Tunisian economy has nevertheless been substantial: it contributes one-quarter to one-third of the country's export revenues.

Tunisia's most prosperous industry remains tourism, the largest earner of foreign exchange. In this arena the country's long-term stability has been most beneficial, for tourism is a fragile industry, and political tension or conflict can do it lasting damage. But the tourists have continued to come in growing numbers, and in the early 1970s they were contributing as much as one-third of all the earnings derived from exports and tourism combined. The ruins at Carthage remain one of Tunisia's leading attractions.

Food processing, textile, leather, and small-scale handcraft industries constitute the bulk of Tunisia's manufacturing; industry suffers from a lack of capital and the mild boom of the 1970s generated a search for investors willing to back new enterprises including chemical and electrical industries, construction materials, and others. The local market, however, is not strong, and industrial growth continues at a low pace.

The Land

The great majority of Tunisians, nearly two-thirds of the population, continue to engage in some form of agriculture, ranging from modern, intensive cash-cropping in the Majardah Basin, the northern Tell slopes, Cape Bon, and the Northern Sahel to traditional subsistence agriculture in the High Tell and Dorsale. As elsewhere in North Africa, lands formerly held by European farmers (nearly 2 million acres or 800,000 ha in Tunisia) have been taken over and converted into peasant cooperatives. At independence, European farms averaged 600 acres (250 ha), while Tunisian peasant families farmed, on an average, less than 15 acres (6 ha). The European settlers did develop and expand the cultivation of certain cereals, citrus fruits, vineyards, olive trees, and market produce. As Fig. 34-1 indicates, vineyards developed especially in the middle and lower Majardah region, citrus groves in the northeast, and olive plantations in the Cape Bon and Sahel zones.

Tunisia's land reform program involved not only the reallocation of the European lands but also the *habou* lands held by various Islamic religious communities and inefficiently farmed. The program of reallocation has not always met with immediate success in the form of sustained or increased yields, but the inevitable difficulties of the transition have been largely overcome and production is growing. Still Tunisia faces an annual food shortage, despite the fact that half its cultivated area lies under cereals—wheat in the more humid areas, barley where it is drier. Problems of excessive land fragmentation in the traditional areas, outdated equipment, and insufficient funds for fertilizers and other necessities keep production below what it could be.

The Majardah Basin

A key to the expansion and diversification of agriculture in Tunisia is the development of the potential of the Majardah (Medjerda) River region. Although this region contains the largest contiguous area of cultivable land in Tunisia, it has always been subject to damaging floods, inadequate drainage, and, in the lower reaches, excessive soil salinization. The Majardah is the only Maghreb river to develop a delta, but for many decades the delta was flood-prone, malaria infested, and unsuitable for settlement and cultivation.

Two thousand years ago the Romans built barrages and aqueducts to regulate the flow of water in the Majardah Valley, for the rainfall in the interior catchment areas is strongly seasonal and water must be stored for the warm summer months. When the French settlers began to arrive, the valley attracted many white farmers and some large estates were laid out; wheat became the chief cash crop. During the colonial period the French Tunisian administration began planning as integrated system of flood control, irrigation, and hydroelectric power supply, but this scheme was designed to support the European farmers and town dwellers and to extend export-crop cultivation, not to make new lands available for Tunisian farmers.

Nefta irrigation project, Tunisia. This government-controlled multi-purpose project is designed to increase wheat and dairy output in northern Tunisia, to create desert oases in the south, and to stabilize once nomadic families. (World Bank)

The French constructed three dams: two in the interior on major tributaries of the Majardah and one (the El Aroussia Dam) approximately opposite Tunis on the Majardah itself (Fig. 34-1). Flow regulation and water storage were the main objectives of these barrages, and little real progress was made in irrigation. When the Tunisian government took control of the country, the Majardah Scheme was revised and reoriented to include major land reform. A development authority was established to promote growth in the Majardah region in all directions, even including local industry.

What Tunisia envisages for the Majardah Valley requires much capital, and it is not surprising that progress has been slow. Nevertheless, nearly 200,000 acres (83,000 ha) of new land have been brought under cultivation, and drainage canals that have been built below the El Aroussia dam have made possible the reclamation of nearly 150,000 acres (60,000 ha) of land in the lower plains and delta; further work on this part of the project is under way.

Most significant, however, has been the impact of the land reform program in the region. At independence, this was an area of large estates and farms (more than two-thirds of the available land was in the hands of only 10 percent of owners, almost all of them whites), absentee landlordism, tenancy, and landless labor working the crops. Reform involved purchase, expropriation, limitation on private ownership (150 acres or 60 ha), a prohibition on fragmentation of land below 10 acres (4 ha), and prescriptions on land use. Landless peasants were awarded parcels of land in certain areas, but elsewhere the large European estates were converted to cooperatives. New cooperative villages were built to serve as administrative centers for the cooperatives as well as village amenities such as schools, infirmaries, shops, banks, all clustered near the houses.

Deforestation and erosion have afflicted the Majardah watershed for centuries, but now the development authority has begun large-scale programs of earth-dam construction, terracing, and tree planting.

Changes in the crop pattern reflect the new occupancy of Tunisia's lands. The wheat variety planted by the French as a cash crop is declining as Tunisians cultivate durum wheat, the hardier cereal destined for local consumption. Citrus fruits, also introduced by the Europeans as large-scale cash farming, are expanding. In general, viticulture has not done well after the departure of the Europeans, and the vines, when they stop producing adequately, are often replaced by citrus or market gardens oriented to the local urban markets, principally Tunis.

Tunisia's rather small cattle herd is confined to the moister northern coastal zone; the sheep that form the pastoralists' mainstay are more widespread and number nearly 5 million, a figure that varies, sometimes sharply, with the fortunes of environment. The goat, which damages soil and cultivated plant alike, was the target of a

restriction in Tunisia's orchard areas after independence and its numbers have declined to about a half million. Expensive dairy products still rank among Tunisia's imports each year.

In a country where calorie intake is low and protein deficiency common, a fishing industry takes on added importance. Tunisia has vigorously promoted its fishing industry after independence, and in the two decades since 1956 its catch has almost tripled (to 45,000 tons annually). The industry is centered on the country's east coast, notably the towns of Sfax, Sousse, Mahdia, and Djerba Island. The fishing fleet has been modernized, and canning factories operate in Sfax, Sousse, and Mahdia.

Tunisia's other sources of income include its exploitation of extensive areas of esparto grasses (Fig. 34-1) and its remaining forests. A paper pulp and cellulose plant at Kasserine processes logs from the High Tell and Dorsale regions. Still another, and by no means insignificant, source of revenues comes from the substantial number of Tunisian workers who are in Europe, principally France (where an estimated 150,000 Tunisians now reside).

Maximizing the Assets

Tunisia in many ways is North Africa's least advantaged country. It has every reason to stagnate: it does not have the oil of Libya or Algeria, the phosphate of Morocco, the farmlands of Egypt. As a protectorate, it ranked low in France's order of priorities; if Tunisia had a sphere of influence prior to the Maghreb's fall to colonialism it certainly benefited not at all from Europe's imposed boundaries. Tunisia was one of Africa's crossroads of history, and so varied were the invasions that a jigsaw of ethnicity and culture might be expected.

But what Tunisia lacks in the gamble of geography it gains in its unity of purpose and its strongly forged and carefully nur-

tured national cohesion. Far greater are the reasons for poverty in Tunisia than in Morocco or Algeria, and yet Tunisia has attacked these causes with considerable success; Tunisian living standards are higher than those of Morocco. With its particular, moderate socialist system and its preference for negotiation (even on the Israeli issue) in a radical Arab world, Tunisia's political fortunes might appear fragile and susceptible to the pressures of change—but internal stability has been Tunisia's hallmark and perhaps its greatest asset as an independent state. Tunisians, it has been said, absorbed the lessons of history more successfully than many other societies. From the Andalusian farmers and their meticulous methods to the ancient Sicilians who peopled the Sahel and its characteristic towns, Tunisian society secured permanent and positive contributions. From the French, apart from a distaste for colonialism, Tunisia retained methods of organization now grafted to traditional objectives. In settling nomads, in attempting the first North African comprehensive birth control policy, in confronting the landlords, and in ousting France from its holdover Bizerte naval base, Tunisia displayed a remarkable capacity to approach difficult issues with a maximum of sagacity—a quality displayed by this North African nation as perhaps by no other.

Bibliography

Becker, M. C. "Quo Vadis Tunis?" *Tijdschrift voor Sociale en Economische Geografie*, Vol. 60 (1969), pp. 34–47.

Clarke, J. I. "Summer Nomadism in Tunisia," *Economic Geography*, Vol. 31 (1955), pp. 157–167.

Clarke, J. I. "Population Policies and Dynamics in Tunisia," *Journal of Developing Areas*, Vol. 4 (1969), pp. 45–58.

Debbasch, C. and M. Camau. *La Tunisie*. Paris: Editions Berger-Levrault, 1973.

Duwaji, G. *Economic Development in Tunisia*. New York: Praeger, 1967.

Harrison, R. S. "Tunisia," *Focus*, Vol. XIX, No. 5 (January, 1969).

Houston, J. M. *The Western Mediterranean World*. New York: Praeger, 1968.

Karabenick, E. "The Medjerda Plan: A Precedent to Agrarian Reform in Tunisia," *Professional Geographer*, Vol. XIX, No. 1 (January, 1967), pp. 17–22.

Karabenick, E. "Djerba: a Case Study in the Geography of Isolation," *Journal of Geography*, Vol. LXX (January, 1971), pp. 52–55.

Stone, R. "Tunisian Cooperatives," *Africa Report*, Vol. 16 (June, 1971), pp. 19–22.

THIRTY-FIVE

Libya is Egypt without a Nile, Algeria minus its Tell: a vast expanse of rocky and sandy Sahara that extends to the very shores of the Mediterranean, broken only by widely dispersed oases and, along the coast, by the slightest of maritime influences. Coastal lands along the Gulf of Sirte receive as little as 5 in. (125 mm) of rain annually, and only where Libya protrudes somewhat into the Mediterranean, in the northwest (the region named Tripolitania) and in the northeast (Cyrenaica), are rainfall totals somewhat higher. Topography plays its major role: Benghazi on Cyrenaica's coast receives only some 10 in. (250 mm), but the slopes of the higher interior around Beida may get as much as 20 in. (500 mm). In Tripolitania, the city of Tripoli records 15 in. (375 mm), but rainfall declines quite rapidly inland, where elevations remain low. And rainfall variability here is extremely high, so that even these low averages are frequently unattained.

When Libya became an independent North African state in 1951, it was one of the continent's poorest countries. Per capita annual income was under $40 per year. The population of slightly over 1 million was perhaps 95 percent illiterate. Some three-quarters of the people were subsistence farmers or pastoralists, many of them nomadic. There was no internal market to speak of, and so no industry of any real dimensions had developed. The list of exports was depressing: esparto grass, some olive oil, and scrap metal gathered from the desert battlefields of World War II. No known, unexploited mineral resources awaited development. Libya appeared likely to remain the prototype of the underdeveloped country with the bleakest of prospects.

And then, in 1958, persistent explora-

LIBYA: THE POWER OF BLACK GOLD

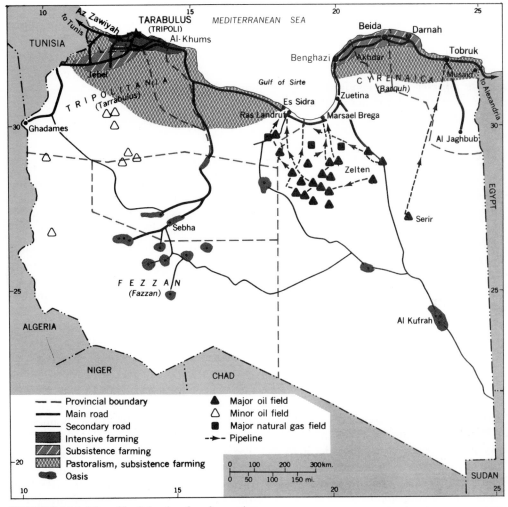

FIGURE 35-1 *Libya. Traditional and modern regions.*

tions by oil companies suddenly changed the situation. The first strike—in the Fezzan region of the southwest—turned out to be but a minor precursor of what was to follow. In 1959 the initial discovery in the Sirte Basin was made at Zelten, soon to be followed by numerous other strikes in the same field (Fig. 35-1). The magnitude of Libya's oil reserves was beyond all expectations; exports began in 1961. In the first full year of oil exports, Libya sent just under 10 million tons to foreign markets; in 1970, a peak year in recent times, exports amounted to nearly 160 million tons, placing Libya among the world's leading producers. Production in the early 1970s declined somewhat as the oil embargo had its effect, but rising prices pushed Libya's enormous oil income to ever higher levels: $38.5 million in 1962, $1.3 billion in 1970, $2 billion in 1974.

The impact of Libya's newfound wealth, both internally and externally, has been enormous. Social and economic reform programs have been initiated, notably in fields of education and agriculture. Formerly poverty-stricken Libya now can afford to send thousands of young people abroad for professional and technical education. It can also afford to buy warplanes and promote ideological causes as far afield as Israel and Uganda; in North Africa it has a powerful voice out of all proportion to its diminutive population (2.5 million in 1977). Prospects are that the oil reserves will continue to sustain the country for at least another three decades; the growth rate of the GNP in recent years has been over 20 percent. Per capita income in Libya is second only to Kuwait in the entire Arab world and first in Africa. In this second half of the twentieth century oil is, indeed, black gold.

Regional Fragmentation

But Libya's wealth cannot overnight turn desert lands green, settle nomadic herders, educate the illiterate, eliminate disease, or wipe out ancient regional contrasts. The oil boom is still an alien intrusion in Libya, and the new facilities and pipelines notwithstanding, life in much of the country has yet to change significantly. For many centuries the country has displayed strong regionalism, a characteristic that still marks it today. The ancient Romans, for whom Libya (then more humid and more productive) was a granary, recognized these contrasts and attached northwestern Libya (Tripolitania) to their African domain centered on Carthage and northeastern Libya (Cyrenaica) to the province of Crete. Even then, Tripolitania was an area of sedentary farming under irrigation, while Cyrenaica's modes of life involved nomadic and seminomadic herding and some shifting cultivation.

During Roman times irrigation was expanded and coastal cities flourished. The Romans had developed centers first founded by the Phoenicians, and Tripoli, along with Sabratha and Leptis Magna, formed the African *Tripolis*. In the fifth century, when the Vandals destroyed Sabratha and Leptis Magna, which had overshadowed Tripoli, the Libyan capital rose to prominence. Benghazi, the modern headquarters of Cyrenaica, was founded by the ancient Greeks but by contrast it declined and remained quite small and unimportant until the modern (European) colonial period.

The Arab invasions of the seventh and eleventh centuries not only changed the region's ethnic makeup and cultural character (through the introduction of Islam) but also altered its economic geography. The Arabs were themselves nomads, and they encouraged nomadism while sedentary farming declined under Arab threat and pressure. Roman irrigation works were abandoned and fell into disrepair. With their herd animals, the Arab tribes damaged the vegetation and caused widespread erosion. The Arab impact was stronger in eastern Libya than in the west, where Berber and Turkish elements survived to a greater degree.

The Turkish period that began in 1835 was one of little change, except that this was the period during which African boundaries were delimited and spheres of influence recognized by treaty: Turkish suzerainty over its province of Tripoli came to include the southwestern region of Fezzan (Fig. 35-1). In this area a third economic system prevails, in further contrast to both Tripolitania and Cyrenaica, for here lie isolated oases where well water provides the means to patches of cultivation.

When Italy took Tripoli and its hinterlands from the Turks in 1911, the colonial regime also recognized Libya's regional fragmentation and administered the country as two discrete dependencies. Tripoli was retained as the capital of Tripolitania, but Benghazi was chosen as the headquarters for Cyrenaica, boosting that town's growth. The Italians approached their colonial objectives with vigor: they fought and overcame local resistance (which was especially strong in Cyrenaica) and began to encourage Italian immigration to the newly acquired lands. For a number of reasons the Italian imprint was much stronger in Tripolitania than elsewhere: the agricultural opportunities were greater, the area remained more stable, while disruptive uprisings constantly occurred in Cyrenaica, and there was greater receptivity to change. Tripolitania had for centuries been the more cosmopolitan sector of the country and by far its most urbanized, and it accommodated the Italian presence most readily.

The Italians' efforts in Libya, however, were designed primarily to benefit Italian colonists, not the Libyans. They made major investments in road building, the construction of villages, irrigation of cultivable land, and the improvement of port facilities, but none of this improved conditions for the traditional farmers. On the contrary, the colonists expropriated some of Libya's better farmland and they reduced the grazing areas of the country's pastoralists. During the 1930s Italy's fascist rulers hoped to create a "second Italy" with as many as 300,000 settlers. By the outbreak of World War II, during which Italy lost Libya, there were 110,000 Italians in the territory, the great majority of them in Tripolitania. As elsewhere in North Africa, independence brought an exodus of Europeans, and fewer than 25,000 now remain, most of them in and near Tripoli. Libya's Jewish community, which numbered about 30,000 before World War II, has dwindled to a few hundred.

Independence

Libya was under joint British and French military occupation following World War II, but these two powers soon sought to abandon this expensive and nonrewarding task. When the USSR showed an interest in assuming a UN Trusteeship in the region, the United States declared itself in favor of local rights of decision on the question of sovereignty. Thus Libya secured independence in 1951 through the support of the United Nations, which approved the establishment of a federation of agricultural Tripolitania, pastoral Cyrenaica, and landlocked Fezzan in a United Kingdom of Libya, a constitutional monarchy. Tripoli and Benghazi were assigned the status of joint capital cities, Tripoli to function as such in the winter months and Benghazi during the summer. This was in acknowledgment of the country's strong regionalism and the widely separated population clusters' provincial allegiances, but for a country as poor as Libya in its first decade of independence, it was an excessive expense. In 1962, it was decided to abolish the three-province system of administration, and the country was divided into 10 *governorates*; it was also decided to build a compromise capital at Beida, on the slopes of Mount Akhdar in Cyrenaica. In the following year the country was officially renamed the Kingdom of Libya, and the federal system was abandoned altogether (the governorates are shown in Fig. 35-1).

In 1969, a group of military officers overthrew the king and established a Revolutionary Command Council, whose chairman became Colonel Qaddafi; Libya accordingly was renamed the Libyan Arab Republic. The country's rather moderate political position changed sharply. Following a period of participation in the Federation of Arab Republics (with Egypt and Syria), Libya and Egypt had differences over the issue of Israel and the union dissolved; Colonel Qaddafi in 1975 accused Egyptian President Sadat of damaging the Arab cause by accepting mediation in the Sinai dispute.

At home, however, the council initiated numerous positive changes and reforms. The costly Beida experiment was abandoned, and Tripoli in effect became the unitary state's

Pipelines leading to the oil-gas separation plant at Zeltan, Libya, one of the country's largest oil producing fields. (Exxon)

Liquefied natural gas facilities, Zeltan, Libya. Petroleum and petroleum products are Libya's major exports and principal sources of national revenue. (Exxon)

single capital. The council moved to nationalize the oil industry by taking control of 51 percent of the operations of all foreign oil firms. The operations of foreign banks also were curtailed and all were obliged to offer 51 percent of their shares to Libyan nationals. When, in 1974, Libya found itself involved in a policy conflict with a major foreign company—Exxon—it proved its new power by forcing the company to shut down its operations. Ironically it was the liberal concessions and favorable conditions that had first attracted the oil companies to Libya for exploratory drilling during the 1950s, in some cases at enormous cost and without result; with the industry in full development the revolutionary Libyan government changed the economic climate.

But the council also proved to have greater concern for the well-being of Libya's population and for the country's future, as the priorities of its development plans prove. No money would be spared, it was announced, to make Libya as green as it was during Roman times; substantial investments were made, for example, in cloud-seeding experiments along the Tripolitanian coast.

More tangibly, the council countered the long-term neglect of the country's agricultural sector by (1) beginning a program to extend the cultivated acreage of Libya, (2) improving living conditions in the rural villages, thereby reducing the migration to the cities, and (3) settling Libya's remaining nomadic peoples in permanent villages and making fodder available by growing and storing it. Pastoral nomadism is viewed by the council as inconsistent with national unity and stable administration.

Agricultural schemes involve areas in the coastal regions of Libya as well as the Saharan interior. One major project envisages the transformation of the Akhdar area in Cyrenaica, where seminomadic subsistence farmers will be settled in newly laid-out olive and almond orchards, afforestation will reverse erosion, new roads will improve communications, and dams will not only store water but permit electrification of the area. Another ambitious undertaking centers

Sand dune control along coastal Libya. Only two percent of the land area is cultivated, and this is threatened by desert encroachment. (UN)

LIBYA: THE POWER OF BLACK GOLD

on the Kufra (Al Kufram) oasis in southeastern Libya. This was a small settlement when, in the late 1960s, a company drilling for oil found, instead, a large source of underground water. The government is now in the process of building irrigation systems to cultivate 24,000 acres (10,000 ha). The systems involve, among other installations, huge circular sprinkler systems of over 3000 ft (1 km) in diameter, each fed by one of 100 wells. This is only the beginning, and the objective is to grow fodder crops so that the sheep of surrounding nomadic herders can be fed here—and their owners settled in a town that may eventually exceed 5000 in population. Other crops, of course, will be grown for local use.

Similar projects are designed to enlarge cultivated acreages in oases of the Fezzan and to improve farming in the established areas of Tripolitania. Libyan farming is a precarious business, with desert encroachment, the hot, destructive Saharan winds (the *ghibli*), unreliable water supply, frequent outbreaks of plant and animal diseases among the inhibitors. But the oil revenues are being put to work to aid farmers in securing fertilizers and equipment, loans and credits, spraying and veterinary services, marketing assistance, and more; fresh water and electricity, as well as roads, are serving places and areas not previously affected by the boom.

Urban Development

The oil boom has also stimulated growth and expansion in Libya's largest cities, and this growth has attracted people from the land—where the Libyan government would have preferred many of them to remain. Urban expansion is not as easy to control and guide as the development of interior oases, even with ample funds, and so Libya's cities developed ugly squatter settlements on their outskirts. Again the government invested heavily in providing apartments for these new city dwellers, but what the country needed in the cities was skilled and technical personnel, not the unskilled arrivals from the countryside. At independence, Libya was 16 percent urbanized, but today more than 30 percent of Libyans live in cities and towns, mainly Tripoli (450,000) and Benghazi (210,000), where over 80 percent of urban Libyans now live.

What drew the people to these cities, of course, was the ripple effect of the oil boom. The oil fields are in the Sirte Basin, not the cities, but the associated developments affected Tripoli and Benghazi quite directly: ports grew busier, transport services were strained, retailing was stimulated, construction increased. Libya now began to develop what it had lacked for so long: a set of local industries including not only petrochemicals, steel pipes, and other oil-related plants but also the manufacture of consumer goods such as shoes, textiles, furniture, and carpets. Certainly there is ample capital; what continues to inhibit the local industries, naturally, is the smallness of the local market. Libyan manufactures have not yet found their place on the world markets.

The Future

Libya's government faces the urgent reality that the opportunity is now and temporary, and that the Libya of the future may have to rely once again on the land, not on the sale of energy. The oil revenues must be used to prepare the country for such a time; but to transform a country of 680,000 sq mi (1,750,000 sq km), even with a population of

Tripoli, Libya's capital and primate city. Minarets of this Moslem city dominate the sky line. (UN)

under 3 million, is a huge task. Libya's oil wealth and its slow response to the initiatives of change is hard evidence of the tenacity of the condition of underdevelopment. Still today, in the late 1970s, Libya must import barley (the staple crop of the countryside), meat, and other foodstuffs, and the country cannot feed itself. The urban migration has left farmlands unattended, livestock herds in decline. Yet these may be the mainstays of a future Libya.

The Revolutionary Council anticipates that its present investments and the priorities of its development plans will in time

have the desired effect. As the potential earnings of farmers increase, a decline in the urban migration is expected; the stream of Libyan laborers returning from European and North African jobs to share in Libya's present fortunes will also decrease. In the meantime, Libya can look forward to decades of sustained high income: its location on the North African coast opposite energy-deficient Western Europe puts the country on the European side of the Middle East's recurrent conflict areas. Additionally, Libyan oil is preferred by Western markets because it has a low sulphur content and is more cheaply refined. Given the rising energy needs of the developed world and the failure of Western countries to push the search for energy alternatives, Libya's position appears secure until, at least, the end of the present century.

The Sirte Basin

To Libya's three traditional regions has been added a fourth: the Sirte Basin (Fig. 35-1). Libya's major oil reserves lie far closer to Mediterranean coasts than those of Algeria, and in the further absence of mountain barriers the construction of a veritable network of pipelines has not presented problems. The whole region has been transformed, not only by the oil installations themselves but also by service roads, settlements, and other related developments. In addition, groups of producing companies each established their own coastal terminals, and the whole Sirte Basin reflects the oil rush that occurred here. Among the settlements generated by the oil boom, only Marsa El Brega has attained sustantial size (but even this town, the major center of the Sirte Basin, counts under 6000 residents).

All the attention that has been given to the Sirte reserves may have resulted in the neglect of another potential Libyan oil source, of which the Serir well and its long pipeline to Tobruk may be early developments. Egyptian oil finds have moved westward, and they may extend into Libya. Similarly, the proximity of Algeria's oil reserves to the Libyan boundary may presage further oil discoveries in western Libya as well (minor finds have already occurred). Libya's black gold may flow even longer than the most optimistic predictions hold.

Bibliography

Allan, J. A., et al. *Libya: Agricultural and Economic Development.* London: Cass, 1972.

Atkinson, K., et al. "Man-Made Oases of Libya," *Geographical Magazine,* Vol. XLV (November, 1972), pp. 112–115.

Beaumont, J., et al. *The Middle East: a Geographical Study.* London: John Wiley, 1975.

Blake, G. H. *Misurata: a Market Town in Libya.* Durham: Department of Geography, Durham University, 1968.

Blunsum, T. *Libya: the Country and Its People.* London: Queen Anne Press, 1968.

Clarke, J. I. "Oil in Libya: Some Implications," *Economic Geography,* Vol. 39 (1963), pp. 40–59.

First, R. *Libya: the Elusive Revolution.* New York: Africana Publishing Co., 1975.

Hajjaji, S. A. *The New Libya.* Tripoli: Ministry of Information and Culture, 1967.

Harrison, R. S. "Libya," *Focus,* Vol. XVII, No. 3 (November, 1966), pp. 1–6.

Hartley, R. G. "Libya: Economic Development and Demographic Responses," in J. I. Clarke and W. B. Fisher (eds.), *The Populations of the Middle East and North Africa,* London: University of London Press, 1972.

Hartley, R. G., and J. M. Norris, "Demographic Regions in Libya: A Principal Components Analysis of Economic and Demographic Variables," *Tijdschrift voor Sociale en Economische Geografie,* Vol. 60 (1969), pp. 221–227.

Heitmann, G. "Libya: an Analysis of the Oil Economy," *Journal of Modern African Studies,* Vol. 7, No. 2 (1969), pp. 249–263.

International Bank for Reconstruction and

Development, *The Economic Development of Libya*. Baltimore: Johns Hopkins Press, 1963.

Khadduri, M. *Modern Libya: a Study in Political Development*. Baltimore: Johns Hopkins Press, 1963.

Wright, J. *Libya*. New York: Praeger, 1969.

BIBLIOGRAPHIES AND REFERENCE MATERIALS

In addition to the references cited at the end of each chapter, there is an abundance of geographical material in yearbooks, government and UN documents, national atlases and the professional journals. The following, of course, is only a partial listing of these materials, but they are some of the most useful and more generally available materials.

BIBLIOGRAPHIES

A Current Bibliography on African Affairs. Washington, D.C.: African Bibliographic Center.

Africa South of the Sahara: Index to Periodic Literature. Washington, D.C.: Library of Congress.

Bederman, S. H. *Africa: A Bibliography of Geography and Related Disciplines,* Third Edition. Atlanta, Georgia: Georgia State University, 1974.

Cumulative Bibliography of African Studies. Boston: G. K. Hall, 1973.

Current Geographic Publications. New York: American Geographic Society. Monthly except July and August.

Duignan, P. (ed.). *Guide to Research and Reference Works on Sub-Saharan Africa.* Stanford: Stanford University Hoover Institution, 1972.

Geographical Abstracts. University of East Anglia. Six series each published six times a year.

Hartwig, G. W., and W. M. O'Barr. *The Student Africanist's Handbook: A Guide to Resources.* New York: John Wiley & Sons, 1974.

International African Bibliography. School of Oriental and African Studies, University of London. London. 1973.

New Geographical Literature and Maps. London: Royal Geographical Society. Twice a year.

Paden, J. N., and E. W. Soja (eds.). *The African Experience.* Vol. III A: *Bibliography.* Evanston: Northwestern University Press, 1970.

Panofsky, Hans E. *A Bibliography of Africana.* London: Greenwood Press, 1975.

Sub-Saharan Africa: A Guide to Serials. Washington, D.C.: U. S. Library of Congress, 1970.

HANDBOOKS AND YEARBOOKS

Africa South of the Sahara. London: Europa Publications, Annual.

Legum, C. (ed.). *Africa Contemporary Record: Annual Survey and Documents.* London: Africa Research Ltd., Annual.

The Middle East and North Africa. London: Europa Publications, Annual.

Morrison, D. G. et al. *Black Africa: A Comparative Handbook.* New York: The Free Press, 1972.

UNITED NATIONS DOCUMENTS

Economic Commission for Africa. *Bibliography: Economic and Social Development Plans of African Countries.* 1968.

Economic Commission for Africa. *Economic Bulletin for Africa.* Semiannual.

Economic Commission for Africa. *Survey of Economic Conditions for Africa.*

Statistical Office. *Demographic Yearbook.* Annual.

Statistical Office. *Production Yearbook.* Annual.

Statistical Office. *Statistical Yearbook.* Annual.

Statistical Office. *Yearbook of International Trade Statistics.* Annual.

AFRICAN GOVERNMENT DOCUMENTS

Most African states publish their development plans, census reports, and annual ministerial reports. Several have published a national atlas.

JOURNALS AND PERIODICALS

Africa Confidential, Africa Digest, Africa Institute Bulletin, Africa Report, Africa Research Bulletin, Africa Today, African Affairs, African Development, African Studies, African Studies Review, African Urban Notes, Annals of the Association of American Geographers, Canadian Geographer, Canadian Journal of African Studies, Current History, East African Geographical Review, Economic Bulletin for Africa, Economic Development and Culture Change, Economic Geography, Economist, Financial Mail, Focus, Foreign Affairs, Geography, Geographical Journal, Geographical Magazine, Geographical Review, International Affairs, Issue, Journal of African History, Journal of Developing Areas, Journal of Geography, Journal of Modern African Studies, Journal of Tropical Geography, Optima, Pan-African Journal, Rural Africana, Savanna, Tijdschrift voor Economische en Sociale Geografie, Quarterly Economic Review, West Africa.

GENERAL REFERENCES

Allan, W. *The African Husbandman.* Edinburgh: Oliver & Boyd, 1965.

Bohannan, P., and P. Curtin. *Africa and Africans.* Revised edition. New York: Natural History Press, 1971.

Bohannan, P. J., and G. Dalton (eds.). *Markets in Africa.* Evanston: Northwestern University Press, 1962.

Church, R. J. H. et al. *Africa and the Islands.* London: Longman, 1973.

Dumont, R. *False Start in Africa.* New York: Praeger, 1966.

Griffiths, J. F. (ed.). *Climates of Africa.* New York: Elsevier, 1972.

Grove, A. T. *Africa South of the Sahara.* Second Edition. London: Oxford University Press, 1970.

Hance, W. A. *African Economic Development.* Second Edition. New York: Praeger, 1967.

Hance, W. A. *The Geography of Modern Africa.* Second Edition. New York: Columbia University Press, 1975.

Kamark, A. M. *The Economics of African Development.* Second Edition. New York: Praeger, 1967.

Kimble, G. H. T. *Tropical Africa.* New York: Twentieth Century Fund, 1960 (2 vols).

Klein, M. A., and G. W. Johnson (eds.). *Perspectives on The African Past.* Boston: Little, Brown & Co., 1972.

Murdock, G. P. *Africa: Its Peoples and their Culture History.* New York: McGraw-Hill, 1959.

Mutharika, B. W. T. *Toward Multinational-Economic Cooperation in Africa.* New York: Praeger, 1972.

O'Conner, A. M. *The Geography of Trop-*

ical African Development. Oxford: Pergamon Press, 1971.

Oliver, R. and J. D. Fage. *A Short History of Africa*. Baltimore: Penguin Books, 1970.

Ominde, S. H., and C. N. Ejiogu (eds.). *Population Growth and Economic Development in Africa*. London: Heinemann, 1974.

Paden, J. N., and E. W. Soja (eds.). *The African Experience*. Evanston: Northwestern University Press, 1970.

Prothero, R. M. (ed.). *People and Land in Africa South of the Sahara*. New York: Oxford University Press, 1972.

Rodney, W. *How Europe Underdeveloped Africa*. Washington, D.C.: Howard University Press, 1974.

Rotberg, R. I. *A Political History of Tropical Africa*. New York: Harcourt, Brace and World, 1965.

Skinner, E. P. (ed.). *Peoples and Cultures of Africa*. New York: Natural History Press, 1973.

Thomas, M. F., and G. W. Whittington (eds.). *Environment and Land Use in Africa*. London: Methuen and Co., 1972.

Thompson, B. W. *The Climate of Africa*. Nairobi: Oxford University Press, 1965.

AUTHOR INDEX

597

SUBJECT INDEX

European population 551
French occupation, 549
origins, 551
as port, 551
Alluvial Soils, irrigation, 47
Al-Morgan, 534, 539
Al-Qusayr, 539
Ambatondrazaka, 406
American Colonization Society, 194
Americo-Liberians, 194
Amharic, 493
Amin, Idi, 116, 461, 464-465
Amin, Lake, 243, 452
Amboseli, 448
Anglo-Boer War, 81, 344
Anglo-Egyptian Sudan, 511
Angola, 325-337
  agriculture, 330-332
  economy 329-334
  and Namibia, 381
  petroleum production, 336
  physical environments, 326-327
  Portuguese policy, 94, 327-329
Angolan Civil War, 286, 334-337, 380
Angolan Independence, 334-337
Ankaratra Mountains, 404, 405
Ankole, 457
Ankole, Kingdom, 73, 455
Ankrah, General, 181-182
Anti-Locust Research Centre, 57
Antisirabe, 406
Anya-nya, 517, 519
Apartheid, 347-349, 352, 368
  in Namibia, 373, 379-381
  theory of, 339
  see also Separate development
Arab aid, Guinea, 212
  Mauritania, 233-234
  Sudan, 520
Arab League, 98, 115-116
Arab traders, 74
Arabic, 577
  and Barbary States, 548
Arabs, in East Africa, 78
  in Madagascar, 406
  in Mozambique, 311
  settlement of North Africa, 67
  ties with West Africa, 71

Archimedean Screw, 528, 529
Arusha, 422, 430, 449, 464
Arusha Declaration, 425, 426
Arlit, 215, 237
Asbestos, 301, 399, 400
Ashanti, ancient state, 72
Ashanti Kingdom, 170, 171, 177
Ashanti Union of Akan States, 170
Ashanti Wars, 113
Asians, 348
  in Kenya, 448-449
  in Mozambique, 320
  in South Africa, 346-347
  in Uganda, 461
Asmara, 109, 492, 493
Assab, 481, 493, 505
Assimilado, 94, 320, 328
Aswan, 534, 539
Aswan High Dam, 515, 526-527, 531, 534, 535, 538, 540
  bilharzia infection, 53
Asyut, 531
Atbara River, 513, 515
Atlas Mountains, 13, 543, 544, 559
  High Atlas, 543, 565, 566
  High Tell, 574-577
  Middle Atlas, 565, 566
  Rif Atlas, 566
  Saharan Atlas, 543, 546
  Tell Atlas, 543, 574-577
Awash Valley, 492
Axum, 479
Axum, Kingdom of, 64, 65, 74, 76
  demise of, 65
  massive dry-stone masonry, 65
  terracing, 65

Bagamoyo, 421
Baganda, 453
Baganda, Kingdom, 435
Bahr el Ghazal Province (Sudan), 507
Baker, Samuel, 83
Bakongo, 73, 325, 334
Bakouma, 269
Balante, 213
Bale, 491, 493
Bamako, 212, 235
Bambata Rebellion, 113

Banana (port), 257
Bananas, 210, 273, 502
Banda, Kamuzu, 287, 291
Bangassou, 268
Bangui, 267, 269
Bangwelu, Lake, 281
Banjul, 233
Bantu Investment Corporation, 361
Bantustans, *see* South African Homelands
Baraka River, 513
Barbary States, 546
Barumbu, climatic data, 24
Basins, significance of, 4-7, 12-13
Basotho Qwa Qwa, 349, 366
Basuto, 341
Bath, Heinrich, 260
Bathurst (Banjul), 233
Battles, Adowa, 87, 482
   Blood River, 79
Bauxite, Cameroon, 271, 274
   Ghana, 176
   Guinea, 210-212
   Sierra Leone, 185, 192
Béchar, 546, 551
Bechuanaland 93, 294. *See also* Botswana
Beida, 584, 585, 587
Beira, 249, 283
   port for Malawi, 288
   port for Rhodesia, 305-306, 312
Belgium, and Belgian Congo, 246
   colonial policies, 90-91
   policies in Congo, 252-253
   and Ruanda-Urundi, 466-468
   territorial claims, 84
Belgian Congo, 90-91, 245, 248-253
   administrative organization, 253
   railroad construction, 248-250
   and Ruanda-Urundi, 466
   See also Zaire
Belinga, 265
Bemba, 281
Bender Ziada, 498
Benghazi, 584, 585, 586
   as capital, 587
   population, 590
Benguela, 78, 334
Benguela Current, 33, 327, 374
Benguela Railway, 103, 249, 286, 333, 334

Benin, 212-217
   ancient state, 72
   demographic data, 211
   political instability, 215
   see also Dahomey
Benin City, 72, 160
Benue River, 146, 148
Berbera, 497
   Soviet missiles, 502
Berberati, 274
Berbers, 67, 546, 548, 559
   Amazigh, 559
   Rifian, 559
   Shleuh (Chleuh), 559
Berlin Conference, 85, 87, 150, 246, 260, 328
Berseem, 531
Bethlehem Steel Corporation, 198
Betsimitatatra Plain, 408
Bhunya, 398, 399, 400
Biafra, 112, 155, 160
Biafra, Bight of, 259
Biafran War, 145, 160, 162
Big Bend, 400
Bihé Plateau, 327
   economic geography, 333
Bilharzia (schistosomiasis), 53
Bir Aouin, 579
Bissau, 213
Bizerte, 579, 582
Bizerte Plain, 577
Black Volta River, 173
Blantyre, 110, 283, 288
Bloemfontein, 110
Blood River, battle of, 79
Blue Nile River, 5, 10, 513
Bo, 188
Boali, 269
Bobo Dioulasso, 236
Bodele Depression, 6, 16
Boers, 79, 344
Boké, 211
Bolgatanga, 173
Boma, 243, 250, 256
Bomi Hills, 197
Bong Ranges, 198
Bophuthatswana, 349, 354
   minerals, 357
   territorial consolidation, 349, 366

Border Industries, South Africa, 360-361
Bornu, 165
Botletle River, 387
Botswana, 358, 383-390
  aridity, 385-388
  cattle economy, 387-389
  ideological links with Zambia, 401
  settlement patterns, 387
  South African influences, 401
Bouaké, 207
Boundaries, 100-104, 226
  geometric, 100-101
  natural, 101
Boundary claims, Tunisia, 578
Boundary disputes, Somalia, 499-502
Bourguiba, Habib, 574, 578-579
Brava, 497
Brazzaville, 260, 261, 265, 266, 269
Britain, and Cape Colony, 79-81
  colonial policies, 93-94
  and the Horn, 498
  and Rhodesia, 302, 305-306
  and Sudan, 511-512
  territorial claims, 84, 86-87
British Cape Colony, 390
British Commonwealth, 115
British East Africa, 434-435
British East Africa Company, 85-86, 435
British Somaliland, 495, 498
British South Africa Company, 281, 282, 294,
    297
British Togoland, 172, 213
Broken Hill (Kabwe), 281
Bruce, James, 81
Brussels Geographic Conference, 245-246
Bu Craa, 564
Buchanan, 197, 211
Buganda, 453-458
Buganda Kingdom, 73, 453-455
Buganda Agreement, 456, 457
Bujumbura, 469
Bukama, 248-249
Bukava, 473
Bulawayo, 294, 304
Bunyoro, 457
Bunyoro, Kingdom, 73, 455
Burton, Richard, 83
Burundi, 464, 466-474

agriculture, 468-472
colonial administration, 466-468
genocide, 473-474
Burundi Kingdom, 73
Bushongo, 73
Bushman (Sarwa), 61-62, 342, 387
  and Hollanders, 79
Bushmanland, 375, 379-380
Busia, President, 182
Busumbura, 473
Butare, 469
Buthelezi, G., 361, 367
Butterworth, 361

Cabinda, 327
  petroleum, 330, 336
Cabora Bassa, 11, 289, 310, 315-317
Cabral, Amilcar, 213
Caillié, René, 81
Cairo (Al Quahirah), 106, 531
  as cultural center, 532-535
  founded, 528
  nodal location, 531-532
  population growth, 537
Calabar, 150
Caliche, 48
Calueque Dam, 334, 380
Cambambe Dam, 332
Cameroon, 261, 264, 269-274, 421
  agriculture, 271-273
  and Chad, 274
  German administration, 88, 271, 561
  mandate system, 270
  manufacturing, 274
Cameroon, Mount, 9, 16, 271
Canada, and Guinea, 212
Canaries Current, 566
Canary Islands, 564
Cape Bon, 575, 576, 580
Cape Colony, British settlement of, 343
Cape Cross, 370, 371
Cape Gardafui, 495
Cape Ranges, 14, 16, 339, 340
Cape Town, 34, 78, 110, 343, 345-346, 348,
    351
Capital Cities, 104-110
  characteristics of, 108
  South African homelands, 362

Caprivi Strip 87, 104, 376, 381, 385
Carter Commission, 440
Carthage, 64, 65, 67, 548, 477, 579, 586
 trans-Saharan trade, 67
Casablanca, 561, 562, 565-567, 571
 industry, 572
 population growth, 572
Casamance River, 232
Cassava, 517
Cattle, 488
 Botswana, 387-389
 Malagasy, 408
Cavalla, 199
Ceao, 230
Cela, 329
Censuses, Nigeria, 153
Central African Customs and Economic
  Union (UDEAC), 274
Central African Federation, 112-113, 280, 293
 economic characteristics, 283
 established, 283, 296
 failures, 297
 opposition to, 283
Central African Republic, 265, 267-269
 accessibility problems, 269
 agriculture, 268-269
 trans-Cameroon Railway, 269
Cereals, 545, 580
Ceuta, 95, 561, 564-565
Chad, 238
 authenticity policy, 238
 and Central African Republic, 274
 demographic data, 223
Chad Basin, 6, 146, 219
Chad, Lake, 6, 13, 271
Chagga, 421
 resistance to *ujamaa*, 428
Chari (Shari) River, 238
Chelif Plain, 544
Chewa, 281
Chilwa-Palombe Plain, 289
China, People's Republic of, and Cameroon,
  274
 and Congo, 267
 and Ghana, 182
 and Guinea, 209
 and Malagasy, 410
 and Mali, 235

 and Mauritania, 233
 and Tanzania, 420, 429, 432-433
Chipata, 289
Chiromo, 289
Chirundu, 285, 293, 301
Chleuh, 559
Chobe River, 385
Chole, 289
Chotts, 577
Christianity, in the Horn, 479-480
Chrome, 301
Church of Scotland, 281
Ciskei, 349, 366
Circumscription, in Mozambique, 312,
  315-316
 in Portuguese Africa, 94
Climate, and agriculture, 36-39
 continental patterns, air masses, 22-24
  barometric pressure, 22-24
  fronts, 22-24
  rainfall, 20-21
  rainfall variability, 22, 30-31
  temperature, 21-22
 South Africa, 340-341
 Types,
  Dry summer subtropical (Cs), 34
  Dry winter subtropical (Cw), 35-36
  Highland (H), 36
  Humid subtropic (Cf), 35
  Low-latitude steppe (BSh), 31-32
  Monsoon (Am), 27-28
  Rainforest, (Af), 24-26
  Savanna (Aw), 28-31
  Tropical desert (BWh), 32-34
  Tropical-wet dry (Aw), 28-31
  Wet equatorial (Af, Am), 24-27
Climate change, Sahel, 224-226
Cloves, 408, 429
Coal, Rhodesia, 302
 South Africa, 357-358
 Zaire, 250
Cobalt, Zaire, 255
Cocoa, 216
 Equatorial Guinea, 270
 Ghana, 175-176, 177
 Ivory Coast, 205
 Nigeria, 150, 157-158
 Sierra Leone, 185

French Somaliland, 505
French Togoland, 172, 213
French West Africa, 92, 202
Friguia (Fria), 211
Front of National Liberation, Algeria
    (F.L.N., 553-554
Fulani, 146, 148-149, 153, 163, 213
Fung Empire, 510, 513
Fustat, 532
Futa Jallon, 7, 184, 209, 212

Gabon, 261-265
  forest resources, 262-263
  manganese, 261, 264
  petroleum industry, 264
Gaborone, 106, 109, 388, 390
Gafsa, 579
Galla, 461, 480, 497
  diet of, 50
Gambia, 233
  boundary establishment, 101
  and Senegel, 233
Gambia River, 84, 233
Gao, 68, 69
  climate data, 32
Gatooma, 305
Gazankulu, 349
Gaza Strip, 534
Gécamines, 254, 256
Geita mine, 420
German Colonization Society, 85
German East Africa, 434-435, 466
Germany, colonial policies, 88-90
  Federal Republic of, and Namibia, 374
  occupation of South West Africa, 370-372
  role in Tanganyika, 421
  territorial claims, 84-86
  and Togoland, 215
Gezira Irrigation Scheme, 38, 512, 513-515,
  519
  Bilharzia infection, 53
Ghadames, 578
Ghana, 169-183, 236
  administrative regions, 172-173
  ancient state, 67-68, 559
  cocoa, 175-176

compared to Nigeria, 170-171, 173
  consolidation of, 170
  ethnic diversity, 172-173
  industry, 177-179
  labor migrations, 135-136
  physiographic features, 173-174
  transport routes, 174-177
  unitary state system, 111
    reason for, 171-172
Ghardaia, 546
Gibraltar, Straits of, 559
Githaka system, 440
Giuba (Juba) River, 495, 497
  as boundary, 499
Giuba Valley, agriculture, 502
Glaciation, ancient, 16
Gobabis, 401
Gojjam, 491
Gold, 301, 338, 351, 357-358, 364-365, 420
  discovered, in Rhodesia, 294
    in South Africa, 80
  Ghana, 176
  South Africa, 357-358
Gold Coast, 78, 97, 169-170
Gold Coast Colony, 149
Golden Stool, 72
Gondwana (Gondwanaland), 14-18
Gordon, Charles, 510
Gorongosa Game Reserve, 318
Gowon, Yakubu, 154, 155
Grande Camore, 409
Grant, James A., 83, 455
Great Dyke, 301-302
Great Escarpment, 3, 4, 5, 279, 293, 310
Great Fish River, 340, 342, 349, 353
Great North Road, 286
Great Trek, 79-80
Groundnuts (peanuts), 203, 222, 233
  East African Groundnut Scheme, 47-48,
    425
  Niger, 236
  Nigeria, 164
  Senegal, 231
Group Areas Act, 347-348, 365
Guinea, 209-212
  agriculture, 210
  bauxite industry, 210-212

Lagos, 106, 156, 224
  as federal capital, 158-159
  as port, 158
Lagos Colony, 149
Lake Chad Basin Commission, 230
Lamu, 450
Land alienation, Kenya, 437-442
  Morocco, 569
  Rhodesia, 282, 294-295
  Swaziland, 396-397
Land Apportionment Act, Rhodesia, 297-298
Lander, Richard, 81
Landlocked states, 101-104
Land Reform, Tunisia, 581-582
Land Tenure Act, 298
Languages, classification of, 138-139
  colonial, 139
  multilingualism, 139
  and nationalism, 139-140
  in Nigeria, 139
  official by state, 140
  use of, in research, 61
La Skhirra, 557
Lavumisa, 401
Lead, 267, 374, 375
League of Nations, 89, 370, 372, 466, 482
  Toto, 203, 213
Lebanese, 189, 213
Lebowa, 349, 357, 366
Leopold, King, 246, 247
Leopold II, King, 245
Leopoldville, 92, 245. *See also* Kinshasa
Leribe, 391
Lesotho, 358, 383-385, 390-395
  agricultural practices, 392-393
  population pressure, 392-393
  soil erosion, 392
  South African influences, 401
Letlhakane, 389
Letseng-la-Terae, 394
Liberia, 84, 193-201, 373
  American investment in, 195-196
  historical geography, 194-196
  iron mining, 196-198
  transport system, 200
Liberian American Swedish Minerals Company (LAMCO), 197
Libreville, 261

Libya, 95, 542, 584-596
  and Chad, 238
  colonization of, 586-587
  historical geography, 586-587
  independence of, 95
  petroleum, 585-586, 588-589, 590-592
Likasi, 250, 258
Lilongwe, 106, 110, 288, 289, 390
  new capital established, 288
Limbe, 283, 288
Limpopo River, 279, 281, 293
Limuru, 446
Livingstone, 245
Livingstone, David, 82, 83
  exploration of Zambezia, 281
Lobamba, 400
Lobatse, 388-389, 390
Lobengula, Chief, 294
Lobito, 249, 250, 327
  outlet for Zambia, 286
  as port, 334
Locusts, 56-57
Loi Cadre (Outline Law), 92
Lomé, 216
Lomé Convention, 204-205, 217
London Missionary Society, 82, 294
London, Treaty of, 499
Longone Valley, 238
Longonot, Mount, 10
Lourenço Marques, 309, 311
  port for Southern transvaal, 312
  See also Maputo
Lower Egypt (Nile Delta), 531
Lower Limpopo Valley Scheme, 317
Luanda, 325, 327, 329
  as capital, 330-332
Luba-Lunda Kingdoms, 73, 281
Lubumbashi, 250, 258
Lüderitz, 371, 372, 375, 376
Lugard, Frederick, 149
Lukenga Swamps, 285
Lundi River, 301
Luo, 442
Lusaka, 110, 285, 291

Maamba, 285, 317
Machel, Samora, 320, 322

Mauritania (*continued*)
  claims to Spanish Sahara, 562-564
  demographic data, 223
  and Morocco, 234
Mayotte, 409
Mayumbe, 251, 384, 399, 400
Mbandzeni, Chief, 396
Mbeya, 422, 431
M'Binda, 264
Mbundu, 325, 334
Mediterranean climate, 34, 566
  Algeria, 543-544
Meknes, 560, 565, 566
  population, 572
Melilla, 95, 561, 564, 565
Memphis, 532
Mende, 186
Menelik, Emperor, 87, 492, 498
  ascent to throne, 482
  and Italians, 482
Menzel-Bourguiba, 579
Merina people, 406
Meroë, 65
Meru, Mount, 10
Mhlume, 398, 399, 400
Mid-Atlantic Ridge, 17
Middle Atlas, 565, 566
Middle Belt, Nigeria, 150, 151, 166
Middle East, and Sudan, 520
Middle Egypt, 527, 531-534
Midwest Region, Nigeria, 154
Mid-West State, Nigeria, 159-160, 163
Miferma, 232
Migrant labor, Ivory Coast, 203
  Lesotho, 390, 393-394
  Namibia, 374
  South Africa, 136, 357-358
  Upper Volta, 203, 236
Migrations, 134-137
  to Africa, 135
  pastoral, 226-227
  in West Africa, 135
Mijurtein (Medjourtine) Mountains, 495
Mineral Zones, 16
Miradi, 221
Mitidja Plain, 544
Mitumba Mountains, 243
Mlanje, Mount, 8

Moanda, 264
Moatize, 317
Mobutu, Lake, 243, 452
Mobutu, President, 254, 336
Moçamedes, 327, 334
Mogadishu, 109, 450, 495, 497, 498, 502
Mohammed V, Sultan, 561-562
Mokanji Hills, 185
Molepolole, 387
Mombasa, 78, 311, 446, 449-451, 453, 473
  port for Zambia, 286
  railroad from, 435
Monrovia, 193, 196, 200
Monsoon climate, 27-28
  Madagascar, 405
  Sierra Leone, 184
Moors, 559
Mopti, 223
Morocco, 92, 95, 542, 559-573, 582
  agriculture, 568-569, 570
  colonial interests in, 560-561
  historical geography, 559-561
  independence granted, 561
  phosphate, 565-566
  population issues, 569, 571-572
  territorial claims, 562-564
Morogoro, 422, 423
Moroni, 409
Moshesh, Chief, 383, 390
Moshi, 421, 422
Moslem Algerians, 553
Moslem Turks, and Barbary states, 548
Mosquitoes, 51-52
Mossi, 69
Mossi Plateau, 236
Mounana, 264
Mountain Ranges, significance of, 13-14
Mozambique, 309-324
  agriculture, 317
  colonial policy in, 94
  diseases in, 53
  forced labor, 316
  physical environments, 310-311
  populations, 319-320
  Portuguese administration, 311-312
  pre-colonial settlement, 311
  relations with South Africa, 321
  settlement schemes, 316-317

Mozambique Convention, 312, 316
Mozambique Current, 35
Mozambique Town, 315-319
Mpanda, 420, 422
MPLA, 334, 336
Mtwara, port functions, 423, 425
Muchinga Mountains, 289
Mufilira, 282
Muhammad Ahmad, 510
Multinational development, *see* Separate development, Apartheid
Mulunje, 289
Murine Plague, 58
Murrua, 317
Musoma, 423
Mussolini, Benito, 95
Muzorewa, Bishop, 306
Mwanamutapa, 73, 74
Mwanza, 422, 423, 428
Mwea Irrigation Scheme, 446

Nacala, 323
  port, for Malawi, 288
    for Zambia, 286
Nachingwea, 425
Nador, 572
Naga, 65
Nagana, 54
Nairobi, 108, 431, 433, 439, 444, 446-449
  industry, 446-447
  population, 446
Naivasha, 438, 447, 448
Nakuru, 438, 444, 447, 448
Namaland, 376, 379-380
Namapa, 317
Namibia, 95, 337, 370-382
  agriculture, 376
  diamonds discovered, 372
  Homelands, 375, 379-380
  independence issue, 381
  minerals, 374-375
  rainfall, 376-377, 380
  and South Africa, 372, 377-380
Namib Desert, 371, 376
  climate, 33
Napata, 65
Nasser, Lake, 526-527, 534, 538
Nasser, President, 530

Nationalism, defined, 113
  and language, 139-140
  in Nigeria, 167-168
  in South Africa, 115
  in Tanzania, 115
National Liberation Council (Ghana), 181-182
National Redemption Council (Ghana), 182
Native Land Husbandry Act, 298-299
Native Trust and Land Act, 366
Natural Gas, 546
Nazret, 492
Nchanga, 283
Ndebele, 341
Ndola, 283, 285
N'Djamena (Fort Lamy), 238
Negritude, 114
Neto Agostinho, 334
"New Valley" (Egypt), 538
Ngami, Lake, 385
N'Gaoundéré, 238, 271, 274
Ngorongoro Crater, 422, 431
N'Gounie River, 261
Nguni, 281, 294, 341
Ngwenya, 398, 399
Niamey, 237
Niari Valley, 266, 267
Nickel, 301
Niger, 229, 236-238
  demographic data, 223
Niger River, 10, 146, 150, 166
  early exploration, 81
Niger-Benue Lowland, 150
Nigeria, 145-168, 274
  agricultural opportunities, 163-167
  civil war, 162
  climates, 147
  cocoa production, 157-158
  colonial policy in, 93
  core regions, 106
  and Equatorial Guinea, 270
  ethnic diversity, 148
  consolidation of, 148-150
  military coups, 154
  and Niger, 237
  petroleum, 161-162
  physiographic regions, 146-147
  population, 154

Sikasso, 235
Simulium fly, 54, 236
Sinai, 525
Sinai Peninsula, Egypt, 534-535, 539
  invasion of, 530
  oil discovery, 535
Sirte Basin, 590, 592
  oil discoveries, 585
Sirte, Gulf of, 584, 585
Sisal, 334, 421, 442
Sishen, 357, 358
Skikda (Philippeville), 554
Slave trade, 71, 158, 194, 259
  Angola, 327-328
  Congo Free State, 246
  East Africa, 73, 311, 421, 450
  Sierra Leone, 186-187
  Southern Africa, 281
  West Africa, 71, 78
Slavery, Cape Colony, 79
  Sudan, 510
Sleeping sickness, 54-55
  effects on human settlement, 54-55
Smith, Ian, 284, 307
Smuts, General, 372
Sobhuza II, King, 383, 400
Sofala, 74, 311
Soil classification, D'Hoore, 48-50
Soil fertility, 46-47
Soils, 46-50
Sokoto, 165
Sokoto-Rima Basin, 146
Somali, 451, 477-479, 497-499
  in Afars and Issas, 497
  in Ethiopia, 497, 501-502
  in Kenya, 497, 499-501
Somalia (Somali Democratic Republic),
    94-95, 464, 477, 493, 495-506
  boundary problems, 499-502
  European partition, 497-499
  locust invasion, 56
  Republic established, 499
Songhai, ancient state, 69-70
Soninke, 68, 234
Sous River, 566
Sousse, 582
South Africa, 282, 338-369

administration of South West Africa,
    372-373
  agriculture, 39, 353-356
  and Angola, 334
  core regions, 106, 351
  federation proposals, 368
  Homeland consolidation, 349, 365-367
  industry, 351-353, 358-361
  industrial decentralization, 359-361
  labor migrations, 136
  migrants from Malawi, 287-288
  mining, 357-358
  and Namibia, 377-380
  natural environments, 339-341
  population, 123, 341-347
  resettlement schemes, 352, 362
  resources, 338, 353, 357
  and Rhodesia, 305-308
  ties with Botswana, 384, 401
  ties with Lesotho, 384, 401
  ties with Swaziland, 384, 401
  urbanization, 350-353, 361-365
  urban population, 344-345
  urban problems, 362-365
South African Customs Union, 401
South African Homelands (Bantustans),
    367-368
  agriculture, 353-355
  areas, 349
  consolidation, 365-367
  government policy, 349
  industry, 361
  mining, 357
  populations, 349
South African Troops, in Angola, 336
South Ndebele, 349, 366
Southern Highlands, Tanzania, 426, 432
Southern Rhodesia, 93, 282. See also Rhodesia,
    Zimbabwe
South-East State, Nigeria, 163
South West Africa, 87, 88. See also Namibia
  German claims in, 86-87
  mandate established, 89, 372
Soviet Union, and Angola, 336
  and Cameroon, 274
  and China, 410
  and Congo, 267

Wet Equatorial climates, 24-26
Wheat, 515, 531, 568, 580, 582
White Nile, 5, 9, 10
   as Sudan unifier, 508-510
White population, Algeria, 554-555
   Angola, 329
   Kenya, 437, 441-442
   Mozambique, 316, 320
   Rhodesia, 294
   South Africa, 342-344
White Volta River, 173
Wilberforce, William, 79
"Wind of Change," 95-98
Windhoek, 34, 372, 375
Wishale, Treaty of, 94
Witwatersrand, 106, 339, 351
   discovery of gold, 344
   industry, 359
   and Lourenço Marques (Maputo), 312, 314,
      320-321
Woina Dega, 36, 487
Woleu River, 265, 270
Wollega, 491
Wollo, 491
Wolof, 234
Wologisi Range, 198
World Bank, 230, 445, 492
World Court, 562

Xhosa, 341-342, 349

Yao, 311, 320
Yaoundé, 110, 271, 274
Yellow fever, 51
Yemen, 540
Yengema, 189
Yoruba, 71, 72, 112, 146, 156, 215
Yoruba Towns, 156
Youssoufia, 565
Yugoslavia, 212

Zagwe (Zague) dynasty, 480
Zaire Basin, 4, 243-244, 250-251, 267
Zaire, Republic of, 243-258, 333
   administrative organization, 253-254

agriculture, 252, 254-255
authenticity drive, 245, 254
colonial era, 245-253
copper, 249-250, 255-256
minerals, 250-251, 254-257
name changes, 245, 254
transport, 244, 247, 248-252, 256
urbanization, 257-258
Zaire River, 10-12, 243-244, 247, 250-251,
   257, 269
Zambezi River, 7, 11-12, 13, 279, 289, 293
   as barrier to settlement, 293
   as divide in Mozambique, 310-311
Zambezia, 87
Zambia, 279-286, 302
   compared with Malawi, 289-291
   copper, 285-286
   economic dualism, 290, 291
   exports through Angola, 333
   historical geography, 281-283
   and Tan-Zam Railway, 432
Zande Scheme, 513, 519
Zanj, 497
ZANU, 306
Zanzibar, 84, 408, 450
   Arab stronghold, 429
   clove industry, 423
   sultanate of, 84, 86, 449-450
   union with Tanganyika, 417
ZAPU, 306
Zaria, 163, 165
Zauditu, 482
Zeila, 497, 498
Zelton, 585, 588
Zimbabwe, *see* Rhodesia
Zimbabwe, Kingdom, 65, 73-75
Zimbabwe Liberation Army, 306
Zimbabwe Nationalist Movement, 306-307
Zinc, 374, 375
Zinder, 237
Zomba, 110, 288
Zulu, 341, 342
Zulu Nation, 73, 75, 79, 396
Zululand, 75
Zulu Wars, 79